THE LITVAK LEGACY

THE
LITVAK
LEGACY

MARK N. OZER

This book was printed in the United States of America.

List of Credits

Map 1.1 "The Yiddish North-South Divide, Courtesy of the Perseus Group Cambridge, Massachusetts

Cover Painting "Self-Portrait" by Samuel Bak Courtesy of Pucker Gallery Boston, Massachusetts

For further information, you may check
www.TheLitvakLegacy.com

To order additional copies of this book, contact:
Xlibris Corporation
1-888-795-4274
www.Xlibris.com
Orders@Xlibris.com
52555

CONTENTS

SECTION III: THE HEBREW SPEAKING DIASPORA

DEDICATION

To those unknown buried in the forests of Lita

ACKNOWLEDGEMENTS

This book has been a labor of love and duty since its inception in the summer of 1997. I made the commitment immediately after leaving the Ponar Forest, adjoining Vilnius in present-day Lithuania. My wife, my brother, and I were now free to travel there after the breakup of the Soviet Union. It was also there in the forest, in the years prior to the revolution of 1905, that I could imagine my grandparents meeting. Along with other young Jews, they met free from the strictures of religious tradition and the eyes of the Tsarist police. They had met and married for love despite the opposition of his father, my great-grandfather. The young man immigrated to the United States in 1912 as part of the Great Emigration from the Russian Empire. The wife—mother of the three remaining children, followed only after the end of World War I. They and their descendants lived in Boston where I had grown up.

But in the summer of 1941, immediately after the German conquest, this forest was a killing ground where shots rang out, and cries had filled the air when thousands of Vilna's Jews were slaughtered. In the years since, by the burning of the bodies on the orders of the Germans, they had tried to obliterate evidence of those massacres. There was the building—still later, in the Soviet Russian period—of several round pits surrounded by low concrete walls. In one of those pits recently disturbed by tractor tracks bent on vandalism, we said the prayer for the dead while mixing my father's ashes with the raw red soil that contained the remnants of some of his fellow Lithuanian Jews. It seemed fitting to bring my father's ashes to the land of his ancestors to be mixed with anonymous others since it was not possible to trace those of his family who had perished in Lithuania during the Shoah/Holocaust.

Leaving the now-silent forest where such horrors had been carried out and had been so poorly memorialized, I was filled with emotion. I decided that I must tell the story of this people,

11

no longer where they had lived but their descendants, like my own family, who had emigrated and had spread over the world. I felt that it was necessary to describe the culture from which they had come; the values of that culture that persisted in many ways although transformed by the subsequent experiences during the successive several generations. It was particularly instructive to consider the evolution not only in the United States but also in how their story differed in other countries where their influence was significant, both in English- and Hebrew-speaking places.

I found, in writing this book, that I tapped into a large extended family that recognized their connection but, like me, were not fully aware of the degree to which they, even unto the third generation, partook of its values. In many cases, I was able to interview some of those descendants whose stories are included. Samuel Bak was most gracious in providing insights into his life and the right to use his painting on the front cover However, most of the material reflects the relatively large amount of published documentation and analysis generated by scholars. The widespread dedication to writing the history of this people itself reflects the impact of the Jewish Enlightenment that created the interest in discerning the factors that affect human life no longer viewed only as the unfolding of a divine design.

I must acknowledge the help received from the staff of the Map Division and the Middle Eastern Division of the Library of Congress, particularly Rachel Becker. Professor Max Ticktin of George Washington University was helpful in the early stages. Each of the chapters was reviewed by one or more persons familiar with the material. These included Dov Levin who provided strong support for the chapter on Lita, Robert Rockaway on the United States (both of Hebrew University), Aubrey Newman from University of Leicester on Britain, Michael Brown of York University in Canada, Milton Shain of University of Cape Town as well as Gideon Shimoni of Hebrew University on South Africa and several academics from the Hebrew University in Israel. The responsibility for the final product, of course, lies with me.

PREFACE

Between the 1880s and the 1920s, a million *Litvak* Jews migrated throughout the world from *Lita*, their home in the western edge of the Russian Empire. This book is the story of the legacy of that migration. What was the character of the culture from which they arose? How did it differ from that of other Jews? What happened to the Jews from Lita and their descendants? What did they contribute to the countries where they went?

The Jewish inhabitants of Lita were called Litvaks (Litvakes in Yiddish) to distinguish them from non-Jewish Lithuanians as well as from other Jews. In their home, they formed a distinct culture that differed in its variant of their language of Yiddish as well as the character of their Judaism. As followers of the Vilna Gaon in the late eighteenth century, in opposition to the spread of Hassidism, *Litvaks* maintained a unique commitment to rabbinical Judaism and intellectual study. They were also unusual in the degree to which arduous and sharp-witted Talmudic study was widespread. The religious tradition continued to evolve in Lita. In response to the challenges of both Hassidism and the Haskalah (Enlightenment), the ethically oriented *mussar* movement became widespread within the Lithuanian yeshivot. *Orthodoxy* evolved out of traditional Judaism. However, relatively few of those traditionally religious chose to emigrate and the Litvak Diaspora was mainly secular although imbued with religious roots.

Lita was also the "greenhouse" of secularism. In the late nineteenth century, particularly centered in Vilna, Lita was a major source of the Jewish responses to modernity such as socialism and the recognition of Yiddish as a language in its own right as well as modern Hebrew and Zionism. The literary and political responses to the breakdown of the Jewish social structure retained the traditional spirit of intensity and sharp-wittedness. The quest for bringing about a better world via *socialism* and

13

Zionism partook of the religious impulse while denying it. The language battles between Yiddish and Hebrew were joined to these ideologies. The characteristic Litvak *intellectual* strand was expressed in the flowering of secular literary and historical studies that also partook of the intensity previously devoted to the sacred writings.

As the Russian Empire containing Lita was broken up following World War I, its inhabitants found themselves living either in Latvia, Poland, the Russian, and Belorussian Republics of the Soviet Union or in the newly independent Lithuania. The entire area, now divided, had a common cultural entity that can be called Litvakia. When the new boundaries were drawn, many of the inhabitants stayed in place and were subject to the Holocaust.

The Great Migration from Lita occurred in the period of the latter third of the nineteenth century and in the twentieth century prior to World War I but extended through World War II. Even beyond the Holocaust/Shoah, the few survivors continued to bear witness to its memory. It is my thesis that there is a distinctive Litvak cultural heritage that can be traced through the maintenance of that culture through several generations and the significant impact it has had on the countries in which the immigrants settled.

Section 1 deals with the evolution of the core in Lita from 1840 to its destruction during the Shoah during World War II. Focus is on the relationship between the developments following 1880 and the ideas carried by the emigrants to the Diaspora from Lita mainly ending in the 1920s. *Section 2* deals with those ideas carried to the English-speaking world and their subsequent evolution mainly in the United States but also in comparison to the United Kingdom, Canada, and South Africa. It was not uncommon for various family members or those from the same area to migrate to each of these several countries.

Focus is on the evolution of the religious strand as well as the secular intellectual, socialist, and Zionist strands derived from Lita and their interaction with the characteristics of each country.

The story of the emigrants is told as exemplified by persons of Litvak ancestry or culture in each of the several generations between 1880-1980. These include the *immigrant generation*, roughly ending in 1920 after the end of World War I; the *acculturating generation*, ending with 1950 with the formation of the State of Israel; and the post-World War II or *integrating generation*, extending to the 1980s. *Section 3* deals with the evolution of these ideas in the Hebrew-speaking Diaspora of Israel. It is highly recommended to read the initial section entitled the "Core" before reading any of the subsequent individual chapters dealing with each of the countries. Although cross-references exist, each chapter devoted to a country has been designed to be self-contained and so can be read separately or in continuity with the others to illustrate comparisons possible between the different settings.

SECTION I

THE LITVAK HOMELAND

INTRODUCTION
LITA—THE NATURE OF THE CORE

This section/chapter deals with the nature of the core—the people and the ideas that they carried to the rest of the world from the portion of Eastern Europe that can be called Lita. It is our thesis that their heritage was not merely genetic but cultural encompassed in the term *Litvakia,* a recent term that serves to define the cultural entity after it ceased after World War I to be a political one within the Russian Tsarist Empire. That heritage has had a significant impact, sometimes beyond what the number of persons would suggest, on the development of the countries to which they went. The Great Migration from Lita occurred primarily in the period in the latter half of the nineteenth century and in the twentieth century, particularly prior to World War I, but extended to the outbreak of the World War II. Even beyond the Shoah, the few survivors continued to bear witness to its memory and contribute to the countries to which they came.

This chapter/section is divided into two parts. The first portion deals with the character of the place, the second with evolution of the strands in the cultural legacy in each era from the 1840s to 1940s reflected in archetypical persons. The Shoah is the major division in the life of this area, but the impact of World War I was a forerunner. Both have had major impact on both Lita and on the Litvak Diaspora.

The word *Diaspora* has traditionally referred to the exile of the Jews from their ancestral land and the Temple in Jerusalem that had been their site for worship. In this book, the term is used in relation to those who left the new *Jerusalem of the North,* the product of a millennium of Jewish life in Europe, to go elsewhere. The core no longer exists although a few Jews might still live in modern Lithuania. Like those in exile from original Jerusalem, those who left Vilna and Lita, which it symbolizes, have also lost what had once existed. The Great Destruction of the Temple has been reenacted in the Shoah/Holocaust of our own time. The horrible extent of the destruction and the story of how those in Lita dealt with their impending destruction reverberate among those who emigrated prior to the Shoah and in the generations that followed.

In summary, the traditional Jewish life of the Pale was dislocated by the Haskalah by new economic forces and pogroms around the turn of the century. By the end of the nineteenth century, the Russian Jewish response coalesced into two major strands. The religious strand was a restructuring of rabbinical Judaism exemplified by the Vilna Gaon into what came to be called Orthodoxy to differentiate from other developments of a Reform nature occurring in Germany and elsewhere. *Mussar* was a development within the Orthodox Lithuanian yeshivot that emphasized ethical behavior along with intensive study. The other major strand translated religious messianism into earthly redemption, one strand through socialism, and the other through nationalism expressed through the choice of language. The Yiddish socialist strand was exemplified by the activities of the Jewish Socialist Bund. The Yiddish nationalist response produced a renewal and flowering of Yiddish culture in the Pale called Folkism. The national strand also led to the Zionist movement and the eventual flowering of a Hebrew-language culture in Israel. Particularly important was the combination of Socialism and Zionism, which led to the renewal of the Jewish nation in Palestine and formed the basis for its early political life. But rivaling all other responses to change in Eastern Europe was emigration, most of it to the United States and to Canada in the New World but also in places such as Great Britain and South Africa, carrying these ideas to these other places.

Table 1

THE EVOLUTION OF LITA DURING THE 19th CENTURY

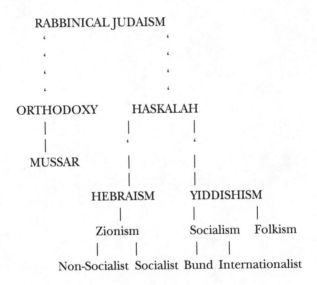

CHAPTER 1
THE CORE OF LITA

List of Maps

Chapter 1.1 The Nature of the Place

This section briefly traces the history of Jewish Lithuania to the early nineteenth century. It was from this background imbued by religion that the vibrant Litvak secular culture of the mid- and late nineteenth century developed. Both the religious and secular culture were carried to the rest of the world by Lita's émigrés and survivors.

1.1.1 The Boundaries of Lita

The kingdom of Lithuania, founded in the thirteenth century, occupied extensive territory in Eastern Europe, between the Teutonic Knights (later Prussia) in the west and Muscovy (later Russia) in the east. At its greatest extent, in the fourteenth century, it stretched from the Baltic in the north to the Black Sea in the south. Its capital city was Vilna (Vilnius).

How then shall we refer to the land and to the Jews who lived there? This study will use *Lita*, the Jewish term for Lithuania, to define the place as part of the Jewish world. This was, historically, where the Lithuanian Jews lived and developed their distinct culture with its center in Vilna. The Jewish inhabitants of Lita were called Litvaks (Litvakes in Yiddish) to distinguish them from non-Jewish Lithuanians as well as other Jews.

As Lita was broken up following the First World War, its inhabitants found themselves living in Poland, the Russian and Belorussian Republics of the Soviet Union, in portions of Latvia or in the truncated twentieth-century Lithuania. Litvakia refers to the homeland of the Litvaks, without reference to political frontiers; while the frontiers shifted, most of the inhabitants stayed in place.

From the early fourteenth century, there were Jewish settlements in all the more important towns in Lithuania. Prior to the introduction of Christianity, these settlements enjoyed a considerable degree of tolerance and even goodwill. In 1386, King Jagiello of Lithuania married Jadwiga, daughter of the king of Poland, and united the two kingdoms. At the same time, Jagiello accepted Christianity and agreed to introduce it to his people. Two years later, the Jews of Lithuania received their first charter modeled on the royal charter previously granted to the Jews of Poland. It safeguarded the rights of the Jews in return for payment of taxes by the community, and it established a system of Jewish self-government that would persist until the eighteenth century.[1] The promise of physical safety and economic opportunity supported a massive eastward exodus of the persecuted Ashkenasi Jews of the Rhineland and Central Europe who then, in turn, formed the basis for the development of East European Jewry and their particular version of the Yiddish language.[2]

The Union of Lublin, in 1569, established a more fully unified Polish-Lithuanian state, with a single executive, a single parliament, and the dominance of Polish language and culture. But although the Lithuanian nobility and middle class were Polonized, the differences between Lita and the Polish Jewish portions of the kingdom persisted and even increased. In 1590, the Council of Lithuania (Va'ad Lita) began to function separately within the Synod of the Four Lands (Va'ad arba ha-aratsot), which had included the Jewish communities of Poland, Lithuania, and Belorussia In 1623, the Lithuanian communities seceded from the overall Synod entirely. The breakaway Lithuanian Council met thirty-seven times, every two to three years, with delegates from the Jewish community councils (kehillot) of the five principal cities of Brisk, Pinsk, Vilnius, Slutzk, and Grodno (Gardinas).[3] A separate Council of Belorussia (White Russia) existed, but it was subordinate to the Lithuanian Council in the crucial matter of taxation. In fact, the Jewish inhabitants of the entire area of Lithuania-Belorussia identified themselves as *Litvaks*. [4]

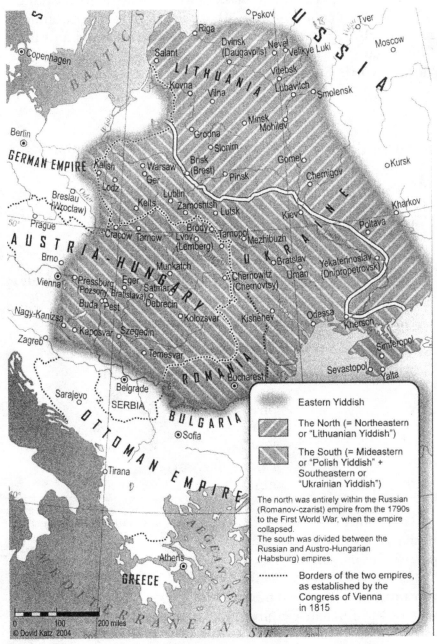

Map 1.1 The Yiddish North/South Divide

The Council of Lithuanian Jewish Communities (Va'ad Medinat Lita) both cooperated and clashed with the analogous Council of Polish Jewish communities. Tensions over tax apportionment reinforced the regional differences—which included a distinct Lithuanian "northern" dialect of Yiddish. (See Map 1.1 The Yiddish North/South Divide and See Table 1.2)

Table 1.2

Northern (Litvak)	Southern (non-Litvak)	Meaning
Ay	a (long -aa)	
Haynt	haant	today
Vayn	vaan	wine
E	ey	
Betyn	beytin	ask
Makhateneste	makhateyneste	in-law (female)
Ey	oy	
Veynen	voynen	live (reside)
Teyre	toyre	Torah
O	u (long or short)	
Matone	matune	gift
Zogn	zugn	say
Oy	oh	
Froy	froh	woman
Kloyz	klohz	little synagogue
U	I (long or short)	
Hunt	hint	dog

There were also increasing differences in religious practice. Both councils were abolished by the Polish state in 1764 due to overwhelming debts.

Following the third partition of Poland in 1795, the Lithuanian provinces in the eastern borderlands of the Polish state became part of the Russian Empire. Lita remained identifiable as the northwestern provinces of the Pale of Settlement, the western edge of the Russian Empire to which Jewish settlement was confined. (See Map 1.2)

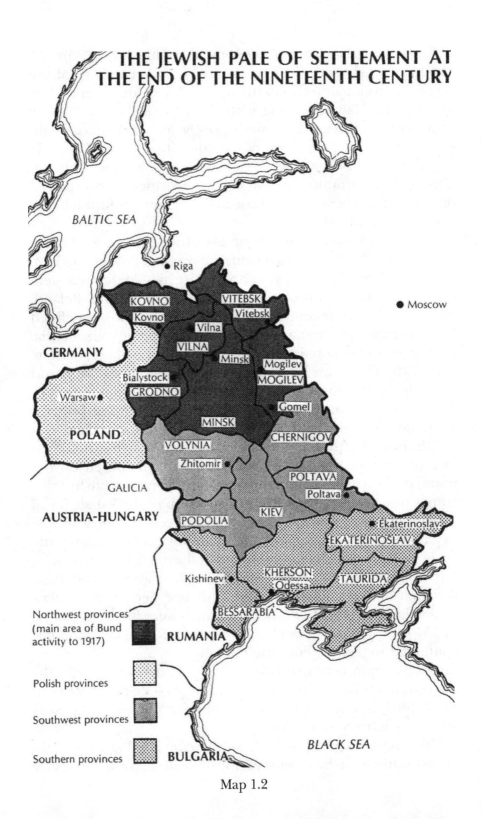

THE JEWISH PALE OF SETTLEMENT AT THE END OF THE NINETEENTH CENTURY

BALTIC SEA

• Riga

• Moscow

GERMANY

KOVNO
Kovno •
Vilna
VILNA
Minsk •

VITEBSK
Vitebsk

Mogilev •
MOGILEV

Bialystock •
GRODNO

Warsaw •

POLAND

MINSK

Gomel

CHERNIGOV

VOLYNIA
Zhitomir •

GALICIA

POLTAVA
Poltava •

AUSTRIA-HUNGARY

PODOLIA

KIEV

Ekaterinoslav •
EKATERINOSLAV

Kishinev •

KHERSON
Odessa •

TAURIDA

BESSARABIA

Northwest provinces
(main area of Bund
activity to 1917)

RUMANIA

Polish provinces

Southwest provinces

Southern provinces

BULGARIA

BLACK SEA

Map 1.2

Lita included the provinces of Suwalki, Vilna, Kovno, Vitebsk, Grodno, Minsk, and Mogilev, generally the area north of the Bug River. Its major towns in the nineteenth century were Vilna, Minsk, and Bialystok along with the capitals of each of the provinces. The area was relatively poorly endowed, marshy with extensive forests. There were other, non-Litvak, areas of the Pale whose soil was better. The Ukrainian or *southwestern* provinces were centered around Kiev; the *southern* provinces were centered on Odessa; and Bessarabia, whose major center was Kishinev, was adjacent to Romania.

Lita was not only distinct from the other parts of the Pale; it also remained differentiated from the original Polish kingdom. The *Polish* provinces of the Russian Empire had a different system of government from the provinces of the Pale; central Poland, including the major center of Jewish life in Warsaw, was defined by the Congress of Vienna following the Napoleonic Wars. Galicia, with large Jewish populations in Cracow and Lemberg, became part of the Hapsburg Empire after the partition of Poland and also remained culturally and religiously distinct from Lita.

The annexation of Lita into the Russian Empire brought about deterioration of communal self-government and a rise in discriminatory taxation.[5] Rabbinical courts lost their jurisdiction in civil matters, residence restrictions were imposed on the population, and discriminatory quotas were established for conscription into the army. The leadership of the kahals (local councils) had become an oligarchy that oppressed those least able to pay the assessed taxes. The moral authority of the communal leadership was severely compromised by the need, under Nicholas I, to fulfill army quotas; the heaviest burdens were placed upon the poor and unconnected. The basis had been laid for class distinctions to flourish. The local councils were finally abolished in 1844. Despite the loss of official status, Jewish communities continued to provide educational, religious, and social services through an unofficial network. The registry of births and deaths was taken over by a government-appointed "state rabbi"; but the town rabbi, appointed by the community, remained the final arbiter in matters of religion.

The cultural center of Lita was the city of Vilna whose first Jewish settlement had been established in 1326. In the early seventeenth century, Vilna was such a celebrated center for Torah study, replacing earlier centers in Poland, that it became known as the Jerusalem of Lithuania. The Great Synagogue, seating three thousand worshippers, was built in 1635. Its courtyard, together with the Strashun Library founded in the nineteenth century and the numerous small shtibelah in the courtyard, formed a major center of learning that continued for the remainder of its history.[6] In turn, many of the residential tenement blocks of the city had a courtyard with its own study hall.

The Tsarist authorities imposed Russian as the official language in the Lithuanian provinces of the empire. The Gentile population found strength both in identification with the Roman Catholic Church and in Polish national consciousness. However, the Polish language never took a commanding hold in Vilna and the surrounding Lithuanian area, no doubt because of the complex ethnic mix of the population—Lithuanians, Poles, White Russians, Russians, and Jews. This worked to the advantage of the Russifiers, but later it also benefited those who promoted the use of Yiddish.[7]

Yiddish was the vernacular spoken by ordinary Jews, both men and women, while the Hebrew of the scripture and particularly the Aramaic of the Talmud were the languages of the very small group of literate men.[8] The choice of language would be a significant issue in Lita, and Vilna was the center of the linguistic-political struggle. The Haskalah (Enlightenment) would pose linguistic options, which will be examined later in this chapter.

1.1.2 The Vilna Gaon and the *Mitnagdim*

The distinction between the *Litvaks* and their fellow Jews was accentuated by the religious-cultural dispute of the late eighteenth century between the Hassidic movement and its rabbinical "opponents" (in Hebrew, the *mitnagdim.*) The clash was a manifestation of divergent religious tendencies: on one side, Hassidic mysticism, spontaneity, ecstatic enthusiasm, and focus on a miracle-working rebbe; and on the other side *mitnagdic* legalism, rabbinical scholarship, and sober restraint. The mitnagdim emphasized intellectual rigor and devotion to Torah learning. The conflict assumed a distinctly regional character as Hassidism, which originated in the Ukraine, spread northward and westward into Galicia. It encountered its fiercest resistance in Lita. Although there were some centers of Hassidism in Lita, the Litvaks and the mitnagdim became synonymous.[9]

Conditions in Lita were quite different from conditions in the Ukrainian provinces of Volynia and Podolia where Hassidism first arose under the Baal Shem Tov (1700-1760). The Chmelnitsky massacres in the Ukraine of the mid-seventeenth century had been followed by recurrent peasant and Cossack insurrections, blood libels, and pogroms. Decades of anarchy had made the Ukraine particularly favorable soil for new social and religious movements despite the terrible experience of a false messiah, Shabbatai Zvi, earlier in the century. Impoverished and without spiritual centers or a responsive rabbinate, Jews in the small towns and peasant villages of the Ukraine had sought comfort in mysticism, fantasy, and miracle healers.

In contrast, the Lithuanian Jews suffered relatively little from pogroms during this time of troubles. Although a poorer country than the Ukraine, the Litvaks lived in larger towns with better protection, access to learning, and strong religious leadership. Not only was their cultural level higher but insulated as well as they were from the brutality of the times; they were less vulnerable to messianic movements. The rabbinical authorities considered it a desecration of religious discipline to place prayer above learning, to criticize the religious traditions and customs, and to alter the content and method of prayer as Hassidim had done. They linked the new movement to the earlier false messianic movements that had threatened Jewish life.[10] Perhaps what also troubled the rabbinical elite was the threat to their status. Rather than the traditional emphasis on trilingualism that included Hebrew and Aramaic, the use of Yiddish in some of Hassidism's most important books represented a "social shift in intellectual power from the intelligentsia to the new populist leaders of the masses."[11]

The leader of the mitnagdic camp was Rabbi Elijah of Vilna (d. 1798), called the Vilna Gaon in recognition of the outstanding quality of his Torah scholarship.[12] Rabbi Elijah embodied the fundamental principles of rabbinical Judaism:[13] strenuous study of the texts, analytic intellectuality, and boundless determination to reach truth through rigorous study.[15] The Vilna Gaon encouraged the study of a wider range of Jewish texts, including the Midrashim and Aggadic literature as well as the Torah, Talmud, and Kabbalah. He reformed the way the Talmud was studied, and he redacted what was to be the standard version to be published in Vilna in large number by the famous Romm Press. The Gaon epitomized what became the traditionally *Litvak* pursuit of the *actual* meaning of the text. On several occasions, the Gaon-directed *herem*, or writs of excommunication, against Hassidism but without total success. In 1804, Hassidism won its right to exist when the Tsarist government issued an edict limiting the power of the local council and the rabbis to prevent the building of more than one synagogue in a town. Rabbi Elijah's commitment to intellectual pursuit was coupled with piety and concern for the development of character. Although he refused to accept an official position as rabbi, the Gaon became the spiritual head of the whole of Lithuanian and, indeed, of Russian Jewry.

Hassidism, however, took a distinctive course in Lita. The indigenous HABAD movement, organized in Belorussia in 1781 by Rabbi Schneur-Zalman of Liadi, became the predominant form of Hassidism with particular influence in the eastern portion of Lita.[16] Its motto combined *Hochma* (wisdom), *bina* (understanding), and *daat* (knowledge), reflecting a dedication to both rabbinical learning and mysticism as a *third way*.[14] Rabbi Shneur-Zalman introduced into Hassidism some of the spirit and character of the Litvaks. Furthermore, unlike the other Hassid sects, he did not consider the head of the community to be a wonder-working tsaddik but, more simply, a spiritual leader.[18] Under his son, Rabbi Dov Baer, the sect became identified with the town of Lubavitch in Mogilev province in Lita. Throughout the nineteenth century, the Habad movement maintained its strict prohibition against the inroads of modernity.[15] Displaced by World War I and the Bolshevik Revolution, the Lubavitcher rebbe, Joseph Yitzsak Schneersohn, lived in Poland during the interwar years before escaping to the United States in 1941. Both the HABAD Lubavitch movement and the scholarly rabbinical *mitnagdic* strand survive throughout the world as part of the religious legacy of Lita.

1.1.3 The Legacy of the Gaon

The Vilna Gaon exerted a powerful influence on Lita during the nineteenth century. The habit of study, considered an act of religious devotion, was inculcated from the earliest years. At the age of four, a boy was taken to a heder (school) in the home of a private teacher, where he would be taught the Hebrew alphabet, to read the Bible, to write and pray in Hebrew as well as basic arithmetic. By the age of ten, boys had usually acquired knowledge of the scriptures and their commentaries and been introduced to the *Shulhan Aruch*, the code of religious law. Often taught by relatively poorly trained and brutal teachers, the heder became one of the favorite illustrations of the aridity of traditional education by nineteenth-century reformers.[16]

After the bar mitzvah, at age thirteen, most students left the educational system to go to work or to become an apprentice. In the tradition of the Vilna Gaon, devotion to religious studies was not confined to rabbis and advanced students but was shared by merchants and artisans. Once their daily work was done, men went to the house of study (beth midrash) to immerse themselves in a page of Talmud, or chapter of Mishna, or a portion of some other volume.

It was more common in Lita than elsewhere in the Pale for talented students to enter into more advanced study of the Talmud, usually in the beth midrash of their own or an adjacent community. Students were supported by the community with meals provided by local families in rotation. At roughly the age of seventeen, a particularly gifted boy would enter the yeshiva, or Talmudic academy, frequently at a distance from his home and sometimes requiring separation from his wife and family. The Gaon had established Vilna as a center of higher learning; and in 1802, one of his disciples, Rabbi Hayyim, founded a yeshiva at Volozhin in Lita where he sought to create an educational response to the spread of Hassidism. The yeshiva at Volozhin became the premiere center for Torah learning with a far greater degree of organization and standards than heretofore. Rabbi Hayyim's students established many other yeshivot where they followed his lead in fusing the intellectual with the spiritual. The major Lithuanian yeshivot drew students from the Russian Empire and around the world. Students found, in the Lithuanian yeshivot, a seriousness and self-sacrifice that pervaded the search for perfection in Torah study.[17] After graduation, these yeshiva students, frequently, were required to migrate to the more prosperous areas in the rest of the Pale where they became the teachers to the young. The Litvak *melamed* became a stock character.

The yeshivas of Lita represented the distinctness of Litvak culture, particularly the devotion to learning as a sacred calling. Students worked alone or in small groups; independent study was the norm. No time limit was set as it was believed that one never completes one's studies. Regardless of these young men's final calling, the years spent in the yeshiva affected their future as Orthodox intellectuals. The elite of Lita was defined by its scholarliness as well as its wealth, and young men who studied in yeshivas were more likely than others to become future communal authorities. Achievement of distinction in one's studies was the best way for a young man to win a bride who possessed the double attractions of a dowry and a pedigree.

Yeshiva students did not train for the rabbinate; rather, the Torah was an end in itself and "not a hoe with which to dig."[18] If, later on, the man reluctantly decided to become a communal rabbi in order to make a living, he left the yeshiva and spent several months studying the *practical Halakha* that was requisite for ordination and a position as a community rabbi. The community rabbi might be appointed by the community council for a three- to five-year term. Rabbinical responsibilities included counseling the community on the observance of Jewish law (Halakha), educating the young (men) with a view to their admission to more advanced Talmudic study, and presiding over the rabbinical court (beth din) consisting of scholars and other judges appointed by the community council. Rabbis also supervised adherence to the laws of kashruth by the ritual slaughterer. In smaller towns, the rabbi's pay and opportunities for further emoluments were limited. During the nineteenth century, the status and income of communal rabbis deteriorated. There was an increase in the number of scholars produced with competition for appointment to community posts while there was concomitant diminution in legal status. The tsarist government established seminaries in

Vilna and Zhitomir and required the "official rabbis" to be their graduates, familiar with Russian, to keep registry of births and deaths.

The students married early, typically by age eighteen. Young couples lived in the home of the wife's parents for the first few years as part of the marriage contract.[19] Such arrangements could lead to many difficulties expressed in the writings of those who later became followers of the Haskalah (Enlightenment), and in response, the age of marriage began to rise by the end of the nineteenth century.[20] The man often earned a meager living by leading a small group of advanced students while his wife ran a store to support the family. The truism was that "the man learned and the woman earned." Education of girls was, on the whole, considered less necessary than that of boys since women had fewer religious duties to perform than men. Nonetheless, there was a strong tradition of training girls for literacy in Yiddish so that they could receive instruction in the religious issues related to household management. In general, girls' education was more practical and the pattern was less consistent and for shorter periods than for boys. The tensions that arose under the pressure of poverty and the large families typical of the era were abundantly reflected in Yiddish popular culture; the irony of Peretz's story "Bryna's Mendl," for example, is illustrative of the role of the hardworking wife.[21]

Thanks to the legacy of the Vilna Gaon, Lita remained distinct from the rest of the Jewish Pale in ways beyond devotion to religious study. What made Rabbi Elijah a transitional figure was his belief that in order to study Torah, one must be well versed in secular knowledge. He taught himself mathematics, geography, astronomy, and anatomy and encouraged the translation of Euclid into Hebrew. The followers of the Enlightenment (Maskilim) invoked the example of the Gaon to validate themselves. Early interest in secular learning came to characterize the culture of Lita to a greater degree than elsewhere in the Pale. The rigor and discipline exemplified by Rabbi Elijah survived in the stereotype of the flinty, scholarly Litvak. Still later, when contempt was expressed for the aridity of the traditional religious education, the appreciation of rigorous secular intellectual study continued. This characteristic

of many nineteenth-century Litvaks became part of their legacy
to their descendants. In addition, many yeshiva students would
be attracted to the secular movements of a later time by the
devotion of those movements to rigorous pursuit of the *truth.*
Many former Talmudic scholars felt at home in radical secular
political movements such as Marxism that stressed such rigor.

The Gaon was transitional in another way too. The Maskilim
founders of modern Hebrew culture invoked him as their mentor
in light of his interest in Hebrew grammar and biblical studies.
Indeed, early in the nineteenth century, a group of disciples of
the Vilna Gaon emigrated to the land of Israel (Eretz Israel) then
in the Ottoman Empire. There they constituted a significant
component of the Ashkenazi Old Yishuv (Jewish settlement) living
in the *holy cities* of Tiberias, Jerusalem, and Hebron on the eve of
the new migration that began in the 1880s. One particular group
derived from Shklov settled in Safed. Religious traditionalists
believed that the conditions for redemption and the return to
Zion were under divine control and would occur only when the
messianic age arrived. But the followers of the Gaon maintained
that redemption could also be contingent on human actions,
at the very least on the maintenance of religious piety, with full
adherence to the mitzvoth. Other traditional religious circles,
mainly Hassidic in character, oppose the ideology of the Zionist
movement even into the present day with the accusation of trying
to "force the end." However, support for return to Zion became
part of the legacy of Litvakia that reappeared later in the religious
Zionist Mizrachi movement that originated there alongside the
secular Zionist movement.

As we turn to the economic, demographic, and political
changes of the nineteenth and twentieth centuries, we will see
that the evolution of the secular culture of Lita was superimposed
upon this strong legacy of Torah study and imbued with it.
The influence of the Vilna Gaon not only strengthened the
intellectual rabbinical tradition, but it appeared to encourage
the development of secular studies as well as the renewal of
Hebrew carried out under the auspices of the Haskalah. Both the
secular and the religious strands were the inheritance of those
who emigrated from this area to the rest of the world, passed on
as a legacy to their descendants.

1.2 The Evolution of the Culture

1.2.1. The Generation of Haskalah 1840-1870

The Haskalah

Haskalah (Enlightenment) is the name given to the movement to bring the Jews of Eastern Europe into the mainstream of European culture, here specifically into Russian life. Modeling themselves on their German predecessors, the followers of the Haskalah, or *Maskilim*, sought a more rational Judaism, less concerned with the Talmud than with the Bible and its historical roots. They believed that reform of Jewish life, particularly in the areas of traditional religiously oriented education and "nonproductive" economic activity, was prerequisite for integration into the larger world. The influence of the Vilna Gaon steered the Eastern European Enlightenment, at least initially, along a course different from the one that Moses Mendelssohn had defined for the German Enlightenment.[1] Mendelsohn's version called for changes in religious practice as a major prerequisite for civic emancipation. But while the adherents of Mendelssohn narrowed the scope of religious life and observance in pursuit of civil identity, the Gaon appeared to define religious life in the broadest terms, even championing secular learning albeit in pursuit of greater understanding of the traditional Jewish texts.

Much as they wished for change, East European Maskilim did not intend to "throw off the yoke of the Torah," as their German predecessors had done, but to renew Judaism in its pure form. Moreover, in the presence of the very large body of Yiddish speakers, the German model of replacement of the "jargon" of Yiddish in favor of German led rather in Eastern Europe to the development of Yiddish as a literary language and to a modern Hebrew literature and eventually to a spoken Hebrew in the Land of Israel.

The Haskalah in the Russian Pale of Settlement began in the 1830s in the city of Vilna. There, small literary circles created a

Jewish subculture that advocated the study of secular subjects while adhering to the Halakha and the mitzvoth. In Vilna they founded a liberal synagogue, with choral music and revised ritual, and schools that would reflect some of their advanced views. Generally upper-class or supported by wealthy patrons, these few young founders of the Haskalah were committed to creating a synthesis between European culture and Jewish tradition. Following the traditional model of text study and responsibility for one's own development, they devoted the same discipline to the study of secular subjects that they had devoted to religious subjects. They read science and learned Russian. They introduced Hebrew as a language for literary expression, and their literary endeavors initiated what was to become modern Hebrew later in the century.

Beginning in the 1840s, the *Maskilim* came under the protection of the government of Tsar Nicholas I and were transformed by it. The government's goal was to Russify the Jews, preparatory to their entry into civil society.[2] A substantial network of primary and secondary *crown schools* was established, as well as the rabbinical seminaries in Zhitomir and Vilna, in which secular subjects and Russian were taught along with Torah. These schools were viewed with great suspicion in traditional religious circles, and the masses in Vilna greeted them with hostile demonstrations.[3] However, the crown schools educated the next generation of Russian-Jewish intelligentsia; many of their graduates returned to the schools as teachers.[4] Most significantly, the Maskilim worked with the tsarist government, placing themselves in opposition to the communal and rabbinical Jewish authorities These early Maskilim were the first self-conscious and self-confident secular intelligentsia dedicated to restructuring the life and culture of Russian Jews.

By the middle of the nineteenth century, the stereotype of the Litvak was established in Jewish consciousness.[5] Modeled on the Maskilim of Vilna, the stereotypical Litvak was "smart, analytical, worldly, skeptical, proud, stubborn, dynamic, and energetic." The reputation of the Litvaks for erudition and worldliness was not appealing to everyone. The Hassids of Poland, for example, felt that beneath their learned exteriors, Lithuanian Jews were hardly Jews at all.

The Mussar Movement:

The government's support of Haskalah affected only a small minority of Jews. More threatening was Hassidism's rejection of purely intellectual religious study. A new educational movement arose within the yeshivot of Lita to meet the challenge of both.[6] The mussar movement was also a response to increasingly widespread economic distress. It introduced an ethical component into traditional religious thought, preaching a doctrine of self-discipline, morality, and right behavior derived from study of particular texts. Mussar maintained the tradition of independent Torah study within Lithuanian yeshivot, but with increased application to daily life and sensitivity to the suffering of the weaker elements in society. By emphasizing the daily aspects of the moral aspects of everyday life, mussar strengthened within its students a commitment to the "healing of the world" (*tikkun olam*).

The founder of the mussar movement was Rabbi Israel Lipkin Salanter, born in Lita in 1810 of a prominent rabbinical line. At age twelve, he became a yeshiva student in Salant, whence his surname. Already learned in Talmud, Salanter came to emphasize also the study of mussar literature—religious texts that emphasized ethical behavior—after a meeting with the humble and learned Rabbi Zundel, the latter with an academic pedigree going back to the Gaon. In the 1850s, Salanter encouraged people to seek perfection by incorporating the ethical norms of rabbinic law into their own behavior such as in business. There was a strong aspect of self-criticism; the goal was to subdue one's "evil inclinations" while working for the benefit of others. The goal of learning was *moral intelligence*. Rabbi Salanter was also not afraid to shock. During a cholera epidemic in Vilna in 1848, for example, he astounded observers by eating at the pulpit on Yom Kippur. He was illustrating the importance of meeting the community's needs even if it meant disregarding the letter of Jewish law. Love of *God* was to be tempered by love of man.

Imbued with the Litvak ideal of study for its own sake, Rabbi Salanter never accepted rabbinical office. When he came under pressure to take a position in the government-sponsored Vilna seminary in the early 1840s, he moved from Vilna to Kovno. It was there that mussar reached its pinnacle. Mussar, with centers at Slobodka (Kovno) and Telz, became one of the leading influences in the Lithuanian yeshivot by the end of the nineteenth century. Yeshiva students were greatly influenced by Salanter and his disciples but so were the students who left the yeshivas to take part in the secular mission to improve the world through socialism or Zionism. They took with them an interest in the problems of human existence, great sensitivity to the material suffering of the lower classes, and belief in the importance of economic activism. Empowered by the teachings of Torah, the individual seemed to have the power to accomplish change without the need to wait for divine assistance.

Through it all, the mussar movement kept alive the Litvak emphasis on the centrality of Torah study and the aristocratic virtues of introspection, seriousness, and restraint. Despite all of its vicissitudes, the Litvak model of the yeshiva as a place for untrammeled Torah study by adult men (*Kollel*) survived the Shoah and would flourish in almost all the countries in the Litvak Diaspora.

The Secular Haskalah/Hebraists

For a short time, in the wake of the reforms of Alexander II in the 1860s, it seemed possible that Jews might enter more fully into Russian society. Selected groups based upon wealth and level of education were permitted to live in cities such as St. Petersburg outside the Pale. In 1863, the wealthy Jewish elite of the capital[7] founded the Society for Promotion of Enlightenment (OPE) among the Jews of Russia. For example, OPE supported translation of the Pentateuch into Russian and the training of Russian rabbis at the relatively enlightened Breslau Seminary in Germany.

Belief in the possibility of integration was powerfully articulated by Judah Leib Gordon, the leading Hebrew poet of the nineteenth century and, for a time, the secretary of the OPE. In the aristocratic Litvak spirit, he believed that it was the duty of the educated "to lead the masses of their people to contemporary civilization."[8] Born in Vilna in 1830, Gordon grew up with close ties of family and friendship to the Vilna Maskilim. In the 1860s and 1870s, he taught in state-supported crown schools near Kovno in Lithuania. His demeanor as well as his ideas emanated from his *Litvak* background. He has been described as the stereotypical Lithuanian Jew, but in a modernist cast. Scrupulously honest, he was disdainful of sentimentality or folksiness in any guise. Moreover, his positions were rigid, and he was unwilling to compromise on either ideological or personal matters.

Gordon epitomized the Haskalah of the second generation, which continued to preach the importance of integrating the Jews into European civilization while championing Hebrew as a national literary language. His narrative poetry was set in the time of King David when Hebrew was a living language. Just as important, Gordon looked to biblical texts for justification of integration. A famous line from his 1862-3 poem "Awake, My People!"—"Be a man in your going out and a Jew in your tents"—echoes the biblical imperative in Deuteronomy, "Rejoice O Zebulon in thy going out and Issachar in thy tents." This line was widely interpreted to reflect the bifurcation between the public and private roles that had been the hallmark of Western European Jewish emancipation. However, for Gordon, it was a celebration of the integration of the two, of being a member of Russian society, while simultaneously maintaining one's Jewish identity in terms of its creative Hebrew heritage. Gordon's championing of Hebrew led him to reject Yiddish as a dramatic example of Jewish separateness and part of the reaction and obscurantism he wished to break down.

In the reactionary 1880s, when the ideal of integration was collapsing, Gordon continued to advocate the reform of Jewish social and religious life. His gaze shifted, however, from integration to an eventual return to Palestine. Although he was an advocate for Jewish colonization there, he was concerned that the obscurantism of the Jews living in the *Old Yishuv* would, without some changes, lead to a theocracy. His hatred of religious obscurantism was so great that at times, he echoed the most extreme accusations leveled against Jews by the reactionary Russian press and by public opinion.

Mid-nineteenth-century Haskalah literature was the work of a group, including Gordon, who consciously began to think of themselves as writers. The core of their contribution was the idea that a secular career as a writer was worthy of a mature Jewish intelligence. These writers, whose origins were primarily in Lita where study of Hebrew text was so intensive, expressed the ferment of their times in the Hebrew press. Never numbering more than several hundred, the influence of the Hebrew literati on Jewish affairs was nevertheless significant.

Short pieces were soon followed by literary efforts on a larger scale. The Hebrew novel was born in 1853 when Abraham Mapu wrote *The Love of Zion*, describing an idealized version of life in ancient Israel. Mapu came from a traditional Litvak background: born near Kovno in 1808, a brilliant student of Talmud, and married by seventeen. Support for study by his wealthy father-in-law was followed by a post in the government school at Kovno. Along the way, Mapu was introduced to modern languages and secular subjects. Mapu's novel was written in biblical Hebrew, but its focus on romantic love made it a bestseller, read secretly by young Talmudic scholars beneath their tomes. Mapu's other writings addressed the hypocrisy of the clerics, their self-proclaimed piety, and the hostility of the older generation to the Enlightenment reforms.[9] Mapu also wrote a novel about the problems of contemporary life in Lita which, though less successful than his earlier books, provided a model for the social realism developed by his successors in Hebrew letters.

The defining focus of the Hebrew revival was the literary periodical. A number of Hebrew journals were created in the era of Alexander II. Between 1856 and 1886, for example, David Gordon published and edited the widely read weekly, *Ha-Maggid* (the Preacher). Gordon was born and educated in Vilna but moved to East Prussia where he could publish more freely. He argued in his writings that the national return to Zion did not, as traditional religion held, have to wait for the coming of the Messiah. Nor did he believe that emancipation required Jews to jettison their traditional religious practices. In the 1880s, his journal became the voice of Jewish nationalism in support of Hovevei Zion (lovers of Zion). He was unique in projecting both a political and spiritual solution to the *Jewish question* with both the *practical* Zionism of the settlements under the auspices of lovers of Zion and its successors and the political Zionism of Herzl.[10]

Another key figure in the Hebrew literary world was Peretz Smolenskin, born in 1842 in the province of Mogilev in Lita. While studying at the yeshivah at Shklov in Lita, he read secular books and learned Russian. Driven out of the yeshivah for his *heresy*, he made his way to Odessa where he published his first novel in 1867. Smolenskin finally settled in Vienna. There he founded the Hebrew monthly *Ha-Shahar* (*the Dawn*), which remained a highly effective platform for Hebrew literature and the early nationalist movement until Smolenskin's premature death in 1885.[11] Like David Gordon, Smolenskin saw in the Haskalah a third path, between the traditionalists on the *Right* and the assimilationists on the *Left*. For example, he published a series of articles in 1876, attacking the rosh (head) yeshivah of Volozhin for his opposition to secular studies. On the other hand, in other writings, he attacked Moses Mendelssohn, the prototype hero of the earlier Maskilim who, in defining Judaism as the observance of commandments, had emptied it of its national elements—its language and history.

The promise of reform and emancipation under Alexander II proved to be short-lived. In 1871, a pogrom took place in the unlikeliest of places, the enlightened city of Odessa. The intrusion of violence into a city that the Jews considered a safe haven marked the beginning of the end of their hopes for integration into Russian society. In 1872, the year after the pogrom, Smolenskin published an article entitled "Am Olam" ("The Eternal People") in which he wrote about the strength and courage that could come to the Jewish people from a land of their own. "Am Olam" was influential in affirming for the next generation the national religious identity of the Jewish people in support of the principles of "autoemancipation."[12]

The trajectory of the life of Moshe Leib Lilienblum also illustrates how the followers of the Haskalah responded to the worsening situation in Russia. Born in 1843 in Kovno, Lilienblum too had a traditional Talmudic upbringing, married young, and found himself living in the home of his wife's family. Desperately unhappy, he began to question the utility of traditional religious training. He began to call for reform during the Lithuanian famine of 1868-9, when suffering was widespread among those whose traditional education had trained them only for nonproductive occupations. Lilienblum was disillusioned not only with traditional education but eventually also with the Haskalah. He was drawn instead to the new radicalism given voice by Chernyshevski in *What Is to Be Done?* In his autobiography, *The Sins of Youth,* published in 1876 and widely read, Lilienblum chronicled his development away from traditional education to outright attack on obscurantism. His narrative of acculturation— from Talmud to Haskalah to social action—was a story that would be replicated by many others in Lita in the next generation.[13]

The response of the rabbis to these attacks marked a milestone in Jewish culture, transforming traditional Judaism in Russia into what came to be called Orthodoxy.[14] There was increasing opposition to the study of secular subjects in the yeshivot despite government pressure. The rabbis refused to consider any changes in Halakha made by "enlightened" rabbis. The Halakha became rigid, with serious consequences for Orthodox Judaism to the present day. Furthermore, the rabbis formed overtly political organizations in Kovno and Vilna to engage in lobbying and informational activities in opposition to Haskalah. For example, the Vilna Orthodox Society for the Defense of the Faith went so far as to accuse Lilienblum and his supporters of heresy and charged that Lilienblum's attacks on traditional religion led to disloyalty to the Russian state.

In 1869, as a result of these attacks, Lilienblum left Lita and went to Odessa—at that time, a haven for dissident Jewish writers. In 1871, he became the editor of the Yiddish weekly journal, *Kol-Mevaser* (the Messenger), founded in 1862.[15] He advocated equal rights for women, reform of the traditional arranged marriage, and political emancipation. Remembering the experience of the Lita famine in 1869, he particularly urged "productivization" of the Jews through changes in the traditional economic roles.

The subsequent pogroms of 1881 in Odessa had a profound effect on Lilienblum, leading him to advocate emigration from Russia to Eretz Israel. He became a nationalist and, with Asher Ginsburg (Ahad Ha'am), represented the leadership of the secular component of the Hibbat Zion (lovers of Zion). He was a founder of the *Odessa Committee* that funded settlements in Palestine. Late in life, in an autobiography, *The Way of Repentance,* he acknowledged the failure of Haskalah to solve the problems of modern Jewish existence.

Yiddish as a Literary Language

The Haskalah's choice for a Jewish national language was Hebrew. The entry into secular studies began to break down the emphasis on the traditional Hebrew used in religious study. Students in the yeshivot began to have access to secular Hebrew writings. Renewed interest in the renaissance of Hebrew also occurred as part of the return to Zion. The development of Hebrew as a literary language was to bear important fruit in later generations, particularly in the development of modern Hebrew in the Jewish settlement in Palestine, but in nineteenth-century eastern Europe, it had a limited market. The Haskalah intellectuals found that in order to reach the Jewish masses, they would have to employ Yiddish—the very language that they disdained as identified with provincialism and obscurantism.

An example of the Haskalah writers torn between Hebrew and Yiddish was Sholem-Yacov Abramovitsch who somewhat reluctantly became the patriarch of Yiddish literature. Abramovitsch was born in Kapuli in Belorussia, in 1836. He received a traditional Jewish yeshiva education and studied at the Vilna Gaon's House of Study. He became a partisan of the more radical Haskalah and taught in a government school, but by 1881, he had moved to Odessa where he was part of the Hebrew literary circle.

In the first decade of his literary life, Abramovitsch wrote in Hebrew such works of scientific content as a textbook on zoology. In the second stage of his writing career Abramovitsch began to use Yiddish, the "undignified" vernacular of the Jewish masses. He used the literary device of Mendele the Bookseller. His first publication in *Kol-Mevaser* in 1864 has been taken to mark the start of modern Yiddish literature. His choice of the device of Mendele the Bookseller supported the principle that the stories were from *real life* and thus had educational value. His use of this device also reflected his detachment from the subjects he wrote about.[16]

During the 1870s, Abramovitsch wrote a series of short novels in Yiddish which, together with the later works of I. L. Peretz and Sholem Aleichem, established *serious* modern Yiddish literature. In the didactic Maskilic tradition, his work remained deeply ambivalent, seesawing between satirical criticism of the ghetto Jew and expressions of love for the Jewish people. During the last decades of his long life, Abramovitsch translated back into Hebrew the works he had written in Yiddish. He struggled to convey in Hebrew the cadences of real dialogue. For this he had to draw not only on biblical Hebrew but on the postbiblical Hebrew of the midrash and even from Aramaic, in order to create a living, spoken language. His contribution to the development of modern Hebrew literature was thus as important as his contribution to Yiddish literature. His book *The Travels of Benjamin the Third*, published in Hebrew in 1896, is the first classic of modern Hebrew literature. Its transformation from its Yiddish version published in 1878 now has the hero recast as reaching Palestine and as a courageous visionary rather than the original quixotic figure of fun. Hebrew literature in this era thus exemplified the new nationalism following the pogroms of the 1880s. Bialik, in response to the pogroms of 1903-1906, carried out a comparable change in Hebrew poetry in his assertion of alienation from Russian assimilation and moral fervor in his "poems of wrath."

In summary, the Litvak religious tradition, exemplified by the Vilna Gaon, distinguished Litvak culture from neighboring Eastern European Jewish cultures. The challenge presented by Hassidism and then Haskalah produced a response within traditional Judaism in the form of reemphasis on intellectual study but also the mussar movement, which added an activist ethical component to religious training. The Haskalah, developing in the Russian Empire primarily in Lita from the 1840s, led to the revival of Hebrew and the beginnings of a secular and integrationist world view. The difficulties of Jewish life in the Pale found expression both in the Hebrew press and in a literature concerned with daily life. In the process were born both literary Hebrew and literary Yiddish. In the interim period during which the hold of religion had begun to decline but the idea of nationality had not yet reached its full flower, literature became the means of collective expression, fulfilling some of the functions of both religion and nationality. As it reported the realities of the life of the Pale, it also nurtured and exalted the collective aspirations of the people. Its mission was to portray Jewish life with uncompromising realism and yet to transcend the terms of the portrayal with an infusion of hope. The stage has been set for the development in the next generation of the secular responses to the plight of the Jews.[17]

1.2.2 The Transitional Generation, 1870-1900

In the 1870s and 1880s, as hopes for integration into Russian life evaporated, elements of the Haskalah were absorbed into a broad *national* response to the continued anti-Semitism. The intelligentsia focused increasingly on Jewish nationhood, a concept that ranged from Jewish culture and identity while remaining in Europe, to settlement in Palestine.

The seeds of Jewish involvement in national programs had been planted in earlier decades. The generation that came to maturity after 1870, however, took a more political stance. Their leaders were younger and more radical, holding populist and nationalist views that were also becoming commonplace among their non-Jewish European peers.[1] Crucial to the understanding of this more radical generation is the population explosion taking place with the expansion of the number of adolescents and young adults coincident with the tripling of the Jewish population between 1825 and 1897.[2]

Not everyone looked to nationalism for inspiration. Many turned to one of the other great nineteenth-century faiths—socialism. They argued that their responsibility was to improve conditions not only for the Jews but for all of the oppressed and the poor; the defining issue for them was class, not religion or even ethnicity. In turning to socialism, these Jews, a great many of them Litvaks, applied the values and familiar structures of their upbringing to new challenges. Both Jewish nationalism and Jewish-led socialism drew on Litvak cultural values to respond to worsening political and economic conditions particularly evident in Lita itself.

The recurrent pogroms in the southern provinces in 1881-1882 and, more particularly, the subsequent *May Laws* that limited Jewish residence in rural areas produced a profound change in Jewish thought and expectations. Promulgated after an investigating commission had found "Jewish exploitation" of the peasants in the small towns at fault for the pogroms, these "temporary" May Laws, in fact, lasted until 1917. They had the effect of nurturing Jewish radicalism throughout the Pale but especially in Lita where they had particular effect in bringing about urbanization. They also destroyed Jewish hopes for a positive future in Russia and in doing so,[3] emigration became the third major response to the worsening conditions as a compelling alternative to life in Russia.[4]

The Populist Movement

Jewish youths began to enter the Russian school system in significant numbers in the 1860s, after Tsar Alexander II decreed that Jews who had a university education could live outside the Pale. But Russian universities in the 1870s were incubators of radical ideas; the many student associations gave birth to a "culture of dissent," consisting of radical discussion groups, workers' cooperatives, and communes. Nor did radicalized students give up their fiery views when they left the university. Many of them went on to become professional revolutionaries.[5]

The first of what would be many radical study circles among Jewish young people across Russia was an informal study group established at the "crown" Vilna Rabbinical Seminary in the early 1870s. In the manner typical of yeshiva study, an independent study circle was formed but now to read and discuss the positivist Russian writers. Chernyshevsky's publication—*What Is to Be Done?*—which identified the need for radical change, had an enormous impact on the youth of that time. The students at Vilna felt a need to devote themselves to social equality and political freedom. Notable at this time for its universal aims, this was the start of a revolutionary tradition among Jewish students.[6]

Circles of radicalized students did not yet constitute an effective organization. Mark Natanson directed the transformation of these discussion groups into a well-structured movement with a programmatic platform, known as revolutionary populism. The son of a well-to-do merchant, Mark Andreyevich Natanson[7] was born in 1850 in the Lithuanian province of Kovno. While attending secondary school, he gave serious thought to effecting his own emancipation while contributing to the betterment of society. In the spring of 1869, Natanson was imprisoned for demonstrating against the tsarist government and was expelled from St. Petersburg Medical-Surgical Academy.

He was the leader of a study circle in St. Petersburg, however, and before he was again imprisoned in 1871, he brought about a change in its direction. Instead of going to the peasants, as the populists did, Natanson's circle went to the intelligentsia; instead of distributing explosives, they disseminated books. They created a network of self-education circles dedicated to the moral and intellectual improvement of Russia's radical youth. Natanson, like so many other idealistic young students, was influenced by Peter Lavrov's *Historical Letters*, published in St Petersburg in 1868-69, which argued that it was the moral duty of privileged individuals to dedicate themselves to the betterment of society. According to Lavrov, progress depended upon collective action by "critically thinking individuals." What was needed was the creation of a revolutionary cadre that would emphasize political organization and strategy. Natanson's program followed Lavrov regarding the importance of an intelligentsia conscious of social conditions who would struggle for civic liberties. A cardinal principle of this movement was the autoemancipation of the revolutionary cadre through acquisition of socially useful knowledge. This was one of the aims of the more radical Haskalah driven by a religiously inspired mission to "heal the world."[8]

By distributing dissident literature to self-education circles, radical students established organizational links all over Russia. The St. Petersburg women's circle was part of Natanson's organization, and a number of women took on leadership roles in it; the woman who became Natanson's wife was a member of this group. By the time of his rearrest and exile in November 1871, Natanson had developed the organizational structure and the ideology of a fledgling political party called the Land and Freedom Party. Faith in the simple Russian peasant, agrarianism, and communalism were the hallmarks of this movement. A network, almost entirely Jewish in membership, grew throughout the northwestern provinces, in Minsk and elsewhere. This network and the parent circle in Vilna constituted a sizable group of social-revolutionary populists. It is important to note that Jewish radicals were assimilationist at this point, but they entered the main stream of the revolutionary movement as a group; and Vilna, the center of Litvak culture, became the center of their revolutionary activity.

Over the next years, there were several permutations of the Land and Freedom Party (Zemlia i Volia). One such permutation, the Will of the People (Narodnaia Volia), provided the base for the terrorist organization that finally succeeded in assassinating Tsar Alexander II in 1881.[9] The viability of this party, despite continuous police harassment, derived in part from the successful operation of an underground printing press within Russia itself. It was run by Aron Zundlevich, one of the members of the first Vilna circle. Vilna itself, due to its location on the main railway line to the west and its proximity to the German border, remained the main point of entry for radical literature and communication with the émigré revolutionaries in London and Geneva.

The Jewish Revolutionary Movement

Although their Jewish background may have shaped their mode of operation in "study circles" and their commitment to social causes, the young Jewish revolutionaries saw themselves as cosmopolitans. They considered the *Jewish question* to be part of a larger problem, namely the liberation of all oppressed groups—Jewish workers included. The pogroms of 1881-1882 led to a moral crisis in Jewish revolutionary circles. The failure of the revolutionary movement to condemn anti-Semitism and, even more shocking, a proclamation by one member of the (Populist) executive committee of the Land and Freedom Party supporting the 1881 pogrom, produced a crisis of conscience among Jewish adherents to the revolution.

Tension would continue between the need to respond to the uniqueness of the Jewish nation and the needs of the wider community. Profound questions were raised: at what point did nationalism become chauvinism or obscurantism, at what point did universalism degenerate into a desertion of one's people in their hour of need? Was Russian or Yiddish or Hebrew to be the language of the Jewish future? This dilemma would recur in the history of Lita, and it would be carried by Litvak emigrants into their Diaspora.

For some, the Jewish masses were a suffering people analogous to the peasants. In the 1870s, Aaron Lieberman had been concerned about "going to the Jewish people." He had grown up in Lita in a family steeped in the Haskalah and Hebrew culture. While enrolled at the (crown) Vilna Rabbinical Seminary, he made contact with revolutionary circles there. Lieberman fled abroad in 1875, eventually joining Lavrov in London where he founded the first short-lived "Hebrew Socialist Union."[10] In 1876, before leaving London, he published *To The Intelligent Young Men of Israel,* a Hebrew socialist manifesto advocating revolutionary activity amongst the Jewish workers. Lieberman also published in Vienna a short-lived Hebrew journal *Ha-Emet* (the Truth), the first Jewish socialist publication. Only later, after the events of 1881, did Jewish students, now repentant sons returning to their Jewish identity, choose to lead the way amongst their own people as Lieberman had advocated.

Some of the students enlisted after 1881 in emigration movements to establish collectivist utopian settlements. One group emigrating to the United States was entitled *Am Olam* (Eternal People), inspired by an article published in Smolenskin's journal.[11] Although small in number and unsuccessful in their utopian agrarian colonies, *Am Olam* was very influential in the establishment of a Jewish socialist movement in the United States. They supplied that movement with its editors and organizers as well as some of its initial cadres. The United States was not the only destination, however. A smaller group, called BILU, an acronym derived from the Biblical injunction in Isaiah ("O house of Jacob, come ye and let us walk"), was the start of immigration to Palestine that was both secular and socialist. The BILU group brought new energy and commitment to the struggling Jewish settlements there. Both migrations were attempts to search for a middle way, both Jewish and collectivistic.[12]

Most Jewish modernizers continued to reject mass emigration; they believed that the solution to the Jewish Question would be found in autoemancipation, a new movement for Jewish renewal, discussed below, which focused not merely on individual self-betterment but the advancement of the community as a whole. With the failure of the liberal and more individualistic efforts at changing the conditions under which Jews lived, more radical and collectivistic ideas came to the fore.

The percentage of young Jews among those enrolled in the university system rose to 14 percent by 1886, with another 9 percent in gymnasia (secondary schools) and 6 percent in professional schools. During this period, the percentage of Jewish student radicals, according to records of arrests, was proportionate to their percentage of the total population of students. This situation changed after 1887, when a *numerus clausus* was instituted, a quota system that severely limited Jewish entry into higher education and the liberal professions.[13] In the generation after 1887, as hopes for social mobility dwindled, the percentage of Jewish radicals rose sharply relative to their percentage of the total population of students. Restrictions on university entry also produced a cohort of "externs," persons studying on their own, and led Jewish prospective students to settle in colonies of exiles in central and western Europe where they were more likely to find opportunities for study. These freer settings became centers for revolutionary thinking.

The joining of the revolutionary student cadres and the Jewish masses would, in the next decades, be the basis for development of the Jewish Labor Movement as well as for commitment to ideologically based renewal in Zion. That these movements developed in Lita was partly due to the severity of the economic distress there, it also drew on the serious religious impulse of the area. The religious tradition of Lita was now directed by the influence of the Haskalah toward improving life in the present rather than awaiting the messiah.

Renewal in Zion

Autoemancipation was the title of a pamphlet written in September 1882 by Leo Pinsker, a physician in Odessa. Pinsker's message (in German) was that "a people without a territory is like a man without a shadow: something unnatural, spectral." In addition, he reminded his readers that in Judaism, there is no personal salvation, but there is only collective salvation that will be achieved by a collective return of an entire people This was a new motif; earlier immigrants to Palestine had been religious Jews who settled in the centers of Tiberias, Hebron, and Jerusalem, dependent on charity from Jewish communities elsewhere. The other new motif, different from that of Western European emancipatory politics, was the focus on nationhood as a unifying factor rather than religion, however ultimately dependent upon quasi-messianic utopian thinking.[14]

Many local committees were formed in Russia to encourage the "productive" settlement of Jews on the land in Eretz Israel. The largest center of activity was in Odessa, evidence of Pinsker's personal prestige, but there were local committees in almost all Jewish communities throughout the Russian Empire. Their members were mainly drawn from the middle classes. In 1887, the name Hibbat Zion (Lovers of Zion) was attached to these committees. However, police repression of all organizational activity forced them to give a charitable cast to their efforts, which limited their effectiveness. Indeed the official name of the society, when legalized in 1890, was Society for the Support of Jewish Farmers and Artisans in Syria and Palestine. It succeeded in establishing a few settlements in the land under Ottoman rule. In addition, it constituted a reservoir of support upon which Theodore Herzl would draw when he called for the creation of a Jewish state in 1897.[15]

Jewish renewal in Palestine required not only a Jewish presence there but an even more difficult psychological transformation. This was seen clearly in the work of Asher Ginsberg. Born in 1856, he grew up on a country estate near Berdichev managed by his father. Ginsberg rejected his father's Hassidism and followed a common trajectory in identifying himself first as a mitnaged and then as a freethinker. He taught himself Russian and the other major European languages and studied their literature. Like many of the freethinkers described earlier, Ginsberg moved to Odessa in 1886.[16]

Concerned about the dangers of assimilation, he became committed to Jewish nationalism in the Lovers of Zion movement. A group of disciples gathered around Ginsberg to form a semi-secret group, the B'nai Moshe Society. [17] B'nai Moshe blended Russian revolutionary and romantic nationalist philosophies. Its members proclaimed the primacy of national consciousness over religious sentiment and of national interest over individual pursuits in ways reminiscent of those who founded later secular collective settlements in Palestine. Ginsberg published his views in Way of Life in 1891. "Not a single Jew should be able to take delight in his personal happiness as long as his nation's fate hangs in the balance . . . A revitalized generation . . . will arise that will . . . take pride in its people, glory in the honor of its nation . . . Such a generation will save Israel."[18]

Under his pen name, Ahad Ha'am (one of the people), Ginsberg published an article in 1889 in the Hebrew journal *HaMelitz* that marked the start of his literary career, carrying him ultimately to a preeminent position in the tiny world of Hebrew letters. Now that the Jewish people had the opportunity to return to its foundations in Palestine, the dominant role played in exile by religion would be nearing its end. Instead, the Yishuv (the Jewish settlement) would be a spiritual and cultural center for the Diaspora. In defining the character of that settlement, battle lines were drawn between the Orthodox and the secularist Jews within the Hibbat Zion, the latter led by Ahad Ha'am and Moshe Lilienblum.[19]

Yiddish Nationalism and Cultural Autonomy

A variety of linguistic and religious communities inhabited these *Lithuanian* lands during the nineteenth century when they were part of the Russian Tsarist Empire. The ethnic mix of Vilna and its surroundings had an impact on the later history of the relationship between the Russian-speaking Jewish intelligentsia and the mass of Yiddish-speaking Jews. The potential for the connection between them was greater in Lita than in rest of Poland, for Lithuanian and Belorussian peasant cultures held no value for the class of educated Jews. Unlike the central Polish provinces where there was a potential for assimilation into a dominant attractive alternative Polish culture, the opportunity for assimilation into a Russian-speaking middle class was less available in the northwestern provinces where there was no indigenous Russian population. With relative loss of the advantages of Russification to facilitate entry into the larger Russian society, Yiddish became the language of choice.

Many Jewish leaders believed that the problems of the Pale would not be solved in Palestine and emigration outside Russia. Chaim Zhitlowsky and Simon Dubnow both sought to provide a basis for Jewish spiritual and cultural survival in the secular world outside of Palestine. Commitment to the existence of the Jewish people arose in the context of the more widespread commitment to humanism to the mutual development of all peoples. The result was a flowering of Yiddish language and culture that came to be known as Yiddishism and that would form a major strand in the Litvak Diaspora.

Chaim Zhitlowsky was born in 1865 in the Vitebsk region of Lita. Eighty percent of the people in his town were Jews, giving Zhitlowsky the feeling of living in a self-contained Jewish land. His father was a wealthy timber merchant. Although affiliated with the Lubavitcher movement, the elder Zhitlowsky would attend operas during business trips to places such as Riga. He also read the literature of the Haskalah and wrote Hebrew poetry and spoke only Yiddish in his home.

Young Zhitlowsky found himself alienated from rabbinical Judaism, but he maintained deep admiration for the prophetic, ethical ideals of traditional Judaism. By 1879, at age fourteen, he described himself as an atheist and revolutionary socialist. Immersed in Chernyshevski's *What Is to Be Done?* he took an active role in the local student group of the People's Will. His early commitment to populism underlay his lifelong support of agricultural transformation of the Jewish people.[20] Zhitlowsky's first essay, published in Russian in 1887, was "Thoughts on the Historical Destiny of Judaism." Focusing on the social and moral ideals of the prophets, he identified the chief dangers to the Jewish people to be rabbinism, assimilationism, and Zionism. He called for Jewish intellectuals to help in the communal effort for national renewal within the boundaries of Russia. He then studied for a time in Germany and Zurich where he received a doctorate in Jewish philosophy. The second version of this essay appeared in 1892, this time published in Yiddish, and thus more accessible to the masses, entitled "A Jew speaks to Jews" ("A Id tsu idn").

Zhitlowsky believed the Yiddish language to be a bridge between the Jewish and socialist worlds. It was also a strong defense against both religious traditionalism and Zionism. Protected against assimilation by the adoption of Yiddish as their language of education and culture, Jews would be free to develop a modern, secular ethos. Yiddishism stressed Judaism as a culture without need for literal belief in the stories of the Bible and with a humanism that all peoples were inherently of equal value that was at odds with the "chosen people" notion of the religious. It became particularly wedded to the concurrent development of socialism.[21] In 1908, he participated in the famous conference at Czernowitz where standards were established for Yiddish grammar and spelling. In the years following his arrival in the United States in 1910, Zhitlowsky had considerable influence in establishing the important role of Yiddish in the class struggle as well as in the emergence of Labor Zionism.

The writings of Simon Dubnow were also influential on the development of Jewish national identity in the Diaspora. For Dubnow, the key to developing a modern Jewish identity lay in understanding, through history, how a people maintained its identity, morale, and ethos over time.[22] Born in 1860, Dubnow was raised in Mstislav, a tiny shtetl in Mogilev province in Belorussia. One of ten children, he came from a long line of rabbis. In his manner of living, as well as in the content of his work, he embodied his intellectual Litvak heritage. Educated in Russian, he was a voracious reader of modern Hebrew literature and of European literature in Hebrew translation. By age thirteen, he was considered to be a *freethinker*. However, due to restrictions on entry by Jews, unable to enter a secondary school and receive a diploma, he could not receive a university education. Instead, he was an autodidact, studying independently the works assigned in courses and replicating the actions of his mitnagdic forbears in their devotion to Torah study by his own ascetic pursuit of secular knowledge.[23]

As early as 1882 he wrote, "My life's task has become clear to me: to spread historical science and work especially on the history of the Russian Jews."[24] In 1883, he joined the staff of the monthly *Voskhod* (*Sunrise*), the major forum of Jewish Russian-speaking intellectuals. In the language wars between the adherents of Hebrew and Yiddish, Dubnow considered Hebrew to be the more important Jewish national language. He valued Yiddish for its role in strengthening Jewish national life in the Diaspora, but unlike Zhitlowsky, he did not advocate Yiddishism as a dogma. With his long view of history, he understood that Yiddish had been in use for only several hundred years and might lose its force in the future.

His ten-volume *World History of the Jewish People* began to appear in 1901. In his historical writings, Dubnow made a crucial distinction between the state on one hand and people or nationality on the other.[24] He argued that *autonomism* was the modern synthesis between the isolation created by religious Orthodoxy and the assimilation of his own day, as seen in Western

Europe. The concept of *autonomy* seemed to be particularly relevant since most Jews lived in multinational empires, such as Russia and Austria-Hungary. Dubnow found his models for self-government in the Lithuanian vaad or council and the community kahals.[25] His theoretical principles were expressed in the *Folkists*, a short-lived Jewish peoples' party after the Revolution of 1905. Skeptical of political Zionism, Dubnow shared the ideas of Asher Ginsberg (Ahad Ha'am), with whom he was associated from 1890 to 1903 in Odessa. After 1903, he lived in Vilna and St. Petersburg before moving to Berlin. When Hitler came to power, he moved to Riga where he was killed by the Nazis in 1941.

Dubnow remained a child of the 1860s and 1870s, a liberal in an age increasingly devoted to revolution, an advocate of the whole Jewish people rather than a Zionist, and opposed to the class divisions of the Marxists and Bundists. His focus on secular Jewish national identity was an important part of Litvakia's legacy of *Yiddishkayt*, which would become particularly important amongst those emigrating. Like Zhitlowsky, Dubnow attempted to establish a new Jewish self-consciousness in order to build collective identity among those alienated from traditional Judaism.[26] His impact can be measured in part by the increased interest in the study of folk culture exemplified by the Russian Jewish Ethnographic Society founded in St. Petersburg in 1908. This society carried out field studies for the collection of artifacts under S. Ansky just prior to World War I. Dubnow was also a participant in the founding of the Yiddish Scientific Institute (YIVO) in Wilno in the interwar period.

The Jewish Labor Movement

The Jews in Lita were predominantly artisans, such as tailors and workers in wood and leather. Jewish workers were concentrated in the cities where they increasingly lost status through becoming factory workers (proletarianized) and where they endured deep poverty. The common bonds of religion and the Yiddish language created Jewish labor solidarity and, at the same time, they distanced Jewish workers from the emerging Russian proletariat.[27] In the 1880s, the many Jewish worker study circles in the area around

Minsk, led by intellectuals, aimed to create a cadre of trained workers who would spread propaganda among their fellow workers. Although the Jewish intellectuals were not initially interested in founding a specifically Jewish movement, the circles they led were attended almost exclusively by Jewish workers. The attendees were mostly advanced craftsmen such as printers, engravers, jewelers, and watchmakers eager for learning. The Jewish labor movement that took shape in the Pale during the following decade of the 1890s was built by these Jewish students organizing socialist activity among their own people.

The Jewish labor movement was, at its beginning, almost exclusively a Lita phenomenon. As it spread to other centers, such as Warsaw, its leaders typically came from Vilna and conducted their activity within the community of workers of Litvak origin. Even at its peak, the movement remained strongest in Lita, where it played a particularly important role in the smaller towns. The strength of the Jewish labor movement in Lita was due to the particular conditions in that region. Proletarianization was proceeding rapidly; there were more unskilled workers and more poorly paid women workers than elsewhere. The new mechanized factories, owned by Gentiles, did not hire Jewish workers. Even when the Jewish-owned plants became more mechanized, Jewish workers were *evicted*. In both cases, Gentile workers objected to the presence of Jews and employers argued that the Jewish observance of Saturday as the day of rest made it impossible to employ Christians and Jews in the same mechanized factory.

Bialystok, the most highly industrialized city in the northwest provinces, was the center of labor agitation. As early as 1882, Jewish weavers staged a successful strike there. The early strike movement was sporadic, however, and failed to develop either permanent organizational features or long-range goals. An organized labor movement developed only when Jewish socialists from the intelligentsia from places such as Vilna established contact with the proletariat. During 1888-1889, in both Vilna and Minsk, these socialist students organized *kassy* or self-help funds within the various craft groups. These new organizations of journeymen differed from the old guild system or *chevra*, which had united masters and journeymen within a craft for religious and social needs. When workers joined a *kassy*, they, in effect, broke away from the masters and declared that the class interests of the workers outweighed their identity as tailors or shoemakers or even as Jews.

The student-led labor movement began to acquire a political cast and an organizational structure. In 1891, a group of young intellectuals organized the Jewish Social Democratic Group (the Vilna Group) in Vilna. This new generation, most of whom had been blocked in their attempts to study for the professions, looked for more radical answers than their predecessors. A majority of these younger leaders were born in Vilna, while the others came from the adjoining provinces of Kovno and Grodno.

The group was still young, the eldest barely twenty, when Marxist ideas began to spread in Russia. George V. Plekhanov, a former populist, reinterpreted Marxism to explain the conditions in Russia in the early 1880s. His work, *Our Differences*, reached Minsk and Vilna by 1887. The scientific cast of Marxism, built on detailed economic theory, appealed to the Jewish socialists in Lita, many of whom had pursued some sort of advanced scientific study.

The earliest published account of the Jewish labor movement, *Four Addresses of Jewish Workers*, was published in Switzerland in 1893. It documented that May Day was celebrated in Vilna for the first time in 1892 when several Social Democrats spoke at a secret meeting in the forest. Several workers spoke who were members of the Jewish Social Democratic circles in Vilna. At least one of the speakers emphasized the distinctive consciousness of a struggle involving a Jewish proletariat.

Around 1893, the focus of the Marxist leadership shifted away from educating small groups of workers to becoming directly involved in their economic struggle. The move from education by the elite toward workers' agitation necessitated a parallel move from the use of Russian to the use of Yiddish. Gozhansky, one of the Vilna Social Democratic group, wrote the next year *Letter to the Agitators*, asserting that Jewish workers, and Jews in general, constituted a distinct group. Since the student radicals' goal was to instill political consciousness, it followed that knowledge of Yiddish was required to reach the workers.

Julius Martov (Tsederbaum), then in exile in Vilna, called—in his 1895 May Day speech—for the development of national as well as class consciousness among Jewish workers. He advocated a separate Jewish workers' organization to act in the struggle for economic, civil, and political liberation This new national-proletarian trend laid the groundwork for the program of what became the Bund. The characteristics of the Jewish intelligentsia in the Vilna region was a factor in the strength of the movement there.[28] Almost all of the intellectuals understood Yiddish, and many of them spoke it (or had wives who were fluent.) From the early days of the labor movement, there was significant cooperation between the intellectuals and worker groups in Vilna. The "semi-intelligentsia" were an influential group relatively unique to Lita. It was drawn from the large number of students once enrolled in the Lithuanian yeshivas. These former students, some affected by the mussar movement, infused the worker movement with Jewish knowledge, spirit, and feeling. These new recruits, far more steeped in Yiddish than the more Russified intellectuals, had a more deeply felt tie to the Yiddish-speaking populace and became a major component of the labor movement

The idea that Yiddish would be at the heart of a Jewish labor movement had already been introduced in England, in the immigrant communities of London's East End. The writings of Lieberman, printed in England, had been smuggled back into Russia. Further, a self-supporting Yiddish press and a Yiddish-speaking trade union movement were flourishing on the East Side of New York. These movements, like the Jewish labor movement in Lita, focused on mobilizing community support and an acute sense of class interest against employers. The organized labor movement grew steadily in Lita between 1894 and 1897. The most dramatic gains were in Vilna where a high percentage of the Jewish population was working class. In the tanning and bristle industries, for example, workers took the lead in developing industry-wide unions. Strike activity increased too. In 1895-96, fifty-six strikes took place in Vilna alone. Despite the fact that free speech and assembly were denied in Russia, both flourished on a small scale; in some cities, particular streets became centers of resistance activity.

Starting in 1894, Vilna activists founded socialist labor groups in other cities, such as Bialystok, and revitalized the organization in Minsk. The Vilna organization became the de facto leader of

Jewish social democracy in the northwest provinces. In August 1897, a Yiddish underground newspaper, *Der Arbeiter Stimme* (*the Worker's Voice*) was founded; it was to be the voice of the Jewish labor movement until 1905. The capstone of all this activity came in October 1897 with the establishment in Vilna of the *General Jewish Workers' Union of Russia, Poland and Lithuania*, known to the world over as the Jewish Socialist Bund.

The backbone of the Bund was the *kassy*, which had begun as workers' self-help groups but had evolved into underground trade unions by the late 1890s. The directorate of each city organization provided centralized control. In Vilna, for example, the original *Vilna group* became the directing committee. Its members, including intellectuals and committed Marxists, lent a political cast to the economic struggle. It is remarkable that these labor organizations survived and even flourished since all worker combinations were strictly prohibited in Russia. The organizational strength created in Lita was unique within the Russian Empire. Economic benefits were not the only objective. Most strikes were fought for a shorter workday and for employee rights. Given the general economic depression and the ready availability of strikebreakers, many strikes had only transitory effects. They did produce one lasting effect, however, a cleavage along class lines between the Jewish employer and employee. The workers became deeply suspicious that the rabbinate was supporting their class enemies, thus establishing an anticlerical cast to the movement that persisted.

Study circles had been particularly important to female factory workers who were cut off from other sources of education. It is estimated that as many as one-third of the members of the Jewish workers' movement were women who carried out the revolutionary tasks of education and propaganda alongside the men and who served as couriers and distributors of illegal literature. Strikes in the clothing and cigarette factories, which employed mostly women, were among the most successful. One of the fruits of the labor movement was greater equality between the sexes; within the movement itself, a number of Jewish socialist groups accorded women equal status with men. This experience was replicated among those emigrating, and female political action was one of the hallmarks of the Litvak Diaspora.[29]

The failure of strike agitation to change the conditions of workers led to other activities more radical in nature, particularly political agitation with a view to political revolution. Jewish workers were particularly responsive since their economic difficulties stemmed from their exclusion from settlement outside the Pale and other political restrictions.

The Jewish labor movement moved onto the national stage in March, 1898, when the Russian Social Democratic Labour Party (RSDLP) was founded. Because of its relative success, the Jewish labor movement could not be considered a mere adjunct to the embryonic RSDLP. The strategic value of the northwest region near the border, so convenient for transporting underground literature from abroad, gave the Bund significant leverage, and it entered the RSDLP as an *autonomous organization*.

It was given complete independence, however, "only in questions which specifically concern the Jewish proletariat."

The culture of the Jewish labor movement had a major impact on Lita and would be carried by emigrants throughout the Diaspora. It offered its followers a new way of life. It had its own institutions and its own ceremonies, infused with a sense of community, such as the singing of the anthem, "The Oath," with the sacred scrolls or the prayer shawl. Its new morality included a strict code of sexual behavior for young men and women, who now met as equals. The bearers of a holy mission, like Zionism, its great rival, it instilled new pride in Jewish ethnic identity. It raised the use of Yiddish to a new level of dignity. In the long run, the Yiddish language became the symbol of the separate quality of the movement. After 1905, the Bund began to champion Yiddishism The Jewish labor movement became a spiritual home for thousands of workers, men and women who firmly believed in its creed of Jewish particularism and Marxist internationalism.

Emigration from LITA

At the time of its only census in 1897, these northwestern provinces of the Pale we call Lita contained approximately 1.5 million Jews.[30] Almost exclusively agricultural and economically backward area, Jews monopolized the minimum of commerce and crafts while there was loss of opportunities as industrialization occurred during the latter half of the nineteenth century. Although the percentage of Jews was greatest in these provinces, its relative proportion of the Jewish population of the tsarist empire had fallen over the years. Migration had occurred both to more prosperous Southern areas of the Pale, to the Polish provinces, and also outside the Russian Empire. Proverbial was the Litvak melamed who went to the more southerly provinces in search of a livelihood. (See Poem by Mani Leib)[30] Beginning in the 1860s, substantial numbers of workers migrated to the new industrial centers in Poland, such as the area around LODZ. As many as 250,000 Litvaks went to central Poland in the last quarter of the nineteenth century.[31] Clearly identified as Litvaks, the newcomers to Warsaw and Lodz disseminated both revolutionary and Zionist ideas. A large proportion of Bundists in these areas were emigrés from Lita.[32]

The earliest large-scale emigration to the west and overseas was also from Lita. In 1868, for example, a particularly severe outbreak of cholera swept northwestern Russia; famine followed the next year, chiefly in the provinces of Kovno and Suwalki in Lita.[33] The Paris-based *Alliance Israélite Universelle* set up a coordinating committee to provide relief. In addition, it offered emigration as an option. This was one of the earliest waves of emigration, though it was small compared to what came later.

Large-scale emigration from the Russian Empire started in the 1880s. The pogroms of Easter 1881 occurred mainly in the southern provinces of the Pale. In the summer and fall, refugees flooded across the Austrian border. The response to the crisis focused on relief, but a small number of the refugees were sent on through Hamburg to the United States. In total, twenty-five thousand Russian Jews entered the United States in 1881-1882. West European Jewry funded organizations that lowered the cost of transit and encouraged emigration, so long as it was to go outside Europe.

There existed widespread opposition to emigration, both in Russia; and in the United States. Russified members of the Jewish community, for example, felt that Jews should remain in Russia in order to fight for rights there. Similarly, opposition to immigration existed within the Jewish communities in the

United States as well as in Western and Central Europe where it was believed that immigrants would jeopardize the position of Jews already settled there. Nonetheless, the stream of emigrants continued to grow and expanded mainly, but not limited, to the English-speaking world. In the absence of subsidized emigration, individual sponsorship took over. The usual pattern was for men already living in a country to support the immigration of family members. When the stream became a flood, emigrants benefited from the competition among steamship companies, which resulted in lower fares.

In the 1890s, the Russian government further tightened the restrictions on Jews. In 1891, for example, Jews who had been allowed to live in Moscow were expelled. In this period, emigration surged once again. Before 1892, Jewish emigration from Russia was prohibited; special permission, which often required connections and bribery, had to be secured. Even after the government legalized emigration, many continued to leave illegally, smuggled across the Prussian border so close to Vilna. It was a less-expensive option; for draft evaders and those escaping the police, it was the only way. The accelerated push toward emigration during the 1890s was also the product of worsening economic and social conditions. The start of industrialization and railway building in Russia in the 1890s caused further dislocation and pauperization of the many Jews who lived in small market towns, increasing moves to the larger towns. These larger towns in Lita had exceptionally high concentrations of Jewish artisans who could not compete with the factories.

Economic hardship increased even more as the population grew. It was estimated in 1898 that 20-25 percent of the families in Lita requested Passover assistance. With increasing poverty, there was also loss of opportunity in the traditional religious structure as many former teachers and rabbinical students faced the prospect of entering the lower social class of artisans At the same time that conditions worsened in Russia, increased awareness of opportunities in the west escalated the pull to emigrate along with the decrease in relocation costs and support from earlier emigrants. Given these factors, the overwhelming number of immigrants leaving the Pale of Settlement before the turn of the century were from Lita.[34] However, large-scale emigration did not markedly lower the population of the northwest provinces of the Pale of Settlement, given the Russian Jews' high birthrate and relatively low death rate. It did, however, change the composition of the remaining population. By removing a large number of people between twenty and forty, it deprived the established Jewish communities of young, enterprising, and skilled members. A report from Kovno noted that "the majority of Jewish artisans left our city to cross the ocean."[35]

The migration of this later period was primarily a movement of families measured by the ratio of females and children under fourteen to males. Those who were well-off, those too poor to pay for passage, and those more traditional in their religious practice tended to remain in Lita. Increasingly, those who had migrated affected those who remained behind in the "core," providing them with financial support and with accounts of life elsewhere.

An active attempt was made to divert immigration to countries other than the United States due to beginnings of restrictions to immigration there. In addition to the ongoing immigration to Britain and France in Western Europe, there was particular interest in South Africa. The Jewish Colonization Association (JCA), founded in 1891 by the wealthy Austrian railroad builder Baron de Hirsch, encouraged immigration to Argentina and Canada as countries seeking agricultural settlers.[36] This was related to the other efforts by the JCA to modify the occupational distribution of the emigrants, emphasizing agricultural skills more widely sought by countries in the New World. In addition, the JCA, in collaboration with Edmond de Rothschild, supported agricultural settlements in Palestine; and funds later went to support agricultural colonies and vocational training in Russia. These and other attempts by the JCA to "productivize" the Jewish masses, while supporting emigration, continued throughout this period.[37]

It is estimated that between 1869 and 1898, 50,000 people migrated from the provinces of Kovno and Vilna alone to the United States. Another 250,000 followed from these same provinces in the interval that ended in 1914. An even larger number came from the entire area of Lita, including the provinces of Belorussia, thus providing a substantial percentage of those emigrating from the Russian Empire, not only to the

United States, but throughout the world. The Jews of Lita brought with them their relatively autonomous cultural life, complete with their two national languages of Hebrew and Yiddish, their developed sense of collective responsibility and their emerging political groupings. They were citizens of what could be called the Vilna-Minsk Fatherland.

1.2.3 The Generation of Revolution and War 1900-1920.

At the turn of the century, Vilna occupied a singular position in the cultural life of the Pale. On the one hand, it was the center of rabbinical religious Orthodoxy; on the other, it was the hub for new developments in Jewish secular life. "Yiddishkayt," Socialism, and Zionism were the secular offspring of the Haskalah. These movements themselves subdivided, creating new strands of thought and action: religious Zionism, secular Labor Zionism, international socialism, and particularist Jewish socialism. These new movements were carried from Lita throughout the world in the large-scale emigration of these years.

The infamous pogrom of 1903 in Kishinev, Bessarabia, was not the only violence experienced by Russian Jews at the turn of the twentieth century. Pogroms continued into the months following the revolution of 1905. The violence and the dashing of revolutionary hopes produced a mighty surge of emigration that continued until the outbreak of the First World War.[1] The wave crested twice, in 1904-08 and in 1913-14; during these peak periods, more than 125,000 Jews entered the United States annually. Canada, South Africa, and Argentina also received record numbers of Jews during this period, though the numbers were much lower than the U.S. immigration figures. A far smaller, but significant, number emigrated to Palestine.

The Hibbat Zion and Herzlian Zionism

The return to Zion was not, as it turned out, accomplished under the auspices of Hovevei Zion. It was Theodore Herzl who created Zionism as a political movement, and at the time he formulated his ideas, he had neither heard of the Hibbat Zion movement nor read Pinsker's work. Herzl interpreted the *Dreyfus* case as a failure of emancipation, defined his program over a short time before publishing his book, *Der Judenstaat* (*The Jewish State: An Attempt at a Modern Solution of the Jewish Question*) in February 1896.

Herzl's goal was to organize the Jewish nation for exodus and resettlement in a country they could call their own. His preferred site was Palestine, but other places, such as Argentina and later Uganda, were seen as possible alternatives. Herzl had counted on rich and influential Jews such as Baron Rothschild and Baron de Hirsch to fund the creation of the state, but he failed to gain their support. Instead, Herzl sought a popular Mandate by convening a congress, presenting it with a program, and establishing the machinery for the mobilization of a mass membership.[2]

Herzl called for a public congress to be held in 1897. The notion was controversial; response from the Russian Lovers of Zion movement was initially negative. Not only were they resentful of a newcomer in a field that they had pioneered, but they were concerned as well about the viability of the few settlements established under the auspices of Baron Rothschild and the Hibbat Zion. In addition, many Eastern European Jews had deep reservations about Herzl's methods; the "noise" he was making in advocating his program was reminiscent of the false messiahs of the past.[3]

Approximately 200-250 people attended the First Zionist Congress in Basle in late August 1897. Many of the attendees from Eastern Europe had belonged to Hibbat Zion. Some of the Russian delegates failed to register officially for fear that they would be arrested on their return home. Most of the participants were educated—middle-class Jews, there were a few socialist Russian-Jewish students from German universities; Orthodoxy itself was barely represented. The result of the congress was the *Basle Program*, which called for "the creation of a home for the Jewish people in Palestine to be secured by public law." Its goals were "purposeful advancement of settlement in Palestine, organizing and unifying all Jewry and strengthening of Jewish national feeling and consciousness [while] . . . obtaining governmental consent as will be necessary to the achievement of aims of Zionism." [4] The program was significant because of two innovations: its political foundation—i.e., the obtaining of governmental consent—and the goal of enlisting world Jewry in support of the settlement in Zion. Major efforts would be launched to *capture the community* across the Diaspora.

Asher Ginsberg, founder of the B'nai Moshe Society, remained cool to Herzl's ideas. Although he attended the First Zionist Congress as an observer, he considered Herzl an upstart.[5] However, even to Ahad Ha'am, it was crucial that "some two hundred Jews from all countries and all tendencies had debated in the open . . . the matter of the foundation of a secure home for the Jewish people in the land of their fathers . . . [T]he national answer had been expounded to all the world aloud . . . and with a straight back—something that had not occurred since Israel was exiled from its land."[6] Lilienblum, his colleague from the secular leadership of the Hibbat Zion, was even more supportive.

Herzl maintained direct contacts with the Orthodox wing of Hibbat Zion. Particularly important was the support of Rabbi Shmuel Mohliver, whose grandson spoke on his behalf at the First Zionist Congress, endorsing the resettlement on the grounds that it fulfilled the commandments of the redemption in Zion. Rabbi Mohliver was born in the Vilna district and became the rabbi of Bialystok. He was unusual in that he entertained the possibility of rabbinical cooperation with Maskilim.[7] Mohliver made his most significant contribution to the development of Zionism in persuading Baron Edmond de Rothschild to commit financial support to the settlers in Palestine. Mohliver was well respected, and his support broadened the social base of Hibbat Zion. In return, the rabbinate was able to ensure that the settlements would observe Jewish law. He now transferred his support to the Zionist movement led by Herzl.

Zionism would later receive support from Rabbi Isaac Jacob Reines of Lida in Lithuania. He was the moving spirit behind Mizrahi (a spiritual center), which would eventually become part of the World Zionist Organization. Rejecting ultra-Orthodox opposition to settlement in Palestine prior to the coming of the messiah, Mizrahi reconciled religion with nationalism.[8] Like Herzl, the religious Zionists placed the political goal first, i.e. the rescue and resettlement of European Jewry. Mizrahi also supported the nonsocialist and neutral stance of the Herzlian program on cultural matters, leaving for later a discussion of the structure and quality of the society to be established. The relationship between religious Jews and Zionism was to have major implications for the evolution of the Jewish settlement in Palestine. Although the main Zionist headquarters were in Vienna, Herzl's message exerted its greatest mass appeal in the East. Herzl himself visited Vilna in the summer of 1903. Despite police restrictions, vast crowds assembled at the railway station and in the streets.[9] Two years later, the central committee of the Russian Zionist movement was moved to Vilna in recognition of its Litvak leadership.

Zionism sought autoemancipation through an exodus from the Diaspora to Palestine. Many opposed Zionism on the grounds that it would discourage involvement in domestic politics. They believed that the distancing of Zionists from local politics would have the effect of strengthening reactionary governments. Thus the Bund attacked Zionism as a reactionary movement that diverted the Jewish masses from the barricades.[10] Zionism's response to the charge that it was abandoning the social and political struggle was *Labor Zionism*. Developed as a means of addressing the needs of Jews in the Diaspora, Labor Zionism was to have a long-lasting and profound impact on the future State of Israel.

The Socialist Strand in Zionism

Nachman Syrkin and Ber Borochov, Zionist historian and economist respectively, studied the needs of the Jewish worker and concluded that the interests of Jewish workers were fundamentally different from those of non-Jews and could not be represented adequately by the broadly based Social Democratic movement.

Nachman Syrkin, born into the middle class in Lita, received a traditional Jewish education but graduated from a Russian secondary school in Minsk. Syrkin joined the *Hovevei Zion* while maintaining contact with Russian revolutionary circles. As early as 1888, before Herzl appeared on the international scene, Syrkin had come to believe that the future lay in a synthesis of socialism and Jewish nationalism. Arrested for his activities, he went abroad to complete his studies; and in Berlin, he helped to found the Russian-Jewish Scientific Society from which many later Zionist leaders, including Chaim Weizmann, would emerge. Moving on to Berne, Syrkin pursued his study of philosophy, psychology, and history in a particularly intense fashion that was reminiscent of traditional Litvak scholarship.[11]

Although he was not an official delegate, Syrkin was one of the few representatives of socialist Zionism at the First Zionist Congress. He was primarily concerned with the form any Jewish settlement would take. His 1898 pamphlet, *The Jewish Question and the Socialist Jewish State*, advocated cooperative mass settlement of Jewish workers in Palestine. It would be both unthinkable and impractical to found a Jewish state on the basis of social inequality. It would fail because it would utilize cheap native labor to the detriment of Jewish labor and, thus, Jewish immigration. Moreover, unlike the utopian vision inherent in socialism, it would fail to respond to the powerful messianic hope that imbued Jewish life.[12] The Marxist explanation of historical development was not however the source of his belief in the ultimate achievement of social justice. Syrkin believed that the prophetic strain in Judaism could now be renewed. Individuals, acting as prophets and visionaries, have the power to affect the future; and Herzl appeared to him to be just such a figure.

The first left-wing Zionist groups appeared in Russia, in Minsk, sometime between 1897 and 1899. They took the name *Poalei Zion* from the Hebrew workers of Zion. Placing themselves in opposition to the Bund, they advanced the proposition that general social and economic progress in accordance with social democratic Marxism could not solve the special problems of Jewish workers.[13] Between 1897 and 1901, groups were formed by Zionist workers throughout the Pale.[14] In 1902, the major groups in the northwest provinces met in Minsk where they adopted a national platform and welcomed secessionists from the Russian social democrats as well as from the Bund.[15] The Poalei Zion, which was active inside Russia, was the only realistic choice for Russian Jewish workers who were interested in Zionist activism.[16] By 1903, Poalei Tzion activists had assumed an important role in the revolutionary struggle against the Tsar; and during the pogroms, they developed and led Jewish self-defense groups in Kishinev and other towns.

By 1906, the socialist wing of the Zionist movement had crystallized into several political parties. The Social Democratic Jewish Workers Party, Poalei Zion, under the leadership of Ber Borochov, was to be the longest-lasting group. It supported settlement in Palestine and rejected other possible territories, such as Uganda. It also emphasized the need for struggle in the Diaspora where Jews now lived. Initially elitist and middle class in its support, Poalei Zion became more working class and militant during the events of 1905; it transferred its leadership from Minsk and the southern Pale to Vilna in order to increase its ties with the laboring class.[17]

Borochov based his synthesis of Marxism and Zionism on a study of the economic conditions of the Jews that was published by the Jewish Colonization Association in 1904.[18] It was clear from this report that Jewish workers were disproportionately relegated to secondary sectors of the economy and were concentrated in technologically backward factories, jobs, and regions of the country.[19] Borochov elaborated a theory of nationality based on the relations between ethnic groups in a multiethnic society, which seemed to explain the detrimental distribution of Jewish workers within the Russian economy. He distinguished between the *territorial* nation, which occupies the primary stages of production (agriculture, mining, and heavy industry), and the *extraterritorial* minority nation confined to secondary and tertiary stages of production (consumer goods, trade, and financial transactions). Immigration without *territorialization,* that is, without control of the primary components of the economy, could only result in the perpetuation of the exploitation of a minority, such as the Jews, and their eventual exclusion. He felt that this problem would not be solved outside of Palestine, the only place where Jews had the opportunity to command the entire economy.[20]

The Bund and the Zionists each represented a vision of Jewish socialism. However, the Bund hoped to see Jewish workers part of an international socialist movement while the labor Zionists hoped to see the Jewish proletariat fulfilling the Zionist dream in Palestine. Syrkin criticized those Jewish socialists to whom "socialism meant, first of all, the abandonment of Jewishness just as liberalism of the Jewish bourgeoisie led to assimilation." The Labor Zionists also considered the Bund's "national" program half-hearted and ambiguous, not totally freed from the Left's well-established belief that nationalism was bourgeois and utopian.

Despite their ideological antagonisms, however, Bundists and labor Zionists resembled each other in their goal to remake Jewish traditional society and in their scorn for the traditional Jewish attitudes of accommodation and nonviolent resistance that had served them in the past but that were inadequate to the conditions of the new century. Zionists and Bundists alike extolled physical resistance and readiness to fight. After the Kishinev pogrom, and specifically in response to the pogrom in Gomel in Lita in 1903, the Labor Zionists began to organize its young men in armed self-defense groups. The Bund did the same. They were both in revolt against Jewish pietism and passive messianic acceptance of Jewish suffering.[21] The idea of self-defense spread from Europe to become a motif of the Jewish settlements in the Yishuv in this era and a major aspect of self-emancipation.

The Zionist movement is part of the legacy of Jews from Eastern Europe and particularly of those from Lita. Both the religious and socialist strands of Zionism found their support in Lita; and Zionist ideology was shaped by the religious, nationalist, and revolutionary traditions of the region. The Poalei Zion, in particular, provided the ideological foundation for the next wave of emigration to Palestine. The Second Aliyah of which they formed the core, starting in 1904, played an enormous role in the economic and spiritual development of the Yishuv. Committed to the worker's life in backward Palestine by their activities on the ground in the Yishuv, the Labor Zionists exerted their own special influence on the evolution of socialist Zionism in the Yishuv and elsewhere.[22]

The International Socialist Movement

The development of Jewish nationalism, whether Zionist or socialist, was markedly different from the nationalism outlined by Lenin in the larger Russian Social Democratic Labor Party (RSDLP), founded in 1898.

The Fourth Congress of the Bund in May 1901, in Bialystok, was a watershed in the evolution of its ideology. At this congress, the Bund resolved for the first time that social democracy should struggle against national as well as class oppression. The congress asserted that the Jews constituted a nation and were entitled to national-cultural autonomy. The Bund needed to distinguish itself from the Zionist nationalists and, at the same time, separate itself from the assimilationist tradition of socialism. Those in the more strongly national branch of the Bund, especially the expatriate student committees outside of Russia, were particularly concerned with *national* interests. Class consciousness remained predominant; however, the delegates condemned Zionist recruitment among workers as "inflaming the national sentiments of the workers, thereby threatening to obstruct the development of their class consciousness."[23]

At the Second Congress of the RSDLP in 1903, the Bund sought to reorganize the Russian party as a federation, reflecting national-cultural autonomy. The Bund itself wished to surpass the limited autonomy it had been given, "in relation to the Jewish proletariat" in 1898. Decentralization, however, was contrary both to Lenin's goal of assimilating national differences and to his short-term plans to forge the RSDLP into an elitist and unified all-Russian revolutionary party.

The role of Julius Martov (Iulii Osipovitch Tsederbaum) in this battle between the RSDLP and the Bund underscores the difficulties faced by Jews in resolving the conflict. His family history illustrates the degree to which a commitment to revolution had become almost universal among educated Jewish youth. Martov was born in 1875 in Constantinople where his father, a confirmed assimilationist, represented both the Russian Steamship Company and a St. Petersburg newspaper. Martov's grandfather, Alexander Tsederbaum, had been instrumental in establishing Hebrew literary life. He had founded a Hebrew weekly newspaper, *Ha-Meliz* (the Mediator) in Odessa, and a Yiddish weekly newspaper, *Kol Mevaser* (a Heralding Voice). *Kol Mevaser* was, for many years, the only Yiddish periodical that the tsarist censors allowed to be published.[25] In addition, the senior Tsederbaum was instrumental in obtaining a Russian charter in 1890 for the Lovers of Zion in the name of the "Association for the Aid in Colonization in Palestine and Syria."[26]

In the 1890s, Martov, along with his siblings and cousins, was active in student revolutionary circles in St. Petersburg. Expelled from university and now a Marxist, he was exiled to Vilna where he worked in the social democratic circles that became the basis of the Bund. It was he who, in 1895, spoke of the need for a separate Jewish workers' organization.[27] Returning to St. Petersburg, Martov was, from 1901 to 1905, on the editorial board of *Iskra* (the Spark), the journal of the Leninist faction. Lenin's mission was to weld together the Russian Social Democrats through "firm ideological unity" by appealing to Marxist Orthodoxy.[28]

Martov was among the Jewish members of the RSDLP who now opposed the Bund's national program. But the two groups were too far apart in another sense too: the focus of the Leninist faction was to develop a cadre of revolutionaries to take power while the focus of the Bund was on the party's broad base. The differences were too many and too deep; the Bund was expelled from the Russian Party at its Second Congress in 1903. The battle was joined, and it would be carried by emigrants from Litvakia into the Diaspora.

Before the end of the long struggle at the RDSDP's Second Congress, Martov himself fell into the same trap as the Bundists. He was not prepared to support the Bund to keep them in the party, but without their support, he was defeated on a separate motion, opposing Lenin's bid for personal domination. In the absence of the Bundist delegates, Martov's faction was transformed from the majority into the minority (or Menshevik) faction. Lenin's faction now became the majority (Bolshevik) faction with far-reaching consequences.[29]

Yiddish Socialist Movement

In December 1904, in the midst of the unrest resulting from the Russo-Japanese War, the Bund issued a proclamation that "the order of the day is the liquidation of the Autocracy." A month later, in January 1905, a delegation of workers assembled to present a peaceful petition to the Tsar was attacked by soldiers in front of the Winter Palace in St. Petersburg. *Bloody Sunday* was followed by strikes in which the Bund took an active role. It enlisted Russian and

Polish workers in general strikes in the northwest provinces around Vilna and Kovno where the Jewish presence was strong.

The tsarist manifesto of October 17, 1905, promised basic freedoms, legislative veto by the Duma, and a broader franchise. Liberal hopes appeared to be on the verge of fulfillment. However, the victory celebrations during the autumn of 1905 provided the setting for a new series of anti-Jewish pogroms.[30] The government, which had stood by during the pogroms of the 1880s, now actively fomented them. All socialist parties now took defense against anti-Semitic violence as one of their central roles, but they suffered heavy casualties when fighting regular army detachments.[31] It was not uncommon for soldiers to fire into crowds, adding to the slaughter.

In November 1905, the ferment continued. "Vilna was boiling like a kettle. Every day new trade unions held their founding meetings and workers clubs were opening."[32] The radicalization of Jewish life spread to include even the St. Petersburg Jewish notables. Their organization (OPE) abandoned its long-established Russification program with the substitution of Yiddish as the main pedagogical language.[33]

Many Jews had believed that relief from their plight would come with an end to tsarist despotism. The outbreak of state-supported pogroms at the very time that the revolution seemed to be succeeding was devastating. The violence weakened the support of the Jewish masses for the Bund. In 1906, the Bundists revealed their weakness by seeking readmission to the RSDLP.[34] During 1905-07, the Bund also began to emphasize its roots in Jewish life. It published in Vilna a very successful Yiddish daily newspaper (*Volkszeitung*).[35] Yiddish translations of secular classics and of political treatises became available. Neighborhood and urban libraries were open to workers, along with special evening celebrations, lectures, and Saturday readings. Yet Yiddish still did not replace Russian as the language of Bund conferences until shortly before World War I.

The influence of the Bund during this entire period was widespread, extending into the smaller towns throughout Lita. One such town was Swislowz in Belorussia near Bialystok in the Grodno district. Its population in 1897 was three thousand, two-thirds of them Jews.[36] The Bund was first organized there in 1900 and, by 1905, had become a powerful organization with membership drawn from all segments of the community. It had called several successful strikes in the leather factories, the major industry of the town. The Bund was also involved in the agitation in the town surrounding the Revolution of 1905. Starting in 1907, however, after the failure of the revolution, the town experienced political oppression, economic depression, weakening of the trade unions, and an increase in emigration. Now families from Swislowz left to escape economic hardship, going to Canada, England, and the United States. It was not incidental that members of the Lewis family, who helped to establish the political arm of the Canadian labor movement, came from this town.

Despite these setbacks, the Bund remained intact throughout the period from 1895 to 1919-1921 when it was finally divided by the founding of the Third (Communist) International. This record can be attributed to a tendency of the Bund to reconcile differences in sharp contrast to the theocratic intolerance that characterized the Russian party under Lenin.

Among those who maintained the direction of the Bund through World War I was Vladimir Medem. He had been a leader of the *national* faction of the Bund in its struggle with the RSDLP in 1903. Medem was born in Courland to Lithuanian-Jewish parents who had converted to Christianity. Raised as Greek Orthodox, Medem was drawn in secondary school to his Jewish classmates. He was expelled from the University of Kiev for political activity and went to Minsk where he joined the Bund and became active in the workers' movement. When he was arrested in 1901, he identified himself as a Jew, and on his release, he went to Switzerland where he became secretary of the Bund organization in Berne.[37]

In 1904, Medem published "Social Democracy and the National Question," advocating a middle path between assimilation and nationalism but advocating that the state permits its constituent nationalities' genuine cultural choice. For Jews, this meant a Yiddish-speaking educational system and recognition of the interests of the Jewish working class in the Russian Pale of Settlement including the right of Jewish workers to rest on the Sabbath.[38] In 1906, the Bundist conferences became officially bilingual with translation of the Russian speeches into Yiddish. At the eighth Bundist congress in 1910, the *national* program was expanded to include more issues relating to language and culture. The Bund also committed itself to support cultural activities such as choruses and drama and literary circles. It was at this congress that the Bund adopted Yiddish as its official language. The Bund particularly led in the sponsorship of Yiddish schools.[39] Medem was arrested in Warsaw at the outbreak of the First World War but was released when the Germans occupied the city in 1915. He remained there until 1920 when he was instrumental in maintaining the Bund's adherence to the Socialist International in opposition to the Third (Communist) International.[40] The Bund's cultural program remained important; in 1921, a conference in Warsaw created the Central Jewish School Organization (known by its Yiddish acronym, Tsisho). This secular, national, and Yiddish-based school system had its largest following in Vilna where it was a pride of the city during the interwar period.

Medem's death in 1924 grieved thousands. His "unique history of returning to the Jewish people and his selfless devotion to the Bund, the austerity of his personal life, his gentleness, modesty and integrity."[41] gave Medem greater stature than most political leaders of his generation possessed. On the day of his funeral, thousands of Jewish workers in Poland left their shops and factories to assemble in the middle of the day in one of the greatest tributes ever offered to a Jewish political figure.

By the early 1920s, the range of responses to the destruction of the traditional society of Lita could be identified. There was Zionism in all its forms, from religious to socialist, based on redemption of the ancestral land. There were also the more doctrinaire socialist responses, derived from Marx, that dealt with the plight of the Jew in the context of redemption within their own setting in Eastern Europe. The Bund, especially, represented commitment to the creation of a Jewish national self-awareness and to the cultural foundations of that awareness in interwar Poland that included the portion of eastern Poland that was part of Lita.[42] However, the dominant response in the late nineteenth and early twentieth centuries to the disintegration of traditional society and to recurrent violence was emigration. The emigrants from Litvakia brought to their new homelands the struggle for a just society and the debates about Jewish self-awareness and national identity. They also carried with them a cultural and religious tradition that would shape the debate from North America to Palestine.

1.2.4 The Interwar Generation 1920-1940

Life in Lita was severely disrupted during World War I when its territory became a battleground between the Russian and German armies. In the spring of 1915, many Jews were deported by the tsarist government from the northwest frontier areas based on the claim that they acted as spies for the enemy. It is estimated that 75-80 percent of the population was expelled, particularly west of the railway line leading to Kovno.[1]

The German occupation of Lita freed the Jews from tsarist oppression and permitted Jewish culture to thrive. When the Russian troops pulled out of Vilna on Yom Kippur 1915, many of the Russified leaders left with them. German authorities recognized the Jews as a nationality and Yiddish as a national language. A Yiddish-speaking drama troupe was established in Vilna along with a Yiddish newspaper.[2]

But the war brought many hardships. The distribution of relief grew beyond the capacity of existing charitable structures to respond, and their inability to meet the need brought about a change in the oligarchic leadership of the community. In 1918, for example, the first democratically elected Jewish community council (kehillah) took office in Vilna, elected by both male and female suffrage.[3]

Following World War I, the entire region we can now refer to as Litvakia continued to exist as a cultural entity, but it was no longer a political entity. The total Jewish population of what had been Lita was approximately one million. Parts of Lita were mainly incorporated into the Soviet Union, Poland, and Lithuania. The separation was complete; political rivalries prevented travel between these several entities. A small portion became part of newly independent Latvia. Under the provisions of the treaties establishing the several successor states of Poland, Lithuania, and Latvia, *national* rights were to be protected "educational committees, appointed locally by the Jewish communities," were granted the right to run primary schools in their own language and at state expense.

The Balfour Declaration and the British Mandate encouraged Palestine as a potential site for immigration. In response to the economic boycotts in Poland, large scale emigration occurred for a time to Palestine that formed the Fourth Aliyah in the 1920s. Opportunities for emigration to countries other than Palestine were limited by the strict quotas adopted by the United States and other English-speaking countries. France and Argentina were relatively open to Jewish immigration from Poland during the 1920s and took place from Lita as well as other parts of Poland. But as the depression took root in the early 1930s, doors closed everywhere—even to Palestine, even while anti-Semitism became more virulent.

The eastern portion of Belorussia, with its capital of Minsk, was incorporated into the Soviet Union. The approximately four hundred thousand Jews of Soviet Belorussia were cut off from the rest of the world. Under Stalin, emigration was no longer possible, nor was it even possible to maintain connections with Jews elsewhere. The experience of the Jews of Soviet Belorussia during the interwar period and the Second World War would parallel the experience of the Soviet Jews as a whole, culminating in the destruction of Jewish communal life.

Another four hundred thousand Jews from the old Lithuanian lands (eastern borderlands) found themselves within the boundaries of the new Polish state. In the new Poland, Jews from Lita were outnumbered by the far-larger Jewish population living in central Poland and Galicia. The Bund continued to be a strong Jewish cultural and political force within Jewish national politics in interwar Poland.[4]

Vilna, in particular, suffered in the early postwar period when it was successively occupied by the Soviets, the Poles, the Lithuanians, and again by the Poles. Its final capture by Poland in 1919 cut off Vilna from the new state of Lithuania that was created after World War I. Vilna, the ancestral capital of Lithuania and center of Jewish Lita, was now just one of several provincial cities in Poland; its name now rendered in Polish as Wilno.

Under the war hero Marshal Pi³sudski, Poland permitted a limited measure of Jewish life. Throughout the interwar period, however, there was considerable Polonization of the schools and of public life with official discouragement of the use of Yiddish and withdrawal of financial support from Jewish education. After Pilsudski's death in 1935, his successors not only encouraged economic boycotts of the Jews but anti-Semitic violence as well. Jewish students were increasingly mistreated by nationalistic Polish students or were excluded from the universities altogether.[5]

The new political state of Lithuania contained only the former provinces of Kovno, Suwalki, and a small part of what had been Courland. About 150,000 Jews were living within the borders of an almost entirely agricultural country, cut off from the ancient centers of Vilna (now within Poland) and Minsk (now within the Soviet Union). Travel between Vilna and Kaunas (formerly Kovno), the new Lithuanian capital, could only be accomplished through a third country, such as Latvia. For the entire interwar period, the Lithuanian government refused to accept the loss of its former capital and the division of its ancestral land. Only in 1939, through the short-lived Russo-German Pact and the partition of Poland at the outbreak of World War II, did Lithuania once again achieve control of its ancient capital, which it renamed Vilnius.

Most Jewish leaders welcomed the creation of a Lithuanian state in which Jews were promised relative autonomy. Minority rights were written into the peace treaty that established an independent Lithuania; it seemed that the Jews would have an opportunity to develop their national life. However, these minority rights were abrogated, starting in 1924. The Lithuanian government encouraged the development of an ethnically Lithuanian urban middle class to compete with, and ultimately to displace, Jewish businesses. Unlike Poland, the Lithuanian government did maintain state subsidies to Jewish schools, which flourished in Lithuania as nowhere else in eastern Europe.[6] In 1935, 80 percent of Jewish children in Lithuania attended Jewish schools, where they were taught either in Hebrew or in Yiddish.[7]

The proletarian centers that had sustained the political Left were now outside the boundaries of Lithuania; and Marxist groups, such as the Bund, were far less prominent in Lithuania between the wars than in Poland. A higher percentage of the Lithuanian Jewish population was Zionist than that of any other nation in Eastern Europe. Among the Zionists, the moderate general Zionists were initially the most important faction, gradually yielding place to the moderate Left Zionist socialists. Between 1919 and 1941, approximately ten thousand Jews emigrated from Lithuania to Palestine to form a substantial portion of the Yishuv. In support of possible emigration, both the Zionist Tarbut school system and the Yavne religious system used Hebrew as the language of instruction, and Hebrew spread from the schools into people's homes.[8] Yiddish education too continued to thrive, and celebrated Lithuanian yeshivot, such as Telz and Slobodka, continued to attract students from outside the country.[9]

The Yiddish cultural and political movement, which had been initiated at the turn of the century as the expression of Jewish national autonomy, continued to develop in Lithuania during the interwar period. But, as in Poland, the Jewish community was divided between the religious and the secular parties, the latter accusing the Agudat Israel of cooperating with the government to further their narrow religious interests.

Religious Political Action

Newly independent Poland was made up of several quite distinct regions: the former Austro-Hungarian province of Galicia, central (Congress of Vienna) Poland, and the Lithuanian-Belorussian borderlands that had been part of Lita. Hassidism had been a major influence in the non-Lithuanian parts of Poland, but the Polish provinces that had come from Lita remained mainly Marxist (Bundist) and Zionist. The religious party had been relatively weak in Lita. However, one of the phenomena of political life in Poland was the continued existence and strength of the religious community now expressed in political action with which the mitnagdim from Lita now joined.

One of its leaders from Lita was Chaim Ozer Grodzinsky. Born in 1863, he was a graduate of the Lithuanian yeshivot of Eisheshok and Volozhin. He was also a prodigy appointed to the rabbinical court (beth din) of Vilna at the age of twenty-four and later its chief judge. He became a central figure in Jewish Orthodoxy called upon to answer queries of both a sacred and secular nature. Opposed both to Zionism and to secular education, Grodzinsky was instrumental in developing political action in the Orthodox community. Rabbinical authorities had been initially averse to the adopting techniques of mass mobilization. They viewed politics as an intricate network of confidential negotiations with the ruling powers. During the course of the nineteenth century, Orthodox Jews had developed an ad hoc and largely informal set of arrangements for communication and mobilization. In the twentieth century, their efforts became more highly organized. For example, in June 1903, the Vilna rabbis issued an antisocialist appeal to the Jewish community to counter the godlessness of revolutionary Jewish youth. The appeal was consistent with the rabbis' long-standing support for authority and their traditional role as intermediaries, seeking mitigation of restrictive decrees from the Russian authorities.[10]

However, in 1914, Grodzinsky became a founding member of *Agudat Israel*, launched significantly in Galicia, a stronghold of Hassidism. Overall, its religious leader was the Gerer Rebbe, a highly influential Hassidic rabbi at that time. Grodzinsky remained a member of the Agudat Israel's Council of Sages and led the effort to expand its influence to the area around Wilno. Although many regional differences remained, this anti-Zionist and antimodern religious party reflected an alliance of the Hassidism in the rest of Poland with the Litvak mitnagdim, resolving their long-standing differences.

The religious party used its strength in the Polish parliament to secure support from the authorities for funding of religious schools and protection of religious rights. Its educational efforts were successful; of all students enrolled in Jewish schools, in a field including Bundist and Zionist alternatives, the largest number went to schools run by the religious party.[11] But the religious party's policy of cooperation with the government was an overall failure. The Polonization of the economy and anti-Semitic agitation, including segregation of Jewish students in the universities, occurred despite all the efforts of the Jewish parties in parliament. Although Poland remained a bastion of traditional Judaism, the process of modernization, secularization, and acculturation accelerated during the interwar years despite the best efforts of Rabbi Grodzinsky.[12] The huge attendance at his funeral in August 1940 during the short period of Soviet rule was seen as the close of the "rich and glorious religious life of Vilna."[13]

Yiddish Cultural Life

Yiddish secular Jewish culture particularly flourished in Wilno during the interwar period. It was the world center of Yiddish literary, linguistic, and cultural studies. In the 1920s, the German writer Alfred Doeblin, traveling in Poland in search of his Jewish roots, remarked that in Wilno, the Yiddish language thrived even among modern Jews. Doeblin inferred the presence of a large Jewish population from the many signs using Hebrew lettering, but he could not distinguish Jews by their appearance as he could in Warsaw.[14]

Jews lived in Wilno as a Yiddish-speaking national minority. "At the Jewish banks, you could write a check in Yiddish . . . Doctors talked to their patients in Yiddish. Political parties competed with each other in Yiddish and posted Yiddish placards on the streets. Young poets wrote their verses in Yiddish and composers set Yiddish songs to music. Nature-study hikes had Yiddish-speaking guides and boxing matches had Yiddish-speaking referees."[15]

Although he remained in Wilno for a relatively short time, Moshe Kulbak was one of the leaders of this Yiddish literary renaissance. Born near Vilna in 1896, Kulbak was given a Jewish education with a modern Yiddish cast. In 1920, he published his first book of Yiddish poems, including "Little Star," which became a popular folk song. From 1920 to 1923, Kulbak was part of a colony of émigré Russian writers and artists living in Berlin. During these years, he experimented with expressionism and produced his first novel, *Messiah, Son of Ephraim.* [16]

Returning to what was now Wilno in Poland, Kulbak taught in the Jewish secondary school and at the teacher seminary. He continued to write literary criticism for *Der Tog*, the newspaper of

the Yiddish-speaking Wilno intelligentsia and published poetry
in *Zukunft*, the important Yiddish literary journal in New York.
The poem that established his international reputation and has
epitomized the city ever since was "Vilna," published in 1926. 'You
are a psalm, spelled in clay and iron . . . Each stone a prayer; a
hymn every wall . . . a dark amulet set in Lithuania."[17] Kulbak's
poetry reflected the character of Vilna, responding to modernity
while demonstrating the influence of religious tradition. Kulbak
was elected president of the local author's group in 1927, but
during the following year, he crossed into Belorussia in the Soviet
Union to join his family in Minsk. There he became a member
of what was still a relatively vibrant Yiddish literary group in that
country.

After the Bolshevik Revolution, Yiddish culture flourished
in the Soviet Union for a while, as part of Lenin's nationalities
policy, while Hebrew and religious studies were suppressed.
During the three years between 1922 and 1925, Yiddish literature
underwent a process of *proletarianization* marked by increased
government censorship and centralized control of publishing. In
1925, the Central Committee of the Communist Party resolved
that literature was henceforth to be in the service of the party,
making the writer an agent of the regime and requiring that all
literature be politically compatible with socialist realism. Between
1925 and 1930, Yiddish literature was *Sovietized*, divorced from
foreign influences and isolated from Yiddish culture elsewhere. To
counteract the appeal of Zionism, there was for a time an official
Yiddish cultural program established in the Jewish Autonomous
Republic of Birobidjan near the border of Manchuria.

The separate Jewish section of the Communist Party was
liquidated in the 1930s as part of the regime's attack on
nationalities. Yiddish writers were imprisoned in the Stalinist
purges of the late 1930s. After a respite during the Second
World War, when the *Jewish Anti-Fascist Committee* was useful to the
regime in its foreign propaganda among Jewish communities, the
campaign against the Jews resumed in the late 1940s. As part of
the Stalinist anti-Semitic policy, almost all of the Jewish writers
still living were executed on the night of August 12, 1952.

Kulbak attempted to satisfy the requirements of socialist
realism, but he found that transforming his style presented

serious difficulties. During his time in Minsk, he wrote a major "Soviet" novel, *The Zelmenianer*, published in two parts in 1931 and 1935. The novel traces the adaptation of a Jewish family to Communism, and it identifies characters by their use of Yiddish, Hebrew, Russian, and other languages. Although the form was socialist realism, the novel's "national" content drew negative notice.[18] Kulbak was arrested while his play, *Boitre the Bandit* was running at the Jewish Art Theater in Moscow. He was sent to the Gulag in 1937 where he died in 1940. He was posthumously "rehabilitated" in 1956.

Although hopes for Jewish national development were disappointed during the interwar years, the Yiddish national cultural movement saw its crowning achievement in the founding in Wilno of YIVO, (Yidisher visnshaftlekher institut or Yiddish Scientific Institute), which brought scholars to Vilna under the direction of Max Weinreich. Thanks to YIVO, Wilno represented Yiddish scholarship during the interwar years just as it had earlier been the center for Talmudic scholarship.

Max Weinreich was from a merchant family living in a town in Courland where Jews were a distinct minority. The Weinreich family, lukewarm in their own observance, enrolled Max in a gymnasium attended by children of Baltic German and Latvian gentry. Max withdrew because of anti-Semitism and enrolled in a private Jewish high school in Dvinsk instead. When the strikes and demonstrations that swept Russia in 1905 reached his town, his interest in politics and the Bund led him to study Yiddish. He made his debut as a Yiddish writer at thirteen as a correspondent for the Bundist daily in Vilna. By the time he was sixteen, he had published his first Yiddish translations of European literature and his first articles on the Yiddish language.[19] After studying linguistics in St. Petersburg and Berlin, Weinreich received his doctorate in the linguistic development of Yiddish in 1923 from the University of Marburg in Germany. He then came to Wilno where he taught Yiddish literature at the Wilno Teachers Seminary and became a leader in the Yiddish scouting movement.

In 1925, Weinreich became a founder and the overall director of YIVO. YIVO was founded upon the principle that East European Jews all over the world shared a peoplehood. The agenda of the institute included the study of the Litvak Diaspora and the problems of Jewish acculturation in the lands where Lithuanian Jews settled. YIVO's scholarship differed from earlier secular Jewish scholarship in Germany and elsewhere. YIVO's span included the entirety of Jewish life: its present and its past; its rabbis and scholars; the language, the literature, and the social lives of the common people. In the spirit of Dubnow, it sought to collect and preserve material mirroring Jewish life to rescue Jewish folklore and to study Jewish problems systematically. Weinreich directed the section on philology and literature with other scholars directing the sections on history, economics, statistics, psychology, and education. One of the latter's tasks was to establish a consistent Yiddish orthography for use in the Yiddish schools. It is scarcely surprising that it did so by using the model of Litvak Yiddish. By 1939, YIVO's collections included one hundred thousand volumes and an equal number of archival documents and manuscripts. It was known as well for its many scholarly publications.[20] With headquarters in Wilno, YIVO maintained branches in Warsaw, Berlin, New York, and later, Buenos Aires. It had correspondents in over fifteen countries,[21] and it proudly included among its patrons Albert Einstein and Sigmund Freud.

Weinreich was in Western Europe at an international conference at the outbreak of World War II and was able come to the United States with his family. The accomplishments of YIVO during the years in Wilno were described by Max Weinreich at its fifteenth anniversary conference held in New York in the dark days of 1941. Weinreich recalled, "[M]ore than everything else [what was important was] the 'myth' [sic] of YIVO. People of our generation experienced elevation and ecstasy in contributing to YIVO a penny or a folkloristic write-down or just in leafing through one of the publications . . . They did these rather in the way their grandfather used to read a passage in a holy book or contribute a coin to the yeshiva at Volozhin or come out, at the reading of the Gemara, with friends in the evening with his own little Talmudic innovation." Weinreich later compared the impact of YIVO to that of "the cabalist who succeeded in drawing the holy sparks out of the broken shells."[22]

Weinreich's use of religious metaphor was deliberate. Weinreich was a secular Jew, international in his outlook, a socialist, and a scientist. Yet he wanted to convey that YIVO, as committed to science though it was, could not flourish unless it put down roots into the irrational layer of the national consciousness into a mythic vision of the institution and its mission. YIVO was based on faith in the continuity and future of the national culture. For those who launched YIVO in 1925, the assumption was that Jewish Ashkenazi culture would continue to flourish, separate and distinct, albeit secular and modern. It was clear by 1941, however, that such continuity would have to take place in the Litvak Diaspora.

It was Weinreich who, by sheer will in his role as director of YIVO's Research and Training Division and as organizer of its Graduate Center for Advanced Jewish Studies, carried the continuity of that culture and its spirit of inquiry to the United States. Weinreich became the first professor of Yiddish at an American university appointed professor of Yiddish language, literature, and folklore at New York's City College. His masterwork, five-volume *History of the Yiddish Language*, was published after his death in 1968.

His son Uriel, a Yiddish linguist like his father, also had an extraordinarily fruitful career before his untimely death in 1967. He was appointed Atran Professor of Yiddish Language, Literature and Culture at Columbia University in 1959 and chairman of the Department of Linguistics. His book *College Yiddish* became the basis for inclusion of Yiddish study into universities worldwide.

Despite the fervent ideological differences in the Jewish community in interwar Poland—between the religious and the secular, between the Yiddishists and the Hebraists, between the Communists and the Bundists—there was an underlying sense of community in Wilno. Many voluntary organizations had been established during World War I; there were over seventy associations of mutual assistance associated with synagogues (of which there were a hundred) and eight major associations of mutual aid. Literally, thousands of concerned individuals devoted their time to voluntary service in orphanages, in old-age homes, subsidizing meals for the needy, and engaging in other humanitarian pursuits. Each ideological group created its own aggressively competing institutions; this was especially true of great many youth groups.[23] However, as the situation of the Jews worsened in the 1930s, the core of dedicated activists turned their attention to the threats to the community from outside. For example, when ghetto restrictions were imposed on Jewish students at the university, the socialist workers went out on strike.

The educational and cultural life of Wilno remained active despite the political and economic difficulties. Wilno experienced something of a literary renaissance with the appearance of many newspapers and other publications. Despite limited support and even opposition at times from the Polish authorities, Wilno supported both a secular Yiddish school system, including a high school, and a Hebrew-speaking school system.[24]

Illustrative of life in interwar Wilno is the story of Hirsch Abramowicz.[25] His father Zelig (Zachariah) owned an estate in the district of Trokai in Vilna province. When the Poles seized Vilna and the Lithuanians broke off all diplomatic relations in 1920, the city and the farm were separated by the border between the two hostile countries. Hirsh Abramowicz was born on the family farm in 1881 and maintained an interest in Jewish agriculture throughout his life. He saw great moral value in working the land and being close to nature. At age fourteen, he was sent to Vilna where he was enrolled in a Russian gymnasium and worked on the family farm during vacations. After two years, he was admitted to the Jewish Teachers Institute. The teachers were Maskilim, extremely loyal to the Russian regime. As a member of the younger generation of Jewish intellectuals, Abramowicz did not agree with his teachers' political convictions. He was initially a Zionist, but he later gave his support to the Bund.

After 1901, Abramowicz was arrested for involvement in the Bund and was thus barred from teaching in government schools. He resumed teaching in government schools only after 1916 with the German occupation of Vilna. Because of his background of physical work on the farm, he was interested in developing vocational education for Jewish youth, and he directed the Help Through Work school until the start of World War II.

Abramowicz was also a permanent correspondent for two Yiddish newspapers between the wars, one in Riga and another in Buenos Aires. He was in Canada in the summer of 1939, visiting his brother, when war broke out. Now a refugee, he managed to eke out a living as a Yiddish writer. After the war, his writings more specifically memorialized the Vilna he knew and the people who made it the "most intimately Jewish" city. To commemorate its past, he wrote biographies of those who represented the qualities he admired, people who showed dignity in representing the community before governmental authorities, dedication and concern for the poor, involvement in relief organizations, schools and cultural institutions, and the struggle to maintain the Yiddish language.

Vilna, the heart of Lithuania, exerted an extraordinary hold on its sons and daughters: [T]he Shekhinah rested in the narrow streets of the Jewish quarter of Vilna . . . [W]hen the Divine Presence . . . abandoned its resting place . . . and left on the road to Ponary to join the Jews on their last journey, Vilna ceased to exist except only in the memory of its people."[26]

1.2.5 The Holocaust

Of the approximately one million Litvaks living at the onset of World War II, only about 10 percent survived. Some escaped into the Soviet Union or fought as partisans. Of those who came under direct Nazi control, only 1 percent survived.[1]

The Soviet-German Pact of August 1939 brought about the dismemberment of Poland whose eastern provinces came under Soviet control. During the two years of Soviet rule between August 1939 and June 1941, official suppression of national minorities had a profound effect on Jewish life. Newspapers were closed down, and Hebrew was proscribed. All national and cultural organizations were abolished.

Wilno, now to be called Vilnius, was assigned by the Soviets to become the capital of the still-independent state of Lithuania. The existence of an independent Lithuania, however, was short-lived. Soviet troops entered that country on June 15, 1940, incorporating it into the Soviet Union later that summer as the Lithuanian Soviet Socialist Republic (SSR). Kaunas was a major Jewish center with three Yiddish daily newspapers and numerous other periodicals, a Yiddish and Hebrew theater, and a multitude of Jewish organizations.[2] With the Sovietization of life, there was official suppression of national cultural and religious

organizations. In the weeks immediately before the German
invasion in 1941, the Soviets banished thirty-five thousand
Lithuanian "enemies of the state," including seven thousand Jews,
to the interior of Russia and placed them in forced labor camps in
Siberia. Zionist and Bundist leaders were among those banished,
leaving their communities without militant leadership.[3]

Germany launched its invasion of the Soviet Union on June 21,
1941. At that time, the Jewish population of Lithuania, including
the newly incorporated area around Vilnius, was about two hundred
fifty thousand, including also additional refugees from German-
occupied Poland. At the time of the German conquest, it is estimated
that about fifteen thousand Jews succeeded in crossing into the
rest of the Soviet Union.[4] Toward the end of 1941, a Lithuanian
Division was created in the Red Army. At its height, about half of
the soldiers in this division were Jews, recruited from the fifteen
thousand mentioned above and from the seven thousand who had
been deported to Siberia. The Jews in the Lithuanian Division took
pride in the Jewish character of the unit; many had been associated
with Zionist youth groups, and Yiddish was spoken freely. Due to
casualties and inability of further recruitment, the proportion of
Jews in the division was reduced to 10 percent by war's end. Of the
total number of Jews in Lithuania in June 1941, approximately
twenty-five thousand survived the war.

During the period between the launch of the invasion and the
completion of the German conquest, several thousand Jews were
killed by Lithuanians in pogroms in cities throughout the country.
The wave of murder swelled with the activity of German mobile
killing squads, which also included ethnic Lithuanians. Jews
were rounded up in each of the towns and brutally transported
to nearby killing sites where they were massacred by gunfire.
The majority of provincial Jews were killed during the summer
of 1941. Most of the Jews in the cities, forced into ghettos, were
liquidated in a similar fashion between September and November.
By December 1941, only some forty thousand Jews remained in
all of Lithuania, with approximately sixteen thousand people in
each of the larger ghettos of Kovno and Vilna and five thousand
people in Shavli. Those remaining were employed as slave labor
in various workshops associated with the ghettos. This period of
relative quiet lasted for approximately eighteen months.

Late in the summer of 1943, the remaining Jews came under the jurisdiction of the SS, and liquidation of the ghettos began. Beginning on August 6 and ending on September 23, 1943, the inhabitants of the Vilna ghetto were deported to concentration camps in Estonia. Between October and December, the Kovno ghetto was halved. Many of its residents were sent to camps in Estonia, but the remainder lived on in what was now a concentration camp around the central workshops in the ghetto. In the Shavli ghetto, deportations to various camps took place in September 1943; an additional eight hundred children, elderly persons, and invalids were massacred there on November 5, 1943. In Kovno, two thousand children, elderly persons, and invalids were killed on March 27 and 29, 1944. With the approach of the Red Army in July 1944, the Germans moved to clear out the ghettos; the remaining four thousand inhabitants of the Shavli ghetto were sent to camps in Germany by June 22 and almost all of the eight thousand Jews remaining in Kovno followed during the week of July 8, 1944. The remains of the Shavli and Kovno ghettos were set afire by the Germans in their retreat from Lithuania.[5] The fires killed those in hiding there, particularly in the Kovno ghetto.

Resistance in the ghettos was of various kinds. Foremost was the effort to maintain life—one's own life and the lives of family and neighbors even of strangers. Since the punishment for smuggling a potato was immediate death, even small actions required great courage. Cultural survival too was a matter of critical importance. Under attack as a people, the Jews took great risks to preserve the culture and the learning that defined them. In the ghettos, they educated their children, and whenever they could, they obtained, read, and shared books with each other. In all instances, they documented their existence as a form of defiance. Armed resistance was planned in each of the Lithuanian ghettos, but was not carried out. The reasons varied, but in each instance, the fighting organizations abandoned their plans because they would not jeopardize the survival of the greater population of the ghetto.[6] Many members of the underground fighting organizations in the ghettos, particularly in Vilna, were able to escape into the nearby forests and fight on as partisans. Fighters from the Kovno and Shavli ghettos, who were unable to escape, maintained their organization and resistance in the concentration camps.

The Kovno Ghetto

During the Nazi occupation, the Jews of Lithuania struggled to maintain their integrity as a people and of their culture. One form of cultural affirmation was the documentation by Jews of their lives and their trials as a form of community resistance. Inside the Kovno ghetto, for example, in a particularly well-organized effort, the Jews wrote their own history.[7] They set up a statistics office and a paint-and-sign workshop; artists and photographers documented their experience despite ever-present oppression. This communal effort produced documentation that survived the destruction of the ghetto.[8]

The Kovno ghetto differed in a number of respects from the ghettos in other Lithuanian cities. A comparison with the Vilna ghetto is particularly striking.[9] The Vilna (Vilnius) ghetto survived only until September 1943. The Kovno ghetto lived on, in the form of a concentration camp, until the summer of 1944. Although the ghettos ultimately suffered the same fate under the Germans, their leaders were chosen in different ways, and both the manner of their choice and their quality as human beings made some difference in the implementation of the German policy. All of the leaders of the Kovno Jewish administration, who were selected by the people of the ghetto, remained until the very end. In Vilna, the Nazis appointed Jacob Gens as head of the Jewish police in the ghetto. The leaders initially chosen by the people of the ghetto were immediately murdered by the Nazis who then appointed Gens to lead the community. In Vilna, suspicion and conflict were endemic between the Fighting Organization and Gens who remained the ruler of the ghetto until its end.

In marked contrast to Vilna, those elected to the Judenrat in Kovno, including its head (Dr. Elchanan Elkes) and his deputy (Leib Garfunkel) had been known and respected in their community before the war. Elkes, a physician in the Russian army during the First World War, became head of the Department of Internal Medicine at Kovno's Jewish hospital. In his private practice, he was personal physician to many government leaders and to the diplomatic community. Although he considered himself a Zionist, Elkes had not participated in political life before the war. His personal stature and devotion to the community inspired an atmosphere of united public struggle.[10]

Elkes and the other leaders of the Judenrat were sustained by their moral authority. Indeed, in Kovno, the ghetto police were part of the underground resistance. Furthermore, the Jewish court in the ghetto operated on the principle of not endangering the life of any Jew who fell into their hands. Elkes dared to remind the Nazis that they could be held accountable after the war for their behavior. Sent to Dachau along with the rest of the Kovno Jews, he chose to share his meager rations with others and, thus, to die.

Elkes illustrates the survival of free will in the face of catastrophe. In the ghettos and in the camps, people held onto the best traditions of Lita, their actions influenced by their sense of Jewish responsibility, their values, and the Litvak tradition of self-organization. Jews chose to act as best they could, and they found the strength to function as an organized community in the midst of chaos.[11]

Abraham Sutzkever and the Vilna Ghetto

Cultural integrity as a form of resistance is seen clearly in the history of the Vilna ghetto and in the career of Abraham Sutzkever. Born in 1913 in Smorgon, Belorussia, Sutzkever and his family were deported to Siberia in 1915 where his father died. They remained there until the end of World War I. In 1920, Sutzkever came to Vilna with his mother. There he set about educating himself, studying literary criticism as an *extern* at the University of Vilna. He was largely immune to the ideological fervor of interwar Vilna, and perhaps as a result, he found only a lukewarm welcome from the literary coterie of Young Vilna. The inspiration for Sutzkever's poetry was nature, and his great wartime poetry is marked by a politics that is distinctly individual, not ideological. Sutzkever's early lyric poetry appeared in 1933 in the *Vilner Tog*. the newspaper of the Vilna intelligentsia. His first book of poetry, *Lider* (Songs), was published in 1937, and a second, a hymn to nature entitled *Valdeks* (Forests), appeared in 1940.

Confined during the war to the Vilna ghetto, Sutzkever was a member of the famous Paper Brigade assigned to work each day in the YIVO building, outside the ghetto limits. These scholars were assigned the task of collating the books confiscated from Jewish libraries throughout Lita, including the holdings of Vilna's Strashun Library. The books were to be shipped to Germany or trashed for the value of their paper. The Paper Brigade secreted books in a hidden section of the YIVO building and smuggled them back into the ghetto where they were buried and saved from destruction. Weapons and ammunition were hidden along with works of art and rare books. The spirit of the Jerusalem of Lithuania was distilled in the role of intellectuals in the preservation of its legacy in the midst of its destruction.[11]

Culture and resistance combined in the Vilna ghetto in other ways too. The ghetto maintained an active artistic and intellectual life although some ventures, such as Gens's project to establish a theater, were compromised by his position as Nazi-appointed dictator of the ghetto. Nevertheless, musical revues became popular; and there were many concerts, literary evenings, and lectures. Full-scale dramas were presented both in Yiddish and in Hebrew, the latter most notably about the Jewish revolt in Rome. By no means all the activities were sponsored by Gens. The Association of Writers and Artists, an organization established by the intelligentsia, sought to improve the economic conditions of its surviving members and to preserve the works of murdered colleagues. It offered Saturday night "evenings," each devoted to a particular cultural theme with speakers and discussants. The Scientific Circle represented the physical and social sciences, along with mathematics and philosophy. This organization awarded a literary prize to Sutzkever and other prizes to artists. Similarly, the physicians of the ghetto-sponsored medical-scientific lectures and teachers offered their own series. The efforts of the doctors produced extraordinary health care in the ghetto, so effective that, despite extreme deprivation and overcrowding, major epidemics were prevented.[12]

Sutzkever was one of the very few creative artists who survived the Holocaust. He was one of the fewer still who lived through it as a writer, producing some of his finest poems between 1941 and 1945, many of them written amid the daily wretchedness of ghetto life. The key to Sutzkever's survival was the redemptive capacity of art. The incorruptible standard of the good poem was the touchstone of a former higher sanity and a psychological protection against despair. "Even when nothing in the universe responds to man, the need for expression is evidence of the determination to resist . . . In the ghetto, the muse is no decorative enhancement of life, but the primitive life-urge, the cry of an almost extinguished self, demanding recognition."[13] Sutzkever's elegies to his mother and his infant son, for example, allowed him to "rescue the dead" and guarantee them a dignified and enduring memorial.

Not only did Sutzkever struggle with his own personal despair, but he enlisted his militant verse against the faint spirit of the Jews around him. His summons to cultural and armed resistance in the Vilna ghetto made him a symbol of heroism throughout the Yiddish world. One of his finest poems of this kind was about the night the Jewish underground broke into the Romm printing house, which had produced the Talmud, and recast the lead type into bullets, refashioning the best of Litvak culture into ammunition against those who would destroy it.

Sutzkever wrote his great dramatic poem, "Kol Nidre," in February 1943. With the last remnant of the Jews bound to the stake and the fires lit, it was clear that only divine intervention could save them. If the Almighty permitted their slaughter, then he must answer for the crime. The setting is a bunker synagogue on Yom Kippur where a father, having already sacrificed four sons, waits in vain for the sign of the ram before sacrificing his fifth and last son. The Jew refuses to free the God of Israel from his pact but rather forces him into confrontation.

Sutzkever escaped from the Vilna ghetto and joined the partisans who were fighting in the surrounding forests. Because of his fame as a poet, the Soviets managed to rescue him from the forest and fly him to Moscow.[14] After the liberation, Sutzkever managed to recover some of the literary treasures that he and his colleagues had hidden during the war. He was able, for example, to save the diary of Zelig Kalmanovitch, a cofounder and one of the directors of the prewar YIVO. In the diary, Kalmanovitch bore witness to the continuation of YIVO's mission even in its destruction and to the vigorous cultural life that had maintained the spirit of the Jews.[15] For example, a note in the diary for December 1942 mentions the celebration of the hundred thousandth book read in the library of the ghetto. Also recovered was the diary of Kruk[16] who had supervised the library assisted by the young Dina Abramowicz who survived to become the librarian of the YIVO library in New York in the postwar period.

Following the war, Sutzkever went to Palestine as an illegal immigrant and fought in the War of Independence. He continued to follow his poetic calling with priestly devotion for the rest of his long life. In doing justice to the great destruction, he became the national elegist, a commanding orator, and one of the great speakers in the Jewish tradition of challenging God.[17]

Holocaust Memory

Samuel Bak introduced his series of paintings, *Landscapes of Jewish Experience*, with a painting entitled *Self-Portrait*.[18] In the foreground, but to one side, a mournful young boy is seated with what appears to be a paintbrush in his hand. Central to the picture, however, is a shadowy image—the famous photo of a child with his arms raised, leaving the Warsaw ghetto to go to his death.[19] It is clear that Bak deeply identifies with the iconic image from Warsaw, that he views his own childhood and later life against the backdrop of the Shoah. In the distant background are belching smokestacks and a community in flames. The other paintings in this series are largely devoid of people but contain emblems of a ravaged civilization. The paintings of Samuel Bak, in his own words, "convey a sense of a world that was shattered . . . of a world that exists again through an enormous effort to put everything together, when it is absolutely impossible to put it together because the broken things can never become whole again."[20]

Bak witnessed the destruction of his family and his own childhood in the Vilna ghetto. Against overwhelming odds, he survived to bear witness, in his life and art, to the million Jewish children who perished in the Holocaust. By an extraordinary coincidence, his surname, BAK, is an acronym for B'ney-Kedoshim (Children of Martyrs), which most likely originated in the Ukrainian pogroms of the mid-seventeenth century.[21]

Bak's works avoid specific horrors and focus instead on emblems of continuity—the Sabbath candles, the Star of David, the Ten Commandments—not entirely vanquished but reflecting the chaos and destruction around them. The candles burn in the shadow of a crematorium chimney. The stone tablets of the Ten Commandments stand but are not intact; their inscriptions now floating in the air. Bak's paintings also reflect the need of the survivors to emerge from the ruins and to continue their historical pilgrimage. The roots of a severed tree, in one of his paintings, do not die but continue to put out shoots.[22]

His history and that of his family represents those whose experiences continue to shape the memories of the Shoah in the Litvak Diaspora. Samuel Bak was born in Wilno in 1933 while it was under Polish rule.[23] His father, Jonas, was a handsome man-about-town in interwar Wilno, successful in his work as a maker of dental appliances and proud of his physical agility and resourcefulness. These traits were essential to the survival of his small family during the Nazi occupation. Several members of the family managed to escape Lithuania before the Nazi invasion, but they did not fare well. His father's older brother, who had been jailed by the Poles for his pro-Communist activism, escaped to the Soviet Union in the 1920s only to be imprisoned in the Soviet gulag and destroyed. His father's sister also escaped from Vilna along with her husband and young child, but they were all killed by the Nazis at Babi Yar, ouside of Kiev.[24] All four of Bak's grandparents were killed in the Ponar Forest.

Bak's family was imprisoned in the Vilna ghetto during the war years, but they received some help from Bak's maternal great-aunt, Hannah. As a young girl, Hannah had been lured away from her Jewish employer and, renamed Janina, was adopted by a Catholic family. She converted to Christianity and was raised under the auspices of the nuns of a Benedictine convent in Vilna. Janina married a well-born Pole, who became an important government official, lived in Vilna during the Nazi occupation, providing a sanctuary to her niece and her family at crucial times. His father, whose skill and strength were instrumental to the survival of the boy and his mother, was killed in the summer of 1944, just prior to the liberation of Vilna by the Red Army. Of the eighty thousand Jews in Vilna in 1939, only a few hundred survived; Bak and his mother were among them.

Young Samuel's precocious skill at drawing was recognized at an early age. He had no formal training, but after the first public exhibition of his work in 1942, in the Vilna ghetto, he became a celebrity. The exhibition was sponsored by the poet Avrom Sutzkever who encouraged young Bak further with the gift of an ancient book, the minutes of a community organization, which had been rescued by the Paper Brigade. Bak used the blank portion of its precious pages as a sketchbook.[25]

After the war, the remaining members of Bak's family were dispersed across the globe. His mother's brother Rachmiel had emigrated during the interwar years to the Yishuv, where he helped found a kibbutz in the Galilee. Her sister survived the Holocaust and migrated to Israel with her daughter, and the youngest brother, who had fought as a soldier in the Red Army, joined them in 1946. The wanderings of Bak and his mother led them out of postwar Soviet Lithuania to a displaced persons' camp in the American occupation zone in Germany where they spent three years. In 1948, they moved to newly independent Israel.

Bak's formal art education began in liberated Vilnius and continued in Munich.[26] He lived in Israel from 1948 to 1959 and studied for one year at the Bezalel Art School in Jerusalem. Bak then moved to Paris, studying at the Louvre and L'Ecole des Beaux-Arts. After experimenting with various forms of art, he then explored forms of expression that would reflect his own experience of the Holocaust. Bak moved once again to Israel and finally moved to Boston where he has remained since 1993. He has personified the wandering Jew in the postwar era. Carrying his art and his experience within himself, he has represented the "desire to present the universality of life and loss and the endurance of man's hope for a 'tikkun.'" The word reflects his role "in reassembling through his art a broken world that still bears witness to the original dislocations."[27] Bak takes pride in his origins in the Jerusalem of Lithuania, and he continues to express both the joy in his early life there and the catastrophes that afflicted his family, community, and people.

* * *

Notes

1.1   The Nature of the Place

1   Masha Greenbaum, *The Jews of Lithuania,* Jerusalem, 1985, 1-85 passim
2   Dovid Katz, *Words on Fire The Unfinished Story of Yiddish,* New York 2004, 11-45
3   Greenbaum, op. cit 1995, 51-53
4   Isaiah Trunk, "The Council of the Province of White Russia," *YIVO Annual* 1956-57 11: 188-
5   Greenbaum, op cit 1985,160-193 passim; Dov Levin, *The Litvaks,* Jerusalem, 2000, 64-70; John Klier, *Imperial Russia's Jewish Question,* Cambridge:2005; John Klier, *Russia Gathers Her Jews,* DeKalb, IL, 1986
6   Samuel Kassow, *Vilna: Jerusalem of Lithuania,* Amherst, MA 1997
7   Lucy Dawidowicz, *From That Place and Time,* New York, 1989, 31
8   Dovid Katz, 2004 op. cit 45-79
9   David Fishman, "Introduction" In *Profiles of a Lost World,* Hirsz Abramowicz trans Eva Dobkin, Detroit,1999
10   Antony Polonsky, "Introduction," In Antony Polonsky, Ed. *Polin Studies in Polish Jewry,* v. 15, Portland, OR, 2002
11   Dovid Katz, op. cit. 2004,161
12   Immanuel Etkes, *The Gaon of Vilna: The Man and his Image,* Berkeley, CA, 2002, 14
13   Louis Ginzberg, *Students, Scholars and Saints,* Philadelphia, 1958, 140
14   Lucy Davidowicz, *The Golden Tradition,* New York, 1967 passim
15   Wolf Rabinowitsch, "Karlin Chassidim," *YIVO Annual,* 1950, 5: 123. 1971 p 33-36)
16   Israel Cohen, *Vilna,* Philadelphia, 1992, 227-253 passim
17   Allan Nadel, *The Faith of the Mithnagdim,* Baltimore, 1997
18   Shaul Stampfer, "Heder Study, Knowledge of Torah and the Mainstream of Social Stratification in Traditional East European Jewish Society," In *Studies in Jewish Education* v3, Jerusalem, 1988, 271-289
19   Immanuel Etkes, "Marriage and Torah Study among the 'Lomdim' in Lithuania in the Nineteenth Century," In David Kraemer, Ed., *The Jewish Family,: Metaphor and Memory,* New York, 1989.164-166)
20   David Biale, "Childhood, Marriage and the Family in East European Jewish Enlightenment," In Steven M. Cohen and Paula Hyman, Eds, *The Jewish Family, Myth and Reality,* New York, 1993
21   I.l. Peretz "Bryna's Mendl," In Ruth Wisse, Ed., *The I.L. Peretz Reader,* New York, 1990, 118-124

1.2   The Evolution of the Culture

1.2.1The Generation of the Haskalah 1840-1870

1   Shmuel Feiner, *The Jewish Enlightenment*, Philadelphia, 2004; Shmuel
      Feiner, "Towards a Historical Definition of Haskalah" In Shmuel
      Feiner and David Sorkin, Eds., *New Perspectives on the Haskalah*, 2002,
      Portland, OR ; Schmuel Feiner, *Haskalah and History*, Portland, OR,
      2002a

2   Israel Cohen op cit 1992, 271-275.

3   Michael Stanislawski, *Tsar Nicholas I and the Jews*, Philadelphia, 1983,
      49-96

4   Ilya Trotsky, "Jews in Russian Schools," In Jacob Frumkin, Gregor
      Aronson and Alexis Goldenweiser, Eds., *Russian Jewry, 1860-1917*,
      New York, 1966, 408-415.

5   David Fishman, op cit, 1999

6   Immanuel Etkes, *Rabbi Israel Salanter and the Mussar Movement*,
      Philadelphia, 1993 206-244; 318-324 "Rabbi Israel Salanter and his
      Psychology Of Mussar," In Arthur Green, Ed., *Jewish Sprituality* v II,
      1987 David Fishman, "The Mussar Movement in Interwar Poland,"
      In Yisrael Gutman, Ed., *Jewry of Poland between the Two World Wars*,
      Hanover, NH, 1989

7   Benjamin Nathans, *Beyond the Pale. Jewish Encounters with Imperial
      Russia.*, Berkeley, 2004

8   Michael Stanislawski, *For Whom Do I Toil*, New York, 1988,. 48-52, 89-92
      and passim

9   David Patterson, *The Hebrew Novel in Czarist Russia*, Boston, 1999, 7-9

10   David Aberbach, "Hebrew Literature and Jewish Nationalism in the
      Tsarist Empire, 1881-1917," In Zvi Gitelman, op cit, 2003

11   Lucy Davidowicz, *The Golden Tradition*, New York, 1967, 119-131.

12   Abraham Menes, "The Am Olam Movement." *YIVO Annual* 1949, 4: 9

13   Shmuel Werses, "Portrait of the Maskil as a Young Man," In Shmuel
      Feiner and David Sorkin op cit 2001, 128-193.

14   Joseph Salmon, "Enlightened Rabbis as Reformers in Russian Society,"
      In Shmuel Feiner and David Sorkin, Eds. Op cit, 2001, 160

15   Dovid Katz, op cit,2004, 200-202

16   Dan Miron, *A Traveler Disguised*, New York, 1973)

17   Eli Lederhendler, *The Road to Modern Jewish Politics. Political Tradition
      and Political Reconstruction in the Jewish Community of Tsarist Russia*,
      New York,1989, 84- Eli Lederhendler, "Politics and Messianism in
      Traditional Jewish Society," *YIVO Annual*, 1991, 20: 1-15.11. Jonathan

Frankel, "Modern Jewish Politics. East and West," In Zvi Goldman, Ed., *The Quest for Utopia in Jewish Political Ideas and Institutions*, Armonk, NY, 2004; Robert Brym, *The Jewish Intelligentsia and Russian Marxism*, New York, 1978, p58 Nora Levin, *While the Messiah Tarried. Jewish Socialist Movements.* London 1978, 387-388)

1.2.2 Transitional Generation

1   Jonathan Frankel op cit, 1981,11; Shmuel Feiner, op cit, 2002

2   David Biale, op cit, 1986)

3   Robert Seltzer, "Jewish Liberalism in late Tsarist Russia," *Contemporary Jewry*, 1988, 9: 47.

4   Mark Wishnitzer, *To Dwell in Safety*, Philadelphia, 1948, 42

5   Robert Brym, op cit, 1978, 50

6   Erich Haberer, *Jews and Revolution in 19th Century Russia.*, Cambridge,1995, 74)

7   ibid 40

8   Elias Tcherkover, "Peter Lavrov and Jewish Socialist Emigres," *YIVO Annual* 1952, 7:

9   Nora Levin, op cit, 1978, 29-39 passim

10 Ber Borochov, "A. Liberman, Father of Jewish Socialism," In Mitchell Cohen, Ed., *Class Struggle and the Jewish Nation*, New Brunswick, 1984, 191-197

11 Abraham Menes, op cit, 1949.

12 David Vital, *The Origins of Zionism*, New York, 1975, 128

13 Ilya Trotsky, "Jews in Russian Schools," In Jacob Frumkin, Gregor Aronson and Alexis Goldenweiser, Eds., *Russian Jewry (1860-1917)*. New York: Thomas Yoseloff, 1966 pp144-171.

14 Gershon Swet. "Russian Jews in Zionism and the Building of Palestine," In Jacob Frumkin, Gregor Aronson and Alexis Goldenweiser, Eds., op cit, 172

15 Lucy Dawidowicz, op cit 1967, 52

16 ibid 367-375

17 D. Weinberg, *Between Tradition and Modernism*, New York, 1996, 217-291

18 Steven Zipperstein, *Elusive Prophet. Ahad Ha'am and the Origins of Zionism*, Berkeley, 1993, 46, 81, 95

19 Lucy Dawidowicz op cit 1967,120-132

20 ibid 411-422; D. Weinberg, op cit 1996, 83-144

21 Lucy Dawidowicz, op cit 1967, 422-426

22 Robert Seltzer, "Coming Home. The Personal Basis of Simon Dubnow's Ideology." *AJS Review*, 1976, 1: 283; D. Weinberg, op cit 1996, 145-216

23 Sophie Dubnow-Erlich, *The Life and Work Of S.M. Dubnow. Diaspora Nationalism and Jewish History*. trans. Judith Vowles, Bloomington, IN, 1991, 52-58)

24 Robert. Seltzer, op cit, 1988, 49-60

25 Koppel Pinson, "The National Theories of Simon Dubnow." *Jewish Social Science*, 1948, 10:335.

26 D. Weinberg, op cit, 1996, 4

27 Yoav Peled, *Class and Ethnicity in the Pale*, New York, 1989 passim; Ezra Mendelsohn, *Class Struggle. The Formative Years of the Jewish Worker's Movement in Tsarist Russia*, Cambridge, 1970, passim; Henry Tobias, *The Jewish Bund in Russia from its Origins to 1905*, Stanford,1972 passim; Ben Halpern and Yehuda Reinharz, "Nationalism and Jewish Socialism," *Modern Judaism*, 1988; Jonathan Frankel, *Prophecy and Politics:Socialism, Nationalism and the Russian Jews 1862-1917*. New York, 1981 passim.

28 Moshe Mishkowski, "Regional factors in the Formation of the Jewish Labor Movement in Tsarist Russia," *YIVO Annual*, 1969, 14:27.

29 Harriet Davis-Kram, "The Story of the Sisters of the Bund," *Contemporary Jewry*, 1980, 5:17

30 Arcadius Kahan, *Essays in Jewish Social and Economic History*. Chicago, 1986; Simon Kuznets, "Immigration of Russian Jews to the United States: Background and Structure," *Perspectives in American History*, 1975, 9: 33

30 a Mani Leyb, translated by Solon Beinfeld (personal communication), *A Folk Song of the Jews of Vilna*: All the way from Vilna/Scholarship's domain/He has brought the Holy Torah/South to our Ukraine. See—his silken coat is shiny/to the threads worn down; bitter poverty in Vilna/drove him to this town . . . A blessing on the Vilna Litvaks, learned folk though poor/who can even teach the Torah /to a Nieshin boor

31 Francois Guesnet, "Stereotypes and Migration," In Zvi Gitelman, Ed., *The Emergence of Modern Jewish Politics*, Pittsburgh, 2003 32 Francois Guesnet "The Change in Jewish Self-Organization in the Kingdom of Poland before 1900 and the Bund," In Jack Jacobs, Ed., *Jewish Politics in Eastern Europe, The Bund at 100*, London, 2001,33 Mark Wischnitzer, op cit, 1948, 29-33;37-45 passim; Zosa Szajkowski, "How the Mass Immigration to America Began," *Jewish Social Studies*,1942,

4: 291; David Berger, *The Legacy of Jewish Migration in 1881 and its Impact, 1983).* Brooklyn, 1983

Elias Tsherikower, "Jewish Immigration to the United States, 1881-1900" *YIVO Annual*, 1951, 6: 157. Ronald Sanders. *Shores of Refuge*, New York, 1988.

34   Simon Kusnets, op cit 1975

35   Dov Levin op cit, 2000, 29

36   Samuel Joseph, *History of the Baron deHirsch Fund*, Philadelphia, 1967, 127-132

37   Theodore Norman, *An Outstretched Arm: A History of the Jewish Colonization Society.* London, 1985, 7-90; Mark Wischnitzer, op cit 1948, 78-93

1.2.3 Generation of Revolution and War

1   Simon Kuznets, op cit 1975

2   Jonathan Frankel, op cit, 1981, 6

3   Eli Lederhendler, op cit 1989, 157

4   David Vital, op cit 1975, 257-262

5   ibid, 364-370)

6   ibid, 339-352

7   ibid, 373)

8   Joseph Salmon, op cit, 2001

9   Walter Laquer, A History of Zionism, New York, 1976, 482

10   Israel Cohen op cit, 1992, 350

11   Ben Halpern and Yehuda Reinharz, op cit 1988).

12   Jonathan Frankel, op cit 1981, 292-293)

13   David Vital, op cit 1982, 394-396)

14   Ben Halpern and Yehuda Reinharz, op cit 1988)

15   Jonathan Frankel op cit, 1981, 311)

16   Yoav Peled, op cit, 1989, 79

17   Jonathan Frankel op cit 1981, 291

18   Itzak Ben-Zvi, "Labor Zionism in Russia," In Jacob Frumkin op cit 1966; Robert Brym, op cit, 1978, 97

19   Mitchell Cohen, *Zion and State. Nation, Class and the Shaping of Modern Israel.* London, 1987

20   Yoav Peled op cit 1989, 81

21   ibid, 87

22   Lucy Dawidowicz, op cit 1967, 62

23   Ben Halpern and Yehuda Reinherz, op cit, 1988

24   Yoav Peled op cit, 1989, 57

25   David Fishman, op cit, 1989

26   Jonathan Frankel op cit, 1981,193

27   ibid, 228)

28   Abraham Ascher, *The Revolution of 1905: A Short History*, Stanford. 1988, 253-262 passim

29   Jonathan Frankel op cit, 1981, 154

30   ibid, 155

31   ibid,160)

32   Gregor Aronson, "Ideological Trends among Russian Jews," In Jacob Frumkin, Ed., op cit, 1966

33   Abraham Ain, "Swislowcz: Portrait of a Jewish Community in Eastern Europe," In Deborah Dash Moore, Ed., *East European Jews in Two Worlds. Studies from the YIVO Annual.* Evanston, IL, 1989

34   Lucy Dawidowicz op cit 1967, 426-434)

35   Jonathan Frankel op cit, 1981,588 ;

36   David Fishman, *The Rise of Modern Yiddish* Pittsburgh, 2003

37   Henri Minczeles *Histoire General du Bund*, Paris 1999, 281

38   Lucy Dawidowicz op cit, 1967, 426

1.2.4 The Interwar Period

1   Dov Levin, op cit, 2000, 107-108

2   Samuel Kassow op cit 1997

3   Arcadius Kahan, op cit, 1986)

4   Ezra Mendelsohn, *The Jews of East Central Europe between the World Wars*, Bloomington, IN, 1983.

5   ibid, 220-224

6   Samuel Gringaus, "Jewish National Autonomy in Lithuania, 1918-1925," *Jewish Social Studies*,1952 14:225.

7   Dov Levin, *Fighting Back*, New York 1995, 28

8   Masha Greenbaum, op cit, 1995, 95-96; Ezra Mendelsohn op cit 1983, 225 passim;.

9   Solon Beinfeld, "Life and Survival" In *Hidden History of the Kovno Ghetto*, Washington, DC, 1997.27

10   Eli Lederhendler Jewish Response to Modernity, New York, 1994, 69-73

11   Dov Levin, op cit, 1985, 29-30

12   Ezra Mendelsohn op cit, 1983,55 and passim

13   Yosef Friedlander, "The Day Vilna Died," *Tradition*,:2003, 37:

14   Alfred Doeblin, *Journey to Poland*. Trans. Joachim Neugroschel, New York, 1991,85

> Born to Jewish parents in 1875 in Stettin, he moved to Berlin after medical training. His magnum opus was *Alexanderplatz 1929* telling the story of a working class German. It became a leading post-War German TV film. During the Hitler period, Doeblin moved to France, became a French citizen and converted to Catholicism prior to his death in 1957

15   Moshe Kulbak *Le Messe fils d'Ephraim* trans Carole Ksiazenicer-Matheron, Paris, 1995.

16   Irving Howe et al, op cit, 1988, 406

17   Lucy Dawidowicz, *The Jewish Presence*, New York, 1977,166

18   Lucian Dobroszycki, "YIVO in Interwar Poland: Work in the Historical Sciences," In Yisrael Gutman, Exra Mendelsohn, Yehuda Reinharz and Chone Shmeruk, Eds., *The Jews of Poland between Two World Wars*, Hanover, NH, 1989

19   Henri Minczeles *Vilna, Wilno, Vilnius, La Jerusalem du Lithuanie*, Paris, 2000, 283

20   Dan Miron, "Between Science and Faith. Sixty Years of the YIVO Institute," *YIVO Annual*, 1990: 19: 1-15

21   N.N. Shneidman *Jerusalem of Lithuania*, Oakville, ON, 1990

22   Arcadius Kahan op cit, 1986.149-160

23   Hirsz Abramowicz op cit 1999, 18

1.2.5 The Holocaust

1   Dovid Katz, op cit 2004, 323

2   Solon Beinfeld, op cit, 1997, 28)

3   Dov Levin, op cit. 1995, passim

4   ibid, p28)
5   ibid, 35-80 passim
6   ibid, 95-99).
7   ibid, 151-157 and passim).
8   Holocaust Museum, *Hidden History of the Kovno Ghetto,* Washington, DC, 1997).
9   Solon Beinfeld, op cit, 1997, 36).
10   Dina Porat, "The Jewish Councils of the Main Ghettos of Lithuania: A Comparison," *Modern Judaism,* 1993, 13: 149.
11   Solon Beinfeld, op cit 1997, 84-85)
12   David Roskies, *Against the Apocalypse,* Cambridge, MA, 1984, 197-229.
13   Dina Porat op cit, 1993
14   Solon Beinfeld, "Health Care in the Vilna Ghetto," *Holocaust and Genocide Studies,* 1998, 12:66
15   Ruth Wisse, "The Ghetto Poems of Abraham Sutzkever," *Jewish Book Annual,* 53:, 95.
16   Ruth Wisse, "Introduction," *Burnt Pearls, Ghetto Poems of Abraham Sutzever,* Oakville, ON, 1981, 23)
17   Zelig Kalmanovitch, "A Diary of the Nazi Ghetto in Vilna,: *YIVO Annual,* 1953, 8:9
18   Herman Kruk, "A Diary of the Nazzi Ghetto in Vilna," *YIVO Annual,* 1965, 13:9.
19   David Roskies, op cit 1984, 225-229.)
20   Samuel Bak, *Painted in Words: A Memoir by Samuel Bak,* Boston,2001,33
21   Lawrence Langer, "Essay" in *Landscapes of Jewish Experience: Paintings by Samuel Bak,* Boston, 1997, 2
22   Samuel Bak, op cit 2001,128
23   Lawrence Langer, op cit, 1997, 3-20 passim
24   Samuel Bak, op cit. 2001, 140-145)
25   ibid, 327-361)
26   ibid,362-420 passim)
27   Alicia Faxon and Irene Tayler, "Shards of Time: Samuel Bak and the Art of Memory," In Irene Tayler, Ed., *Between Worlds: The Paintings and Drawings of Samuel Bak from 1946-2000,* 2002, Boston

SECTION II

THE ENGLISH-SPEAKING
LITVAK DIASPORA

INTRODUCTION

Three basic strands of Litvak culture—religious Orthodoxy, Jewish national consciousness, and social and economic justice—were developed in Lita and were carried by its survivors throughout the world.

The great migrations, which began in response to the pogroms of the early 1880s, accelerated in the 1890s as the situation in Eastern Europe deteriorated. Restrictive tsarist policies, a hostile environment, and the general deterioration of opportunities for Jews convinced many that the future lay elsewhere. After the renewal of pogroms in Kishinev in 1903 and throughout Russia in the wake of the 1905 revolution, emigration became a flood that only ceased with the start of World War I. Ultimately about two million Jews emigrated from the Russian Empire, comprising two-thirds of the total emigrating although only 5 percent of the population. Mainly at least initially from the northwest provinces of the Russian Pale of Settlement, ultimately one may estimate that about one million persons were from the area of Lita with its particular religious orientation and culture as well as character of response to the economic and social stresses of the time.

Most went to the United States, yet significant numbers settled in Britain, in Canada, in the Western Hemisphere, and most specifically in South Africa. These other mainly; but in the case of Canada and South Africa, not entirely English-speaking countries, had a similar evolution but with the sometimes-marked differences from the United States that their specific characteristics created.

One may argue that all these countries share a structure that permitted political and economic opportunities to uniformly poor and oppressed immigrant Jews of the early twentieth century. There was similarity in the experience of the closure of immigration by the start of World War I in Britain after partial restriction in 1905, essentially by the mid-1920s in Canada and the

United States, extending to 1930 in South Africa. The interwar era was similar in all characterized by economic dislocations and the rise of anti-Semitism—exclusion in face of the acculturation of the children of the immigrant generation. The impact of World War II and the foundation of the Jewish state was experienced by all; all were also bystanders to the Holocaust.

Yet the differences they offered are instructive. For example, the "capture of the community" by Zionism varied in extent and onset. It was most marked overall and of earliest onset in South Africa, also quite early in Canada, later in Britain, and last—not until the postwar period—in the United States. One factor may have been that the last two countries had, prior to the East European immigration, a relatively large and influential existing Jewish community that opposed Zionism. Yiddishism expressed in the diffusion and extent of maintenance of Yiddish use and literature also varied. It was least supported and persistent in Britain; rather widespread in the United States, given its large population, but not lasting beyond the mid-1930s; remarkably maintained in South Africa even into the postwar era; and most persistent in Canada, particularly in Montreal.

Labor unionism was also universal, particularly in the garment trade, in all countries in the immigrant generation and the interwar era. Most extensive and most lasting was Jewish influence in the United States labor movement. In South Africa, class-based organization foundered on racialism. The frequent corollary of Yiddishism and labor unionism was the secular expression of a better life via a belief in democratic socialism as well as Communism. In all countries, although relatively few in actual number, Jews were heavily represented during the immigrant generation in the Communist Party and its congeners. Stalinism, by the end of World War II, weakened the attraction of the Communist Party as the bearer of freedom from anti-Semitism dating from the Russian Revolution. Despite the most severe suppression, remarkably persistent was the adherence to the Communist Party of those few Jews in the context of the color bar in South Africa.

Jews mainly found expression in Democratic Socialism most significantly in the Labour Party in Britain, and in several provincial legislature in Canada. Some Socialist ideas found support in the mainstream Democratic Party of the United States to which Jews have continued to adhere despite their middle-class status. The prominence of Jews in the 'New Left' and early civil rights movement can be considered a more revolutionary remnant of that impulse. The "white liberal" impulse of the Jews of South Africa persisted to a remarkable degree but foundered in its political expression in the context of apartheid. Emigration to Israel as well as the other English-speaking countries became its answer.

The persistence of *Orthodoxy* was most notable in Britain where it found its home in the mainstream United Synagogue under a chief rabbi; his influence has also extended strongly to South Africa where nonobservant Orthodoxy is most followed. Orthodoxy has been less followed in Canada where American forms of Conservative and Reform Judaism have also taken hold. The latter two strands are strongest in the United States where they have accommodated Judaism to the American setting. Reform in the United States and Canada also adapted to its East European membership in the post-World War II era. Most innovative has been the Conservative and Reform accommodation of Judaism to the involvement of Jewish women and, to a lesser degree, the revolutionary impulse of Jewish counterculture. These expressions of vitality in Judaism have not been experienced as much elsewhere.

Perhaps most noteworthy have been the differences in the public recognition of the significance of the Holocaust. It has been recognized in the public spaces of cities throughout the United States and in the sacred precincts of the capital. In Canada, although Holocaust Memorial Day is proclaimed on a provincial basis, almost all memorials lie within Jewish settings such as cemeteries and community centers. There is a Holocaust Memorial Center in Cape Town with a monument in Johannesburg's West Park Cemetery. Its recognition has been particularly least in Britain where Holocaust Memorial Day has been recently opposed by Muslims.

The commitment to learning "for its own sake" as a cultural ideal might be considered as a part of the legacy of the Vilna Gaon and the Litvak yeshivot, secularized but still potent. It had particular impact early on in the United States with free access to nonsectarian public schools with relatively less expression in Britain where secondary school and university education was less widely available and was initially sectarian. Education was freely available at a university level in South Africa but was mainly sectarian at a secondary level in private schools. Sectarian schools were a recurrent problem in Montreal in Canada where Jewish day schools have flourished in the context of a continuing sectarian system in Quebec.

The integration of Jewish experience in the literature of the mainstream language was one product of the post-World War II generation, particularly in the United States, to a lesser extent in Canada but still quite marked. The limited amount of South African literature has been heavily affected by Jewish sensibility. British literature has been affected, but least so reflective of the deep-seated, anti-Semitic strain of British culture. Another was the recognition in the post-World War II period of the particularistic Jewish experience as an entity to be studied in the universities primarily of the United States but also in Canada and Britain and at the University of Cape Town in each of the other countries.

Those settling in Palestine in what became a Hebrew-speaking Israel are the subject of a separate section. Smaller numbers settled in France with a quite different history, including the Holocaust, and in Argentina in the Western Hemisphere. In the latter, the history of the contribution of the Litvak strand is less clearly defined although many of the strands to be followed elsewhere are also evident in Argentina such as a legacy of secular Yiddishism and socialism.

The Jews who emigrated during the early years of the twentieth century expected to rekindle elsewhere the hopes that had been extinguished in Russia. They carried with them the experience of political struggle and a heady sense of partial victory and the necessity of self-defense. They had experienced the development of Jewish socialism as part of an international socialist movement. Although there was a marked weakening of traditional religious commitment, religious motifs—still powerful—were transposed onto secular activity.

Despite the disruption of World War I and its aftermath of poverty, the various strands of Orthodox religion, national consciousness, and social and economic justice continued to arouse passionate commitment. The story of the maintenance of organized Jewish life in Litvakia during the interwar period and the Shoah continues to resonate. Even in its destruction, Litvakia left a legacy of self-consciousness and integrity. The survival of Lithuanian Jewish culture and its evolution in the Diaspora is the rest of the story.

CHAPTER 2
THE UNITED STATES OF AMERICA

2.1 The Character of the Place

2.1.1 A Nation of Immigrants

Immigration is one of themes of America. The largest migration in recorded history occurred to the present boundaries of the United States. Between 1820 and 1920, the new American republic welcomed over thirty-five million Europeans from many different countries, more than all other nations combined.[1] The Statue of Liberty, standing at the entrance to New York Harbor, has become the symbol for the asylum that the United States represented for generations of immigrants. The poem by Emma Lazarus continues to welcome the "huddled masses yearning to breathe free."

America's existence was further defined by revolt from the *mother country* and a commitment for self-conscious evolution of new ways of life. It preaches the liberation of the self from all would-be fetters. Hector St. John Crèvecœur defined, in his 1782 book *Letters from an American Farmer*, what Americanization entailed. "Individuals of all nations were to be melted into a new race of men . . . Leaving behind . . . all his ancient prejudices and manners, [he] receives new ones from the new mode of life he had embraced." Casting off the old for the new was seen as an improvement: "Everything has tended to regenerate them . . . Here they become men." By embracing the new life, the immigrant could fulfill his destiny as a human being.[2]

However small the Jewish population (estimated as 2,500 in 1785 in a population of 3 million), it had participated in the American Revolution, probably mainly on the side of the colonists and probably in a higher ratio than their percentage in the population.[3] The foreign-born were eligible for all political offices in the republic aside from the presidency. As an example of such openness, the first Naturalization Act, passed in 1790, required only a two-year residency for the conferral of citizenship. The issue of Jewish civil rights was never explicitly mentioned in the Constitution or Bill of Rights. However, there was a sense of a new beginning in the famous Letter to George Washington by the Jewish citizens of Newport in Rhode Island. Their letter refers; and in his reply, he echoes, to the new "government which to bigotry gives no sanction, to persecution no assistance, but generously affording to all liberty of conscience and immunities of citizenship."

Before the American Revolution, the legal status of American Jews was equal to that of the other inhabitants mainly because the laws drew no formal distinctions. Although not singled out as Jews, their political rights were limited, along with all others, in those colonies such as Virginia and Massachusetts where membership in an established church denomination was prerequisite. The Bill of Rights adopted in 1792 expressly forbade Congress to enact any law that might make it possible for any one denomination to dominate others or to forbid the free worship of any sect. The laws of the various states all eventually came into conformity with this federal law with Maryland the last to do so in 1826. Jews thus enjoyed full civil, religious, and political equality as a matter of general principle.[4]

The obverse of the full rights enjoyed by Jews was the voluntary nature of religious life in the United States. No formal, legally established Jewish community existed with its traditions, controls, and taxes as existed in Europe. There was no official collective Jewish existence but rather an individualistic one.

2.1.2 The Existing Jewish Community

Starting after the end of the Napoleonic era, the second wave of Jewish immigration took place in America along with the more general, large-scale immigration at the same time. It continued into the late 1860s with 150,000 Jews coming from a widespread area mainly throughout Central Europe.[5]. The *German* component, prior to German unification, actually reflected origins in Bavaria, Württemberg, and Posen. Posen, for example, although part of Prussia, was actually Polish with Yiddish as the language of its Jews. Starting as peddlers, many advanced to become storeowners and, in some notable cases, owners of department stores. The vast majority, however, remained peddlers and petty merchants with their activities centered in the "dry and fancy goods" areas. They were widespread throughout the major commercial cities and smaller towns both in the North and, to a considerable degree, in the South.

Recurrent appeals for assistance to indigents belie the assumption that all America's Jews in mid nineteenth century were prosperous.[6] A kind of Jewish subeconomy existed in the interstices of the larger economy where capital was not readily made available. Jews dispensed "free loans" to each other; family and kin networks served to support each other.[7] Many, if not all, had reached a degree of prosperity different from what they experienced on their arrival and different from the poverty-stricken compatriots who were to start coming from Eastern Europe.

The increased visibility of Jews at the time of the Civil War had aroused anti-Semitic attacks both in the Confederacy and in the Union. Judah P. Benjamin was a leading figure in the Confederate government in Richmond. He was singled out as a Jew and blamed for their defeats. On the Union side, General Grant singled out Jewish traders and banished all Jews living in the Department of Tennessee by means of the notorious General Order No.11 in December 1862. It affected the removal of Jewish residents of towns such as Paducah in Kentucky before being revoked by Lincoln's direct command in March 1863. This order was an instance when official anti-Semitism was sponsored by an arm of the United States government and may be taken to reflect widespread feelings within Grant's officer corps.

Social anti-Semitism was exemplified by the episode in 1877 when Jesse Seligman, the principal of an international banking house, was turned away from the Grand Union Hotel in Saratoga Springs in New York on the basis of being *Hebrew*. There was to be increasing social ostracism and exclusion from clubs and other markers of the social elite to which they had previously belonged. Despite or perhaps because of their prosperity, *German* Jews could be concerned about their status in their new country.

Reform Judaism was the primary form of religion affiliation of this group that had achieved middle-class status in the United States. Traditional religious services seemed unseemly with each worshipper racing through the prescribed prayers, often without understanding the Hebrew. Another perhaps even more meaningful problem was how to function in a more secular world. Judaism was to become a religion among other religions rather than an all encompassing way of life.

Starting in Charleston in South Carolina in 1830s at Beth Elohim, the elements of *Reform*, already begun in Germany, were introduced into American Jewry. Reform societies and then congregations spread throughout the country associated with the principle of maintaining the spirit rather than the letter of Jewish law (Halakha) in response to the character of modern life. Also implicit was the acceptance of living in the Diaspora as a proper place rather than waiting for a return to the Land of Israel. The messianic age was to be the millennium for all mankind, and the essence of their Judaism was moral and ethical rather than based upon outward observance of what could be considered outmoded traditions.[8]

Jewishness, for most men and women in America, had come to involve little systematic thought or even traditional study. The entire tradition of textual analysis and commentary played little or no role in their lives. Those who were involved in the study of Jewish texts in Europe did not normally come to America. A German-trained professional leadership eventually became available from European seminaries. However, innovative rabbis found themselves stymied by their lay boards who acted as "Americans," asserting the right of citizens to determine policy. Religious authority played only a small part in founding and shaping communal life.[9]

Isaac Mayer Wise, a native of Bohemia, was the rabbi at Cincinnati's Plum Street Synagogue (Bene Jeshurun) and the leader of American Jewry. In the model of several Protestant denominations, Wise founded the Hebrew Union College in 1875—its rabbinical training center—and the Union of American Hebrew Congregations in 1873. The term *union* connotes an attempt to welcome a range of differences in ritual and theology and to unify all Jewish congregations. Reflecting a great degree of cultural homogeneity prior to the start of the East European immigration, a large number of congregations joined, particularly in the Midwest and South.[10]

Nineteen mainly Midwestern rabbis gathered in Pittsburgh in 1885 to establish the Pittsburgh Platform that was to serve as the credo of "classical Reform" for the next generation.[11] The Pittsburgh Platform emphasized the evolutionary possibilities of Judaism, adapting itself in each age "according to the postulates of reason." The development of this platform served to distance their program from the more traditional East Europeans as well as the new interest in Zionism.[12] Reform Judaism was to be considered a religious confession rather than the expression of peoplehood or nationality.[13] The leaders of *Reform* stigmatized East European religious practices variously as "orientalism, Talmudism, or rabbinism." Yiddish was despised as a jargon "that created an spirit of antagonism to American institutions."[14] There was emphasis on Judaism's moral laws and its idea of *God* in support of these laws, that is, ethical monotheism. The mission was to bring this message to the world and a commitment to act in accordance with ethical monotheism to eradicate social injustice.

Membership in a B'nai B'rith or a Masonic lodge, as opposed to a congregation of any sort, could also be fully compatible with maintaining notions of Jewishness as group identity.[15] Outside the orbit of the synagogues, an entire network of organizations developed to deal with education, philanthropy, group defense, and recreation. They published newspapers, wrote books, and founded societies which demonstrated that Jews did more than pray differently from other Americans.[16] Just prior to 1880, it was estimated that the Jewish population was 250,000 within a total population of 43 million Americans (.50 percent).[17] There was thus a significant number of Jews already living in the United States when the larger scale East European immigration began to take place.

Millions of immigrants had arrived in the United States since 1820. However, during the mid-nineteenth century, when Catholics became more numerous, the *Know-Nothings* were merely one of the recurrent nativist efforts that sought to close the gates. In post-Civil War America, potential immigrants extended beyond the original sources in Northern Europe, southward to Italy, and eastward to the Habsburg and Russian empires. These "new" immigrants were attracted, and indeed recruited, to fill the jobs available with industrialization and the opening of the Great Plains to agriculture.[18] However in 1882, for the first time, Congress passed a law that barred immigrants from the United States on the basis of race or nationality. The Chinese Exclusion Act in 1882 forbade the immigration of Chinese and prohibited their naturalization. It was the start of a concerted movement for the restriction of immigration that would stress racial and cultural homogeneity.

There was polarization between native Americans and the newer immigrants and between capital and labor. The earlier welcome to revolutionary ideas carried by immigrants, such as republicanism, did not extend to more fundamental social changes exemplified by such doctrines as anarchism and socialism. The labor movement was particularly seen as a threat to American verities smuggled in from abroad by the immigrants.

It was in this era that East European Jewish immigration became part of stream of immigration and reinforced this sense of subversion and alienation from American principles in the minds of the native-born. The new far-larger Jewish immigrant population seemed as inassimilable as any group could be. They seemed bent on preserving, not abandoning, their "ancient prejudices and manners." At question was the possibility of the Jew's *regeneration* as an "American." Their identification, along with other of the "new" immigration, as the bearers and breeders of socialism and anarchism had some basis in reality.

2.1.3 The Great Migration

The source of the newer Jewish immigration was primarily from Russia. In the 1870s, it was estimated that approximately thirty-four thousand Jews emigrated from the Russian Empire out of an overall total of fifty thousand Jews. Thus from the start, the major component of East European immigration to the United States was from the Russian Pale. Approximately the same ratio persisted throughout the following decades. From 1870 to 1900, approximately four hundred fifty thousand Jews immigrated from the Russian possessions. Of those Jews emigrating from Russia, the major source during this initial period was from Lita, the northwest provinces of the Pale of Settlement.[19]

Within each of these decades, there were substantial annual variations that reflected to some degree the activities in the tsarist empire. An initial rise in 1881-1882 reflected the pogroms of that year. A rise in 1887 reflected the implementation of educational and residence restrictions. The latter can be credited with the extraordinary rise in 1891 and 1892, following the expulsion of Jews from Moscow.[20] In the following decade, ending in 1910, there was a huge increase reflecting the Kishinev pogrom in 1903 and the disruptions associated with the Revolution of 1905 and the pogroms that followed. Emigration entailed an act of emancipation as an alternative to continuing to participate in the widespread-but-unsuccessful revolutionary movements. In this decade just prior to the start of World War I, the Russian Empire still accounted for 77 percent of the total but now from the larger area of the Pale than the Northwest provinces alone.[21]

In the decades following 1880 ending in 1925, over 2.5 million Jews arrived. The Jewish percentage of the American population rose to over 3 percent of the total. A high birthrate and relatively low death rate additionally contributed to the growth in population from immigration. The number returning back to Europe was also lowest of any other major ethnic group. Among Jews, there were an almost equal number of men and women and a large number of young children, indicating that immigration was that of families. It was common for the man to arrive first, find a means of earning money and subsequently send for the family.[22]

There was a greater concentration than before in the cities of entry in the North Atlantic region of the country such as New York, Boston, Philadelphia, and Baltimore. There was particular growth in the Jewish population of New York. In 1877, its Jewish population was 73,000. By 1905 it had risen to 672,000, and its Yiddish-speaking population alone was 862,000 in 1910 with marked concentration in the Lower East Side. From the start, there were concerns expressed about urban concentration on the East Coast and New York in particular .[23] (See Map 2.1 New York's Lower East Side)

Map 2.1 New York's Lower East Side

American life had changed. The opportunity for an unskilled, unlettered Jewish immigrant in the earlier period of the *German* immigrants was literally "on the road." In this later period, the opportunities that existed were within the cities. The burgeoning garment industry and the process of urbanization replaced peddling or small-town merchandising.[24] The larger number entering also allowed those Jews who did come to find themselves in large-enough concentrations to permit the possibility of a full-scale Jewish culture. Whole neighborhoods spoke the same language and facilitated an entirely Jewish life. Public schools in these neighborhoods often became Jewish schools, not in curriculum, but in clientele. Jewish ethnicity could flourish.

The largest number of the earlier immigrants came from Lita from an area in which arduous and *sharp-witted* Talmudic study had been far more widespread with a tradition of intellectuality to an unusual degree. However, relatively few of the traditionally conservative chose to emigrate. Lita was also from what could be called the "greenhouse" of secular Judaism, the source of literary, nationalistic and socialist responses to the breakdown of the traditional Jewish social structure while retaining this spirit of intensity derived from the pervasive religious environment.[25] These were the strands coming from Lita that would evolve in the next generations in the context of the opportunities and limitations within the United States.

2.1.4 The Response to the Migration

The existing Jewish community was concerned about the impact the East European migration could have on the attitudes of the non-Jews. At stake was the historical Jewish communal responsibility to assume care for needy fellow Jews. One example is the situation in Boston where not a single Jew had been on relief. Yet with the arrival of 415 Jews on one ship in 1882, the local community was overwhelmed with the burden of caring for them.[26] The presence of a host of destitute Jews on the streets and the occasional intervention of non-Jewish charities, primarily to repatriate Jews to Russia, was felt to discredit the existing Jewish community.

The Jews of the 1880s were uncomfortable with the poverty, the Yiddish, the Orthodoxy, and the socialism of the new arrivals. The columns of the *American Hebrew*, a leading English-language periodical, reflects this attitude toward the immigrants by the existing community.[27] In 1882, it stated "Nothing but disgrace and lowering of the opinion in which American Israelites are held . . . can result from the continued residence among us of these wretches."[28] There was antagonism toward West European Jewish organizations who were "dumping" Eastern European immigrants on American Jewry. The New York Russian Emigrant Relief Fund wrote to the French-based Alliance Israélite Universelle, at that time still supporting immigration, that "the position of Jews is not such that they can run any risk of incurring the ill feeling of their fellow citizens."[29]

Jews from Eastern Europe were being singled out as a particular threat. They were characterized in a State Department report to the Committee on Immigration of the U.S. Congress as "filthy, un-American, and often dangerous in their habits . . . physically and mentally deficient and economically as well as socially undesirable." When described as un-American, they were described their very nature "unfit to become Americans: that their physical and mental makeup and social characteristics were inimical to American values and the American Way of Life." Particularly problematic was the nativist attitude toward the *Russian Jews* as a class as carriers of disease expressed in the typhus and cholera epidemics of 1892-1893.[30]

This attitude was translated into successive attempts to control immigration. Throughout this period, restrictions on immigration was supported by organized labor such as the American Federation of Labor.[31] A series of bills were passed starting in the 1890s to require a literacy test as the initial wedge for an eventual total reversal of immigration.[32]

Most Jews, although actively disliking the new immigrants, were not prepared to prevent their entry and, in the tradition of *tzedakah*, strongly supported relief. The *Hebrew Emigrant Aid Society* (HEAS), formed in 1881,[33] was the forerunner of more lasting organizations such as the *Hebrew Sheltering Society*. After 1891, the desperate straits of the Jews in Russia began to transcend even the worries about the rise of anti-Semitism. While the general population moved toward restriction in immigration, Jewish leaders committed themselves toward support of open immigration and helping even more those who did immigrate. For example, the New York United Hebrew Charities began to maintain an agent at the port; a free employment bureau in places like Boston provided jobs. There was active and sometimes effective opposition to overzealous public health officers turning away immigrants on entry for "mental deficiency" on the basis of linguistic difficulties or on the basis of an inappropriate diagnosis of communicable disease. The editors of the *American Hebrew* now opposed legislative efforts to curtail immigration. Such groups as the B'nai B'rith, primarily reflecting the German Jewish community, campaigned to maintain immigration. They ensured that Yiddish as well as Hebrew were recognized as a *literary language* enabling Jews to meet tests of literacy designed to exclude immigrants.[34]

There were concomitant efforts to "empty the ghettos"; to divert immigration from New York to other ports of entry, such as Galveston in Texas; and to settle immigrants in agricultural colonies in the countryside rather than the urban ghettos. Funds were provided by the de Hirsch trusts starting in the 1890s. For example, the Baron de Hirsch Fund established the *Jewish Agricultural and Industrial Aid Society* that financed agricultural settlements. Particularly successful was the concerted effort to establish Jewish farming in southern New Jersey. Land was bought in Woodbine, New Jersey, in 1891 and an agricultural training center established there in 1895. This same society, in its Industrial Removal Office (IRO), also attempted relocation in smaller communities throughout the country.[35] Although there were individual successes, the absence of Jewish fellowship and limited opportunities in the hinterlands limited the success of all these efforts as significant ways to divert immigration or to defuse American support for restrictive legislation.[36]

The other avenue that was pursued was to help bring about "melting" of the immigrants into the general stream of American life, to give up their cultural distinctiveness. At first seen as a "leveling' in the hands of outsiders, Americanization evolved to the concept that a multiethnic society could exist consistent with American principles enabling the continued existence of Jewish distinctiveness.

The public schools, such as those of the Lower East Side, were major instrument of Americanization. The use of Yiddish was discouraged not only to avoid a Jewish accent but a Jewish intonation to speech.[37] Access to an education in the free nonsectarian public elementary schools was limited by poverty. Leaving school occurred for the large majority, by age fourteen, regardless of the grade completed. Until 1900, schools were crowded with half-time attendance common compounded by truancy. Secondary school, although free, was not widely used until the first decade of the twentieth century. In New York City, Townsend Harris and Hunter High School were examples of select academic high schools that could lead to entry for the few to the tuition-free City College for men and Hunter College for women.[38]

The Educational Alliance, founded in 1891 in the *downtown* Lower East Side by *uptown* notables such as Isidor Straus of Macy's department store and the banker Jacob Schiff was the prototype of what became a national movement. The name marked the "alliance" of such groups as the Hebrew Free School Association and the YMHA-YWHA. The name chosen reflected its early ostensibly nonsectarian character with devotion primarily to its goal of Americanization. As an example of that goal, at first, the use of Yiddish was forbidden as a language of instruction. It was only with the appointment David Blaustein as director in 1898, himself a recent immigrant from Lita who had graduated from Harvard, did Yiddish come to be used. The large building was filled, serving as the "People's University" with a wide range of classes. The art classes trained such artists as the Soyers, the sculptor Jacob Epstein, as well as Ben Shahn and many others.

Blaustein, also trained as a rabbi, brought a religious school and "People's Synagogue" into the "Alliance," thus exemplifying the combination of religious, social, and educational components that was the forerunner of the "Jewish center' of the next generation.[39] The immigrants, suspicious of the efforts initiated by the rich "uptowners," also initiated their own version of education and Americanization, focused on the socialist ideology of social justice and communal solidarity in the "Educational League."[40]

Jacob Schiff was the acknowledged leader of American Jewry. The wealthy head of the leading *Jewish* banking house of Kuhn, Loeb & Company, he was unique in the degree of acceptance both *uptown* and *downtown*. He was a firm supporter of Americanization while also using his political connections to make it possible for Jewish immigration to continue. Adhering to his background in Judaism and despite his own official connection with *Reform* congregations, he was instrumental in the development of the Jewish Theological Seminary (JTS) under Solomon Schechter to create a format more compatible with traditional Judaism. His search for recognition of Jewish contributions to culture involved him in almost single-handed support for the Semitic Museum and the Department of Semitics at Harvard to be discussed further in the next section.[41]

Schiff also supported Lillian Wald who, in 1893, founded the *Henry Street Settlement House.* Starting with nursing services to the Lower East Side, it extended its services to a full range of social and educational programs. This same process went on in Chicago, Philadelphia, Boston, and elsewhere.[42] All these organizations served as a bridge between the elder immigrant generation and their Americanizing offspring as well as between the German Jews and those from Eastern Europe. Nevertheless, the patronizing quality of the help provided and the general arrogance toward the immigrants was not forgotten. As soon as possible, the immigrants developed their own parallel institutions. For example, in both Denver and Los Angeles, Jewish communities built two national institutions devoted to the treatment of tuberculosis. In Cleveland, where there was a *Russian Relief Society* and the *Hebrew Temporary Home*, the newer immigrants built their own *Hebrew Shelter Home* in 1897 "as the only institution in town which asks no questions of its clients."[43]

The process of Americanization by people such as Schiff, in his own image, was considered as compatible and even supportive of Jewish values and culture. Americanism became a faith evolving alongside the other secular ideas of Jewish liberation, that is, socialism and nationalism.[44] It was perhaps the most widespread creed among the Jews of the new immigrant generation. The more rapid rise in economic and professional status achieved by Jews in New York, when compared to a similar group in London, can be considered to be the result of the assimilation of such American values as self-help and initiative expressed in extraordinarily high levels of entrepreneurship.[45]

The concept of *Americanism* came to be regarded as consistent with the entire range of ideologies that the Jews espoused. One can

be a good Jew and adhere to "American" values. Indeed one would
be a better American by being consistent with one's Jewish identity.
That identity was, however, one of acting with dignity and pride
as a "free man in a free country" rather than as in a *ghetto*. This
was the rhetoric of the Haskalah, of emergence from the ghetto,
of emergence from oppressive forms of Judaism. Liberation from
their own past was an ideology that resonated in America where
self-invention was encouraged. The issue to be faced was whether
opportunity to "become a man" in America could be based upon
creative survival of the ethnoreligious community. One must be
alive to the dangers of artificial Americanization that may destroy
old values without building up new values in their stead.[46]

Even the socialist Yiddishist Chaim Zhitlowsky found shelter
in his concept of Americanism. "Immigrant Americanism was
based upon the following syllogism: America deserves Jewish
love and loyalty because America is free; America is free to the
extent that it allows its citizens a liberal measure of self-esteem
and self-expression, that is, insofar as Jews may remain true to
themselves; therefore, Jewish allegiance to America may be taken
as a measure of America's faithfulness to itself."[47] If the essence
of Jewishness was its folk-ethnic basis, this was a far cry from the
formulation of Crèvecœur that emphasized the "leaving behind
of all ancient prejudices and manners."

Judah Magnes, in 1909, in his role as rabbi of New York's
Temple Emanu-El, the bastion of Reform, also opposed the
concept of Americanization as conformity. Rather, he defined a
multicultural America as a better place; America was not, after
all, the melting pot. The aim was to establish the legitimization of
pluralism, that is, Jewish distinctiveness within American society.
One way to have pride was to identify with the Judaic lineage
that had been claimed for the American Republic "a people
that adopted the very principles of justice and human dignity
proclaimed by Israel's lawgivers and prophets." The fulfillment
of Jewish prophetic hope appears in American form.[48]

In the context of the social changes following World War I and
the Russian Revolution, the bill eventually passed in 1924 limited
total immigration to 150,000 persons with a quota system based
upon the 1890 census. This reduced the proportion available
to persons coming from Southern and Eastern Europe and

brought about the end of the tradition of open immigration upon which the nation had grown. Until the 1960s, the law, with its quotas, would blatantly reflect the prejudices and fears of those intimidated by urban and industrial change and threatened in its folkways by the felt presence of exotic ethnics.[49]

This sentiment not only affected those who wanted to enter, it reflected on the foreign-born in the United States. Restriction gave official sanction to the assertions that the immigrants were separate from and inferior to the native-born. The "new" immigrants were somehow second-class citizens.

2.2 The Evolution in America

2.2.1. The Immigrant Generation

The first "immigrant generation" is most active roughly between 1880 and 1920. The basic shaping element is the immigration experience and their distance from it. There had been an overturning of the social pyramid that had existed. The genteel scholars of Lita were no longer the leaders in this new country. They became factory workers, particularly in the needle trades, because they had no choice. That first generation could be characterized as having anxiety along with hope. Anxiety was inevitable for those so uprooted. Even when Judaism itself was denied, the persistence of a sense of community rooted in Jewish ethics and commitment to social justice provided hope for a better world for many. There was continuity of the cultural strands that had been brought by the immigrants from their experiences in Eastern Europe that would grow even more evident in interaction with the character of the country.

American Socialism

One of the most salient characteristics of Lita had been the development of socialism, the particularistic Jewish Socialist Bund within the context of a more universalistic Social-Democratic movement. Its development in the northwest provinces, particularly the cities of Vilna and Minsk, has been attributed to the higher degree of urbanization and the proletarianization of the Jewish artisans that occurred in these provinces. The Jewish radical intelligentsia in Russia that joined with the artisans were not engaged in a class war against a ruthless industrial capitalism. Industrial capitalism did not exist in the Pale. Their economic goals had been modest: a twelve-hour day, the right to organize, to be paid a living wage. When they arrived in America, their previous political goals in Russia for the right to vote and a constitutional government were already in place. Unlike the situation in Lita, politics in America was at most a seasonal phenomenon at election time.

They continued to fight for an economic utopia. Although they couched their battle in terms of distributing wealth, in practice, they fought only for union recognition. That fight was compatible with the American ethos of the dignity of man, of the dignity of the worker, and parity with the boss as a human being. The labor movement provided a sense of community for those who remained within the working class. However, they made sure that their children would not also be workers. They formed a one-generation working class, "neither the sons nor the fathers of workers."[1] In 1900, 60 percent of Jews were factory workers; by 1930 only 14 percent, far outpacing class mobility in the general population.[2]

Particularly difficult was the plight of the intellectuals among the immigrants. "Unused to physical labor, they were pressed into the only means of survival: the garment-making shop and peddling . . . One, who came [early in the 1880s] as a member of the Am Olam group describes his first seven years in America. 'I worked in tobacco, canning, paper collar, iron and textile factories and in a sawmill. Then I tried my hand at some crafts: making pillows, chairs, sewing shirts. I dug ditches, worked on a farm, was a railroad inspector, opened a grocery, worked in a bank, spent some time as a medical student, a sanitary inspector, dealt in real estate, taught in a public school, edited a weekly and have ended up doing reporting for a number of large American newspapers.'" Most went to work in the garment industry.[3]

Russian Jews raised to a high art the "section-work" which broke down the various segments of an article of clothing moving it along a variant of the assembly line. The *tailor* became a *garment worker* and sewing machine workers became *operators*.[4] The industry was undergoing a rapid expansion at the time when East European immigration was at its height. The growth in product value for both men's and women's clothing tripled in the years 1870-1900. The number of workers doubled. New York City was the fashion center of the United States with 65 percent of the value of all women's wear produced in 1899. This continued into the 1920s when 78 percent of the value was in New York City.[5]

Immigrants were typically recruited by their compatriots when they arrived. Exploitation was rampant. Pay was low. The work was seasonal. The *slack periods* when there was no work lasted for several months each year. Many had to pay to get their first jobs and were frequently required to work several weeks without pay for the "learning." Workers were often charged for the needles, the electricity to run their machines, and overcharged for mistakes and fined for lateness. The factories were dirty, the windows nailed shut; safety was ignored. Injuries were common. In addition to the problems of the factories, the lofts and tenement rooms converted to garment shops were even worse. The entire industry could well be called a sweat shop in terms of its intense competition. The small-shop character of the industry was further fragmented by contracting, subcontracting, and homework.[6]

The Jewish labor movement was a unique result of the joining of the Russian principle of the intellectual "critically thinking individual" with the proletarianized immigrants. The radical intellectuals stemming from the educated class imbued with either anarchist or Marxist critique of capitalism were able to find a fertile ground.[7] Socialism was a means of bringing about a better world consistent with their religious traditions.[8] This religious aspect was inherent in the character of the labor movement that was to evolve. The similarity in the Jewish background of both the worker and the boss enabled them to eventually find common ground. The Jewish tradition of arbitration and conciliation had been enshrined in the rabbinical courts that had long dealt with issues within the community. These same principles were to be put into place in the American garment industry as a major site for Jewish jobs.

One of the factors which maintained the immigrants on the Lower East Side in the midst of their turmoil and general disorder was the proliferation of small synagogues (five hundred before 1914), landsmanshaften (organizations of persons from the same East European town) of which there were two thousand by 1910 in New York[9] and fraternal orders such as the socialist Arbeiter Ring (Workmen's Circle). Synagogues were sited not only in specific houses of worship but in landsmanshaften meeting places and even workshops. Affiliation was based not only on place of origin but on occupation since many jobs derived from family or communal connections.[10] The immigrant organizations provided mutual aid funeral and cemetery benefits—important in the absence of an organized community or a burial society. It was estimated that eventually there were three thousand such landsmanshaften with a membership of five hundred thousand in New York.[11]

The *Workmen's Circle* provided access to medical care and insurance, particularly burial insurance. Cast in spirit of the Bund, it reflected the experience of those arriving in the wake of the failure of the Revolution of 1905.[12] The later development of the labor unions, particularly in the garment industry, would provide this same quality of fraternal, even family-like, support even beyond the issues of wages and hours. Socialism and the class struggle resonated with the traditional concepts of social justice derived from the Biblical prophetic writings and the injunction to improve the world.[13] The menage of anarchism, socialism, and Russian populism brought by the radical intellectuals represented the path to modernity in which, hopefully, Jews would be fully accepted, where class interests would supercede religious and ethnic divisions.

The *Jewish Workingmen's Verein* (association), formed in 1885, was the first of several attempts by Jewish intellectuals to organize what was clearly a Jewish proletariat and to identify it as such. The name of the association had evolved from that of a previous organization which had incorporated *Russian* in its title.[14] Nevertheless, the numerous successive socialist newspapers published during the 1890s maintained their use of Russian and remained oriented to Russian issues. Although the writers were Jewish intellectuals, they did not acknowledge their identity or commitment to *national* Jewish interests.[15]

These intellectuals gradually discovered the existence of a Jewish proletariat, particularly in the needle trades. They were to make that labor movement somehow reflect their own idealism based, as for their members, ultimately on their Jewish traditions.[16] The unions were not merely concerned with wages and hours, the "bread and butter" issues of the existing American unions, such as the American Federation of Labor. They once again provided the social and fraternal network that had been shattered in the immigration to the new country. The union hall began to play the same function as the *beth hamidrash*, the house of study, had played in the old country. Instead of the revered rebbe, there was the socialist intellectual labor organizer. The doctrines of socialism substituted for the Torah, and the zealousness of their previous beliefs were transferred to a secular system.[17]

Abraham Cahan led the integration of socialism into an American social democratic action model that adapted the Jewish socialism of the Bund and made it compatible with the American national ethos of regeneration.[18]

Born in a shtetl in Belorussia in 1860, he moved to Vilna at age six. His father was a relatively poor shopkeeper and Hebrew teacher. Being groomed to be a rabbi like his more illustrious grandfather, the boy began his education in a *heder* and continued on to study the Talmud. Mainly by self-study, he mastered Russian and gained admission to the Jewish Teachers Institute in Vilna in 1878, the hotbed of revolution.[19]

By 1880, he underwent his "conversion' to socialism, affected by his reading of *The Call to Youth*, the pamphlet written in Hebrew by Aaron Lieberman that had been smuggled into Russia.[20] He speaks about the experience in religious terms. "It was a forbidden object [published] by people who live together like brothers and [are] ready to go the gallows for freedom and justice . . . I took the pamphlet in hand like a holy thing . . . All this became part of my new religion."[21] Cahan enrolled in a revolutionary "circle" where students were united in seeking a new world. Eluding the police for his revolutionary activity in the wake of the 1881 assassination of Tsar Alexander II, he emigrated to America in 1882.[22]

He came as one of the Am Olam, the first of the Jewish student groups that committed themselves to setting up communal agrarian settlements in the New World. He was in the vanguard of the large-scale Jewish immigration that he came to exemplify and influence. Working in a cigar factory and then in a tin shop, he taught rudimentary English to his neighbors at night. Lecturing in Yiddish and English in 1884-5, he helped organize a Jewish tailor's and cloakmaker's union. In concert with the trends in Russia, the intelligentsia who happened to be Jewish had not yet committed themselves to "going to the people," specifically with the use of Yiddish rather than Russian. Soon after his arrival in New York in the summer of 1882, Cahan was the first who chose to address the workers in their native Yiddish.[23] The use of Yiddish was the exemplar of joining with the workers for "agitation" analogous to the direction taken almost a decade later in Lita. Cahan's evolution from agrarianism to anarchism to socialism and then to participation in the Jewish labor movement was the pattern of many of the Am Olam idealists. During the 1880s, this group, numbering as many as one thousand, stood apart from the masses and harkened back to the dreams they had held in Russia.[24]

The development of the Yiddish press was an important ingredient in the joining of the Jewish masses to political action within the Socialist Party and the formation of the Jewish labor movement. The first Yiddish daily, *Yiddishe Tageblatt* (Jewish Daily News), Orthodox-Zionist in orientation, had been founded in 1885. However, in 1890, Abe Cahan, with others, founded a Yiddish weekly reflecting their socialist ideology called the *Workman's Times* (*Arbeiter Zeitung*), adding a daily version in 1894. The voice of the organized workers, this publication was affiliated with the United Hebrew Trades, the labor organization founded by the Socialist Labor Party. In 1897, Cahan cofounded the competing, eventually preeminent, *Jewish Daily Forward* (*Vorverts*). It was to be the organ of the Jewish labor movement, more eclectic than the sectarian Socialist Labor Party, more attuned to America, and ultimately most lasting. Cahan framed contemporary issues in the context of a morally intense Judaic heritage.[25] The Yiddish press and its readers had their primary goal to help immigrants adjust to a new life in a new land and only secondarily the perpetuation or enlargement of Yiddish culture. Under Cahan's dictatorial control, he saw the newspaper become means to educate the masses in Yiddish culture but to simultaneously tear them away from it in fulfillment of American opportunity.[26]

To a unique degree among immigrants, Cahan was also trained in mainstream New York journalism. A prolific writer, he wrote several novels of which *The Rise of David Levinsky*, published in 1917, was the best known. It can be seen to express Cahan's own ambivalence about his socialist identity in the context of capitalist success exemplified by the ten-story building housing his newspaper erected during that time.[27]

Cahan's memoirs were his major work in Yiddish. Howe[28] describes him "as having a certain Litvak dryness to his Yiddish, [just] as [in] his memories, and [in] his very soul . . . to allow himself to have spontaneity of expression might [also] threaten his role as the mentor of immigrants and guide into the new world." His *Litvak* ancestry also expressed itself in his ongoing focus on practicality in his political and cultural leadership via his newspaper along with his outbursts of spiritual passion.[29]

Over his long life, Cahan was a unique figure in forging a bridge between the two worlds of America and the East European immigrant. In addition to his newspaper, he was also instrumental in the development of the *Arbeiter Ring* (Workmen's Circle) and the United Hebrew Trades, both housed in the Forward Building at 175 East Broadway. His reportage on his trip to Palestine in 1925 led to a more sympathetic approach to Zionism by Jewish socialists. His opposition to Russian Communism was consistent even when not fashionable. His turn to Roosevelt in 1933 at a Socialist rally in Madison Square Garden was crucial in the future development of Jewish politics and marked the demise of the Socialist Party as an effective political force.

Jewish sections were organized within the Socialist Labor Party, the guiding force in immigrant socialism until the turn of the century.[30] The trend was to encourage entry into the wider community via learning of English and general Americanization. Illustrative was that during the 1890s, the Jewish socialist section of the *Socialist Labor Party* met under a banner that proclaimed that they were not Jews but rather Yiddish-speaking proletarians.[31] This commitment to assimilation, cosmopolitanism, and anticlericalism were characteristic of a *secularist ideology* that reflected the experience in the Pale of Settlement and, particularly, in Lita.

There the Jewish religious establishment was joined in many ways to the government under which the workers suffered oppression. Their revolt against the latter also included the former.

The *United Hebrew Trades* was organized by the Socialist Labor Party in 1888 under the auspices of Morris Hilkowitz (Hillquit), partially in response to hostility within the labor unions such as the AFL representing the native born.[32]

Hillquit, born in Riga in 1869 and initially German speaking, acquired Yiddish to address the East European masses on the Lower East Side. The Jews there provided a major component of the Socialist vote in New York. The Socialist Party welcomed Yiddish-speaking immigrants into its ranks as equals unlike the majority parties. The Democratic Party leaders were mainly Irish and made few overtures to the immigrant Jews. In 1901, now English-speaking, Morris Hillquit, together with Eugene Debs, put together a coalition of the more moderate groups that became the Socialist Party of America.[33] They succeeded in 1910 in electing Meyer London as a Socialist congressman to represent the Lower East Side in Washington. Moreover, Socialism also provided a sense of a "moral community" that "promised an enlightened and blessed time" compatible with the messianic religious roots of the immigrant.[34]

Yiddish Literary Life

The term Y*iddishkayt* is used to describe the primarily secular culture based upon the prevalent use of the Yiddish language. The Jewish socialist intellectuals used Yiddish as their medium of expression to elevate and educate rather than merely entertain the Jewish masses. Periodicals, such as the monthly *Zukunft*, also sought to provide a general education as well as deal with both Russian and Jewish issues. Founded in 1892 by the United Hebrew Trades, it accepted a wide range of articles and stories. *Die Freie Arbeiter Stimme* was another long-lived weekly, representing anarchism. The periodicals offered a cultural, secular Jewishness without religious content. The newspapers joined the literary journals in providing an outlet for Yiddish writers. They both published original Yiddish literary works such as those of Peretz and Sholem Aleichem as well as translations of Russian and other non-Yiddish authors.[35]

At their height in 1915, amplified by interest in the First World War, the overall circulation of Yiddish newspapers was over 500,000.[36] At its peak, the *Daily Forward* had a circulation over 250,000 in the New York area alone with regional editions throughout the country. The *Tageblatt* incorporated the *Morning Journal* in the 1920s. *De Tag* (the Day), founded in 1914 as a liberal, pro-Zionist, and literary nonpartisan daily, was forced to combine with the *Morning Journal* in the 1950s before its demise in 1973. The *Freiheit* was the Communist newspaper starting in 1922 that was most active in the 1920s and 1930s.[37] No longer Socialist, the *Forverts* continues in the twenty-first century as a weekly in English and Yiddish versions. Regardless of affiliation, the role of the newspapers was not only to entertain but to educate. They provided their readers with guidance to the adjustment to the new country as a vehicle for Americanization.[38]

Foremost among the Yiddish literati of this era was Abraham Liessin, born in 1872 in Minsk. He came from a family with a distinguished rabbinical pedigree. He showed great gifts as a student, beginning his study of the Talmud when only seven. He showed an independent streak early when he was expelled from his yeshivah at age fourteen for conducting study sessions on secular subjects. He then moved to Vilna where he took up with a group of progressive Jewish intellectuals. Even before the formation of the Bund, he had a reputation as a young Yiddish writer working toward a synthesis of socialism and Yiddish nationalism. Political trouble due to his work with the Bund forced him to leave for America in 1897. Soon thereafter, he started to write a series of articles for the *Forverts* where he continued for many years. In light of his background with the Bund in Lita, he began to represent the *Nationalist* camp among the *Forverts* writers. For example, in 1898, he came out in support of the bourgeois Dreyfus, contrary to the usual Socialist focus on the class struggle. Even more, after the 1903 pogrom in Kishinev, his columns accepted the idea that cooperation in support of "national" interests across class lines would be necessary.[39]

Liessin served as editor of the *Zukunft*, from 1913 until his death in 1938. It was the leading Yiddish monthly combining socialist reflection with literary breadth. Although it remained socialist and secular in orientation, it was open to all sectors of opinion in Yiddish life and served to elevate the material published in that language. It published the work of almost every Yiddish writer in the United States and many from other parts of the world. It was one of the most widely respected journals in that era of critical thought, literary creativity, and Jewish survivalism.[40]

Liessin wrote narrative poetry about the martyrs of the past such as Bar Kochba. Called the Yiddish national poet, his role was analogous to that of Bialik in Hebrew. He connected the socialist martyrs of his time with those of the past in a way to make Judaism and the Jewish experience in the past relevant for the masses of Jews struggling for justice and dignity in their own time. He also treated Yiddish as a unique language which deserved respect.[41]

Chaim Zhitlovsky, a cultural nationalist when living in *Lita*, first visited America in 1904. At that time, the intelligentsia that led the East European labor movement in the United States were mainly influenced by assimilationist ideas.[42] Zhitlovsky played a key role in raising the issue of Jewish cultural nationalism. He had been one of the participants in the famous conference in Czernowitz in 1908, which served to recognize Yiddish as an official language.[43] On his return to New York in 1909, he founded a magazine called *Neue Leben* (New Life) which proclaimed Yiddish to be the equal of any other language. His emphasis remained that of the role of the *developed* intellectual bringing Yiddish to bear on writing accurately about sophisticated subjects.[44] For example, in 1910, he published the first book on philosophy in Yiddish as if to quash doubts as to the vernacular's capabilities of dealing with complex subjects.[45]

Zhitlovsky brought together all the different ingredients of Jewish culture—socialism and nationalism, universalism and resistance to assimilation, religious sentiment and modernist rationalism. By synthesizing these elements, he reflected the common immigrant experience and helped to mold it as one which integrates all of the above.[46] He was closely associated with the Poalei Tzion (Labor Zionist) party where he, as a Yiddishist, was able to unite with Nachman Syrkin, a Hebraist to make Labor Zionism acceptable to American Jewry and gain respectable reception within the entire spectrum of the Jewish community.[47]

The group founded a Yiddish weekly in 1907 called *Der Yiddisher Kempfer* (the *Jewish Fighter*) and a mutual benefit association called Jewish National Workers Association (Yiddishe Nationaler Arbeiter Farband). As representative of the non-Bundist Zionist Left, the Poalei Tzion was more successful than its small number of members would lead one to suppose.[48]

The development of secular schools in which Yiddish was taught to the children of immigrants was one of the products that continued in Zhitlowsky's name both by the Labor Zionists (Folkshule) and, later, by the Bundist element represented in the Workmen's Circle as well as other groups.[49] Several secularist educational strands developed characterized by devotion to Yiddish language and culture that were ideologically differentiated by the degree of commitment to Hebrew and/or religion. This ideological divisiveness undermined the ability of such an ethnically based educational program to compete with the overwhelming power of the Americanization ethos once the number of Yiddish-speaking immigrants declined.[50]

Alexander Harkavy was born in 1863 in Novogroduk in Belorussia, grandson of the town rabbi. After a traditional Jewish education, he also took an interest in languages other than Yiddish and Hebrew. Coming to Vilna in 1878, he wrote his first book in Yiddish under the sponsorship of the early Yiddish author Isaac Meir Dick.[51] He joined the Vilna contingent of the *Am Olam* movement, immigrating to America in 1882.

His difficulties in finding a vocation were typical of the entire group of Russified intellectuals who had emigrated in search of a life to be dedicated to the service of their people.[52] After living in Montreal, he returned to New York in 1890. There Harkavy wrote a series of successful books addressed to new immigrants. One helped to learn English, another to write correspondence correctly. He also translated a number of literary classics such as *Don Quixote* into Yiddish. Others of his works included a translation of the King James Version of the Bible, presenting the Yiddish alongside the English. His major work was a widely accepted Yiddish-English dictionary and, later, a Yiddish-Hebrew-English dictionary. He lectured widely on Yiddish literature and grammar in places such as the Jewish Teachers College at the Jewish Theological Seminary.

By the time of his death in 1939, Harkavy's life and work exemplified the impact of the early immigrant cohort coming from a learned background in *Lita* to the "development" of the Jewish masses. That "development" was not necessarily in the direction of developing intellectuals but rather strengthened the trend to Americanization and the eventual disappearance of Yiddish.

New pogroms in the aftermath of the Revolution of 1905 was a catalyst for American Jewry to organize, but all the various organizational efforts were frustrated by lack of unity. The various radical political groups then active among the Jewish immigrants included not only Bundists but also anarchists, socialist-revolutionaries and Labor Zionists. Unity was also made difficult by incessant mutual attacks between the various elements of the Left carried out in the Yiddish press.[53]

Most notably, there was the formation in 1906 of the *American Jewish Committee* as the representative of the "uptown" German Jews under the leadership of Jacob Schiff. Agreement was reached regarding the use of money for relief efforts in Russia between the *plutocrats* and the socialists. This was the basis for the *Joint* in the name of the long-lasting Joint Distribution Committee. In addition, the *Jewish Defense Organization* was formed to include the spectrum of the community in order to provide arms with which the Jews of Russia might defend themselves. This effort at political unity broke down. At stake was the issue of representation of the entire spectrum on the basis of democratic politics. A *democratic* mode of organization would give power to the masses of Russian Jews. The notion of a democratically elected "American Jewish Congress" arose only fleetingly.[54]

The economic and the political agitation in Lita after the Revolution of 1905 and its subsequent pogroms brought this second wave of immigration to create a more "nationalist" view than the earlier more "cosmopolitan" socialists. The flow of new immigrants that were devoted to the labor movement as a folk mission inspired a massive labor revival at the end of the first decade of the twentieth century. The immigrants united their revolutionary romanticism with the practical experience of veteran unionism to bring renewed energy and status to the Jewish labor movement.

The Jewish Labor Movement

The Jewish Labor Movement that arose in the large urban centers in conjunction with the garment industry was similar to that of the other urban centers throughout the Diaspora and brought to fruition the struggles that had gone on in Lita. Its success was greatest in the United States in influencing the evolution of American labor and the political life of the mainstream. The revolutionary and secular tradition expressed in Yiddishkayt withered as elsewhere over the next generations; but the religious roots, in seeking redemption on earth rather than heaven, still has the power to drive behavior even unto the third generation.

The oft-expressed idea was that Jewish workers were considered "very bad unionists . . . but very good strikers."[55] There was a tradition of "labor unrest" and spontaneous strikes based on a sense of injustice and ethics that characterized the Jewish workers. Jewish immigrants invoked their rights as workers on the basis of equity for protection against the tyranny of the bosses. Mainly unskilled, they were more easily subject to replacement by "scabs," and communal support for strikers was a crucial component of their success.[56]

The Bundists had direct influence on the evolution of the American Diaspora derived from their experience with *agitation* and strikes. The connection between socialism and the Jewish labor movement was to be the basis for its evolution. It gave Jewish unions an idealistic character that distinguished them from the "purely business proposition" of the American Federation of Labor.[57] The idealistic character of the Jewish labor movement arose by emulating the model of the Bundists in visibly combining some of the values of the modern world and some of the transmuted values of traditional Judaism. In the context of strikes, speeches resonated with imagery drawn from historical and religious experience. Egyptian slavery under the Pharaohs was a symbol invoked for the toiling garment workers in opposition to their bosses. Enslavement under the Romans was invoked in association with the fast days in memory of the destruction of the Second Temple.[58] Immigration and union organization together created the Jewish worker's personality.

The first involved the desire for change and the aspiration to a new and better place for himself and for all Jews in the New World; the second process was development of an institutional structure through which he could work out a new identify and be acceptable to native Americans.[59]

Only just prior to the First World War, when employers began to cooperate in the collection of union dues, could the trade unions grow into the powerful organizations they later became. Sidney Hillman was among the union leaders that brought about that transformation. He was also instrumental in bringing to fruition in the era of the New Deal the responsibility of the labor movement for political action derived from its early roots in Lita.

Sidney Hillman was born in 1887 in a small town near Vilna, the son of an Orthodox flour merchant and the descendant of a line of rabbis. After a traditional *heder* education, he was sent, at age fourteen, to the yeshivah at Slobodka in Kovno, a center for the *mussar* movement. There he rebelled against both his father and his religious training by taking Russian lessons. He later joined a circle of students who would discuss natural science subjects and became involved in revolutionary socialist politics.[60] In 1903, he joined the Bund. He was arrested during the Revolution of 1905 and imprisoned before emigrating, going first to England and then to America in 1907.

He settled in Chicago, working at the large Hart, Shaffner and Marx (HSM) men's clothing factory. In 1910, he was a leader in the ultimately successful citywide strike of the Chicago garment workers. There he demonstrated his organizing skills and, more importantly, developed an understanding of the role labor unions could play in bringing stability to the industry. He also connected to the progressive community in Chicago where he became known to Progressive reformers such as Jane Addams, Clarence Darrow, and Harold Ickes.[61]

Before this strike in Chicago, there had been successes in New York. In 1907, the strike in the relatively small and homogeneous children's clothing industry had eventually succeeded. After seven weeks, the strike was settled after all the resources of the labor movement had been brought to bear, and outside community forces, including rabbis, had sought settlement. The strike settlement freed workmen from having to pay for needles and other supplies and required employers to provide sewing machines and, perhaps most important, instituted the "closed shop." The closed shop required employees to join the union and provided stability to union organization. The methods at work in achieving this settlement were to be the pattern for the other achievements in the coming years.

In 1909, strikes in a few shops in the women's shirtwaist industry occurred. On November 22 at Cooper Union, a number of supporters, including Cahan, Meyer London, and Samuel Gompers of the AFL, addressed a waist maker's mass meeting. The audience was electrified by an impassioned plea delivered by a young girl in Yiddish for a "general strike," affecting the entire industry. Twenty thousand waist makers participated in the first great strike by women in American history. In the context of the revived women's suffrage movement, the waist-maker *uprising* aroused appeal among the social elite as well as the Yiddish press and the trade unions. Nationally renowned attorneys from Columbia University joined the usual labor lawyers such as Morris Hillquit and Meyer London. The settlement was incomplete, but the strike had broken down ethnic and even racial boundaries within the workers and set the stage for widespread community support for unionization.[62]

One of the icons of both radicalism and feminism in the early twentieth century was Emma Goldman. She was born in Kovno in Lita in 1869 and lived there and in adjacent Courland and East Prussia before immigrating in 1885 to Rochester, New York. She was the eldest of the three children and the only daughter. Her father, Abraham, born in 1845 in Shaulei in Lita, moved to Kovno where he married. He was highly educated, speaking four to five languages, but could not advance because of being a Jew. His frustration vented itself in harsh treatment of his family, particularly his independent-thinking daughter. Her mother, Taube, was a widow with two daughters when she remarried. She worked alongside her husband, managed the finances of the family after immigrating, and became very active in philanthropic work in the Rochester Jewish community. She was quite literate despite having little formal schooling. Emma Goldman attributed to her parents the legacy of "my ability to think for myself and a considerable mental capacity."[63]

There were two elder half-sisters. Helene, the eldest child, took the role of a mother to Emma. She also introduced her to the revolutionary literature circulating among students in the 1870s and 1880s. The paternal grandmother, eventually widowed, immigrated in her sixties to Rochester where she lived into her nineties. She is remembered by her radical granddaughter as a "resilient, courageous and spirited woman." She was devoted to her granddaughter as a "good Jewish daughter" because "she gave everything to the poor." Goldman attributed some of her own revolutionary fervor to one of her maternal uncles who had been imprisoned because he had "advanced ideas and talked [about] them."

When she arrived in the United States, Goldman had already a commitment to a "passionate ideal" engendered by her reading of Chernyshevsky's *What is to be Done?* She patterned herself after the nihilist heroine of that book.[64] Goldman educated herself after immigrating and became a skilled public speaker. She was the prototype for an entire generation of women in both the Jewish and wider community of commitment to radical political action as well as personal freedom. The pages of *Mother Earth* that she edited from 1906-1917 were filled with Yiddish stories and tales from the Talmud. As an adherent to anarchism in both her personal and political life, she considered the state to be a coercive force that destroyed genuine freedom in its role of creating conformity but, in her emphasis on universalism, did not cast off her Jewish identity.[65]

Beyond such notables as Emma Goldman, the commitment by women to political action and unionization was widespread. In New York City before World War I, female Jewish workers formed the majority of unionized women workers. They emerged as union leaders during the strikes that established the basis for the eventual unionization of the garment industry. In the strike in 1909 of those workers making shirtwaists, for example, "it was mainly women who did the picketing, who were arrested and fined, who ran the risk of assault, who suffered ill treatment from the police and the court."[66] Young working-class women in the garment unions also provided the initiative for intensive activity in support of women's suffrage in New York City and elsewhere. Rose Schneiderman exemplified women who were active both in trade union and suffragist activities.[67] After the suffrage amendment was ratified, Jewish women registered to vote in large numbers.[68]

In addition to the revolutionary tradition, Jewish women's interest in increased work opportunities reflect their greater opportunities for education. Even in the immigrant generation, females were able—because of compulsory attendance laws—to carry on their education longer than had been possible in Europe. Like Jewish men, Jewish women internalized the value of education, so prominent a part of East European culture. Those immigrant families who came from the same more secularized revolutionary tradition retained the tradition of intellectual pursuit, transmuted from the Talmudic studies of the yeshivot of Lita. Among Jewish families who had a commitment to education, the opportunities available to Jewish sons also extended to their daughters. Fathers as well as mothers committed to "modernization" maintained the tradition of pursuit of learning, which thus overcame the other tradition of the inequality of daughters.[69]

In the Spring of 1910, the International Ladies Garment Workers Union (ILGWU) called the first general strike in the garment industry. New York's entire cloak industry closed down, affecting what is variously estimated at sixty to seventy-five thousand workers. The Ethical Culture Society led the way in seeking a settlement eventually enlisting Louis Brandeis, the brother-in-law of Felix Adler, the leader of the Ethical Culture Society. The major sticking point was the issue of the "closed shop," which Brandeis solved with the term "preferential shop." Jacob Schiff, mindful of the reputation of the Jewish community, finally intervened. On Labor Day eve, just prior to the High Holidays, the greatest strike in the city's history ended. The settlement, designated as the Protocol of Peace, laid the foundations for a comprehensive health and safety program, including representatives of the public such as Lillian Wald. A board of arbitration would serve to settle major disputes, and a board of grievances for the continuous adjudication of minor disputes was established. Despite evasion, the principle had been established that employers, together with union and public representatives, would all accept responsibility for industrial peace.[70]

Just three weeks after the settlement of the women cloakmakers, nearly a thousand workers struck at the HSM factory in Chicago to protest wage cuts; in less than a month, there were thirty-five thousand, mostly Jewish workers, on the picket lines in the men's clothing industry with Hillman a key player. Permanent arbitration machinery was set up that eventually led to agreements recognizing the respective interests of employers and workers and binding upon both. After his success in Chicago, Hillman moved to New York where he became the president of the independent *Amalgamated Clothing Workers*. This union had been formed in 1914 after having split from the American-born AFL-affiliated *United Garment Workers of America* (UGWA) in 1912.

Both public support as well as the labor militancy seemed necessary to achieve even a modicum of success in this era of bitter class war. Certainly the moral stand of the unions seemed irrefutable particularly in light of the tragic Triangle Shirtwaist Factory fire of March 26, 1911. Late Saturday afternoon, after all union shops had already closed, a fire broke out on the eleventh-floor shop of the city's largest nonunion shirtwaist company. About 850 people, mainly young girls, were trapped behind locked doors with inadequate fire escapes. About 146 died, and many more were disfigured for life by burns. Memorial meetings took place downtown at Cooper Union addressed by Meyer London and uptown at the Metropolitan Opera House addressed by Rabbi Stephen Wise. There were fifty thousand silent marchers in a solemn mass parade. Laws were passed, dealing with safety, hours of labor, and working conditions.[71] In light of the tragic fire and the justice of their cause, further strikes in 1913 by women garment workers attracted widespread public support. For example, Theodore Roosevelt spoke out in support of the strikers at that time.

During the First World War, Hillman won a forty-four-hour week for his union in 1918 and the union shop in 1920. Between 1915 and 1920, the membership of the Amalgamated rose from 38,000 to 177,000.[72] He had close contact with the Progressives such as Brandeis, Walter Lipmann, and engineers dealing with scientific management and industrial efficiency. His union led in having a role in negotiating and enforcing production standards. The Amalgamated also pioneered banking services and sponsored cooperative housing. His interest in maintaining purchasing power during the 1930s brought him to support an increased government presence and made him a leading figure in the New Deal. In the 1930s, Hillman led his union into the CIO and into the highest circles of the Democratic Party. A succession of political creations, starting with the American Labor Party, the Liberal Party, and the Political Action Committee (PAC) of the Congress of Industrial Organizations (CIO) reflected his interest in labor participation in politics compatible with the tradition of Jewish Labor Movement that had originated in Lita.[73] The "divine spirit" that spoke to the Bund in alleys of Vilna was to prove contagious on the plazas of Union Square."[74]

It is important to recognize that initially both the employers and the workers parties were mainly Jewish. With the cessation of large scale immigration soon after the end of the First World War, the overwhelmingly Jewish membership of the garment worker unions began to recede. The unions ceased to be Jewish but the leadership continued to be so; and the unions continued to reflect the values that had been so important in their formation. In the context of the Second World War and the early knowledge of the Holocaust, Hillman, who had been an *internationalist* and non-Zionist, recognized his early roots. He provided significant support in international labor settings for the recognition of the Histradut Labor movement and for the National Home in Palestine.[75]

The Jewish labor movement and the American labor movement, of which it increasingly became a part, was one of the major legacies of the immigrant generation. The Jewish unions brought to the American labor movement a tremendous optimism, youthfulness, and energy as well as self-consciousness. The establishment of the concept of arbitration in the garment industry was a significant contribution to industrial relations. There was also support for a sense of unity and a set of socially minded values evoked by the term *labor movement*. The unions became a way of life, encompassing health clinics, credit unions, housing, insurance funds, and educational and cultural programs. Political action, first directed to the Socialist Party, became increasingly pragmatic and directed to application to more mainstream electoral politics.[76]

The other major secular response that developed in Lita was that of nationalism. Its development in the United States required the concept of "cultural pluralism" to become consistent with Americanism.

American Zionism

The Zionist program in the United States at its start paralleled its development in Eastern Europe. Pinsker's essay on autoemancipation following the pogroms of 1881-82 provided the basis for the Hibbat Zion groups that developed in America just as in Europe. Although their number was small, their presence compelled opponents both in the Reform movement and in the more universalist labor circles to signify their opposition. The American movement already has its infrastructure in place when Herzl came on to the scene in the 1890s. The Federation of American Zionists, (FAZ) founded appropriately on July 4, 1898, attempted to unite the various groups. It was officially committed to Herzlian Zionism with its emphasis on the removal of Jews to Palestine. In practice, it functioned as source of funds for land acquisition and colonization in Palestine for other than Americans.

The pogroms in Kishinev in 1903 marked a turning point in the reception of Zionism. Palestine became more prominent as one of the possible solutions for resettlement. However, American Zionism was distinguished from that elsewhere. There was not the "negation of the Galut." Rather, the aphorism was "Zionism plus diaspora, Palestine plus America."[77] The difference was expressed by seeing America as an alternative to Palestine rather than as a place for temporary sojourn. This was to be the hallmark of the American response to the Zionist movement.

The Zionist strand that appeared to reflect the Litvak influence was that of Labor Zionism. The acceptance of its principles as one of the segments of the total spectrum arose from the influence of Nachman Syrkin who had immigrated to the United States in 1907. His outlook was "consciously voluntaristic, populist and prophetic in nature." Although militant and self-consciously proletarian in the Pale, Poalei Tzion in America adjusted its outlook to fit the exigencies of Jewish life in that country by emphasizing the voluntaristic nature of its social democratic ethos.

Horace M. Kallen was among the young intellectuals who saw Labor Zionism as a fusion of Jewish idealism and American progressivism. The son of an Orthodox rabbi of Latvian background, Kallen was born in 1882 and brought to Boston as a youngster. He rejected his father's insistence on the primacy of religious training in favor of secular education, eventually graduating from Harvard. He also rejected his father's Jewish religion in favor of what he later called *atheistic humanism*.[78] Nonetheless, he did not discard his Jewish identity. Under the influence of one of his Harvard teachers, Barrett Wendell, Kallen reconciled his Hebraic inheritance to his American identity. He believed the development of America was based on the effect of the Hebrew Bible on the Puritan mind.

In 1906, he helped found the Harvard Menorah Society, the first of its kind in the United States serving to sponsor Jewish cultural events among college-level students.[79] His initial academic career, after a short period at Harvard, was at the University of Wisconsin from 1911-1918 where he failed to achieve tenure. His major academic position was at the New School for Social Research, which he helped found in New York and where he taught from 1919 until his retirement in 1952.

Kallen's interest was in the secular, nontheological aspects of Jewish tradition. Ethnic identity, he asserted, can provide the individual with the will to persist in the rootlessness of modern life. Zionism, as a secular Hebraic ideal to renationalize the Jewish people, became his replacement for the religious tradition he no longer accepted. It was also a means by which he could reconcile his membership among the Jewish people with his adherence to American principles. Becoming a Zionist was fully compatible with being an American since the Bible was the foundation for the formation of a free society with guarantees of liberty and justice for all—the American idea. Support for the formation of a new society in Palestine devoted to these same ideas would make one a better American as well.

He used the same thinking as part of his justification for cultural pluralism as an alternative to the idea of the *melting pot*. In America, he stated, Jewish Emancipation is not the suppression of differences as was the case in Western Europe. In accordance with the Declaration of Independence, it is the liberation of differences. He reiterated these ideas, toward the end of his long life,[80] America represented to him "right to be different . . . That law and government are devices to secure this right . . . to convert feelings of exile into sentiments of freely belonging . . .

It is Emancipation for rather than from, creative rather than defensive."

Kallen similarly developed the ideology of early American Zionism in a Labor Zionist format. Kallen saw in the Halutzim (pioneers) a new ascetic vanguard, an elite symbolizing the ongoing Jewish struggle for social equality, dignity, and autonomy. They were evidence of the specific role of the Jews, revolutionary and humanist in orientation, whose larger goal was the elevation of humanity's condition.[81] It was the *mission* of the Jews to provide "gifts to the world." "Through national freedom, the Jewish people would be in a position to render service to mankind. And this service and freedom may best come out of Palestine."[82]

In 1913, Kallen set up a short-lived society called the Perushim (Pharisees) whose function was similar to the B'nai Moshe by Ahad Ha'am (see chapter on Lita). He then founded Zeirei Zion, an offshoot of the relatively utopian non-Marxist branch of the Labor Zionist Party, which brought together a number of educated American Jews who later served to implement these ideas. Kallen's way of thinking also enabled Louis D. Brandeis to resolve his concern about "dual loyalty" and commit himself to the leadership of the American Zionist movement.[83]

The principles of Labor Zionism as defined by Kallen were adopted by the American Zionists in 1918. It emphasized provisions for civil and political equality, national ownership of land and resources, universal public education, and the use of the "cooperative principle in all enterprises." Despite conflict within the American Zionist movement and the resignation of Brandeis, the other recommendations for establishing modalities for investment in Palestine were implemented during the 1920s in the Yishuv.

Even beyond its influence in the overall Zionist movement, Paolei Zion succeeded in winning support within the general American labor movement for Zionism by its support of involvement in World War I. In 1917, for example, the American Federation of Labor publicly endorsed the Balfour Declaration. Labor Zionism during World War I was also identified with the formation of the Jewish Legion. Although primarily symbolic of the commitment to fight for the Jewish National Home, its members eventually provided a major percentage of American

Jews who settled in Palestine during the early postwar Third Aliyah of 1919-1923. David Ben-Gurion and Yitzhak Ben-Zvi, future leaders of the Yishuv (Jewish settlement in Palestine), were in America recruiting for the Jewish Legion. Although relatively few in number, Labor Zionism also became an important factor in the campaign during 1914-1918 to elect the American Jewish Congress as a democratic assembly, representing all of American Jewry. The maneuverings that finally led to the meeting of that body in December 1918 brought about a realignment of the forces in the Jewish community with a greater acceptance of Zionism within the Socialist-Bundist camp led by Cahan.[84]

Histadrut, the workers' organization in Palestine, sent emissaries to the United States in 1923 who appealed directly to Jewish workers in America. The United Hebrew Trade union (UHT) found common ground with Histadrut by focusing on the support of workers in Palestine rather than ideological battles. This alliance ended the organized labor monolithic opposition to the Yishuv. Soon after, the visit of Abe Cahan to Palestine led to his adoption of a pro-Labor Zionist position. During the 1920s, the principle of support for the Yishuv had become part of the American Jewish ethos along with joining immigrant societies, attending synagogue, sending their children to religious school, and belonging to a trade union.[85] A premium was placed on Palestine as progressive society in the making. Emphasis was on the pioneers, the cooperative spirit, and the rebirth of the Hebrew language. "Labor Zionism became the Zionism of mainstream American Jewry . . . [it] validated the moderate spiritual and liberal political character of American Jewry."[86]

The secular strands of socialism and Zionism did not totally obscure the continuity of religious life, but the rabbinical religious strand carried from Lita required major modification in America. The "voluntary" nature of religious life prevented the organization of Jewish life to achieve the level of other countries with a tradition of a more "collective" existence. Ultimately, Jews in the United States could choose to be Jews. The identification of religious and linguistic identity in Canada and South Africa to which the Jews had to respond was not found in the United States; nor the identification of the country with a single established church such as the Anglican church in the United Kingdom.

The Religious Strand in America

Religious authority had been eroded by the urbanization that had already occurred for many of the immigrants while still in Lita. In individualistic America, the *trefe medinah,* Jewish piety was very much under attack. For the majority, Sabbath non-observance was common. While there was stretching of the range of permissiveness, there remained widespread support for traditional mores and folkways. Particularly on the High Holidays, congregations could not accommodate all those who wished to attend. For example, in 1917 in the Lower East Side, it was necessary to create hundreds of temporary synagogues prior to Rosh Hashanah. Even many socialists fasted on Yom Kippur and could be seen in shul.[87]

Most Orthodox congregations throughout the country were without permanent rabbis or buildings. The few rabbis who immigrated were poorly paid. The traditional roles of the rabbi and savant as the most respected members of the community were overthrown. Efforts were made to replicate the situation in Eastern Europe: to set up a "chief rabbi" to oversee *kashrut* in the various cities. The initial effort in New York was ultimately unsuccessful although the rabbi invited had been one of Vilna's highly regarded ecclesiastical judges. The chief rabbi of Kovno in Lita was particularly instrumental in encouraging graduates of Lita's best yeshivot to come to America. Between 1889-1892, rabbis trained in Kovno and Volozhin came to towns such as Des Moines and Rochester as well as Boston and Philadelphia.

The role of the rabbinate in America was quite different from what had been the case in Lita. Raising up scholars and writing technical tomes on Jewish law seemed out of place in America where rabbis were expected to be inspirational to their congregants and to be communal leaders. One such rabbi in Omaha came from a distinguished family with excellent credentials and tried to combine communal responsibilities while also striving to maintain traditional contribution to scholarly enterprise.

Zvi Hirsch Grodzinsky was a cousin and classmate of the famed Hayyim Ozer Grodzinsky who had been described in the section on interwar Lita. Descended from a collateral line of famous scholars, Zvi Hirsch was born in 1857 in the western

Lithuanian town of Tauragé several years before his cousin. Zvi Hirsch came to live in the home of Hayyim Ozer's father before going on to study in Vilna and probably also at the yeshiva at Volozhin. In 1880, as customary, he had married the daughter of a wealthy family in his hometown, thus providing support for the ten years of his continued learning while in Europe. In 1891, Rabbi Zvi Hirsch arrived in Omaha just prior to the High Holidays. On his arrival, the *Litvishe shule* was reorganized, expanding into a newly remodeled building.[88]

Rabbi Hirsch initially received an honorarium of $50 per month from the two Orthodox congregations and supervised the kashrut at the city's slaughterhouses. His choice of Omaha, a relatively small Jewish community, was colored by his wish to pursue his scholarly endeavors without the need to deal with the political tensions between rabbis in the larger cities. He nevertheless maintained connection with rabbis in the eastern cities and was involved in setting up, in 1901, the Union of Orthodox Rabbis to maintain the religious traditions in America. In a further development in 1904, The Union of Orthodox Rabbis named the Rabbi Isaac Elchanan Theological Seminary in New York as its institution for rabbinical training and ordination in America.

Although Rabbi Zvi Hirsch possessed the gifts of a scholar, he nevertheless saw his fundamental responsibilities to his congregation as a rabbi. That is, as the *chief rabbi* of Omaha, he recognized his role in dealing with the practical concerns of his community. Unlike most Orthodox rabbis, he preached sermons regularly in Yiddish throughout the year. He presided over a group studying the Mishna. He served as counselor to his community when persons sought advice on a variety of spiritual and personal matters. Nevertheless, in the early 1920s, in what became the usual pattern, he was not reappointed. His place was taken by an English-speaking rabbi who would lead what was to become a more modern congregation.

Rabbi Hirsch's interpretation of various segments of the Mishna was published in learned journals in Palestine as well as Europe as were several of his books. However, most of his work remained unpublished. His decision perhaps reflected the characteristic modesty of the greatest exemplars of his rabbinical tradition. He chose not to publish most of his work during his lifetime on the grounds that too many scholarly books were being published already. Public respect for the Torah was being degraded, he felt, since congregants of the authors may feel compelled to purchase such books merely to support the writer. Within his local community, it was probably the case in that many, if not most, Omaha purchasers did not read his books. On his death in 1947, although praised as one of the leading scholars of his generation, most of his congregants saw him merely as "an old-time rabbi" with little to contribute to their own lives. "Replete with learning and invested with the right to decide the greatest complexities of Jewish law, Grodzinsky still served at the pleasure of his congregations' leadership. An active, accessible leader in all segments of Jewish living, he was nevertheless put aside by a flock which wanted a leader more attuned to the general culture."[89]

The efforts to meet the religious problems of children of immigrants on their own American terms had been initiated during this same period. The Union of Orthodox Jewish Congregations of America, founded in 1898, represented attempts to develop what was to become "modern" Americanized Orthodoxy. Young people's synagogues had English liturgy, orderly rituals and, the late Saturday afternoon service as the major one, rather than the morning service, in acknowledgement of the reality of working on the Sabbath.

Still another aspect of addressing the religious needs of the next generation was the resuscitation of what had become a moribund Jewish Theological Seminary (JTS). It was originally founded in 1886 as an alternative to the Hebrew Union College as a site for rabbinical training in response to the Pittsburgh Platform of the Reform movement. The name chosen was a direct translation of the name of the rabbinical seminary in Breslau in Germany, which had been the center for the idea of a historically evolving Judaism but less radical than either German or American Reform. Solomon Schechter, the reader in rabbinics at Cambridge University, was recruited in 1902 to lead the JTS in a direction blending tradition and innovation that was to become the American Conservative movement.[90] He recruited a faculty who were products of East European schooling but had continued their studies in more modern German or American universities. In the minds of his supporters, generous "uptown" German

Jews, the goal was to help immigrants cross over to American Judaism and the American mainstream more compatible with their background than *Reform*.[91] The JTS began to shape its own identity and, in 1913, formed the United Synagogue of America comprised of congregations compatible with its principles.

The first and perhaps most lasting faculty appointment made by Schechter at JTS was Louis Ginzberg as professor of Talmud at the newly reorganized institution. Ginzberg was to provide the transition between the traditional religious training exemplified by his Lithuanian ancestry and the American setting.

Louis Ginzberg was born in 1873 in Kovno in Lita, the scion of a family of scholars which counted among his ancestors the renowned Vilna Gaon.[92] His father was a substantial businessman but also a scholar. He regarded himself as a disciple of Rabbi Salanter with regard to ethical behavior and disciplined living. Young Louis went to the yeshivot of Telz and Slobodka for Talmudic studies starting at age eleven. At age fourteen, he came to Vilna to study Talmud. Illness forced him to leave Lita in 1889 to pursue a modern education as well as Judaic studies. He completed gymnasium in Frankfurt and studied at the University of Berlin and then Strasburg. He received his doctorate at Heidelberg and did postgraduate studies at University of Amsterdam. At age twenty-six, he was fully equipped by pedigree as well as breadth and depth of scholarship to establish in America what was to be the center for Jewish scholarship in the Litvak Diaspora.

He came to the JTS in 1902 and remained there until 1948. He trained 650 rabbis who would lead congregations throughout the country. He shared Schechter's vision of making it a training site not only for rabbis but for scholars and teachers. He was the reigning Halakhic expert of Conservative Jewry and became of one of the principal architects of the Conservative movement. He recognized that the Jewish legal tradition had evolved in the past in response to external economic, social, and political changes as exemplified by the differences between the Babylonian and Palestinian Talmud. He was thus an adherent to the *historical* school of modern Jewish thought. He saw Halakha, the law, as other than a simple function of divine inspiration and subjected it to analysis in accordance to the scientific theory. However, he refused to consider how the law should continue to evolve in contemporary times.

His concern for the quality of scholarship led to his founding and acting as president of the American Academy of Jewish Research, established to stimulate and set standards for Jewish scholarship. He was recognized as the foremost Jewish scholar of his time, and when Harvard University honored him in 1936, it thereby recognized rabbinic scholarship as an academic discipline.[93] The depth of his learning and his aristocratic approach to the development of Halakha was the basis for his "antipathy towards the modern rabbinate and his opposition to any 'tinkering with the [Law] by those who, by personal attainments, are not competent and expert."[94] This created a tension in the Conservative rabbinate, which respected their teacher for his learning and the sanctity with which the law must be approached but nevertheless sought to adapt to the exigencies of American life rather than to encourage, by default, wholesale disregard of the law by their congregants.[95]

Through his student and disciple, Louis Finkelstein, native-born son of a rabbinical Lithuanian family, Ginzberg continued to exert influence on the evolution of the JTS and Conservative Judaism in the next generation.[96] Conservative Judaism stressed not only the loyalty to Halakha and reverence for the Jewish past but most of all the unity of the Jewish people. The outstanding difference between the Conservative movement and the other strands of Judaism that existed at that time was its commitment to Zionism. Conservatism was unlike Reform whose universalism led it to the point of anti-Zionism. It was also unlike the Orthodox who were opposed to the secular quality of Zionist nationalism. Conservatism, with its emphasis on catholic Israel and Jewish peoplehood, was the most comfortable home for Jewish nationalism and Zionism.[97]

2.3.2 The Acculturated Generation

This period ranges from the close of large-scale immigration in 1920 to the end of the Second World War and the founding of the State of Israel in 1948 in the context of the Shoah and the destruction of the core civilization in Lita.

Large-scale immigration ceased with the passage of the successive Immigration Laws in 1920 and in 1924; the bill passed in 1924 particularly established quotas on the basis of the census of 1890 prior to the largest number of entrants from Eastern Europe. The inter-war generation was now the generation for whom English was their primary language. The relationship between the immigrant and the succeeding acculturated generation is a struggle between "fathers and sons," a repudiation of the synagogue, the flight from the parents' language, and rejection of their authority. The second generation has been described as one that felt "shame and guilt."[1] Many of the more openly alienated became radicals. Moreover, their opportunities were limited by the widespread anti-Semitism as well as the Depression.

The acculturation process in the major urban centers where the immigrants had congregated led to secondary areas of almost totally Jewish neighborhoods. This further migration had occurred continuously even during the period of active immigration. For example, during the peak years of 1905-1915, approximately two-thirds of those living in the Lower East Side left the area.[2] In New York City, the move was from the Lower East Side to various sections in Brooklyn and the Bronx. This process continued and was accelerated in the 1920s. In cities outside New York, patterns of secondary, mainly lower-middle-class, settlement in the 1920s followed the same pattern. For example, in Boston, it was from the North and West Ends to Roxbury, Dorchester, and Mattapan along the spine of Blue Hill Avenue.

The several cultural strands brought from Lita had begun to be adapted to the character of America. If Americanization was the major new culture to which all else would reflect, the melting pot did not always work. The socialist dream of assimilation via cosmopolitanism was another avenue that continued to maintain itself but was now rent by factional struggles between the Communist and non-Communist Left. American Zionism derived its identification with Americanism in the context of democratic pluralism. Compatible with the Wilsonian ideals of self-determination was the commitment within Zionism to also transplant democratic American ideas to national homelands.

Religion was central to Jewish identity in America. It, like Zionism, was the method to delimit the process of acculturation and perpetuate Jewish identity. There was a spate of synagogue building in these new neighborhoods. Although only a minority of Jews were affiliated, the synagogue served as the symbol of maintenance of Jewish collective life. However, the character of the synagogue did not remain static. The form of the synagogue in the centers for immigrant life had been numerous small *chevras* reflecting commonality of experience in one's hometowns. They would foster both social, including social welfare, and religious needs. "As the secular Jews found in their fraternal lodges and landsmanshaften, religious Jews found in their chevras."[3] Although they were numerous, their membership was usually quite small and in actuality, the Jewish ghetto was an overwhelmingly secular place.[4]

With the move to new neighborhoods and mainly lower-middle-class status, second-generation Jews would design a synagogue as a center that would serve families, not merely the immigrant men. Rabbis would become communal leaders, largely leaving behind the intensive scholarship of their predecessors. "The new 'Jewish Synagogue Centers' remained an institutional bulwark of middle-class ethnicity no longer based on the town of origin."[5] Yet they maintained the original pattern of fulfilling both the social and religious needs of their members. They were classically the "shul with a school and a pool."

Judaism as a Civilization

At the center of this evolution in response to the American setting was Mordecai Kaplan. Israel Kaplan, Mordecai's father, was born in 1848 in the Kovno area. He studied in a yeshiva in Vilna starting at age twelve and then in the great yeshivas at Volozhin and Kovno, becoming a follower of Israel Salanter and the mussar movement.[6] Israel Kaplan obtained rabbinical ordination from the famed rabbi, Yitzchak Elhanan Spector of Kovno. Although trained in the best traditions of mitnagdic Litvak scholarship, Israel Kaplan was also interested in secular subjects. The father's Litvak background as a mixture of piety, Talmudic study, and Enlightenment was to find expression in the life and work of the son.[7]

Mordecai was born in 1881 in the small town of Sventsian in Lita where he started traditional heder at age five. In 1889, he was brought to America by his father who had become associated with the religious establishment forming around the chief rabbi newly imported from Vilna to New York.

Mordecai M. Kaplan's life and work mirrored the evolution of traditional Judaism as it responded to the character of Jewish life in America. He was appropriately enrolled initially in the Etz Chaim Yeshiva set up on the Lower East Side to replicate the schools of his native town. It was an all-day school where the language of instruction was Yiddish. He was later enrolled in the public schools with an after-school tutor who was a mathematician and physicist as well as principal of a fledgling Talmud Torah. His father also became his teacher who taught his son regularly for the rest of his (Israel's) life.[8] At age twelve, in 1893, young Mordecai enrolled in the Jewish Theological Seminary (JTS) in its early days, pre-Solomon Schechter. Instruction was in English, and Kaplan learned to speak English without a foreign accent.[9] Kaplan simultaneously received his bachelor's degree from City College and MA from Columbia. While a student at the seminary, he was also leading religious services in a more modern format by delivering sermons in English as well as lectures dealing with a varied curriculum of Bible, history, and Hebrew grammar.[10]

He was beginning to shape the development of a new form of Orthodoxy. As early as 1904, he used the term *reconstruction* to refer to the concept that traditional views needed to be examined and perhaps discarded.[11] He was particularly influenced by the ideas of the Darwinian Herbert Spencer in his studies at Columbia University. By accepting the idea of evolution, he could no longer adhere to the notion of a divine source of the Torah. His sociological training helped him to focus on the character of the "collective consciousness" which could reflect folkways and cultural traditions. His concept of Judaism as a "civilization" reflected this broader viewpoint of Jewish peoplehood.

He was like Dubnow[12] for whom the sociological and cultural dynamics of Diaspora peoplehood were central. Unlike Dubnow, Kaplan was a Zionist but of the Diaspora in that Zionism served to protect against assimilation but did not necessarily lead to aliyah.

The future of the Jewish people required a strong Diaspora, but in accordance with the thinking of Ahad Ha'am, the Diaspora would lack an essential source of inspiration without its vital center in Eretz Israel.[13]

As an English-speaking graduate of the seminary, he was selected to lead Kehilath Jeshurun, an uptown Orthodox synagogue on East Eighty-fifth Street in Yorkville. Its impressive architecture and size represented the modern Orthodox synagogue based not on source of congregants like the old *chevra* but on class and common interests.[14] In 1909, displaying the influence of Ahad Ha'am's cultural Zionism, Kaplan claimed that nationalism was the key to Jewish survival and that "all Jewish teaching and practical activity [must] be based on the proposition that the Jewish religion existed for the Jewish people and not the Jewish people for the Jewish religion."[15]

In 1909, Schechter offered Kaplan the principalship of the newly established Teachers Institute of the reconstituted JTS. He would remain at JTS for the next half century until 1963 despite disagreements with more traditional faculty members. In the early part of those years, he took a major role in the development of what was to be increasingly identified as Conservative Judaism. For example, in 1913, he helped found the United Synagogue of America, the congregational arm of the Conservative movement.

During the second decade of the century, many who had been the mainstay of Kaplan's former Yorkville congregation migrated to the Upper West Side of Manhattan. They saw the need to replicate, in their new setting, a modern Orthodox synagogue that would be more attractive to Jewish families and youth. The new concept was an expanded *Jewish Center* incorporating social and educational components while retaining the centrality of the synagogue.[16] Kaplan served from 1918 to 1922 as the leader of the Jewish Center being built on West Eighty-sixth Street to embody these principles. This Jewish Center was the model for a series of such centers built during the prosperous 1920s throughout the United States.[17] The goals of their founders were not entirely realized in integrating the twin issues of the religious and social needs of the acculturating generation but reflected the transitional nature of that generation.[18]

In 1920, in speeches and articles, Kaplan advocated a third movement with its own newly formulated "modern code of Jewish practice" to be distinguished from both the "religious anarchy of the Reform movement" and the "spiritual despotism of Orthodoxy."[19] After his resignation as rabbi of the center, Kaplan founded the Society for the Advancement of Judaism (SAJ) which was to be his vehicle for continued innovation in prayer and ritual. Mordecai Kaplan, in the absence of sons, trained his eldest daughter, Judith, who then went on to perform the first female coming-of-age ceremony, a *bat mitzvah* in 1921. This was the forerunner of a more egalitarian congregational life that SAJ sought to develop. It was also part of a much more open attitude toward the role of women that was to be one of the major developments in Judaism in the following generation. [20]

Kaplan's major book, *Judaism as a Civilization,* published in 1934, summed up his design for meeting the spiritual needs of the American-born generation that attempted to reconcile Jewish and American values. "Judaism is, and always has been, a human-directed civilization with sets of significant symbols . . . traditions that have changed over time as Jews responded to different cultures and political realities. The problem was . . . how to respond to the new worlds of freedom, rationalism and science . . . He did not believe that God had spoken to Moses on Mount Sinai."[21] Even more iconoclastic was his notion that one must reject the concept of *election* as the central theme of the Jewish faith. An alternative is to consider one's *vocation* and the commitment to adherence to a higher ethical standard as the mark of Judaism.[22] The existence of the Sabbath, the holidays and the special value of the Hebrew language continued to have relevance even without the invocation of a supernatural being.

His continued adherence to the spiritual aspects of Zionism would be consistent, he felt, with the character of Jewish communities within countries such as America. For Kaplan, statehood was not as important as peoplehood. "Nationalism is not a political but a cultural concept." Zionism was a resource for maintaining Jewish life in the Diaspora, particularly in America where the trend toward Americanization was so strong.[23]

For a long time, the Orthodox had considered Kaplan anathema. In 1945, the Rabbinical Council of New York even went to the length of excommunicating him and burning his new version of the prayer book. There had been ongoing rejection of Kaplan's philosophy by other faculty members at the JTS, particularly Ginzburg. Kaplan's disciples, particularly his son-in-law Rabbi Ira Eisenstein, led in founding the Reconstructionist Fellowship of Congregations in 1955, thus forming what became a fourth strand in the Jewish religious tapestry. Finally, in 1968, Reconstructionism declared itself a denomination when it opened its own Reconstructionist Rabbinical College (RRC).[24]

"Kaplan's mind had its roots in the world of his father, which despite his radicalism, he never abandoned. His rational-analytical temper and his obsession with ethical issues are both evident in the world of Lithuanian Jewry from which he came. Though thoroughly Americanized, he lived in two civilizations. He was the [Talmud] scholar . . . and the sociologist—become-theologian. His secular training enabled him to become the primary spiritual spokesman for second-generation Jews in America who were torn between their need to relate to their past and their craving to be part of the land in which they were growing up."[25]

American Jewish Scholarship

The adaptation of Jewish religious tradition to American values also permitted the entry into the intellectual life of America of those with Jewish values and thinking. The emphasis on rigor of the pursuit of knowledge represented a transfer into the area of secular knowledge of the same spirit which had previously pervaded their pursuit of Talmudic study in Lita.

This transformation of the Litvak spirit from the yeshiva to secular settings was clearly evident in the life of Harry Wolfson, the first incumbent of the first chair in an American university completely devoted to Jewish studies. As the professor of Hebrew literature and Jewish philosophy at Harvard, he was the forerunner of the renaissance of Jewish scholarship to emerge within the secular, non-Jewish university in the next generation.

Harry Austryn Wolfson was born Zvi Hirsch (Hershel) ben Mendel Wolfson in 1887 in a small town near Grodno in Lita—the town from which he derived his middle name. The first son, he was recognized early as having a sharp mind. He was sent to a yeshiva in Grodno to live with his maternal grandparents who were leading Zionists. At age eleven, he was enrolled in a yeshiva in Bialystok. Subsequently, between age thirteen and sixteen (1900-1903), he was enrolled in the important yeshiva in Slobodka in Kovno, the center of the mussar movement. At Slobodka, Wolfson was the leader of a sub-rosa Zionist society. After leaving Kovno, he spent six months reading classical and modern Hebrew literature at the Strashun Library in Vilna. "Wolfson's later life-style and scholarship would show . . . the imprint of his Lithuanian experiences."[26]

In 1903, along with his family, he immigrated to America where he continued his Talmudic studies until 1905, at the newly formed Rabbi Isaac Elchanan Theological Seminary (RIETS), the nucleus of what was to become Yeshiva University. He then took a job teaching Hebrew in Scranton, Pennsylvania, for the next several years during which he completed high school and learned English. He was enabled to enter Harvard on scholarship in 1908. Horace Kallen was at Harvard during this time and befriended Wolfson as well as enrolling him in the Menorah Society there. His extracurricular activities centered around that society, and he continued to write in the *Menorah Journal* well into the 1920s. Having received a scholarship underwritten by Jacob Schiff, Wolfson earned his bachelor's degree in 1911 and doctorate in 1915.

Starting in 1889, Schiff had been on the Visiting Committee of the Department of Semitics. Over the years until 1914, Schiff donated a substantial portion of the money required for the building of the Semitic Museum and its acquisition fund as well as the support of faculty. The replacement of Eliot, a philo-Semite, by Lowell, an anti-Semite, as president of Harvard led to the starvation of the department and severely limited the prospects of Wolfson.[27]

Unrecognized and initially not accorded tenure, yet Wolfson remained constant in his commitment to remaining at Harvard rather accepting an offer to become a faculty member at Hebrew Union College. His meager salary as an instructor in Jewish literature and philosophy was underwritten by members of the Jewish community and his appointment subject to the uncertainties of a requirement for annual reappointment. He achieved a level of security only in 1925 when he became the holder of the chair funded by Lucius Littauer. Important was his appointment in the Department of Philosophy as well as the more traditional site in the Department of Semitics. He remained at Harvard and in Cambridge until his death in 1974.[28]

Wolfson chose to work in philosophy rather than the Hebrew letters that was his first love. He benefited from the methodological affinity between the Talmudic texts and the esoteric philosophical documents. In his focus on mediaeval philosophy, he explored the times when Jewish philosophers writing in Hebrew were central to both Latin and Arabic cultures.[29] Wolfson positioned medieval philosophy between his other work on Philo, the first-century Jew of Alexandria and Spinoza, the seventeenth-century Jew of Amsterdam. He saw Hebrew as the language of the great achievements in rational Jewish philosophy and spoke disparagingly of Yiddish that had been his native tongue.

Despite his long tenure and eventual recognition and honors, he remained alien to the university. His work was his life. He is described as being the first to enter the stacks of Widener Library and the last to leave. He was the mitnagid, the gaon, the austere preeminent scholar. In the words of his successor and student Isidore Twersky, "He was reminiscent of an old-fashioned 'gaon' transposed into a secular university setting, studying day and night, resisting presumptive attractions and distractions with a tenacity which sometimes seemed awkward and antisocial."[30] The connection to his ancestry may be seen in Wolfson's view that "scholarship is by nature a priestly craft. It is only right that its guardian be zealous for its purity and fearful of its being contaminated by the gaze and touch of the uninitiated."[31]

Jewish faculty had not been appointed other than the one chair at Harvard and one at Columbia that was held by Salo Baron. Entry into academia was still very difficult and was to remain so for this generation. Yet Wolfson's example and influence marked the emergence of Judaica in great universities as a respectable, self-sufficient discipline with its own integrity, autonomy and comprehensiveness.[32] In recognition of this, at the time of formation of the Association for Jewish Studies (AJS) in 1969, he was selected as the first honorary member.

American Literary Life

The crucial issues of the 1930s for this generation were the Depression and the continued rise of anti-Semitism in the United States as well as throughout Europe. The American cultural and literary scene had migrated back to New York from the *Lost Generation* in Paris. In the 1930s, a large number of authors came from working class backgrounds for whom[33] growing up Jewish was their basic experience. The Bronx or Brooklyn (and the equivalent areas of other cities in which they grew up) was an immigrant ghetto in which their parents had settled. Maturing in a half-English, half-Yiddish environment, the young sons came in time to reject and abandon this world as they entered the city, the New York of their dreams. "Culture," and especially modernist culture, replaces the older Orthodoxy of their fathers.

The circle that would gather around the the *Partisan Review* (PR) in the 1930s adopted a literary outlook that assumed the possibility of an American cultural maturity based upon a commitment to "cosmopolitanism."[34] Its first incarnation, starting in 1934, was an offshoot of the New York John Reed Club. John Reed had been the Harvard graduate, a Byronic hero whose book *Ten Days that Shook the World* eulogized the Bolshevik Revolution. The editors of the PR, Phillip Rahv and William Phillips, were members of the John Reed Club and of the Communist Party. The second incarnation, starting in 1937, was anti-Stalinist but Marxist in its inspiration while affirming the autonomy of art aside from its political origins. It retained initially its radical commitment but evolving over its life into Cold War liberalism. Its story is that of the entry of second-generation Jews into American intellectual life.

The ethnic identification of the largely, but not entirely, Jewish membership of what was to be called the New York Intellectuals was ambiguous.[35] Ethnicity was not the primary source of identity nor was there the vision of a common humanity leading to the ultimate disappearance of ethnicity. Rather "Cosmopolitanism" implied support for openness and opposition to what appeared close-minded or parochial. The excitement of entering the wider world of intellectual inquiry and literature for this Americanized generation can be compared to the excitement experienced during the earlier Haskalah. This process of Jews entering into the larger world of secular literature while in the Pale that had been the story of Lita during the latter part of the nineteenth century.[36] Entering into the secular world now, in America, was a similar opportunity for entry into the nonethnic or at least, some would argue, the pluralist world.

In the 1930s, capitalism was in apparent collapse and a new socialist or communist order was anticipated. The Soviet Union was an egalitarian society that seemed to provide fair treatment for Jews. Radical politics and commitment to modernism would appear to go together. The young writers considered themselves as the young American *intelligentsia*, a self-conscious group committed to the future.[37] These young Jewish intellectuals did not address directly the plight of the Jews as a people. They sought release from their own Jewishness in the context of modernism and Marxism that rejected narrow national preoccupations.

The issue was to maintain the distinction between literary judgment and political judgment.[38] The original PR ceased to exist in May 1936 in the era of the *Moscow Purge Trials*. The original editors, joined by others such as Mary McCarthy and Dwight McDonald, started in December 1937 "an independent Marxist journal emphasizing literature, philosophy, [and] culture in general."[39] PR equated Stalinism with fascism and the antithesis of true Marxism.[40] Even before the Hitler-Stalin Pact in 1939, the PR had evolved to represent a center for not only anti-Stalinism but for a critique of liberal intellectuals who supported the Popular Front. The New York Intellectuals of the PR continued to evolve over the next several decades. The issues of their Jewish identities arose more clearly in response to the impact of the Shoah and the founding of the State of Israel in the post-World War II era.

The life and career of Lionel Trilling was the "representative man" of this development. Trilling associated himself with PR during the late 30s and early 40s, contributing regularly and substantially.[40] He mediated between the two worlds of the "downtown," represented by PR, oriented as it was to ideas of radical politics and culture as well as literature; and the "uptown" of academic literary studies between the general culture and the university.[41] His life and his work were one; he developed his work in response to his early experiences and in conflict with them.

Lionel Trilling was born in New York City on July 4, 1905. The father, destined for a rabbinical career, was sent in disgrace to America when he failed to perform his reading from the Torah during his bar mitzvah. At first, successful in the garment and fur business, his father assumed the manners and appearance of a gentleman. He continued to act in this way even after the Depression had brought about his financial ruin and the family was dependent on Lionel for its precarious support. The mother was a strong, ambitious woman. Born in London's East End to an East European immigrant family, it had been her lifelong dream that her son would receive an Oxford doctorate. From age five, Lionel was made aware of his destiny for that role. She had a passion for Victorian literature and took pride in her English accent. Her single-mindedness and strength of will is illustrated when Lionel was first refused admission to Columbia; her direct intervention helped reverse the decision.[42]

Lionel grew up in an Orthodox home where kashrut was observed. His bar mitzvah was an elaborate one that took place at the Jewish Theological Seminary and for which he was prepared by a disciple of Mordecai Kaplan. He graduated from DeWitt Clinton High School and then Columbia in 1925. He received a master's degree in 1926. Married in 1929, he taught evening courses at Hunter College to support his parents and wife. In 1932, he was appointed an instructor in the English Department at Columbia.

Clearly "on trial" as the first Jew to be appointed, he successfully confronted the anti-Semitism that had contributed to his failure to receive reappointment in 1936. He was finally able to complete his dissertation on Matthew Arnold and received his doctorate in 1938. His crucial promotion to assistant professor in 1939 came about only after the personal intervention of Columbia's president, Nicholas Murray Butler, overcame the objections of the faculty.[43] Trilling became professor in 1948.

Starting in 1925, he became associated with a group of young Jewish writers published by the *Menorah Journal*. Its purpose was to promote Jewish ideas and learning to offset the negative effects of anti-Semitism. The possibility of careers in college teaching for this group of young writers was highly unlikely. The editor, Elliot Cohen, was characteristically unable to achieve an academic position after a brilliant career at Yale. Trilling explored his ambivalent feelings about his Jewish identity in many of his articles and stories written for the *Menorah Journal*. He reflects his conflict, as an acculturated Jew, toward those who were unacculturated. Also in his reviews of books, he emphasized the need to divest treatment of Jewish themes from any form of parochialism. In his last fictional contribution, he seemingly deals with his own life at University of Wisconsin when he writes of a young Jewish teacher living in a Midwestern town. The teacher in the story isolates himself from participating in the wider world around him by cultivating an excessive Jewish sensibility. After leaving the *Menorah Journal* in 1931, Trilling never again had any connection with specifically Jewish settings and later denied that he was to be regarded as a "specifically Jewish writer." He did not deny his Jewish origin nor that his Jewish identity had influenced his intellect and temperament.[44]

For Jewish students at Columbia and elsewhere, Trilling was an important social and intellectual role model. By being at Columbia where Jewish students living at home made the daily transition from Brooklyn to Morningside Heights, Trilling served to facilitate the entrance of Jews into the American literary academe and made their presence there a matter of course.[45]

He was the cicerone of the continued evolution from communal to individual-oriented thinking that was the hallmark of the Haskalah. Further, his culture was apparently consistent with his Litvak ancestry. "One can see Trilling as a descendent of . . . rationalist Jewish culture . . . his refusal to [think] . . . in terms of a transcendent religious perspective . . . [or] to explore deeply the demonic side of the psyche. These and other positions are hardly surprising in a man of mitnagdic sensibility."[46] His achievement was to make the transition from his father's world, which had originated in a rabbinical family in Bialystok to Columbia's Morningside Heights without paying the price of complete intellectual assimilation. In doing so, Trilling introduced the viewpoint of the Jewish rationalist into American literary criticism.[47]

Although religion was not part of their daily lives, Diana Trilling, in her biography of their marriage, emphasizes that he was "fully conscious of his religious heritage and of what, in difference from non-Jews, it might account for in the attitudes he brought with him into the world."[48] He was fundamentally interested in what literature does, rather than the fashion of the *New Criticism* of his time concerned about what literature is. He was interested in the intersection of literature with society.[49] This same predilection was expressed by Trilling in his work. Observing and "text centeredness" remained constant. Trilling was a son of his father's, of the rationalist rabbinical tradition of Lita. He was also a pioneer for the Jewish critics who came after him and those who entered academia. His professorship was a victory. Now the way into the heart of American culture was open to be followed in the next generation.[50]

We have been following the evolution, in the context of acculturation, of the rabbinical and intellectual tradition of Litvakia and its increasing attenuation and secularization. Particularly evident was the secular response as expressed in the socialist revolutionary movement. The political strand expressed within the Socialist Party ceased to be a force after the World War I. The Socialist Party's antiwar stance was one factor. In New York State in 1921, the Republicans and Democrats carried out a concerted bipartisan attack. The New York Assembly refused to seat an elected Socialist assemblymen. The Lower East Side district that had elected a Socialist congressman was gerrymandered out of existence. The Jewish immigrant vote, as well as the vote of the acculturated, increasingly was Democratic rather than Socialist.[51] During the 1920s, under the governorship of Al Smith, the Democratic Party in New York supported a number of social welfare issues and welcomed Jews into political life.

In the 1930s, with Roosevelt and the New Deal, Jewish voters became even more identified with the Democratic Party's mixture of social reform and internationalism, even to the detriment of ethnic identity. The formation of the American Labor Party in 1936 gave those who tended to vote Socialist (or against Tammany) a way to support the nominees of the Democratic Party. The latter became the political ideology of most second-generation American Jews by the 1940s. For many, there was a continued commitment to Marxism and to the concept of Social Democracy. One might consider that the New Deal, and the role of the Democratic Party under Roosevelt was a partial fulfillment of the social democratic idea. The state had the role to alleviate the excesses of capitalism. "Issues of social welfare and civil liberties, of internationalism and civil rights had become Jewish issues."[52] Liberalism had become as intrinsically Jewish as radicalism had been in the immigrant generation. In rejecting the old bonds of class and ethnicity itself, they still remained devotees of ethnic ideology.[53] The entire issue of ongoing Jewish political support for liberal, even radical, causes into the next generation may be considered one of the residues of the secularization of the messianic commitment to making the world a better place arising in the late nineteenth century in Lita.

With the Bolshevik Revolution, the former "left wing" of the Socialist Party joined the newly formed Communist Party. With the *Bolshevization* of the Communist Party during the 1920s under Stalin, internecine ideological warfare between the two segments of the Left exhausted both. Communist Party members formed an organized cadre made up of many full-time revolutionaries in the Russian tradition.[54] In the 1930s, the wave of strikes and the formation of trade unions enabled these cadres to take over a number of unions with a large percentage of Jewish members. The teacher's union in New York was one, another was the union of social workers and others working in Jewish Federation agencies. Communist strength was not based generally on large numbers but on the activity of the "Communist faction," which acted as a disciplined group.[55] Membership and association with both Socialism and Communism found resonance in the acculturated generation coming from a radical background.[56] There was particular impact on the newly educated acculturated generation whose opportunities for entry into jobs were limited not only by the Depression but ongoing anti-Semitism.

The continued attachment of Jews to the Left, even despite their rise into middle class status, can be explained.[57] Their European experience had been that "no Conservative Party in Europe . . . could reconcile itself to full Jewish political equality . . . Jews supported the Left . . . because they had no choice. As far as the internal life of the Right was concerned, Emancipation [of the Jews] had never taken place, and the Christian religion remained a prerequisite for political participation . . . Radical Leftism . . . was the only political movement . . . in which Jews could become the spiritual brethren of non-Jews . . . radical Leftism—eschatological

Socialism in particular—began to constitute itself as a new religious faith in which no separation between the sacred and the profane occurred . . . the religious differences between Christians and Jews became totally irrelevant in the new faith . . . The decisive difference between the intellectual and dynamic aspects of Leftism [that is, between liberalism and radicalism is that] the former offered a wholly rational and [but relatively] [sic] superficial admission to the larger society; the latter involved a measure of real spiritual communion." Adherence to the revolutionary Left remained despite the conflict in Jewish identity buffeted by the line taken by the Communist Party in response to the dictates of the Comintern and Stalin.

Yiddish Literature

For secular socialists and nationalists who resisted Zionism, the Yiddish language and the emerging Yiddish culture were central. Yiddish was also part of the Labor Zionist culture as a reflection of the Jewish working class whose language it was. There was a Jewish working class, albeit increasingly eroded for its children by opportunities for public higher education particularly in New York's City Colleges. With the close of immigration and the almost total commitment to Americanization, Yiddishism per se became less and less evident. There was, however, a literary flowering that occurred within Yiddish that extended into the 1920s that may be considered as a response to America.

They were originally young poets who had been touched by the revolutionary ferment in Russia and by the socialist ideals of the Bund. The failure of the Revolution of 1905 brought about a rejection of inflated rhetoric and a sense of weariness. Coming to America—working as waiters, shoemakers, and other menial jobs—they would meet in cafes after work. They sought to free themselves to express their personal struggles. Starting in 1907, a group of immigrants calling themselves Die Yunge (the Young Ones) started to publish a small periodical called *Jugend* (Youth) that became the forerunner for an entire series of "little magazines" and anthologies. "As the first mindful poetic group among the Jews, the Yunge were also the first to establish that Yiddish had an indigenous . . . poetry worthy of respect."[58]

Unlike their immigrant poet predecessors, this new generation denied the obligation to speak only in terms of national ideals and collective sentiments. They wanted to make their work more than "the rhyming department of the Jewish labor movement."[59] These poets were a "Sect . . . apart from everyone, not only from other writers but from everyone . . . to be separate [from] the false sounds, the cheapened literature [of the Yiddish press]. In their high seriousness, these writers appeared as though, in religious imagery, to be seeking an artistic 'holy place.'"[60] To live by the senses seems commonplace in twentieth-century literature, but it was unheard of in Yiddish. It seemed frivolous, even decadent. Like modern poets of every culture, they suffered the burden of isolation. As their audience began to disappear, they had no successors.[61]

A visionary figure, H. Leivick (pseudonym of Leivick Halpern) was at the center of modern Yiddish poetry along with the entire coterie.[62] Born in 1886 in a small town near Minsk in Belorussia, he was the eldest of what were to be twelve children of a poor teacher. A brilliant yeshiva student, he soon discovered Hebrew Haskalah writings. Expelled from the yeshiva, he joined the Jewish Labor Bund as his contribution to the dream of redemption. In 1906, he was sentenced to six years of hard labor for his revolutionary activity and sent to Siberian exile. He refused to claim clemency on the basis of his youth or to have the services of counsel. His words were, "I do not wish to defend myself. I do not want to deny anything. I am a member of the Jewish revolutionary party, the Bund. I do everything I can to overthrow the . . . Tsarist regime of bloody hangmen."[63] He escaped by literally walking from Siberia to European Russia from which he came to America in 1913. Although recognized as a gifted Yiddish writer throughout the world, he had to continue to work as a paper hanger. Suffering from tuberculosis, he spent several years in the 1930s recovering in Denver.[64]

He sought a basis for Jewish spiritual strength in the legends of Talmudic and mediaeval periods.[65] He was a prolific writer both of poetry and plays. One of his more widely produced plays called *Der Golem* was produced in 1924 by the Habimah Theater in Moscow. He was instrumental in producing an annual anthology of Yiddish literature in New York starting in 1936. Although peripheral to the *yunge* group in their emphasis on aestheticism, he was compatible with them in that the seriousness with which they approached their work made Yiddish writing an almost religious experience.[66]

The theme of suffering runs throughout his work. His metaphor is that of the binding of Isaac and the insecurity of the possibility of the "angel coming too late." In an intensely personal way, he also shares in the ordeal of his generation and his people. The mission of suffering was to purge the soul and achieve redemption. Redemption could not, however, be associated with violence but with social justice in the prophetic tradition of the Hebrew Bible. He identified, in his personal sufferings in childhood, with the story of Isaac and with the fate of the Jews in the Shoah. In 1957, speaking in Israel near mount Moriah, the putative site of the "Binding of Isaac." "To me, six million slaughtered Isaacs is an incomprehensible thought. I can, however, conceive one Isaac who waits to be slaughtered and while waiting experiences the horror of six million victims as if he himself had been slaughtered six million times."

In his identification with all those injured, he is the poet of exile, raised to the ecstatic mystique of martyrdom."[67] During his lifetime, he became a culture hero within the Yiddish-speaking world. His poetry seemed to echo the ethical concerns of the *mussar* movement of Rabbi Israel Salanter. "He expected words to behave morally."[68] A word has a living soul with consciousness and responsibility of whom moral demands could be made.

Although the Shoah could not be imagined in detail during the 1930s, there was a sense of forboding of danger and of defenselessness in face of that sense of danger. The Shoah was the horror that, in turn, pervaded the lives of the postwar generation. America's Jews were pervaded by guilt for their impotence to have prevented it and their relative security and survival. Leivick expressed these same motifs. He wrote with great intensity about the Shoah but also saw in the Israeli the redemptive sequel.

American Zionism

Zionism was then the other major strand to be followed into this generation. Its increasing acceptance during the course of the late 1930s and particularly during the 1940s formed one of the important bases for the continued evolution of the Jewish community. The safety and security of the remnant of Jewry in the State of Israel was to be one of the foci of the postwar generation.

The thrust of American Zionism during the 1920s and 1930s, as before, focused on financial support for Palestine for settlement of Jews from elsewhere and for economic development. The Palestine Restoration Fund, immediately after World War I, exemplified these efforts. The United Palestine Appeal (UPA) was established in 1925 by Zionists to assure support for activities in Palestine. The founding of Histadrut, the General Federation of Jewish Workers in the Land of Israel, provided an alternative method for Zionist fund-raising that bypassed the usual sources among the wealthy contributors to the United Palestine Appeal. Cahan, upon his return from Palestine in 1925, encouraged support to come from the wider range of the Jewish immigrant community, from the Jewish labor unions and mutual aid associations.[69] With disenchantment in Stalinism and the erosion of possibilities of the Jewish colonization in Soviet Birobidjan, Labor Zionism seemed to offer an alternative social democratic model.

The group publishing in the Labor Zionist *Jewish Frontier* in the 1930s provided the intellectual basis for this movement. It would regularly publish articles by Horace Kallen and Mordecai Kaplan among others. The heir to Nachman Syrkin, its original theoretician, was his daughter Marie, who would be the doyenne of Labor Zionism.[70]

An only child, Marie Syrkin, was born in 1899 in Switzerland when both her father and mother were studying medicine. They had met at the Second Zionist Congress in Basle in 1898. Her mother was a "headstrong revolutionary activist" and strong feminist. Her father had just written his seminal *The Jewish Socialist State*, the synthesis of Socialism and Zionism that was the program of the eventual founders of the State of Israel. The family finally moved to the United States in 1908. Marie initially planned a life devoted to poetry. In addition to writing poetry throughout her life, she was one of the first to translate Yiddish poetry into English. She graduated from Cornell in 1920 with an MA in 1922. In 1930, she finally married the Yiddish poet Charles Reznikoff. Although detesting it, she taught high school English in New York City until 1948.

In 1933, she made the first of many trips to Palestine. She became a close friend to Golda Myerson (Meier), a fellow feminist. Syrkin assumed a position on the editorial board of the newly established Labor Zionist monthly, *Jewish Frontier*, where she continued for the next thirty-five years. She wrote not only about Palestine. Particularly notable was her indictment of the *Moscow Trials* of 1935-36, at a time when Communism still seemed to be the answer for many Jewish intellectuals. After the war, she broadcast in English for the clandestine Kol Israel on behalf of Haganah. She wrote her moving book about the stories of the Jewish resistance including the story of Hanna Senesh. Her translation of Hannah Senesh's poem "Blessed is the Match" became one of the classics of Zionism.

Only at the age of fifty-one did she receive the opportunity to achieve the career she had long wanted. As professor of English, she was appointed the first female professor at newly founded Brandeis University. She instituted the one of the first courses in Holocaust literature and in American Jewish literature at any American university. She continued to lecture widely and write in a variety of journals such as *Commentary*, *New Republic*, *Saturday Review*, and *New York Times Magazine*. She became a speechwriter for her friend Golda Meier when prime minister. Living until ninety, in her old age, she wrote in opposition to the "politically correct" "New Left" as she had been in opposition to the "Old Left" in the 1930s.

We have explored how Mordecai Kaplan had emphasized the centrality of Eretz Israel and the Yishuv to American Jewish life. Kallen earlier had connected the pioneer movement and the socialistic framework of the Yishuv to Americanism. Marie Syrkin continued to maintain the strand of Labor Zionism that had emanated from the Pale. During the 1930s, in the midst of the Depression and in response to the heightened anti-Semitism both in Europe and America, it had not been possible to loosen immigration quotas. With the war and enormity of the *Final Solution* increasingly evident, the response of the Jewish community remained fragmented. There was a clear need to develop support for a political solution that would enable free immigration to Palestine.

The State of Israel

Abba Hillel Silver was perhaps most associated with both the widening of the Jewish American role in the political process and the subsequent establishment of the independence of Zion. He used mass politics rather than the personal emissary-like relationship that had been the hallmark of his predecessors like Rabbi Steven Wise. This association between the State of Israel and organized American Jewry was to be one of the salient aspects of the next generation.

Silver was born in the Lithuanian village of Neustadt-Schirwindt in 1893, the third of six children and the younger of the two sons. His father, Moses, a descendent of many generations of distinguished rabbis, received ordination in 1886 after a lengthy course of Talmudic study. He joined the nascent Zionist movement in the era prior to Herzl and taught his son spoken Hebrew in childhood. The mother was unusual for her time in having gone to a government-sponsored Russian school and thus able to converse in Russian, German, Polish, in addition to her native Yiddish.

The father worked as a Hebrew teacher after immigrating to New York in 1898 with the family following in 1902. The son, at this time called Abraham, went to public school in the morning and Yeshiva Etz Chaim (the forerunner of RIETS and the nidus for the Yeshiva University) for Hebrew studies in the afternoon. In 1904, along with his elder brother and other students at the Yeshiva, he founded the Dr. Herzl Zionist Club in memory of the newly deceased leader, a hero to his father. One of the requirements of the club was the use of Hebrew for all deliberations. Abraham became president of the club soon after his bar mitzvah and, despite his youth, addressed a national Zionist convention. Exposure to the pro-Zionist oratory each Friday night at the Educational Alliance of Zvi Hirsch Masliansky, the outstanding Jewish orator of his time was one of the formative influences of his later life. Abe went to Townsend Harris Hall (high school) where he excelled in literature and composition and did well in history and language. From 1911 to 1915, he pursued both a rabbinical degree at Hebrew Union College and a simultaneous degree from the University of Cincinnati.[71]

When he entered the Hebrew Union College (HUC), Reform still adhered to the anti-Zionist plank of the Pittsburgh Platform of 1885. Despite this, Silver organized and led student discussions and debates on Zionism and arranged for prominent Zionists to address the students. He wrote and edited both a monthly literary magazine for the university and an equivalent journal for the Hebrew Union College. Serious in all that he did, he appeared polished and physically impressive.[72] Now called Abba, his exposure to Reform had strengthened his emphasis on prophetic justice and social ethics as well as confirming his previous passion for Zionism and the Hebrew language.

His first rabbinical post in 1915 was in Wheeling, West Virginia. In addition to his congregational duties, he was active in the larger community—a pattern he was to follow throughout his life. For example, he was a founder, and vice president, of the West Virginia Conference of Charities and Corrections, on the Board of the Wheeling Associated Charities and active on behalf of Woman Suffrage. In 1917, he became the rabbi of the Cleveland Temple (Tifereth Israel), one of the largest Reform congregations, despite his Hebraism and Zionism. He was to remain there for the rest of his life with his role as a rabbi central. Silver returned home to Cleveland to preach and lecture on Sunday mornings despite all his efforts on a national and international level.[73]

Coming from his doctrinal background in prophetic Judaism, he also addressed issues of civil liberties and social injustice in his community. He was particularly involved in an industrial city such as Cleveland with the rights of labor and the justice of their cause in the post-World War I era In the 1930s, he led the fight to introduce unemployment insurance at the state and later at the national level.[74]

His Zionism through much of his early rabbinical career was based upon Ahad Ha'am, seeing Palestine as a spiritual rather than merely a political center. Although not identified as a Labor Zionist, he supported its principles in that the social vision of the "pioneer" was the mark of the national redemption that was in accordance with biblical prophetic mission. He accepted the position of classical Reform Judaism that the mission of the Jews to bring their message to the world would seem to require their continued dispersion as a value rather than only an "exile."

However, he emphasized that the development of the center was necessary to strengthen Judaism in the Diaspora. He would return to the Herzlian political Zionism of his youth in the context of Nazism.

Crucial to the evolution of American Zionism were the changes that occurred in traditionally anti-Zionist Reform Judaism. The transformation of the Reform movement occurred over the years as its membership began to reflect increasing participation by Americanized Jews of East European background. There was a beginning of softening of the original doing away of the customs, ceremonies, and rituals that the rabbis at Pittsburgh has seen to "obstruct rather than further spiritual elevation." Like the membership, there had also been a demographic change within the Reform rabbinate, the student body of the HUC, and its faculty.[75] A new generation of rabbis, like Silver, themselves children of East European immigrants, helped bridge the gap between North American Reform and the immigrant's religious background.

There was greater receptivity to Zionism. As early as 1928, HUC was prepared to offer an honorary degree to Chaim Weizmann, the president of the World Zionist Organization. Each year, Silver—along with other Reform rabbis, such as Steven Wise—sought to modify the movement's position on Zionism. Finally, in 1937, only after much conflict, the CCAR (Central Conference of American Rabbis) adopted a new set of "guiding principles" in what was called the Columbus Platform after the city where it was approved. The term *the Jewish people* replaced the earlier *religious community*. Palestine was not only a "land hallowed by memories and hopes," but there was an "obligation" to make it a *Jewish homeland*. This term evoked the wording of the Balfour Declaration although it did not go to the political issues of a Jewish state. Palestine was to be "haven of refuge for the oppressed" and "center for Jewish culture and spiritual life."[76] The governing laity represented in the UAHC remained non—if not anti-Zionist. It was only in 1946 that the UAHC adopted the stronger stance taken in 1943 by the CCAR that "there was no essential incompatibility between Reform Judaism and Zionism."

The phenomenon of *philanthropy* as a major unifying force within the entire Jewish community was also part of the acculturating process. The successive crises in Europe served to unite American Jewry at least temporarily to succor their fellow Jews. For example, earlier, the response to Kishinev served to form the American Jewish Relief Committee as a coordinating group although a separate group still functioned to solicit funds from the immigrant community. The American Jewish Joint Distribution Committee signified, by its name in 1914, its role in the distribution of funds drawn from all sources. By 1918, in response to the dislocations of the world war, the then large sum of $15 million was allocated. Techniques were developed that would continue to serve as a prototype for national campaigns to follow. The model was that of the "war chest" campaigns going on in the wider community.[77]

With the Depression and ongoing needs abroad, there was need to regularize the solicitation and distribution of funds. However, the German Jewish American community was willing to contribute to the Joint but not to Palestine. Several attempts during the 1930s did not succeed in bridging these differences. Finally, in 1938, in response to Kristallnacht, it became clear that, despite the ideological differences, it was necessary to unite and find what was to be a permanent United Jewish Appeal (UJA). For example, the Federation (for the Support of Jewish Philanthropic Societies of New York City) became increasingly, during the interwar era, a collective enterprise rather than only that of the rich. It served "to reach across class lines to unite Jews into a nonsectarian community of interest with moral dimensions."[78] Raising money for Jewish causes was consistent with the tradition of *tzedakah*. It could provide a vehicle for even the most nominal Jew to retain some connection with the collective. It also offered recognition to East European Jews to enter into some connection with the "uptown" elite. It emphasized the American character of Jewish distinctiveness. By the start of World War II, there has now been experience with means by which there could be coordination and unity to deal with the enormous demands to be made. The priorities for the distribution of funds not only for local needs but for refugee needs in Europe as well as Palestine was to be an important issue in the succeeding generation.

Silver's activities in the crucial days of the war and its aftermath built upon these organizational and somewhat democratizing trends. He also brought his extraordinary personal skills and unusual political connections. On Mother's Day, May 10, 1942, at the Biltmore Hotel in New York City, the Emergency Committee for Zionist Affairs met, representing all the segments of American Zionism. These included the Zionist Organization of America (ZOA), Hadassah, the women's Zionist organization, Mizrachi (religious) and Poalei Tzion (Labor). The aim was to develop a unified strategy that will win the support of the entire range of American Jews as well as the wider community.

Most America's Jews were indifferent to Zionism prior to the late 1930s. Few joined the movement or were active in its projects. Hitler changed the situation by making it absolutely necessary for there to be a place for Jews to find refuge. No country, particularly America, was willing to take Jews. Even for those connected to the movement, the goal for most—if not all—American Zionists had always been to support Palestine as a cultural or religious center, a "homeland," under a British protectorate rather than an independent state. However, in response to Arab agitation, Britain had severely limited immigration to Palestine to fifteen thousand persons each year. The White Paper of 1939 envisaged a cutoff of all immigration within a few years.[79]

Despite increasing knowledge of the extent and enormity of the Nazi war against the Jews, American Jewry was impotent to influence events. "Their attempts to bring more refugees into the United States were thwarted by anti-Semitism in the issuance of visas in the State Department. In their efforts to force rescission of the British White Paper limiting immigration to Palestine, they found themselves confronted by both the War and State Departments which feared the effects such actions would have on the Arabs and Middle Eastern oil supplies. Their appeals to the president met with constant sympathy and expressions of support but absolutely no concrete results."[80]

The response of Zionists to the British actions reflected their divided leadership. Chaim Weizmann, the president of the World Zionist Organization (WZO), had been instrumental in achieving the Balfour Declaration upon which Jewish settlement had occurred under the British Mandate. He was committed to maintaining a relationship with Britain. Steven Wise, the leading figure of American Judaism, had deferred to Roosevelt's advice to postpone Zionist demands until after the war. David Ben-Gurion, the chairman of the Jewish Agency, the shadow government in the Yishuv, had decided that only with political independence could immigration occur. Silver distrusted both Roosevelt and the British. He wanted American Zionists to pressure both governments to permit immigration to Palestine.

Together with Ben-Gurion, Silver led the militants in issuing the *Biltmore Declaration* that the goal was to seek immigration and for Palestine to be established as a *Jewish commonwealth*.[81] This Biltmore Declaration was to be the touchstone for developing support for Jewish statehood over the next several years. The American Jewish Committee (AJC), the bastion of "uptown' Jewish establishment, was non-Zionist although supportive of Palestine as a cultural and religious center but not statehood. The B'nai B'rith was the other major non-Zionist group. Under the auspices of its president, Henry Monsky, a meeting was called in January 1943 in Pittsburgh.

This then led to a *democratically* elected *American Jewish Conference* that met at the Waldorf-Astoria in August 1943. The analogy was to the meeting of the American Jewish Congress during World War I when Zionism contributed to a democratic attempt to replace the leadership of the American Jewish Committee (AJC). The objective was to bring about unity in the American Jewish community in support of a Jewish state. In order to do so, this unity would occur under the auspices of Zionists by drawing upon a more democratic base than heretofore. The elitist AJC felt the need to participate in order to reclaim its previous leadership role. All agreed on the need for open immigration if not statehood.[82] Silver, with magnificent oratory, moved the meeting to endorse the concept of a "Jewish commonwealth," the wording of the Biltmore Declaration, and established Silver as "the dominant spokesman for American Jewry."[83]

The AJC then seceded from the implementation of that endorsement but, in doing so, increased its isolation from the remainder of American Jewry. Aside from the anti-Zionist *American Council for Judaism,* all other organizations involved in the conference maintained their support for the Jewish Commonwealth concept. This resolution was the goal to which American Zionism had devoted its efforts, since Basle, and signified the high point of the "capture of the community."[84]

Membership in Zionist organizations across the ideological spectrum increased substantially over the next several years. It is estimated that as many as 1.5 million directly, and another 1 million indirectly, had endorsed the conference and thus, the Biltmore Declaration.[85] Reorganized as the American Zionist Emergency Council, Silver was drafted to take complete charge of what was to be an extraordinary grassroots effort throughout the country to achieve support for the "commonwealth" concept. For example, it enlisted political support from over four hundred members of Congress. Massive petitions and letter writing campaigns enlisted such groups as 150 college presidents and 1,800 faculty members from 250 universities in forty-five states. Pro-Zionist resolutions were approved in forty-one state legislatures and hundreds of municipalities representing 90 percent of the population. Both the AFL and CIO passed resolutions in support of a Jewish commonwealth in Palestine.[86] Both major parties in 1944 adopted pro-Zionist planks in their platforms with the Republican endorsement affected by Silver's personal connection with Ohio's Senator Taft.[87] During this period, much of the anti-Zionist sentiment in the Jewish community was neutralized. The large mass of American Jewry endorsed the idea of a Palestine homeland. In all this, Abba Hillel Silver played a crucial role.[88]

In the immediate postwar era, much of the focus was on the persons displaced by the war. Many, but by no means all, were Jews who had survived the concentration camps but fled the persistent anti-Semitism of Eastern Europe to the displaced persons (DP) camps in the western zone of Germany. For the Zionists, the issue went beyond the immediate relief of the DPs. A Jewish state would take in the refugees, but the goal of the movement extended far beyond . . . Zionism aimed at giving the Jewish people new pride and self-reliance. The ethos was that Jews would never again have to rely on the mercy of an indifferent world.[89] The first postwar Zionist Congress confirmed the militant stance of Silver, representing American Zionism along with Ben-Gurion, for statehood as the goal separated from halfway measures dealing with refugees. Silver had, in the meantime, displaced Steven Wise who had been the leader for so long. Weizmann was also displaced from the presidency of the World Zionist Organization he had headed for the past twenty-five years.[90]

The British finally moved the Palestine question to the United Nations in 1947. In a series of maneuvers in which Silver played a major role in presenting the Zionist case and gaining support from President Truman, partition was approved on November 29, 1947.[91] The founding of the State of Israel in May 1948 can be taken to mark the start of the postwar Jewish life.

2.2.3 The Integrated Generation

The postwar era from 1950 to 1980 was affected by both the Shoah and the founding of the State of Israel to find anti-Semitism less evident and the opportunities more available for entry into the cultural and political life of America. Important to a sense of integration in American life was the experience of Jews who had served in the military during World War II. and the validation of the *Judeo-Christian* basis of American life.[1] The commitment to radical politics that lasted through the interwar period became attenuated, but its residue was expressed in the student revolt of 1960s and the experimentation with new forms of politics as well as new modes of Jewish life. The relative openness of American society led to an intellectual and literary efflorescence that ranks alongside the great eras of Jewish life in the Diaspora.

Several of the main tenets of American Jewish life in this next generation had already come into the foreground during the previous era. The organizational skills extending into all walks of life throughout the community was to be called upon for support of philanthropy for Jews in need both at home and abroad. Particularly strong will be the connection between political action and support for Israel. Israel was the place where the remnant surviving the Holocaust continued to need support and, moreover, seemed to represent the values compatible with America. An American brand of Zionism became the unambiguous test of Jewish affirmation. A Jewish homeland would give Jews respect in the eyes of their Gentile neighbors while saving themselves from the demoralization and self-hatred that are the by-products of anti-Semitism which still continued to pervade American life.[2] The evolution of American Jewry was tied very closely to the events going on in the new center in Israel. However, the other major center was America. American Zionism ultimately did not mean aliyah for any but a small number. Its evolution continued, influenced and occasionally influencing, but apart from that of Israel.

The immigrant experience, still shared in part by the first American generation, had become attenuated but still existed. The number of Yiddish speakers fell to less than a million by 1960, and the number of students in the secular Yiddish-language schools continued to fall. The circulation of secular Yiddish dailies continued to decline. However, YIVO, transplanted from Vilna, reflected the possibility of further development with the assumption at Columbia University by Uriel Weinreich of the newly established chair of Yiddish Language, Literature, and Culture.[3] Discrimination still existed, but changes occurred in the areas of housing and education if not, until later, in employment. The GI Bill and Truman's effort to put an end to discrimination in higher education, coupled with the demands for scientists in the Cold War, opened new educational and occupational opportunities for Jews. Opportunities to enter American intellectual life, both in academia and general culture, became more available.

However, the character of the "integrated generation," that of the postwar era in America, carried with it some of the same strands of singularity in its political and cultural life that had evolved from the original sources. The secular expressions of the intellectual and political tradition originating in Lita continued to provide part of the ideological bases of American Jewish life. The secular strands of socialism and social democracy continued albeit further transmuted by integration into the wider culture and in the need to differentiate itself from the Communist Left. The intellectuality reflected in literature as well as scholarly pursuits remain evident even if sometimes expressed in irony and in opposition to the mainstream. Indeed, the openings in the professions and in universities may have reinstated some of the old social hierarchy overturned in the immigrant generation. Many of the men becoming eminent in academia and letters had genteel immigrant fathers and rabbinic forbearers.[4] The religious pattern also continued to evolve and to influence the non-Orthodox majority and even to, once again, receive sustenance from the original sources in the religious tradition of the yeshiva culture.

In the postwar era, with increased prosperity and abandonment of restrictive covenants limiting Jewish residence, by 1965, about one-third of Jews left the big cities to establish themselves in suburbs. In New York, Jewish neighborhoods persisted but were under siege as the population left the city for the suburbs.[5] Hundreds of new Jewish communities were established, defined by new synagogues but also by membership in a Jewish Center rather than the more traditional synagogue of the previous generation. For example, in 1965 the eight hundred synagogues identified as Conservative, the largest single American denomination, were double the number at the end of the War in 1945.[6] There were also approximately 650 Reform congregations in that same period.[7] The rate of synagogue affiliation rose from 20 percent in the 1930s to nearly 60 percent, particularly high in these smaller communities.[8]

The synagogue served primarily as a meeting place, a center of community life. Jewish schooling was after regular school or *Sunday schools*. There was little return to traditional values such as rituals or study of sacred texts. In a survey of board members of Conservative synagogues, only one-third participated in the main Sabbath service, with any regularity.[9] One-third kept a kosher home. Only a quarter read Jewish books or magazines.[10] Membership in the synagogue was assertion of their Jewishness and not their faith in Judaism. It was less an expression of religiosity than ethnicity.[11] Questioned even at its zenith in the immediate postwar era was whether a commitment to ethnicity is a sufficient basis for continuity.[12] This issue has become even more salient with the rise in number of intermarriages. The focus on energies devoted to *survival* as the major theme of American Jewry in memory of the Holocaust or devotion to the security of Israel will be questioned even more in the evolution of this generation. There was, however, at the start of the postwar period, the promise of entry into an America where Judaism was accepted as one of a trifaith culture of *Judeo-Christianity*.

The career of Philip Klutznick and the role of the B'nai B'rith can be seen as representative of this entry into the mainstream society while maintaining ethnicity.

American Politics and Jewish Ethnicity

Philip Klutznick was born in Kansas City, Missouri, in 1907, the second child and first son. His parents had immigrated there from Belorussia soon after the Kishinev pogrom in 1905. The father, Morris, came from Grodno, a leather center, which may explain his early work as a cobbler in America. He could read Hebrew, read and write Yiddish, and was at home with "folk level" of Yiddish culture. The mother, Minnie, was from the area around Bialystok. She could read Yiddish and recite Hebrew prayers by heart. She never learned how to read or write English.

Their immigration to Kansas City via Galveston, Texas, had been part of an effort to divert immigrants from New York and to settle Jews away from the Eastern Seaboard. Sponsored by the Industrial Removal Office (IRO) of the Baron de Hirsch Fund, this effort was also supported by B'nai B'rith chapters who helped settlement. That was how the Klutznicks were drawn to Missouri. Their background from one of the more industrialized towns may have better prepared them for life in the Midwest where it was necessary to live within a mainly non-Jewish setting. Klutznick also attributes to their background an idealized commitment to Zionism as well as certainty about their religious identity.[13] The small Orthodox shul to which his family belonged governed itself and functioned without a full-time rabbi. Tzedakah in the form of contribution to charity was an integral part of daily life with the prominent blue-and-white collection box for buying land in Palestine.[14] His life in a small Jewish community in the Midwest made his experience very different from the large majority of his generation growing up in the much larger Jewish immigrant communities.

Klutznick was aware that the B'nai B'rith lodge in his town as the bastion of the German Jews from which his father, as an East European small merchant, was barred. Morris Klutznick was later only able to join a second lodge that was formed. However, the life of Phillip Klutznick was intimately connected with B'nai B'rith. He was one of the founders in 1924 of the B'nai B'rith boys group called AZA. As president of the fledgling organization, he had, by 1926, organized twenty-three chapters mainly in the Midwest. He also moved to Omaha where AZA had its early headquarters and he was given a part-time job as executive secretary of the organization. He enrolled at the same time in Creighton University, a Jesuit school, and then its law school from which he graduated in 1930.[15]

As a young lawyer, he became involved in Omaha City reform politics and worked for the city's Corporation Counsel who had been the dean of his law school. With the Depression and the availability of Federal funds, he began to organize the building of public housing. During the war, he came to Washington to organize emergency housing for defense workers. After the war, he left the government to become involved in the building of housing for veterans. He had a successful business career building what were "new towns" such as Park Forest near Chicago and, later, large-scale projects elsewhere.[16] This eventually enabled him to carry on volunteer work in relation to the Jewish community as president of B'nai B'rith during an important period of its development, government service including Ambassadorial level in the Kennedy era, and eventually a cabinet post in Carter's administration. His story is an important one in the realization of the American Dream but also in the range and importance of the organization with which he was associated for most of his life.

Founded in 1843 by German immigrants in New York, B'nai B'rith (Sons of the Covenant) became the oldest and largest Jewish service organization in the world. International in scope, its strength has mainly been in North America. Indeed, it was the first indigenous American-Jewish organization to cross the Atlantic in a reverse journey from that of its immigrant founding fathers.[17] As a secular Jewish fraternal order, its functions were mutual aid, social service, and philanthropy. The initial impetus for its formation was to "reduce the chaos and anarchy of Jewish life."[18] At its founding, the animosities engendered by the several warring religious congregations were to be submerged in an organization in which Jews of all types could work together for a common purpose. As the first secular Jewish organization, it provided Jews with an alternative way of affiliating with the Jewish community. However, it gave its officers Hebrew titles; by emphasizing the inherently Jewish nature of the organization, it tied a religious past to a secular future.[19] Its ongoing principles have been to help achieve unity among American Jews.

Its original emphasis was on burial insurance and support for hospitals such as the National Jewish Hospital in Denver for those with tuberculosis. Their philanthropic efforts were unusual in that they were for the entire community and not only for their own members. In 1913, the Anti-Defamation League (ADL) was founded to counter caricatures and other degrading portrayals of Jews.[20] Defending the rights of Jews became a larger part of its mission than the earlier focus on philanthropy. It arose in the context of the nativism and racism of the 1920s represented by Henry Ford's *Dearborn Independent* and the Ku Klux Klan.[21] In addition to the youth group which Klutznick helped start, Hillel Foundations on college campuses was first started at University of Illinois in 1923.

In the early decades of the twentieth century, B'nai B'rith took on once again its initial role in attempting to bring about unity. Neutral in respect to Zionism and increasingly open to immigrants and their descendants, it began to bridge the gap between German Jews and the recent immigrants. The election of Henry Monsky from Omaha as president in 1938 was an important milestone as the first from an East European background. A law graduate of Creighton University like Klutznick, he belonged to synagogues of all three denominations and was an ardent Zionist. He sought to make the organization a mass-membership organization and take a leading position in American-Jewish communal affairs.[22] He moved his organization from its *non-Zionist* stance in accordance with the general trend in American Jewish life during the late 1930s. For example, he was responsible for calling the meeting in early 1943 in Pittsburgh that preceded the American Jewish Conference at the Waldorf-Astoria where Abba Hillel Silver was successful in gaining widespread support for the Zionist position.

The ADL and B'nai B'rith's battle against anti-Semitism in the 1940s extended toward working for a free society and opposing discrimination against all groups. The work of the ADL was to promote an ideology of Americanism based upon acceptance of group differences.[23] Support for Israel was also legitimatized as consistent with American principles of fostering self-determination. The protection of Israel could be construed to be part of a foreign policy of the United States that was bound up with strengthening the democratic West in opposition to Communism.

Phillip Klutznick's election in 1953 brought new life to the organization. Able to work almost full-time, he saw the presidency of B'nai B'rith as one of the leaders of American Jewry.[24] He played an active role in establishing the Conference of Presidents of Major Jewish Organizations as a means of establishing a unified approach particularly on political issues. Formed in reaction to the anti-Israeli policies of the Eisenhower Administration in the 1950s, the conference has provided an ongoing structure for Jewish unity. In 1966, Klutznick described the character of his organization as a "movement for all Americans of the Jewish faith . . . It is the synthesis of the American Jewish search for a genuine compatibility of a great Jewish heritage with the inspirational qualities of the American dream itself."[25]

The World of Our Fathers

The transformation of utopian messianism into Socialism was transmuted into Liberalism in this generation. In a survey, a commitment to social equality remained the most important quality defining Jewish identity. Voting patterns continued to reflect an overwhelming commitment to liberal candidates even to the detriment of those who were Jewish. The liberalism of the Democratic Party in issues of social reform and as an immigrant party continued to engender Jewish loyalty. The commitment to social action during the immediate postwar period extended beyond purely Jewish interests to an active role in American civic affairs. Community Relations agencies lobbied for legislation directed against racial discrimination for social welfare programs as well as for a strict interpretation of the separation between church and state. Organizations such as the American Jewish Committee, rather conservative in its origins, along with the Reform and Conservative religious movements as well as B'nai B'rith, took on social justice agenda as inherent in Judaism. Being Jewish in America meant fighting for open housing and fair employment practices for social welfare and prounion legislation.[26]

This Social-Democratic strand continued to exert commitment into the 1980s exemplified by "an active governmental role in relation to social welfare needs, belief in the importance of equality as assuring civil rights; a quest for individual freedom manifested in protection of civil liberties and a general internationalist orientation."[27] There was a historical basis for this continuity. The important experience for the immigrant was that socialism was the point of entry into secular politics in the Pale with the Bund as a prototype.[28] The premise was that a new order could be constructed based upon the principle of equality, to be governed by a new "enlightened" state. This was the premise of the French Revolution and then of Russian revolutionary thinking. There was an emergence of a messianic sensibility in political, economic, and social matters. There was an expectation of universal regeneration. The strength of this ongoing Jewish commitment derives from religious thinking but also reflected historical experience in the nineteenth century. The French Revolution led to the emancipation of the Jews as a product of the Enlightenment.

"Normative" Judaism contained a balance between its two elements. As a result of the experience of the French Revolution, the *prophetic* element in Judaism acquired a greater degree of autonomy freed from the *rabbinical.* There was a breakdown in traditional control as the Haskalah, the Jewish version of the Enlightenment, took hold. In traditional Judaism, "hastening the end" to achieve a messianic era was always a temptation to be controlled against. With the breakdown of traditional Judaism, a secular version of Judeo-Christian messianism arose, whose prophetic vision had even greater validity since it was rooted in science. Why not hasten the progressive movement toward its predestined end—the universal regeneration of mankind? The ascendancy of the prophetic element in Judaism merges with secular humanism to create a peculiarly intense Jewish secular humanism that characterized the commitment to socialism.

Herberg[29] similarly placed the ongoing commitment to liberal, if not radical politics, within the Jewish religious tradition. To be Jewish in any way is to have an orientation to "what is to come," the essence of Messianism. This principle derives from the belief that history is the medium of man's encounter with God, that such history will be characterized by eventual fulfillment away from the present state of alienation. Even with the crumbling of the adherence to Halakha among Jews, messianism remained but now directed into secular paths. Marxism derived its power to motivate people by the sense that there was a "wrongness" to present existence that required rectification. In the absence of faith in God, history acquired a transcendental value with redemption to be achieved by man within current time. Socialism brought a sense of destiny and a hope for the future to the displaced workers and intellectuals of the modern industrial age. Although a false prophet with messianism sundered from its transcendental roots, Marx was nevertheless a prophet.

The trajectory of Will Herberg's own life illustrates his theme.[30] He was born in 1901 in a village near Minsk. The father brought the family to the United States where a younger brother was born in 1904. The parents, *passionate atheists*, were committed to their faith in socialism. Will received no training in Judaism. The mother, divorced, supported her sons by housework and with a single-minded devotion to their education. Will went to Boy's High School in New York City where he began a period of intense intellectual activity in the study of science, mathematics, and languages. Graduating in 1918, he entered the College of the City of New York (CCNY). Due to various administrative problems, he was suspended from college in 1920 and never pursued any further formal education. Soon after, he entered the Communist Young Workers League and, in 1925, rose to its executive committee and writer for its *Young Worker*. Married that same year to a fellow activist, the couple decided to remain childless in order to devote their energies to the party. Herberg, along with many others, was purged from the mainline American Communist Party in 1929 by Stalin's Comintern. Until 1941, he remained active in the Lovestonite faction, CPO (Communist Party Opposition), claiming adherence to the original Leninist line and in opposition to both Trotsky and Stalin. As editor of its *Workers Age*, he continued throughout the 1930s to write and lecture extensively in favor of the growth of labor unions such as the CIO, maintaining his faith in Marxism while increasing opposition to Stalinism. Starting in 1934, he became the educational director of Local 22 of the ILGWU (International Ladies Garment Workers Union) where he continued until 1952.

In 1938, he began to prefer the terms *socialism* and *democratic socialism* to *communism* and question the validity of Marxism from an ethical viewpoint. Remaining committed to the ideals of freedom and social justice, he could no longer find a basis in the materialism of Marx. From 1940, under the influence of the writings of Reinhold Niebuhr, the Protestant theologian, he questioned the moral basis of his previous thinking. He experienced a crisis that led him to theology as a basis for his continued belief in *democratic socialism*. His turn to religion ultimately led him to Judaism and the study of classical Jewish texts as well as modern Jewish thinkers. In *Judaism and Modern Man*, published in 1950, he saw the relationship between the Hebrew God and the Jew, as expressed in the scripture, the basis for the libertarian ethos to counteract the secular and the collectivistic pitfalls to which he, along with his generation, had succumbed.[31]

Socialism was the "religion" of much of the immigrant generation, an integral part of its *Yiddishkayt*. As exemplified by Herberg and many others, the second generation was not entirely at home either in the Jewish ethnic group of their parents nor the larger American community. Anxious about anti-Semitism and the Depression, social radicalism became characteristic of this generation. The man most identified during this generation with this Yiddish socialist background was Irving Howe. In its disappearance, his work examined, and perhaps crystallized it for the ages.

Irving Howe, an only child, was born in the Bronx in 1920 to David and Nettie (Goldman) Horenstein. His father ran a grocery store initially in the West Bronx but later became a presser in a dress factory after the store failed in 1930. This was a "great event" in the life of the boy. In poverty, the family moved to the poorer East Bronx where life was much rougher. His mother also worked as an operator in the dress trade. They were faithful union members for whom the success of the great strike of 1933 meant that life could be easier. *Solidarity*, the motto of the ILGWU, was part of the family ethic and remained that of Howe throughout his career. Yiddish was the predominant language of the entirely Jewish neighborhood and was his own earliest language. Starting in the public school, English became his language although initially quite foreign to him.

After sporadic attendance at a heder and bar mitzvah in a storefront shul, Irving was drawn to the secular Workmen's

Circle, the successor to the Bund, that emphasized things Yiddish along with things Socialist. While in high school he joined, in 1934, a socialist youth group. From then on, the *movement* was his home. Marxism, moreover, seemed to provide a key to the understanding of history and a ready answer to what was to be done. Everything seemed to fall into place, a life was shaped by purpose analogous to a religious faith.[32] At City College starting in 1936, he began to use a "party name." *Howe* was his eventual choice as a surname. He rarely attended class but was commissar of Alcove 1 in the lunchroom as the headquarters of the Left sectarians, the anti-Stalinists, next door to the Stalinist Alcove 2. Along with many other radicals who were also Jewish, he became a Trotskyite in opposition to Stalin and the purge trials.[33] After graduation in 1940, no longer a follower of Trotsky, he continued to blame all the world's ills on capitalism as editor of the *Labor Action*, a publication of the splinter Worker's Party.

He spent the war years stationed in Alaska. He was able to carry on his self-education, freed somewhat from the turmoil of his previous political life. His interests became clearly literary. His postwar stance began to differentiate his newfound role as a literary critic from the purely political evaluation of a work. In 1946, Howe began to contribute to the *Partisan Review*, which continued its ongoing non-Stalinist Marxist commitment along with its commitment to literary modernism. Howe, in 1968, applied the term *New York Intellectuals* to the group as meaning "intellectuals of New York who began to appear in the 1930s, most of whom were Jewish" and who also published in the *Partisan Review*.[34]

PR continued to be a place where one could be proud to see printed "one of [T.S.] Eliot's 'Four Quartets' side by side with Marxist criticism."[35] Howe, like most of his colleagues on PR, ignored their own Jewishness in their wanting to embrace "universalist" values, however anti-Semitic were the values of those such as Eliot. Finally unacceptable to Howe and calling into question "esthetic autonomy" was the bestowal of the Bollingen Prize for Poetry on Ezra Pound in 1949. Highly relevant for Howe was the centrality of the anti-Semitism of the *Pisan Cantos* and Pound's activities on behalf of Fascism in the context of the Holocaust.[36] Even more crucial for Howe was the response led by Harold Rosenberg, one of his colleagues at PR, to Sartre's essays on anti-Semitism published in 1948. Sartre defined Jews in terms of the anti-Semitism of the non-Jewish culture. In the rejoinder, what was affirmed was the creation over the past two thousand years of the unique being, the Jewish intellectual, who arose from the tradition of the "lifelong student." What spoke to Howe, "partial Jew" as he then was, was "the insistence upon the integrity of the inner history of the Jews despite the absence of governments, armies, and diplomacies." His stance reflected that held by the non-Zionist Yiddishists who celebrated the years of exile from Zion as the very opposite of a historical emptiness, as a higher form of Jewish civilization than had existed in the Land of Israel.[37]

Howe began his literary career in the early 1950s with books published about Sherwood Anderson and William Faulkner. It was unlikely that he would receive an appointment in academia in light of the absence of a graduate degree and his Jewishness. These factors were fortunately in his favor for his appointment at the newly opened Brandeis University in 1953. The turning point in his career, was, in 1954, the publication of the first of a series of anthologies of Yiddish literature published with Eliezer Greenberg. It was dedicated to the six million who died in the Holocaust. He was also affected by the murder of all the Russian Jewish poets on an August night in 1952 in Lubyanka prison.[38] He refound his Jewish identity editing the translation of Yiddish stories and poems into English.[39] Out of this effort came also the discovery by Howe of I. B. Singer and his first publication in English in the *Partisan Review* in a translation by Saul Bellow of "Gimpel the Fool."[40]

With the impasse in the hopes for socialism in America, Howe began to consider himself more primarily as a Jewish intellectual.[41] The work with Yiddish brought Howe back to his childhood memories of hearing it spoken. It also brought him back to his own father now grown old and alone. "My own hope was to achieve some equilibrium with that earlier self that had started with childhood Yiddish . . . and then turned away in adolescent shame . . . Yiddish poetry helped me to strike a truce with, and then extend a hand to, the world of my father."[42] The beauty of Yiddish literature for Howe was also its consistency with his socialist principles. It had its sources both in the religious tradition and the rebellion against that tradition. It was a "'modern' literature but one still imbued with the traditional sense of communal responsibility and fraternity with the poor."[43]

His commitment to politics persisted in maintaining the role of democratic socialism in its critique of capitalism, yet eschewing the anti-Communism of the Cold War liberals. He founded the quarterly called *Dissent* in 1954 and continued as its editor throughout the rest of his life.[44] In the early 1960s, the differences between the Dissenters and the Students for a Democratic Society (SDS) became more evident particularly in relation to the latter's anti-anti-Communism and support for third world leaders such as Castro. Howe was highly critical of their ahistoricism and was attacked in turn.[45]

He crystallized the Jewish immigrant experience in *The World of Our Fathers*, published in 1976 during the American bicentennial year. It represented the values he found missing in the New Left—a sense of history, institutions of fraternity and freedom, and a rigorous commitment to democratic values.[46] The book also arose in a personal way as he recognized the depth of his father's loyalty to him and in his description of his father's slow death. His most successful book, it was the elegy for the culture that had been so fruitful and with which he ultimately identified. In 1993, just prior to his own death, he summed up the losing cause for which he had fought in his generation. "We are witnessing the end of a major phase in Jewish history, the phase of Yiddishkayt and with which is interwoven the rise and fall of Jewish secularism. With the Enlightenment, there was a distinction made between one's 'fate' and one's 'faith.' One could choose whether or not to live as a Jew. What occurred was the rise of secular Jewish culture, though with strong religious elements. Secular Jewish culture was based mainly on Yiddish as the language that mirrored the common suffering, and the transcendence of suffering in the Diaspora. It enabled the rise of secular ideas, a whole segment of Jews who abandoned religion yet who remain utterly Jewish. Social liberalism remained the 'secular religion' of many American Jews . . . the salvage of their immigrant and East European heritage."[47]

"Yiddishkayt," the culture which had nourished the Bund in Vilna and in turn been nourished by its adherents on its transfer to America seemed to have come to an end in its original form. It nevertheless lived on in a number of writers who transferred their sensibilities to their new vernacular. Writing in English, they continued to speak to their fellow Jews but also to the larger number of educated Americans.

American Literary Life

Sometime in the early 1960s the implications of secularization and cultural pluralism became more evident. John Kennedy's election in 1960 is taken to mark the end of the Protestant hegemony in America. Another defeat of the traditions of religious conformity was the Supreme Court decision barring the recital of prayer. Christianity no longer had a privileged place in the public culture.[48] At this same time, the increased number of Jews on many faculties became statistically significant. The longtime barrier to Jewish intellectuals within academic institutions seemed to collapse. In 1969, a survey indicated that they formed a substantial percentage of the faculty particularly in the most prestigious universities. Most highly represented in the social and physical sciences including biomedical, they still represented about a fifth of faculty in the humanities from which they had been most persistently excluded.[49]The reasons for this had been prefigured in the earlier postwar period when the pervasive genteel anti-Semitism became less acceptable in wake of Hitler; there was increased opportunity for entry into higher education. This was coupled with increased publicity to the continued existence of restrictive quotas and the passage of the first of the antidiscrimination laws.

The impact of *freethinking* Jewish intellectuals was particularly significant to the detriment of the *Christian* character of American life. That had been the fear of T. S. Eliot expressed in his famous University of Virginia lectures published in 1934. At the turn of the century, a pervasive transdenominational Protestantism influenced the nation's cultural institutions controlling public education, scholarship, literature and the arts.[50] So pervasive was this influence that what appeared "universal" actually arose out of what was a parochially Anglo-Protestant perspective. Immigration restrictions gave that hegemony a new lease on life. The opportunities for others to enter the public intellectual life of the nation through literature and the universities eventually came about. Rather than speaking to a specifically Jewish constituency, these *freethinking* Jews spoke to the wider issues.[51]

In a much-quoted 1944 Commentary Symposium, Lionel Trilling declared, "as the Jewish community now exists, it can give no sustenance to the American artist or intellectual who is born a Jew." By committing themselves to the ideal in culture and politics, the intellectuals were invoking a culture that was more demanding in its austerity and morality than the ordinary pursuit of material comfort. The roots were in the austere culture of Torah study "for its own sake" that had characterized the ideal represented by the Vilna Gaon. In the postwar generation, American Jewish writers, each very much an individual, formed a literary renaissance that seemed to burst forth to fill almost all of American literature. There is frequently a polemic against the shallow values of post war America, as well as the Jewish community that partakes of it, in the fashion of the prophet who came down from the hills to excoriate the cities of the plain.[52] The concerns are mainly ethical and social rather than the metaphysical and theological. In the face of man's alienation from man as well as from God the ancient tradition recurs in the focus on the "prophecy of the heart, the centrality of love in the reconstruction of the social order."[53]

Saul Bellow and Cynthia Ozick helped to define some of the variety and range of this literary flowering. The work of Saul Bellow established the centrality of the Jewish experience.[54] He not only wrote almost exclusively about Jews but did so with a prose style that was unashamedly influenced by the rhythms of Yiddish. Yet "it was through Bellow's efforts that Jewish literature became American."[55]

Solomon (Saul) Bellow was born in the working-class town of Lachine in Quebec, brought up in Montreal, in what he described as a *mediaeval ghetto*, and then in Chicago. His father had been a rabbinical student in Vilna. The mother had been the daughter of a rabbi from a relatively more prosperous family near Riga. Living in St. Petersburg without a legal residency permit, the family was forced to emigrate in 1912 and come to Canada to join some relatives. Solomon (Saul) was born in 1915, the youngest of four, and the only one born in the New World.[56] Bellow was trilingual, speaking Yiddish as well as French and English. As a boy, he wore a *tallith katan* or scapular under his shirt.[57] He went to traditional religious school starting at age four. Pivotal in his sense of destiny was a long hospitalization in 1923, separating the bookish boy from his family. Poverty-stricken, the family joined relatives in 1924 in the Jewish area of Chicago near Humboldt Park. Sol, his mother's favorite, was to be a rabbi like his maternal grandfather.

In the fervent literary and political atmosphere of his high school, he became close friend and also rival to Isaac Rosenfeld, later a New York editor and writer. The atmosphere of the high school carried on at the University of Chicago in the 1930s where he spent a year before then going to Northwestern University in Evanston. It was there that he felt his talent was fostered. However, there were few opportunities for Jews on the faculty of Northwestern, and none in Department of English, still under Anglo-Saxon "protection." Despite the gibes of his now more prosperous family, he felt that he was to be a writer to follow his singular destiny. At the time of his graduation from university in 1937, he changed his name to Saul as a reflection of his break with his family and their philistine life.[58]

His ambition to be a writer was first recognized by the publication of a story in the Partisan Review in 1941. His first published novel was *Dangling Man* in 1944, written about *Joseph*, a man like Bellow, awaiting induction into the army. The character epitomized himself and his heroes, fighting to stay independent in the face of the demands of society or domesticity.[59] In justification of his persistent search for recognition, he likened himself to his grandfather, the Talmud scholar, in being supported by his wife while working on his writing. His first book to break out of relatively restricted readership, *The Adventures of Augie March*, won the National Book Award in 1953. It established a Jewish-American perspective at the very center of American letters. The story is of a resilient man with an unquenchable hospitality toward experience, a *larkiness*, a bounce and rhythm.[60] Although he plays many games, there comes a point at which he digs in his heels and claims independence of what others may want for him, to find his own "axial lines."

The internal dialogue, so much a part of Yiddish literature, is the characteristic of his first best-selling *Herzog*, published in 1964. The character writes a series of unmailed letters to various famous people. It is in the format of Talmudic study. In that format, the scholar recites aloud to himself, in singsong, the arguments of one then the other disputant, alternating in performing each of the roles. Herzog is the heir of the prototype of the ineffectual Jewish intellectual.[61] "Herzog's Jewishness is the one thing about him that goes deep . . . it emerges solidly, naturally, authentically from the family experiences that . . . [are] the main province of his temperament."[62] The Bellow hero struggles to reconcile his Jewish upbringing and recollections of immigrant family life with being an uprooted intellectual. The dominant question is the moral one. Given the existence of the Holocaust, to what extent does traditional Mosaic morality exert claims on human behavior?

Bellow insisted in calling himself an *American* writer who is Jewish.[63] Yet the characters in his books seemed to reflect the qualities of the immigrant Jewish experience. "They convey an eager restlessness, moral anxiety, an openness to novelty, a hunger for dialectic, a refusal of contentment, an ironic criticism of all fixed opinion."[64] The specifically *Jewish* content of his work lies in its "moral optimism . . . a Jacob representing his limping protagonists wrestling with life itself." In an after-Auschwitz world, Bellow affirms the sanctity of life, the world's need for morality and a bond of humanitarianism.[65] He was awarded the Nobel Prize in Literature in 1976 in the context of *Humboldt's Gift*, evoking Chicago as well as the death of a poet patterned after Delmore Schwartz, and his nonfiction *To Jerusalem and Back*, written while his then mathematician wife was on a sabbatical in Israel. On the faculty of the University of Chicago, his work became synonymous with that city and the Jewish immigrant story that was his own.

His was the literary generation based on the New York Intellectuals who had helped to bring the Jewish immigrant experience into the American mainstream. In Bellow's last book, *Ravelstein*, based on his friend Alan Bloom, the character's older brother was named Shimon, unlike the equivalent character called Simon in *The Adventures of Augie March*. It is suggested that the Hebraization of the name reflected the transformation of the once-hyphenated *Jewish-American* into *Americans* who could now acknowledge their origins without apology.[66]

In the next generation, Cynthia Ozick almost single-handedly moved Jewish-American fiction beyond the "dare" of ethnic Jewishness to a more complicated, more demanding "double dare" of a fiction firmly couched in Jewish ideas and rendered in liturgical rhythms."[67] As the emotional and aesthetic distance from the immigrant experience widened, there may be expectation that there would be a lessening of the literary efflorescence that Bellow as well as others represented. There has been, however, a staking out into new territories. It was Ozick who led the way in imagination as witness to the shadow of the Holocaust.[68] She has advocated a new language couched in English that would be the "New Yiddish."[69]

Cynthia Ozick was born in New York City in 1928, the younger of two children and the only daughter. Her parents Celia (Regelson) and William Ozick were owners of the Park View Pharmacy in the Pelham Bay section of the Bronx, then suburban in nature. She worked in the store along with her parents who put in fourteen-hour days. Despite the Depression, the family pharmacy gave a sense of comfort and prosperity, yet poverty was immanent. Her parents came from the northwestern provinces of the Pale. Her father was a discreet, quiet man; wrote beautiful Hebrew; and had a Talmudist's rationalism. Ozick's Litvak background is important in explaining her temperament. She identifies herself as a mitnagid. Even when she describes a Hassidic rabbi, he seems such a reasonable man that one might think him a Litvak. Central to her art, as in her own life, is the awareness that the sources of the life of her characters lies in the tradition from which they arose.[70]

Ozick entered *heder* at age five and remained there despite the initial opposition of the teacher to the enrollment of a girl. A sense of membership as a woman in the religious tradition was illustrated by those such as Cynthia Ozick already introduced to Jewish learning and able therefore to participate in worship. She was both "almost always the only girl" in her *heder* and "almost always the only Jew" in her public school. She knew Yiddish from her grandmother. In the public school, the only Jewish child in her class, she was not recognized for her intellect and was publicly humiliated for refusing to participate in singing carols at Christmas. Books magically transformed her into "who she was," that is, a reader and the writer she dreamed of being.[71] The example of her maternal uncle, Abraham Regelson, a well-known Hebrew poet, paved the way for her family to accept such a "frivolous" career choice. A student at Hunter College High School, she immersed herself in Latin poets. In 1946, she entered New York University where she discovered from the start the "gods of the Partisan Review," the house on the north side of Washington Square where Henry James was born, the nearby residences of the poets Marianne Moore and W. H. Auden.[72] At Ohio State, she wrote, in 1950, her master's thesis on Henry James with whom and whose *mandarin* style she then identified herself with. It was not until 1963 that she would finally complete *Trust,* her first book.

Her reentry into Judaism came to her in her adulthood as an *autodidact.* In 1954, she discovered the work of Leo Baeck who emphasized the distinction between Christianity as the "romantic" religion and Judaism as the "classical" religion in which man finds holiness arising from ethical responses to the concrete realities of everyday life. "Our business is to go about making an ethical civilization."[73] Even within Judaism where there is a conflict between mysticism of Hassidism and rationalism of the *mitnagid,* she sides with rationalism.

Starting with the publication in 1971 of her first collection *The Pagan Rabbi and Other Stories,* she views as central to both Judaism and her own work the struggle to deal with the prohibition against "idolatry." Her subsequent work has dealt with the relationship of her characters to the assumptions of Jewish history, most notably to the Holocaust. Her stories and essays reflect the deep moral seriousness that contradicts the modernist aesthetic in that she has felt that "a story must not merely be, but mean [something]."[74]

Ozick has insisted on the essential Jewishness of Jewish American literature. To be a Jewish writer is to be committed to the *liturgical* in its concern with history, the echo of the voice of the lord of history, attentive to the implications of the covenant and the commandments.[75] The struggle is between Jerusalem and Athens, between Judaism and Hellenism, between monotheism and paganism. When a Jew is seduced by the secular world and venerates natural beauty, he is damned to the loss of his dignity and even his soul. Reflecting her Litvak temperament, she had been insistent about history, about memory, about law, about restraint. She has been in a way almost self-abnegating, concerned about the responsibility of the writer. "Whoever writes a story that includes villainy enters into and becomes the villain."[76]

While Judaism in Bellow's work is a source of nostalgia and also of guilt and anxiety rather than pride and pleasure, for Ozick it is the safeguard of the future, a source of moral insights, dignity, and gratification. It is the Jew's attraction for the Gentile world that leads to moral destruction.[77] Her characters have roots in the past yet uncertain about reliance on a God who is conspicuous by his absence.[78] However, they can never achieve escape by acculturation. Rather than dwelling on that fate, she sees the return to the faith as the only way to solve the problem of alienation and to find a new homeland for the disturbed soul.

Ozick not only represented a shift in American Jewish literature by her grounding in Judaism, she also represented a shift in her description of Jewish women.[79] Her character, Ruth Puttermesser, unlike the female characters of Bellow or the other male Jewish American novelists, is a more fully realized person of greater intellectual and spiritual depth. Like her character, for whom she is an *alter ego*, Ozick has described herself as a *classical feminist*. For her, feminism should not sponsor but fight the idea of gender difference. She views the value of feminism in the striving for personhood, which perceives women as well as men as ends in themselves. She also sees the personhood of women as consistent with the basic sources of Judaism. One example is derived from the Bible wherein the woman was seen as a person in her own right as distinct from one who merely bears children. The story of Hana and Elhanan in Samuel I seems to her to provide support for this attitude. In that story, Elhanan maintains Hana as his wife although she is childless, and he has had sons by a concubine.

The *New Left*

In the 1950s, the political life of the Left appeared to go underground in the wake of the Cold War and the attack of McCarthyism. The intellectual leadership of the *Old Left* had included the largely Jewish "family" associated with the Partisan Review along with the socialist journal *Dissent*, edited by Irving Howe, and the short-lived anarchist *Politics*, edited by Dwight Macdonald. Its writers identified with the rich heritage of Western civilization.

The *New Left* was a great political surprise. It seemed to defy all the expectations of the social scientists who, in their surveys, found students politically apathetic. It defied the *Old Left* which had declared America to be the graveyard of radicalism.[80] The failure of America to polarize into two warring camps in accordance with Marxist theory, led ex-Marxist sociologists such as Max Lerner and Seymour Lipset to find explanation in de Tocqueville. America was indeed an "open class" society. The concepts of status in relation to one's social and professional role seemed to supercede the view that the worker was defined only in relation to the means of production. Further, in the context of the extraordinary productivity of the postwar American economy, it appeared that the old socialist goal of equality could be ignored. Wealth had no longer to be distributed but could be expanded. "The spectacle of affluence had replaced the specter of scarcity, making consumption the new opiate of the people."[81]

Young radicals of the 1960s were mainly the children of parents who had come of age during the '30s and the '40s. The parents had survived the privations of depression and war to enter into a life of relative abundance. Beneath the façade of material comfort, there appeared to these young a spiritual impoverishment and unconscionable remnants of poverty. The young particularly identified hypocrisy in denial of the poverty that existed based on racial segregation. They emphasized the dark side of the affluence and the need for social reform. Democratic America seemed to fail to keep its promises, and the civil rights movement in the early 1960s enlisted white students to come to the South in what clearly seemed to be a moral crusade.

Marxism had proposed to solve the problems not only of equality and justice but also of power. The idea of a classless society implied that political power would be democratized. Rather than being democratized, new oligarchies arose in the form of postrevolutionary bureaucracy. Political theorists of the Left vainly sought an explanation for the totalitarianism of Stalin. Stalinism, unlike Fascism, could not be explained as the product of either monopoly capitalism or the decadence of the middle class. Marxism had also failed in its claims of historical inevitability. It did not predict the failure of the proletariat as the carriers of democratic values and the rise of totalitarianism. The New Left defined itself in opposition to the classical texts and reasoning that formed the basis for Marxism in its various forms. The young students would substitute faith in the role of participatory democracy as a means of overcoming a sense of powerlessness arising out of the increasing role of technology and large organizations and the centralization that marked the Leninist tradition. The previous Marxist focus on the role of the working class and the rise of labor unionism shifted to the dispossessed, both black and white.

The failed connection between the editors of *Dissent* led by Howe and the then new student leaders of the Students for a Democratic Society is exemplified in a famous meeting in 1962.[82] Indeed, Howe became the exemplar of the conflict between the two in his focus on the need to of the *New Left* to separate from authoritarianism. What mainly discredited the Old Left and caused it to lose moral authority in the eyes of the younger generation was the Cold War and its anticommunism. *Counterinsurgency* seemed to be one more example of where America's Cold War interests seemed to be paramount. It was particularly directed to the third world and the guerilla movements in Latin America that were led by the example of Cuba. The young radicals saw in Castro's Cuba the embodiment of a "new humanist socialism." Young, bearded, and defiant, Castro became a symbol for rebellious young Americans. In the liberation movements of the third world, there seemed to be the possibility for an alternative both to the corporate and the statist bureaucratic ethos of both American capitalism and the Soviet systems. There once again was the search for millennialism but now based upon a new set of values

Jews were greatly over represented among the leadership and activists of the several phases of student movement. For example, it was estimated that one-third to one-half of the student volunteers on the Mississippi Freedom Summer Project in 1964 were Jews. The murder of three civil rights workers in Philadelphia Mississippi in 1964, two of whom were whites and Jews, epitomized the era before the transformation of the civil rights movement into the radical *Black Power* movement that excluded whites. Initially in the context of the civil rights movement, the *New Left* emerged in the college campuses of Ann Arbor, Madison, and Berkeley, Starting in 1965, the Students for a Democratic Society (SDS) led the way toward a range of radical student activities in opposition to the draft and the Vietnam War affecting campuses throughout the country. Increased commitment to violence characterized the movement in the early 1970s before its destruction.[83]

Although in opposition to many of its features, the student movement saw itself as heir to an older American radicalism. The young radicals were not necessarily turning away from their parents. The family of typical student activist was leftist with considerable parental support for their activism.[84] The rationale for such continued commitment among Jewish youth to universalist social justice, sometimes antithetical to their own more particularistic personal interests, can lie in the tradition of the immigrant radicals and the revolutionary tradition of Eastern Europe. The existence of traditions of radicalism and dissent in Jewish families is but one factor. Even when families were not radical, ever-present in the background for many was the sense of taint of survivorship of the murder of one's family members in the Shoah and the recurrent Passover message of liberation from slavery.[85] More specifically, it was continuity with the revolutionary traditions that had characterized the politics of Lita. Its recurrent strength into this third generation derived from its religious fervor of redemption channeled into secular pursuits.[86]

The hope was that a socialist consciousness would develop as the victims of society who liberated themselves through autonomous community action. Although community action was achieved only in part, significant changes did occur. Starting with blacks, the new modes of protest became the vehicle for successive groups to gain rights.

The Counter Culture

In its élan and anarchistic bravado, one aspect of the New Left belied ideology by poking fun at its pretensions. The change in consciousness was perhaps the greatest legacy of the era. One could claim that no major transfer of wealth or power occurred in the 1960s despite all the disruption of the universities and the eventual ending of the Vietnam War. However, values were inverted and symbols transformed.

Cultural revolution was what the '60's were about and Abbie Hoffman was its best known instigator, one might say 'actor.' By being so gifted a clown, he ended up worthy of being taken seriously.[87] Hoffman deflated the historic danger of an elite imagining itself to be a revolutionary vanguard or posing as the moral benefactors of humanity as had some of the other student revolutionaries in the Students for a Democratic Society (SDS). His *yippies* (Youth International Party) represented but one of the activities spawned by the questioning of all that seemed sacred. His fame was the result of fusing the cultural radicalism of hippie youth with the anti-Vietnam War movement and the political agenda of the left.

Abbie Hoffman was born in 1936 in Worcester, Massachusetts, the firstborn of three children and the elder son. His father had been born in Russia and immigrated with his family as a one year old in 1906.[88] The father founded a pharmaceutical supply house and prided himself as a hardworking successful businessman and a proper member of Worcester's small Jewish community. There were frequent beatings in an attempt to bring Abbie's behavior under control.[89] His increasingly wild exploits made him the stuff of legends even in high school.[90]

In a society where people were becoming more faceless, Hofmann affirmed his own individuality.[91] He enrolled at Brandeis University, in the 1950s an oasis of intellectual freedom and a haven for radical intellectuals. There was a spirit of nonconformity at Brandeis that suited Hoffman. He tested ideas, overturned them, and gave himself permission to think what may have seemed unthinkable. He was particularly influenced by the teaching of faculty members such as Abraham Maslow that social rebellion was not necessarily a sign of maladjustment. When society needed changing, Maslow taught that acts of rebellion could be a positive sign of mental health.[92] One of Hoffman's touchstones to be that individuals are free agents: that men "are not the keys of a piano."[93] He decided to major in psychology in college and then went as a graduate student to Berkeley but did not get a graduate degree.

He spoke in public for the first time after he witnessed the police attack on students protesting the hearings in San Francisco of the House Un-American Activities Committee (Black Friday) in 1960. The police violence was what seemed un-American. The young white rebels in San Francisco and Berkeley had "an almost religious sense of purpose and conviction . . . Abbie shared in this spiritual sense, as he identified with . . . the belief in the need for a social order of justice permeated by love and a redemptive community."[94] Back in Worcester, he became active in civil rights issues and worked in Mississippi first in the summer of 1965. In the next year, he became involved in the early protests against the Vietnam War. He also began to use LSD and marijuana. Moving to New York's East Village in the Fall of 1966, he entered that bohemian, hip milieu. The East Village, being resettled by artists and others seeking cheap rent, was the new term for the Lower East Side of the immigrant generation.[95]

Young high school and college dropouts, "baby hipsters" or "hippies" began to appear in the East Village around this time. They had broken with their past and had become outlaws because of their use of drugs. The hippies appealed to Hoffman's own sense of being an outlaw and to his political organizing instincts. The hippie rebellion seemed to point to those life-affirming qualities of friendship, community, and self-expression that marked the self-actualizing apex of his mentor Maslow's pyramid.[96] The march on the Pentagon with the *flower people* in 1967 and the confrontation at the Democratic Party Convention in 1968 are the stuff of history.

Hoffman joined that line of resisters seeking to wriggle out of the shackles of the "nice Jewish boy" along with others of his time such as Norman Mailer, Lenny Bruce, and Joseph Heller. Their activities, in tune with a revolutionary tradition, were of those who had become part of a generation more at home in America. Abbie felt secure as an American. Unlike his parents, he never tempered the assertiveness that he considered crucial to his Jewish identity.[97] Hoffman liked to flaunt the insignia of the Jewish subculture he flouted. He repudiated the norms of middle-class mobility and success. Yet no radical was more eager to assert a sense of peoplehood. He took pride in his ancestry and the Jewish reputation for cleverness; he cherished his affiliation with the sort of intelligence that is at once subversive and sensible.[98] He claimed descent from the Jewish revolutionary tradition. Noteworthy was his invocation of his Yiddish background in his confrontation during the Chicago conspiracy trial with the presiding Judge Hoffman. Abbie Hoffman's culture was in confrontation with that of the more conservative German Jewish culture of the judge. The book he said that affected him most was *Diary of Anne Frank*. Singularly, while hiding from arrest on a drug charge in the 1970s, he made the decision to sign his own name in the visitor's book when visiting the house in Amsterdam.

Hoffman's radicalism showed tenacity and durability. Even as his influence waned in the '70s and '80s in reaction to the excesses of the 1960s, his so seemingly frivolous a spirit turned out to be the least corrupted, the most resilient and dedicated radical of all. In the eulogy after his death, the rabbi of his family's congregation in Worcester implanted his career "in the Jewish prophetic tradition, which is to comfort the afflicted and to afflict the comfortable."[99]

The New Left fragmented in the context of black power. Many Jews walked out from the 1967 Conference on New Politics when the black caucus demanded acceptance of an anti-Zionist platform in the wake of Six-Day War. This was the beginning of the New Left's crusade, branding Israel as an oppressor and support for the Palestinians. The days preceding Six-Day War in June 1967 also called forth for Jews the possibility that Israel could be destroyed and occasioned an outpouring of support. In turn, the victorious results helped arouse a sense of militancy and triumph. In addition, the moral stance of Russian Jews choosing to identify themselves as Jews in opposition to the Soviet government touched a vein of idealistic support.

Jewish Renewal

Out of the New Left experience, a movement of young Jews arose whose focus was directed at the renewal of Jewish life in tune with the cultural revolution going on elsewhere. In addition to their radical political stance was their connectedness to Judaism.[100] They can be described as Jewish radicals rather than radicals who happened to be Jews. They successfully lobbied for Jewish Studies programs in their universities and an increased commitment to Jewish education on the part of Jewish Community Federations.

The support for Jewish scholarship had come about in a limited way at the turn of the century in the context of Departments of Semitic Studies in a handful of settings.[101] The rise of anti-Semitism in the universities in the interwar era had jeopardized the status of scholars such as Wolfson at a bellwether place such as Harvard. The Six-Day War and the student unrest of the 1960s brought about a greater degree of Jewish inwardness. In the 1970s, particularism took hold in the university. The "Ethnic studies" movement opened a new avenue of university access through the creation of separate departments or programs sponsored by Jewish philanthropy concerned with communal survival. The role of these courses in maintaining the survival of Jewish identity among undergraduate students is problematic. Its main legacy in the inclusion in the American university of Jewish studies as a model for other settings elsewhere. Jewish learning found its sanctuary in a setting that was no longer based upon the previously dominant Protestantism that viewed its parochial interests as universal.

The Association of Jewish Studies (AJS) was founded in 1969 to provide opportunities for scholarly communication and to encourage the appointment of properly qualified faculty to the burgeoning field. The AJS has continued since then in providing support for the maintenance of integrity of standards of scholarship as academic Jewish programs have proliferated in American universities in the subsequent generations.

The continued growth of the AJS reflected the fact that by the 1970s, Jewish learning would be offered in one-sixth of all four-year colleges and universities. The sites were particularly those with more developed library and other resources as well as larger enrollments.

A Jewish counterculture also emerged in which they sought to create an alternative Jewish lifestyle contrary to "extravagant buildings, Friday night fashion shows, bar mitzvah and weddings smothered in wealth."[102] Its members rejected the impressive buildings but did not reject Judaism but rather their parents' version of it. They understood themselves to be "observant" and differentiated themselves from Reform Judaism in that they recognized that rules must exist that extended to the entire range of their lives. They used the rituals of traditional prayer but differentiated themselves by their informality, lack of formal leadership, and active participation.[103] Judaism became more meaningful to them because it was made to assimilate contemporary political and social values.[104] In reconstructing a Jewish identity for themselves as students and young people, they were functioning as members of the "third generation" in America.

Arthur Waskow, in the context of the 1968 Washington riots after the death of Martin Luther King, founded the *Freedom Seder*, drawing parallels between the exodus from Egypt and contemporary liberation movements. His interest in civil rights dates from his high school days in Baltimore then a segregated city. He recalls the excitement he felt when the Supreme Court decision was announced desegregating schools. A historian, his dissertation was on the race riots immediately post World War I. He was an early member of Jews for Urban Justice in Washington, D.C., that picketed Jewish organizations on behalf of improving the conditions of blacks in relation to their Jewish landlords. The opportunity was to use the abundance all around them in the 1970s to enable all to share. Even more, his manifesto from the start was founded in religious prophecy: "The conditions exist that make it possible . . . for us to break through to the 'era of freedom,' the Messianic Age."[105]

Immigrating to New York in 1891, the Waskow family eventually settled in Baltimore. He was born in Baltimore in 1933. His paternal grandfather, a socialist tailor, was particularly influential in his life. His father, American born, was a high school history teacher who was active in the teacher's union. Waskow describes his childhood home in Jewish Baltimore as centered around the Orthodox shul although his own family was nonobservant. Like so many others of his generation, he was *bar mitzvah* in the neighborhood shul, having learned to recite the Hebrew, not to read it. His strongest memory of his Sunday school lay in his role as one of the sons of Hannah, the mother of the Maccabees. Hannah was also the name of his own mother.

It seemed right to him that the mother of the Maccabees was willing to sacrifice her sons in civil disobedience against the idolatrous tyrant Antiochus.

At university at Johns Hopkins, he studied in university departments where there were many other people who were "Jews more or less," but merely by habit. He describes his university life as one when he learned to think with a Jewish fervor but empty of Jewishness. Once again, after graduate study in history at Wisconsin, he moved in a "neighborhood" of Jews in the civil rights movement and the struggle for peace and social justice. Living in Washington, he wrote about arms control and politics. Yet he was only dimly aware that what they were calling for had Jewish roots. "Justice, justice shall you pursue . . . Seek peace and pursue it" were commands of the Torah. It was in the context of Passover in 1968 that he describes that connection being made between his universalism and his Jewishness.[106]

In the years between 1968 and 1972, Waskow shifted his life direction to lead to his work in "Jewish renewal" where he has continued since. His goal was to create within his life and those of others in America a renewal of the sense of Jewish community that had been shattered by modernism.[107] The spirit of community he advocated as part of the nonhierarchical counterculture existed in groups such as the *Fabrangen*, founded in Washington in the late '60s." It is a group that "came together" as the Yiddish name indicates.[108] Ongoing, the group, along with others, has tried to create "a modern path of life that draws authentically from Jewish tradition but is expressed in new ways."[109] Becoming more widespread, the new form emerged of the chavurah or fellowship rather than a professionally led synagogue. Built around Shabbat as a day of meditation and rest, it combined the study of Torah and a sense of community as well as a commitment to social justice. There was also an extension of its living in harmony with Judaism throughout the week and in one's totality of life.[110] By his sense of the possibility of renewal, he came to see deeper meaning of the very word *yisra-El*, that is, "God wrestler."

Waskow drew upon the Kabbalist concept that the world had become broken; the "holy sparks" existed only in isolation. These sparks of holiness had become obscured in their alienation from one another. It was our task to work with God to bring together once again these bits of holiness, to reunite them into a unified "way of life" a Halakha. In his most recent book dealing with the Jewish renewal, he harkens back to the revolutionary tradition of the Bund when he met some of its survivors one day in New York in the 1970s.[111] Perhaps more important was the story of his own grandfather who, throughout his life in America, still retained his belief in the need for economic fairness. A tailor, he became a shop steward in the Amalgamated Clothing Workers union and an organizer for the Socialist Party.[112] In his background, being Jewish was always somehow entangled with being progressive. Waskow has called for a new set of Halakha—of law that would encompass, as did the old, politics, religion, culture, and the family—that life is a path in which all is fused.[113] Once more there is the ancient dream of Judaism, that there can be a messianic age, that, coming out of its religious tradition, has been the ongoing spark of the history of the Jewish people in the twentieth century.

The best-selling successive *Jewish Catalogs* expressed the concept of Jewish spirituality that had been one of the salient features of the early movement. Greater support for Jewish education in the United States was another new direction. The political stance of many chavurah toward Israel was one of "open dissent" toward some of its policies in Lebanon and in respect to Palestinians. These developments broke through the monolithic support for Israel that had been characteristic in the past. Although Israel is a center for Jewish life, it is not the only one. The Diaspora is also a center and must develop in its own right alongside Israel.[114]

One of the most lasting movements for Jewish renewal that arose out of the counterculture was that of the role of women in Jewish communal life and worship. These developments were in many instances derived from their role in the more universalist feminist movement starting in the late1960s. The realities of sexual inequality became even more obvious when, in the civil rights struggles and antiwar activism in the late '60s, women were clearly delegated to second-class citizenship. In the late '60s and early '70s, women consciousness raising groups led to the organization of health collectives, women's shelters, abortion counseling services

Published in 1963, Betty Friedan's widely read *The Feminine Mystique* dealt with educated women such as herself who felt denied the use of their skills in a public role and condemned to the monotonous chores of housework and child-rearing. The solution would be a "culture that did not narrow the acceptable image of women to the . . . housewife, that expanded the vision of female students rather than shoving them into home economics courses and women who recognized that they deserved expanded horizons."[116] In 1966, Betty Friedan helped organize and was the first president of the National Organization of Women (NOW). Impetus for its organization was the continued existence of sex-segregated want ads. There was, in addition, the need for expanded efforts seeking the implementation of Title VII of the Civil Rights Act dealing with discrimination on the basis of sex. NOW's goal was "to take action to bring women into full partnership in the mainstream of American society now, exercising all the privileges and responsibilities thereof in full partnership with men."[117]

Betty (Goldstein) Freidan was born in Peoria, Illinois, in 1921, the eldest of three children. She was favored by her father for her intellect. Her father, born in Russia, had come to St. Louis with his family when aged six. At age thirteen, he came to Peoria on his own and eventually founded a leading jewelry store on one of the main streets. Her mother was born in Peoria, the daughter of an immigrant physician. Prevented from going to Smith College by her family, the mother was a fashion plate and led an active social life. Betty was not pretty and suffered from the social ostracism endemic in the anti-Semitic character of small towns of that era. Redeeming her mother's thwarted ambition, she found Smith College more congenial and gloried in its relative intellectuality. She was a crusading editor of the newspaper and was recognized for her brilliance as well as her aggressive ways. She identified with labor unions and radical politics that connected with her immigrant family origins and the social snobbery that excluded her as a Jew and an intellectual.

Graduating from Smith College in 1942, she went to Berkeley for graduate study in psychology but, in a personal crisis, declined the opportunity to go on to a doctorate and a professional career. Moving to New York, she worked at the newspaper agency that provided articles to labor newspapers and then, until 1952, for the newspaper published by the leftist Electrical Workers Union. She met and married Carl (Friedman) Freidan. Born in the industrial town of Chelsea near Boston, he was the second of three sons of poor parents who had immigrated from Latvia. He graduated from the Boston Latin School but did not finish college. Their marriage was stormy with frequent fights but also three children. In the 1950s, Betty was a freelance writer of articles for the women's magazines with particular emphasis on describing her experiences in a multiracial and multiethnic community near the United Nations in Queens. Dealing with her own conflicts about her role as a wife and mother versus a professional career, her book published in 1962 brought her fame and the start of the "most far-reaching social revolution of the century."[118]

She went on to become an icon for women throughout the world. Her experience as a Jew in Peoria was the mainspring of her passion for justice. Also evidence that she never abandoned her heritage was her equal passion for the value of ideas.

In 1967, at a meeting of *New Left* political groups, a women's caucus was refused the opportunity to bring up a women's rights resolution on the grounds that it was "trivial" and would interfere with dealing with important world issues. This was the same meeting that insisted on an anti-Zionist platform from which a Jewish caucus also seceded from the New Left. The male-dominated socialist organizations assumed that the problems women faced would be righted by attacking the issues of private property and capitalism. The socialist feminists at first continued to accept their subordinate role in the radical political movement. Others, radical feminists, saw the subjugation of women as due to men's need to dominate, as the basic form of exploitation of one human by another.[119]

In the fall of 1967, Shulamith Firestone was one of the organizers of Radical Women in New York. The Radical Women's protest at the Miss America pageant in Atlantic City in September 1968 was the first to gain widespread attention. Although many of these women came from socialist backgrounds, they did not think that Marxism dealt adequately with female subjugation, nor did they trust the male dominated Leftist organizations. In 1971, The National Women's Political Caucus was founded by Congresswomen Bella Abzug and Shirley Chisholm along with Betty Friedan.

The organizing meeting in July was the introduction to the movement for Lettie Pogrebin, who was then writing a column for the *Ladies Home Journal* entitled Working Women. *Ms.* magazine was founded in 1972 by Gloria Steinem and Lettie Pogrebin, among others with experience as writers. It was a breakthrough for a national magazine to reflect a feminist viewpoint unlike the traditional women's magazines.[120] A full range of feminist activities was now in place. In all these efforts, Jewish women were in the forefront.

Although a higher percentage of immigrant and second-generation Jewish women were enrolled in high school and college than other immigrant groups, their gender did not permit initial parity with their brothers. This discrepancy began to disappear by 1950, at least in respect to high school training.[121] In 1970, at the start of the modern women's movement, the percentage of Jewish women with one to three years of college was almost twice that of total of other white women. Those with college degrees was almost two and one-half times as frequent. Moreover, those with postgraduate training were four times as many.[122] It was this pool of trained women that provided the basis for seeking, and succeeding to some degree, in achieving some early gains in employment in response to the claims of the women's movement.

The large number of Jewish women in the vanguard of the women's movement has been a truism.[123] Their number was even greater than their membership among the educated class. Schneider attributes this to "the Jewish drive toward social justice and equality." Betty Friedan founded her passion for women's rights on her sense of injustice originating in the injustice of anti-Semitism. The extraordinary contribution of Jewish women to the feminist movement can be attributed at least in part to the revolutionary secular tradition that arose in Eastern Europe and particularly in the northwest provinces in Lita. Significant numbers of women were evident in the Jewish revolutionary movements. For example, young unmarried women were about one-third of the membership of the Bund. They were instrumental in holding that organization together after the mass arrests in 1898. In the 1900s, increasing and disproportionate numbers of Jewish women were arrested for political activities. This revolutionary tradition then flourished in the earlier immigrant generation in America particularly in the Jewish labor movement.[124]

The story of Lettie Cottin Pogrebin is illustrative of the need to reconcile her feminism and her Jewish identity. She was born in 1939. Unlike her European-born mother, her father had been born in the United States in New Haven in 1900, soon after the arrival of his parents. He had learned Hebrew from his paternal grandmother and studied Talmud with his own father. He had graduated from City College and NYU Law School. He seemed to know about everything and treated his daughter "as though I could get it on the first hearing."[125] He was said to contrast his own Litvak family tradition of educated women to that of his wife's non-Litvak background (Pogrebin personal communication). Treating her seriously "like a son," her father brought all his facility and fervor to her bat mitzvah lessons.

She came to know him as selfish and uncaring about her mother during a terminal cancer illness. Part of her persistent anger was his apparently offhand way with which he did not permit her to complete the minyan for the Kaddish on her mother's death. She describes the basis of their relationship: "to be called I had a good 'kepele', a smart head, was the ultimate compliment; brains were all that mattered."[126] There was transmittal of the father's intellectual tradition to the daughter, particularly in relation to religious training, traditionally a male prerogative. Unfortunately, there was not an equivalent recognition of her emotional needs. That failing may not only be a personal one. It may be claimed to be inherent in the pursuit of knowledge tempered only by its value in relation to God that was characteristic of the *mitnagdim*. She came to feel that she could not identify with a Judaism so intertwined with her now so negative feelings about her own father. "Merge the Jewish patriarch with patriarchal Judaism and when you leave one, you leave them both."[127]

As the message of women's liberation has spread to both working class and minority women, criticism has been of the white and middle-class character of the movement. To an important extent, this criticism has been directed at Jewish women who had been in the vanguard. The *universalistic* gender aspect has been attacked on the basis of *particularistic* issues of class and race. Symptomatic was the response within the women's movement as a whole to the anti-Zionist resolutions at Mexico City in 1975 and Copenhagen in 1980 in United Nations-sponsored conferences on women. Feminists who were Jewish felt that anti-Semitism was being masked by the anti-Israel political stance so prevalent in the United Nations. This has led people like Lettie Cottin Pogrebin in the 1980s to respond to anti-Semitism in the women's movement.[128] Her publication of *Mexico City* marked for her a need to identify herself as a Jew as well as a feminist. She identified with Golda Meier in the secular political arena as well as the judge Deborah in the religious arena.

The transition experienced by Lettie Pogrebin to that of identification as both a feminist and a Jew has been replicated by many others. The founding of Lilith as a Jewish feminist quarterly in 1976 has served to bridge the two.[129] The quest by Jewish feminists has brought about an extraordinary renewal in the character of American Judaism.[130] Girls in many Orthodox and Conservative day schools study on equal level with boys. Conservative and Reform movements ordain women as rabbis. Women take an active role in prayer services in those settings. Even in Orthodox circles, women have set up their own prayer groups. Baby-naming ceremonies for girls are now almost standard procedure. Bat mitzvah services are almost universal.[131] Other new rituals have been developed to connect with activities unique to women such as Rosh Hodesh, ritual associated with the new moon.[132]

American Orthodoxy

Coincident with this opening up to women in Conservative and Reform Judaism has been a contrasting and equally extraordinary resurgence of Orthodoxy after 1950. Traditional Judaism had seemingly been permanently left behind in the rush to secularism in Lita and later in America in the generation seeking acculturation. To the contrary, in 1968, there were 310 Orthodox day schools with seventy-five thousand students. In 1981, there were 489 such schools in thirty-six states in the United States, one-third of these high schools with far more students.[133]

The Daf Yomi movement encourages thousands of Jews to read one page of Talmud each day, culminating in the enormous number of persons participating in a completion ceremony every few years at places such as Madison Square Garden.[134] Particularly noteworthy has been the success of efforts to create *eruvim* in the 1980s in communities throughout the country. The establishment of "boundaries" surrounding these communities enable Orthodox families to carry objects as though they were "private places" thus fulfilling the strictures of the Talmud in regard to Sabbath observance.[135] In general, there has been a greater punctiliousness in the observance of kashrut and the Sabbath and a greater distinction made between the level of observance between those who consider themselves Conservative and Orthodox.

It may be noted that the original immigrants tended to be those without status. It was relatively uncommon for the well-established rabbinical authorities of Lita to migrate to what they considered to be *trefe medinah.*[136] America was a difficult place to maintain Sabbath observance, kashrut, and the entire range of traditional observance. For example, it was not easy even in New York to find a mikveh, the ritual bath required of a traditional woman after menstruation before returning to marital intercourse.[137] The synagogue was normally controlled by the laity who were also far less learned than the norm in the Pale in Eastern Europe.

The traditional communal structure could not be reinstated in the large American cities such as New York or Chicago. In the smaller cities, there was usually one rabbi who towered over the Orthodox community supervising kashrut and presiding over the local Jewish court. The role of the communal rabbi successively declined as rabbis became representative of their individual congregations and with a proliferation of other forms of organization. An authoritative figure who could answer questions of religious law became less often called upon. The life of Zvi Hirsch Grodzinsky in Omaha illustrated this incongruity between the Litvak religious scholar and deterioration in the communal role of the rabbi in the acculturating generation.[138]

Several attempts were made within Orthodoxy to deal with the disaffection of American youth with the old style synagogue and rabbinate. In recognition of the widespread problem of Sabbath observance, attendance at the evening service became for many an alternative to the morning one. Among the initiatives maintaining Orthodoxy in the interwar generation was the Americanized

Young Israel movement. Starting in 1915, it was lay-led for most of its existence until postwar World War II period.[139]

In the early postwar period, it appeared that Orthodoxy was "an anachronism."[140] It was predicted that Orthodoxy would have no permanent place in the free atmosphere of America. Orthodoxy was correlated with the foreign born, elderly and poor.[141] Later, there were those who were young, educated, and affluent who, in increasing number, observed kashrut and Sabbath observance within the Orthodox framework. The five-day week made such observance more easily accomplished. "Modern Orthodoxy" has been able to transcend its identification with the immigrant Jewish culture of East Europe and to withstand the pressures of modernization and secularization."[142]

Yeshiva University has provided the Americanized religious leadership for the movement as well as secular education for the faithful. Its charter from the first was to combine the learning of Talmud along with the language of the land. The Rabbi Isaac Elchanan Theological Seminary (RIETS) was founded in 1892. The first rebbes were of Lithuanian origin and training.[143] In 1922, Rabbi Solomon Polachek was recruited on the basis of being a disciple of the famed sage Rabbi Hayyim Soloveitchik. The recruitment of the latter's son Rabbi Moshe Soloveitchik to RIETS in 1929 contributed even greater stature to the Seminary.[144] Growing out of the RIETS, Yeshivah College was established in 1928 as a four-year liberal arts college.

Orthodox revitalization has been generally attributed to the influx of Orthodox immigrants around the time of World War II. Particularly after the war, many of the refugees from the Holocaust were Orthodox Jews who had previously regarded America as a spiritual wasteland. Particularly influential in the evolution of modern Orthodoxy among those immigrants and others in America has been the leadership of Rabbi Joseph B. Soloveitchik. His followers refer to him as The Rov. He was the one figure who commanded respect not only in the Orthodox movement but was also recognized as a spokesman for Orthodoxy in the wider Jewish community. He was fluent in English as well as Yiddish and Hebrew. As chairman of the Halakha Commission, he was the leading personality in the Rabbinical Council of America (RCA), the organization of rabbis of Orthodox congregations. He succeeded his father as a teacher of Talmud in 1941 at RIETS and served as professor of philosophy at the graduate school of Yeshiva University. Like his father, but unlike other descendents of his famous grandfather, he also identified with the religious Zionist organization (Mizrachi) of which he was honorary president. However, he rejected the proffered position of chief rabbi in Israel and chose never to visit that country. He was of the Diaspora.[145] His writings and lectures have exemplified an exploration on the nature of one's relationship to God within Orthodoxy that was part of a new trend in Jewish theology in America.[146]

Born in 1903, Rabbi Joseph Soloveitchik was the scion of a preeminent Lithuanian rabbinical family. His father, Moses, was originally the rabbi of a town in Belorussia. His grandfather, Hayyim, had been noted as the founder of a method for Talmudic study, named Brisker after the city of Brest where he was the rabbi. Joseph Soloveitchik grew up in a household where intellect was a supreme value. Until his early twenties, he devoted himself almost exclusively to the study of Talmud and Halakha under his father's tutelege and mastered his grandfather's mode of study. His mother, a descendent of another strand of the Lithuanian rabbinate, encouraged him to study secular subjects. Private tutors provided him with the equivalent of a secular high school education. In 1931, he received his doctorate at University of Berlin majoring in philosophy. Berlin at that time represented for many young scholars from Orthodox backgrounds a place to relate their religious tradition to ideas that challenged their validity.[147] He was thus not only a master of Torah learning but conversant with Western philosophy and the world of science and technology. In his study of philosophy, he brought its terminology to bear to "the world view implicit in his progenitors critic-conceptual method."[148] In 1931. he married a woman with a doctorate in education from another German university. The faithful and loving relationship to his wife had a profound effect on his teaching. It provided him with the experience of the communication and communion possible between two people.[149]

Emigrating to America in 1932, he became the rabbi of Boston's Orthodox community, a position he maintained for his entire active life. His local activities included the founding of the Maimonides School, the first Orthodox day school in New England. By virtue of his activities at Yeshiva University, he was the teacher of many of the modern Orthodox rabbinate. His annual Halakhic discourse delivered at Yeshiva University at his father's "Yarzheit" attracted thousands and was regarded as the major academic event for the American Orthodox community. Speaking and writing much, he published little, in accordance with the family tradition of perfectionism.

His most widely read book was originally published in Hebrew in 1944 and in English translation as *Halakhic Man* in 1983.[150] His theological position was that only through observance of Halakha could life be sanctified and brought into a relationship with God. Observance of the law enables man to become a master of himself in control of his thoughts and actions and thus one's life becomes sanctified. However, he stressed that it is man by his actions who helps create the sacred. The example is given that the Torah scroll itself derives its holiness by the contribution of the scribe who writes it in a spirit of sanctity in observance of the Halakhic requirements. It is the connection between his training in Western philosophy and his mitnagid Litvak Yeshiva background that produced his intellectual and highly analytic approach to the Halakhic system.[151] One must struggle as a person with one's emotional self. Passion for learning was the only emotion permitted to exist.[152]

His later *Lonely Man of Faith*, published in 1965, reflects the feeling of alienation that one might have as a man of faith and the clearest statement of his theological intentions. "He seeks to reconcile the two, conflicting, divine Mandates: one, to subdue the earth, the other to crave redemption. Both have their legitimate place."[153] His neo-Orthodox theology seeks to reconcile in a dialectical way the modern and the biblical into a third way. Awareness of one's uniqueness causes loneliness and insecurity. In that state of isolation, one yearns for a redeemed existence. In order to achieve redemption, one must provide room for another in a "covenantal faith community," a community in which God is a partner. The covenant consists of God's commandments crystallized in the Halakha. His will expressed in these teachings answers the need for communication with others and nearness to God that helps to transcend the loneliness. Prayer is the means for achieving both these needs. Devout prayer is distinguished from mysticism by its clear stress of a religious ethical norm.[154]

Rather than drawing upon the characteristics of his ancestors for support of his theology, Soloveitchik actually was original in his inspiration.[155] His mitnagdic ancestors were fundamentally pessimistic and viewed spirituality as ultimately only possible with death.[157] Soloveitchik departed in emphasizing the spiritual significance of Halakhic study and observance as an optimistic alternative. Although harkening back to his Litvak predecessors, perhaps to provide legitimacy, Soloveitchik has transmuted their pessimism into its opposite. This transmutation, while retaining the value of the law, may be a response to the experience of America as differentiated from the character of its Litvak roots.

Fundamental to Soloveitchik's values and that of the mitnagdim, from whom he arose, was the focus on the very act of study itself. This was in addition to the fruit of such study being its value in learning about the divine will. All study, regardless of its purity and motives, is inherently the most exalted form of human behavior.[157] This enthusiasm about the greatness of scholarship resulted in the development throughout the nineteenth century of an uniquely great network of Lithuanian yeshivot initiated by the disciples of the Vilna Gaon. With the destruction of East European life during the Holocaust, there has been an extraordinary proliferation of such yeshivot in the United States. There are about twenty *major* Lithuanian-style yeshivas with twice that number of smaller schools with an estimated enrollment in the 1980s of five thousand students.[158]

For example, the famous yeshiva in Telz was able to evacuate its faculty just before the war and was re-established in Cleveland in 1941. It is particularly noted as retaining its methods and replicating them in America as carriers of a noble and ancient tradition Beth Medrash Govoha, the largest and most prestigious, "the Harvard of yeshivas," was established in Lakewood, New Jersey, in 1943 by Reb Aaron Kotler. Like his colleagues, he had been trained in Slobodka and later became head of the yeshiva founded by his father-in-law at Slutsk. He chose Lakewood in accordance with the need he felt to establish a place of study, in the Litvak model, that was in a small city away from distractions. His rationale was based not only on the utilitarian needs to produce rabbis, teachers and educated laymen but ultimately to learn Torah for its own sake, *Torah lishma.* He was also instrumental in establishing and maintaining separation of the Orthodox rabbinate from other denominations within American Judaism, thus marking the split between the *modern* (such as represented by RIETS) and *right-wing* Orthodox communities.[159]

The purpose of the course of study in these yeshivot is not necessarily ordination or religious teaching. Rather, in the Litvak tradition, it is to produce pious persons who carry on their lives in the context of their primary profession but do so well versed in the laws and customs of Judaism. Ideally, what has been instilled is a love for and commitment to learning. There are thousands who study Talmud in small groups on a part-time basis along with their regular work.[160] This is in accordance with the tradition of mitnagdim which in exalting study, in raising learning to greater heights, sought to make "the common man into the uncommon scholar."[161]

Holocaust Memory

The two central events of postwar Jewish history have been the rebirth of Israel and the Holocaust. The Holocaust has affected American Jewish life in the most fundamental way. It initially brought about the unification of Jews in the founding of Israel as a haven for the East European remnants as exemplified by Rabbi Abba Hillel Silver. It has been a basis as well for the political commitment to the continued defense and prosperity of Israel in the world community as exemplified by the role of Philip Klutznick entering into American government. Both issues seemed to come to the fore in June 1967 when American Jews seemed to be reliving the Holocaust in the possible mortality of Israel.

The success in the war by exemplifying Redemption seemed to provide the opportunity for the Holocaust to become an event as well.[162] The primacy of the Holocaust had already been foreshadowed in the early 1960s in the writings of Elie Weisel and others. However, it is since 1967 that those have been widely heard who have struggled to confront and respond seriously to the experience of the Holocaust. They have sought to consider a conception of human dignity and of some notion of God and covenant in light of Auschwitz.[163]

The Holocaust has cast a huge shadow over the lives of American Jews. There are those who feel that the rise in intermarriage in the recent decades reflect the ultimate answer to the horror it engendered. Most profound has been the role memorializing the Holocaust has played in the reordering of priorities in the entire range of Jewish life in the United States. The first question is how the Holocaust and its memory has affected Jews living in America; the second question is how American Jewry has affected the memory of the Holocaust. American Jews can in most instances view it not only as survivors but as bystanders. Their impotence in affecting American policy during the 1930s and during the war itself can only lead to guilt. This guilt has been partially expiated by protestation of solidarity with Israel and adherence to giving witness to memory.

The Day of Remembrance (Yom Ha-shoah) is marked annually in many American communities. It is noteworthy that Day of Remembrance is connected with the Warsaw Ghetto Uprising as the time of resistance. Although there are religious aspects, it is primarily a secular commemoration. Memorials and museums have been built throughout the country with the most salient the National Holocaust Memorial Museum adjacent to the Mall in Washington in the center of American life.

In 1978, almost a full generation following the end of the Second World War, President Carter created a presidential commission on the Holocaust devoted to recommending a national Holocaust Memorial. The timing was related to the thirtieth anniversary of the State of Israel and a visit to Washington of the then Prime Minister Menachem Begin as well as even more narrow political issues. Stuart Eizenstat, born of Litvak family in Atlanta, was the key person in the White House assigned as liaison. The commission made a deliberate decision to place the memorial in a larger American context by building, in Washington, a museum with an educational mission. By functioning under governmental auspices, a process was initiated that led to some degree of universalization of the event. It became necessary to recognize not only the Jews but other victims of the war and, potentially, of other past and future genocides. The language used by Elie Weisel, the chair of the commission, sought to protect the uniqueness of the Holocaust: "All Jews were victims but not all victims were Jews." There were constant battles about the membership of the Holocaust Memorial Council that replaced the Commission and was responsible for the implementation of the Report.[164] Concern was always that the central Judaic core of the Holocaust would be obscured.[165]

In 1979, there was also the beginning of the annual ceremonies commemorating the Jewish Holocaust, but also others, in the Capitol Rotunda in Washington. This public ceremony is echoed in the various states along with hundreds of towns.[166]. Once again, in entering the larger political arena, there is the struggle to maintain the integrity of the memory in a sea of contradictions. Particularly problematic in the museum as well as Memorial ceremonies are the claims of ethnic Poles and Ukrainians for recognition, given the anti-Semitism that imbued their nationalism and their roles during the Holocaust.

In the Americanization of the Holocaust, the effort remains to retain its significance to Jews by the process of differentiating their experience from those of other victims whilst recognizing both. However, in the American public schools, the teaching was related to American values. It was taught that the Holocaust was an example of the abrogation of the principles of pluralism, respect for differences and freedom from prejudice.[167] In 1993, the United States Holocaust Memorial Museum was officially dedicated by the President and other high officials. It stands adjacent to the Mall and within sight of the Washington Monument. It has taken its place in the itinerary alongside the other museums and monuments of the busloads of high school students and families visiting Washington from all over the country, the majority non-Jewish. For those who come, there is "a new recognition of the tenets of American Constitutional democracy: a belief in equality and equal justice under law, a commitment to pluralism and tolerance . . . For American Jews it is a place of pilgrimage and a source of pride . . . it represents the arrival of the American Jewish community as confident and self-assertive. A generation ago, the museum would have been built in New York, not in Washington . . . [they] would have preferred to keep their bereaved memories private, parochial . . . A generation ago, Jews had internalized the rule of emancipation 'be a Jew in your house, a man in the street.' No public life as a Jew was permitted to them. Now, in pluralistic America, the most painful of Jewish memories can be brought to the center of American life."[168]

The life and work of Rabbi Yitz Greenberg has represented the entire range of issues in the evolution of American responses to the existence of Auschwitz. He was born in Brooklyn in 1933 to Orthodox parents in whose home there was both learning and piety. His father was an immigrant who was a Talmud scholar in the mitnagid Litvak tradition and had the greatest influence on his development.[169] The father is also described as a rebel against injustice and a "fierce fighter for the underdog." He was a teacher in the synagogue. His mother was an unusually pious woman. Yitzsak was sent to a modern Orthodox day school and then to an equivalent Orthodox high school (Yeshiva University High School in Brooklyn). He also joined a religious Zionist youth group. After high school, he enrolled in a transplanted "mussar" yeshiva (Novardok) in Borough Park. The mussar Litvak tradition had a major impact on his view toward the Jewish role of *tikkun olam*. Along with religious training, he pursued secular studies in history at Brooklyn College.

In 1955, while a graduate student at Harvard, he "came out" by wearing a *kippah*. In 1959, he became professor of history at Yeshiva University. In doing so, he describes this decision "as opting for a career in which Jewish expression would be central."[170] A Fulbright Scholar in Israel in 1961, his attention to the Holocaust at Yad Vashem represented a further religious turning point. On his return, he was successful in establishing one of the first courses on the Holocaust at Yeshiva University. Comparing himself to Rabbi Israel Salanter, the founder of *mussar* in the mid-nineteenth century and whose works he had translated into English, he felt he could not live only a fulfilled personal religious life while Judaism needed to deal with the forces of assimilation and modernity. He founded the Department of Jewish Studies at City College. In 1979, he left City College to became full-time at CLAL, later called the National Jewish Center for Learning and Leadership, in order to promote intra-Jewish dialogue. Its mission was to provide leadership for this new postrabbinic era of Judaism in response to the Holocaust and the State of Israel. One of CLAL's key sections was "Zachor: Holocaust Resource Center" to encourage the development of Holocaust memorials as "sacred spaces," albeit in secular settings, that would transmit the memory of the Holocaust while doing justice to its meaning. Stuart Eizenstat, later a key advisor to President Carter in relation to the Holocaust Museum, was one of those affected by CLAL.[171]

In 1979, Greenberg was appointed director of the newly formed Holocaust Memorial Commission whose chair was Elie Weisel.[172] With the fruition of the Holocaust Memorial Museum in Washington in 1993, he felt his work still remained incomplete. Particularly necessary remained the task of renewing Jewish education and community in light of the high level of intermarriage and assimilation.

The question remains as to the extent the story of the destruction and resistance and subsequent postwar renascence of the Jewish people reverberates within America in light of the Litvak tradition that Greenberg represents. Most crucial perhaps has been the focus on the historical events of Israel and the Holocaust that has called into question one's stance in relation to historicism. The question has been asked throughout the post-Enlightenment period. However, it has now become even more sharply drawn. That is, to what extent are the features of Jewish belief and conduct determined by the historical context or is there a core that remains unchangeable, that transcends history?

Greenberg had come from the Orthodox tradition but had grown up in America. His yeshiva training had been heavily influenced by Salanter in terms of an ethical response to the law. In the introduction to his first book, *The Jewish Way*, along with his own father, he found his mentor in J. B. Soloveitchik. He credits the latter for introducing him to the pattern of the law rather than being lost in its thousands of details. "It was a system by which to live humanely, a way to seize life whole, a confrontation with the dilemmas and anxieties of existence . . . Rabbi Soloveitchik went on to show a personal model of open encounter with modern culture and a willingness to influence and be influenced by it."[173] Rooted in modern Orthodoxy, Greenberg in CLAL sought to maintain a dialogue with other components of American Jewry.

Unlike his ultra-Orthodox Litvak colleagues in the yeshivot, he maintains that, although a covenant with God is the character of Judaism, the great events of our time must be incorporated into the ongoing Jewish way.

That covenant is, in this *post-Rabbinical era*, a different one in light of Auschwitz. In his profound and incisive work dealing with the Holocaust, *Cloud of Smoke, Pillar of Fire*, Greenberg states, "No statement, theological or otherwise, should be made that would not be credible in the presence of the burning children."[174] His purpose is to retain the tradition by enabling it to incorporate the events of our time. The covenant at this time can be thought of as a "voluntary" one. Jews have chosen to remain Jews. They renew the covenant "so in love with the dream of redemption . . . that they volunteered to carry out the mission . . . [of tikkun olam]." The task of Jewish existence is to respond to death by creating life and to continue the Jewish people's journey in history.[175]

The circle has come around since the heady exploration of the Haskalah and the breakdown of the communal structure. The story is told that one of the great rabbis in the early nineteenth century petitioned Napoleon not to emancipate the Jews for fear that equal rights would start a process that would lead to apostasy and disintegration of the religion. But Napoleon and the processes of modernization that he represented were not deterred. The vast majority would not choose to return to poverty or pariah status in order to avoid the temptations of acceptance and assimilation. The secularized responses to industrialization and nationalism have had their influence. Particularly in America but elsewhere as well, with all the drawbacks and problems, never have Jews ever enjoyed this level of freedom during the past two thousand years. In the context of America over the past one hundred years, the energy and ideologies that arose in Lita have affected life in America and been transmuted by it. The future is uncertain; the covenant remains and is renewed in each generation. "Each generation is enjoined to feel a responsibility to those who came before and to those who come after, and to study the past as a way of apprehending the purposes of the God of the Covenant."[176]

*   *   *

END NOTES

2.1 The Nature of the Place

1   Moses Rischin, *Immigration and the American Tradition*, Indianapolis, 1976 pxx
2   Eli Lederhendler, *Jewish Responses to Modernity: New Voices in America and Eastern Europe.*, New York, 1994 p 105
3   Jeannette Baron, Ed., *Steeled by Adversity: Essays and Addresses on American Jewish life* by Salon Wiittmayer Baron, Philadelphia, 1971, p98
4   Lloyd Gartner, "Immigration and the Formation of American Jewry,1840-1925" In Marshall Sklare, Ed., *The Jew in American Society*, New York, 1974
5   Jeannette Baron, op cit, 1971, 276
6   Henry Feingold, *The Jewish Experience from Colonial Times to the Present*, New York, 1974, 76-80
7   Hasia Diner, *A Time for Gathering. The Second Migration, 1820-1880.*, Baltimore: 1992,
8   Lloyd Gartner, op cit, 1974
9   Hasia Diner, op cit, 1993, 26
10   Alan Silverstein, *Alternatives to Assimilation*, Hanover, NH, 1994, 46-70
11   Marc Raphael, *Profiles in American Judaism: The Reform, Conservative, Orthodox and Reconstructionist Traditions in Historical Perspective*, San Francisco, 1984, 9-16
12   Alan Silverstein, op cit, 1994,116-120
13   Marc Raphael, op cit, 1984,17
14   ibid,
15   Hasia Diner op cit, 1993
16   Hasia Diner, op cit, 1993, 28
17   Jeannette Baron, op cit, 1971, 271
18   Esther Panitz, "The Polarity of American Jewish Attitudes Toward Immigration," In Abraham Karp, *The Jewish Experience in America*, New York, 1969, 33-36
19   Simon Kusnets, "Immigration of American Jews to the United States: Background and Structure," *Perspectives in American History*, 1975, 9: 35.
20   Samuel Joseph, *Jewish Immigration to the United States, 1881-1910*, New York, 1967,98-100
21   Jeannette Baron, op cit, 1971, 278)

22   ibid, 281

23   ibid, 276

24   Hasia Diner, op cit,1993

25   Lloyd Gartner, op cit, 1974

26   Jeannette Baron op cit, 1971, 283

27   Charles Wyszkowski, *A Community in Conflict*, Lanham, MD, 1991,5-20

28   Gerald Sorin, "Mutual Contempt, Mutual Benefit, The Strained
      Encounter between German and East European Jews in America
      1880-1920." *American Jewish History*, 1993-94, 81: 34.

29   ibid 34.

30   Howard Markel, *Quarantine! East European Jews in New York*,
      Baltimore,1997

31   Melvyn Dubovsky, "Organized Labor and the Immigrant in New York
      City, 1900-1918," *Labor History*, 1961, 2: 182.

32   Elias Tcherikower, "Jewish Immigration to the United States, 1881-
      1900" *YIVO Annual*, 1951, 6: 157

33   Gilbert Osofsky, "The Hebrew Immigrant Aid Society of the United
      States1881-1883," In Abraham Karp, *The Jewish Experience in America*,
      New York, 1969, 73-85

34   Esther Panitz op cit, 1969

35   Robert Rockaway, Words of the Uprooted, Ithaca, NY, 1998,13-33

36   Gerald Sorin, *The Prophetic Minority*, Bloomington, IN, 1985, 43

37   Stephan Brumberg, "The One-Way Mirror: Public Schools on the
      Lower East Side in the Early Twentieth Century," In Hasia Diner,
      Jeffrey Shandler, and Beth Wenger, Eds., *Remembering the Lower East
      Side*, Bloomington, IN, 2000, 137

38   Selma Berroll, *East Side-East End*, Westport, CN, 1994 60-108 passim

39   David Kaufman, *Shul with a Pool*, Hanover, NH, 1999, 103-127

40   Hadassah Kosak, *Cultures of Opposition: Jewish Immigrant Workers, New
      York City 1881-1905*, Albany, NY, 2000, 92-99

41   Naomi Cohen, *Jacob Schiff: A Study in American Jewish Leadership*,
      Hanover, NH, 1999, 47-81

42   Gerald Sorin op cit 1985, 47-53

43   ibid, 56

44   Eli Lederhendler op cit, 1994, 111

45   Andrew Godley, *Jewish Immigrant Entrepreneurship in New York and
      London 1880-1914*, New York, 2001, 51-60

46   Eli Lederhendler op cit, 1994,120

47   ibid, 123

48   ibid, 116
49   Moses Rischin, op cit, 1976, xli-xliii

2.2   The Evolution in America
2.2.1 The Immigrant Generation

1   Lucy Dawidowicz, "The Jewishness of the Jewish Labor Movement," In Jonathan Sarna, Ed., *The American Jewish Experience*, New York, 1986
2   Jacob Lestchinsky, "Economic and Social Development of American Jewry," In Isaac Graeber and Stuart Butt, Eds., *Jewish in a Gentile World: The Problem of Anti-Semitism*, New York, 1942
3   Elias Tcherikower *The Early Jewish Labor Movement in the United States*, trans Aaron Antonovsky, New York, 1961, 120
4   Nancy Green, *Ready to Wear, Ready to Work*, Durham, NC, 1997, 29-34
5   ibid, 48
6   Gerald Sorin *A Time for Building: The Third Migration, 1880-1920*, Baltimore, 1992 57-63
7   Charles S. Liebman, *Jews and the Left*, New York, 1979
8   Gerald Sorin op cit 1985, 26 &&
9   Gerald Sorin op cit, 1992, 81&&
10   Hadassah Kosak, op cit 2000, 87-92
11   Elisa Tcherkower, op cit, 1961, 133
12   Maximilian Hurwitz, *The Workmen's Circle*, New York, 1936
13   Gerald Sorin, *Tradition Transformed*, Baltimore,1997 107-110
14   Steven Cassedy, *To the Other Shore: The Russian Jewish Intellectuals Who Came to America*. Princeton, 1997, 65
15   Ibid,5-76
16   Ezra Mendelson "The Russian Roots of the American Jewish Labor Movement, *YIVO Annual*, 1976, 16: 394.
17   Henry Feingold, *A Midrash on American Jewish History*, Albany, 1982, 99
18   Eli Lederhendler, op cit, 1994, 134-137
19   Gerald Sorin, op cit 1985, 89
20   Steven Cassedy, op cit, 1997, 46
21   Gerald Sorin op cit, 1985, 29
22   Ronald Sanders, *Downtown Jews*, New York, 1969, 28-39
23   Irving Howe, *The World of Our Fathers*, New York, 1976, 103
24   Ezra Mendelson op cit, 1976
25   Gerald Sorin, "Tradition and Change: American Jewish Socialists as agents of Acculturation." *American Jewish History* 1989, 79: 37,

26 Irving Howe, op cit, 1976, 524
27 Richard Pressman, "Abraham Cahan, Capitalist, David Levinsky, Socialist," In David Walden, Ed., *The Changing Mosaic: From Cahan to Malamud, Roth and Ozick*, University Park, PA, 1993
28 Irving Howe, op cit 1976, 526
29 Ronald Sanders, op cit, 1969, 29
30 Jonathan Frankel,. *Prophecy and Politics:Socialism, Nationalism and the Russian Jews 1862-1917.* New York, 1981, 454
31 Isaiah Trunk, "The Cultural Dimensions of the American Jewish Labor Movement," *YIVO Annual* 1976, 16:342.
32 Melvyn Dubovsky, op cit, 1961
33 Gerald Sorin op cit, 1985, 79
34 Arthur Liebman, "The Ties That Bind; Jewish Support for the Left in the United States," *American Jewish Historical Quarterly*, 1976, 66: 285.
35 Charles Madison, *Jewish Publishing in America*, New York, 1976, 129-140
36 Mordechai Soltes, *the Yiddish Press: An Americanizing Agency*, New York. 1950, 1-29
37 Charles Madison, op cit, 1976, 102-128
38 Mordechai Soltes, op cit, 1950, 175-181
39 Jonathan Frankel, op cit, 1981,478
40 Steven Cassedy, *Building the Future: Jewish Immigrant Intellectuals and the Making of 'Tsukunft'*, New York, 1999, passim
41 Nathaniel Goldsmith, "Abraham Lyessin, National Poet of Yiddish Literature," *Jewish Book Annual*, 1994, 52: 163
42 Emmanuel Goldsmith, "Zhitlowsky and American Jewry," In Joshua Fishman, Ed., *Never Say Die*, The Hague, 1981
43 Joshua Fishman, "The Sociology of Yiddish: A Forward," In Joshua Fishman, Ed., op cit
44 Steven Cassedy, op cit, 1999, 98
45 Moses Rischin, op cit, 1967, 166
46 Irving Howe, op cit 1976, 506-507
47 Mark Raider *The Emergence of American Zionism*, New York, 1998, 20
48 Isaiah Trunk, op cit, 1976
49 Bezalel Sherman, "Nationalism, Secularism and Religion in the Jewish labor Movement," In Irving Howe and Eliezer Greenberg, Eds., *Voices from the Yiddish, Essays, Memoirs, Diaries*, Ann Arbor, 1972
50 Sandra Parker, "An Educational Assessment of the Yiddish Secular School Movement in the United States" In Joshua Fishman, Ed., op cit

51 Alexander Harkavy, "Chapters from My Life," In Uric Hershen, Ed., *The East European Experience in the United States, American Jewish Archives*, 1983,53 ibid

52 Zosa Szajkowski, "Impact of the Russian Revolution of 1905 on American Jewish Life," *YIVO Annual*, 1978 17: 54.

53 Jonathan Frankel op cit, 1981,494-495

54 Ibid, 458

56 Hadassah Kosak, op cit, 2000,114-125

57 Gerald Sorin, op cit, 1997,108

58 Hadassah Kosak, op cit, 2000,110

59 Bernard Mergen, "Another Great Prize: The Jewish Labor Movement in the Context of American Labor History," *YIVO Annual*, 1976, 16: 394.

60 Henry Soule, *Sidney Hillman*, New York, 1945, 7

61 Stuart Kaufman, "Labor Will Rule," *American Jewish History*, 1994, 82: 382

62 Moses Rischin, op cit,1967,247-250

63 Alice Wexler, *Emma Goldman, An Intimate Life*, New York, 1984, 5-13

64 Gerald Sorin, op cit, 1985, 7

65 ibid, p8

66 Paula Hyman, 'Gender and the Immigrant Jewish Experience in the United States In Judith Baskin, Ed., *Jewish Women in Historical Perspective*, Detroit, 1991

67 Linda Kuzmack, *Women's Cause*, Columbus, OH, 1990, 151-156)

68 Paula Hyman, op cit, 1991

69 Gerald Sorin, op cit, 1985,127

70 Moses Rishlin op cit,1967, 200-252 passim.

71 ibid, 254

72 Roy Helfgott, "Trade Unionism Among the Jewish Garment Workers of Britain and the United States," *Labor History*, 1961, 2: 202.

73 Moses Richlin, op cit, 1967, 194

74 Stuart Kaufman op cit, 1994)

75 Gerd Korman, "New Jewish Politics for an American Labor Leader, Sidney Hillman, 1942-1946," *American Jewish History*, 1994, 82:, 195

76 G.B. Hardman, "Jewish Workers in the American Labor Movement," *YIVO Annual*, 1952, 7: 229-235.

77 Mark Raider et al, *Abba Hillel Silver and American Zionism*, Portland, OR, 1997, 20

78 Sarah Schmidt, "Messianic Pragmatism: The Zionism of Horace M. Kallen," *Judaism*, 1976, 25: 217

79 William Toll, "Tthnicity and Freedom in the Philosophy of Horace Kallen," In Moses Richin, Ed., *The Jews of North America*, Detroit, 1987

80 Horace Kallen, "The Bearing of Emancipation on Jewish Survival, *YIVO Annual*, 1959, 12: 9.

81 Mark Raider op cit, 1997, 152

82 Alon Gal, "The Mission Motif in American Zionism, 1888-1948," *American Jewish History*, 1985, 75: 363.

83 Mark Raider op cit, 1997, 27

84 Jonathan Frankel, op cit, 1981, 546-547

85 Mark Raider, op cit, 1997, 43

86 ibid, 29

87 Gerald Sorin op cit, 1992, 175-180

88 Jonathan Rosenbaum and Myron Wakshlag, "Maintaining Tradition: A Survey of the Life and Writings of Zvi Hirsch Grodzinsky," *American Jewish History*, 1994, 84: 263.

89 Marc Raphael op cit, 1985, 88

90 Gerald Sorin, op cit, 1997,133-136

91 Pamela Nadel, *Conservative Judaism in America; A Biographical Dictionary and Sourcebook"* New York, 1988, 98-102

92 ibid

93 Herbert Parzen, *Architects of Conservative Judaism*, New York, 1964, 129

94 ibid, 143).

95 Marshall Sklare, *Conservative Judaism: An American Religious Movement,'* New York, 1972

2.2.2 The Acculturating Generation

1 Daniel Bell, "Introduction," *The Winding Passage*, 1980

2 Deborah Dash Moore, *At Home in America: Second Generation New York Jews*, 1981, 110

3 ibid,126-127

4 David Kaufman, op cit, 2000.

5 Deborah Dash Moore op cit, 1981, 129

6 Mel Scult, *Judaism Faces the Twentieth Century: A Biography of Mordecai M. Kaplan*, Detroit, 1993, 22

7 Jeffrey Gurock and Jacob J. Schacter, *A Modern Heretic in a Traditional Community*, New York, 1997, 10)

8 Mel Scult, op cit, 1993, 30

9   ibid, 49)

10   Jeffrey Gurock op cit, 29

11   Mel Scult, op cit, 1993, p61

12   Robert Seltzer, "Kaplan and Jewish Modernity," In Emanuel S. Goldsmith, Mel Scult, and Robert Seltzer, Eds., *The American Judaism of Mordecai Kaplan*, New York, 1990,

13   Jack J. Cohen, "Reflections on Kaplan's Zionism," In Emanuel S. Goldsmith, Mel Scult, and Robert Seltzer, Eds., op cit,402

14   Jen Joselit, New York's Jewish Jews, Bloomington, IN, 1990, 25-31

15   Jeffrey Gurock and Jacob Schacter, *Modern Heretic and Traditional Community. Mordecai M. Kaplan, Orthodoxy and American Judaism*, New York, 1997, 55

16   David Kaufman, op cit, 1999, 216-228

17   ibid, 242-274

18   ibid, 275-283

19   Jeffrey Gurock and Jacob Schacter op cit, 1997,109

20   Kessner, 1990 p347

21   Jeffrey Gurock and Jacob Schacter, op cit, 1997, 137, 140

22   Arnold Eisen, *The Chosen People in America*, Bloomington, IN, 1983, 74-83

23   Arthur Goren, "Spiritual Zionism and Jewish Sovereignty," In Robert Seltzer nad Norman J Cohen, Eds., *The Americanization of the Jews*, New York, 1995

24   Deborah Musher, "Reconstructionist Judaism in the Mind of Mordecai Kaplan, Transformation from a Philosophy into a Religious Denomination" 1998, *American Jewish History*, 86: 397.

25   Mel Scult, op cit, 1993, 365

26   Suzanne Klingenstein, *Jews in the American Academy, 1900-1940, The Dynamics of Intellectual Assimilation*, New Haven, 1991,21

27   Paul Ritterband and Harold Wechsler, *Jewish Learning in American Universities*, 1994, Bloomington, IN, 102-107

28   ibid,111-116

29   ibid,113

30   Leo Schwarz, *Wolfson of Harvard: Portrait of a Scholar*, Philadelphia, 1978, xx

31   Arthur Hyman, "Harry Austryn Wolfson, 1887-1974," *Jewish Book Annual*, 1975-76, 137-145

32   Leo Schwarz, op cit, 1978, xxii

33 S.A. Longstaff, "Ivy League Gentiles and Inner-City Jews Class and Ethnicity around 'Partisan Review' in the Thirties and Forties," *American Jewish History*, 1991, 80: 325

34 Terry Cooney, *The Rise of the New York Intellectuals: Partisan Review and it Circle*, Madison, WI, 1986, 70

35 Terry Cooney, 'New York Intellectuals and the Question of Jewish Identity," *Jewish Social Science*, 1991, 80:344

36 Terry Cooney, op cit, 1986, 15

37 ibid, 25

38 ibid, 88

39 ibid,127

40 ibid,139

41 ibid, 217

41 Mark Krupnick, *Lionel Trilling and the Fate of Cultural Criticism*, Evanston, Il, 1986,6

42 Diana Trilling, *The Beginning of the Journey*, New York, 1980; Alan Wald, *The New York Intellectuals*, Chapel Hill, NC, 1987, 33

43 Alan Wald op cit, 1987,35

44 ibid, 36

45 Suzanne Klingenstein, *Enlarging America, The Cultural Work of Jewish Literary Scholars*, Syracuse, NY, 1998, 216

46 ibid, 140

47 ibid, 141

48 Diana Trilling, op cit, 1993, 143

49 Nathan Scott, *Three American Moralists, Mailer, Bellow and Trilling*, South Bend, IN, 1973,156

50 Suzanne Klingenstein, op cit, 1998,198

51 Deborah Dash Moore, op cit, 1981, 204-208

52 ibid, 223

53 ibid, 229

54 Nathan Glazer, The Social basis of American Communism, New York, 1961,4

55 ibid, 116

56 ibid, 143-147

57 ibid, 167

58 Ruth Wisse, *A Little Love in Big Manhattan*, Cambridge, MA, 1988, 228

59 Irving Howe, op cit, 1976, 25

60   Ruth Wisse, "Di Yunge and the Problem of Jewish Aestheticism," *Jewish Social Studies*, 1976, 38, 265

61   Charles Madison, op cit, 1976, 159-176

62   Ruth Wisse, op cit, 1988

63   Nathaniel Goldsmith, op cit, 1994,198-99

64   Charles Madison, op cit, 1976,195-199

65   Nathaniel Goldsmith op cit, 1994

66   ibid 206

67   Irving Howe op cit, 1976, 38

68   Nathaniel Goldsmith op cit, 1994,207

69   Mark Raider, op cit, 1998, 48

70   Carole Kessner, "Marie Syrkin: An Exemplary Life," In Carole Kessner, Ed., *The 'other' New York Intellectuals*, New York, 1994, 51-70

71   Marc Raphael, Abba Hillel Silver. *A Profile in American Judaism*, New York, 1989, 1-10

72   ibid,10-14

73   Alexander Schindler, "Zionism and Judaism: The Path of Rabbi Abba Hillel Silver," In Mark Raider et al, Ed., *Abba Hillel Silver and American Zionism*, Portland, OR, 1997

74   Raphael op cit. 1989, 59-62

75   Marc Raphael, op cit, 1985,39-40

76   ibid, 441-46

77   Marc Raphael, "Origins of Organized National Jewish Philanthropy in the U.S. 1914-1939," In Moses Rischin, Ed., *The Jews of North America*, Detroit, 1987, 213-223

78   Deborah Dash Moore, *B'nai B'rith and the Challenge of Ethnic Leadership*, Albany, NY, 1981,150

79   Melvin Urofsky *We are One. American Jewry and Israel.* Garden City, NY, 1978, 5-7,

80   ibid, 44

81   ibid,11-12

82   ibid, 27-30

83   Marc Raphael op cit, 1989, 89

84   Naomi Cohen, *The Americanization of Zionism, 1897-1948*, Hanover, NH, 2003,165-170

85   Melvin Urofsky op cit, 1978, 33

86   ibid, 115-120

87   ibid, 58

88 Marc Raphael op cit, 1989, 92-95

89 ibid, 103

90 ibid, 115-120

91 Marc Raphael op cit, 1989, 155-164

2.2.3 The Integrated Generation

1   Deborah Dash Moore, *GI Jews*, 2004, ix-xi

2   Melvin Urofsky op cit, 1978, 126

3   Eli Lederhendler, *New York Jews and the Decline of Urban Ethnicity 1950-1970*, Syracuse, NY, 2001, 28-30

4   Judd Teller, *Strangers and Natives*, New York, 1968, 231

5   Eli Lederhandler, op cit, 2001, 89-92

6   Marc Raphael op cit, 1985,19

7   ibid, 71

8   Arthur Hertzberg, *Jews in America*, New York, 1989, 323

9   ibid, 325-326

10 Deborah Dash Moore, op cit, 1986, 261-263

11 Nathan Glazer, op cit, 1990, 35-41

12 Phillip Klutznick, *Angles of Vision*, Chicago, 1991, 17-25; 26-28;33-34;58-61 passim ;

13 Deborah Dash Moore, op cit, 1981, xi

14 Edward Grusd, *B'nai B'rith. The Story of a Covenant*, New York, 1966, 12

15 Deborah Dash Moore, op cit, 1981, 7

16 ibid,150-156

17 ibid, 116

18 ibid, 120

19 ibid, 127

20 ibid, 215

21 Edward Grusd, op cit, 1966, 297

22 Charles Leibman, op cit, 1973,138

23 Arthur Goren, "A Golden Decade for American Jews 1945-1955," *Studies in Contemporary Jewry*, 1992. 8::3

24 William Spinrad "Explaining American Jewish Liberalism Another Attempt," *Contemporary Judaism*, 1990, 11: 107.

25 Irving Kristol, "The Liberal Tradition of American Jews," In Seymour Lipset, Ed., *American Pluralism and the Jewish Community*, New Brunswick, NJ, 1990

26   Will Herberg, "Socialism, Zionism and the Messianic Pasion," In David
     Dalin, Ed., *From Marxism to Judaism: The Collected Essays of Will Herberg*,
     New York, 1989,110-126

27   David Dalin, "Will Herberg's Path" In Robert Seltzer and Norman
     Cohen, Eds., *The Americanization of the Jews*, New York, 1995

28   Harry Ausmus, *Will Herberg: From Right to Right*, Chapel Hill, NC, 1987,
     1-107 Passim

29   Gerald Sorin, Irving Howe. *A Life of Passionate Dissent*, New York,
     2002,-14)

30   Irving Howe, "The New York Intellectuals," *Commentary*, October,
     1968, 46:29

31   Seward Alexander, *Irving Howe, Socialist, Critic and Jew*. Bloomington,
     IN, 1998, 1-6

32   quoted by Alexander, op cit, 1998, 31

33   ibid, 62-79

34   Irving Howe, *A Margin of Hope*, San Diego, 1982, 194

35   Ibid, 195

36   Ibid, 275-276

37   Ibid,198

38   Gerald Sorin, op cit, 2002, 134

39   Ibid, 103-142 passim

40   Ibid, 188-210 passim

41   Ibid, 230.

42   Irving Howe, "The End of Jewish Secularism," *Occasional Papers in
     Jewish History and Thought*, 1993

43   Stephen Whitfield, "The Stunt Man: Abbie Hoffman (1936-1989)," In
     Barbara Tischler, Ed., *Sights on the Sixties*, New Brunswick, NJ, 1992

44   David Hollinger, *Science, Jews and Secular Culture*, Princeton, 1996,8-26
     passim

45   Abraham Chapman, *Jewish American Literature, An Anthology*, New York,
     1965, 665-667, 689

46   Norman Podheretz, "The Rise and Fall of the American Jewish
     Novelist," In Gladys Rose, Ed., *Jewish Life in America Historic Perspectives*,
     1978 p 147)

47   James Atlas, *Bellow. A Biography*, New York, 2000, 129

48   ibid, 6-10

49   Steven Rubin, *Writing Our Lives*, Philadelphia, 1991, 166

50   James Atlas, op cit, 2000, 26-56 passim

51   ibid, 93-102

52 Nathan Scott op cit, 1973, 120

53 Judd Teller, op cit, 1968, 266

54 Theodore Soltaroff, *The Red Hot Vacuum*, New York, 1970, 99

55 Sanford Pinsker, *The Uncompromising Fiction of Cynthia Ozick*, Columbia, MO, 1987, 8)

56 Harold Ribalow, "Saul Bellow, Jewish Writer," *Jewish Book Annual*, 1977-1978, 35:157 L.H. Goldman, "The Jewish Perspective of Saul Bellow," In L.H. Goldman, Gloria Cronin and Ada Aharoni, Eds., *Saul Bellow: A Mosaic*, New York 1992,

58 James Atlas, op cit, 2000, 599

59 Sanford Pinsker, "Dares, Double Dares and the Jewish American Writer," In Hilda Raz, Ed., *The 'Prairie Schooner' Anthology of Jewish American Writing*, Lincoln, NE, 1997, 282-284

60 Ruth Wisse, "Cynthia Ozick as an American Jewish Writer," In Harold Bloom, Ed., *Cynthia Ozick. Modern Critical Views.* New York, 1986, 35-45

61 Joseph Lowin, *Cynthia Ozick*, Boston, 1988, 2

62 Elaine Kauvar, *Cynthia Ozick's Fiction*, Bloomington, IN, 1993, 239-241)

63 Lawrence Friedman, *Understanding Cynthia Ozick*, Columbia, SC, 1991,2-3

64 Victor Strandberg, *Greek Mind, Jewish Soul*, Madison, WI, 1994, 22

65 Sanford Pinsker, op cit 1987, 3

66 Bonnie Lyons, "Faith and Puttermesser: Contrasting Images of Two Jewish Feminists," In Joyce Antler, Ed., *Talking Back*, Hanover, NH, 1998

67 John Patrick Diggins, *The Rise and Fall of the American Left*, New York, 1992, 220

68 ibid, 190

69 Irving Howe, op cit, 1982, 291-294

70 Stanley Rothman and Robert Lindner, *Roots of Radicalism. Jews, Christians and the New Left*, New York, 1982, 3-45 passim)

71 Nathan Glazer, *Remembering the Answers. Essays on the American Student Revolt*, New York, 1970, 222-244 passim

72 Todd Gitlin *The Sixties, Years of Hope, Days of Rage*, New York, 1987, 24

73 Steven Whitfield, *American Space, Jewish Time.* Hamden, CT, 1988,106-128

74 Steven Whitfield, op cit, 1992, 108

75 Marty Jezer *Abbie Hoffman, American Rebel,* New Brunswick, NJ, 1992, 3

76 Jonah Raskin, *For the Hell of It. The Life and Times of Abbie Hoffman,* Berkeley, 1996, 8-22

77 Marty Jezer op cit,1992, 69-77

78 ibid, 8

79 Steven Whitfield op cit, 1992, 112-113

80 David Glantz, "An Interpretation of the Jewish Counterculture," *Jewish Social Studies,* 1977, 39: 117.

81 Paul Ritterband and Harold Wechsler, op cit, 1994, 210-236 passim

82 Jack Porter, *Jewish Radicalism,* New York, 1973, xli

83 Riv-Ellen Prell, *Prayer and Community. The Havurah in American Judaism.* Detroit, 1989, 15-17

84 op cit, 23

85 Arthur Waskow, "Judaism and Revolution Today," In Jack Porter and Peter Drier, Eds., *Jewish Radicalism,* New York, 1973, 27

86 Arthur Waskow, *These Holy Sparks,* New York, 1983 p13)

87 ibid, 3

88 George Johnson, "Fabrangen : A Coming Together," In Jacob Neusner, Ed., *Contemporary Judaic Fellowship in Theory and Practice,* New York, 1972 p 185)

89 Arthur Waskow, *Down-to-Earth Judaism,* New York 1995, 195,

90 Norman Friedman, "Social Movement Changes. The American Jewish Counterculture 1973-1988," *Jewish Social Studies* 1988-1993, 50: 127.1988-93)

91 Edward P. Morgan, *The 60s Experience. Hard Lessons About Modern America,* Philadelphia, 1991, 222-227

92 Barbara Sinclair Deckard, *The Women's Movement,* New York, 1983, 324-328

93 Judith Hennessee, *Betty Friedan Her Life,* New York, 1999, 1-79 passim

93 Mary Thom, *Inside Ms,* New York, 1997, 1-43)

94 Paula Hyman op cit 1991, 232-233)

95 Susan Weidman Schneider, *Jewish and Female,* New York, 1984, 504

96 Gerald Sorin, op cit, 1997, 117-118

97 Lettie Cottin Pogrebin, *Deborah, Golda and Me,* New York, 1991 32-45; 202-239 passim

98 Sylvia Barack Fishman, "The Impact of Feminism on American Jewish Life," In Jeffrey Gurock, Ed., *American Jewish Life 1920-1980,* 1998, New York,

99   Francine Klaysbrun, "Changing Roles of Jewish Women," In Irving
     Levitz and David Schnall, Eds., *Crisis and Continuity, The Jewish Family
     in the 21st Century*, Hoboken, NJ, 1995,67-69

100 Paula Hyman, "Ezrat Nashim and the Emergence of a New Feminism,"
     In Robert Seltzer and Norman Cohen Eds., *The Americanization of the
     Jews*. New York: New York University Press, 1995 284.

101 Marc Raphael op cit, 1985 168-170

102 Reuven Bulka, *Dimensions of Orthodox Judaism*, Hoboken, NJ, 1983,
     40-45

103 Jeffrey Gurock, "A Generation Unaccounted For" *American Jewish
     History*, 1987-88, 77: 247.

104 Edward S. Shapiro, "The Missing Element: Nathan Glaser and Modern
     Orthodoxy," *American Jewish History*, 1987-88, 77: 263)

105 William H. Helmreich, *The World of the Yeshivah*, New York, 1982,
     20-23

106 Charles Leibman, *The Ambivalent American Jew*, Philadelphia, 1983,
     59-71

107 Robert Goldy, *The Emergence of Jewish Theology in America*, Bloomington,
     IN, 1990

108 Hillel Goldberg, *Between Berlin and Slobodka*, Hoboken, NJ, 1989,92-95

109 Ahron Singer, "Soloveitchik's 'Lonely Man of Faith'" In Raphael
     Patai and Emmanuel Goldsmith Eds., *Thinkers and Teachers of Modern
     Judaism*, New York, 1994, 113

110 Robert Goldy, op cit, 1990, 78-82

111 Ahron Singer, op cit, 1994, 105-109

112 Alan Nadler, op cit, 1997, 132

113 ibid, 140

114 ibid, 155

115 William Helmreich op cit, 1982, xi-xiii

116 ibid, 45

117 ibid, 5

118 Edward Linenthal, *Preserving Memory*, New York, 1997 p10)

119 ibid,42-51; 82-103

120 Michael Berenbaum "Transforming the Void," In Carol Rittner
     and and John K. Roth, Eds., *From the Unthinkable to the Unavoidable*,
     Westport, CN, 1990, 11-39

121 ibid, 188).

123 Irving Greenberg, *The Jewish Way. Living the Holidays*, New York, 1988
     p7-8)

124 Irving Greenberg In John K. Roth and Michael Berenbaum, Eds., *Holocaust: Religious and Philosophical Implications*, New York, 1989,315

125 John K. Roth and Michael Berenbaum, op cit, 1989, 303

126 Steven Whitfield, op cit, 1988, 191

CHAPTER 3
THE UNITED KINGDOM

3.1 The Nature of the Place

3.1.1 A "Christian State"

Britain is an island. The British have seen their insularity as one of its strengths. They did not welcome *foreigners*. Contrasted with Irish Catholic internal migration, Jewish immigration was external and clearly foreign in many ways. Suffusing its political structure was a sense of order derived from the Christian religious establishment with the Sovereign at the apex. Since the time of Henry VIII, religious disloyalty in some way must also involve political disloyalty.[1]. Jews were not disadvantaged expressly because they were Jews but because they were not members of the Church of England. Most of these disadvantages also burdened Catholics and Protestant Dissenters.

Moreover, Jews in Britain do not have a continuous history of settlement. They were expelled in 1290. Yet even in their absence, the image of "the Jew" was deeply embedded as related to usury and the *blood libel*. The *resettlement* of Jews in Britain began to take place in the seventeenth century. The long emancipation debate that ensued was based on the grounds of the "foreignness" of the Jew and his low moral character bent on financial gain with a stereotype such as Shylock remaining in the popular mind.

Coincident with the *Glorious Revolution* of 1688, there was regularization of establishment of permanent Jewish residence. John Locke's *Letter on Toleration* written during this period mentioned Jews only as an extreme example of the lengths to which tolerance might go.[2] "Jews were acceptable unlike atheists, whose godlessness would invite anarchy or Catholics whose intolerance of other men's opinions was the very negation of their own claims to tolerance."[3] Although it was now clear that there would not be any threat of their expulsion, no special laws were enacted to establish a legal basis for their position. They were not permitted to hold public office, take a degree in the major English universities of Oxford and Cambridge, vote or be elected to parliament. All these disabilities were connected to requirement that oaths be taken on the New Testament.

It should be noted that British *nationality* was based upon birth. Those Jews born in England as children of alien Jews would thus be citizens based upon a principle dating from feudal times.[4] Those born abroad, classified as aliens, were not permitted to own land and were subject to a number of other restrictions.[5] There was no easy provision for naturalization aside for Anglicans since there was a *Sacrament Test*, the requirement to provide a certificate of having received communion from a priest of the Church of England. The passage of the Jew Bill in 1753 was an attempt to remedy this situation for those Jews born abroad. It was almost immediately repealed because of a widespread outcry, probably motivated by economic self-interest as well as religious bigotry.[6] Opposition against relaxing restrictions was based on the widespread sense of their "foreignness."[7]

Social exclusion, aside from some of the wealthy notables as well as political exclusion, persisted during the remainder of the eighteenth century. There was retention and reinforcement in the public mind of the widespread connection between Jews and criminality.[8] In 1818, when seeking openly to establish the rights of Jews, a case was brought for a Jewish girl denied the benefits of a legacy established originally under Edward VI. The Jewish child sought an apprentice fee based on the argument that "On their readmission to this country after the *virtual* repeal of . . . the act of injustice which had banished them, the Jews were restored to the privileges of other subjects."[9] The judge held for the opposing counsel on the basis that "it is the duty of every judge presiding in an English court, when told that there is no difference between worshipping the Supreme Being in chapel, church or synagogue to recollect that Christianity is part of the law of England."

During the early nineteenth century, notwithstanding Dickens's *Oliver Twist*, published in 1838, the public image of Jews began to change, exemplified by such novels as Sir Walter Scott's *Ivanhoe*, first published in 1819. John Murray published in 1829 *A History of the Jews* that portrayed them in positive terms recognizing their remarkable endurance despite their oppression. Jewish boxers, such as Daniel Mendoza, became renowned for their success in the ring.[10]

Anglo-Jewish political emancipation did not come from the top downward, emanating from the state. Rather, it grew in small steps out of changing social and economic conditions that then served as a basis for the changes in political equality.[11] In 1826, Parliament did pass a bill that abolished the certification of the Anglican sacrament before naturalization thus fulfilling the objectives of the *Jew Bill* of 1753. However, in 1828, the requirement to meet the test of swearing "on the true faith of a Christian" was inserted in a bill thus enfranchising nonconformists but not Jews. This was followed by emancipation of Catholics in 1829. With this last measure, the relation of the state to religion had clearly began to change.[12] Heresy, the holding of religious views at variance with those of the established church was apparently no longer tantamount to treason.

There then began a series of unsuccessful efforts to bring about open removal of Jewish political barriers by statute in Parliament. Concomitantly, there were partial breaches in the wall of discrimination, both social and political. The first Jewish barrister was admitted to the bar in 1833, swearing on what is described as a *rabbinical* Bible; the University College of the new University of London, incorporated in 1837, allowed students of any faith to study and take their degrees, thus bypassing Oxford and Cambridge. When a special act spared use of the Christian oath for those offices, municipal offices were opened to Jews, including eventually election as the lord mayor of London in 1855.[13]

Parliament remained the last bastion. In 1847, Lionel de Rothschild was elected as a Liberal for the first time. Unwilling to take the required oath as a Christian, he was not permitted to sit. From that year onward, as he was recurrently reelected, bills were introduced annually to remedy this burden, always ending in failure. The battle became conflated with party politics as well as issues of principle. The Tory party represented the landed class. Its stance was based upon the nation's Christianity as providing one of the bonds between those governing and the governed and the basis of its hierarchical nature. The battle was about what appeared to be a surrender of national

Christianity as it connected with the legitimacy of established political authority.[14]

Finally in 1858, the Jewish Relief Act passed both Houses, and on 26 July 1858, Lionel de Rothschild took his place in the House of Commons. The final resolution ironically came under a Tory government but was not definitive. What was permitted was for each House to determine its own procedures, thus freeing the Commons to permit a Jew to take an oath on the Hebrew Bible. In turn, the refusal of Queen Victoria in 1869 to confer a peerage on Lionel de Rothschild was a reflection of the persistent disdain of the upper class toward Jews.[15] Lionel's son, Nathaniel de Rothschild, was eventually appointed the first Jewish peer in 1885, taking his place in the House of Lords. Official recognition had finally occurred, symbolic of the principle that Jews could now enjoy all the rights that accrued to native-born Englishmen.[16]

The religious diversity of the nation had thus led to a solution of pluralism rather than uniformity.[17] Toleration and equality were part of the agenda of both Protestant Dissenters and Roman Catholic groups seeking recognition vis a vis the ruling Protestant establishment. Jews were not demonized as uniquely evil or alien or illegitimate. Anti-Semitism, although widespread on a social basis, tended to be more marginalized and not politicized as on the continent.

The bargain that seemed to be struck for Jews to be treated as Englishmen extended to their commitment to become like Englishmen. Anglo-Jewry had been willing to fit in, to be "English."[18] The absence of the extreme elements of continental anti-Semitism created a Jewish culture of conformity and assimilation without disappearance based upon being a "community of faith." Conversion was relatively infrequent. The Jewish community remained within the political and religious center.

It had taken nearly two hundred years. Equality on the basis of law required surmounting an entire set of barriers built around the Anglican state religion originally designed to disenfranchise Catholics but used to disenfranchise all those who differed, including Jews. The slowness of the process, particularly following

Catholic emancipation in 1829, signified the radical alteration of thinking that was required to contain a Jewish minority on equal terms. Britain was a self-consciously Christian nation. The implicit, and frequently explicit, "bargain' was that Jews could maintain their religious difference at the cost of their "national" difference.

Despite the acceptance of Jews in political life in the mid-nineteenth century, their position remained tenuous. For example, attacks on Disraeli's pro-Turkish policy during the Russo-Turkish War of 1877-78 were couched in terms of anti-Semitism, despite his Christian baptism.[19] Later, it also became widely accepted that Jewish capitalist interests in South Africa rather than British interests might be at work in the Boer War in 1899-1902.

It is against a background of hard-won rights that the East European immigration coming late in the nineteenth century was superimposed. The "bargain" was to change with the relatively large-scale East European immigration with its foreignness of language, culture, and political interests.

3.1.2 The Existing Jewish Community

At the mid-nineteenth century, just prior to the start of the large East European immigration, the Jewish population is calculated at thirty to thirty-five thousand with the overwhelming majority living in London.[20] Small provincial communities in the range of one to two thousand existed in Liverpool, Manchester, and Birmingham.[21] No ghetto existed, and Jewish settlement was not limited to a single area even in London. Within the major area of settlement east of the City of London were the Sephardic original synagogue of Bevis Marks and the several Ashkenazi synagogues including the Great Synagogue as well as other institutions such as the Jewish Board of Guardians (JBG). The *East End* that came later to be the area of greatest Jewish settlement signified areas east of the Tower of London, including Whitechapel and Spitalfields. (See Map 3.1 The East End of London)

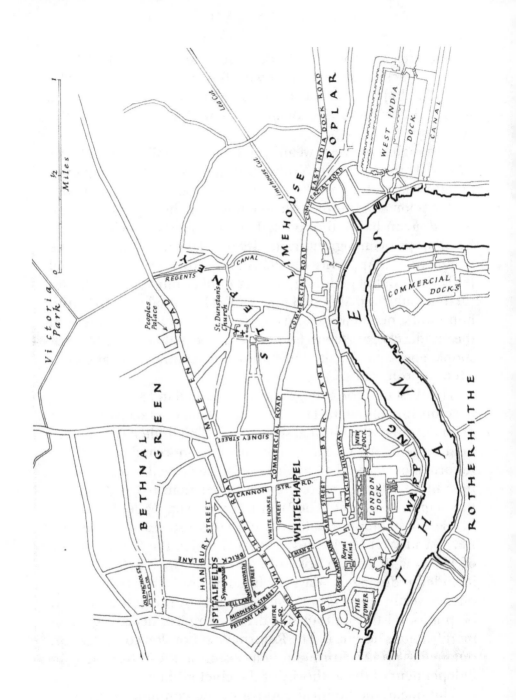

Map 3.1 The East End of London

The area west of Temple Bar, the *West End*, also had been a major nucleus of settlement with four to five thousand. The great Anglo-Jewish dynasties settled in the fashionable areas such as Kensington and Belgravia as well as Bayswater in the West End.[22]

Although there were wealthy Jews, at least half were "of lower classes," barely surviving. A substantial number of those employed in industrial settings worked in cigar and cigarette manufacture under poor conditions with low wages including child labor. *Sweatshop* conditions thus preceded the appearance of the larger East European immigration after 1880 and the introduction of the needle trades. Apprentice systems under JBG served to channel Jewish boys out of peddling, with its air of criminality, into trades such as tailoring, shoemaking, and cabinetmaking; girls into housework, needlework, and cooking. The proportion of Jews in the middle classes grew as Jews ceased to be peddlers and became shopkeepers, participated in commerce, manufacture, and even a few in professions.[23]

The West London Synagogue was founded in 1840 responsive to complaints about the lack of decorum and the excessive length of services in the traditional synagogues. This limited response to modernity did not take the direction of the more radical German Reform movement. The service should be more decorous rather than more rational; more genteel rather than based upon any theological changes.[24] The West London synagogue did issue a new Forms of Prayer developed under the auspices of its minister, Rev. David Wolf Marks and Hyman Hurwitz, the first professor of Hebrew at University College in London. The changes included reducing the days for holiday observance from two to one. Nevertheless, a *declaration* was issued by the grand rabbi to be published throughout the British Empire, declaring these modifications heretical. The Reform West London congregation retained its position throughout its history as the only synagogue independent of the authority of the chief rabbi.[25]

The oligarchic political control of the community was wed to conformity in religious life. The religious leadership was expressed through the chief rabbinate, evolving out of the rabbi of the Ashkenazi Great Synagogue in Duke's Place.[26] Under Nathan Marcus Adler, appointed in 1844, the chief rabbinate took on substance as well as form. Adler used the opportunity to centralize control given by his consultative position in relation to the Board of Jewish Deputies (BJD). The latter conferred the right of Jewish congregations to maintain marriage registers. Further, Chief Rabbi Adler issued Laws and Regulations for all the Synagogues in the United Kingdom by which he was to superintend religious services, sanction the building of new synagogues and the formation of new congregations. His influence, if not writ, later extended over congregations elsewhere to the settlements in Australia, New Zealand, and Cape Town as chief rabbi of the British Empire.[27]

The old requirements for the rabbi to interpret the law was replaced by attention to pastoral duties and preaching in conformity with the form of Protestant clergy.[28] These developments required changes toward a preacher-minister format, native English speakers rather than foreigners. The conflict over the character of the clergy was finally determined at the time of the establishment in 1855 of the Jews' College in London. At the request of the wealthy laity and, in accordance with the chief rabbi, the curriculum of the college did not include provision for training *rabbis* in the traditional sense, equipped to deal with issues of Halakha. Resolution of such issues was to be reserved to the beth din chaired by the chief rabbi.[29]

By 1870, several communal structures were in place. First and foremost was the Board of Jewish Deputies (BJD). It derives its name from the *diputados* occasionally appointed in the early eighteenth century by the original Sephardic congregation to deal with political matters. It traces its institutional origin from 1760 when the Elders of the *two nations* (Sephardic and Ashkenazi), having made separate expressions of loyalty to the new king George III, agreed to hold joint meetings in the future to discuss any relevant public matter. In 1835, it began to take more formal shape: meeting more consistently and claiming to represent the entire community including provincial congregations as well as those in London. In 1836, by Act of Parliament, BJD assumed responsibility for the registration of marriages. In 1852, it was given responsibility for supervising educational grants allocated by Parliament. In accordance with the stand of Sir Moses Montefiore, the crucial lay leader of the BJD from 1835 to 1874, the principle was established to uphold the Orthodox character of British Jewry and centralized communal institutions. It was as a religious community that Jews maintained their identity but also as worthy of the full rights of citizenship. The pervasiveness of religion in Victorian public life, particularly in its Orthodox style, made the equivalent in Judaism consistent with the normality of Victorian life.

Montefiore was but one, although the exemplar, of the closely inbred group of wealthy families (the *cousinhood*) with a highly developed sense of responsibility for the Jewish communal institutions they led.[30] They ultimately considered the community their dependents. The relationship of patron and retainer was reflective of the class structure of English life. Further, the pattern was replicated within the religious structure similar to that of the established church. The United Synagogue was established by an Act of Parliament in 1870. It combined the main Ashkenazi synagogues in London in an English-style instrument against deviation from ritual and liturgy. The United Synagogue structure served mainly as a method for maintaining communal responsibility for the financial well-being of its constituent congregations.[31] However, by statute, it enabled the religious administration, in a form analogous to the episcopal character of the Anglicans, to be under the sole control of the chief rabbi. This arrangement under Hermann Adler, his father's successor as chief rabbi in 1891, was consistent with the controlling lay leadership of families such as the Rothschilds, to whom he was related by marriage. Like the Anglican church, to which it could be compared, the "native" acculturated members were satisfied "with the public forms of piety and the non-ideological spirit of their performance . . . deference to established authority."[32]

Emancipation was based upon the Jews as a religious community and not as a *nation*. Although the integrity of the communal religious structure was maintained and even enhanced, problems were to arise in the wake of the large scale immigration, particularly for those immigrants for whom *religious* identity was no longer the only basis of community. There would be the conflict between membership in the Jewish nation as well as the English nation.[33]

3.1.3 The Great Migration

Because of the large element of transshipment and temporary sojourn, it is difficult to estimate the actual net immigration. It is estimated that a total of one hundred fifty thousand East European Jews settled in the United Kingdom between 1870 and 1914 during this period of heavy immigration.[34] Prior to the passage of the Aliens'Act in 1905 there were about one hundred thousand Jewish immigrants actually settling in Britain itself (rather than those in transit) between 1881 and 1905 with eight thousand in that last peak year. An additional fifty thousand arrived in the nine years between 1906 and 1914.[35] The high birth rate and low child mortality rate added to the demographic impact far exceeding the number of original immigrants.[36]

However, nearly three times that number might disembark even for short periods on their way elsewhere. There might therefore be a substantial albeit temporary impact on the limited number of localities affected. Great Britain served as a major staging area for transatlantic emigration.[37] It was estimated that only 12 percent of those entering via London might be found there thirty days after arrival. Even those who did remain after a month retained a sense that they were transient and were likely to eventually go on to America.[38] Those who stayed did so because of family ties or lack of funds rather than a sense of having arrived where they wished to be.[39]

The "pull" exerted by the large number of previous immigrants in the United States was strong. America was the *goldene medina* (the golden country). When unemployment was a problem in the United States, immigrants with welcoming relatives in Britain may have still chosen to leave Eastern Europe and go to Britain since it was relatively easily reached.[40] One could later choose to move on if conditions improved in the United States. Of those who eventually crossed the Atlantic, it is estimated that four hundred to five hundred thousand did so as English natives or East Europeans having spent several years in Britain.[41] Even a relatively short sojourn had impact on those who later emigrated to other places such as Canada and South Africa as well as the United States.[42]

The reputations of the two destinations may also have contributed to the decision to settle in either place. There was the anti-Semitism of the British working class and the more rigid class structure. On the other hand, there was concern about the spiritual health of those going to the *trefe medinah* of New York, with the more observant more likely to remain in London where it was known that traditional Judaism still existed.[43] The reputation was that England was a free country where one could work very hard and earn very little but also where someone, like Rothschild, had become rich and influential.

Most immigrants from the northwestern provinces of the Pale would travel across Germany to Bremen, Hamburg, or Rotterdam where they arranged for an Atlantic crossing. At times, it was cheaper to travel from Europe to England and then to travel to America via Liverpool than from Europe directly. London was the main port of arrival for those transshipping. Unless they were able to leave London right away, they moved directly to the East End. In 1914, no city other than New York and Chicago contained more East European immigrants than London.[44] Immigrants going eventually to America might also transfer from Hamburg to towns such as Hull on the East Coast, then cross to Liverpool on the west. In addition to the area of old settlement in the East End, there was the enhanced development of new provincial centers. Leeds particularly increased its population along with the other centers of Manchester and Birmingham as well as Liverpool.[45]

Jewish immigration to Britain, like that to America, initially came mainly from Lita, the northern provinces of the Pale of Settlement in the tsarist empire.[46] Immigrant marriage registers confirmed the origins of brides and grooms.[47] The preponderance of Litvaks was to have an impact not only on the political life of the immigrants but their religious life. Their Judaism tended to be of a more intellectual and less pietistic nature than the Hassidim.[48] The story of the evolution of the East European immigrants during the following years was a function of the interaction of the cultural components they brought with them, mainly from Lita, tempered—unlike the United States—by the existing relatively monolithic and hierarchical setting to which their relatively small number remained unwelcome and expected to conform.

Like Jewish immigration to America, it was common for families to emigrate rather than single men and to move away from Eastern Europe permanently.[49] In response to pogroms and economic dislocation, there was a peak in 1881-1882 then again in 1891, another peak in 1896 before declining until 1899. London became an early center for Yiddish-language culture and politics. Following 1900, there was a steady rise to an all-time peak in 1903-06. After this, the passage of the "Aliens Act" in Britain caused a check before an increase just prior to World War I.

Within just over a generation, the East European immigrants and their children outnumbered the previous Jewish population by a factor of 3:1. By 1914, the estimated total Jewish population was in the range of three hundred thousand with 60 percent (180,000) in London. There was a major increase in the industrial centers in the North. Manchester and Leeds were closely matched and, together, comprised half of those outside London followed by Liverpool and Birmingham. Of the ten thousand Jews in Scotland, the large majority were in Glasgow. In all these places, their percentage of the population was quite small: 3 percent in London rising to a high of 5 percent in Leeds.[50] Within each of those cities, an immigrant Jewish quarter developed. They were generally near the railroad terminal or docks adjacent to the central business district.

The East End of London was the exemplar. There were the early beginnings of a Jewish industrial proletariat in the East End by 1880. The largest group was tailors with bootmakers and cigar and cigarette makers next.[51] *Immigrant* and *Jew* came to be synonymous in the public mind because the East End was a particular focus for all those interested in studying social problems.[52] In the first decade of the twentieth century, crowding reached its peak with about 125,000 people in Whitechapel and adjacent areas. The density of Jewish population reached 50 percent in Whitechapel, called Jewtown.[53] By 1914, there had been some dispersal of the Jewish population to secondary centers in the north and northwest parts of London with a reduction of the population density.

The occupational structure of those immigrating consisted mainly of the mechanically skilled and unskilled workmen. A census of 1901 showed almost half in tailoring, approximately one-eighth in boot and shoemaking and about the same in furniture making. Leeds, as a center for clothing manufacture, particularly attracted tailors. The three major areas of occupation were those already established with Jewish employers already in place. They could provide employment to the new immigrants where Yiddish could be spoken and accommodation made for observance of the Jewish Sabbath. Other employment opportunities were limited by discrimination.[54] Besides these manufacturing trades, there was petty commerce in hawking and market trading. In the smaller towns, there was a higher percentage of small traders and shopkeepers with pawnbrokers particularly prominent.[55]

Like the East Side of New York, the East End became a center for small workshops under poor conditions. The contracting system led to the *sweatshops* characterized by long hours, low wages, and unsanitary conditions.[56] Work was frequently seasonal and irregular. Earnings were low. Cabinetmaking paid somewhat better than the others, with shoemaking particularly low paid, competing as it did with an increasingly mechanized factory production. The relative paucity of movement into the entrepreneurial class by self-employment among the immigrants in London in comparison to New York has been attributed to the existence of a "craft" mentality in Britain. This can be expressed by "If I can't have it, neither can you" attitude. [57]

Yet some of the East European immigrants eventually developed large-scale enterprises throughout Britain such as Marks & Spencer, Britain's largest store chain and Burton clothing stores.[58] The story of Ephraim Sieff was not common but did serve as a model. The son of a village miller in Lita, he came first to Hull and then to Manchester. He started as a collector of scraps of cloth. Within eight years, he bought out the English company to which he had sold the scraps. His son became a partner of Simon Marks whose father, Michael Marks, had founded Marks & Spencer. The Sieff and Marks families became particularly important in their support of Zionism in the following generation.[59]

3.1.4 The Response to Immigration

In general, the Jews already settled in Britain objected to the immigrants. The established community wished to stress its qualities as British citizens who happened to profess Judaism. The manners, culture and the politics of the immigrants all skewed the overall character of British Jewry in an opposite direction.[60] Exemplary of the rejection was that of the language of the immigrants, the "corrupt jargon" of Yiddish.[61]

During the wave of immigration from Eastern Europe at the turn of the century, the term *alien* was shorthand for the Jew in a country where few other foreigners existed that were so clearly different. When applied to the poor East European immigrant, the label of *economic man* was coupled with his undercutting the health of the community with his willingness to work under the terrible conditions of the *sweatshops*. Jews were seen as unwanted and incompatible elements in British society coupled with their being so evident, clustered in the East End so close to the center of the capital.

The Jewish tradition of "caring for our own" meant that every effort was made to ensure the Jewish poor did not enter workhouses established by the state or seek relief from secular authorities. The leading Anglo-Jewish families organized the Jewish Board of Guardians (JBG) in 1859 to deal with these problems within the communal structure. The governing board consisted of the usual Anglo-Jewish magnates.[62] Their preoccupation was to avoid attracting paupers and to differentiate properly between the "deserving" and "undeserving" poor. Much of their relief was in the form of small loans to enable individuals to acquire sewing machines in order to earn their own way.[63]

In 1882, almost a quarter of the Jews of London were paupers and another fifth were in the poorer working class. The JBG became overwhelmed and began to carry out an advertising campaign to discourage immigration and to encourage repatriation to Eastern Europe.[64] Over the years of large-scale immigration, fifty thousand persons (17,500 cases) were either persuaded to return to Eastern Europe or offered financial assistance to settle elsewhere—mainly the United States, but also Canada, South Africa, and Argentina. Advertisements in the Russian press discouraging immigration to England emphasized that the board would do nothing to support immigrants during their first six months residence.

In accordance with this same policy, the BJG opposed any facilities for receiving immigrants. Despite their opposition, the Poor Jews Temporary Shelter was opened in November 1885. The shelter's policy was also quite restrictive. The rule was to permit no one to stay more than two weeks and to provide two meals daily, but no money. The JBG continually tried to restrict further the criteria by which people might be helped in order to discourage immigration as much as possible.[65]

To the chagrin of Anglo-Jewry, Jews became news. They were the objects of surveys. The places they lived such as the East End became objects of curiosity but also became identified as "problem areas." Select committees of both Houses of Parliament were set up to look at various issues. Housing was a major problem that was attributed to the alien Jewish presence. There had been destruction of housing due to the building of railway marshalling yards and large warehouses. The borough of Stepney, of which Whitechapel was a part, lost 4,000 houses while gaining 40,000 people between 1881 and 1901. Whitechapel itself, the core of *Jewtown*, lost 2,500 houses while gaining 3,300 people ending with a density of six hundred people per acre.[66] Jews did not move to less densely populated Irish areas in St. Georges in the East where they were clearly unwelcome. Baron Nathan Mayer Rothschild set up a company in 1884 to build low-rental tenements for the poor. For example, the Rothschild Dwellings offered two-room apartments in six-story buildings. These towering barracklike tenements would mark the character of the East End for the next generation.[67]

This was also a time of recession and unemployment in Britain. Britain was no longer the "workshop of the world." Protectionist sentiment developed against foreign goods and labor. The sense was that "the nation was overstocked, that resources were fixed, and also the nation had reached if not passed the zenith of industrial development."[68] The alien influx was identified as a menace to English values and to social norms. "Sweating" was joined to the existence of Jews in particular trades such as tailoring although the system of small unsanitary workshops had preceded Jewish immigration and extended to trades in which Jews did not participate.[69] It was commonly believed that it was the alien presence that made "sweating" come about—that it was the character of these "aliens" that made sweating possible—that these people were naturally "filthy" and came from a background "beyond the pale of civilization."[70]

Even as some of these issues were alleviated, and objective evidence failed to support impressions, anti-Jewish and antialien feeling continued to rise. Some went further, seeing the problem as racial. During the 1890s, the issue of "a people apart" became politicized. The British Brothers' League was organized to press for restrictive legislation. Members of the league would march through the East End in uniform shouting anti-Semitic slogans. Both left-wing anticapitalism and right-wing jingoism coupled with the Boer War seemed to unite in mounting countrywide anti-Jewish prejudice during this time.[71] The remedy was exclusion. Within society at various levels, that exclusion manifested itself in widespread social snobbery despite, if not because of, the concomitant entry of the few into prominent positions in the government and onto the society pages.[72]

Nevertheless, most communal leaders wanted to keep Britain's doors open. The principle of *free trade* in goods and persons was one of the credos of the Liberal Party, and opposition to antialien legislation was not limited to Jews but had a wider constituency.[73] There was support for the reception of refugees from persecution and pogroms that transcended and even preceded the charitable impulses of the Jewish communal leadership. One manifestation was the Mansion House meeting in 1882 called to protest the pogroms of that year in Russia. Cardinal Manning, the leading Catholic prelate, and the archbishop of Canterbury joined in developing what was called the Mansion House Fund to support refugee immigration from Russia. It evolved into the Russo-Jewish Committee, which together with the Jewish Board of Guardians, remained active in the settlement of refugees. The Conjoint Committee of these two organizations continued to function during the years of immigration with much of its effort devoted to screening those who could be encouraged to move on to other countries.[74]

A Royal Commission was established in 1902 to consider the issue of alien immigration. A number of influential Jews joined in opposing immigration of "undesirables." The Jewish communal leaders could point to their actions over the years of restricting

Jewish immigration by their own policy of repatriation.[75] The bill initially introduced in 1904 sought to exclude the entry into Britain of such widely drawn criteria as "persons of notoriously bad character" and "persons likely to become a public charge." The longstanding issue of *overcrowding* and the shortage of housing was reflected in a provision to restrict settlement in certain areas. The Jewish Board of Deputies did not oppose the bill in its entirety but sought modifications, giving the right of appeal to any expulsion order. In addition, Rabbi Hermann Adler, the chief rabbi, reflecting the stance of the Jewish elite, chose not to condemn the legislation as it made its way through Parliament.[76]

The implied commitment made at the time of emancipation, and subsequently reinforced, was that Jewish members of Parliament would not reflect a *Jewish interest*. Unlike other religious groups, there was denial of a *Jewish vote*. Indeed, of the twelve Jewish MPs, four voted for the Aliens' Bill, four were against and four abstained.[77] Outright opposition came only from a group of radical Liberals and the immigrants themselves. The immigrant opposition was related to the Jewish Workingmen's Club and the recently formed Poalei Zion, the socialist Zionist party.[78]

The *Aliens Act* came into force in January 1906. Immigration continued at the rate of five thousand a year during the years prior to the start of the war in 1914. But by knowledge of its existence, the Aliens Act had considerable impact in achieving its goals of reducing the potential number of immigrants during that period when immigration surged elsewhere. The Aliens Act also changed the overall character of those entering Britain as compared to other countries. The particularly heavy emigration after 1905 was from throughout the Pale rather than primarily from the northern provinces. Those leaving the Pale of Settlement in the later period were also more likely to be touched by new political movements of socialism and Zionism that continued to evolve there. They were more likely to avoid Britain in light of its more restrictive immigration policies.[79] The early preponderance of those from Lita, the northwest provinces of the Pale of Settlement, was maintained.

Although Britain was the epitome of liberal democracy, it was also a place where social and cultural barriers remained almost impenetrable to outsiders. Beyond the issue of immigration came the obstacles to naturalization. *Alien* status was not easily overcome. The Naturalization Act of 1870 had required the payment of a fee, five years' residence and testimonials of good character. In 1880, the fee had been raised to the rather large sum of five pounds with another sum required for the various affidavits.[80] Starting in 1905, a literacy test was also instituted that could be variously interpreted to the detriment of the applicant.[81] All these reduced the ability of immigrants, particularly the poor, to enter more fully into British life.[82] For example, at the time of the passage of National Insurance Bill in 1911, aliens were originally to be denied benefits. It was the Jewish "friendly societies" (landsmanshaften) that lobbied successfully for their own interests in dealing with this issue.[83]

To complete the control over immigrants, in 1914, in conjunction with war, registration of aliens and power for deportation came into effect.[84] In 1919 in conjunction with the Red Scare after the Bolshevik Revolution, there was an increase in power to deport undesirable aliens as well as increased obstacles placed in the way of those seeking naturalization.[85] In 1920, the Home Secretary directed that Russians and other East Europeans be given the lowest priority for processing the backlog of applications accumulated during the war just ended. Various other barriers included requirement for far longer duration of residence than other aliens.[86] In these laws Jews were targeted as "undesirables" in a culture that tended to dismiss aliens altogether.[87]

Because of the large number of immigrants, London Jewry, initially in large part lower middle class, had become largely working class as well as alien. The same trends characterized the major provincial cities. In addition to limiting the number of immigrants lay the policy of bringing about the acculturation, if not the assimilation, of the "foreign element." There was the conviction, fostered by the *Jewish Chronicle,* the newspaper of Anglo Jewry, that the majority culture would not tolerate that which made the immigrants different.[88] For example, the Jewish Workingmen's Club was founded by Sir Samuel Montagu in 1872 in London to "eliminate foreign speech, habits and views . . . repugnant to English feeling and to imbue the newcomers with

English sentiments and notions."[89] In general, *Anglicizing* was defined as the "act or process by which persons learn to conform to English modes or usages in speech, in manner, in mental attitude, and in principles."[89]

The major vehicle for acculturation must be education. Prior to 1870, there were no state schools. All schools were denominational although receiving state funds. The Jews Free School (JFS) had been founded in 1817 to provide religious education for the children of poor Jews. By 1870, it was the largest Jewish school in Britain providing elementary education as well as a Jewish one to several thousand students.[90] Its aim throughout its history, under one headmaster for fifty-one years, had been to anglicize the children. In 1873, he testified that "their parents were the refuse population of the worst parts of Europe; [the children] were [to be] Anglicized or humanized ... [They] knew neither English nor any intelligible language." They were weaned away from Yiddish as quickly as possible. Their Yiddish cultural background and lifestyle were derided. Starting in the 1880s with the development of state schools, Jewish day schools were discouraged.[91] Traditional *chederim* conducted by Hebrew teachers were a particular target.

A similar process went on in the provincial centers.[92] In Manchester, a daughter of immigrants attending the Jews' school there was told by the headmistress to change her name to one more "English." It was clear that Yiddish was disdained. Many aspects of the school curriculum also contributed to Anglicizing the children. In the state schools, holidays such as Empire Day were celebrated as well as Christmas. Neatness and tidiness were emphasized as well as manners to the detriment of "cleverness." The message was that the culture and the language they had were clearly inferior—uncivilized and backward—while the English culture was enlightened and modern. The loss of Yiddish by the younger generation contributed to an extraordinary lack of communication between the generations. In the process, there was also a lack of religious spirit among Jewish youth. Judaism, in its conventional mode, was no longer something that provided the basis for organizing one's life.

In actuality, the primary schools in the East End were run as a subsystem with modifications consistent with Jewish practices such as early closing on Friday.[93] Secondary schools were not entirely free in Britain as they were in the United States. Entry to secondary schools (grammar schools) with fees paid by scholarship was contingent on passing an examination. The number making this transition was very limited since there were few scholarships made available to East End Jewish students along the need to earn money to help support the family.[94] The use of schooling as a means of upward mobility was less available in London than New York with its free municipal university system. Access to University of London was an alternative to the more costly Oxford or Cambridge but not widely used. The more rigid class structure of the British educational system as well as the lesser economic opportunities were important differential factors in accounting for the slower rise for immigrant Jews that occurred via the educational ladder compared with the United States.[94]

A number of organizations was set up for young men and women patterned after those in the non-Jewish community to encourage acculturation, if not assimilation. The Jewish Lads' Brigade (JLB), for example, was founded in 1896 to follow the model of the equivalent Christian Lads' Brigade in its combination quasimilitaristic and patriotic spirit. The Jewish Lads' Brigade aimed to "iron out the ghetto bend" into a strong and manly Jewish youth. Boys would learn such exemplary English characteristics as good comradeship and playing the game. Its founder was Albert Goldsmid whose family was a member of the Jewish "cousinhood." He had been a Sandhurst-trained officer in the British Army who converted to Judaism, thus reclaiming his Jewish ancestry. Under his direction, JLB officers were drawn from the English-born Anglo-Jewish upper classes analogous to the more general phenomenon of the educated classes going to the East End "to elevate the condition of the people."[95]

The efforts to modify the immigrant religious structure was particularly important. The proliferation of small *chevras* provided both a social and a religious function for the immigrants. Housed in storefronts or tenement rooms, they traditionally functioned as houses of study and prayer as well as meeting social needs such as funeral benefits. Part of the process of Anglicizing was to bring the religious life in the immigrant community under the control of the elite's communal leadership.

The United Synagogue was the expression of middle-class Anglo Jewry. Its synagogues increasingly clustered in the newer areas of settlement in the north and northwest suburbs. There was but one synagogue in the East End and costs of membership excluded all but the most prosperous living there.[96]

Sir Samuel Montagu, the Liberal MP representing the East End, was unusual among the Anglo-Jewish magnates in his religosity and belief in the literal interpretation of the Bible. Although very wealthy, he was a self-made man who had been the son of a small tradesman in Liverpool. Yiddish-speaking, he saw something of great value in the religious intensity of the chevra. Montagu was a member of the Liberal Party while his rival in communal leadership, Lord Rothschild, was intimately connected with the Conservative Party.[97] Their political and communal rivalry played out in a number of areas, particularly in the religious arena. Montagu sought to mold the chevra into an organization analogous to the United Synagogue in terms of its fiscal responsibility and organizational stability. His Federation of Synagogues was to be doctrinally Orthodox, culturally quasi-Anglicized, and incorporated into the structure of Anglo-Jewry under the general aegis of the chief rabbi. However, unlike the United Synagogue, East European rabbis were recruited, and those already in place were included within the *beth din* and other religious structures. Although it encouraged the study of Hebrew and set up Talmud Torah schools, English rather than Yiddish was to be the language of instruction. The abandonment of Yiddish was the hallmark of the acculturation process.[98] The Federation of Synagogues was, in actuality, probably the largest single instrument of Anglicizing that Anglo-Jewry had.[99].

The religious, political, and cultural characteristics of the East European immigration reflected the fact that so many found their roots in Lita. They had experienced the development of a revolutionary ethos along with a sense of nationhood within a far more pervasive rabbinical religious setting. The differences between them and the already existing Jewish community led to the development over the subsequent generations of what is now Anglo-Jewry.

3.2 The Evolution of the Culture

The Anglicizing process could not efface the ethnic particularity of the immigrant culture. There was more than differences in religious practice but an entire spectrum of customs and lifestyles that were a source of pride rather than embarrassment. They sought to maintain their distinctiveness.[1] Their sense of peoplehood would be expressed in the evolution of their socialism and Zionism as well as a more fiery commitment to improving the world associated with the differences in class and political identification. The legacy of the immigrants included a devotion to radical politics, to the renewal of Jewish life in Palestine through labor expressed in the Poale Zion and to a tradition of intellectual rigor relatively absent within the wealthy business people who had represented the ethos thus far.

Despite the differences between the immigrants and Anglo-Jewry, the communal structures would eventually encompass the acculturated children of the immigrant generation. In so doing, those structures also changed. The evolution of that culture in the context of Britain is the story of the next several generations in which those coming from Lita played an unusually prominent role.

3.2.1   The Immigrant Generation

The major avenue by which Jewish immigrants eventually entered English life was in conjunction with their working class status. The earliest record of a Jewish worker's organization was the short lasting union of Lithuanian Tailors founded in London in 1872. The founder was one of the series of politically educated elite, frequently derived from Lita, who would become involved with Jewish workmen in London prior to moving to America. The tendency among these radicals was to view socialism in a more universalistic way. They regarded the fight for betterment of the Jewish proletariat as part of the struggle for the working class as a whole.[2]

Jewish Socialism

In 1876, another tailoring union was formed in London as an offshoot of the Hebrew Socialist Union under the leadership of Aaron Lieberman. He was to be the founder of the principle of both socialism and trade union movement directed specifically to Jewish interests.

Aaron Lieberman was born in 1849 in Grodno Gubernia (Province) in Lita. After a religious education, he was thoroughly conversant with the Talmud and had a great love of Hebrew literature. He dropped out of the Vilna Rabbinical Seminary where he had been introduced to revolutionary thinking. He had been inducted into the Vilna circle of revolutionaries in 1872 by Aron Zundelevitch, one of its early founders. His strongly anticlerical attitude was forged in his experience during this time when the Vilna rabbis preached against the socialists to ingratiate themselves with the tsarist authorities. In the words of one of his associates: "We had broken . . . from the culture of Russian Jews . . . from their bourgeois and Orthodox sections . . . As for the Jewish working masses, we believed that the liberation of the Russian nation would also liberate all the other nationalities in Russia."

Threatened by arrest by the Tsarist police after the breakup of the Vilna Circle, Lieberman fled abroad. In August 1875, he was eventually welcomed to work with Lavrov in London as a typesetter and lithographer. Although a freethinker, he was occupied with questions of the Jewish people. Interested in propagating socialism among the Jews, in May 1876 he became one of the founders of The Hebrew Socialist Union, essentially a small study group committed to socialist principles. Despite his universalist notions, he nevertheless maintained some notions of Jewish identity. This was reflected in the decision led by Lieberman to postpone a meeting scheduled to take place on the ninth of Av, the fast day commemorating the destruction of the Temple. The ten founders were all either intellectuals or so-called semi-intellectuals of the *Maskilim* type. As a *Maskil* seeking a new direction for the Haskalah in Lita, Lieberman had chosen socialism as a forerunner of what became a significant strand in the subsequent decades.[3]

There was conflict between the aims of the various leaders reflecting the conflict going on at the same time in Lita from which they had just come. The "enlightened politically conscious" leadership was unclear whether to form a broader workers' organization or to build up initially a Jewish socialist grouping working in liaison with its non-Jewish counterparts. The issue of universality versus particularism was a recurrent one in the left wing movements in each of the countries of the Litvak Diaspora as it was in Lita itself.

Lieberman was one of those who called for the Jewish intelligentsia to commit themselves to the class war among the Jewish workers. It was necessary for the educated Jewish intelligentsia to recognize and deal with their alienation from the Jewish masses by virtue of their educated status. He wrote the first manifesto in Hebrew toward the task of working with one's own people. "Going to the people" was in the tradition of the populist People's Will, but now going to one's own people meant the Jewish worker. He wrote for Lavrov's journal in July 1876 a pamphlet a *Call to Jewish Youth*, the first Jewish Socialist manifesto in Hebrew. This appeal and the formation of the Hebrew Socialist Union in London as a study group for workers qualifies Lieberman as the founder of Jewish Socialism, the progenitor of the Bund, and, in the long term, Poalei Zion, Socialist Zionism.[4] The style of Lieberman's writing, his use of Hebrew, and his notion of a socialist journal in Hebrew (*Ha-Emet*) indicate the direction of his work as a *Maskil*. His circle was primarily the group of enlightened intellectuals and yeshiva students with radical tendencies rather than the masses of Jews.[5]

Lieberman's group became committed to "agitation" among Jewish workers leading to the formation of a clothing workers union in London. It was still ambiguous whether Jewish workers were to be organized so as to enter the broader English working class movement or to be a specifically Jewish labor organization. The goal of the first meeting on August 26, 1876, was to enlighten the Jewish workers about socialism. It was the first Jewish socialist public meeting with its handbills written in Yiddish. Lieberman rose to speak in his "arrogant and caustic way." He attacked both the Jewish financial aristocracy and the local rabbinate in England. The latter became the basis for his downfall.

At the second meeting, infiltrated by the opposition organized by religious authorities, a fight broke out between the more religious and those workers supporting the socialists. The *Jewish Chronicle* aided in branding the socialist leadership group as being sponsored by Christian missionaries in light of the attack on religion. Divorcing itself from the Socialists and without leadership, the Tailors' Union quickly fell apart.[6]

Because of the failure of the Tailors' Union, the Hebrew Socialist Union also fell apart. Lieberman was blamed for the poor results and left London. While on the continent, he began to also translate some revolutionary material into Yiddish. Eventually he recognized that agitation among Jewish workers required the use of Yiddish rather than Hebrew. He returned to London in 1879-80, destitute after having been imprisoned in Germany. He became enamoured of a woman who denied his advances. Unsuccessful after following her to New York, he committed suicide in Syracuse in November 1880.[7] The significance of his transient and premature appearance on the scene lies in the depth of the hostility he generated from the Jewish press, the clergy, and the employers. The major immigration that would have provided him with a larger base from which to recruit followers was soon to come with the pogroms and May Laws of 1880-1881[8] Particularly in the 1880s, London was the "Jerusalem" of Jewish radicalism and influenced the Jewish labor movement the world over.[9]

One of Lieberman's successors was Morris Winchevsky, born in 1856 at Yanova near Kovno in Lita. At thirteen, he entered the Vilna Seminary and later underwent the usual conversion from piety to radical atheism. He was nevertheless able, in his writings, to summon up a rich variety of religious images. He responded to Lieberman's *Call to Jewish Youth* and left Russia in 1877. He settled in Konigsberg where he worked as a bookkeeper and then a writer for a Hebrew journal. Threatened with arrest, he left for London, arriving in 1879.

His life in Whitechapel convinced him of the importance of socialist principles in improving the life of the Jewish masses. He was both a Yiddish writer and socialist philosopher of great eloquence. The newspaper he founded would be in Yiddish, the language of the masses. In 1884, he founded the *Polishe Yidl* (the *Little Polish Jew*), the first Yiddish Socialist newspaper with a nationalist-radical orientation anywhere in the world. Features included local, national, and world news with political analysis, correspondence from the other great Jewish centers such as Leeds, and dramatic criticism of the Jewish theatre. Its role was didactic, evaluating the harsh conditions of Jewish life with practical suggestions for improvement but also criticizing the Jewish workers for their vices such as gambling.

A committed socialist, he published in 1884 what was the first Jewish socialist Yiddish pamphlet called *Let there be Light*, a parody on Maimonides's *Thirteen Articles of Faith*. He went on to found in July 1885 the world's first openly socialist Yiddish periodical called *Arbeiter Fraint* (the *Worker's Friend*). It remained the main left-wing Yiddish periodical for many years, albeit under anarchist sponsorship.[10]

In the same year in 1884, an organization named International Workers Educational Club was formed on Berner Street in the East End that later took over the management of the newspaper, making it a weekly. The title of the organization reflected the maintenance of a universalistic rather than particularistic Jewish character to the movement. It was at these clubs in London and elsewhere that the first contacts were made with British Socialists. There was particular contact with William Morris, the leader of the Socialist League, which preached education toward revolution. There was eventually the formation of an East End branch of the Marxist Social Democratic Federation (SDF) in the mid-1880s and, in 1905, a League of Jewish Social Democratic groups, the forerunner of the Labour Party.[11] It was difficult to maintain the nonpartisan stand of the newspaper as well as the Berner Street Club among the various factions, both socialist and anarchist. Despite ongoing factionalism, the club celebrated its fifth anniversary in 1890. At the festivities, Winchevsky was recognized "as the man, who, more than any other Jew, symbolized for his audience the root yearnings of the immigrant poor, and the nobility of the Socialist cause."[12]

Eventually, both the newspaper and the club came under the control of the anarchists. Although there was variation among their adherents, in general the anarchists or Libertarians were opposed to participation in elections and committed to terrorism rather than trade unionism. In reality, the issues of participation in elective politics seemed irrelevant since few had become citizens. By 1891, Winchevsky was deposed from leadership in the club. He departed for America in 1894. Despite support by Abraham Cahan, visiting from New York, the socialist group did not remain active.[13] Socialism in Britain was to succeed only as part of the mainstream trade union movement or within nationalist Labor Zionism.

In 1886, writing for the *Arbeiter Fraint*, Winchevsky argued against the Lovers of Zion by claiming that they would re-create in Palestine a society based on charity and transplant the conditions of the Pale. His stance was that the Jewish masses would attain relief only by a program based on socialist principles in concert with their Gentile comrades and by bringing about the redemption of humanity at large.[14] Winchevsky eventually joined the Socialist Zionists.[15] as the expression of both his socialism and particularistic Jewish interests. Like others active in the in 1880s in London, he continued to carry on his work in the United States, participating in the formation of the *Forverts* (Forward) in New York in 1897.

Starting in the 1890s, with the advent of the dominance of the anarchists in Jewish radical circles in London, the radical movement in the United States became independent of Britain and pursued a more social-democratic Marxist direction. Bundists played an important role in energizing the Jewish labor movement in the United States, following their immigration after the Revolution of 1905. The Bund had less influence on the evolution of socialism and unionism among Jews in Britain. With the Aliens Act and the possibility of being returned to tsarist Russia, radicals tended to avoid Britain and go directly to America at a time when the number of immigrants there was at its height.

Unlike the experience in the United States with the success of the *Forverts*, the Yiddish press in England suffered from factionalism. Many newspapers would be founded, but last only for short periods. Beginning in 1907, the *Yidisher Journal* (Jewish Journal) was the longest lasting. It was edited by its founder Anshel Levy until 1913; and then for many years by Morris Myer as *Di Tsayt*.[16] It continued under his son Harry Myer until 1950.

The major developments in Jewish labor in the era ending in 1914 were under the auspices of the anarchists under the leadership of Rudolph Rocker, a German Gentile who committed himself to the Jewish cause.[17] The opening of a club on Jubilee

Street in 1906 became a center for adult education along with the presses of the *Arbeiter Fraint* that functioned intermittently as a monthly or weekly until 1932.

The Jewish Labor Movement

All these rivalries seemed to have no relationship either to the masses of Jewish workers nor the development of stable unions. It was clear that attempts by the politically enlightened to harness the unions to the overthrow of capitalism would not succeed. Particular problems arose by the injection of the antireligious aspects of the radical ideology such as Yom Kippur Balls organized by the libertarian anarchists. The unions would need to meet more immediate goals for shorter work days and increased wages. In England, given the legal freedoms and the concomitant growth of other labor unions, the thrust was to create a Jewish trade union movement rather than its politicization.

Illustrative was radical support for the large scale London clothing workers' general strike in 1889 seeking a twelve-hour day that lasted five weeks. The workers received support from non-Jewish trade unions as well as from Sir Samuel Montagu serving as a mediator to achieve a settlement in tune with the workers' demands. The employers soon violated the settlement. Nevertheless, this strike, and one in 1890 by the bootmakers, have significance beyond their relatively limited immediate results. They marked the birth of a Jewish labor movement and the beginning of an exchange across boundaries of nationality, religion, and skill.[18]

By 1906-07, there were many small Jewish unions in the garment industry competing with each other for jobs and members. It proved to be impossible to develop stable unions among the tailors in London or to maintain any concessions won during the strikes that took place. This recurrent failure was attributed to the existence of many small workshops with intense competition, unemployment and the ready supply of new immigrants. The "sweated" hoped to become entrepreneurs and escape their lot by "sweating" others. It was possible to make changes only with the passage of the Trade Boards Act in 1909, establishing minimum wages. In 1912, the strike of East End tailors lasted thirty-six days but was finally successful in establishing the crucial closed union shop and an increase in wages. The entire East End community supported the strikers with Rocker, the Gentile anarchist, providing leadership. There was also for the first time a level of cooperation with the Gentile dock workers who were also on strike.

By 1920, the Jewish unions were absorbed by the United Garment Workers Trade Union with a Yiddish-speaking local. During the subsequent interwar period, there was a further cleavage along political lines between Socialists and Communists rather than religious lines. Jewish unionism ended with amalgamation in 1939 with the dominant National Union of Tailors and Garment Workers. Unlike the United States, there was a dearth of immigrant intellectuals who remained in England to lead the unions.[19] The weakness of the Jewish labor movement in the garment industry mirrored that of the "English" section wherein unions were also relatively ineffective in organizing workers.

Unlike the experience in London, the Leeds workers had managed to form a viable union for many years. The relative success of the Leeds Jewish trade union can be attributed to multiple factors. One aspect was responsiveness to the local conditions of the tailors there and their relative freedom from politicalization. The founding in 1876 of Leeds Jewish Working Tailors' Society was attributed to the workers' own desire to avoid exploitation. Another important factor was that the larger scale workshops in Leeds reflected a focus on wholesale rather than the smaller scale, more fragmented, structure of London that weakened the ability to combine. The Leeds Jewish immigrant population was less likely to be transient with ongoing fresh immigration. People had come directly to Leeds from a small area around Kovno in Lita with the sole intention of settling there in the clothing industry. Proximity to the indigenous tailors and the need for interaction led to a greater degree of integration in action with the local branch of the Amalgamated Society of tailors (AST). Although refused membership in the English AST craft union, the Jewish union joined the Leeds Trades Council in 1884. Further, a member of one of the Jewish tailoring unions was a founder member of the local branch of the Socialist League. There were recurrent attempts to unite with the general trade union movement, leading to the eventual amalgamation of the two clothing unions in Leeds in 1915 into the first national clothing workers' union. This same fusion was not carried out until 1938 in London.[20]

The cultural strands brought to Britain with the East European immigration included not only the secular developments of socialism and labor unions. The immigrants who were religious preferentially came to Britain and brought with them the religious traditions of Lita.

The Religious Strand

In each of the immigrant areas in London as well as the provincial cities, synagogues, and smaller chevrot arose as alternatives to already established synagogues. For the first time, there had also been migration of rabbinical scholars of high repute trained in the great yeshivot of Eastern Europe.

One of the leading examples was Abraham Abba Werner who arrived in London in 1891 to take the post of rabbi for the "truly Orthodox" Chevra Machzike Hadath (Society of the Upholders of Religion). Born in 1837, he had been trained in the Telz Yeshivah in Lita and had been appointed as a Dayan in the rabbinical court in Telz. An ardent follower of the Vilna Gaon, he was an opponent of both Haskalah and Hassidism. He was one of the few enabled by training and reputation to function in the traditional role of East European rabbis as a mediator and interpreter of law. It was to the *rav* that the more Orthodox came with their religious questions or problems of a personal nature.[21]

Under Werner's leadership, the Brick Lane Talmud Torah was the first institution in Britain to give instruction in Yiddish and whose standard was high enough to warrant a class in Talmud for its senior students.[22] The Spitalfields Great Synagogue became the center for immigrant opposition to Adlerian and United Synagogue Judaism. It was the principal synagogue in the East End, with both worship and study in contrast to the original Ashkenazi Great Synagogue in Duke's Place. The selection of a rabbi such as Werner with proper credentials was the result of dissatisfaction with the role of Chief Rabbi Nathan Adler in relation to the rules as to kashrut. The appointment of Rabbi Werner was a challenge both to Adler, and the Anglo-Jewish lay leadership that supported the role of chief rabbi with his concomitant control over religious life through his authority over the marriage registries. Unlike the chief rabbi, Werner was also unique in his support for Zionism as an attendee at both the Second Congress in Basle and the Eighth in The Hague in 1908 reflecting his East European constituency.[23]

In time, after a number of court actions, the office of chief rabbi could no longer claim exclusive jurisdiction to certify meat as kosher. The beth din, the rabbinical court also acquired some recognition as a counter to the dictatorial rule of the chief rabbi with the appointment of a "minister" representing the Federation of Synagogues. The schism was further healed in 1905 when Sir Samuel Montagu negotiated the admission of Werner's synagogue into the Federation of Synagogues to be ultimately under the authority of the chief rabbi.[24]

In addition to issues as to authority, the Spitalfields Great Synagogue, in following the model of the Great Synagogue in Vilna,[25] represented for the readers of the *Jewish Chronicle* in 1905 a new concept of religion integral to the life of its community. "It is a curious sight that this place of worship presents to the visitor day or night. From [early morning] to midnight or later, there is always something going on . . . [For example] At half past six in the evening, there were about a hundred persons assembled . . . At the same time, both a large and small [House of Study] each contained their complement of students . . . going through a course of study. The members are in the large part, of the working classes. The Talmud Torah [provides] instruction for 1000 children in Hebrew and Talmud, the instruction given in Yiddish. While the kind of teaching that is given can hardly be approved of from an English standpoint, one cannot but admire the enthusiasm of the foreign poor that sustains them in the sacrifices they make to give their children what they regard as a suitable Hebrew and religious training."[26]

The friendly but patronizing attitude evidenced by the *Jewish Chronicle* was a comment that reflected the contrast with the usual lack of attendance at the "established" synagogues. This same focus on the differences between the native-born and foreign-born Jew continued to be the theme in the Jewish press. In an interview with Rabbi Werner just prior to his death in 1912, the *Jewish Chronicle* describes the changes that might have occurred under his auspices. "The weak spot of Judaism in England is the lack of study. Judaism was stronger in England than it was twenty years ago at the time of his arrival. This could be attributed to the arrival of Russian Jews who brought a greater commitment to rabbinical study derived from their roots in Lita."

British Literary Life

The existence of a separate culture amongst the immigrants in the East End had been the subject of surveys documenting its horrors. Israel Zangwill was the first writer in England to represent the Jewish immigrant in fiction and in a relatively sympathetic way that would be acceptable to the majority culture.[27] His most famous book, *Children of the Ghetto,* centers on the generational conflict between the Orthodoxy of the parents and Anglicized children. This same split between one's *English* more universalistic and *Jewish* particularistic sides characterized both his life and his writing.

Zangwill was born in Whitechapel in 1864, the eldest of three sons and the second of five children of a father who had emigrated earlier from Latvia. His father, Moses, had been pressed into the Russian Army at age twelve and managed to escape from its barracks to come to England in 1848. Moses is described as "being steeped in tradition." On his arrival in London, he enrolled in the study of the Talmud. The mother was also a recent immigrant from the area near Brest-Litovsk in Belorussia.

After their marriage in 1861, having no practical training, the father became a pedlar and trader in old clothes. He wanted a quiet life, prayer, and study. The mother was described by one of her sons as a *Tartar,* angry about her husband's lack of success and passivity. The family lived in Bristol until 1872 when they returned to London. Israel was enrolled in the Jews Free School, eventually becoming a pupil-teacher there. He understood spoken Yiddish and was able to read it somewhat but could not speak or write it well. Although an ardent student of Hebrew language and traditions, when in 1884 he graduated from the University of London, his honors were in English and French. He hoped that "in one soul Greek may meet Hebrew with no tug-of-war, moral aspirations may wed with artistic and conscience be reconciled to culture."[28]

Zangwill began by writing short stories and articles for the Jewish press. Starting in 1890, he began to write humorous short stories for the English press. His 1889 article on "English Judaism" in the *Jewish Quarterly* was an attempt to combine the "scientific morality of Moses with the emotional morality of Christ." It brought him to the attention of Judge Mayer Sulzberger in Philadelphia who arranged for a commission from the Jewish Publication Society to write a book about the East End ghetto. His 1892 book *Children of the Ghetto* described the life of the Ansell family, patterned after his own. He had two contradictory impulses. One was to present the East End to the wider world. In doing so, he was presenting images which were in line with communal expectations to portray the "alien" as God fearing and law abiding. The other aspect was his universalising ideals. For example, the heroine confesses her interest in the New Testament. The themes of the book are the transition and conflict between tradition and change, between the new generation educated in English schools and the old. All the characters seek to escape from the ghetto but nearly all wander back in the end returning to its spiritual comforts. Generally treated in a derogatory way were interspersed Yiddish words.

Devoted to the values of the Jewish past expressed in the ghetto, he also sought to escape from its restrictiveness and that of Judaism as a religion. His play *The Melting Pot* gave its name to the entire phenomenon of the assimilative transformation that would occur to the immigrant both in London and in New York. His marriage in 1903 to a non-Jew who was both a writer and a feminist made him to look for a world religion of brotherhood and love, a fusion of Judaism, and Christianity.[29] The split between the two poles of the ghetto and the melting pot illustrate Zangwill's inability to recognize the possibility of any reconciliation that would enable an Englishness that could accommodate a Jewish past.[30]

A territory where Jews would be preponderant was for Zangwill the only alternative to the "melting pot." His meeting with Theodore Herzl in 1895 marked the start of his very active involvement with Zionism. He was particularly involved with the Uganda Plan as a possible site for Jewish settlement. Urgency for relief after the Kishinev pogrom in 1903 and the impossibility of significant Jewish settlement in Palestine under Turkish rule led Zangwill to seek to establish a "state for Jews" wherever possible even if devoid of particularistic Jewish content. With the defeat of this "territorial" approach by the Zionist Congress in 1905, he nevertheless organized the Jewish Territorial Organization (JTO) to pursue this goal.[31]

English patriotism combined with his Jewishness. The universal mission of fashioning a new world would be led, he believed, by England. He was both a child of the ghetto and the "bargain" made at the time of nineteenth-century emancipation.[32] His domination of Anglo-Jewry's intellectual life prevented the recognition by others of any literary attempt to construct a useable Jewishness separate from one's Englishness.[33]

Unlike the small number devoted to socialism and anarchism, the other major thrust for enlisting energy for moral renewal would flower in Zionism. However, the thrust was middle class. It comprised respectability, Jewish cohesion and an enthusiastic (but not chauvinistic) patriotism. It maintained that the revitalized nation of the Jews would contribute to the advancement of humankind.[34] Crucial to the developments in Zionism was the connection with Britain.

As early as 1895, Herzl was well received in London by a group of Jewish professionals under the auspices of Israel Zangwill. In January 1896, the *Jewish Chronicle* published Herzl's ideas that were later to be incorporated unto his *Judenstaat*. One of the most extraordinary episodes in Herzl's early career was the near-messianic reception in Whitechapel where, in July 1896, he delivered his first public address on political Zionism.[35]

Unlike his experience elsewhere, Herzl found the concept of Zionism in England had considerable support among Gentiles. There was a philo-Semitism based upon the British sense of their connection with the Hebrew Bible that provided underpinning for a movement to Judaize the Holy Land. For many Christians, the restoration of the Jews to the Holy Land was seen as a preliminary to the conversion of the Jews and the Second Coming. Similarly, the Biblical connection underlined the importance of settlement in Palestine and the symbolic importance of Jerusalem. British politicians also saw Jewish interests wedded to British Imperial interests in the Middle East.[36]

The English Zionist Federation (EZF) was founded in 1898 after the First Zionist Congress in Basle. It incorporated many of the members if not the leadership of the extant Lovers of Zion groups. The latter had been founded in 1890 in Britain under the auspices of many of the members of the establishment. It was in tune with the long standing connection of Anglo Jewry with good works in Palestine exemplified by Sir Moses Montefiore. Its leadership, including such as Chief Rabbi Adler, had been committed to the gradual development of settlements and cultural renewal. The Anglo-Jewish leadership of the Lovers of Zion did not support Herzlian Zionism nor did the leaders of the other communal organizations, such as the Board of Jewish Deputies or the Board of the United Synagogue.[37] The loss of support of religious personages such as Rabbi Adler for political Zionism was counteracted somewhat by the support of immigrant rabbis such as Abraham Werner.[38] However, a Mizrachi religious Zionist organization did not appear in Britain until 1918. Agudat Israel, the Orthodox movement to its right, was far less accommodating to Zionist views.[39] However, particularly helpful to the Zionist cause in Britain was the influence of the *Jewish Chronicle* now under Leopold Greenberg, an avowed Zionist, editor from 1906 onward.

Emphasis on the formation of a Jewish state had serious implications for seeing the Jews as a national grouping, in potential conflict with their position in Britain.[40] Political Zionism clearly challenged the assumptions on which Anglo-Jewish institutions had been constructed and goals that they pursued. The Jews, they claimed, constitute a religious community, not a nation; distinctiveness is derived from their particular beliefs and practices, not from their national or racial characteristics. This was generally the stance of the United Synagogue pastorate susceptible to the will of their lay boards. Particularly anti-Zionist was the stance by the Liberal branch of Judaism. Its founder, Claude Montefiore, saw evolution of Judaism in terms of a spiritual destiny in the Diaspora rather than as a national entity.[41]

Herzl, in setting up the first Zionist Congress in Basle in 1897, had established a revolutionary concept in Jewish life. He had designed the Zionist Congress as a means of developing a widely based movement.[42] There would need to use a public Mandate and not merely a group of notables to "conquer the communities." However, the leaders of the English Zionist Federation followed an approach consistent with their generally middle-class character and wedded to their own personal aims for recognition within the communal structure. Rather than trying to develop a mass following among the immigrant community and develop any more widespread political base, they chose to infiltrate the various existing communal organizations.[43]

The other campaign initiated by Herzl was to seek an international charter for a Jewish state. Particularly crucial was the support of Britain and therefore the activities by the Zionist groups in Britain as they might affect governmental policy. It can be argued that the greatest legacy that Anglo-Jewry gave to the Jewish world was to pave the way for the creation of the State of Israel. The path to the Balfour Declaration and the British Mandate lay from Manchester to Whitehall and in the person of Chaim Weizmann.[44] Weizmann, along with the acculturated members of the East European immigrant community, was the moving force rather than the Anglo-Jewish magnates accustomed to be the representatives working with the government.

British Zionism

Chaim Weizmann was born in 1874 in a shtetl near Pinsk in Grodno Province. He was the third child and the second son of a family that ended up with twelve living children. He was born and bred in a completely Jewish milieu. He was particularly favored by his maternal grandfather with whom he lived as a child in the house adjoining his own. His father, Azer, was a timber merchant but descended from a distinguished rabbinical family. Thoroughly rooted in the unbroken historical continuity of Jewish tradition, Azer bequeathed to his children the conviction that all that comes can be turned to positive advantage and a clear-eyed pragmatic approach to issues.[45]

Chaim was educated in a heder under a teacher from whom he learned a love of the Bible and Hebrew literature. He was then sent to Pinsk to a secondary school where he acquired a secular education in accordance with his father's *Maskil* tendencies. He, along with his siblings, were all enrolled in secular studies and not in yeshivot. However, he continued his Jewish studies while enrolled in the secular gymnasium. He described his early memories as slogging through the mud and snow in Pinsk to collect money for the newly established Lovers of Zion. Pinsk was a mainly Jewish city with an active industrial as well as cultural life and almost uniquely associated with support for Zionism. Central to Weizmann's role in the Zionist movement was his lifelong and deep sense of Jewishness derived from his experience in growing up in the very essence of the Pale of Settlement. Despite his eminence, nurtured as he was in the uniquely Jewish nature of the Pale, he gave voice to the sense of identity of the Jewish masses and their ties to the Land of Israel.[46]

Because of the *numerus clausus* limiting Jewish places in Russian universities, Weizmann continued his education in Germany. He eventually graduated from the Institute of Technology in Berlin in biochemistry in 1898. While there, he joined a Zionist group with such others as Nachman Syrkin and where his mentors included Ahad Ha'am, in Berlin at the time.[47] He received his doctorate at the University of Fribourg and his initial academic appointment at the University of Geneva in 1901. While there, he helped organize a Zionist student group among the East European students in competition with the more general interest in socialism among the students. He never lost his detestation for the Russian socialist leaders for detaching from the movement of Jewish liberation some of the ablest sons of his people.

He also remained active in international Zionist work during this time. As a member of the Democratic faction, he advanced a more deliberate emphasis on cultural development with education as well as Hebrew revival as a basis for the Jewish settlement in Palestine.[48] This led to dissension with Herzl who was concerned that focus on cultural matters would lead to dissatisfaction with Zionism by the religious who provided only tenuous support for Zionism.[49]

Weizmann came to England from Switzerland in 1904 to pursue his career in chemistry with an appointment at the University of Manchester. His choice of Britain was a crucial one as it was at that time the world greatest political and financial power. In addition, for Weizmann as for many of his generation,

England stood for a settled democracy, legal equality, respect for individual rights, and a religious tradition founded as much on the Old Testament as the New.[50] His choice of Manchester was based on personal needs for a secure position but was fortuitous. Although primarily concerned with his career, he nevertheless also involved himself in Zionist affairs where he was appointed to the national committee in 1905. Trading on his base as being outside of London, his Mancunian connection enabled Weizmann to rise to the vice presidency of the English Zionist Federation (EZF) in 1914.[51]

Weizmann represented the *practical* approach to Palestine, that is, increasing colonization and the founding of institutions such as a university. Since both now lived in England, Weizmann was to continue his relationship with Ahad Ha'am. Despite his withdrawal from active Zionist work, Ahad Ha'am continued to epitomize the importance of spiritual renewal as a prerequisite for the development of the Jewish people in Palestine. Weizmann also could draw on his connections with Manchester. In addition to the financial support of the Sieff and Marks families of Marks & Spencer living there, Manchester was a center of nonconformist, Liberal Britain with its biblically derived culture and sympathy for the underdog.[52] C. P. Scott, the editor of the *Manchester Guardian*, was a consistent and influential ally. By 1914, Weizmann was about to become not only the leader of British Zionism but the key figure in world Zionism.

The entry of Turkey into the World War against the Allies brought Zionism into the sphere of practical politics. Palestine was now the object of planning for the sharing of territory after the hoped-for victory. Zionism and British Imperial interests could possibly coalesce. Weizmann was able to approach directly members of the government as early as 1915 aside from the normal channels. The Conjoint Committee, consisting of members of the Board of Deputies and the Anglo-Jewish Association, was the usual vehicle for intervention with the Foreign Office. The Conjoint, however, opposed the grant of special Jewish rights in Palestine and any recognition of Jewish nationality and published in the *Times* a manifesto to that effect.

This caused a split in the Jewish community with the Board of Jewish Deputies in a seemingly crucial vote on June 17, 1917, repudiating their own members of the Conjoint Committee. Henceforth, Weizmann could claim supremacy vis-à-vis the anti-Zionists. The Jewish *parliament* had indicated that the anti-Zionists of the old establishment could no longer claim that they were speaking for the Anglo-Jewish community. The June 17 vote can be seen not as much as a Zionist victory per se since opposition continued to political Zionism. This vote, important as it was, reflected a continuing effort to increase the degree of representative government within the board both in terms of regionalism and antagonism to influence of a privileged coterie that had acted without prior consultation with its parent body.[53]

Following the June vote, Weizmann and his political committee of the EZF, with Lord Walter Rothschild at its head, worked on getting a public declaration of British support. The Balfour Declaration in November 1917 was the fruit of Weizmann's labors, starting in 1915. In late 1916, the accession of Lloyd George as prime minister placed a person with Zionist sympathies in power with whom Weizmann had had direct contact. It was appropriate that Balfour's name as foreign secretary was attached since he had been "steeped in the Hebrew Bible since birth." To him, the Jews were not tools of the Christian millenium or agents of imperialism, but exiles who should be given back their homeland.[54] Despite the strong opposition of Edwin Montagu, one of the sons of the late Sir Samuel Montagu (1st Lord Swaythling) and a cabinet member, the Balfour Declaration was issued in the form of a letter to Lord Rothschild. The key term of the establishment of a "national home" was taken by Balfour to refer to protectorate in which the Jews would be able to "build up . . . a real centre of national culture and focus of national life."

The determining factors for its issuance in the wartime crisis was not the strength of British Zionism. There was the feeling that the American Zionist movement was powerful and issuance would strengthen American commitment to the Allied cause as well as possible positive impact on Jews in postrevolutionary Russia.[55] The San Remo Conference in 1920 incorporated the Balfour Declaration as part of the British Mandate of Palestine. This was the highpoint for Weizmann who believed that it was in the context of a British Palestine that a Jewish Palestine was to be developed.

Although the EZF membership rose dramatically and large-scale meetings took place in recognition of these successes, Zionism did not "capture the community." Immediately after the Balfour Declaration, the influential group of anti-Zionists formed the League of British Jews whose membership was limited by its name to nonaliens. The majority of the Jewish opinion leaders were non-Zionist, and the strength of the Zionists vis-à-vis anti-Zionists reflected the enlistment of Gentile Zionists. As the latter became less influential during the interwar years, the political support for implementation of the Mandate became problematical.

Nevertheless, the interests of Britain and of British Jewry were intimately related to the issue of Palestine during the Mandate years, and the headquarters of the World Zionist Organization with Weizmann as president were in London. The British connection that Weizmann represented was clearly problematic following the Arab Riots of 1929. Following the Passfield Report and the White Paper that followed, severe restrictions were to be imposed on the Zionist program in Palestine under the auspices of the Labour government. This policy was overturned by a direct intervention with the Labour Prime Minister Ramsey McDonald. This was Weizmann's final personal victory. Despite the victory, his position in the Zionist movement was undermined because of his moderate stance toward the British. He resigned as president of the WZO in 1931. When reinstated, it was in tandem with Ben-Gurion.

Weizmann was the product of the encounter between East European Jewry and the West. His passion for England was central and caused him to invest much of his emotional capital in his English political connections that eventually failed to support Zionist aspirations.[56] He however consistently emphasized the distinction between him and the British Jews. Despite his acceptability on the basis of acculturation, he nevertheless remained authentically the Eastern Jew.[57]

3.2.2 The Acculturated Generation

Reduced immigration followed the Aliens Act along with successively more stringent application of its principles brought about cessation of immigration. The interwar period was one in which the acculturated immigrants and their British-born descendants entered into positions within the communal institutions as a measure of the democratization of those institutions.

There was a marked weakening of the power of the old Anglo-Jewish elite. There was the postwar reduction of London's role in world finance from which they had derived their wealth.[1] Since the entire communal structure and governance was based upon voluntaristic dispensation of philanthropy, high office was dependent on wealth and standing among the majority culture. The reigning ideology of the old "elite" was *assimilationism* combining a commitment to British citizenship and culture with adherence to Judaism and Jewish tradition. The identification of Jews as an ethnic entity was the result of a newer way of thinking reflective of the immigrants and their descendants.

The limited effectiveness of the Jewish communal leadership in the face of anti-Semitism and native fascism during this period led to the rise of alternative political groups outside the existing conservative Jewish community structure. By the end of the interwar period, the relatively centralized structure ceased to exist with the proliferation of other organizations. Anglo-Jewry's unusually sensitive role in the implementation of the British Mandate in Palestine made Zionism an important factor in internal communal politics. Zionism became more acceptable at least partially because the acculturated immigrant cohort was reaching positions of prominence. This was the result of democratization in a broader sense of which Zionism was part of ethnic identification.[2] However, the original convergence of Zionism with British imperial interests in the Middle East as expressed by the Balfour Declaration became increasingly less evident. By the end of this period, Britain ceased to be the world power uniquely identified with Zionist aspirations.

The religious tradition brought by the immigrants persisted into the interwar era but eventually succumbed to the more latitudinal United Synagogue structure that had been a product of the original Anglo-Jewish ascendancy. There was continued growth in both the Federated and United Synagogue camps with the total number rising to 350 in 1940. However, the general trend toward increased synagogue membership was particularly evident in the United Synagogues.[3] The integration of the children of the immigrants into the *native Orthodoxy* of the United Synagogue came about by the body's financial and administrative resources and the still-dominant social prestige of its leaders.[4]

As the Jewish population during the interwar period increasingly became British-born, there was a comparable change in demographic patterns in terms of later age of marriage and fewer children than the pattern in the immigrant generation. Upward mobility occurred despite the depressed state of the British economy. Consumer industries in the south of England, in which Jews were more prominent, were less seriously affected. With some improved prosperity as well as acculturation, there was concomitant movement into secondary areas of settlement from London's East End. Lower-middle-class and skilled artisans moved to boroughs to the north of the East End and then, in the 1930s, to the more prosperous suburban areas to the West. By the early '30s, seven of the eleven elementary schools in Jewish areas of the East End had been put to other uses. Enrollment at the Jews' Free School, which had been full to overflowing, at the turn of the century had been halved. In a 1929 survey, the Jewish population of East London had fallen to eighty-five thousand, less than 40 percent of the total in Greater London.[5] Nevertheless, to be Jewish was not only an ethnic identity but a class one since for most it meant to be working class and relatively radical. It was a poor community in the East End, even poorer than the surrounding non-Jewish one due to the largely seasonal or part-time nature of the clothing and furniture trades, the largest employers of Jewish labor. There was assimilation to the English working class in terms of lifestyle but the maintenance of connection with their Jewish ethnic identity, albeit without a religious component. The immigrants and their British-born children entered into English politics on their own behalf, primarily via the Labour Party. The commitment to socialism was one of the persistent strands derived from the experience of the immigrants in the old Pale of Settlement. After 1920, the Labour Party had to compete with the Communists for support by the relatively radical Jewish trade unions.[6]

A migration similar to that of London occurred in the provincial centers where there were secondary areas in which Jews clustered with growth of synagogues in those areas.[7] The Zionist movement as well as the B'nai B'rith and the "friendly societies" served to structure Jewish ethnic middle-class life in these new areas of settlement along with synagogue membership.[8]

There was a higher but still small number able to go beyond elementary school into secondary education and grammar school as preparatory to white-collar jobs or possible university entrance. The overwhelming majority still left school at age fourteen. Given the elitist structure of British higher education, the relatively small number going to university was consistent with the experience of those who were middle class in the general population. More than half in universities were studying medicine or dentistry, with law the next highest. The choice of profession reflected the opportunities available where it was possible to be self-employed. Nevertheless, the contribution of the immigrant group to the highest reaches of academic rank can be measured by fellowship in the Royal Society wherein the percentage who were Jewish in 1940 was six times that of 1910.[9]

There was movement into a greater diversity of occupations although tailoring remained the largest single activity with particular increase in female employment. There were fewer Jewish men clothing workers in what had been the largest single source of jobs. Boot—and shoemaking almost disappeared with furniture manufacturing still an important area. Much of the increase took place in the area of shop assistants and office work among the women and salesman and clerks among the men. The service industries were expanding with young Jews employed in family shops. There still remained vestiges of the Jewish labor market in which Jews worked for other Jews in a small number of industries such as clothing. Small workshops predominated as before with the poor working conditions little changed.[10]

During and after the First World War, Jewish trade unions became amalgamated with the appropriate British unions sometimes as identifiable separate sections. Nevertheless, there remained a degree of independence with a Jewish Labor Council still possible to be set up in 1934 to combat fascism. The Jewish clothing workers' union in London remained independent, using Yiddish for its union business into the 1920s and not amalgamating with a British union until 1938.

There was relatively little Zionist interest among the Yiddish-speaking working class of the East End aside from Poalei Zion, the Labor Zionist faction. Dr Nachman Syrkin, the intellectual leader of Poalei Zion, addressed his *Call to Jewish Youth* in London in 1901. Founded in Whitechapel in 1904, there were Socialist Zionist groups identified with Poalei Zion in several cities with large immigrant working-class population such as Leeds, Manchester, and Liverpool. British Poalei Zion was formally constituted in a meeting in Liverpool in 1906. The movement helped to generate support for Zionism in the Yiddish-speaking community by maintaining a Jewish Cultural Society. The visits of Chaim Zhitlovsky in 1912 and by Ber Borochov in 1914 were energizing. In 1917, even prior to the Balfour Declaration, the Labour Party issued, as part of its War Aims Memorandum, a clause supporting a Free State in Palestine. It was the first official expression of sympathy for Zionism by any British political party. Poalei Zion distributed copies in Yiddish, announcing this statement and campaigned actively for Labour candidates in the elections in 1918.[11] Poalei Zion was instrumental in organizing the Jewish trade union membership into Jewish National Labor Council, combining with trade unions' and Workers' Circle branches.

The full impact of the working-class alliance would come about with the adhesion of the Labor Zionists to the Labour Party in 1920. Poalei Zion officially affiliated to the Labour Party in the category of Socialist Societies alongside groups like the Fabian Society. It was via the Labour Party that the political integration of the immigrant generation and their offspring would come about in the next generation with Labor Zionism providing a significant bridge.[12] The local British Labor Zionist organization functioned alongside the World Confederation of Poalei Zion that was also headquartered in London in recognition of the importance of Britain as the Mandatory Power. The main branch of the Poalei Zion remained with the social democratic socialists of the Labour Party with a smaller number splitting to join the Communist International in 1919.

The franchise reform of 1918 removed *rate paying* as a barrier to voting and increased the number of Jewish voters who were eligible by virtue of British birth. The increased difficulties placed in achieving naturalization restricted voting by those who were foreign born. With the break up of the old Liberal Party, the Labour Party seemed to be the only viable alternative for the working class Jewish voter. In 1918, the Labour Party came out from under the control of the English Trade Unions that were neither militant nor socialist. Labour was now committed to the nationalization of the means of production. There was also the creation of local Labour Parties in each constituency which individual members could join providing an alternative to membership via trade unions. Thus its membership could now include radicals and intellectuals. It had become a political party rather than a loose association of trade unions and socialist associations.

The conflict within the Left was between the social democratic Labour Socialists and the British Communist Party over the souls of the newly enfranchised with the British Communist Party providing the main working class opposition to Zionism.

The Stepney Labour Party, founded in 1918, was an expression of the long-established Jewish connection both to trade unionism and socialism. The East End, with its socialist tradition, also had links to the Russian revolutionary movement as well as family connections with those still in Russia. During the war years, the Bolshevik-led antiwar and anticonscription agitation mainly involved Jews. Starting in 1916, with the carnage on the Western Front, conscription was introduced into Britain. As "friendly" aliens, Russian Jews became liable for conscription into the British Army or deportation to Russia. Their opposition to conscription in support of a tsarist government drove a wedge between the aliens and the native born. For example, the Jewish Board of Guardians refused to give assistance to the dependents of those deported for failure to enlist in the British Army. Opposition to identifiably *Jewish* units in the British Army such as the Zion Mule Corps and the Jewish Legion also split along the usual communal lines with opposition by established Anglo-Jewry and support by immigrant-based Zionist groups.[13]

After the end of the war, British government intervention was occurring on the side of the White Armies who were, at that very time, perpetuating pogroms in Russia on the basis that all Jews were Bolsheviks. There were manifestations of anti-Semitism, now cloaked as anti-Bolshevikism, in the press. The issue of the association of Jews and Bolshevism was an extremely sensitive one. The Jewish communal authorities felt under attack. Illustrative of a departure during this time from the "quiet diplomacy" of the past by the Board of Jewish Deputies was their founding of a press agency. Its functions were analogous to the Anti-Defamation League of the American B'nai B'rith.[14]

Socialism was tarred as being a foreign import along with Bolshevism in the wake of the post-World War I unstable political climate.[15] Antialienism could now be joined not only with anti-Semitism but with anti-Bolshevism. In actuality, the newly won votes of East End Jewry backed the Labour Party in relation both to the continuation of the war and its attitude toward the earlier liberal February Russian revolution. The Yiddish press was pro-Bolshevik after the October revolution only in opposition to the intervention of British forces supporting the White Armies and in favor merely of recognition of the new regime. The Conservative Press nevertheless used "Bolshie" indiscriminately to label anyone with leftist political preferences whether socialist or Communist.[16]

The *Jewish Chronicle* published a seemingly positive series of articles discussing the hopes that the Bolsheviks had engendered for emancipation of the Jews of Russia as well as commenting on the dangers of their rise to power. The "letter of the ten" in 1919 to the arch-Tory *Morning Post* was in response, dissociating the signatories, all drawn from the communal establishment but acting as members of the anti-Zionist League of British Jews, from the connection apparently being made between Jews and support of the Bolsheviks. The Yiddish press along with the *Jewish Chronicle* accused those signing the letter of betraying their fellow Jews to curry favor with the anti-Semites. Their letter was used to strengthen the hand of those antialien forces that could now equate Jews with the new shibboleth of Bolshevism in addition to those arguments used heretofore. A motion passed by the Board of Jewish Deputies deprecated the letter as making a distinction between foreign and "British" Jews while also appending a repudiation of Bolshevism. The effect of the "letter of ten" forfeited for the old leadership much of the trust or respect from those who had previously followed their lead. This became more evident during the interwar period when their authority came under attack from what was becoming an increasingly more variegated Jewish community.[17]

The Labour Party was the vehicle for Jews to enter political life during the interwar era. It was compatible with their socialist as well as national leanings. In 1922, a Labour candidate won the seat for Whitechapel for the first time. By 1924, support for Labour was respectable among Jews.[18] Labour was the only party to announce support for the implementation of the Mandate in Palestine. Yet the connection between socialism in Britain and Zionism was always an ambiguous one. Sympathy with Jewish suffering and condemnation of anti-Semitism went together with a reluctance to acknowledge Jewish nationhood. Zionism was viewed as a product of bourgeois ideology and middle class rather working-class interests.[19] Nevertheless, based on the connection with their fellow socialists, the Labor Zionists in Britain took an active role throughout this period in cementing the relationship of the Labour Party to the Jewish cause in Palestine.[20]

British Socialism

The 1922 election saw the election of the first Jewish Labour MP, Emmanuel Shinwell. Throughout his life dedicated to Labour, Manny Shinwell exemplified the commitment of some Jews to their working class origins although he did not always identify himself with what might be considered "Jewish" interests. His career also can represent the evolution of the Jewish population of Glasgow as the major Jewish settlement in Scotland. Like those other provincial centers such as Manchester and Leeds, the large majority of the immigrants that formed the Jewish settlement were from Lita. Rapid growth in population occurred in the era between 1891 and the outbreak of the First World War attributed in part to the greater involvement of Scottish shipping firms in the transmigration trade. Opportunities existed in such "Jewish trades" as the clothing, furniture, and tobacco industries. Peddling continued to be a major occupation, with pedlars going to the mining villages, long after this had been less common in other provincial centers. There was particular focus on the manufacture and selling, through peddling, of picture frames.[21]

As in London, union activities were hard to organize given the small size of the sweated workshops. A Jewish Tailors Union was set up in 1890. There was a Workers Circle center where a branch of the United Garment Workers union was also based and where socialist activities went on such as support of Loyalists in Spain during the 1930s. The Depression had particularly serious impact in Glasgow with unemployment in the industries in which Jews were more likely to be found. For example, in 1937, 10 pecent of the Jewish population was receiving welfare from the communal agencies. The poverty of the Jewish settlement in the Gorbals was extreme. Illustrative is the story of a son of a garment worker who had emigrated from Lithuania in 1902. Leaving school at age fourteen, he became a presser before having the undreamed of opportunity to go to Oxford.[22]

Emmanuel Shinwell was born in London in 1884, the eldest of thirteen children of a tailor. Brought up in Glasgow in the Gorbals, he joined the Independent Labour Party (ILP) at age nineteen in 1903 and became active in trade union work. He became a member of the Glasgow Trades Council in 1906 when merely twenty-two years old. He had a reputation as a boxer. During the World War, he was an official of the Seamen's Union. He was arrested and imprisoned in conjunction with the Glasgow Strike Committee in 1919. In 1921, he became a member of the Labour Party National Council.[23]

The following year, he was the first Jewish Labourite elected to Parliament from a Scottish mining district outside of Glasgow where there was probably not a single Jew. Clydeside and Scotland were Labour bastions where unemployment was high in the post-World War period. Shinwell's parliamentary seat was held intermittently, varying with the fortunes of his Party during the interwar years. He was a junior member of the first Labour government of 1929-1931. When approached at that time by a Labor Zionist emissary from Palestine to enlist him in opposition to the Labour Party's stance in relation to the Jewish National Home, he was apologetic but claimed he had little interest in Jewish affairs.[24] In the cabinet following the Labour victory in 1945, he remained true to the traditional party policies supportive of Zionism by supporting partition and thus a Jewish state but for pragmatic rather than ideological reasons.[25] In the conflict over Suez in 1956, he deliberately abstained rather than support the Labour stand in opposition to Israel.

Though never officially associated with Jewish or Zionist causes and resolutely antireligious, he nevertheless always prided himself on his Jewish origins. He provided one of the most memorable moments of Jewish self-assertion when his background was insulted while giving a speech in the House of Commons. He punched to good effect the man who had been the heavyweight boxing champion of the Royal Navy.[26] He was made a life peer in 1970 with a career in national Labour politics spanning sixty years until his death in 1986

A greater compatibility of Zionism and Jewish identity with the Labour Party was exemplified in the career of Morris (Morry) Davis. His father, Joseph, was born in 1868 in Minsk in Belorussia. He immigrated to London in 1889 and became naturalized in 1896. He was a founder of the Cannon Street Synagogue (later affiliated with the Federation of Synagogues) and a Talmud Torah and active in the Jewish Friendly Society movement. Initially a bootmaker, he became a publican. Morry, born in Whitechapel in 1894, became an East End Labour Party leader as well as leader of the Federation of Synagogues. It was significant that he was born and had his early schooling in a neighborhood that bordered an Irish Catholic one and moved easily in that world. He was the earliest of the new East End immigrants to play a major role in Anglo-Jewish life.[27]

Davis's career was associated with the Stepney Labour Party. When first organized in 1918, it brought together Jewish and non-Jewish socialists and trade unionists. The alliance in 1919 of the Jews and the Irish brought about Labour control of the Stepney Council with Clement Attlee as the borough's first labour mayor. Heavily involved in politics, Davis became the vice president of the Stepney Labour Party in 1922, a Stepney Councilor in 1924, and member of the London County Council (LCC) in 1925 as the representative of Whitechapel and St George's. His work on the LCC was particularly important as the leader in a new more activist spirit of Jewish politics. The LCC, under control of antialien forces, had limited the availability of council scholarships to secondary school to children not only born in Britain but whose fathers were also born in Britain or the Dominions. Thus almost all Jewish children in the East End were excluded. Davis's other activities in the interest of his Jewish constituents were in employment and housing, In 1928, he was successful in leading a deputation of the Board of Jewish Deputies in removing the restriction on educational opportunities. This action took place despite the reluctance of many of the Old Guard in the BJD to taking such a stand.[28]

Davis was also active in Jewish communal affairs. He was at the head of the growing dissatisfaction with the British lord who ruled over the Federated Synagogues. One of the signatories of the "letter of the ten" in 1919 had been Louis Montagu, the second Baron Swaythling, also the heir of his father in his leadership of the Federated Synagogues. He lacked his father's piety. He was also high-handed in his actions. Davis represented the embittered Yiddish-speaking membership when, in November 1925, he moved and carried the resolution permitting the use of Yiddish in its deliberations. In so doing, Louis Montagu, who did not understand Yiddish, was deposed as president. In1926, Davis was chairman of its meetings and its third president in 1928. The federation henceforth, in contrast to the anti-Zionist stance of the Montagu family, became the first major non-Zionist group to contribute to the Jewish National Fund for redemption of the homeland. In addition to the Federation of Synagogues, Davis was involved with the London Jewish Hospital and a manager of the Jewish Free School and member of the Board of Jewish Deputies.[29]

Davis went on to become mayor of Stepney borough in 1930 and leader of the council in 1935. Catholic support for Franco during the Spanish civil war was the solvent, destroying the Jewish-Irish alliance upon which Davis's position depended.[30] During the 1930s, Davis was attacked by the more radical Communist union leaders as being passive in relation to the threat of fascism. The Communist request for a popular front with Labour in Stepney was refused. Given his political alliances with the Catholics, Davis did not support the development of any of the confrontational Communist-led antifascist initiatives in the East End.[31]

He had become increasingly dictatorial as well as corrupt. In a bizarre incident arising out of a ticket on the London Underground, falsification of an identity card led to imprisonment in 1944. The method of his fall as well as his actions while in power led to strengthening of Communists in the Stepney Borough Council.[32]

Barnett Janner was still another Jewish politician of the interwar period who maintained his connection to Jewish communal affairs and advocacy of Zionism while in Parliament. He was born in 1892 in Barry in South Wales in what was then a coal-exporting town near Cardiff. His father had reached this place by a circuitous route that reflected the pereginations of the Litvak immigrant of this era. Joseph Janner originated from a town in Kovno province in Lita. Having joined the gold rush to South Africa, he then went to Chicago before finally landing in Barry Dock in Wales as the first Jew. At some point, he had married a woman from Telz, the center of Jewish learning in Lita.

Joseph was also learned and taught his son Hebrew as well as his native Yiddish. The second child and the only son, Barnett's happy childhood was cut short by the death of his mother in 1902 and her replacement by an unpleasant stepmother. His schooling under a benign headmaster, Edgar Jones, was an antidote to his unhappy home life. Having chosen law, he went to what later became the University of Cardiff while also a clerk with a local solicitor. He was active in debating and theatre before entering the army in 1917 as a private. He was gassed while in the trenches. After discharge, he set up as a solicitor in Cardiff. He ran for municipal office in Cardiff while taking an active role in the Cardiff Hebrew Congregation and the local branches of the Zionist Federation and the Board of Guardians. He moved to London in 1929 after his marriage.

The Liberal Party leanings of his headmaster mentor determined Janner's own initial political allegiance. He ran unsuccessfully as the Liberal candidate for Parliament in 1929. He ran again in 1930 as a Liberal in a by-election in Whitechapel that was fought in the context of the Passfield Report issued in 1930 by the then Labour government.

The Passfield Report and the subsequent White Paper was one of a series of attempts by the British in the 1930s to scale down the implications of the Balfour Declaration.

The Labour seat had previously been won by a substantial majority by a pro-Zionist Gentile who had just died. Now after the

White Paper, the seat was much less secure in a constituency in which one-third of the voters were Jewish. The Labour candidate was an Irish Catholic called James Hall. The Liberals put up Barnett Janner.

The English Zionist Federation worked on behalf of Janner, the Liberal candidate. The Poalei Zion group (Labour Zionist) continued to support the Labour candidate despite their opposition to the White Paper. Hall did win, but with a much-reduced majority of only a thousand votes. This election came to be considered the first expression of ethnic politics. The reduction of the Labour majority could be claimed by the Zionists to reflect Janner's strong identification with opposition to the Passfield Report. The Zionists could also claim that Hall's victory was based on his assurance of opposition to the implementation of the White Paper. It would appear that Zionism was a factor affecting Anglo-Jewish political behavior, although not necessarily enough to overcome class interests in favor of Labour. Janner was elected as a Liberal to Parliament from the same Whitechapel district in the 1931 general election. Contributing to his victory was his ability to address his constituents in "fine Yiddish."[33]

Janner continued in Parliament until 1936, taking the lead in the organization of the Parliamentary Palestine Committee to develop nonpartisan support for implementation of the Jewish National Home under the British Mandate. He spoke about the problems of German Jews under Hitler at a time when other Jewish MPs felt constrained from doing so. He attacked the Board of Jewish Deputies for their inactivity on behalf of the German boycott and other activities opposing Hitler's policies. Simultaneously, he opposed restrictions to immigration to Palestine. Defeated by the Labour candidate in Whitechapel, and with the Liberal Party no longer a force, Janner joined the Labour party. In 1936, he became president of the Association of Jewish Friendly Societies, representing the immigrant community. It was only in 1945 that another election occurred when he was elected to a seat in Leicester that he held until 1970 as a Labour MP. During this period, he remained active in seeking British recognition of the State of Israel and issues of restitution for those who suffered under the Nazis. From 1955 to 1964, he was elected as president of the Board of Jewish Deputies. In recognition of his status, he received a knighthood in 1961.[34] He eventually became a life peer and was elevated to the House of Lords as Baron Janner. His son Greville succeeded him in his seat in Leicester as well as the presidency of the Board of Jewish Deputies.

Throughout his long career, he retained his concerns not only for the Jewish people but for the needs of his constituents for adequate housing and opportunities to temper the problems they faced in their everyday life. He dedicated his life to deal with social injustice in the spirit of his ancestry.

If the Labour Party was associated with the interests of the Jewish working and lower middle classes during the interwar period, Harold Laski was the best known Socialist. At the London School of Economics (LSE) from 1920 and professor of political science there from 1926 until his death in 1950, he straddled the entire interwar era. He was the most important Socialist intellectual in the English-speaking world. He tempered the abstractions of continental Marxism with faith in democracy to become the principal theorist of a Democratic Socialism identified with the British Labour Party. He never wavered in his commitment to the replacement of economic individualism and the profit motive by an egalitarian society based on cooperation and public service.

He was also a Labour Party activist, member of its National Executive Committee from 1937 to 1949 and party chairman during the election year of 1945. Even when his membership on the National Executive brought Laski within the party's leadership, he still maintained his role of outside critic. Much of his energy throughout his life would be devoted to managing this outsider/insider ambivalence so central to his identity as a Jew in Britain.[35] Laski's Jewishness and his attitude toward it shaped his life. In his allegiance to universalist socialism, he nevertheless was reminded of his Jewishness by opponents both of the right and the left. As Laski worked with other English Socialists to realize the dream of a New Jerusalem "in England's green and pleasant land," he was conscious of being one of the few Jews among the Labour movement's earnest Christian leadership. Socialism in Britain had its strongest roots in the elimination of selfishness and greed by service and cooperation. British "ethical" socialism was shaped more by the nonconformist chapel than by Marx.

During the Nazi era, Laski became an outspoken advocate of Jewish rights and critic of British policy in Palestine. Yet he found it difficult, because of his hypersensitivity to anti-Semitism, to be outspoken as he might have felt in opposition to Bevin's actions in postwar Palestine in maintaining restrictions on Jewish immigration.[36]

Harold Laski was Manchester "born and bred." His father, Nathan Laski, had been born in 1863 in Brisk in Belorussia. Immigrating to England, he was eventually naturalized in 1901.[37] Raised in Middleborough, he lived in Manchester and made his fortune in the cotton trade with India, the major Manchester industry. The Laskis lived in an almost exclusively Jewish quarter. Despite wealth, the father refused to follow the tide of fashion to move to a more genteel suburb.[38]. The dietary laws of kashrut as well as the sanctity of the Sabbath were strictly observed.[39] Although of East European background, Nathan Laski became one of the Anglicized elite who functioned to acculturate those who came in the subsequent wave of immigration. Considered the head of the Manchester Jewish community, he was president of the Manchester Great Synagogue, Jewish Board of Guardians, Council of Manchester and Salford Jews, the local Zionist Central Council and of the Jewish Hospital.[40] Recognized beyond the confines of his city, he was the first provincial Jew to serve on the Board of Jewish Deputies. Nathan Laski was also a prominent Liberal and his wife Sarah Laski was a member of the Manchester City Council for many years.

Harold's elder brother Neville, born in 1890, was a lawyer and judge. As the son-in-law of the Rabbi Moses Gaster, *haham* of the Sephardi Synagogue, Neville was actively involved in Jewish communal work. It is appropriate, given his father Nathan's pioneer membership on that body, that Neville in turn was the first of the immigrant group descendents to be elected president of the Board of Jewish Deputies in 1933.

Harold Laski was born in 1893. He was a precocious student at the famous Manchester Grammar School and a voracious reader. A book by William Morris, a founder of the Socialist League in the 1880s, provided him by his headmaster was particularly influential as a source of his socialism. He later also attributed his socialism to his Jewish upbringing, the sense it conferred of being treated differently from other people for no apparent cause.[41]. In 1910 he won a scholarship to New College at Oxford. Before going there he spent some months in London studying genetics. An article by him on genetics for the *Westminster Review* brought him to the attention of Sir Francis Galton, the founder of the field. Meeting a woman called Frida Kerry, they eloped to avoid the strictures of both families opposing the marriage. The marriage was kept secret, and the couple mainly kept apart during the years at Oxford as a condition for an allowance from his family.[42]

At Oxford, Laski received honors in history in June 1914. He particularly excelled at debating. A short man, he was described as a "gamecock," energetic in his activities particularly in the cause of women's suffrage. While at Oxford and less than twenty years old, it is instructive to that he completed an essay that was never published. Entitled "The Chosen People," it deals with his own conflict with his father in relation to his marriage to a non-Jewish woman. In many ways, he recapitulates Israel Zangwill. He describes himself as having an "intensely Jewish spirit . . . that tinged all he thought and knew . . . [not that] he had any belief in the religion." It was rather in the nation itself that he believed. He was immensely proud of the men it had produced such as Disraeli, Heine, and Spinoza, incidently all either converts or exiles from the Jewish community. "I cherish love for the Jewish nation because I believe its continuance is necessary for the existence of civilization. I want its spirit of intense determination to achieve a mighty end." He goes on to develop a universalist philosophy which would supercede and embrace all former faiths. Like himself, the person described does so in the context of meeting a woman older, purer, more spiritual than himself who admits her undying love for him.[43]

The writing of this essay apparently helped Laski to deal with the turmoil in his mind relating to his marriage. Despite its adolescent quality, it may have provided him with a philosophy that affected his future career. His dedication to the principles of Socialism was not entirely foreign to his Judaism. Despite difficulties with his family as a result of his marriage, Harold remained influenced by the strong sense of unity that existed among the Manchester Jews but could not assume that he had the right to be admitted to the Gentile's club. On a more personal level, he later reconciled with his family. In May 1945, in the wake of the Holocaust, at a convention of Poalei Zion, Harold Laski expressed his personal conversion to Zionism.

Laski's contribution to the evolution of British Socialism was to provide for Labour in Britain the path to "revolution by consent." His landmark book *The Grammar of Politics* in 1925 had reflected a Fabian Socialist gradualism. The state is the organ both of government and reform but there remains the decentralization of power by the existence of cooperatives and other organizations that can affect the implementation of the welfare state. Ramsey Macdonald's Labour government in 1931 had been deposed by the actions of the capitalist class under siege. Although now more clearly Marxist in orientation in terms of the necessary evolution from capitalism to socialism, Laski was not Marxist in terms of process. Unlike the Communists, he did not advocate the small disciplined revolutionary party that would seize power and establish a dictatorship.[44]

In the context of the world war starting in 1939, Laski saw the possibility of the foundation of a new social order to take place after the war and for a peaceful transition to a Socialist Britain. His efforts were devoted to making this possible both during the war and in the subsequent election that was successful in bring Labour to power. "Laski was a scholar and political philosopher; he was a politician, orator and journalist . . . all were knit together by his conception of the task of an intellectual in society."[45]

British Communism

It was in the context of the crises of the 1930s that the Communist party had its greatest effect. Fascist violence and the threat of such violence was a major issue of Jewish and particularly working-class Jewish life in the 1930s and a threat that continued even during the war being fought against the fascists.[46] The British Union of Fascists (BUF) under Sir Oswald Moseley was only the largest of a number of Fascist and anti-Semitic groups active during this period. Analogous to what occurred in Germany, they carried out terror in the Jewish areas such as the East End but also reinforced the widely held feeling that Jews were too powerful and that they were incompatible with Britain. Official anti-Semitism was expressed in the successive Aliens Act, deportations and administrative restriction to naturalization. This was a continuing phenomenon as expressed in the internment in May 1940 of refugees from Nazism, almost entirely Jewish, on the basis of their alien status. Underlying British policy was the sense that Britain was not a land of immigration and, at best, only for temporary refuge and limited even in that respect.[47] The overall response to permitting entry of refugees as well as policies during the Second World War toward Jews reflected the sense that anti-Semitism was the responsibility of the Jews as a result of their actions.[48]

The Jewish East End persisted as an entity throughout this interwar period and even through the heavy bombings of the Second World War. The Yiddish press, particularly *Di Tsayt* (the *Times*) founded in 1913 under Morris Myer was still active. Particularly active on the cultural front was the Workers' Circle (Arbeiter Ring). A "friendly society," it provided health and death benefits and was made up of a variety of leftist groups descended from the Bund in Eastern Europe. Yiddish language was part of the cultural legacy they upheld. Founded in Britain in 1909 following the formation in the United States, it maintained a "Yiddishe shule," a Yiddish language school

The Workers' Circle coming from a Bundist background was instrumental in organizing the opposition to the BUF through the Jewish People's Council against Fascism and Anti-Semitism' (JPC). It was a combination of Jewish trade unions and socialist societies with the active support of the Communists. Despite the stance of the Board of Jewish Deputies (BJD), a decision was made to confront the planned march of Oswald Moseley's BUF through Stepney in the East End. The action of the JPC in bringing a petition to the Home Secretary requesting cancellation of the march was a direct threat to the Board of Deputies The BJD then went to extraordinary lengths to delegitimatize the JPC in the eyes of the government. Instead of uniting the Jewish community, the threats from the fascists once again highlighted the social, economic as well as ideological differences within the community.[49]

The slogan "They Shall Not Pass" reflected the Spanish Civil War and the Loyalist response to the Fascist attack on Madrid. The Battle of Cable Street in October 1936 was a time when the march of Moseleyites was prevented. The Irish dock workers came to the aid of the Jews in opposing Moseley and the British fascists reflecting earlier support by the Jewish unions of the docker strikes.[50] The issue for many was not only anti-Semitism but antifascism and the protection of democratic values. Jews came to support the JPC despite its anti-Zionist and antireligious stance.[51] There was a confluence of Jewish and Communist interests based not only on "bread and butter" issues but on the role of the Soviet Union in fighting Fascism as well as the local fight against anti-Semitism in Stepney. For many acculturating East End Jews, Communism took the place of traditional Jewish religosity and was a secularized substitute for it. Marxism was a modern secularized version of Judaism, but one universalistic rather than particularistic and a faith offering immediate solutions to some of the most pressing questions of the day.[52]

In 1945, the Communist candidate won the parliamentary seat in Mile End, the most heavily Jewish constituency. In the autumn of that same year ten Communists were elected to the Stepney Borough Council. In the late 1940s, the circumstances which had given rise to the Jewish-Communist alliance began to dissipate not only in Britain but elsewhere too. The Soviet support of the State of Israel turned into hostility and the revelation of Stalin's own persecution of the Jews became evident. Zionism came to be in the ascendant within the Anglo-Jewish community.[53]

In 1945, the Labour Party stated its renewed support for a Jewish National Home and Jewish immigration in contrast to the 1939 White Paper—only to disregard that stance following the formation of the Labour Government after that election. The 1945 election had the largest number of Jewish MP's ever returned, almost all members of the Labour Party. Despite the British policy in Palestine, it would appear that the Labour Party was open to the sons of the immigrant generation as their entry to political recognition.[54]

The Religious Strand

During the interwar period, only two modes of Jewish identity appeared to be growing in strength in Britain. In contrast to the political identification with socialism was the bundle of patriotic and conservative attitudes connected with United Synagogue Anglo-Orthodoxy. The expansion during the interwar period reflected not only a large number of new synagogues and increased membership but the dispersion of population into suburban areas.[55] Particularly representative of the enduring Litvak tradition while continuing to adapt to British conditions was the example of the Daiches rabbinical family.

The father of the founder of the family in Britain was Loeb Hirsh Aryeh Zevi, who was a judge in the rabbinical court and head of a yeshiva in Kovno. The family was one of a long line of rabbis and scholars that stretched back many generations. The son, Israel Hayyim, was born in 1850 in Lithuania. Studying at a Lithuanian yeshiva, he was supported by his father-in-law while living a life of pure scholarship and meditation. He then came to Leeds in 1901, becoming rabbi of the Beth Hamedrash Hagodol, the principal immigrant synagogue. The Leeds community was the creation of the immigrants since there was barely a minyan prior to the 1880s. He was regarded as the leading East European rabbi in the provinces.[56] He founded the Union of Orthodox Rabbis in England and published responsa as well as collections of his sermons. He was also responsible for the only periodical dealing with rabbinical scholarship to be published in Britain in his time, *Bet Va'ad la Hahanim* (Assembly House of the Wise). His early support for Herzl along with other immigrant rabbis imparted strong sense of religious respectability to the English Zionist Federation. His two sons then made their own contributions to the evolution of traditional Judaism in Britain.

The elder son, Samuel, was born in Vilna in 1878. He studied with his father and at a secondary school in Koenigsberg in adjacent East Prussia where both he and his younger brother acquired a secular education. This decision by the father for his sons to acquire a secular education is said to have scandalized the local Jewish community. The sons both also attended the Berlin Rabbinical Seminary. After serving as rabbi in Sunderland in England, Samuel became lecturer in Bible, Talmud, and Midrash at Jews' College, London in 1908 where he remained for forty years. His coming to the Jews' College was part of a renewal in direction and elevation in level of scholarship that occurred in response to the impact of the East European immigration and criticism of the low level of Hebrew knowledge.[57] His scholarly work dealt mainly with Babylonian antiquity and its influence on Judaism. He also took an active role in Jewish communal organizations. These include B'nai B'rith as well as the Board of Jewish Deputies.

The younger son, Salis, was born in 1880 in Vilna. He recalled his study of Talmud while a young boy by the light of candles stuck in the wall. Like his brother, he was educated at home, at Gymnasium in Koenigsberg, and then at Hildesheimer's Berlin Seminary. That seminary represented the combination of strict Jewish Orthodoxy and sound training in traditional rabbinics with knowledge and appreciation of secular Western culture. He then received a PhD in Hume's philosophy at the University of Liepzig. As a young man in England, he continued to pursue philosophy in relation to Kant and Judaism and eventually wrote a book called *Aspects of Judaism.* He also was one of the translators of the Soncino Talmud. He spoke English well. Although Yiddish was his native tongue, he preferred Hebrew as the language of Jewish culture.[58]

Daiches was first rabbi at Hull and then Sunderland before becoming the rabbi in Edinburgh in 1918. The Edinburgh Jewish community had mainly arisen out of the East European immigration. Most arrived through the port of Leith. Some were recruited from elsewhere such as Manchester and Leeds to work in various factories. In comparison to the larger Glasgow community, it was more prosperous and more cultured. The presence of Rabbi Salis and his reputation for erudition gave it the unity and renown far greater than its size would warrant.[59] The Graham Street synagogue, housed in a converted chapel, contained the English-speaking congregants. Another Yiddish-speaking smaller house of study also existed. When Rabbi Salis accepted the position, he insisted that he be invited by both the Yiddish-speaking as well as the more modern congregation. In 1932, he succeeded in bringing them together in a new building. Indeed, the single Edinburgh Hebrew Congregation he created remains unique in Britain. That year marked the watershed of his career. He had been optimistic both about the importance and viability of British Orthodoxy and the emergence of Judaism as a proud part of a pluralistic European culture.

Daiches was active in B'nai B'rith and the Zionist movement. Characteristic of his thoughtful ways was his criticism of Zionist activities as too focused on fund raising to the detriment of its educational focus.[60] While in Edinburgh, although but a rabbi of a relatively small congregation in one city, he became the spiritual leader and spokesman for Scottish Jewry. He took a very active role in maintaining the good name of the Jews in Scotland and was well known for his letters to the editor of the leading newspaper the *Scotsman*. He always assumed the closest natural sympathy between Scottish Presbyterianism and the Jews. In his letters to the press and in his talks to a variety of organizations, he acted with dignity and authority as the official spokesman of his people. In his view, the role of a modern Orthodox rabbi was to speak up for his people with dignity and equality before his fellow citizens. He nevertheless maintained some of the more traditional roles in adjudicating matters of Jewish law. As such, he represented the transition from the scholarly role of his father's immigrant generation to the development of modern Orthodoxy in Britain. He combined a pastoral and scholarly role with that as a spokesman of his people to the wider community.

Although there were individual exceptions, it has been said that the offspring of the immigrant generation in Britain had not yet left its collective mark on cultural or intellectual life during the interwar era. The limits imposed by poverty on artistic development among the British-born generation in the immigrant era is belied by the appearance of the poet Isaac Rosenberg, whose life was cut short by death in the war. He can be considered as a member of the acculturating generation in that English was his language, although he did not live into the interwar period. Indeed his reputation was limited and known only to a few until after World War II. Although his existence was wound up with his Jewishness, his poetry was his personal yearning for the Gospel of Beauty.[61]

The Gospel of Beauty

Isaac Rosenberg's father, Barnett, was a native of Lita and a student of the Torah. He had been born in 1859 in Kovno province to a family of rabbis and scholars. Starting school at five in the cheder, he continued his studies toward a life of scholarship in a neighboring town. Married at age twenty, he remained the naïve scholar, unsuccessful in dealing with the requirements of earning a living. He immigrated to England in 1886 to avoid conscription. He eventually came to Bristol where he staked out the pedlar route through Devon and Cornwall that he was to follow for the rest of his life. Unhappily married, his wife nevertheless followed him to England with their one child. Isaac was the next born in 1890 in Bristol, the second of a twin who had died at birth. He was so tiny that it was doubtful whether he would survive. There were to be a total of six living children.

Moving to London's East End in 1897, the family lived in a single room in back of a rag shop on Cable Street near the docks. With the father lacking ambition and devoted to his learning, the family's condition was tenuous. Isaac was enrolled in a state school. He was encouraged by the English headmaster of his school to draw and write. Art and English literature were to become the dominant interests of his life to the exclusion of religion, the stringencies of daily life, and the political ferment of the East End. Reading was his delight, and drawing his pastime.[62]

Isaac went to the Arts and Crafts School in Stepney after regular school. Leaving school at age fourteen, he was apprenticed to an engraver. He hated his work there and succeeded in going to art classes that enabled him eventually, with the aid of patrons, to enroll in the Slade School of Art in 1911. Particularly noted for its emphasis on drawing, the Slade's unrelenting emphasis on the sharp clear line was an important lesson not only in his painting but in his verse.

His earnestness and awkwardness never left him as well as bouts of depression. Ambitious and determined, he sought advice; but stubborn and sensitive, he would always be on the defensive. Shy in his speech, he would increasingly express himself in his writing. He had been intent in being an English poet in the line of Keats and Shakespeare. Encouraged to read the English romantic poets by his mentor at the Whitechapel Public Library, they nourished his longing for nature. His instincts for light and harmony and freedom made him hate the ugliness of his surroundings, its noisiness as well as its poverty of spirit.[63]

He had found some patrons who, in buying his art, enabled him to publish some of his poems in 1915 at his own expense without much success. Indecisive and despondent, he enlisted in the army despite his ill-health, awkwardness, and small stature.[64] He wrote a major verse drama "Moses" while in training in preparation to go to France. It reflected his increased awareness of his poverty as well as his Jewishness. Like Moses, he was "of halt tongue" but found a new power of expression in his writing. He continued to write some of his greatest masterpieces while on the front lines. He was killed on the Somme on April 1, 1918.

The struggle to establish his reputation after his death paralleled his own efforts while alive. His sister Annie was his faithful literary executor. He failed to achieve recognition in the wake of other more fashionable war poets such as Wilfred Owens. It was only in 1937 that a definitive *Collected Works* was published with an introduction by Siegfreid Sassoon to little notice. In the 1950s, a reissue appeared in the United States with subsequent further continuing recognition in the *Jewish Quarterly* under Jacob Sonntag. A memorial exhibition at Leeds University in 1959 finally established Rosenberg as having "arrived."[65]

The scholarly Litvak religious strand became transmuted into more secular scholarly and literary pursuits to a limited degree in Britain. The number of British Jews that moved outside the usual range of Jewish occupations and the number going to university was quite small by comparison to what was happening in the United States during this same period. Advanced secondary and university education was a luxury available only to the upper classes.[66] As an example, the readership in rabbinics at Cambridge was allowed to lapse in the 1920s because English Jews were not willing to contribute the few hundred pounds necessary to support it. The offspring of the immigrant generation were conforming to well-established pattern of behavior in their relative indifference to the liberal arts.

Jewish Scholarship

However, in a culture in which precedent and history is so important as a basis for legitimacy, the writing of Anglo-Jewish history was a scholarly pursuit to support such legitimacy. This was embodied in the formation of the Jewish Historical Society of

England (JHSE) in 1893. It was organized originally in response to the planned destruction of the Bevis Marks synagogue. It continued in the context of the large-scale East European immigration and the development of national notions of "Englishness."[67] The mission of JHSE was to overcome not only the impact on the existing community of the "alien" immigration but to attempt to deal with the image of "the Jew" as a moneylender so engrained in English history since mediaeval times. The mission was to show the rootedness of Jews in English society, their contributions to English life, and their patriotism.

The formation of a Society followed the success of the Anglo-Jewish Exhibition in 1887 celebrating the fiftieth anniversary of the accession of Queen Victoria with an exhibit illustrating the history of Jews in Britain.[68] It was noteworthy that the initial meeting of the society in 1893 was called by Lucien Wolf on November 11. It was the anniversary of the meeting between Cromwell and Menasseh ben Israel in preparation for the conference to arrange for resettlement of the Jews in England.[69] The JHSE organized an annual event celebrating "Resettlement," culminating in 1906 in the celebration of the 250th anniversary of the Whitehall Conference of late 1655 called by Cromwell to consider resettlement. There had just been passage of the Aliens Act of 1905 that reflected agitation to limit Jewish immigration. By focusing on the period leading from resettlement to Emancipation, one could avoid the appearance of ingratitude when dealing with the persistent anti-Semitism and also counteract the "foreignness" of the East European immigration.[70]

During the interwar period, Cecil Roth was the prime representative of this school of Anglo-Jewish history with Emancipation its culmination. His classical *History of the Jews in England* was but a portion of his far-ranging concern with general Jewish history as well as general history including that of Italy. His first major published work in 1925 was *The Last Florentine Republic* derived from his doctoral dissertation.

Cecil Roth was born in Dalston, a suburb of London in 1899. His immigrant Maskil scholarly father was a builders' merchant.[71]. Cecil was the youngest of four boys. The family was meticulously observant. He learned Hebrew originally from his father but then with tutors including Morris Vilensky, a product of the renowned

Yeshivot of Telz and Volozhin in Lita. He learned Hebrew as a living language then an avant-garde approach. His scholarship, however, was that of Oxford rather than the traditional world of the yeshivah and Talmud. He did carry on and urged for others the basic commitment to study for its own sake that derived from the yeshivah culture of Lita.[72]

As did his brothers, he studied at the City of London School, a fee-paying, non-Jewish day school favored by rising Jewish families. Following army service as a private on the front line in 1917-18, Roth enrolled at Merton College at Oxford. During 1921, he spent his vacation in Florence, beginning his work on Renaissance Italy as well as the history of the Jews in Italy. Having obtained a doctorate in 1924 dealing with a non-Jewish subject, he had nevertheless become interested in Anglo-Jewish history while at Oxford. He worked there with Herbert Loewe, then reader in rabbinics at Exeter College. An Orthodox but liberally minded scholar, Loewe held one of the few academic appointments dealing with Jewish subjects. Roth read his first paper in 1920 before the JHSE with which he was to be so closely identified.

At the time of his graduation from Oxford, there were no opportunities for an appointment in Jewish history. Unable to receive an academic appointment in his major field of Italian studies, he nevertheless eventually sought his professional future within Jewish scholarship. A temporary appointment at the newly organized Jewish Institute of Religion in New York brought him to the attention of the editor of the American *Menorah Journal* where he set out in articles published in the late 1920s his vision for the study of Jewish history. He emphasized the importance of the history in the English-speaking world rather than the Teutonic focus of Graetz and East European focus of Dubnow. His one-volume *Short History of the Jewish People,* published in 1935, marked his transition to acceptance as a Jewish historian.[73] However, his acceptance as an academic historian remained problematic. Only in 1939 did he become reader in Jewish studies at Oxford where he remained until his retirement in 1964. His last achievement was as editor in chief of the *Encyclopedia Judaica,* which appeared in 1971 after his death in 1970.

Roth was intimately connected with the JHSE, serving as its president for nine terms. In his presidential addresses in 1936 and

1938, he laid out in an eloquent manner the role of Anglo-Jewish history. Since Jews were being attacked not for their religion but for their race with its basis not in theology but history, it was history that must be a weapon with which to fight. To counter the attacks based on *alienism* in Britain, there is the history of the Jews in mediaeval Britain. To counter these attacks based on the Jewish life being limited to the capital, there is Jewish life in towns throughout England as well as Ireland. In his review of contributions by Jews in all fields to British life, he also emphasized the support given by British governments dating back to George II to intervention on behalf of Jews abroad. He emphasized as well the long-standing interest in Zionism, placing the Balfour Declaration as but a recent manifestation.[74] Characteristic of this school of history is that Roth's book on Anglo-Jewry leads to the Emancipation in 1858. In the third edition published in 1964, there is a short epilogue with merely a paragraph or two dealing with the East European immigration of which Roth himself was an outstanding product.[75]

Roth remained a traditional observant Jew in the United Synagogue tradition with a lifelong interest in Jewish liturgy and art as well as history. He was, for example, interested in illustrated Haggadot and edited, along with the artist Arthur Szyk, the famous 1940 edition noted for its illustrations. His style of life was not merely that of a Jew but eminently an English Jew as peculiar to his time and place.[76] A diaspora-centered historian, he saw Jewish history to be understood as a result of Jewish-Gentile interaction colored by his life as a patriotic Englishman.

British Zionism

Individual exceptions of university-trained academicians, of course, occurred. The life of Selig Brodetsky represented the unusual attributes of an academic career combined with a dedication to the Jewish communal organizations.

Selig Brodetsky was born in the Ukraine in 1888, the third of six living children, and brought to London with his family in 1893. There were good scholars on both sides of the family. The father was self-taught in mathematics as well as skilled in rabbinics but was unsuccessful in business, finally becoming a beadle. Selig went to the Jews Free School in London's East End where one of the advantages was provision of suit of clothes and a pair of boots each year.[77] At the same time, he attended a Talmud Torah run by an Orthodox rabbi. He became known as a Talmudist and went on to study with his father after going beyond the curriculum of the school. Although born in the Ukraine, in his memoirs, he describes himself as "remaining the Jewish student who loved study for its own sake" in the Litvak cultural tradition.[78]

He earned a London County Council scholarship to secondary school in preparation for higher education. His exceptional mathematical ability earned a scholarship to Trinity College at Cambridge. His career there led to the post of senior wrangler in 1908. The title is given to the person who scored a top *first* in the mathematics tripos. The use of the unusual term *wrangler* derived from having been a successful disputant in defending one's thesis. He continued his studies in mathematical astronomy at the University of Leipzig, earning a doctorate there in 1913. In 1914, he was appointed to his first academic post at the University of Bristol and then in 1920 appointed rofessor of applied mathematics at the University of Leeds where he continued until 1949. He prided himself in his teaching and was a leading figure in the Association of University Teachers. Specializing in theoretical aerodynamics, he wrote on the development of the airplane. As an educator, he wrote books on mathematics for the general audience as well as a life of Sir Isaac Newton, reflecting his interest in astronomy and his membership in Trinity, Newton's College at Cambridge. However, he never achieved eminence in his academic career consistent with his early promise, attributed in part to his commitment to communal affairs.

His career in communal politics has been taken as a signal of the changes that took place in the Jewish communal leadership during the 1930s, culminating in 1939 in the presidency of the Board of Jewish Deputies.[79] He has served to epitomize the "capture of the community" by Zionism as well as by the immigrant acculturated generation. As senior wrangler, he became a celebrity with headlines in the newspapers.[80] His academic achievement in 1908, so soon after the passage of the Aliens Act, served as an exemplar of the potential available by opening up universities to children of the immigrant generation.

He recalls his father being present at Herzl's first public meeting in Whitechapel in 1896 and then going with his father to meetings of the first Zionist society in England. Later, while at Cambridge, he helped found the Zionist society there. Brodetsky's activity at Cambridge was but an example of the spread of Zionism among university students that aroused concern at that time among the anti-Zionist communal leadership of the Board of Deputies.[81] To the detriment of his development as a mathematician, young Brodetsky became a public figure, in demand to speak to Jewish groups mainly about his Zionism.[82]

In 1928, Brodetsky became a member of the executive committee of the English Zionist Federation and, subsequently, the head of the Political Department of the Jewish Agency in London.[83] He was particularly involved in the successful efforts to counteract the findings of the Passfield Commission and the White Paper that followed in 1931 that recommended a restriction in Jewish settlement in Palestine. The response to this White Paper led to the first open political confrontation between the Zionist movement and the British Government. A public protest took place at the Kingsway Theatre in the West End and then a monster rally at the Pavilion Theater in the East End. These events ended the concept of "patriotic Zionism" that saw the building up of Jewish Palestine as compatible with the expression of British imperialism.[84]

The events in Germany under Hitler now gave an edge to the Zionist message. The militant anti-Zionism of the ruling elite softened into a non-Zionist stand that supported the development of Palestine as a refuge without necessarily dealing with the issue of a national entity. The election of the respected barrister Neville Laski, the son of Nathan Laski (and the elder brother of Harold Laski), as president of the Board of Jewish Deputies in 1933 turned out to lead to only limited acceptance of Zionism. When confronted with the rise of Nazism in Germany, Laski counseled against public protests and boycott of German goods. Both Zionists and many others representing organizations outside the Board criticized the relatively passive stand of the ruling hierarchy. An example the appearance in 1933 before the Board of Simon Marks, of Marks & Spencer and a wealthy backer of Zionism, recommending the withdrawal of Neville Laski as president in favor of Chaim Weizmann.

Throughout the 1930s Neville Laski made the clear distinction between support for Jews settled in Britain and those seeking refuge from Germany then later Austria and Czechoslovakia. At no time did thinking about refuge extend to Jews from Poland and Eastern Europe. The limited and cautious response of the board to entry of aliens was in direct collusion with the limits placed by the British government. These activities were conditioned by the government's fear of stirring up even further anti-Semitism. Antagonism to entry had become even more widespread with the immigration of educated professionals who were seen to compete for British middle-class jobs.

Even less satisfactory was the response of the Board of Deputies to the anti-Semitic British Union of Fascists (BUF) and other groups that arose during the 1930s in sympathy with Nazism. The Defence Committee of the board tried by informational material to counteract the anti-Semitism that was becoming ever more widespread with the BUF. The board maintained a conservative anticonfrontational approach and opposed public protests to the native fascists. In their efforts to maintain a uniformity of approach, they sought to suppress dissent within the Jewish community as well as regional differences. The Battle of Cable Street in October 1936 marked the breakdown of that strategy. Thousands of working-class Jews acted in defiance of the upper-class leadership to oppose the provocation of the planned march of Moseley's blackshirts through the East End.[85]

Neville Laski and the board generally accepted the defensive premise that anti-Semitism was the problem of the Jews and created by their behavior. Ultimately "vigilance committees" were formed to investigate complaints made against Jewish landlords, employers, and traders and bring to bear the communal authority to change their behavior. This was a signal that British Jews were not, after all, just like other British citizens. In taking on policing duties, the board was essentially validating the attitudes of those attacking the Jews. Laski appeared to urge his fellow Jews to accept second class status as a price to pay to dampen anti-Jewish prejudices.[86]

Fear of inciting further domestic anti-Semitism was a major constraint in any attempt to act on any issue in the Gentile world to improve welcome for refugees or suggest the existence of a

"Jewish vote." There was widespread antipathy within British society to "foreigners" that Anglo Jewry also shared to some degree. Nevertheless, after Kristallnacht and the Anschluss, a significant number of refugees, including children, were admitted to England on the basis of guarantees provided by the Jewish community. However, there was no effect in enabling immigration to Palestine where the White Paper of 1939 sealed off the escape route from Europe.[87]

The Board of Jewish Deputies was no longer the sole voice of British Jewry. In the absence of what appeared to be an effective stand in favor of refugees from Nazism as well as native Fascism, other groups began to develop. One was the British Section of the World Jewish Congress (WJC). A number of organizations adhered to the WJC despite the opposition of the Board of Deputies. Opposition was based on WJC's claim as representative spokesman of Diaspora Jewry made up of national bodies. Its very existence and mode of organization seemed to give credence to one of the anti-Semitic shibboleths about an international Jewish conspiracy. Still, another strand was the Jewish People's Council in the East End, representing a left-wing alliance with Communists. The other nationalistic strand particularly among the younger people was identification with Zionism. Cultural Zionism was an expression of ethnic separatism for those no longer closely connected to synagogue membership and observance. Zionism was becoming more fashionable, displacing both traditional religious values and the Yiddish-based communal structure.

Illustrative of his generation is the story of Morris Beckman, growing up in the interwar period in Hackney, a London suburb adjacent to the East End settled by Jewish immigrant families.[88] Running out of money on his way to America from Lita, his father remained in London. Beckman's mother had come from Vilna; they married in 1904 in the East End. The youngest of six, Morris was born in 1921 in Hackney where they owned a five-storey "terrace" house with a front yard unlike the tenements of the East End. His father was a wholesale textile merchant in the East End, just managing to keep the business afloat during the Depression in the 1930s. Beckman describes his brothers' ceasing to go to synagogue with their father as they became acculturated to English life. His own schooling was interrupted by frequent street battles with the fascist thugs who were everywhere in the areas of Jewish settlement of Hackney and Stoke Newington during the '30s. He went to the famous Hackney Downs Secondary School where he played cricket and football.

Habonim was the largest of the Zionist youth organizations directing its members to kibbutz life in Britain. Summer training camps became a large part of Beckman's adolescence. Some went on aliyah to Palestine although he did not. Habonim had been established in 1929 in an attempt to weld scouting with Palestine culture. In the mid-'30s there were forty such groups, each about twenty-five to thirty-five young people twelve to sixteen years old increasingly focused on Socialist-Zionist pioneering. It provided a "sense of dynamism, the quality of life distinguishing it from its surroundings, a quasi-religious emotional experience shared by its members."[89]

In addition to the impact of Zionism on the youth, there was a rise in Zionist membership on the Board of Deputies, but still a minority. Moreover, the Zionist Federation did not have its own representatives on the board. It was necessary for Zionist members to be deputies of various synagogues and other institutions.[90] As late as the spring of 1939, Neville Laski, as board president, published a book condemning statehood. The British government effectively abandoned the Balfour Declaration in the infamous White Paper of 1939. Jewish immigration was limited to seventy-five thousand over the next five years thus also ending the principle of Jewish sovereignty in Palestine by condemning the Jews to a minority status. In the turmoil surrounding the start of the Second World War, Laski resigned.[91] Selig Brodetsky, only recently a member as a delegate of the United Synagogue of Leeds, an avowed Zionist as well as an immigrant, was elected unopposed.

This action has been considered as a milestone of the acceptance of Zionism within the Jewish communal structure.[92] Brodetsky's election was also the recognition of the entire acculturated generation of the post-1880 immigration. He was the first academician to hold that post as well as the first Jew originating from the East End. His successive elections during the course of the war reinforced the *Zionization* of the board. The board's issuance in November 1944 of statement on postwar policy was opposed by the non-Zionists. It supported unlimited immigration and future statehood or commonwealth status for Palestine within the British Commonwealth, the crucial stance of the Biltmore Conference in New York City.[93]

The conflict within the communal bodies concerning Zionism as well as personal animosities led to several bodies, seeking to speak for Anglo-Jewry vis-à-vis the government. The government could then, by pointing out the discrepancies between the several approaches recommended, choose to discount all and mute any response to the ongoing destruction of European Jewry.[94] The pervasive anti-Semitism continued even during World War II that was ostensibly being fought against Nazism. The ongoing anti-Semitism affected governmental policy in the response to knowledge of the Holocaust.[95]

The Holocaust profoundly changed Jewish historical geography, making British Jewry the largest in Europe outside of the Soviet Union and, for a time, the fourth largest in the world. Although Anglo-Jewry was one of the largest communities to survive and had not been directly affected by the Holocaust, it was caught up in a situation where its interests were at odds with its government as well as the country at large. In 1945, Britain had just managed to survive the war that had been won. Resources were depleted. It retained the Mandate in Palestine but considered it a burden to be dropped. Brodetsky was the head of the Board of Deputies and a Zionist. Nevertheless, there was little that Anglo-Jewry felt it could do in the context of British anti-Semitism in the wake of the King David Hotel bombing and the attacks on the British military in Palestine.

Whereas Britain had been a central player at the end of World War I, it became increasingly peripheral to the decisions made by the United States in reference to Palestine. Any "British" solution offered by Weizmann was superceded by that of Ben-Gurion and the Americans, leading not only to free immigration but to an independent state. In the United States, Zionism and the commitment to the creation of a Jewish State became an objective of Jewish communal life with widespread non-Jewish support. Unlike the active role of the United States at its birth, British recognition of the State of Israel as de jure came only in 1950. This can be taken to mark the end of the British story as uniquely connected with Palestine and the start of the postwar period for Anglo-Jewry.

3.2.3 The Integrated Generation 1950-1985

In the post-World War II era, the increasingly middle-class and educated nature of the immigrant stock helped Anglo-Jewry take on a coloration more consistent with their entry into the larger society. Nevertheless, the persistence of disdain for Jews has colored the ability of Jews to defend Jewish interests. Jews were generally validated on the basis of their conformity to the values and manners of middle-class British society and not in their Jewish identity. Even the most assimilated were considered as never to be purely and simply "English." Economic advancement has been remarkable and has erased the class bound traditions of the immigrant. Entry to educational opportunities has become far more available as a mode of advancement in the postwar generation. The major institution of Anglo-Jewry has remained the *Orthodox* synagogue, but that institution has lost its strength with greater degree of assimilation coupled with greater adherence to traditional, separatist, religion by others.

Even more recently, Britain began to experience a wider ethnic and racial character. Jews were no longer the sole marginalized minority. There was also an opportunity to see a Jewish contribution more integral to British history and modern literature. True "integration" can become possible, if still difficult, with recognition that the old arrangement of cultural assimilation in return for emancipation need not be required.[1]

The dispersion of the immigrant stock from the East End and adjacent boroughs was accelerated by wartime conditions. Both increased upward mobility and the bombing of the East End near the London Docks contributed. By the mid-'80s the East End, the boroughs of Tower Hamlets and Hackney contained just over one-eighth of London Jewry with the overwhelming majority now living in the middle-class, outer-London north and northwest suburbs. The total London Jewish population was estimated at 217,000 from a total of 330,000 thus maintaining the relative ratio of London to the provinces of 2:1. Distribution within the provincial centers of Manchester, Leeds, and Glasgow similarly had occurred in the direction of their outer suburbs.[2]

This dispersion reflected a more middle class occupational structure with a drastic fall in those in the classical immigrant trades and those working in unskilled or artisan occupations.[3] There remained a clear segment of working-class Jews who now worked in a greater variety of occupations and were frequently self-employed. Taxi drivers were one such self-employed entity in London. Another was hairdressing.[4] Concomitantly, there has been decline in the Jewish trade unions and the Jewish units of the amalgamated trade unions. The traditional Jewish trades, such as clothing and furniture, retained Jewish owners although no longer likely to have Jews as workers. Those families who had small businesses now had the potential for larger aggregations of wealth during the postwar boom. Jews were generally more highly represented in the professional and higher social classes. For example, in the mid-'70s, as much as 80 percent of the Jewish males in Glasgow were self-employed in comparison with circa 30 percent of the non-Jews.[5] The number in the professions continued to rise given the wider educational opportunities for university education in postwar Britain with new Redbrick universities as well as the expansion of existing ones. Entry into the professions was the mode of upward mobility particularly for the descendants of the later immigrant families who were originally manual workers rather than shopkeepers.[6]

The Freeman Family

The various branches of the Freeman family can illustrate this process of gradual movement through middle class British society and diffusion from the original immigrant setting.[7] Jane Bragovsky was the eldest of six children born in Yanover in 1870 in the area around Kovno in Lita. Jane arrived in London's East End in 1890 and, in 1895, married a fellow immigrant from the Kovno region in the East London Synagogue. Although connected with the United Synagogue, it was the most popular site for immigrant weddings because of its low cost. Born Indorsky, the family name was changed to several variants of Freedman or Freeman in the ensuing generations. The couple lived in Bethnal Green in the Jewish East End. The groom was described as a "bootfinisher" on the marriage certificate. He thus was in one of the "Jewish trades" but one which was particularly subject to low wages in competition with the factory production of shoes and boots. He later became a market trader, selling household linens. Jane ran a drapery store on their house premises. After her husband's death in 1935, Jane moved in with her elder unmarried daughter and then-still-unmarried youngest son, David.

Six surviving children were born of that marriage. The first native-born generation followed the pattern of acculturation during the interwar period, took part in the war, and then the postwar diffusion into other parts of Britain but in "Jewish trades."

A daughter, Becky, married a man she met coming out of a dance hall in Hackney. He had fought in the Jewish Legion during World War I. Owning a barber and hairdressing business, the family lived in Hackney and moved to Glasgow during World War II "after a close encounter with a bomb." Portions of the third generation after the Second World War moved into white-collar and professional jobs, but others did not. Of Becky's three children, the eldest, a daughter, was in the WAAF and in the Army of Occupation in Germany. She trained as a secretary and worked at Barclay's Bank before marrying a physician. He was in general practice in Essex. One of their sons, in turn in the fourth generation, has continued in medicine, rising to a consultant status as a radiologist.

Of Becky's other children, Stanley married a Glasgow girl, became a cook, and ran a successful patisserie in the West End after serving in the military in Egypt. His daughter, in turn in the third generation, married a hairdresser and lived in Elstree, in Essex near London. Two of her four children attend the Jews Free School. Stanley's son was an accountant who worked for an international finance company. In turn, his two sons went to Haberdashers' School, a "public" school. Becky's younger son Tony, a bachelor, was a hairdresser like his father and minicab driver.

Simon, Jane's second son of this first native-born generation, was apprenticed to a cabinetmaker after primary school. He had a series of marriages and eventually ran a poultry business in Petticoat Lane in the East End and then in Edgeware. His eldest daughter, Doris, married a non-Jew she met originally in the ATS during the war. They lived in Birmingham. Their son, Tony, of the third generation, visited Israel and later moved there in 1978 and became interested in Judaism. He has been in the Golani infantry brigade on several tours of duty and lived on a kibbutz.

Nathan was born in 1904 in Britain and was also apprenticed to a cabinetmaker. Unlike the others, he retained the *d* in the name. Married to a girl from Cardiff, he settled there after wartime service in the Royal Artillery. He worked first as a cabinet maker before going into the drapery business with his wife's family. His son Dennis grew up in Cardiff and married a girl who had also grown up there. He eventually became director of the Midland Bank's venture capital section. He and his wife organized their own group of companies in association with Midland Bank. One of their daughters was a marine biologist and the other was a teacher and ski instructor as well as a single parent.

David, the youngest son of this first native-born generation, was born in 1915. He was a member of the Jewish Lads' Brigade and played in their band. Leaving school at fourteen, he worked in various aspects of retail trade. After returning from the war, he had a ladies' wear shop in the London Bridge Station of the London Underground. He lived in East Finchley and Ilford in the farther reaches of the migration north and northeast from the original East End home. Of his two children, one son has lived in Israel since the 1970s and worked with computers there. A daughter also lived in Israel, married a Sephardic Jew from Tunisia before emigrating to the United States.

Saul (Syd), Jane's eldest child, was born in 1896. He went to the Jews Free School on scholarship before being apprenticed to a tailor. He was wounded by a shell in France just prior to the armistice. He remained a bespoke tailor the rest of his life, working in clothing factories associated with such high-class firms as Simpson's. Living in Stoke Newington during the war, to escape the bombing he successively moved to Glasgow and then to Leeds where he remained even after the war. He married a London woman who was of Russian and Dutch background. The couple were active in the Reform Temple in Leeds. There were two children born of that marriage.

The son, Cecil, born in 1926, was first evacuated to Warwickshire from Stoke Newington in 1941 before joining his family when they left London. He entered the army in 1944 and was stationed in India in the Royal Corps of Signals. After discharge, he went to University of Leeds. Trained as a textile engineer, he actually worked in various sales capacities before spending the major part of his career with the *Yorkshire Post*. Of his two children from the first marriage, both daughter and son moved to Israel. The daughter remained there since 1988, and the son has since emigrated to the United States. The son of his second marriage went to the prestigious Leeds Grammar School before going to the University of Leeds where he trained as a crop scientist.

The other of Saul's children was Elise, born in 1922. She was thwarted by parental disapproval in her ambition to be a ballet dancer. She took a commercial course and remained a secretary her entire life, eventually working for the chief executive of a company. She married, in 1942, Alfred Kersh when he was on leave. He was originally from Glasgow. They lived in Leeds where he worked as a cinema manager and then in the retail furniture business. There were two daughters born of that marriage. The younger, Wendy, was with Habonim and spent time on a kibbutz before training as a hairdresser. She married a Leeds salesman. The elder, Gillian, trained as a teacher. Her Zionist background was also in Habonim and also spent a year in Israel. Working as a primary school teacher in London, she married Robert Bernard. Bernard's grandfather had taken his given name to substitute for the original surname of Fishberg. Bernard's father had not been permitted to go to university despite having gone to a grammar school. He became a successful importer of Italian textiles. Robert, the only child, had grown up in Finchley in the postwar era and gone to grammar school there before then going to the University of Hull. Trained in applied physics, he worked in areas such as the measurement of air quality for the London County Council.

The Bernard family lived in a good-sized semidetached house in Edgeware and belonged to the Edgeware and District Reform Synagogue. Edgeware has a substantial Jewish population. There were strong connections to family members who lived in Israel with frequent and sometimes long-lasting visits. Both sons in turn had gone to the "public" City of London School where an official minyan existed and a substantial number of students were Jewish. Both were drawn to a more observant form of Judaism as evidenced by public wearing of the kippah and membership in the Masoriti branch of Judaism, closer to the American Conservative movement. Both sons were now at university, Adam at Oxford and Timothy at University of Bristol. The latter intended to train at the Jewish Theological Seminary for a career in the rabbinate although not as a communal rabbi.

This family illustrated the trajectory of many of the original immigrants who came from Lita in the great migration. Like most, they settled in the East End as immigrants. The next English-born generation spread to the eastern and then northwestern boroughs. World War II hastened the dispersion of one branch to Leeds, another to Glasgow, still another to Cardiff, also areas of Jewish settlement. Poor and with a large family, they entered the *Jewish trades* with the eldest apprenticed as a tailor even prior to World War I and others in cabinetmaking. Others went into retail trade, hairdressing, and cab driving in the interwar generation. There was little representation in the professions until the postwar era with greater opportunity for university education and greater level of prosperity. Zionism seemed to be a significant component in the postwar generation with aliyah, especially after 1967, although not apparently of a strong ideological bent. Several of those in turn left Israel to emigrate to the United States. The choice of surnames and given names reflected the acculturation that occurred. It is the most recent postwar generation that has returned to a more open religious identity.

British Politics

Coincident with the shift in demographics and residence was a political shift away from Labour. Bevin, as foreign secretary in the postwar Labour government, acted to maintain the White Paper of 1939, opposing immigration to Palestine even in light of the Holocaust. He also opposed the development of a Jewish State. The many Jewish Labour MP's elected in 1945 were unable to break ranks to affect British policy in the abandonment of the Mandate, the subsequent Partition and the War of Independence. Labour's anti-Israel stance in the Suez crisis in 1956 once again served to distance Jews from that party. This time, there could not be an excuse of governmental policy since Labour was in the opposition. Once again, when Harold Wilson's Labour government was in power during the Six-Day War in 1967, the British went to great lengths to distance themselves from Israel.

Yet the earlier allegiance to the Labour Party persisted even into the mid-1970s when the number of Jewish MP's remained as high as 10 percent of all Labour members. Fourteen of the Labour members of Parliament were members as well of the sister Poalei Zion Israeli party.[8] However, increasingly in the 1970s, left-wing anti-Zionism in the Labour Party caused deviation from "support for Israel is a given fact."[9] The increasingly left-wing and doctrinaire quality of the Labour Party, in its minority status during the 1980s, tended to support anti-Zionist rhetoric.[10]

The Conservatives under Margaret Thatcher were the beneficiaries of these factors in Labour Party policy along with identification by middle-class Jews with her policies, attuned to entrepreneurs and homeowners. Margaret Thatcher has had personal connection with Jews who formed a large part of the constituency she long represented in the northwest London suburbs. Noteworthy has been recognition of her social policies by the Chief Rabbi Jacobovits to whom she granted a peerage.[11] In the late '70s, Jewish Conservative Party members began to appear in Parliament.

The post-World War II generation has had the opportunity to feel at home in Britain, enough to consider the possibility of recognizing its Jewish roots as a means of entering the mainstream of English culture in the arts and literature.

British Literary Life

Arnold Wesker represents even more than most the postwar generation. He has been the most socially minded of the new crop of British playwrights that appeared in the early postwar era. He was considered as "one of the angry young men" in his working class origins and lack of university training. Politically active, he was imprisoned for a short time in 1961 for participating in the Ban the Bomb demonstrations. From 1961 to 1970, he went beyond his work in the theater to try to organize, with some support from the trade unions, Centre 42. It was a cultural movement to make the arts more widely accessible. He withdrew from these efforts, learning the futility of group efforts that submerge the individual in the name of ideology.[12]

Arnold Wesker drew from his East End Jewish left-wing background the essential material of his own rebellion. Jewish characters people many of his plays, and he identified his Jewish origins as central to his life and work.[13] His characters reach universal meaning by retaining their Jewishness. Theirs is the failed socialist dream transformed into the insipid mellowness of good salaries and suburban life.[14] In speaking with the rhythm of Jewish dialect, his characters do so without any sense of inferiority but as a valid currency for expression.[15]

He defines his Jewishness as being in the prophetic tradition, in the spirit of justice and tolerance, and the energy for action to change the world.[16] His socialism was "more emotional than intellectual" and in the utopian tradition more than Marxist. Although not a practicing Jew, the messianic dream of the salvation on earth appeared everywhere in his plays.[17] In what he considered one of his most important plays, *The Merchant*, his figure of Shylock is that of the free spirit. It was that spirit that Wesker viewed as the quintessential Jewish character.[18] In contrast to Shakespeare's character, Wesker's is moral and principled with his commitment derived from his immersion in his Jewish studies. When Shylock gives his word, it is binding, as in the Torah.[19] Refusing to accept things as they are, he becomes a target but remains unintimidated. So is Wesker. His willingness "to step out of line" reflected his very deep individualism. His mother was a fighter all her life, and he identified strongly with her. He was brought up to fight the machinery, to fight by getting up petitions and write letters.[20]

Arnold Wesker was born in 1932 in the East End on what he identifies somewhat sarcastically as Empire Day. The paternal grandfather who immigrated to England from Russia was described as "well versed in the Talmud." First living in Swansea, the family then moved to London. The grandparents lived in the famous Rothschild Dwellings built to house Jewish artisans at the turn of the century. Arnold lived there with his paternal aunts along with his sister when his parents separated, and even when they were once again together, so that his mother could go out to work.[21] His aunt Sara was one of the organizers of the Jewish Tailor and Garment Workers Union. His father, Joseph, was a tailor described as a "lovable but weak personality who was more intelligent than his work required, which he hated." He was not interested in making money.[22] His mother, Leah, worked as a cook among other jobs. They met while singing in a Poalei Zion choir before she went on to be a believer in Communism.

Arnold was the younger by six years of two children and the only boy. An earlier infant brother died from meningitis. Wesker attended Jewish schools and elementary school in Stepney and Hackney. Evacuated during the war from age seven to thirteen, he lived with foster parents but returned to London whenever he could. Unlike his sister, he failed the examination that provided entry into the academic track. He went to a technical secondary school that emphasized clerical studies such as bookeeping, typing, and shorthand but was encouraged by an English teacher to continue writing. After leaving the Young Communist League, he joined Habonim, the Zionist youth group, at age fourteen to which he attributed the deepening of his Jewish consciousness.[23] He eventually quit the latter to join an amateur theatre group. Leaving school at age sixteen, he worked at odd jobs before going into the RAF for his National Service. After discharge in 1952, he worked at more odd jobs, including working as a farm laborer in Norfolk where his sister and brother-in-law lived, finally as a pastry cook in London and then Paris. All these experiences became part of his early work.

His first play, *Chicken Soup with Barley* opened in Coventry in 1958 before moving to London's Royal Court Theatre. It took place in a tenement flat patterned after the two-room flat where he had lived with his family. He achieved widespread recognition as a playwright with his second play *Roots* in 1959, which went on to the West End commercial theater. *I'm Talking About Jerusalem* in 1960 completed the trilogy about the Kahn family, patterned after his own. The first play in the trilogy spanned the years 1936 to 1959, charting the gradual fading of the Communist faith and youthful energy of a group of members of a Jewish family from the East End. The opening act of that first play takes place on October 4, 1936, the day of what became the almost mythical Battle of Cable Street. The energy derived from the struggle against Moseley's Fascists is dissipated in the postwar Stalinism of the Hungarian Revolution and the victory of Conservatism in Britain in the 1950s. The second play deals with the hero Ronnie, but in relation to a Norfolk farm family. The woman Wesker later married came from a working-class family in Norfolk. The third play deals with the attempt to escape from industrialized consumer-society life to the Norfolk countryside of Ronnie's sister and brother-in-law, patterned after equivalent real family members.[24] His sister, Della, had married a man who served as Arnold's mentor. Working as a carpenter, he was a young Communist who was literate and dreamt of being a writer. Although, aside from *Roots*, the plays are about failure, they are also about defiance, about a refusal to accept defeat.[25]

It is through his working-class and Jewish roots that Wesker found his truth. Yet his later work has moved even further from his belief in the possibilities of socialism to a greater emphasis on questioning the ideologues of the Left and more connected with his Jewish roots. His shift was from finding his voice in his working class to his ethnic roots.

The London-based *Jewish Quarterly,* under Jacob Sonntag, strove to develop a literary journal equivalent to *Commentary* in the United States. Starting in 1953, it offered a new and uniquely Jewish vehicle for young Jewish writers, recalling for some the literary interests derived from the legacy of intellectual pursuit "for its own sake." There was not the large Jewish readership in Britain as in the United States. Nevertheless, there was an extraordinary effloresence of Anglo-Jewish writers in the 1950s. This flowering came about in those writers forced to deal with their Jewish identity in positive terms in response to the problem of dual allegiance. There had to be realization that, if cut loose from their Jewish roots yet they were unaccepted as Jews in English society. The adherence to British norms by the acculturated Jew growing up in the middle-class suburbs was stronger yet the degree of ostracism was even greater than that in America in the private schools and golf clubs.[44]

Harkening back to the East End where there had been a sense of community was one focus as exemplified by Wesker. The other aspect which freed the Jewish writer is epitomized by Emanuel Litvinoff who found in the Holocaust the pride of bearing the badge of suffering.[45] It marked the difference between the Jewish writer and his contemporaries as well as his predecessors. Published in the *Jewish Quarterly,* he was described as the first avowedly Jewish poet of interest to write in English.[46]

His "Jewish" character is the acceptance of a unique situational predicament of "otherness" plus a sense of a joy outside the core of sadness. A comparison is made to the art of Chagall as a poet who expresses that sensual joy and the Sabbath in the context of almost unbearable tragedy.

Emanuel Litvinoff was born in London in 1915. His father had landed in London on his way to America but was unable to go on. As an alien, he disappeared when deported to Russia around the time of the Bolshevik Revolution. Supporting her children by her sewing, his mother eventually remarried to a man unsympathetic to the boy.[47] The second of four boys with subsequent half-siblings, he grew up in the Jewish East End in a two-room flat in a tenement building. He was sent to the Cordwainers' Technical College to learn bootmaking where he was the butt of both the students and teachers. Failing to win a scholarship for secondary school, he left school at age fourteen and worked in tailoring, cabinetmaking, and the fur trade. He served in the British army in West Africa and Egypt during the Second World War. When first published in 1942, he became noted as a war poet. Another volume of poetry was well received when published in 1948.[48]

He writes about the death and frustration but does so addressed to the Jewish predicament. His poetry is the poetry of protest, protest against a civilization that sent him to war as well as one that has committed pogroms against his race for thousands of years. Since the early 1960s, he has published drama and fiction concerned with the destruction of European Jewry. He also edited a newsletter on behalf of the Soviet Jews. He described his adolescence and the process of coming to terms with his Jewishness and his social commitment.[49]

His is the conflict of dual allegiance, his Jewish roots, and the temptation of Christianity reflected in his intermarriage. Yet thinking himself English, he is confronted by T. S. Eliot's anti-Semitism. In his poem, "To T.S. Eliot," famously read aloud in the poet's presence, Litvinoff proudly rebukes Eliot.[50] He recognizes his roots with tenderness and, for the most part, is bitter and angry; for wherever he looks, he is haunted by the human tragedy of which the Jewish story is but a part.[51]

Jon Silkin, born of mixed Jewish-Christian parentage, is another self-consciously Jewish poet although he would deny that identity.

He was born in 1930 in suburban London. He was evacuated to Wales during the war where he experienced alienation from self and community. In his poem about his evacuation, he used the metaphor of Shylock as describing himself as the outsider Jewish boy in the pastoral surroundings. After his military service, he abandoned his comfortable background to work as a laborer in London. In 1952, he founded *Stand* as a magazine of committed writing that he coedited. In 1958, he was appointed to a poetry fellowship at Leeds University. For him, the advantage of his Jewishness was his membership in a persecuted minority that enabled him to speak to the rest of humanity.[52]

Exploring his own sense of Anglo-Jewish poetry,[53] Silkin saw English Jews as partaking in the art of exiles, belonging neither wholly to England nor to Israel. One theme is that of rootlessness. Another is the Messianism in the care of humanity. Silkin has been particularly involved with bringing Isaac Rosenberg to the attention of the postwar generation as the epitome of the aspect of rootlessness and the concern for assimilation that is one of its products. His concern was universal in dealing with a society in decay by virtue of losing its national and religious values without anything that could replace them. Like Rosenberg, Silkin saw himself as a cosmopolitan arising from Judah but preaching a humanitarian universalism.

Silkin's post-Holocaust stance was to see the relationship to nature, to animals, and even plants as fraught with danger. One must find a language that is not debased. One must safeguard the clarity of language and morality from the media which, like the Nazis employs vulgarity and jargon to obfuscate live issues.[54] Like others, such as Sutzkever in his poetry while living in the Vilna Ghetto, only the purity of language can serve as a requiem for the absent dead. One of Silkin's more recent poems deals with the martyrdom of the Jews of York, England, in 1190. They chose a Masada-like fate of suicide rather than conversion. He has also identified with modern Israeli poetry that he has translated. Despairing of the Judaism found in the synagogue, yet he acknowledges the mystic's ascribing meaning to the blank spaces in the Torah where one seeks the divine presence.[55]

These writers had to come to terms with an identity forgotten or unknown in the context of assimilation in a society largely complacent about the fate of those killed. The postwar generation of Anglo-Jewish writers, in dealing with the Holocaust, have gone beyond the marginality that characterized Jewish writers in England in previous generations. The former conflict between Jewish roots and assimilation has been succeeded by a reassessment of identity with a reevaluation of morality.[56]

Notwithstanding the efforts these writers represent, there was a recurrent theme of inadequacy of English letters to adequately reflect the uniqueness of Jewish life in England. Even more recently in 1989,[57] relative feebleness of the Anglo-Jewish literary tradition is compared to the American Jewish cultural one. English philistinism and the sense that being "clever" as bad form continues to be an important part of the explanation. Still another recurrent explanation is the lack of the pluralist culture in Britain unwelcome as it is to any deviance.

The postwar generation of the East European immigrants has taken its place in Britain in the "elite" of its intellectual life. This is particularly noteworthy since such membership had not been as characteristic of the wealthy elite prior to 1914. Prestige, as evidenced by presence in the Edwardian Court society, had been based on wealth and not on ideas. It was the East Europeans who brought about the commitment to the world of ideas in Britain the tradition that had been theirs in Lita. This academic tradition was exemplified by Isaiah Berlin.

Isaiah Berlin stood for one basic idea, that of liberalism forged by the integration of his background and the opportunities offered in Britain for their expression. His father Mendel, was born in 1883 in Vitebsk in Lita. As a boy, Mendel recalled his own grandfather as an "other-worldly rabbi who devoted all his waking hours to the study of holy books."[26] After schooling in his native town in a cheder, he went to gymnasium in Riga. He was taken into his great-uncle's timber firm and was soon travelling to London and Paris on business. Mendel would consult with the Lubavitcher rebbe to whom he was related. Isaiah's father, to the dismay of the son, would attribute his son's extraordinary memory and scholarly achievements to his rabbinical ancestors. His mother, Marie, grew up in an Orthodox home in Riga's Jewish quarter but received a secular education. It was to her that Isaiah attributed his strong identity as a Jew and his Zionism.

Isaiah, born in Riga in 1909, was named after the adoptive great-grandfather. The latter had been the first to leave the Pale of Settlement to move to Riga, married the daughter of the important Schneerson family of the Lubavitcher dynasty, and founded the large-scale timber firm, which Mendel had just inherited. Isaiah was an only child, born after a difficult delivery with a resultant limp left arm and was doted upon all his life.

Leaving Riga in the throes of the world war, the family moved to a small town in the midst of the forests they owned. Here, Isaiah first started school in the local cheder and learned his never-forgotten Hebrew letters. They then moved to Petrograd in 1916, to Riga in 1920, and England in 1921 to escape the Bolshevik Revolution. The marks of exile remained with him in wanting to belong to his sense of the best of what England stood for, in his Zionism, and in his fascination with the marginal excluded figures of history who did not yield to the need to "fit in" as he had. Judaism remained one of the major strands in his life, following an Orthodox style of religion on Rosh Hashanah and Yom Kippur and the annual Seder.[27]

He went to St Paul's School in London and then studied classics at Corpus Christi College at Oxford. Alongside these influences, starting as an adolescent, he was mentored by an extraordinary savant. Shmuel Rachmilievitch was the prototypical prerevolutionary Russian intellectual who turned Isaiah toward philosophy. At Oxford, he came under the influence of Maurice Bowra, the famous classical dean who freed him to be the voluble person he had always been. In 1932, at the age of twenty-three, he was selected to be a fellow at All Souls, the first Jew to be elected. This was the very Parnassus of all academic appointments. Berlin began to develop on his own the interest in the philosophy of history, and the theory of liberty he was to make his own.

His basic principle was that pluralism is both possible and desirable. The state as well as any controlling institution should be sensitive to minority feelings. The evolution of individuals is dependent on their being self-directing and, in varying degrees, responsible and free and not reducible to statistical analysis or mechanistic system.[28] Equality and freedom are both ends but cannot exist to the detriment of the other. Pluralism extends beyond politics to the acceptance of a multitude of ideas appropriate for different situations and for men of different callings.[29] This stance does not extend to relativism, the denial of objective standards of behavior. There are universal, or nearly universal values. "Spontaneity and security . . . mercy and justice are ultimate human values . . . yet may be incompatible and choices need to be made "[30]

A lifelong Zionist, Berlin was closely associated with Weizmann and, although supportive of Israel, not willing to identify himself as anything but a British Jew. In his essay published in 1951 in the *Jewish Chronicle* entitled "Jewish Slavery and Emancipation," he claimed for Jews the freedom for the first time to choose from a fuller range of possibilities while also saying that full assimilation was not a true possibility. The existence of Israel provided the alternative of living a purely Jewish life undeformed by the repression by non-Jews. However, for some like himself, he could find his identity in Britain but in the defence of Israel as a necessary condition for Jews to have that freedom to choose.

He eloquently expressed his own position in British society when he described the role of the Jew as the outsider who cannot escape his difference from the "native." The accuracy of his observation of the native society reflected his distinctiveness and nonbelonging.[31] He was speaking of himself as being like "an anthropologist studying a tribe . . . [who] could prosper if he made himself more of an expert on the customs of the tribes than the natives." His own social success was due to such finely tuned radar, but he could see his own sensitivities as a deformation . . . too eager for Gentile approval."

As the most-respected Jewish figure in British intellectual life, Berlin was able to get support from Isaac Wolfson in building a new college at Oxford from 1966 onward. The intersection of Berlin with Wolfson as the premier philanthropist of postwar Britain represented the coming of age of the East European contribution to British cultural life. Wolfson College was the largest single philanthropy of the Wolfson Foundation, the source of much of the private funding of hospitals and universities in Britain in the postwar era.[32] Wolfson's father, Solomon, had migrated from Bialystok in Lita in the 1880s. A cabinetmaker, he settled in the Gorbals in Glasgow. One of thirteen children, Isaac left school at age fourteen. Moving to London in 1920, his success in business was legendary. His wealth was not his only legacy. He remained a man of almost simple piety, beginning and ending the day with prayer. He ate only in accordance with the laws of kashrut even when dining at Queen Elizabeth's table. He was the first president of the United Synagogue to be a practicing Jew. Charity has been a moral obligation for him in accordance with his Jewish identity.

Unlike Berlin who remained observant and connected to his Jewish roots even as a member of the Mandarin establishment, the route taken by David Daiches was entry into the literary and academic life as an Englishman. His life as the son of the rabbi was one that he did not at first see as incompatible with his life as a boy growing up in the wider society of Edinburgh. Indeed, his father had attempted to synthesize Orthodox Jewish and British culture. The entry of David Daiches into a career as a literary critic and university professor exemplifies the secular expression of the life of Torah study that his forbears brought to Britain.

David Daiches was born in Sunderland in 1912, the younger of two boys and with a younger sister. The family moved to Edinburgh in 1919 where his father became the rabbi who came to represent Scottish Jewry to the surrounding community. David grew up as a relatively lonely child; most sure of his membership in a family whose pedigree went back for generations of scholars including Rashi, the great commentator of the Scriptures in eleventh century. His life on the streets and parks of his beloved Edinburgh was distinct from the family life with his rabbi father on the Shabbat and holidays. The "two worlds" did not seem separate in his childhood. His father's role as a respected leader in the Jewish community, compatible with its Scottish Presbyterian surroundings, provided a sense of rightness. He and his brother picked up Hebrew as intrinsic to their daily life without much in the way of formal training. It was expected that, being the descendant of the countless generations of scholars, he would be able, as he did, to read with understanding any part of the Hebrew Bible.

In his adolescence, and particularly while at the University of Edinburgh, he began to experience his two worlds as distinct. Daiches chose agnosticism rather than some form of Judaism other than his father's Orthodoxy. As he could no longer believe in the divine origins of the Hebrew Bible and the Oral Law, he began to dissociate himself from his Jewish identity to immerse himself in the larger world of his literary interests. In his marriage to a non-Jewish woman, he wrestled with his love for his father and for his heritage and his ultimate respect for his father's dedication to his ministry.[33]

His career, first in the United States and then back in Britain, has reflected his split heritage. His extraordinary literary career has ranged from studies of Virginia Woolf to Willa Cather, his Scottish heritage in studies on Burns, Scott, Boswell, and Stevenson as well as Scotch Whiskey. He has also written on Milton, the King James Bible, and Moses. In the last, he explored, in an erudite fashion the man, Moses, and his role in the evolution of the Jewish people as expressed in the Torah and in the context of historical scholarship.[34] Daiches draws upon his childhood knowledge of Hebrew as a final tribute to the generations of scholars that preceded him.

For Jewish writers, the Holocaust has required them to reexamine their humanity as well as their Jewish identity. Particularly difficult to tackle for Jews in England was their safety while their brethren were being burned across the narrow stretch of the channel. Despite abundant information about the extent of the extermination going on, the powerlessness of the Jewish community in Britain, no less than the United States, precluded action. The powerlessness bred despair.[35] During the war, the British government was reluctant to emphasize the fate of the Jews, and the communal authorities were unable to have any significant impact.[36] By the end of the war, the particular fate of the Jews was of little concern to the British public at large. There was a general sense that the Jews had suffered badly, but such knowledge reinforced the belief that anti-Semitism was of the Jews' own making. The Holocaust made little impact on British society. As elsewhere, there was no widespread educational, artistic, or cultural attempt to confront the subject until the 1970s. With regard to the Holocaust and the pre- (and post) war British racism, there has been a conscious desire "to remember to forget."[37]

Compounding the issue of powerlessness in the face of the Holocaust and indifference to the fate of the Jews was the tension caused by the limited role of the intellectual in Jewish life in Britain. In 1964, in the American journal that had just published Philip Roth's "Writing About Jews," Dan Jacobson wrote a comparable article dealing with issues in "Jewish Writing in England."[38] Despite the defensiveness of the Jewish community in the United States to some of Roth's work, it was clear that there was an extraordinarily widespread acceptance of writing by Jews who were American. The contrast was made to the relative inhibition of Anglo-Jewish experience in contribution to the English literature. This has been an ongoing issue. Somewhat later, in 1970, Chaim Bermant[39] explored the marginality of the Jewish writer or artist to the Anglo-Jewish community. The high standing of Dan Jacobson, born and bred in South Africa rather than England, confirmed the issue of marginality of the Anglo-Jewish intellectual. In South Africa as in America, the Jew was not a "latecomer" as in Britain.

Jacobson suggested that there has "not been a place in England for the Jews." The awareness of this on the part of the Jews has inhibited the development of the feeling that their experience has been in any way central to the society. Such marginality reflected the peculiarly English sense of unity in terms of homogeneity and long-standing inheritance in which precedence has such power. The metaphor is of a family "in whose very being" and in whose literary tradition, riddled with anti-Semitism, the Jew is "the outsider." In England, the Jew is still an identifiable and distinct accretion. In the absence of integration in British society, it remained difficult for the Anglo-Jewish writer to speak to the wider society in his particularity. Because of the small number of Jews, the Jewish writer who writes in English on Jewish themes must write for more than his own people.

The Religious Strand

The interwar years had seen the success of the United Synagogue in maintaining the centralizing structure established in the nineteenth century despite the large number of immigrants. The postwar era saw a lesser level of affiliation along with a greater split between the various branches. In 1964,[40] the basic fact was that the great bulk of the community "has only the slightest concern with Judaism." During the interwar period, synagogue marriages were overwhelmingly carried out in the United Synagogue. In the late postwar era, 1976-1980, there has been a large absolute decrease in the number of synagogue marriages, reflecting the secularization of the community and outmarriage. There was a rise in marriages in the more "progressive" synagogues identified as Liberal or Reform (from 3 ppercent to nearly 22 percent) and in the right-wing Orthodox, from less than 1 percent to over 7 percent with an overall fall to 68 percent in the United Synagogue whose adherents are more in the provinces.[41]

The synagogal religious structure had been the traditionally major unifying force. Its stresses came to public notice in the context of the *Jacobs Affair* in the 1960s with the impact felt in the subsequent decade in the figures reflecting decline in synagogue connection. The latitudinal nature of normative British Orthodoxy became less of a tent with the rise of both Progressive and Liberal Judaism as well as more restrictive Orthodoxy. Nonetheless, the original impetus for the more religious to opt for Britain rather than America remains with the persistence of the greater strength of "normative" Orthodoxy versus other denominations.

Louis Jacobs was born in Manchester, the son of working-class, British-born Jews.[42] He studied at a local grammar school. At fifteen, he joined the Manchester Yeshivah and graduated at age twenty-two with a rabbinical diploma. He then went to the center of higher Talmudic studies at Gateshead near Newcastle-on-Tyne, the heartland of Orthodoxy. He received recognition there for his Talmudic learning. After graduation, he became the assistant to the rabbi at the ultra-Orthodox Golders Green Synagogue while getting a doctorate at University College at the University of London. From there, he moved to the Manchester Central Synagogue and then to the New West End Synagogue in London. It was the latter that had first, in the nineteenth century, sought the minor changes in the liturgy that had aroused the ire of the then chief rabbi. It had now become the premier pulpit in the United Synagogue. While there, he was widely admired as a teacher, preacher, and thinker. His books included a translation of the *Tract on Ecstasy* written by the son of the founder of Lubavitch Hassidism. He appeared to represent a person eminently qualified to be a potential chief rabbi.

Published in 1957, his book *We Have Reason to Believe*, was a popular book designed to defend modern Orthodoxy. However, he appeared to discern a human agent in the composition of the Torah. Despite concern as to his heretical leaning on the part of some Orthodox leaders, he was nevertheless appointed in 1959 by the then Chief Rabbi Brodie to the faculty of the Jews' College. As the training institution for the rabbinate of Britain and the British Commonwealth, it was in need of rejuvenation. Despite his success as a tutor at the college, he was not appointed to fill the vacancy as its principal in 1961. The chief rabbi chose to follow the concerns of the more Orthodox members of his beth din in failing to confirm Jacobs as principal. Considerable public notice began to appear in the newspapers of this controversy with support for Jacobs by the *Jewish Chronicle*. When in 1964, the position of rabbi at New West End again became available, Jacobs was invited to come back to his previous pulpit. Chief Rabbi Brodie, for the same reasons, now refused to certify him as was required under the United Synagogue rules. When nonetheless reappointed by the congregation, the battle had become one of the authority of the chief rabbi. The chief rabbinate was one of the most revered elements of the established order, and Brodie was upheld by the Council of the United Synagogue in a hurried vote led by Sir Isaac Wolfson.[43] The hurried nature of the vote reflected the extent of publicity and the concern of communal leadership that any notice outside the community was "washing our dirty linen in public."

Dr. Jacobs then organized another synagogue, the New London Synagogue, with considerable support from his former congregants. Jacobs had hoped to excite the Jewish public about its faith, to make them think anew. This was not successful beyond his personal adherents. Several other attempts to extend such thinking onto a larger group in Glasgow and in Hendon in Northwest London did not succeed. Once again, the centralizing tendencies of organization on the Anglican model failed to enable the rejuvenation of the faith, to enable modern Judaism to be taken seriously by the mainstream of Anglo-Jewry.

Anglo-Jewish History

That the lack of recognition of Anglo-Jewish history remains is evidenced by work done in the development in 1990 of a National History Curriculum for the schools in response to the more varied character of the postwar British population. Even in respect to buildings, the recognition of British "heritage" has limited itself to Christian churches and cathedrals to the exclusion of other religions. The Holocaust as one of the central events of the twentieth century had been initially kept out of the National Curriculum.[58] Britain in general and Anglo-Jewry in particular has, unlike other countries with sizeable Jewish populations, taken very little notice of the Shoah. The only monument, for example, is a small one in Hyde Park.[59]

In 1956, the tercentenary of the Jewish Resettlement was marked with an Anglo-Jewish Historical Exhibition that represents a watershed in the representation of Anglo-Jewish history. For the first time, there were exhibits of Yiddish culture and immigrant life in the period 1880-1918. There remained the exclusion, even in the historical record, of the informal small synagogues or the immigrant's radical politics. The publication of Lloyd Gartner's book in 1960 *The Jewish Immigrant in England*[60] explored what had been relatively unexplored subjects such as the religious and political life of the immigrants. Noteworthy is that Gartner, an American, was the first to explore these subjects. It was only in 1987 that the celebration of the Jewish East End marked the coming of age of the new generation of historians of Jewish Britain.[61]

There has been a greater recognition of Jewish studies as an appropriate field of study by the academic community particularly at a graduate school level. A specific Jewish intellectual life at Oxford has continued to progress with the formation in 1972 of the Oxford Centre for Postgraduate Hebrew Studies under the leadership of David Patterson and with support from the Wolfson Family. The premier Department of Hebrew Studies at University College founded in 1827 was renamed in 1967 the Department of Hebrew and Jewish Studies and offers the full range of programs from undergraduate to doctoral.

As an early example, the program at Leicester University has been successful in incorporating elements of Jewish history into the general history degree. Aubrey Newman was its founder. Coming from an East European Litvak background via Glasgow, he was trained at the University of Glasgow and Oxford. He has organized several symposia under the auspices of JHSE dealing with the East End.[62] He has had particular interest in the factors affecting the largely Litvak immigration to South Africa as well as the United Kingdom. His election as president of the Jewish Historical Society of England from 1977 to 1999 can also be considered a milestone in the evolution of that organization in acceptance of the centrality of the study of the East European immigration.

The historians of this post-Holocaust generation do not consider themselves as successors to Cecil Roth. Unlike the more defensive interwar generation, focus is not on covering up the fissures based on class and other social issues but placing these at the center of intracommunal conflict transcending the undoubted ethnic bonds.[63] They have assessed anti-Semitism as being both more deeply rooted and less peripheral to the existence of the community and its needs. As a corollary, the impact of the disdainful attitude toward Jews has been understood to undermine the ability of the community to act in its own behalf and ultimately its long term survival.[64] More than in the past, focus has been on the period of immigration and acculturation lasting until the close of Second World War. It has been suggested that their celebration of those antiestablishment traditions of trade unionists, anarchists and Communists reflects their own political preferences.[65]

There also has been the concomitant development of university programs that have added legitimacy to what had previously been considered as too parochial an interest to warrant entry into the precincts of academia. Underlying the increased interest of Anglo-Jewish history in its own right is the possibility that Britain might be moving toward a more multiethnic society with the postwar immigration from the Caribbean as well as Asia. There has been a questioning about the fate of Jewish culture in Britain and the reasons why Anglo-Jewry was mired in self-effacement and apologetics.[66] There has thus been a reconnection with the broader stream of British life while recognizing that those junctures present problems as well as successes.

The conditions under which the relatively few Jews entered into the political life of the nation in the mid-nineteenth century were shaped by the fact that Britain was an explicitly Christian country with an established church. The Anglo-Jewish Liberal bargain was severely threatened by the far greater number of East European immigrants in the latter part of that century, mainly derived from Lita, the northwest provinces of the Russian Pale of Settlement. Their relatively intellectual religiosity as well as secular *Yiddishkayt* and Socialism evolved somewhat differently in Britain from elsewhere in the Litvak Diaspora. Although actually small in number and in percentage of the population, the immigration was widely thought to be alien and excessive. Attempts to anglicize the immigrants and bring them under social control were based upon the relatively great financial and political resources of the upper class Jewish Establishment and were consistent with the general tenor of class-based British life. Nevertheless, London was for a time the center of Jewish radical politics even before New York in the person of Aron Lieberman and Morris Winchevsky, literature with Israel Zangwill, misnagdim religiosity with Rabbis Werner, and Zionism with Chaim Weizmann.

With the reduced immigration following the Aliens Act in 1905 and the ever more stringent application of its principles, the immigrants and their British-born children entered into political life on their own behalf, primarily via socialist Labour rather than the Liberal Party. Anglo-Jewry's unusually sensitive role in the implementation of the British Mandate for a Jewish National Home in Palestine made Zionism an important factor in internal communal politics. During the interwar period, the defensiveness of the organized Jewish community in face of native fascism and anti-Semitism led to the rise of alternative political groups outside the existing structure. These included both increasingly acceptable Zionism as well as generally unacceptable Communism. The old class-based communal structure leadership opened to a somewhat broader constituency as Britain simultaneously ceased to be the world power uniquely identified with Zionist aspirations. Much of the new leadership in cultural as well as political life arose from the new immigrant stock in persons such as Isaac Rosenberg, Cecil Roth, Selig Brodetsky, Harold Laski, and the Rabbis Daiches.

In the postwar era, the increased opportunities in education helped Anglo-Jewry make a transition to now-secularized intellectual and cultural East European roots. Writers like Arnold Wesker and Emmanuel Litvinov, poets such as Dannie Abse and

Jon Silkin and their expression through the Jewish Quarterly were limited but did succeed in dealing with both their British and Jewish attributes. For David Daiches, his ancient connections remained but transformed into mainly secular and non-Jewish areas; Isaiah Berlin represented the entry of Jews into the intellectual establishment while retaining his connection with Judaism. There has been exploration of the old Anglo-Jewish "bargain" by the group of New Historians and the recognition in academia associated with the development of centers for Jewish studies in several universities.

The metaphor of "The Exodus" has been used to describe the evolution of Jewish life in Britain since 1967.[67] The biblical language does not infer a religious revival but rather the ongoing adaptive nature of the Jewish people so soon after the Holocaust, the ultimate "Egypt." This is evidenced in a variety of alternative ways of expressing one's spiritual roots in Judaism such as Louis Jacobs in Anglo-Orthodoxy, of revival of Jewish learning, of Jewish feminism, and of continuation of the commitment to *tikkun olam,* of healing the world. All this still harkens back to the sense of messianism that pervaded the religious world rooted in Lita that was the main cultural as well as the genetic source for the British branch of the Litvak Diaspora, limited in its expression by the character of the larger British culture.

Notes:

3.1   The Nature of the Place

1   David S. Katz, *Philo-Semitism and the Readmission of Jews to England,* Oxford, 1982, 161

2   ibid, 175

3   M.C.N. Salbstein, *The Emancipation of the Jews in Britain,* Rutherford, NJ, 1982, 36

4   ibid, 45

5   David Katz, op cit 1994, 241

6   Todd Endelman, *The Jews of Georgian England,* Philadelphia, 1979, 24-27, 90-92

7   David Katz, *The Jews in the History of England, 1485-1850,* Oxford, 1994, 246

8   ibid, 240-254

9   ibid, 364

10   ibid,358-363

11   Geoffrey Alderman, "English Jews or Jews of the English Persuasion," In Pierre Birnbaum and Ira Katznelson, Eds,., *Paths of Emancipation,* Princeton, 1995, 129

12   David Feldman, *Englishmen and Jews, Social Relations and Political Culture, 1840-1914,* New Haven, 1994, 4

13   David Katz, op cit, 1994, 386

14   David Feldman op cit, 1994, 31-34

15   M.C.N. Salbstein, op cit, 1982, 217

16   David Katz, op cit, 1994, 384-389

17   Abraham Gilam, *The Emancipation of the Jews in England, 1820-1860,* New York, 1982, 149-153

18   Todd Endelman and Tony Kushner, "Introduction," In Todd Endelman and Tony Kushner, Eds., *Disraeli's Jewishness,* Portland, OR, 2002

19   Jaime Bronstein, op cit, 2000

20   Geoffrey Alderman, *Modern British Jewry,* Oxford, 1992.3

21   ibid,20-29

22   ibid,13-17

23   Vivian Lipman, *A History of the Jews in Britain Since 1858,* New York, 1990, 5-7

24 Todd Endelman, "The Englishness of Jewish Modernity in England," In Jacob Katz, Ed., *Towards Modernity*, New Brunswick, NJ, 1987 p 231-33

25 Stephen Sharot, "Reform and Liberal Judaism in London, 1840-1940," 1979, *Jewish Social Studies*, 41:211

26 Cecil Roth, *Essays and Portraits in Anglo-Jewish History*, Philadelphia, 1962, 250-261

27 Geoffrey Alderman, op cit. 1992, 40-45

28 Steven Singer, "The Anglo-Jewish Minority in Early Victorian London," 1985, *Modern Judaism*, 5: 279.

29 Michael Goulston, "The State of the Anglo-Jewish Rabbinate, 1849-1914," *Jewish Journal of Sociology*, 1964, 10: 55

30 Chaim Bermant, *The Cousinhood*, London, 1971 passim

31 Aubrey Newman, *The United Synagogue, 1870-1970*, London, 1976, 17-35, 112-121

32 Israel Finestein, *Anglo-Jewry in Changing Times*, London, 1999, 92-7

33 Vivian Lipman, op cit, 1990,12; David Feldman, op cit. 1994, 69-71

34 Leonard Prager, *Yiddish Culture in Britain*, Frankfurt-on-Main, 1990, 85

35 David Feldman, op cit, 1994,141

36 ibid, 171

37 Lloyd Gartner, *The Jewish Immigrant in England, 1880-1914*, 2nd ed, 1971, London, 121

38 Lloyd Gartner, "Eastern European Immigration in England: A Quarter Century View," *Transactions Jewish Historical Society of England*, 1982-86, 29: 297

39 Stuart Cohen, "How Shall we Sing of Zion in a Strange Land? : East European Immigrants and the Challenge of Zionism in Britain, 1897-1918," *Jewish Social Studies*, 1994-1995. n.s. 1:66

40 Andrew Godley, *Jewish Immigrant Entrepreneurship in New York and London, 1880-1914*, New York, 2001, 86-87

41 Lloyd Gartner, "North Atlantic Jewry." In Aubrey Newman, Ed., *Migration and Settlement*, 1971, London, 18.

42 Leonard Prager, op cit, 1990, 85-88

43 Selma Berrol, *East Side/East End. East European Jews in London and New York 1870-1920*, Westport, CN, 1994, 11

44 Lloyd Gartner, *The Jewish Immigrant in England, 1870-1914*, 1st ed, London. 1960, 17

45 Vivian Lipman, op cit, 1990,14-16
46 Vivian Lipman, op cit, 1990, 44 ; David Feldman, op cit, 1994,155; Geoffrey Alderman, op cit, 1992, 111; Lloyd Gartner, op cit, 1960, 33
47 Andrew Godley, op cit, 2001, 65-66
48 Chaim Bermant, *Troubled Eden*, New York, 1970, 221-222
49 David Feldman, op cit, 1994, 159
50 Vivian Lipman, op cit, 1990, 49-50
51 ibid, 20
52 Bernard Gainer, *The Alien Invasion. The Origins of the Aliens Act of 1905*, New York, 1972, 3-4
53 David Feldman, op cit, 1994, 166
54 Harold Pollins, *Economic History of the Jews in England*, Rutherford, NJ, 1982, passim
55 Vivian Lipman, op cit, 1990, 56-59
56 Harold Pollins, op cit, 1982, 142-151
57 Andrew Godley, op cit, 2001, 127-129
58 Vivian Lipman, op cit, 1990, 60-61
59 Harold Pollins, op cit, 1982, 150
60 Geoffrey Alderman, op cit, 1992, 120-124
61 Leonard Prager op cit, 1990, 2-8
62 Geoffrey Alderman, op cit, 1995, 140-141
63 Nancy Green, "The Modern Jewish Diaspora.: East European Jews in New York, London and Paris," In Todd Endelman, Ed., *Comparing Jewish Societies*, Ann Arbor, 1997
64 Severin Hochberg, "The Repatriation of East European Jews from Great Briatain, 1881-1914," Jewish Social Studies, 1988-92, 50:49.
65 Geoffrey Alderman, op cit, 1992, 120-124
66 Selma Berrol, op cit, 1994, 26
67 Jerry White, *Rothschild Buildings: Life in an East End Tenement Block: 1887-1920*, London, 1980, 7-30
68 Colin Holmes, *John Bull's Island: Immigration and British Society, 1871-1971*, Basingstoke, Hants, 1988, 69
69 Jay Pilzer, "The Jews and the Great 'Sweated Labor' Debate, 1888-1892, 1979, *Jewish Social Studies*, 41: 257
70 Geoffrey Alderman, op cit, 1992, 122-125
71 Claire Hirshfield, "The British 'left' and the 'Jewish Conspiracy': A Case Study in Modern Ant-Semitism," *Jewish Social Studies*, 1981, 43: 95; Geoffrey Alderman, op cit, 1992, 133-134
72 Colin Holmes, *Anti-Semitism in British Society*, New York, 1979, 116-120

73 Todd Endelman, "Native Jews and Foreign Jews in London, 1870-1914," In David Berger, Ed., *Legacy of Jewish Migration, 1881 and its Impact*, New York, 1983, 120-121

74 Eugene Black, *The Social Politics of Anglo-Jewry, 1880-1920*, Oxford, 1988 p254-257

75 Severin Hochberg, op cit, 1988-92

76 Geoffrey Alderman, op cit, 1995, 148

77 Vivian Lipman, op cit, 1990, 76

78 Geoffrey Alderman, op cit, 1992, 136-137

79 David Feldman, op cit, 1994, 157

80 J.M. Ross, "The Naturalization of Jews in England," *Transactions of the Jewish Historical Society of England*, 1970-73, 24:59.

81 Peter Stansky, "Anglo-Jew or English/British? Some Dilemmas of Anglo-Jewish History," *Jewish Social Studies*, N.S. 1995-96, 2: 150

82 Eugene Black, op cit, 1988, 317-320

83 David Feldman, op cit, 1994, 370-378

84 Vivian Lipman, op cit, 1990, 73-75

85 David Cesarini, "Joynson-Hicks and the Radical Right in England after the First World War," In Tony Kushner and Kenneth Lunn, Eds., *Traditions of Intolerance*, Manchester, 1989, 118-139

86 J.M. Ross, op cit, 1970-73

87 Nancy Green, op cit, 1997

88 David Cesarani, *The 'Jewish Chronicle' and Anglo-Jewry: 1841-1991*, Cambridge, 1994 p75

89 Nancy Green, op cit, 1997

89 Selma Berrol, op cit, 1994, 37

90 ibid, 49

91 Geoffrey Alderman, op cit, 1995, 143-145

92 Rosalyn Livshin, "The Acculturation of the Children of Immigrant Jews in Manchester, 1890-1930," In David Cesarini, Ed., *The Making of Modern Anglo-Jewry*, Oxford, 1990

93 Selma Berrol, op cit, 1994, 50-54

94 ibid, 98-99

95 ibid, 146

95 Sharman Kadish, "Ironing Out the 'Ghetto Bend': The Impact of the Jewish Lads'Brigade on the Jewish Immigrant in England, 1895-1914," In Aubrey Newman and Stephen Massil Eds., *Patterns of Migration*, 1850-1914, London, 1996

96 Stephen Sharot, op cit, 1973

97 Daniel Gutwein, *The Divided Elite: Economics, Politics and Anglo-Jewry*, Leiden, 1992, 145-288
98 Eugene Black, op cit, 1988, 61-62
99 Geoffrey Alderman, op cit, 1992, 165

3.2 The Evolution of the Culture
3.2.1 The Immigrant Generation

1   Geoffrey Alderman, 1995, In Pierre Birnbaum and Ira Katznelson Eds, op cit, 149
2   Vivian Lipman, op cit, 1990, 101
3   Peter Elman, "The Beginnings of the Jewish Trade Union Movement in England," *Transactions of the Jewish Historical Society of England*, 1951-52, 17: 53.
4   William Fishman, *Jewish Radicals*, New York, 1974, 98-111
5   Elias Tsherikower, *The Early Jewish Labor Movement in the United States*, New York, 1961 p179-183
6   Anne Kershen, "Trade Unionism Among Jewish Tailoring Workers of London and Leeds 1872-1915," In David Cesarini Ed., op cit, 1990,42; William Fishman, op cit, 1974,114-122
7   William Fishman, op cit, 1974, 121-134
8   Geoffrey Alderman, *The Jewish Community in British Politics*, Oxford, 1983, 49
9   Leonard Prager, op cit, 1990, 21
10   William Fishman, op cit, 1974, 140-151
11   Geoffrey Alderman, 1990 op cit, 179
12   William Fishman, op cit, 1974, 194
13   ibid, 150-164
14   Stuart Cohen, op cit, 1982, 59
15   Geoffrey Alderman, op cit, 1983, 59
16   Lloyd Gartner, 1960, op cit, 257-260
17   William Fishman, op cit, 1974, 229-302
18   David Feldman, op cit, 1994, 216-226
19   Roy Helfgott, "Trade Unionism Among the Jewish Garment Workers of Briatain and the United States," *Labor History*, 1961 2:202; Vivian Lipman, op cit, 1990, 102-105; Tcherikower, op cit, 1961, 196-199
20   Kershen, op cit, 1990, 43-52
21   Bernard Homa, *Orthodoxy in Anglo-Jewry, 1840-1940*, London, 1969, 21
22   Leonard Prager, op cit, 1990, 172-173

23 Geoffrey Alderman, "Not Quite British: The Political Attitudes of Anglo-Jewry" In Ivor Crewe, Ed., *Politics of Race*, New York, 1975

24 Geoffrey Alderman, op cit, 1992, 144-150

25 W.D. Rubinstein, *A History of the Jews in the English Speaking World, v. I Great Britain*, Basingstoke, Hants, 1996 p240; Bernard Homa, op cit, 1969 p27

26 Nancy Green, op cit, 1997, 195-197

27 Bryan Cheyette, "The Other-Self: Anglo-Jewish Fiction and Representation of Jews in England, 1875-1905," In David Cesarini Ed., op cit, 1990

28 Maurice Wohlgerenter, *Israel Zangwill: A Study*, New York, 1964 p11-19

29 Elsie Adams, *Israel Zangwill*, New York, 1971, 19-24

30 Bryan Cheyette, *Modernity, Culture and the 'Jew*, Stanford, 1998, xvi-xx

31 Stuart Cohen, *English Zionists and British Jews*, Princeton, 1982, 85-104

32 Maurice Wohlgerenter, op cit, 1964, 14

33 Bryan Cheyette, op cit 1995

34 Michael Berkowitz, *Zionist Culture and West European Jewry Before the First World War*, Cambridge, 1993, 2-6

35 Stuart Cohen, op cit, 1982, 32

36 W.D. Rubinstein, op cit, 1996, 164-166

37 Stuart Cohen, op cit, 1982, 48

38 Lloyd Gartner, op cit, 1960, 265-267

39 Stuart Cohen, op cit, 1982, 202

40 Vivian Lipman, op cit, 1990, 122-125

41 Stuart Cohen, op cit, 1982, 163-183

42 Michael Berkowitz, op cit, 1993, 12-13

43 Stuart Cohen, op cit, 1982, 67-75

44 Isaiah Berlin, *Personal Impressions*, New York, 1980, 38

45 ibid,. 41-42

46 Yehuda Reinharz, *Chaim Weizmann. The Making of a Zionist Leader*, New York, 1985, 10-25

47 ibid, 32-42

48 Michael Berkowitz, op cit, 1993, 43

49 Yehuda Reinharz, op cit, 1985, 65-91

50 Isaiah Berlin, op cit, 1980, 52

51 Stuart Cohen, op cit, 1982, 112-123

52 W.D. Rubinstein, op cit, 1996, 168-169

53 Stuart Cohen, op cit, 1982, 243-276; Geoffrey Alderman, op cit, 1992, 247-249;

54   Barbara Tuchman, *The Bible and the Sword*, New York 1984, 312
55   Vivian Lipman, op cit, 1990, 129-133
56   Isaiah Berlin, op cit, 1980, 54-57
57   Yehuda Reinharz, op cit, 1985, 403-406

3.2.2The Acculturated Generation

1   W.D. Rubinstein, op cit, 1996, 229
2   David Cesarini, "Communal Authority in Anglo-Jewry," In David
     Cesarini, Ed., *The Making of Modern Anglo-Jewry*, Oxford, 1990
3   W.D. Rubinstein, op cit, 1996, 235; Vivian Lipman, op cit, 1990, 218
4   Barry Kosmin, "Localism and Pluralism in British Jewry 1900-1980,"
     Transaction Jewish Historical Society of England, 1981-82, 28: 111
5   Todd Endelman, *Radical Assimilation in English Jewish History, 1656-
     1948*, Bloomington, IN, 1990, 182
6   Elaine Smith, "Jews and Politics in the East End of London," In David
     Cesarini, Ed., op cit, 1990
7   Vivian Lipman, op cit, 1990, 208-210
8   David Cesarini, op cit, vide supra1990
9   Vivian Lipman, op cit, 1990 p210-215)
10   Harold Pollins, op cit, 1982, 191-103, 186-188
11   Gideon Shimoni, "Poale Zion: A Zionist Transplant in Britain,
     1905-1945," In Peter Medding, Ed., *Studies in Contemporary Jewry*,
     Bloomington, IN, 1986
12   Geoffrey Alderman, op cit. 1995 In Pierre Birnbaum and Ira
     Katznelson, Eds., op cit, 151
13   David Cesarini, op cit, 1990
14   Sharman Kadish, op cit, 1988-92
15   John Callaghan, *Socialism in Britain Since 1884*, Oxford, 1990, 76-77;
     Keith Layborn and Dylan Murphy, *Under the Red Flag: A History of
     Communism in Britain 1849-1991*, Phoenix Mill, 1999, 76-92
16   Sharman Kadish, *Bolsheviks and British Jews: The Anglo-Jewish Community,
     Britain and the Russian Revolution*, London, 1992 p229-241
17   Sharman Kadish, "The 'Letter of the Ten, Bolsheviks and British Jews,"
     In Jonathan Frankel, Ed., *Studies in Contemporary Jewry*, Oxford, 1988, 96
18   Geoffrey Alderman, *The Jewish Community in British Politics*, Oxford,
19   83 p102-107
19   Joseph Gorny, *The British Labour Movement and Zionism*, Totowa, NJ,
     Routledge 1983, xii

20 Gideon Shimoni, op cit, 1986
21 Kenneth Collins, "Scottish Transmigration and Settlement," In Aubrey Newman and Stephen Massil, Eds, op cit 1996
22 Ralph Glasser, *Growing Up In the Gorbals*, London, 1999, 26-34
23 Emmanuel Shinwell, *I've Lived Through It All*, London, 1973, 20
24 Joseph Gorny, op cit, 1983, 55
25 Ibid, 214
26 Michael Berkowitz, *The Jewish Self-Image in the West*, New York, 2000, 127
27 Geoffrey Alderman, op cit,1992, 255
28 Ibid, 255-258
29 Elaine Smith, In David Cesarini, op cit, 1990
30 Geoffrey Alderman, "M.H. Davis: The Rise and Fall of a communal Upstart," *Transactions Jewish Historical Society of Britain*, 1988-1990 31: 249
31 Elaine Smith, "But What Did They Do? Contemporary Responses to Cable Street," In Tony Kushner and Nadia Valman, Eds., *Remembering Cable Street,: Fascism and Anti-Fascism in British Society*, London, 2000
32 Geoffrey Alderman, op cit, 1992, 217; Geoffrey Alderman, op cit, 1988-1990
33 Michael Berkowitz, op cit, 2000, 128; Geoffrey Alderman, op cit, 1992, 265-270; Geoffrey Alderman 1 "The Political Impact of Zionism in the East End before 1940," In Aubrey Newman, Ed., *The East End*, London, 1981
34 Elsie Janner, *Barnett Janner: A Personal Portrait*, 1984, 1-43 and passim
35 Isaac Kramnick and Barry Sheerman, *Harold Laski: A Life on the Left*, New York, 1993, 1-4
36 Joseph Gorny, op cit, 1983, 227
37 W. D. Rubinstein op cit, 1996, 477 n.44
38 Kingley Martin, *Harold Laski*, New York, 1953
39 Isaac Kramnick and Barry Sheerman op cit, 1993, 10
40 Bill Williams, "East and West: Class and Culture in Manchester Jewry, 1850-1920," *Studia Rosenthalia*, 1989, 23: 88
41 Isaac Kramnick and Barry Sheerman, op cit, 1993, 19
42 Kingley Martin, op cit, 1953, 1-14
43 Ibid, 14-18
44 Ibid, 77-94
45 Ibid, 243
46 Tony Kushner, "British Anti-Semitism. 1918-1945, In David Cesarini, Ed., op cit, 1990

47 Louis London, *Whitehall and the Jews: 1933-1948*, Cambridge, 2000, 5

48 Tony Kushner, in David Cesarini, op cit 1990,

49 Elaine Smith, In Tony Kushner and Nadia Valman, Eds., op cit, 2000

50 William Fishman, East End Radicals, 1875-1914, 1981

51 Henry Srebrnik, *London Jews and British Communism*, Portland, OR, 1995, 53-57

52 W.D. Rubinstein, op cit, 1996, 245

53 Sharman Kadish, op cit, 1992, 246-247

54 Geoffrey Alderman, op cit., 1983, 117-127

55 Aubrey Newman, op cit, 1976, 112

56 Lloyd Gartner, op cit, 1973, 216

57 Michael Goulston, op cit, 1964; *Albert Hymanson, Jews' College, London, 1855-1955*, London, 1955, 82

58 David Daiches, *Two Worlds. An Edinburgh Childhood*, Tuscaloosa, AL, 1989, 82-105

59 Chaim Bermant, op cit, 1970

60 Geoffrey Alderman, op cit, 1992, 262

61 Jon Silkin, "Isaac Rosenberg," In Jon Silkin, *Out of the Battle: Poetry of the Great War*, London, 1972

62 Joseph Cohen, *Journey to the Trenches. The Life of Isaac Rosenberg*, London, 1975, 7-20

63 Diana Collecott, "Isaac Rosenberg: A Cross-Cultural Study," In Aubrey Newman, Ed., op cit, 1981

64 Joseph Cohen, op cit, 1975, 67-122 passim

65 ibid, 174-187

66 Todd Endelman, op cit, 1990, 187-189

67 Lucien Wolf, "Jewish Historical Society: A Plea for Anglo-Jewish History," *Transactions Jewish Historical Society of England*, 1893, 1:1; Lucien Wolf, "Origins of the Jewish Historical Society of England, *Transactions of the Jewish Historical Society of England*, 1911-14, 7:206.

68 Peter Stansky, op cit, 1995-96

69 Stephen Massil, "The Foundation of the Jewish Historical Society of England," *Transactions of the Jewish Historical Society of England*, 1992-93, 33:225.

70 Jaime Bronstein, "Rething the Readmission: Anglo-Jewish history and the immigration Crisis," In Neville Thompson, Ed., *Singular Continuities*, Stanford, CA, 2000

71   Geoffrey Alderman, "The Young Cecil Roth," *Transactions Jewish Historical Society of England*, 1994-96, 34:1

72   Leonard Prager, op cit, 1990, 557

73   Frederic Krome, "Creating Jewish History for our own needs: The Evolution of Cecil Roth's Historical Vision, 1925-1935," *Modern Judaism*, 2001,21:216

74   Cecil Roth, "The Jewish Historical Society of England: The Challenge to Jewish History," *Transactions of the Jewish Historical Society of England*, 1935-39, 14: 1

75   Cecil Roth, *A History of the Jews in England*, Oxford, 1964, 269-270

76   Chaim Raphael, "In Search of Cecil Roth," *Commentary*, 197022:75

77   Selig Brodetsky, *Memoirs: From Ghetto to Israel*, London, 1960, 28-29

78   ibid, 48

79   Gideon Shimoni, "Selig Brodetsky and the Ascendancy of Zionism in Anglo-Jewry, 1939-1945," *Jewish Journal of Sociology*, 1980, 23:125

80   Selig Brodetsky, op cit, 1960, 61

81   Chaim Bermant, op cit, 1970, 112

82   Selig Brodetsky, op cit, 1960, 68-71

83   Aubrey Newman, *The Jewish East End, 1840-1939*, London, 1980

84   Geoffrey Alderman, op cit 1992, 265-270

85   Tony Kushner, op cit, 2000

86   Geoffrey Alderman, op cit, 1992, 282-300

87   Bernard Wasserstein, Britain and the Jews of Europe, 1939-1945, London, 1999, 17-35

88   Morris Beckman, *The Hackney Crucible*, London, 1996 passim and, 155-172

89   Tony Lerman, The 'Habonim' Story: The Formative Years," *Jewish Quarterly* 1978, 25:33.

90   Gideon Shimoni op cit, 1980

91   David Cesarini, op cit, 1990

92   Gideon Shimoni, op cit, 1980

93   ibid,

94   Richard Bolchover, *British Jews and the Holocaust*, Cambridge, 1993, 31-37

95   Tony Kushner, "The Paradox of Prejudice: The Impact of Organized Anti-Semitism in Britain in an Anti-Nazi War," In Tony Kushner and Kenneth Lunn, Eds., op cit, 1989

96   ibid

3.2.2 The Post-War Generation

1   Todd Endelman, *The Jews of Britain*, 1656-2000, Berkeley, 2002
2   Geoffrey Alderman, op cit, 1992, 321-331
3   Ernest Krausz, "The Economic and Social Structure of Anglo-Jewry," In Julius Gould and Shaul Esh, Eds., *Jewish life in Modern Britain*, London, 1964
4   Harold Pollin, op cit, 1982, 209-217
5   Geoffrey Alderman, 'Jewish Political Attitudes and Voting Patterns in England, 19451987," In Robert Wistrich, Ed., *Terms of Survival: The Jewish World Since 1945*, 1995,
6   Harold Pollins, op cit, 1982, 218-235
7   Sylvia Budd, *The Road from Janova: A Family History*, 2001 passim; Personal communication, Timothy Bernard
8   Geoffrey Alderman, op cit, 1975
9   Geoffrey Alderman, op cit, 1992, 339-350
10 W.D. Rubinstein, op cit, 1982, 157
11 Geoffrey Alderman, "The Political Conservatism of the Jews in Britain, In Pater Medding, Ed., *Studies in Contemporary Jewry*, XI, New York, 1995
12 Reade Dornan, *Arnold Wesker Revisited*, New York, 1994, 16
13 Harold Ribalow, *Arnold Wesker*, New York, 1965
14 Stephen Tabatchnick and William Baker, "Reflections of Ethnicity in Anglo-Jewish Writing," In Jacob Sonntag, Ed., *Jewish Writing Today*, London, 1974
15 Robert Wilcher, *Understanding Arnold Wesker*. Columbia, SC, 1991, 1-21
16 Arnold Wesker, *Distinctions*, 1985, 255
17 Heiner Zimmermann, "Arnold Wesker and the Desire for Utopia: Utopia's Enemies and Wesker," In Reade Dornan, Ed., *Arnold Wesker*, New York, 1998, 55
18 Arnold Wesker, op cit, 1985, 252-283
19 Reade Dornan, op cit, 1994, 103
20 Reade Dornan, op cit, 1998, 76
21 Arnold Wesker, *As Much As I Dare*, London, 1994, 15-25
22 Reade Dornan, op cit, 1994, 11-13
23 Ronald Haymen, *Arnold Wesker*, London, 1970, 5
24 Glenda Lemming, *Wesker, The Playwright*, London, 1983, 1-44
25 Reade Dornan, op cit, 1998, 81
26 Michael Ignatieff, *Isaiah Berlin*, New York, 1998, 13 ibid, 292, 14-35 passim

27 Isaiah Berlin, 1980 op cit, li-liii ibid xv-xxiii ibid, 21-23 ibid, 162-185

28 Chaim Bermant, op cit, 1970. 141-144

29 David Daiches, op cit, 1989, 142-150 passim

30 David Daiches, *Moses; The man and his Vision*, New York, 1975, 240-251.

31 Richard Bolshover, op cit, 1993, 7-20

32 Colin Holmes, "Britain and the Jews of Europe," *Jewish Journal of Sociology*, 1980, 22:59

33 Tony Kushner, "Remembering to Forget: Racism and Anti-Racism in Post-War Britain," In Bryan Cheyette and Laura Marcus, Eds., *Modernity, Culture and the 'Jew',* " Stanford, 1998

34 Dan Jacobson, "Jewish Writing in England," *Commentary*, 1964, 37: #5, 46 50

35 Chaim Bermant, op cit, 1970, 168-177

36 Norman Cohen, "Trends in Anglo-Jewish Religious Life," In Julius Gould and Shaul Esh, Eds., op. cit, 1964

37 Barry Kosmin, op cit, 1981-82

38 Chaim Bermant, op cit, 1970, 239-253

39 David Cesarini, "David Kessler and the 'Jewish Chronicle,'" In Alan Crown, Ed., *Noblesse Oblige: Essays in Honour of David Kessler, OBE*, London, 1998

40 Efraim Sicher, *Beyond Marginality : Anglo-Jewish Literature After the Holocaust*, Albany, 1985, 24-25 ibid, 35

41 Dannie Abse, "Portrait of a Jewish Poet," *Jewish Quarterly*, 1954, 1:16

42 Emmanuel Litvinoff, *Notes for a Survivor*, Newcastle-on-Tyne, 1972 ibid ibid

43 Efrai Sicher, op cit, 1985, 34-39

44 Dannie Abse, op cit, 1954

45 Efaim Sicher, op cit, 1985, 143

46 Jon Silkin, "Some Reflections on Anglo-Jewish Poetry," In Jacob Sonntag, Ed., *Caravan: Jewish Quarterly Omnibus*, New York, 1962

47 Efaim Sicher, op cit, 1985, 160 ibid, 143-149 ibid, 154

48 Stephen Brooks, *The Club: The Jews of Modern Britain*, London, 1989, 319-331

49 Tony Kushner, *The Jewish Heritage in British History*, London, 1992, 1-20

50 Stephen Brooks, op cit, 1989, 421-425

51 Lloyd Gartner, op cit, 1960

52 Tony Kushner, op cit, 1992, 1-20

53 Aubrey Newman, *The Jewish East End 1840-1939*, London, 1980; *Patterns of Migration*, London, 1996

54 Lloyd Gartner, op cit, 1982-86

55 Todd Endelman, *The Jews of Britain*, Berkeley, 2000, 257-269.

56 Todd Endelman, "English Jewish History," *Modern Judaism*, 1991, 11:91

57 David Cesarini, *The Making of Modern Anglo-Jewry*, Oxford, 1990, 1-11

58 Howard Cooper and Paul Morrison, *A Sense of Belonging: Dilemmas of British Jewish Identity*, London, 1991, 105-155

CHAPTER 4
CANADA

4.1 The 'Main' of Montreal

4.1.1 A Bicultural Society

Canada now prides itself as a country that is a "mosaic," reflecting its heterogeneity. However, for most of its history, it was a bicultural society rather than a multicultural one. It has been called a *society* rather than a nation in that it has never become a centralized nation-state in the classic European model.[1] Its character lies in its both its European roots and its North American connection.

Its population centers are mainly strung along the southern tier close by its larger neighbor. Each of its major geographic regions has a natural affinity, looking south toward the United States whereas there are important difficulties in communication between east and west within Canada itself.[2] Hence comes its North American identity. Canada also looks to Europe in its origins. The important southern tier contains a French entity that has maintained its distinctive character. Its other European major entity is British, nurtured from the eighteenth-century remnants of the Loyalists exiled during the American Revolution. This ancestry has provided a degree of persistent *Toryism* that was absent in the United States. Its English-speaking segment has also been augmented by the European immigration of the nineteenth and early-twentieth centuries that were initially mainly from the British Isles.[3] As a settler nation within the nineteenth century British Empire like Australia and New Zealand, it evolved toward greater degrees of independence but has remained mainly tied to the Anglo-Saxon traditions of both Britain and the United States.

Canadian national character also derives from its regionalism. It is a federation of provinces split from its start by language, culture, and religion. *Confederation* in 1867 encompassed initially the major provinces of Upper (Ontario) and Lower Canada (Quebec) whose names derived from their position on the St. Lawrence River. Quebec City was founded by Champlain in 1608, and Montreal was founded in 1642. The first peasant farmers were brought from Normandy and Brittany under Cardinal Richelieu to become the pioneer "habitants" of New France. In 1663, the

absolutist regime of Louis XIV established direct royal control
with appointment of an intendant and governor to share power
with the bishop. The three pillars of the community were the
autocratic royal government, the adaptation of the feudal system
of land tenure under the rule of the seignior, and the Catholic
church.

The prototype ecclesiastical power was Bishop Laval who
arrived in 1659 and died in Quebec in 1708. The church was
committed to the establishment of a French Catholic colony in
the New World where both the religious and national elements
were inextricably intertwined. It had been established from the
beginning that education as well as religion was the province of
the Catholic church. French Canada was unique in the integration
of the church in the daily life of its inhabitants.[4]

The British victory on the Plains of Abraham in 1759 led to
the cession of Canada to Britain in 1763 at the end of the Seven
Years' War. The Quebec Act in 1769 reinforced the role of the
church and the feudal relationship to be the basis for British rule.
This was contrary to the direction being taken by the American
colonists that led soon after to the American Revolution.[5]

One residue of the American Revolution was to increase the
English-speaking population of Canada. The migration of United
Empire Loyalists led to the development of Upper Canada. There
was continuing migration of Americans into the farmlands of
Upper Canada with the spread of Protestant evangelical sects,
particularly Methodism. Kingston and York, later called Toronto,
were the towns of Upper Canada while Montreal was, by far, the
largest metropolis. English-speaking merchants who settled within
the boundaries of Lower Canada in Montreal were a minority but
retained their economic and political ambitions for hegemony.[6]
The Constitutional Act of 1791 divided the colony into the two
provinces of Lower and Upper Canada, one predominantly
French and the other English. The latter was to evolve consistent
with "freehold" mode of land tenure while the former could
retain its traditional character. Each was to have its own assembly.
The character of the linguistic, national, and religious divisions
within Quebec and between Quebec and the Western English-
speaking areas continue to define the evolution of Canada until
the present day.

The first Jews to arrive in Canada came in the 1760s with the British conquering army. Under the previous French regime, all non-Catholics had been forbidden. No professing Jew lived there, notwithstanding the major investment in colonization of New France provided by the Gradis family from the Sephardic Jewish community of Bordeaux. The positive Jewish view toward the Anglo-Canadian connection was colored from the start by this association with open immigration as well as Britain's reputation during the nineteenth century of political and moral virtue.[7] Many of the Jews who came in the wake of the British army had come from England or the British colonies on the eastern seaboard. Naturalization was thus not an issue. If they were foreign-born, the Naturalization Act of 1740 for the Colonies had given Jews rights in the British Colonies equal to non-Jews.

Aaron Phillip Hart was the most noteworthy of those early Jewish settlers. Born in London of German parents, he came to New York. He arrived in Canada as a commissary officer with General Amherst's army in 1762.[8] He settled in Trois-Rivières in Lower Canada. His family prospered, particularly in the fur trade.[9] Jewish merchants, such as Hart, identified with the British merchant class that had become powerful in Montreal and opposed the French *Parti canadien*. The governor was British as was his executive council while the popularly elected assembly was largely French.

After an election in 1808, caught up in the religious and sectional differences within the Assembly, Ezekial Hart, the second son of Aaron, was denied his seat on the basis that the oath required was "on the true faith of a Christian." After election, once again the following year, he was again expelled. Even further, a bill introduced by the French members to "disqualify Jews from being eligible to sit in the House of Assembly" was averted only by the dissolution of the assembly by the British governor, a friend of the Hart family. This fight to bar Jews was led by the French nationalist leader in the assembly who was also the founder of the first French-Canadian newspaper *Le Canadien*. Jews were now officially second-class citizens, unable to take office when an oath was required.[10] Other cases of discrimination appeared in the wake of this episode. A brother of Ezekial Hart was denied a commission in the militia on the basis of his religious affiliation.

A 1828 petition was successful for Jews to be recognized as a community with permission to maintain the register of births, marriages, and deaths. Ezekial's son Samuel Hart succeeded eventually in 1832 in the passage of the Jew Bill that established in a positive fashion the rights of Jews as of "all other natural-born British subjects.[11] Beyond the issue of political rights was the ongoing problem of the confessional nature of education.

In company with the far larger European immigration to the United States in the post-Napoleonic era, there was a substantial diversion that flowed to the provinces of Canada. The English-speaking population was augmented by about equal number of English and Scots. The massive Irish emigration of the famine era made them the largest of the three Anglophone "British" immigrant groups. By mid-nineteenth century, there had been a doubling of the population of Upper Canada, now known as Canada West whose total was now greater than what was now called Canada East. These two major segments along the St. Lawrence Valley had been united in a single entity called Canada and had autonomous parliamentary government since 1841. It was also during this time that the beginnings of French-Canadian cultural development occurred. The publication of the *Histoire du Canada* in 1845 was the start of the celebration of the virtues and achievements of the French-Canadian race.

There was a political deadlock based on sectional differences. The conservative elements of both sections united. The Catholic hierarchy and the other magnates united with the English mercantile class to form the basis for a government to take power. Under the leadership of John Alexander Macdonald and George-Étienne Cartier, the Liberal-Conservative Party became the basis for Confederation.[12] The British North America Act of 1867, the enabling Act that established confederation, reflected the legacy shared with Britain of constitutional monarchy, parliamentary institutions, and responsible government. There was no written Bill of Rights, but Canada was heir to the rights and privileges in continuity with British common law.

The largely Francophone provinces held about one million persons and the Anglophone provinces about two million in the 1871 census close to the time of Confederation. The French Canadians were an entity but felt themselves under siege as a minority overall.

Anglo-Canadian homogenization was unacceptable to the French Canadians. The French linguistic and religious minority was protected within the provincial structure of Quebec. There was a collectivistic approach to the notion of rights within each of the linguistic-religious communities. To the extent that the concept of *bi*nationality was held to, there was no notion of the country as a place for multiple races, nations, or religions. Only a century later did Canadians came to a notion of "ethnic mosaic" that would allow greater diversity.

Confederation permanently enshrined sectarian interests ultimately reflected in the organization of education. In Quebec, there was public support of sectarian schools identified either as Catholic and Protestant. In Ontario and Maritime provinces, there were state-supported secular schools but also a state-supported Catholic system. Universities were also denominationally based.[13]

The question of Jewish rights became intertwined with the confessional nature of education, particularly in Montreal, where the largest concentration of Jews lived during the period of large East European immigration. The history of the struggle in Quebec concerning the education of Jewish children reflects both the lack of options for alternatives to the originally confessional nature of Canadian life and the class divisions within the Jewish community. This issue will be discussed in the section of this chapter dealing with the immigrant generation when it came to the fore.

4.1.2 The Existing Jewish Community

Like the American colonies, the first Jewish congregation in Canada followed the Spanish and Portuguese rite and took the same name as its New York predecessor. *Shearith Israel* was founded in Montreal in 1768. As late as 1857, the bylaws of the Montreal congregation specified "fixed prayers shall be read in Hebrew according to the customs of the Great Portuguese Synagogue in London."[14] Actually, mostly Ashkenazi in origin rather than Sephardic, the community was transient and numbered only ninety people in all of Lower Canada in 1825. Questions of religious law were referred to the chief rabbi of England. The elders of the synagogue had autocratic powers over the rest of the community, levying fines for any infraction. Aristocratic in tone, the elders upheld every tenet of Orthodoxy even as to their dress.[15]

Abraham de Sola, of a distinguished British Sephardic family, arrived in 1847 as rabbi of Shearith Israel, the mother congregation. He was the first ordained rabbi to come to Canada. He became one of the most active and best-known intellectual figures in North America. Teaching Hebrew and Spanish at McGill, he was also awarded an honorary degree from that institution in 1858. The Hebrew Philanthropic Organization was also founded by Abraham de Sola in 1847 to deal with the needs of poor Jews. Although short lasting, it was the forerunner of other more lasting efforts to deal with the needs of newly arrived immigrants as well as others needing help. Establishing a dynasty in Montreal, de Sola remained rabbi for thirty-five years to be succeeded by his son, Meldola for another forty years.

During the 1840s, there was an increase in the number of immigrants from central Europe as well as Britain with the formation of a second and Ashkenazi congregation in 1846 in Montreal called Shaar Hashomayim.[16] Some of the members of this earlier congregation followed the trend in the United States in founding in 1882 Temple Emmanu-el as the first Reform congregation. In Toronto, the first Hebrew congregation was *Holy Blossom* in 1852, later to become associated with the Reform movement. Other nineteenth-century pioneer synagogues were established in Hamilton, Ontario, and Victoria, British Columbia. Particularly noteworthy to these developments was the contribution of immigrants from Lithuania who arrived in the 1860s and 1870s.[17]

Although few in number, the immigrants were soon almost entirely middle class. Some became wealthy with interests in the development of utilities in Montreal and Quebec City in shipping as well as the fur trade with acceptance in the upper-class society of the times.[18] In addition to the religious organizations, Montreal, in 1863, saw the foundation of the Young Men's Hebrew Benevolent Society (YMHBS). It contained members from both of the existing congregations. Its *relief committee* united both factions in dispensing charity. Its focus was on small amounts of emergency type aid and in providing funds to enable immigrants to move on. The Ladies' Hebrew Benevolent Society was founded in Montreal in the mid-1870s to help women and children in the pattern of an earlier organization with a similar mission in Toronto. The burdens placed on these organizations in Montreal led to complaints in the 1870s addressed to the London Ladies Emigration Society for their policy of encouraging immigrants to come to Canada.[19]

Even when political rights and economic security were achieved, there were still major problems in the degree of acceptance by the Francophone community in Quebec driven by its militant Catholicism. Theologically based anti-Judaism was part of the teachings of the church. The catechism published in 1750, used until 1890, reinforced the teaching of the punishment of the Jews for the crucifixion. This teaching was also tied in the popular mind with the legend of the "Wandering Jew." This fable was widely believed by pietistic peasants. The story arose in mediaeval times of the Jew condemned to wander for taunting Jesus on his way to death.

Drawing upon the nineteenth-century French Catholic teaching in opposition to the French Revolution, the Jew was among the elements such as the Masons determined to destroy Christendom.[20] As both the traditional Antichrist of theology as well as the symbol of the modern, secular world, Jews became the focus of Catholic animosity. In French-Canadian literature, as in French literature, the Jew was an outsider and a caricature. The anti-Semitic writings of Edouard Drumont, author of *La France Juive*, were widely known in Montreal as well as Paris. The most respectable paper of the nationalist Quebec intelligentsia, *Le Devoir*, featured Drumont. The *Dreyfus Affair* brought to the fore in Montreal the differences between the segments of the population. The English-speaking press was unanimously in favor of Dreyfus, and the French press was anti-Dreyfus. Belief in the guilt of Dreyfus was a nationalist credo in Canada as in France.[21]

At the time of the Great Migration occurring at the turn of the twentieth century, it was clear that the English-speaking community in Quebec was the more open to Jews and more attractive to them than becoming French speaking. Government and business even in Montreal, the largest French Canadian city, was conducted in English. English was the language of the rulers, and French the language of the subservient class. French was closely associated with the Catholic faith, and its intimate connection with the religious body in Canada made it unattractive to the non-Catholic immigrant. However, the entry of Jews into the Anglo community was also somewhat problematic. In Quebec where the Anglo community was in the minority, and particularly in Montreal, the actions of the Protestant School Board indicated that the Jews were not entirely welcomed by the Anglo community. In Ontario in turn, the existence of Jews could be seen as a threat to the Christian character of the Protestant hegemony in that province. Confederation had established Catholicism in Quebec and Protestantism in Ontario in relation not only to schools but to other aspects of official life such as access to jobs. The formation of Canada was intimately tied to religious identity and that religion was Christianity. The concept of a "Christian Canada" also underlay some of the activities of the Christian sects intent on proselytizing among the Jews.[22]

Even prior to the great migration from Eastern Europe, the influence of Goldwin Smith supported exclusion of Jews in Anglo-Canada. A former professor at Oxford, he came to the University of Toronto in the late nineteenth century where he became the arbiter of Anglo-Canadian culture. He expressed anti-Semitic views on many occasions, providing respectability and authority to those views. Although based on religious grounds, he extended his diatribes against Jews on economic and social grounds as well. He drew upon the writings of the French and German anti-Semites who invoked the racial and secular bases for Jew hatred. It is interesting that his strong views remained in the long-term memory of his student Mackenzie King, a man who was to have a profound effect on Canada.[23]

4.1.3 The Great Migration

In order to safeguard the British nature of Canada, it was desirable to encourage immigration and to make naturalization easy. Between 1815 and 1850, over 800,000, mainly British, immigrants came to British North America. A new rise occurred after Confederation in 1867. Immigration became a concern of the federal government. It was necessary to seek immigrants from parts of Europe beyond the British Isles. However, no significant German Jewish immigration occurred. The Jewish population in 1871 had risen only to around 1,300. They were relatively widely dispersed in twenty-nine different centers of population, mainly in Ontario with a lesser number of sites in Quebec.

The East European phase started around 1870. At the end of that decade, there were 2,500 Jews in Canada contrasting with circa 280,000 in the United States.[24] The earlier East European immigration in the 1870s provided a prosperous class that was called upon to support the immigration of their confreres later in the century. It is estimated that around 15,000 Jews came to Canada during the period ending in 1900 at the same time 600,000 came to the United States. Unlike migrants from several other countries, Jews came mainly as families.

The major East European immigration occurred after 1890 through to the outbreak of World War I. The sources of this Jewish immigration were similar to the much larger number going to the United States. Seventy percent came from the Russian provinces of the Pale of Settlement. The sources within those provinces cannot be absolutely determined. As early as 1857, immigrants began to appear from Lita. They tended first to settle in rural districts in the St. Lawrence Valley, later moving to Montreal and other cities where they became the mainstay of the existing community. In response to the cholera epidemic in Lita and other problems, there was a further increase in the decade 1868-78 from this same area of the Pale of Settlement. It can be assumed that the large preponderance coming to the United States from the northwest provinces, particularly in the early phases of immigration prior to 1905, may also be the case in Canada. The Litvak component was prominent in the secular Yiddish and Labour Zionist strands particularly noticeable in Winnipeg but evident also in the Yiddish literary and educational movement in Montreal and least of all in Toronto. As in the United States, immigration subsequent to 1905 came from many of the areas of the Jewish Pale of Settlement as well as Galicia in the Hapsburg Empire and Romania.[25]

Many of the Jews who came to Canada had first lived in the United States as well as having entered via New York or Boston. Noteworthy was the movement back and forth across the open border with the United States. During the years between 1900 and 1914, there was a net gain to Canada of approximately twenty thousand Jews from the United States, a substantial percentage of the total immigration during that period.[26] Others came directly to Halifax or the Port of Montreal.[27] The minimum cost for passage from Europe was about $20 to Halifax. The cost of reaching Buffalo or Toronto via New York City would be $25, substantial sums for the poverty stricken.[28]

The Kayfetz family in Toronto illustrates this transfer of Jewish immigrants to and from the United States. The father, Mottel, had been born in Vilna Gurbernia (province) in 1879 and came to Canada in 1904 to join an elder brother in Toronto. Each of the several branches of the family in North America transformed the name somewhat differently in their attempt to adapt the Hebrew letter with the initial ch sound to the Roman alphabet. Kayfetz was the spelling that some adopted. The famous violinist Jasha Heifetz, also from Vilna, was a relative who chose to maintain the softer second part of the initial sound. For example, another branch settled in Detroit. His children spelled their name with an initial C and grew up as Americans in the Detroit area.

The mother, Leah, was born in 1887 in a portion of the Northern Ukraine adjacent to Belorussia. She identified herself as a Litvak. She was one of four siblings who eventually came to Canada. Leah, the second child, came in 1907 to join her elder sister. That sister, Chessia, had settled in Windsor, Ontario. Of her nine children, seven moved to various sites in the American Midwest as well as California. Another sister, Manya, came before 1914. After marrying a widower with two children, she eventually had four additional children, all of whom emigrated to the New York City area. Her one stepdaughter Norma remained in Toronto. The stepson emigrated to West Virginia. One brother, Ora, immigrated to Canada only in 1920, after having gone to Palestine and served in the Jewish Legion in the First World War that had been organized by Ben-Gurion and Itzhak Ben Zvi. Several of his children and grandchildren settled in New York. Still another brother had remained in Haifa and raised a family there, after immigrating there during Ottoman times prior to the British Mandate.

The increase after 1870 in those who were destitute began to overwhelm the established organizations such as the YMHBS (Young Men's Hebrew Benevolent Society) founded in 1863 to "assist needy co-religionists." The problem was initially greatest in Montreal as the main port of entry from Europe.[29] Immigrants first landing in New York also entered Canada at Toronto and other cities along the border such as Hamilton. In response, immigrant aid societies were founded in these several cities in the 1870s.

In 1882, in response to the pogroms in the Pale of Settlement and the May Laws in Lita, immigration began in earnest. The Mansion House Committee Fund set up following the meeting in London, protesting the pogroms, had particular influence in Canada. One of the activities of the Russo-Jewish Committee, set up by the Fund, was to insure the movement of immigrants to the New World. The Canadian high commissioner in London at that time, Sir Alexander Galt, became involved with the Fund in encouraging Jewish immigration as part of his overall role in encouraging immigration of all kinds. For example, in 1882, a large contingent was sent to Winnipeg under the auspices of the Mansion House Fund, albeit without adequate preparation. This marked the beginning of the substantial Jewish presence in that city.

In 1890, Baron De Hirsch sent a contribution to the Montreal YMHBS to aid in their work. A building was purchased to be called the DeHirsch Institute.' This support was augmented by a bequest by the Baroness DeHirsch in 1900 that led to a new much larger building. The choice of honored guests at dedication of the new building of the institute in 1902 was emblematic of the dichotomy between the existing established community and the immigrants it served. At its gala opening, there was no representative of the latter. Following this, a group met with the leaders of the institute to warn that they were not content to be treated as "objects of philanthropy" and wanted a role in the decision-making bodies of the Jewish community.[30] The institute became the first central address of the community and the focus of the Jewish quarter, the home of a night school for those working and a Jewish day school for immigrant children, to prepare them for entry into the English-speaking Protestant Schools.[31]

The Jewish Colonization Society (JCA), also set up by DeHirsch, took on responsibility for a time to support the work of the Institute. After 1906, the JCA set up its own organization in Montreal to more specifically focus on the support of agricultural colonies in Canada.[32]. The work of the JCA has been credited with the increase in Jewish immigration that took place after 1901.[33] The first agricultural settlement, set up originally by the Mansion House Fund under the auspices of Sir Alexander Galt in 1883, was in Moosomin, Saskatchewan. Underfunded but also subject to recurrent disasters ending with a fire, it was abandoned as a failure in 1889. Another Jewish colony established near by in Wapella in 1888 lasted far longer. One of its members was the founder of the Bronfman family in Canada, originally from Romania.[34] The JCA began to participate in this effort and supported the colony of Hirsch, also in Saskatchewan, founded in 1892 as well as another called Lipton in 1901.[35] More successful was JCA support by loans and technical advice for a number of other settlements made up of individual farmers who, in turn, created their own communities.[36]

Despite the existence of a number of farmers, the occupational distribution of the East European Jewish immigrants to Canada was generally similar to those going to other countries. They settled mainly in the major towns. Starting as peddlers, some were able to move up to storekeepers. Mainly artisans and semiskilled, they entered trade and manufacturing. They worked as carpenters, bakers, painters, machinists, and bricklayers. The more skilled entered small manufacturing such as upholstery, furniture making, and jewelry trades. As elsewhere, Jewish workers predominated in the clothing trade.[37]

Starting in 1896, government subsidies were given particularly for those likely to become agriculturists. By 1906, the total number of immigrants had become a torrent. Four hundred thousand entered in 1913 and a total of 3.4 million in the two decades following 1900 from a large variety of peoples, including Ukrainians and other non-Jewish inhabitants of the Russian Empire. Settlement occurred in Manitoba and the *Prairie Provinces* of Alberta and Saskatchewan. While subsidies were paid for possible agriculturists, Jews were specifically excluded from such bonuses.[38] Jewish immigration was felt to conflict directly with public policy dedicated to diverting immigrants into rural areas.[39]

Data to the extent and distribution of the Jewish population is collected as part of the decennial Dominion census. It has thus been available for review and planning purposes by the Jewish community.[40] By 1901, the Jewish population had reached 16,700, highly dispersed in 113 centers.[41] The major immigration occurred in the two decades following 1900. The Jewish population in 1920 had reached 125,000 settled in 573 different communities. Although widely distributed, two-thirds lived in the three largest cities of Montreal, Toronto, and Winnipeg. Montreal alone had more than one-third of the total. It is estimated that an additional 20,000 net immigrants entered Canada in the decade, ending in 1931, when immigration was drastically curtailed. An estimate is that a total of almost 200,000 Jews entered Canada during the years from 1880 to 1930. There was an emigration of circa 75,000 during that same period to the United States with a net immigration of around 120,000.[42]

Overall, Jewish immigration to Canada was one-twentieth of that to the United States and only one-fortieth of the total immigration to Canada from all sources.[43] When in 1914, Jews represented 3 percent of the population of the United States; they represented about 1 percent in Canada. The choice of Canada rather than the United States for even those relatively few Jews who did ultimately come there was conditioned by several factors.[44] One was the connection with England since many of London's Jewish organizations dealing with migration were more likely to maintain ties with Montreal than with New York. Many of those passing through England therefore had Canada as a destination.[45]

The harsh climate and more limited economic opportunity all may have contributed to this discrepancy between Canada and the United States. Also likely was the awareness of the Canadian ambivalence toward their existence. Canada was a country based upon a Christian religio-communal identity that contrasted with the opportunity for individual equality in the United States.[46]

4.1.4 The Response to the Migration

In 1921, despite the increased variety of immigrants, the ethnic distribution of the population remained strongly binational with 55 percent Anglo-Saxon, 28 percent French, and only 17 percent "alien races." Only in the Prairie Provinces were those of British ancestry in the minority in respect to those "of alien races." Restrictions against Oriental, and later Indian immigrants had already come into effect.

The French Canadian community was never in favor of immigration, feeling that it would dilute their influence in maintaining the autonomy of Quebec and its particular culture. As power shifted to English Canada with the increase in immigrant population as well as economic development, French Canada clung more defensively to its rights under the original Confederation binational idea. In that setting, there was no provision for outsiders. Montreal, the largest Jewish community, was the focal point of this confrontation. For the first time, the city was receiving some thousands who were neither French nor British in a city where the two groups both resided. It was also, of course, the first group that was not Christian. As the Jews there identified with English Canada, they became a target of animosity directed specifically against them but also as part of the animosity against English Canada.

The old differences within the Jewish population between the Sephardic and Ashkenazi rites were now superceded by the social cleavage between the settled and the new immigrants. There was the usual conflict between the already settled "uptowners," and the subsequent, far-larger number, poor "downtown" immigrants—mainly peddlers and artisans. The well-established residents were much disturbed by the alien behavior and appearance of the immigrants. They were clearly "too conspicuous." Particularly prominent in Montreal, *uptown* and *downtown* became precise terms of social differentiation. In the 1880s, each of the well-established synagogues had followed their members to the more fashionable upper and west end of Montreal.[47]

Despite the social differences, some uptowners took an unusually active role in helping their coreligionists. This was particularly true for those who had arrived in the previous generation from Eastern Europe that were now prosperous. Amongst them was Lyon Cohen, owner of one of the largest men's clothing firms in Montreal. He would personally go down to the docks to meet immigrants and labored in many charitable causes along with his close friend Sam Jacobs, both identified with the original Ashkenazi synagogue. The Montreal charities such as the Baron de Hirsch Institute and the Ladies' Hebrew Benevolent Society were dominated by those who had arrived between the 1840s and 1870s.[48] This concern for the new immigrants extended even to Clarence de Sola, a son of the original rabbi of the Sephardic mother congregation. An outstanding example of the uptown crowd, he set up the Montreal branch of the "Anglo-Jewish Association" to aid immigrants.[49]

By a law enacted in 1870, Jews were free to pay their school taxes into either of the two systems. In Montreal, each of two congregations maintained their own cheder where children received instruction in Jewish subjects. Abortive efforts were made to establish a full Jewish day school, combining both English and Hebrew subjects under their dual sponsorship.[50] In the 1880s, the Spanish and Portuguese Congregation eventually established a day school under the direction of Meldola de Sola. It was to be the source of major controversy starting in 1889.

In accordance with the collective nature of Canadian society, funding for the school system was based on taxes levied on the various adherents to the religious bodies. The funds collected from Jewish property were largely those of the well-established members of the Spanish and Portuguese Synagogue. They had an arrangement by which these monies passed through the Catholic School Board to their own school. A much larger number of children of poorer and nontaxpaying Jews were enrolled in a school attached to the Baron De Hirsch Center, serving the Jewish immigrant community. In addition, the even larger number of Jewish children attending the schools administered by the English-language Protestant School Board were not entirely supported by monies raised by taxes or school fees among the Jewish community. The only category available for Jewish children was the nonexistent religion of "non-Catholic, non-Protestant." This issue came to a head in the case of Jacob Pinsler, a ten-year-old whose scholarship to high school was denied on the basis that his family, a renter, did not cover his costs in the Protestant system.[51]

In 1903, only after a struggle were Jews to be counted as Protestants in the per capita allocation of general funds as well as from Jewish rate payers. An agreement was made to enable Jewish students to be included under the Protestant banner. But the Protestant Christian nature of the schools was retained. Jewish students could be excused from religious instruction, but no Jewish teachers would be hired since the classroom teachers were responsible for Protestant religious instruction. Thus it was felt that Jewish teachers acting in that role would obscure the sectarian nature of the system. Even when the absolute prohibition of Jewish teachers was removed, in practice, they were not hired. In addition, despite the large representation of Jewish students in the "Protestant" schools in 1909, there was defeat of efforts to have elected rather than appointive commissioners of the school board. With the possibility of being elected, Jews would presumably have more opportunity to affect policy, given their substantial presence in the system. Still later, with election still not possible, opposition also prevented the alternative option of direct appointment of Jews to the board by the Montreal City Council.[52]

Those well-off remained opposed to the development of an alternative Jewish educational system. They were concerned that they would be required to fund it and opposed a separatist parochial system that would separate Jews from others and retard their entry into Canadian life. The controversy was ongoing. The organization in 1912 of a People's Conference in response to the school-funding issue led eventually to those same elements of the immigrant community supporting the more democratic grouping of the Canadian Jewish Congress in 1919. The conflict within the community was to be renewed in the post-World War I era. Its eventual rather unsatisfactory resolution at the hands of the establishment, and in accordance with their wishes, led to the withdrawal of support for their leadership by those whose children were actually involved.[53]

The social and class differences were also expressed in religious life. The newer immigrants were shy of the older congregations with their impressive buildings and use of English. Many small congregations sprang up in storefronts or apartments in the east-central portion of the city where the new immigrants clustered. For example, a new congregation of Russians (B'nai Jacob) filled the old building left behind by the original Ashkenasi synagogue (Shaar Hashomayim) in its move to the more fashionable uptown area. Similarly, when, toward the end of the nineteenth century, the number of Russian Jews in Toronto had increased, they organized their own congregation.

Each group did the same in each of the large centers, leading to the proliferation of 125 synagogues in Canada by 1920.

Immigrant aid was one unifying force in the Jewish community. The number of immigrants was so great at one time that it became necessary to hire several warehouses in Montreal to house immigrants awaiting settlement. Similarly in Toronto in 1882, the Anglo-Jewish association in that city leased a hotel to provide lodging and food while immigrants awaited transit to points farther west. Like the de Hirsch Institute, the center for Jewish immigrant communal life in Montreal, charitable organizations in each town were founded in response to the need to care for immigrants.[54] These immigrant aid societies, at first, saw their role as primarily philanthropic to deal with a short-term emergency. Only later did they begin to see a role that extended to social integration. *Landsmanshaften* (kinship groups) were helpful as well as families themselves. Free loan associations also served to provide an alternative to alms for those too proud to accept the latter.

In 1897, the first Anglo-Jewish newspaper, the fortnightly *Jewish Times,* appeared in Montreal. It was founded in the context of the rising anti-Semitism associated with the *Dreyfus* case and its impact on the nationalist French Canadian movement. Supported by Sam Jacobs and Lyon Cohen, it continued as a public service until superceded by the commercial *Canadian Jewish Chronicle* in 1914.[55] The latter remained the newspaper of middle-class community of the western suburbs. It promoted Canadianization and the ways of the British empire.[56] Any reference to the activities of the downtown Jews was couched in condescending terms that emphasized their poverty and the need for those better off to be generous in giving them assistance.[57]

Yiddish was, however, the primary mode of communication within the immigrant community. In addition to the leading daily Yiddish *Kanader Adler* (*Canadian Eagle*) in Montreal, the Toronto daily was *Der Yiddishe Zournal* (*Jewish Journal*), starting in 1912 as a weekly and converting in 1913 to a daily. It came out six days a week well into the 1960s. In Winnipeg the daily, *Kanader Yid* (Canadian Jew) became in 1917 the weekly *Dos Yiddishe Vort* (the Jewish Press).[58]

In 1893, "moved by the first large-scale Jewish immigration there was the formation of L'Association Catholique de la Jeunesse Canadienne" (ACJC), French Canada's premier youth group and also a spearhead of the nationalist battle against a Jewish presence in

Quebec. Anti-Semitism was also expressed in the Catholic press and within the nationalist political movement. *Racial* as well as religious homogeneity were conflated and were even more zealously asserted than in the past.[59] Most regressive was the accusation in 1910 by a Quebec City notary and journalist, Joseph Plamondon, of the Jewish blood murder libel in a lecture to the ACJC chapter. Following its wider dissemination in the form of a pamphlet, Jews were attacked on the streets and synagogue windows broken. Sued for damages by several Jews, the case was eventually won in a cause celebre that echoed the blood libel trial of Mendel Beilis in Kiev.[60] The seeds thus planted of an active anti-Semitic movement were to be expressed even more openly in the interwar era.

Immigration policy ultimately reflected an act of the federal Parliament. However, a provision in the act permitted regulations to be issued in a more direct fashion by Orders in Council on the advice of the minister of immigration. Thus administrative restrictions could be easily imposed. In 1900, the opportunity to turn away "undesirable immigrants" was invoked to turn away a shipload of Romanian Jews. Sufficient funds to certify that they would not become public charges, so-called landing money, was a recurrent problem that led to detention and possible deportation, particularly during the economic setback of 1908-1909.

Any possible discretionary restriction was applied to Jews with particular severity. In 1908, immigration assisted by philanthropic organizations was prohibited with particular potential impact on the poor Jewish immigrant. The Order in Council in 1910 increased the discretionary power of inspectors to turn away immigrants whose "racial characteristics" could be the basis for exclusion. Other restrictions were placed that could selectively affect Jews, although billed as impartial on the surface. One forbade entry to those who interrupted their trip to North America by a stopover. This was characteristic of much of the immigration pattern from Eastern Europe. Another order in 1910 required a valid passport from the home country, difficult if not impossible for those fleeing Russia for political reasons.[61] Initially, selectively enforced to exclude immigrants from southern Europe, it applied after 1914 to Jews as well.

Following World War I, with the general economic turndown, as immigration officials sought to cut down immigration, Jews were again selectively excluded. A series of administrative edicts successively put greater obstacles to Jewish immigration. A "money test" introduced in 1921 was far higher than before. Further, in 1923, the government closed out immigrants from eastern Europe except "bonafide agriculturists." In 1927, a series of restrictions were embodied in the Revised Immigration Act. It prohibited admission except for certain categories. Countries in the "nonpreferred" category included most of the countries in Eastern Europe from which Jews were likely to emigrate. In addition, all Jews were lumped in a "special permit" group even aside from their country of origin. For example, although Germany was ordinarily a country on the "preferred" list, Germans who were Jews could only enter by "special permit." Jews were thus distinguished from their German fellow citizens by Canada, predating the Nazi racial laws. An effort to admit a selected number of refugee Jews stranded in Romania after World War I was poorly handled. It provided the officials bent on restricting immigration the ammunition to never again relax the restrictions on immigration of Jews throughout the interwar period.[62] The issue of safeguarding the possibility of immigration became a major preoccupation of the Jewish community during the interwar era. In addition to issues of immigration, naturalization became more problematic after the First World War. Following the war, applicants must meet certain criteria such as being of "good moral character" and be able to read English or French. Nevertheless, over 80 percent of all Jews were citizens with the highest percentage of aliens in Quebec.[63]

War relief during World War I illustrated the split in the Jewish community. In the fall of 1914, the Jewish Relief Campaign Committee was established in Montreal, mainly by the uptowners. During the following spring, the Canadian Jewish Alliance, known as the People's Relief Committee, represented labor organizations and fraternal societies directly reflecting the newer immigrants. It arose in opposition to the distribution of the previously raised funds carried out unilaterally by the uptowners. In turn, the Canadian Jewish Conference arose in opposition. It was made up of the notables along with the Zionist Federation and formed what was called the Canadian Jewish Committee. Still other groups formed. In the fall of 1915, the Central Relief Committee derived its support from the synagogues and Orthodox organizations. Finally in 1919, the Associated Jewish War Relief Societies of Canada came into being to unite the various campaigns.

The Canadian Jewish Alliance also sought a more democratic organization that would represent the entire range of people in contrast to the traditional leadership of the established and wealthy. A meeting of the Canadian Jewish Congress (CJC) occurred in March 1919 based upon the initiative of the alliance but finally with the cooperation of the Zionist Federation. A strictly democratic organization, one delegate was to be chosen for every 750 Jews (both men and women), and nearly every adult Jew voted.[64]

Although the CJC did not survive as an entity at that time, it was clear that immigration could no longer be handled merely as a settlement issue. In light of the restrictive governmental policies and the urgent need for relief after the war, an organized national effort was necessary that would also have a political role. An organizational meeting took place with representatives of the CJC, landsmanshaften, and the Association of Jewish Relief Societies along with the JCA. The Jewish Immigrant Aid Society of Canada (JIAS), founded in 1920, would be a communal immigrant rescue and rehabilitation effort. In its first year, although not always successful in preventing deportation, an agent of the JIAS at the Port of Quebec succeeded in intervening in the hundreds of cases in which immigrants were detained for infraction of the several restrictive regulations.[65]

Although in close proximity to the United States, Canada is different. It is less secular, less democratic and nationalistic. But like its neighbor, it was still a place where there was freedom from persecution and an opportunity for economic advancement. Membership in the world Jewish community, in relation the far larger Jewish community of the United States, presented difficulties similar to those experienced by Canadians in general. It was necessary to express their distinctiveness both as Canadians and as Canadian Jews. One way that had been done was the relatively strong national voice expressed in the Canadian Jewish Congress (CJC). This unity has not been possible in the United States. Yet the organization of the community that resulted in the establishment of the CJC reflected the bar to full equality that was experienced in Canada. Emblematic is the cross that surmounts the hill overlooking Montreal to which the main street of the Jewish community led. This can be contrasted to the Statue of Liberty, welcoming the immigrants of all sorts to New York and to the United States.

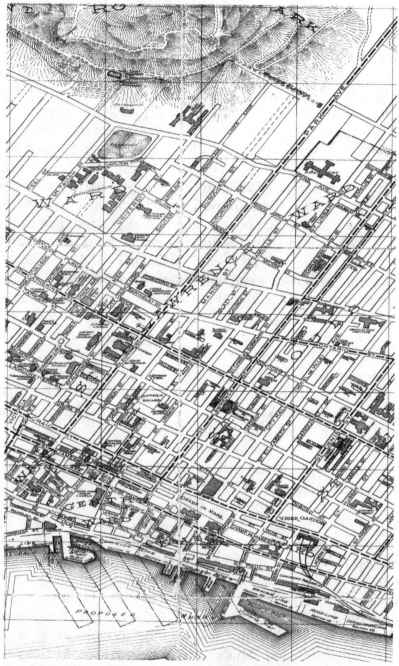

Map 4.1 The "Main" of Montreal runs between the docks
to the hill where a cross overlooks the city.

4.2 The Evolution in Canada

The experience in Montreal in the province of Quebec was different from that of Toronto in Anglo-Canada and different as well in the smaller communities with a relatively strong Jewish culture such as Winnipeg. Litvaks formed but a portion of the total East European immigration. It is our thesis that they formed a particularly significant portion not merely because of their relative early preponderance but by their leadership in many facets of political and intellectual Canadian life reflective of their roots.

The immigrants from Lita to Canada brought with them a strongly rationalistic religious tradition that had become transformed in the context of the political and economic conditions of the late nineteenth century. The more secular ideological trends, nevertheless, maintained their religious and ethical sources in the search for a messianic age. These trends continued to manifest themselves in the adherence to socialism, both particularistic and internationalistic, and Zionism, particularly in its socialist variant as well as devotion to an intellectual and literary tradition. Particularly noteworthy was the development of the Montreal School of Yiddishists, secondary only to the much larger community of New York City. All these strands were to become increasingly modified by the Canadian context but remained identifiable unto the third generation.

Like South Africa, Zionism had a particular attraction in a country where national identity and confessional identity were so basic. The response to Zionism was heightened by its acceptance among the existing Jewish establishment and the need to identify in terms of one's nationality in a Canada that was riven by the differences between its two "founding nations." Again, like South Africa, Zionism in Canada was conditioned by a connection to the British Empire while it was in its ascendancy. The British connection was enhanced by identification with the English-speaking component of a bilingual and binational country with the British element in the majority aside from Quebec.[1] Increased adherence to a multicultural ethos in Canada in the post-World War II era provided a unique opportunity for the development of the Jewish entity.

4.2.1 The Immigrant Generation

While Montreal's total metropolitan population grew by 55 percent in the 1880s and by 25 percent in the 1890s, its Jewish population rose an average of 300 percent in each of these decades. Montreal's Jewish population reached nearly 29,000 in 1911. Toronto's Jewish population grew slightly more than 100 percent starting from a lower base during the 1890s and by 600 percent by 1910. The rates for the next decade ending in 1920 were a more modest 60 and 70 percent. There were even larger percentage increases in the West with Winnipeg growing by 800 percent. In these larger centers, there was a range of occupations with a significant working-class component. There were also a number of smaller communities throughout Canada where Jews had a different experience, primarily entering the commercial occupations with small stores.[2]

Jews particularly entered the garment industry both as entrepreneurs and workers. Production of ready-made clothing became the second largest industry in Quebec by 1900. Governmental reports on conditions in the clothing industry documented the sweatshops. Workers were poorly paid, frequently underage, in unsanitary and poorly ventilated settings. The Jewish character of the industry was commented upon in these reports. The *Jewish Times* criticized the conditions provided by the Jewish manufacturers as leading to discredit of the Jewish community as a whole.[3]

In Montreal, some of the immigrants worked as peddlers in the city and the surrounding countryside. Small-scale shops with Yiddish lettering arose along the Saint Laurent du Main that bisected the city. The name was changed to Boulevard Saint-Laurent in 1905. The *Jewish quarter* stretched north about six blocks on either side of the Main from the docks. (See Map 4.1). Each successive decade saw the movement farther north away from the original area of settlement. In dividing the French-speaking section east of the Main from the English-speaking sections to the west, the Jewish area of settlement was symbolic of the precarious marginality of the Jewish presence to both communities.[4] Jews formed a majority of the population of this

St Louis city ward and the federal Cartier riding extending into the interwar period.

Comparable immigrant settlements appeared in Toronto in the St. John's Ward in a narrow downtown area. Like the Main of Montreal, this Jewish quarter was adjacent to the principal shopping street and to the heavily traveled street car lines. A slum by the standards of the time, nearly half the city's Jews lived in crowded unsanitary conditions. In 1912, 87 percent of the children in the areas two elementary schools were Jewish. It was convenient to the city's garment factories, particularly the large one run by Eaton's, the large department store chain. Synagogues abounded with the most impressive Goel Tzedec, the Lithuanian shul. Mutual benefit associations reflected those who could not afford synagogue membership or were secularists. By 1925, there were thirty such organizations, equally divided between those representing a same area in the "old country" (landsmanshaften), those who were ethnically mixed and those who were affiliated with the secular labor socialist Arbeiter Ring (Workmen's Circle). There was a predominant working-class identity to all these associations, providing strike benefits as well as health and burial benefits.[5].

The comparable site in Winnipeg was the North End of town. The Jews were in close approximation to other ethnic communities, particularly the Ukrainian. In one North End school in 1911, Jewish pupils were the largest single group but a minority among the children of Christian immigrants from a large variety of places. The old animosities arising from Europe reappeared in the competition for political power in the larger society of the city dominated by the Anglo-Saxons.[6]

There were Jewish workers in the various factories including meatpacking, sheet metal as well as clothing with the latter a majority of women workers. Each of the several ideological components of the community established their own schools, both day schools and those supplementary to the public schools. The religious established what was called Winnipeg Hebrew School—Talmud Torah. The radicals established first a literary and cultural club then the Workmen's Circle School with a Yiddish and Socialist cast to the curriculum.

Illustrative was the story of Aaron Gurvitch who came to Winnipeg from Vilna Gubernia in 1909 to join a cousin who had come there in 1905. He landed in Halifax before taking the rail to Winnipeg. An only son of a melamed, he studied for a short time in a Yeshivah after having been tutored by his father. Being groomed to be a rabbi like his grandfather, he soon left religious training when he began to read secular books such as Plato and heretical books such as Spinoza. He, however, remained an avid reader his entire life and kept a large library of Yiddish and Hebrew books. His commitment to his Yiddish literary background was vouchsafed by the choice of name for one of his sons, that of the famous writer Sholem Aleichem. Aaron's fiancee joined him from Vilna in Winnipeg to marry in 1910. She was a seamstress. Originally a worker in a meat packing plant at twenty-five cents an hour, Aaron soon opened a wholesale fruit-and-produce business which, whatever else, "assured his family enough to eat."

Two of his sisters later joined him in Winnepeg. Rose, the younger one, was young enough to enter elementary school in Winnipeg. Coming under the close tutelege of a teacher who encouraged her, she became a schoolteacher herself. Her husband, Ben Victor, surmounted the high barriers to Jewish students entering the University of Manitoba Medical School to become a physician. One of their sons, Maurice, in turn became a professor of neurology in the United States and coauthor of the leading neurology textbook of his time.

Canadian Political Life

Montreal was the largest city in the country and the capital of Canadian Jewry. Closely associated with all the activities during this crucial time was Sam Jacobs as both one of Montreal's notables and a representative of Montreal's immigrant masses in the federal parliament. He was also an exemplar of the longtime connection between the Jewish community and the Liberal Party in Quebec.

Sam Jacobs was born in 1871 in a rural enclave in Ontario settled by a group of Lithuanian Jewish families. His father,

William Jacobs, had come to Lancaster in the 1860s. In 1867, William had been married by Abraham de Sola in the Spanish and Portuguese Congregation in Montreal. His wife, Hannah, was the daughter of a Hebrew teacher. Having a good Hebrew education, she was able to teach her children in the absence of a teacher in the small town where they lived. A dealer in horses, William became prosperous as the purveyor to the Montreal tramline owned by Jesse Joseph, the brother-in-law of Rabbi de Sola. There were six sons and two daughters. The family moved to Montreal in 1881 when Sam was ten. He was bar mitzvah at the Shaar Hashomayim Ashkenazi Synagogue they had joined. Their home was in the fashionable part of town across the street from the new synagogue built in 1885. Sam graduated from the Montreal High School and then the law school of McGill University, the latter in 1893. He was unusual in also attending the French-speaking Laval University. Now admitted to the bar, he formed a successful law partnership with persons whose background was in high legal circles of both the French and Anglo communities. He was emblematic of his generation of acculturated Jews in his lack of Yiddish although fluent in both English and French.[7]

Jacobs carried out his Jewish communal activities concurrently with the development of his legal career. In 1890, while still in law school, he became the recording secretary of the YMHBS. He remained associated with its successor Baron de Hirsh Institute, becoming president in 1912-1915. In 1906, he became secretary of the governing body of Canadian branch of the de Hirsch-funded Jewish Colonization Association. In 1897, with Lyon Cohen, he launched the *Jewish Times*. It opposed anti-Semitism but also any efforts to develop separate Jewish organizations. The aim was to "become British subjects and Canadians in all things, while remaining true to their religion and the support of their benevolent institutions."[8]

Jacobs was active in almost every issue that affected the Jewish community of Montreal. He was a member of the delegation to the Dominion Minister of Justice in 1906 in reference to Sunday closing. After the passage of the federal law, he was instrumental in the passage of the law in Quebec provincial legislature, excusing those who observed Saturday as their day of rest. He was the lead lawyer in the litigation dealing with the status of Jewish students in the Protestant schools leading to the law in 1903. He was also the lead lawyer in the *Plamondon* trial in Quebec City in 1913 in which Jews had been accused of the *blood libel.*

In 1917, he was elected in the "downtown" Cartier constituency to the federal parliament from Montreal on the Liberal Party ticket. He assured his election and the ascendancy of the Liberal Party by insuring the naturalization of five thousand immigrants in his district. Henceforth, this district with a substantial Jewish population generally continued to return Liberal Party candidates in both provincial and federal elections.[9] To Jacob's great disappointment, the Liberal governments in the interwar period under Mackenzie King did not open up immigration. In the succeeding years until 1937, Jacobs remained in Parliament as the person representing Jewish interests without the recognition of a cabinet post. Although he failed to accomplish the goals of his constituency in respect to immigration, he nevertheless maintained his commitment to the integration of Jews in Canadian society.[10]

Canadian Zionism

The first national organization of Canadian Jewry was Zionist. As early as 1887, a short-lived branch of the Lovers of Zion (Hovevei Zion) organization was founded in Montreal by Alexander Harkavy who was living there at the time. An offshoot of the American organization, the Lovers of Zion enlisted the mainly Lithuanian immigrants who had arrived in the 1870s. It initiated an abortive settlement of Canadians in Palestine.[11] Following the Zionist Congresses led by Herzl in 1897 and 1898, Zionist groups sprang up in the major centers of Jewish life. In 1899, a national organization was set up in Canada. The Federation of Zionist Societies (FZS) had branches throughout Canada, particularly prominent in the smaller centers of Jewish life where almost all the male Jews would be members. It served to cement those communities as well as join them to a national Jewish movement when none else existed.

Although most, if not all, the membership was made up of new immigrants, the Zionist movement in Canada was closely identified with Clarence de Sola, the third son of original rabbi Abraham de Sola. He remained head of the FZS of Canada until 1919.

The FZS was an ardent supporter of the Basle Program and the principles of political Zionism. The issue of dual loyalty did not arise with so prominent a man as de Sola speaking for the place of Zionism in Canadian life. For him, Palestine was a place to which those who were oppressed could come, even perhaps as an alternative to immigration to Canada. Identification with Palestine was also highly consistent with patriotic identification with British-Canadian nationalism and imperialism starting with the Boer War and rising even higher during the First World War. Some of this manifested itself in recruits for the Jewish Legion where about a fifth of the American Legionnaires were Canadian.[12]

The largely middle-class leadership of the Zionist organization determined that the meetings of the Zionist organization be conducted in English rather than the Yiddish of most of its members. This echoed the stance of the *uptowners* expressed in the *Jewish Times* when it also opposed the use of Yiddish in political gatherings. Several Yiddish-speaking Zionist organizations appeared in the three major centers of new immigrants enrolling those who had been Zionists in Europe. One called Doreshi Zion was founded in Montreal in 1903; another called Bnei Zion in the other centers. However, the thrust of the immigrant interests became even more manifest in the development of the Poalei Zion, the Labor Zionist movement, that first appeared in Canada in 1906. It served to combine the revolutionary aspirations of the Jewish proletariat and their survival as a national entity. It injected a spirit of radicalism and social justice.

The Labor Zionist strand was in the leadership among the Jewish workers in Canada to a greater degree even than the United States. Those coming to Canada, particularly Montreal, during 1905-06, provided the leadership for a revolutionary Yiddish-speaking component that enlarged Canadian Zionism. It was especially in

Montreal that this wave included Jews from the northwest provinces of Lithuania and Belorussia as well as Romania.[13]

In 1910, the Montreal chapter of Poalei Zion hosted the general meeting of the Labor Zionist organization throughout Canada. It organized demonstrations in support of Beilis, accused of blood libel in Kiev. Similar activities took place in Toronto and Winnipeg. The Labour Zionists took an active role in the short-lived publication starting in 1912 of the Volks Tzeitung, the first Yiddish socialist worker's publication in Canada. In 1913, The National Radical School, named after Peretz, combined the teaching of both Yiddish and Hebrew in a framework that focused on the ideas of social justice. In 1914, Poalei Zion helped establish in Montreal the Jewish People's Library along with a center for popular education. They also participated in the development of the Garment Workers Union and supported the 1912 garment workers' strike. In opposition to the Federation of Zionists, Poalei Tzion were among the initiators of the Canadian Jewish Congress.[14] All these efforts were interconnected through the Yiddish literary movement most easily expressed in the daily Yiddish newspaper to which they all contributed.

Poalei Zion combined both Yiddish and Hebrew. However, both the anti-Zionist (but nationalist Bundists) and the internationalist Socialists saw Yiddish as the language to foster. The Bundists made Yiddish an essential tenet; the Socialists did so as the language of convenience among its Jewish components. The Jewish youth had to choose between these different means of instituting messianism, between ways of bettering society and of ensuring the survival of the Jewish people in a modern progressive world.[15]

Yiddish Literary Life

The immigrants were traditionally cheder and yeshivah educated. Few had the benefits of more universal education prior to immigrating. In Canada, their options were for self-study and informal education in organizations based on ideology or in unions or mutual aid associations. The Yiddish press served as a medium of both self-expression and of intellectual growth. The Montreal School was a Jewish intelligentsia that could compete in some ways with New York.[16]

A year after arriving in Montreal in 1902, M. Hershman opened a Jewish bookstore that became a political and social center. His upstairs dining room became a free library and reading room. H. Wolofsky, the first to have a Yiddish linotype machine, founded what became a Yiddish daily. Der *Kanader Adler* (*Eagle*) began in 1907 as a weekly but became an eight-page daily in 1908. The Eagle Publishing Company in 1914 also took over the successor of old English-speaking *Jewish Times*. The contributors to the *Kanader Adler* also contributed to its progeny during the next decade including *Der Veg* and the *Volkszeitung*. Unlike the *Forverts*, the leading newspaper in New York, the *Adler* and *Der Weg* however both chose to support the main parties rather than the Socialists.

The *Eagle* became a weekly in midcentury and ceased publication finally in the 1960s.

One of the most long-lasting contributors to the *Adler* was Benjamin G. Sack. Although born with a form of muscular dystrophy, he was long-lived. He remained a contributor for sixty years and eventually wrote the first history of the Canadian Jewish community. Born in Lithuania in 1889 in a small village in the Kovno province, his parents were descendants of a long line of Talmudic scholars. Despite Sack's poor health, he was an outstanding student at the heder. The only secular education he received was from a visiting teacher when he was fourteen years old. In a short time, he mastered Russian and German and began to study mathematics, French, and English by himself.

Aged sixteen, he joined his father in Montreal in 1905. His elder brother, Mendel Leib, a student in the famous yeshivah at Volozhin, became a principal of the Talmud Torah at the Baron de Hirsch Institute in Montreal and also one of the founders of the Labour Zionist movement in the city. Under his brother's influence, Benjamin began to write poetry in Hebrew and Yiddish. He continued to write for the *Adler* from its start until it closed in 1967. At various times, he was its editorial writer and editor. He wrote for a number of other publications including the *Winnipeg Yid* and the *Volkzeitung*. He continued his studies in French, translating French poetry for publication in his newspaper and remained interested in the history of French Canada. He wrote about Canadian affairs for his readers with some breadth and depth despite the grind of daily journalism and his extraordinary physical limitations.[17]

Still another Yiddish writer who combined his work with his ideology was Solomon Haim Schneour. He was born in Vilna in 1884. He went to the Vilna Yeshivah and had an intense Jewish education. He was one of the youth of the city who, in a burst of joy, unharnessed the coach of Theodore Herzl on his historic visit in 1903. He opposed the anti-Zionist Bundists in the name of Jewish Socialism in the Land of Israel. Arriving in Montreal in 1907, he was recruited at the start of the *Adler* to write a column and editorials for the paper. He was instrumental in organizing the first Montreal Poalei Zionist group. He was a founding member of almost all the Jewish community organizations in Montreal during the immigration era. He attacked the lack of support for Jewish immigration by the existing craft labor movement and the similar stand by the Canadian Socialist Party.[18]

Contributing to the efflorescence around the *Adler* was the presence of one of the leading Hebrew scholars of his time. Reuben Brainin was born in Belorussia in Lita in 1862 in Liady to a very poor and religious family.[19] He was seventeen before he read his first secular book and began to move away from his traditional roots. He left Russia in his twenties to enroll first at the University of Vienna and then the University of Berlin. A journalist by profession, his great love was the revival of Hebrew as a living language. He wrote extensively in the Hebrew journals of his time about art and music, about travel and love. A central theme of Brainin's work was Hebrew literature in the Haskalah period with essays on such writers as Smolenskin and Mapu. He also wrote extensively in Yiddish.

Brainin was recruited from New York where he edited a Hebrew magazine to become editor in chief of the *Adler* in 1912.[20] Already fifty at the time of his arrival in Montreal, he had enormous impact on the community despite his short stay. He made the *Adler* the organ of new ideas while he himself became the focus around which the intellectuals of all political persuasions grouped themselves. He set up a Hebrew center where he gave lectures on a wide range of topics. His most lasting work was his success in helping to establish Montreal's Jewish People's Library (JPL), renamed the Jewish Public Library in 1932.[21]

Reading rooms had been characteristic of the immigrant community. A Zionist reading room had been set up in Montreal initially in 1887 by the Hibbat Zion. Other Zionist reading rooms also arose later both in Montreal and Toronto. The more radical arrivals after the turn of the century set up their own such as one created by Hershman above his bookstore. From the start of the Poalei Zionist group in the spring of 1905, there had been interest in establishing a *library*. The plan was to set up in 1912 a People's Library in collaboration between the Jewish Labour Farband, the Workmen's Circle as well as the various struggling union groups. Brainin was invited to be the president of the new library and its associated People's University. It finally opened its doors in 1914 in rented quarters with books, half in Yiddish, assembled from Poalei Zion and Dorshei Zion collections. It was representative of the entire immigrant community rather than any particular party. Its activities were patterned by Brainin after the Educational Alliance established on the Lower East Side of New York.[22] Activities included, as a major fundraiser in 1915, a program involving the famed writer Sholem Aleichem.[23] Its twentieth anniversary in 1934 featured the Yiddish poet Haim Leivick. It has grown over the years in terms of its collections and cultural offerings in English and French as well as Yiddish and continues even into the twenty-first century.

Brainin championed, during World War I, the cause of democracy in Jewish public life. He was president in 1915 of the Canadian Jewish Alliance made up of representatives of people's organizations that served as the eventual basis for the first Canadian Jewish Congress. In 1915, he left the *Adler* to found his own competing Yiddish newspaper *Der Weg*. After its closure in 1916, he returned to New York. His contribution to the initiatives leading to the Canadian Jewish Congress was recognized when he was a featured speaker at its inauguration in 1919. Although his stay was short, Brainin broadened the social and intellectual scope of the community.[24] He looked back on his Canadian stay as a high point in his life and, on his request, was buried in Montreal after his death in 1939.

The Jewish Labour Movement

The Jewish Labour movement sprouted directly from the terrible conditions in the garment industry. Piecework at home under bad conditions was the pattern in Canada as in all the other settings. Newly arrived immigrants could be recruited to undercut any attempt to organize a union or win a strike. The garment industry, particularly in Montreal, was dominated by Jews, both as employers as well as employees. The enemy was identifiable by class. For example, a bitter strike in 1900 at the Mark Workman factory in Montreal carried over to the angry strikers, filling the seats in the synagogue he was dedicating in his role as president of the congregation

In Toronto, there were fewer opportunities to find work in Jewish settings where Sabbath could be properly observed. Peddling and the salvage trades were thus more common. With the increase in immigration after the turn of the century, the smaller Toronto community became more industrialized. Unlike Montreal, almost all the firms in the clothing industry in Toronto were non-Jewish. There were also some large-scale firms in Winnipeg. In all three centers, efforts to organize workers did not last, nor were strikes effective. For example, in 1907, an unsuccessful attempt was made among the men's clothing workers to organize the United Garment Workers Union (UGWU) in Montreal. Several of the Poalei Zion members, along with other socialists and anarchists, were involved.

The examples of successful strikes in New York fed the militancy in Canada. In 1909, a group in Toronto finally formed the Toronto Union of Cloakmakers that joined the International Union of Ladies' Garment Workers (ILGWU) in 1911 after the latter's successes in New York. 1912 saw the massive industry-wide strike in Montreal against the men's clothing factory owners. It was the first general strike in the men's clothing industry in that town. Many, if not most, of the owners were the leaders of the Jewish communal organizations. The owners were frequently related by marriage or business ties going back to the 1860s and 1870s in the Litvak colony in the Lancaster area of Ontario. There were twenty important factories employing five thousand workers, almost all Jewish.

The fiery Leon Chazanovitch led the strike. He was the editor of the more radical Yiddish weekly *Volkszeitung*. Spending less than a year in Montreal during 1912, Chazanovitch began several important initiatives that bore fruit after his departure.

Born in Lita, Chazanowitch fled the yeshivah to become an *agitator* for the Poalei Zion. He adopted his name while in America in 1908. Going to Argentina, he defended the settlers against the Jewish Colonization Society. His deportation at the behest of the JCA made him even stronger in his opposition to bourgeois Jewry. While in Montreal, he clearly identified the political parameters of the school board issue. In calling together the *peoples conference*, a meeting of twenty organizations on schooling, he provided the model for the organization of the Jewish community that would bear fruit in 1919 with the Canadian Jewish Congress.[25]

The strikes of 1912 went on both in Montreal and Toronto. In the former, after seven weeks, the union was only partially successful in reducing working hours but did not succeed in replacing piecework or in establishing a union shop. Nevertheless, the degree of unity engendered by the strike action was one of its even more important results. In his leadership of the strike through the *Volkszeitung*, Chazanovitch brought into the class struggle legitimization of his emphasis on Jewish nationalism that Poalei Zion represented. The Montreal locals of what was the United Garment Workers of America (UGWA) identified with the Poalei Zion. Its messianic message provided them with the ideological basis for their union militancy. They were battling not only for improved wages and working conditions but for social justice and recognition of the dignity of labour.[26]

Unlike Montreal, the Toronto women's clothing industry was dominated by Eaton's, the large department store chain. The failure of the strike at Eaton's in 1912 made even more difficult the further development of unions in that city, and Eaton's remained nonunion. However, its monopoly of the women's garment trade was broken by the development of small Jewish-owned firms in the area of Spadina Avenue.

In 1916-17, a further series of strikes took place but now under the auspices of the Amalgamated Clothing Workers of America (ACWA) led by Sidney Hillman. Bitterly fought and lasting several months, the findings of an arbitration panel were finally accepted that included a forty-six-hour week, time and a half for overtime, and the equivalent of a union shop. Although focused on wages and working conditions, there was an underlying spirit that motivated the Jewish labour movement. The unionism of the ACWA incorporated some of the ideology of the immigrants' search for social justice, reflecting the leadership of Sidney Hillman, the head of the parent Amalgamated Clothing Workers in the United States.

The needle trades and the search for justice in the class struggle was in Canada, as elsewhere in the Litvak Diaspora, the context where the messianic ideology intersected with the labour movement and contributed to its development beyond the original concept of trade unionism. The messianic belief in the possibility of a New World order on earth lay behind the militancy with which the unionization was carried out. Their common bond was a sympathy for the working classes, an adamant secularism, and a belief in the necessity to maintain that secular culture through the Yiddish language.

In each of the several Canadian centers, one expression of this secular socialist strand was the development of cultural, mainly literary, societies and schools to offer an alternative to assimilation and the very limited education offered by the traditional religious cheder.[27] One example in Toronto was the National Radical School founded in 1911. It evolved by 1916 into the I. L. Peretz School under the auspices of the Workmen's Circle.[28] Similarly in Winnipeg, the secular-minded socialists established in 1912 a Yiddisher Jugend Farein affiliated with the Workmen's Circle. It also became known by the name of the Yiddish writer I. L. Peretz. Relevant was the fact that the percentage of the Jewish population reporting Yiddish as their mother tongue was higher in Winnipeg than any other Canadian city. It was 90 percent in 1941.[29] Ideological differences between the Labour Zionists and the socialists expressed themselves in the degree to which there was use of Hebrew as well as Yiddish as languages of instruction. In 1920 in Winnipeg, these various schools evolved into the first Yiddish day school in North America that retained the name of Peretz.[30] In Montreal, the evolution of the Yiddish-speaking schools came about under similar auspices of the Poalei Zion and the Workmen's Circle. Separation occurred between these two strands, depending on the emphasis to be placed on Hebrew versus Yiddish as a reflection of the relative Zionist motifs of the curriculum.[31]

The Religious Tradition

The messianic secular movements of Socialism and Zionism that arose out of Lita did not entirely diminish the religious identity that remained. The relatively conservative nature of Canadian society served to maintain the adherence to Orthodoxy. The most difficult adjustment was required of the religious scholars. There was no opportunity for support while they spent their lives studying. A few found work in Jewish schools or were able to form small congregations. Forced to earn a living, many worked in the needle trades.

The institutions within the existing Jewish community prior to the great migration sought English-speaking rabbis from Britain or the United States. There was a relatively small Reform Temple Emmanu-el in Montreal along with relatively large Holy Blossom Temple in Toronto. Each of the Reform temples, including a third in Hamilton, expressed to a differing degree their identification with the very large Reform movement in the United States.[32]

The influence of the United States was particularly manifest in the development of an offshoot of the American Conservative movement in *Shaar Hashomayim*, the premier Ashkenazi synagogue in Montreal. Its longtime rabbi was Haim (Herman) Abramowitz. Abramowitz was born in Vilna in 1880. He recalled having been brought to its yeshivah as a youngster by his father. At age eight, after his father's death., he emigrated to the United States with his mother but remained committed to becoming a rabbi. He graduated in 1902 from New York's Jewish Theological Seminary soon after its reorganization under Solomon Schechter. Appointed immediately after graduation to the Montreal synagogue, he was the voice of the conservative religious tradition as its rabbinate evolved to participate as a representative to the larger community. Illustrative of his many appointments of a wider nature was that of Jewish chaplain in the Canadian army during the First World War.[33] The *Shaar*, as a Conservative synagogue, was the leader in the Montreal community extending through into the post-Second World War era.[34]

The religious leaders of the immigrant community reflected the Litvak heritage. The Orthodox leaders in all three major centers derived from roots in the great yeshivot of Lita. To an unusual extent, they were Zionists. Non-English speaking, their activities focused on the development of Jewish education in the East European model.

The dean of Toronto's rabbis was Jacob Gordon. He was born in 1877 in Danilovitz in the Pale of Settlement. He was educated at rabbinical academies in Minsk, Kovno as well as the world-famed Volozhin in Lita. But recently ordained as a graduate of the Yeshivah of Volozhin, he arrived in Toronto in 1903. He became the rabbi of the largest synagogue there, remaining the senior rabbi until his death. He was succeeded as chief rabbi by an English-speaking rabbi in 1917. His synagogue, Goel Tzedec, known as the Litvak shule was organized by East European Jews in 1884 who also employed their own butcher to assure kashrut. They did not want to depend upon the services provided by the Reform-minded *Holy Blossom Temple*. In the East European tradition, Gordon became the rabbi whose authority was accepted by the large number of Orthodox congregations. He acted as the judge on religious issues. Under his auspices the first substantial Talmud Torah was organized. It was staunchly Zionist and used Hebrew as the language of instruction in the model of the Tarbut schools of Lithuania. He lectured and taught the Talmud in Hebrew as well as writing books on commentaries.[35]

Perhaps even more in the classical East European tradition was the role of Rabbi Israel Isaac Kahanovitch as chief rabbi of Western Canada. He was born in Grodno in Lita in 1872. Educated at the yeshivah of Grodno and Slobodka in Kovno, he was ordained in his twentieth year. He came to North America in 1906. After about a year in Scranton, Pennsylvania, he came to Winnipeg where he remained for his entire career.[36] He was the first ordained Orthodox rabbi in Winnipeg and Western Canada who could deal authoritatively with questions of Jewish law. He eventually established a system for *kashruth*. He organized Talmud study circles in the Orthodox Beth Jacob synagogue to which he had been appointed. He supported the interest in the building of a Talmud Torah where modern spoken Hebrew would be the language of instruction. This was the forerunner of what became one of the largest such educational programs in North America. A day school was founded in 1944 along with a secondary school and school for higher Jewish studies called Maimonides College.[37] Kahanovitch was one of the leaders in Western Canada in supporting the convening of the Canadian Jewish Congress and topped the list of delegates from Winnipeg after receiving the largest number of votes.[38]

The concept of a "congress" had been in use within the Zionist world since the First Zionist Congress in Basle in 1897. This revolutionary idea was a more democratic method of organization than the more traditional use of well-connected persons to interact with the powerful. Solomon Schneour, in the *Adler* as early as 1908, had broached the idea of a *parliament* of Canada's Jews. Other suggestions for the formation of an equivalent to the British Board of Jewish Deputies was opposed in 1909 by the directors of the Baron de Hirsch Institute.

The issue came to a head in the context of the distribution of funds raised for relief activities during World War I. The basic issue was the failure to consult the wishes of the majority. The Zionist Federation, under the longtime leadership of de Sola, was the only existing national body. It opposed the action of the "Alliance" as competitive with the already existing role of the Zionist Federation. De Sola called a group together in the fall of 1915, under Federation auspices called the Canadian Jewish Conference. This new group known as the Canadian Jewish Committee, led by notables such as Lyon Cohen and Sam Jacobs, carried out its own relief activities. In the meantime, the calling of the democratically elected American Jewish Congress in the United States served as a powerful example. The issues seemed to go beyond those of war relief and Zionism to the protection of the civil rights of Jews in the countries to be formed at the Peace Conference as well as organization of Canadian Jewry to deal with restrictions on immigration. The differences were not ideological but institutional, perhaps even personal.

The Zionists eventually adhered, under the leadership of the newly chosen Archie Freiman, to the principle of a democratically selected "congress." This compromise was for a "congress" to be called with the Zionists rather than by them. It led the way to the Canadian Jewish Congress in March 1919.[39]

The East European immigrant generation had become the majority of the Jewish community. Their impact ultimately manifested itself in the political arena within the more democratic governance of the Jewish community itself. The founding and short-term operation of the Canadian Jewish Congress was an important measure of that development. However temporary was the unity achieved of the wealthy, the Zionists, and the immigrant community, it was to be reestablished in the interwar period when its necessity became even more urgent. Unlike the experience in the United States, the Canadian Jewish Congress remained a relatively strong national voice.

4.2.2 The Acculturating Generation

There was a net increase of approximately 20,000 immigrants, mainly occurring before 1926 when restrictions began to be applied with even greater stringency. The Jewish population increased more slowly since it was now far more dependent on natural increase. In 1941, the 170,00 Jews continued to form approximately 1.5 percent of the entire population.

Despite the great effort by the JCA, in 1921, the grand total of the Jewish farming population was variously calculated between 2,500-3,500. There had been the widespread departure of children of the original farmers to the cities in search of war jobs during World War I.[1] Only 4 percent of Jews were living in rural areas. The three urban centers continued to increase. The percentage living in cities was twice that of non-Jews in Canada. The population was split almost entirely between the provinces of Ontario, Quebec, and Manitoba with its greatest density in the last, albeit only holding one-eighth of the total.[2]

By the early 1930s, the percentage of Jews, either foreign-born achieving citizenship status or Canadian born, exceeded 80 percent and exceeded other non-British ethnic groups.[3] In 1941, for the first time, slightly more than 50 percent were Canadian-born and the percentage that held Canadian citizenship reached 85 percent.[4] Circa one-third of Jews were engaged in trade, having fallen about 10 percent from the previous census. The one-third in manufacturing was twice that of the rest of the population reflecting the large number still engaged in the manufacture of clothing. The number of clerical workers had nearly doubled, and those in the professions had increased two-thirds with the latter still less than the percentage in the total population. There was thus a major increase in the acculturated Canadian-born moving into clerical and professional groups. However, the generation of Canadian-born Jews seeking to enter the professional classes was opposed by both the existing Anglo-Celtic and the rising French-Canadian middle class.[5]

The religious and secular strands, both Socialist and Zionist, brought to Canada by the immigrant generation continued to evolve during the interwar period differentiated somewhat between the several centers.

Evolution in Winnipeg

During this interwar era, Jews formed a higher percentage of the total population in Winnipeg as well as of the professional classes in that city than elsewhere. The Gurvitch/Gurvey family, whose origins were described earlier, can illustrate the evolution of the Jewish community in that city and its relative adherence to Yiddishkayt.

The Gurvitch family continued to live in the North End of Winnipeg in what was an almost entirely Yiddish neighborhood. They identified themselves with the Bundist Workmen's Circle (Arbeiter Ring) and a belief in socialism. They were not religious or Zionist. The four sons all went to Yiddish school in the afternoon, either at the Peretz Schule or the one run by the Arbeiter Ring after going to public school. They did not belong to a synagogue although the boys were all bar mitzvah. The children changed the family name to Gurvey during the 1930s when "no one with a Jewish-sounding name could get a job."

There were four sons. The eldest, Morris—born in 1911—after high school, went to Toronto where he went into the export-import business. He married a Toronto girl. Another of the sons, named after Sholem Aleichem but called Samuel Nathan, born in 1917, married a Winnipeg girl and worked as a pharmacist. The youngest brother, Gerald, born in 1919, married a Winnipeg girl. A high school graduate, he worked as a booking agent for films.

Harry Gurvey, the second son, was born in 1915. Like his brothers, he went to Yiddish school after the day spent at public school. A Yiddishist like his father, he read and wrote Yiddish rather than Hebrew. He became a pharmacist after studying at the University of Manitoba and owned a small retail pharmacy in the West End of Winnipeg in an Icelandic neighborhood near downtown.

He married, in 1956, a woman born in Winnipeg in 1931 and trained as a librarian. She had a religious background, and it was on her initiative that the family belonged to a Conservative synagogue, *Rosh Pinna*, from the time of their marriage. There were no longer any Yiddish schools in Winnipeg, and the children went to Hebrew schools after completing the public day school. The family also had moved from the north end to the more fashionable south end.

There were three children. Their elder son, Martin, born in 1957, went to Herzlyia Academy for Hebrew training after public school before going on to School of Chiropractic in Toronto. Living in Winnipeg after marrying a Toronto girl, Martin had three children with the single son, Harlan, going to an Anglican day school. Harry's only daughter, Gayla, was born in 1959. After training as an occupational therapist at the University of Manitoba, she lived in Toronto where she married a psychiatrist. Her five daughters all went to Bialik School, a Hebrew day school. The younger son, Alan, born in 1962, trained in law at University of Manitoba after undergraduate training at Brown University in the United States. Unmarried, he lived in Southern California.

Harry Gurvey credited his consciousness of his Vilna background as giving his upbringing a greater flavor of *Yiddishkayt* than others might have. Vilna represented a greater grounding in the literary character of Yiddish life, in a commitment to learning for its own sake. The family thought of themselves as better educated and more respectful of learning. They also identified with the sense of making the world a better place in the spirit of socialism and in the spirit of the Bund, secular and non-Zionist.

The story of Winnipeg since the great migration was one of a close-knit Jewish community that was a relatively large percentage of what was at that time a small-sized city. The original settlement in the North End has dissipated with the move to the more fashionable South End. The city has grown considerably in size while many of the descendants of the original Jewish families have migrated elsewhere, particularly to Toronto but also to the United States. Jews were prominent in Winnipeg politics, and the family supported the election of CCF candidates in general although not active in politics themselves. Coming from a Yiddish secular background, the subsequent generation learned Hebrew. They were also more likely to go to the local university, in this instance the University of Manitoba. Pharmacy in the first generation and medicine and law in the second generation were the measure of professional status. The grandchildren living in Toronto went to a Jewish day school with an emphasis on Hebrew. The single grandson went to a fashionable private Anglican school in Winnipeg while his sisters went to the public school.

The Yiddish language schools were part of an even more generalized Jewish educational system in Winnepeg during the interwar period. The city's Jewish community had the strongest representation of the secular Yiddish socialist ethos. The schisms and mergers that occurred mirrored the history of the movement to maintain Yiddish national culture during this generation. In 1916, the Labour Zionists combined with the Socialist Territorialists to develop the long-lasting Peretz School. This school combined both Yiddish and Hebrew to accommodate both tendencies. Starting in 1920, the Peretz School began to develop a Yiddish day school, the first of its kind in North America. Haim Zhitlovsky was appropriately the featured speaker at the graduation of its first class in 1925 since its character was in accordance with his teachings. In 1930, the Labour Zionists split off to establish their own Volks Shule to emphasize Hebrew in accordance with their Zionist commitment. The Arbeiter Ring Shule, founded in 1920, reflecting the more internationalist social democratic strand, split in 1926 as the Workmen's Circle expelled those Marxists that followed the Communist Soviet Union. This schism then created the Sholem Aleichem Shule under the auspices of the Communist International Workers Order (IWO) whose Jewish Peoples Fraternal Order (JPFO) was the Yiddish branch.[6]

Coincident with these developments, the Yiddish press also became established. The *Dos Yiddisher Vort* (the *Israelite Press*) was the Winnipeg newspaper in the interwar era. It was supportive of the Canadian Jewish Congress at the time of the latter's formation. The newspaper took a nonpartisan approach supporting both the Hebraists and the Yiddishists in the cultural wars. In the 1920s, English-language weeklies began to appear, reflecting the acculturation in the readership.[7]

Illustrative of the energy behind these developments were men such as Alter Cherniack. Born in Northwest provinces of the Pale in Belorussia, he arrived in Winnipeg in 1905 at age twenty having repudiated his yeshivah education by membership in the Socialist Territorialist movement. He was militantly conscious of social inequities. He remained particularly interested in problems of immigration, having experienced mistreatment along with his mother and younger sister when immigrating to Canada via Halifax. In 1914, for example, he was one who protested against the Order in Council that was to be applied to Jewish immigrants, requiring them to carry a passport issued by the Russian authorities. This requirement would be impossible to meet for the large group who were leaving Russia after having transgressed any of the numerous regulations designed to harass Jews.[8]

Cherniack worked as a watchmaker on his arrival in Winnipeg, but his major interest was in his commitment to the movement he believed would help change the world. Despite being penniless, he was a delegate to Socialist-territorialist conventions in Boston and Cleveland. He was, along with his wife Fanny, one of the founders of the Peretz School in 1916. She worked as a seamstress to support them as he gained an undergraduate degree at St John's College and then a law degree at Manitoba Law School (University of Manitoba). He campaigned for the principle of a democratically based congress and was selected as a delegate to the Canadian Jewish Congress (CJC) from Winnipeg in 1919. He was involved in maintaining the Jewish Immigrant Aid Society (JIAS) whose branch in Winnipeg was the most active during the interwar era and in the Labour Zionist Jewish National Workers Alliance (Farband).

Cherniack was involved in politics, first with the Independent Labour Party and then the CCF. For example, he served as A. A. Heap's first campaign manager in 1926 in his election as a socialist member to the federal parliament from the heavily Jewish North End. He and his family remained a supporter of the Yiddishist initiatives. His wife was instrumental in bringing about the expansion of the Peretz School into a day school to which their own children and grandchildren went.[9, 10]

Evolution in Toronto

The population of the two major eastern provinces was approximately equal signifying the increased growth of Toronto as the major centre in Ontario during this interwar period. In that city, Jews were the largest single non-Anglo-Celtic ethnic group. The Jewish population had spread beyond the old central district into the area of Spadina where the garment industry had also migrated.

The route taken by the Kayfetz bamily in Toronto, with their origins described earlier, illustrates that taken it was by many others. The parents, Leah and Mottel, married in 1908. The latter worked in a number of different factory jobs. Mottel became ill in 1919, eventually paralysed due to some unknown cause, and died in 1927 while at a nursing home. The burden of caring for the family fell upon the elder brother, Dave, who ran a successful newsstand adjacent to one of the resorts in Toronto. The mother, Leah, would take in work at home from the garment factories and would also, at times, work in the garment factories to help out. There was little interest in politics beyond municipal issues. Toronto politics were the bailiwick of the Protestant Orangemen.

The family lived in the Bathurst area of Toronto and ran a variety of different stores on the ground floor of their house. They owned a free-standing house bought for $5,000 in the early 1920s that was sold for the same price some years later. Both daughters moved to California after relatively low-level jobs. Dave joined the Canadian army during World War II but was unable to reclaim his profitable newsstand upon his demobilization. He had a number of relatively successful businesses. His four children included the son who was a successful criminal lawyer and a daughter with an administrative position in the Ontario public high school system.

The younger son, Ben, was the first of his family to finish high school, graduating from Harband Collegiate High School in 1934. He worked as a newsboy to pay his way to the University of Toronto where he studied English, French, and German. His first regular job was as an editor and all-around worker on the English-language weekly *Jewish Standard* in Toronto and later in Chicago under Meyer Weisgal, the Zionist publicist. Not accepted by the military for health reasons, he worked as a teacher in Huntsville in northern Ontario during the war. Due to his skill with languages, he was hired by the Canadian government to censor German POW mail and continued in a similar role in Berlin in occupied Germany from 1945-47. While still there, he was recruited for a job at the Canadian Jewish Congress where he spent the remainder of his career.

Under direction of Saul Hayes, the executive director, he was responsible for the CJC's work in conjunction with the Anti-Defamation League of the B'nai B'rith in the area of combating anti-Semitism and passing antidiscrimination laws on a provincial and federal basis. Ben considers himself a Litvak not merely by ancestry. He harkens back to the Mussar movement of Rabbi Salanter as his cultural ancestor. The Litvak devotion to ethical standards and their "obstinancy" are the touchstones of his identity. They have helped to sustain him in his life of service to the Canadian Jewish community and in his literary work.

Evolution in Montreal

During the interwar period, the population of Montreal was still the largest in Canadian Jewry with movement toward the west and north portions of town. Jews were the third largest ethnic group in that city next to the French and the Anglo-Celts. English was clearly the dominant language in Jewish Montreal with Yiddish continuing to be used as well in the majority of families.[11]

The British connection to the implementation of the dream of Zion in Palestine reinforced the commitment of Canadian Jewry to their Anglo identity in Quebec.

The problem facing the Jews of Montreal in light of the confessional nature of its schools remained unresolved for the entire decade of the 1920s. Litigation was carried to the highest level of the Privy Council in London. In 1922, the 1903 law under which Jewish students were placed under the Protestant School Board was declared unconstitutional at the behest of the Protestant Board. Their concern was to maintain the Christian nature of the Protestant school system by the exclusion of Jewish representation on the teaching staff or the governance of the system. The problem was compounded by the differing interests of the two major segments of the Jewish community. The uptowners advocated an "integrationist" position of remaining within the Protestant system. The "separatist" alternative of a Jewish school system was supported by the Jewish Worker's Conference, representing the clothing workers union, the Arbeiter Ring, and a number of Yiddishist groups as well as those concerned with the uneven quality of Hebrew religious education.[12]

The "David" law passed in 1930 authorized the appointment of a Jewish school commission that could go about creating a Jewish school system. It became the touchstone for vicious attacks by the anti-Semitic press as bowing to Jewish pressure and making the Jews equal to the French Canadians by legitimizing the Jews as an official minority. The very significant opposition of the Catholic hierarchy weighed in. Their concern was the possibility of a religiously neutral school system being established. The government exerted great pressure on the Jewish school commission to negotiate an arrangement with the Protestant School Board rather than establish an independent system. The compromise was essentially a return to the 1903 law but without all the rights accorded under that law. Those who were of Protestant religious and Anglo-Canadian national identity remained in control of the education of the Jewish students. There was to be no Jewish representation in the management of the Protestant School Board. The Jewish "nationalistic" position was undermined by the opposition of the "uptowner" appointees to the Jewish school commission opposed to the development of a Jewish cultural option. The resultant disunity continued in 1930s when even more difficult challenges would exist.[13]

To a considerable extent, the "nationalists" represented the group that had supported the development of the secular radical schools in the period following the 1910 Montreal Convention of the Poalei Zion. The Poalei Zion established the Jewish Community Council that led the fight for Jewish day schools in Montreal as part of the attempt to create a Yiddish environment. In the 1920s, Montreal was unique in its commitment to Yiddish and Hebrew teaching in its secular schools. The full range included the I. L. Peretz School, the Jewish People's School as well as the Abraham Reisen School run by the Workmen's Circle. They lasted into the post-Second World War era. The Volk Shule established in 1928, and still in existence, is an expression of that utopian commitment by people such as Schlomo Wiseman, the chief theoretician of the Yiddish day school movement.[14]

The evolution of the Garmaise family in Montreal illustrates the move into professional self-employment as well as the more religious identification characteristic of that city. Saleh Garmaise was the founder of the family who came around 1895 from a small village near Vilna. It is likely that he married in Canada since all of his seven children were born there. The family name was an adaptation to the French of the original name. Other branches of the family chose Garber as their surname. Quite learned, Saleh was a quiet man who busied himself with his cronies, playing chess and held a number of low-paying jobs such as a watchman. The family lived on Saint-Urbain Street where Mordecai Richler also placed his characters.

The three eldest daughters remained unmarried and lived together. The eldest became an elementary school teacher in the Devonshire School run by the Protestant School Board in what was an immigrant district. Initially Jewish, the school district was the successive home of those most recently immigrated over the forty-five years she remained. When she finally retired, she had reached the status of being the so-called Dutchess of Devonshire. Her two younger sisters held clerical jobs, one a bookkeeper for her brothers Max and Maurice in their law practice.

Max was the eldest son born in 1908. In 1910, he suffered polio and required crutches to get around for his entire life. Despite his disability, he had a full life, both personal and professional. He had extraordinary perseverance, walking to school despite the icy sidewalks of the Montreal winter. Max's tuition was paid by a cousin who had immigrated earlier, enabling him to be both an undergraduate at McGill and then a law graduate. He qualified as a *notary*. This profession is unique to the law as practiced in Quebec. It deals with real estate transactions and other business contractual aspects. His career was thus sensitive to the business climate and particularly problematic in 1932 when he entered practice. The Depression was a particularly severe one in Montreal.

Max Garmaise married, in 1934, Anne Richler who had grown up in a Chassidic family from Galicia, devoted to their rebbe. The extent of their devotion was the burial of her father, Jacob Richler, in a grave adjacent to the rebbe. Unlike the Garmaise/Garber family derived from Lita, Jacob Richler did not encourage his nine children to go to school. Only the youngest brother graduated from McGill. Having met his wife at the Orthodox Young Israel, Max and his branch adhered to a religious identity to an unusual degree. Their residences echoed the drift of Jewish life, moving west. Starting in an area close to Boulevard Saint-Laurent, they moved to Outremont and then to a duplex house in Côte-des-Neiges, following the peregination of the Young Israel congregation with which they were closely involved. All the three children were schooled in Orthodox Jewish day schools. Anne's first cousin was the father of the famous author, Mordecai Richler. The family was proud of their famous member but disturbed by his intermarriage and, unlike their continued adherence to Orthodoxy, his decision not to raise his children in the Jewish tradition.

After qualifying as a notary, his next brother, Maurice, joined the practice after return from overseas duty in the Canadian army during World War II. Like his younger brothers, he was identified with socialist causes. To an unusual degree, his children were associated with Habonim and Hashomer Hatzair, the Labour Zionist youth groups. One remains a "carpenter in the Galilee" on a kibbutz. Another son had joined a moshav but returned to Canada.

The next brother, Avram, also suffered from the effects of childhood polio and trained at McGill as an accountant. Highly cultured, he was active in left-wing causes particularly in sponsorship of avant-garde films. His son became a librarian. His daughter became a supporter of the separatist Parti Québécois, very unusual among Anglophone Jews.

The youngest brother, David, trained as a chemist, earning a doctorate from McGill in an accelerated wartime program at an unusually early age. His identification with left-wing causes stunted his career by disqualifying him from the security clearance required for other than civilian sector jobs. He worked at McGill. His children lived both in the United States and Canada. One of the Garmaise cousins, also called Max, was a close colleague of Abraham Klein in the latter's short-lived legal career in Rouyn Quebec. Later a judge, his daughter married Klein's son.

Jewish Farm Life

Despite the small rural population, the promise of Canada as an opportunity for Jewish renewal on the prairies was not entirely lost. Even as late as 1941, after a decade of drought and falling farm prices, there were some hundreds living on the farms. The number of second-generation sons still on the land was in the range of 45 percent, somewhat higher than the percentage of those sons of non-Jewish farmers.[15] The JCA continued to support, by loans, those who tried to stay on the land despite recurrent crop failures and low prices.[16] Of all the Jewish farm colonies in Western Canada, Edenbridge in Saskatchewan was the most successful. It is described in 1939 as "a living monument to the courage, enterprise and adaptability of the Jew."

Edenbridge was set up in 1906 in the Carrot River region in northern Saskatchewan. The first portion of the name derived from the Yiddish *Yidn*. Imbued with radical ideas, they sought a *productive* Jewish life by working the land analogous to the spirit inspiring the pioneers in Palestine at that same time. The colonists would work all day and then debate and study all night.[17] It was founded originally fourteen miles from the nearest railway in an area of dense swamp and forest. The settlers cut the forest to provide logs for sale and then lumber to build their houses.[18] The settlement lasted through the interwar period but the droughts of the 1930s and the inevitable migration of the young to the cities weakened it from its height in the 1920s. Its success for nearly forty years may be attributed in part to the ideological basis its Litvak founders brought to it.

The Vickar brothers were its first settlers. They came to the prairies of Canada in 1906 after having migrated to South Africa from Lita some years before. They were the leading family in the southern end of the settlement. They owned the general store and built the synagogue as well as farming a large number of acres. Many of the other newcomers aimed to prove that Jews could succeed in "noble labour." They did not want to succumb to capitalistic exploitation nor to the role of *nonproductive* labour. They were left-wing socialists and antireligious. In the north end of the settlement, they built their own International Hall and Free Library with Mike Usiskin, their leader. Each segment in the settlement had its own school with two sets of teachers and two school boards.[19]

Usiskin had come to Edenbridge in 1911 from the East End of London, after having emigrated originally from the Vitebsk region in Lita in 1906. There the Usiskin family lived in the countryside as tenants on a lord's manor where the father earned his living as the innkeeper and distiller. The grandfather had been the rabbi in the district. Like his brothers and sisters, Mike was educated by tutors who came to their village. Educating himself, he went far beyond the usual in the study of nature as well as languages. His family was not fanatically religious and encouraged him to pursue secular subjects. Working as a fur cutter in the East End of London, he looked for a solution to the exploitation he saw around him. From the beginning, his dream was a farming colony in which the farmers would buy their supplies and sell their produce cooperatively "to live and work together in friendship."[20]

At a meeting of the farmers in Edenbridge under Usiskin's leadership, they agreed to begin a life concerned with cultural and spiritual values even as they were trying to conquer a wilderness. There would be a meeting hall, a free-lending library, a drama club.[21] Usiskin himself brought with him two hundred books and periodicals. At Edenbridge, he organized the Yiddish school, the lectures, and theatre that were well attended despite the twelve to fourteen hours of farmwork each day.[22] They were always arguing about their various ideas. What had been created on the prairies did not depart from concern for the world of ideas that had been nurtured in the urban settings of Lita.

Yiddish Literary Life

The continued cultural evolution of Yiddish on the North American continent was clearly under siege in the context of the acculturation of the immigrant generation and their offspring.

Abraham Roback worked for the recognition of Yiddish as a language within the community of languages of the world. Born in 1890 near Bialystok in the northwest Pale, he was brought to Montreal at the age of two. He continued to identify with his birthplace by publishing, even as a teenager, under the nom de plume of Goniandzer, his hometown. His father, Isaac, worked in a clothing factory. Uneducated, he was described by his son as a fiercely independent man who never hesitated to insult his employers and never asked for favors. Abraham's elder brother, Moses, had been trained in a yeshivah in Europe but also worked in a clothing factory as a cutter. There were a total of four children, including two sisters, before the parents were divorced. Abraham, as the youngest, remained with his mother who was described as a "fanatically religious person." She encouraged her son to stay with his prayers to the extent that he was frequently late for school. She also had an unusually rich Yiddish vocabulary that provided a source for her son's initial interest in the variations to which Yiddish was prone.

Roback received his education in Montreal in the Talmud Torah and with private teachers. He began Talmud training at age nine. On his own, he pursued studies in philology and Latin, Greek, and Arabic as well as Hebrew and Yiddish. He began to publish in the *Adler* at its very start in 1907 and worked as one of its early editors while at McGill. At age seventeen, one of perhaps sixty Jewish students, he entered

McGill, graduating in 1912. While there, he argued for Yiddish as the Jewish national language and recognition of its literature and folklore. When he went to Harvard for graduate study that same year, he already was one of the foremost authorities in Yiddish, battling for its recognition and preservation. Several hundred persons under the chairmanship of Reuben Brainin honored young Roback at his departure from Montreal. At Harvard, he studied philosophy and psychology. His subsequent academic career in the Boston area was in psychology at Emerson College, not a major university.

A polymath and scholar in the Litvak tradition, he published extensively in the entire range of the Yiddish daily press and periodicals. The historian of Yiddish folklore and literature, he published in English under YIVO auspices *The Story of Yiddish Literature* in 1940 and 1958. He was the principal organizer of the Yiddish collection of the Harvard College Library and of the first Yiddish course at an American university while at Emerson. Not part of the Yiddish establishment, he nevertheless carried on his fight for recognition of Yiddish throughout his life. Published in Paris in 1964 was his major tome *Der Folks Geist in der Yiddisher Sprach* just prior to his death in 1965.[23]

The Yiddish literary initiatives of the early immigrants continued to flourish to an unusual degree in Montreal during the interwar era. It was the only city on the continent other than New York that had enough Yiddish writers to form a Yiddish Writers Guild.[24] Unlike New York as the other center for Yiddish writers in North America, the Montreal school reflected a relatively strong cultural base, albeit a far smaller population. The Montreal Yiddish renaissance of this era was incubated by the Jewish Public Library and the Arbeiter Ring where public readings would take place. There was the development unique in North America analogous to the secular Yiddish culture of Eastern Europe.[25]

Noah-Isaac Gotlib was born in Kovno in Lita in 1903. He came to Montreal in 1930. A left-wing Zionist, he became part of the Yiddish scene. He published a dozen books in Yiddish with the last called *Montreal* published after his death in 1968. This long poem deals with his impressions soon after his arrival, his meeting with the others in the literary circle, and bringing to the streets and parks of the Jewish quarter a sense of similarity to his origins in Lithuania.[26]

Yabob Yitzhak Segal was born in the Ukraine in 1896. He was the sixth of seven children and his father, a cantor and scribe, died when he was three. Segal was of scholarly ancestry on both sides of his family. He was raised in an observant household in Korets, a Chassidic center. The town had a major role in his poetry. He came to Montreal in 1911. His first job was a pants stitcher alongside his brother and one of his sisters. He began to contribute poems to the *Kaneder Adler* soon after his arrival and became its literary editor. In 1920, he became a teacher in the Folk Shule. He lived in New York from 1923 to 1928 in search of friendship with other Yiddish writers there. Upon his return to Montreal, he continued to work as a teacher at a Poalei Zionist school as well as working on the Yiddish newspaper. A prolific writer, he published a dozen volumes of his work. His writing reflected the alienation and loneliness he felt in Montreal. He always remained an outsider in the Christian city. Yet the city reminded him of the shtetl from which he had come. Relatively unknown during his lifetime, he wrote mainly for the small literary circle of fellow Yiddish writers. Although born in the Ukraine, he reflected a scholarly tradition and a commitment to the secular Yiddish tradition that led him to describe Montreal his home as "the Vilna of Canada."[27]

Ida Maza (Massey) was both a writer and a catalyst for others by providing the place where writers could meet. She was born in a hamlet in Belorussia in Lita. Her poetry was "suffused with the aromas of forest and field."[28] Described as the *mother* of Canadian Jewish poetry, she maintained, in her apartment near the Jewish Public Library, a "poetry workshop" where people informally would bring their productions for criticism. The group would include all the artistic lights of Montreal Jews and those visiting writers such as the Yiddish poet Leivick. The Dworkins, the parents of Miriam, later known as Waddington after her marriage, were among the visitors to the Massey's summer place in the Laurentians.[29]

The Jewish Labor Movement

Compounding the disunity created by the cultural issues between the Hebraists and the Yiddishists were the class differences that continued to be expressed most clearly in the clothing industry. In Toronto in 1931, roughly one-third of all Jews were employed in that industry. The Jewish workers were concentrated in the men's coat and suit branch and in the women's cloaks and suits as well as furs. These workers were more likely to be male and older than the frequently young and single women in the dress factories where non-Jews were clustered. By this time, the majority of the garment shops were also Jewish-owned.

Activism in the Jewish community reflected not only class interests but drew from their experience as Jews. A working-class culture pervaded the Jewish community. Community organization made it difficult for strikebreakers. The support for strikers was widespread, extending from the Yiddish newspaper to the landsmanshaften. Occasionally both the employer and the striking workers were both members of the same organization. It was not uncommon for the manufacturer to recruit his workers among his own kin or landsleit. Pressure put on him to settle the strike might include expulsion from the organization where the employer belonged. Class interests had become paramount on both sides of the conflict.[30]

The Arbeiter Ring and the Communist Labour League provided social support and a wide range of cultural activities to the workers. The mission of the unions went beyond economic interests. They served as a movement in pursuit of an ideal of a new way of life, one with dignity and pride. Worker solidarity came about in the context of the union's broad mission. The commitment was to socialism as a fairer way of life. Many of the members had religious training although adamantly secular. They found their strength ultimately in the principles of social justice in the Bible. Religious ideas of social justice and communal responsibility inherent in Judaism were in conflict with capitalistic materialism and individual nature of their society.[31]

During this interwar period, the same problems in the clothing industry existed as they had before. Speedups, piecework, low wages, seasonal unemployment, and unsanitary conditions persisted even in "inside shops" such as that of Eaton's.[32] Those who worked at home were even worse off. Contractors would compete to offer the lowest price and would squeeze their profit from the workers. Even lower wages prevailed in Montreal than Toronto due to the easy availability of French-Canadian female workers.[33]

The International American-based Amalgamated Clothing Workers (ACW) had succeeded in 1919 in establishing a mechanism to avoid strikes and lockouts by binding arbitration and mechanisms to establish wage rates and a preferential union shop. Although the union existed, it did not prevent many of the problems caused by harsh working conditions particularly during the 1930s and the Depression. The women's garment union (ILGWU) had even less success during this entire era. Other *international* unions connected with American counterparts existed in the fur industry and among cap makers with somewhat greater success. Canadian-based unions also existed. One, Communist-led, was the Industrial Union of Needle Trades Workers (IUNTW) mainly concentrated in the dressmakers and thus in competition with the ILGWU for members. There was also the National Clothing Workers of Canada (NCWC) associated with the All-Canadian Congress of Labour (ACCCL). Its formation reflected not only a Canadian nationalism but a differentiation from the strongly Jewish ACWA not salved by an Anglophone local.[34] There were thus several unions that were competing with each other. There was little opportunity to improve conditions via unionization.[35]

The disunity within the labor movement in the needle trades reflected differences between the ethnic groups that made up the union. Various locals existed based upon language and ethnic differences as well as concomitant skill differences. The "joint board" responsible for collective bargaining sometimes could not function to supercede the differences between the skill levels as well as ethnicity of the different "locals."[36] The Jews had a fundamentally different philosophy in the role of the union. For Jews, the union was not merely concerned with economic issues. It was to be involved in political action, and that political action was frequently to work toward a better world via socialism. The further issue that divided the labour movement was the choice of political group to which any particular union was to adhere, if one were to identify with any one.

The Jewish labor movement, as expressed in the needle trades, was part of an even larger Canadian labor movement that had its major strength in the Prairie Provinces. The success of the Bolshevik Revolution in Russia seemed to be a harbinger of the possibility of revolutionary changes in other countries.[37] There had been discussion in Calgary at the Western Labour Conference in early spring 1919 of forming what was called One Big Union (OBU) organized along industrial rather than craft lines. The dream was that OBU would eventually take power and reorganize society.[38]

On May 15, 1919, a local strike in Winnipeg by metal workers seeking higher wages and right to collective bargaining became a general strike there when other workers also walked out. Other strikes also took place throughout the country. The Dominion government looked upon the Winnipeg strike as the work of the Bolsheviks and the opening gun of revolution. An attempt was made to connect the strike with Bolshevik agitators who were "foreigners" with particular emphasis on those who were Jews.[39]

Almost all the leaders were actually of British extraction in the tradition of British industrial unionism but not revolutionaries. A group of strike leaders were arrested, among whom was Abraham A. Heaps, then an alderman belonging to the Social Democratic Party. Most were released on bail aside from several with Jewish names who remained in prison and possibly subject to deportation. A mounted charge by the military of a peaceful assembly of strikers and their supporters broke the strike on June 21, 1919. When it was crushed, Jewish cultural and socialist organizations were raided as were the homes of individual Jews. The Winnipeg Yiddish newspaper *Die Volk Stimme* was ordered to cease publication and its successor also threatened. Of the five "foreigners" arrested, three were Jews.[40] *Bolshevism* was equated with the recent East European immigration, and support grew for a quota system to limit immigration similar to the one recently set up in the United States.[41]

The major conflict within the political parties of the Left within the Jewish community as well as elsewhere was between the Communist Party and the various "social democratic" parties.

Those belonging to the Communist Party and its Labour League were provided with a total social environment. The Jewish branch developed its own schools named after the poet Winchevsky who had been one of the early socialists in London's East End. A weekly Yiddish newspaper was called the *Vochenblatt*. The Yiddish-speaking United Jewish People's Order (UJPO) was the Communist fraternal order.

The split in the Left was translated into conflict within the Labor movement and was particularly expressed within the garment industry. Initially, Communists tried to exert their influence within the existing unions. Under Stalin, there was a change in policy, and separate unions were set up. The Industrial Union of Needle Trades Workers (IUNTW) was founded in 1928 under the auspices of the Workers Unity League of the Canadian Communist Party. It tried to draw members from the Hatmakers, the Furriers, ILGWU and ACWA. Most successful among the dressmakers, there was continual conflict with the ILGWU in its efforts to organize the other aspects of the garment industry. The IUNTW was eventually dissolved in 1936 in the context of the further change in Communist policy, leading toward the formation of a *popular front*. Following the dissolution of the IUNTW, the ILGWU was more successful in organizing the dress industry.[42]

Joe Salsberg was the leader of the IUNTW after having previously been an officer in the Toronto Hatmakers local and then vice president of the international union headquartered in Chicago. Salsberg was born in 1902 in Poland. He came to Toronto in 1913 and was raised in an ultra-Orthodox family. He was a serious student of the Torah. Leaving school to work at age thirteen, he became involved in politics soon after. When he joined the Labour Zionists as a youth in 1917, his father was horrified by his reading of secular material, such as the writings of Sholem Aleichem. While still in his teens and an active member of the Poalei Zion, Salsberg led its youth section and edited its newspaper in New York. Later, when the Poalei Zionists split, he went with the Left faction into the Communist Party in 1926.[43] His conversion to Communism was part of the pattern of belief shared by many at this time that one stood at the crossroads of history. The Russian Bolshevik Revolution seemed to bring justice and equality to all, including the Jews. In its secular as in its religious form, the messianic dream was a light that flickered in the distance, keeping hope alive.[44]

The Communist Party of Canada eventually became prey to the internecine battles of the Soviet Communist Party with the expulsion of Trotskyites starting in 1928.[45] Although initially expelled as "unprincipled" and accused of "right-wing deviationism" in 1929, Salsberg returned to the fold of the Stalinists. As the trade union director of the Communist Party, Salsberg established locals in Montreal and Winnipeg as well as Toronto among the garment workers. As in other countries, there was to be conflict with the social democratic groups and the building of separate unions, carrying out independent political action.

The split between the rival labour unions in the garment industry was also reflected in the politics where Salsberg's candidacies were opposed by the socialist CCF led by David Lewis. Salsberg was a popular politician.[46] He was eventually elected to the Toronto City Council in 1942.[47] At the height of the euphoria surrounding the victory of the Red Army in Stalingrad, he was the first Jewish Communist elected to the Ontario Provincial Legislature in 1943 and was reelected until 1955. While there, he was active in the passage of laws providing for nondiscrimination in housing and employment.

Ultimately, revelations made by the Khrushchev speech at the 1956 Communist Party Congress led to Salsberg's disillusionment and resignation from the Communist Party.[48] In response to the revelations of the anti-Semitic character of the Russian Communist Party, he led a group out of the UJPO to form a left-wing fraternal order free of ties to the Kremlin.[49]

Canadian Socialism

The Winnipeg General Strike in 1919 was a watershed event of the Canadian labour movement. Its failure was to have significant implications for the ultimate political activities of labour in the interwar era. It became the touchstone for the existence of democratic socialism during the 1920s that coalesced in the early 1930s in the wake of the Depression.

The aborted OBU had been opposed to participation in politics. Now following the trial of the union leaders after the general strike, the entry into political action led to the formation of the Social Democratic Independent Labour Party (ILP) in 1920.[50] The ILP drew support from socialists like Heaps, trade unionists and Christians committed to the Social Gospel. The long struggle of the general strike had created a sense of labour solidarity. The prosecution of the strike leaders also ensured their popularity. Several, while in prison, were elected to the Manitoba Provincial legislature. Woodsworth, an ex-preacher and one of those who had been imprisoned, was repeatedly reelected to the Federal Parliament from Winnipeg North Centre from 1921 until 1941.[51] He was the leader of the Labour contingent and its allies from the western provinces during the interwar period.

Abraham Heaps, who had been tried for sedition but acquitted, was elected from Winnipeg North from 1925 until 1940 as one of the few Jewish MPs. He came from a Jewish working-class family in Leeds, a center of immigration from Lita to England. The eldest of seven children, he left school at age thirteen and was trained to be an upholsterer. Coming to Winnipeg in 1910, he was an active member of the upholsterers union and joined the Independent Labour Party and its later incarnation as the Co-operative Commonwealth Federation (CCF). Self-educated, Heaps became noted for his meticulous collection of facts and reasoned argument. He was instrumental in the passage of old age pensions and unemployment relief.[52]

Particularly partisan was his reelection on the CCF ticket in 1935 when running against Tim Buck, the head of the Canadian Communists. Buck's support included the organization of the cloakmakers in Winnipeg under the auspices of the Communist-led United Industrial Needle Trades under Joe Salsberg. Heap's eventual defeat in 1940 marked the end of an era in Winnipeg. It was related to the appeal made by the Liberal Party to the prosecution of the war and the turning away by Winnipeg Jews from class as well as ethnic identification.

The ultimate fruit of all these developments was the combination of the agrarian and labor protests in the formation of the Co-operative Commonwealth Federation (CCF) after 1933.[53] There were several radical parties in each of the provinces of western Canada, representing a group of either farmers or urban workers. The onset of the Depression after 1931 brought about a coalition of these groups to deal with problems of both farmers and workers in the national political arena. The League for Social Reconstruction (LSR), originally made up of university intellectuals in Toronto, organized branches throughout Canada, hoping to function as the intellectual wing of a Socialist Party not unlike the relationship of the Fabian Society to the British Labour Party.

Woodsworth, the leader of CCF, exemplified the principles of socialism, pacifism, and humanitarianism that the new party represented. At its organization in Calgary in 1932, the credo was "the establishment . . . of a co-operative commonwealth in which the basic principle . . . will be the supplying of human needs instead of the making of profits."[54] The Manifesto presented and adopted at the Regina Conference in 1933 reflected the work of members of the League for Social Reconstruction (LSR) and was frankly socialist advocating public ownership "of all industries and services essential to social planning."[55]

In accordance with its socialist principles, the CCF was a movement rather than merely a political party. It provided its members with their social life both in the prairies and the cities. Its ideological basis provided a sense of unity of purpose. Its belief was that socialism was both a more moral and efficient alternative to capitalism. But like the British Labour Party, the CCF accepted the rules of parliamentary democracy and their ideas were thus accepted, if not their ideology, and incorporated in legislation passed by the majority party. Although their caucus had few members, under the lead of the visionary Woodward, they were the true opposition to the ascendancy of the Mackenzie King Liberals in the 1930s. They spoke in support of those whose interests were being ignored and in favor of civil rights. For example, they led the repeal of the section of the Immigration Act instituted in 1919 that permitted the deportation of "aliens." In 1939, under the prodding of the CCF caucus, the Liberal government introduced the law that finally guaranteed the rights of employees to establish unions.[56]

With the organization of the CCF party, its center shifted from the western Prairie Provinces eastward to reflect urban socialists. It was the belief in the essential rightness of the cause that brought men such as David Lewis to continue under adverse conditions and low pay. He never lost his driving passion about the essential immorality of capitalism.[57] Consistent with his own background and interests, he sought cooperation with the albeit still relatively undeveloped labor movement. During the early years, much of his effort had to deal with the Communists in their opposition, under the dictates of Stalin, to social democratic parties throughout the world. This conflict then extended into the Labour unions as they became more powerful during the 1930s with the formation of "industrial" unions in the pattern of the American CIO.

David Lewis had been born in 1902 in a mainly Jewish shtetl of Swislocz in the Grodno Gubernia in Lita as the eldest of three children and the elder son. His paternal grandfather owned a flour mill and a store on the main square. The maternal grandfather was a poor but devout and almost saintly man who earned his meagre living as a peddler. Maishe, David Lewis's father, although destined for the rabbinate after training in the yeshivah, became a socialist and agnostic. He dropped out of school to work in one of the leather factories in the town. Refusing the opportunity to work in his father's business, he had deliberately chosen to become a member of the proletariat. He was an active member of the leatherworkers' union and the Bund. The leather factories were the mainstay of the town, and several general strikes took place under the auspices of the Bund during the years preceding World War I.[58] The boy David was part of the adult circle which came to his house to discuss politics; the terms justice, working class, and equality were familiar words to the young boy.

Their village was successively occupied by the Germans then the Bolsheviks and finally the Poles. The father's Bundist activities and Menshevik politics led to his arrest by the Soviets during the years immediately after World War I. His execution was imminent but not carried out. This experience was said to be a basis for Lewis's profound distrust and antipathy to Communism. In May 1921, both his father and maternal uncle emigrated to

Montreal where another maternal uncle had settled around 1900. The family followed in August 1921. The family name was changed from Losh to Lewis. The father carried out his Bundist associations by becoming a member and then city chairman of the Workmen's Circle. Disabled by a heart attack in the late 1930s and no longer able to work as a garment worker, Moshe Lewis became the Canadian Secretary of the Jewish Labour Committee set up to coordinate work to help victims of the Nazis. Like a rabbi in the shtetl, he would help people to resolve their differences by emphasizing the need for personal integrity.[59]

David Lewis taught himself English so as to progress through school rapidly enough to catch up with his age group. He was able to enter high school by 1924. The Baron Byng High School was in the center of the Jewish quarter on Saint-Urbain Street when it was founded in 1921. It served to nurture an entire generation of immigrant boys. It was there at the almost totally Jewish high school that Lewis and A. M. Klein became close friends. That friendship left Lewis with a lasting love of literature that tempered his almost exclusive devotion to politics.[60] Lewis managed to graduate from high school in 1927, barely six years after coming to Montreal and then entered McGill. During the Depression, his father was on short time, and David earned money by tutoring other students. Nevertheless, he received recognition at McGill as an outstanding debater. He was encouraged to join in the discussion groups with several of his professors who formed the League for Social Reconstruction (LSR). As secretary of the tiny Montreal Labour Party, he would be invited to address meetings of the local unions. He was a delegate to the Young People's Socialist League convention in New York City where he met Walter Reuther, later president of the United Auto Workers.

To the surprise of all, he was chosen as a Rhodes Scholar after graduation from McGill and its law school in 1932. While at Oxford, he was recognized as one of the most outstanding men and elected president of the Oxford Union, the debating society. He also became close to a range of such luminaries of the Labour Party as Jennie Lee and Stafford Cripps. The latter was described as his mentor secondary only to his own father.

David Lewis returned to Canada in 1935 at the time the Co-Operative Commonwealth Federation (CCF) had just fought its first national election. Working as a law clerk in Ottawa, he was appointed in 1936 as unpaid national secretary by Woodsworth, the CCF leader in Parliament. He became full-time in 1938. He remained in that position until 1950 followed by other positions including national chairman and then president from 1958 to 1961 of the successor New Democratic Party (NDP).[61]

In the political arena, Lewis himself was defeated in a contest for the Parliamentary seat in the largely Jewish Cartier riding in Montreal in 1943 by the Communist Fred Rose. Lewis's defeat in a constituency in which he had grown up was particularly difficult to accept and kept him from running in other places where he might have won a seat much sooner than when he was eventually successful.[62] He was finally elected to the Federal Parliament in 1962 from the Toronto riding of York South and reelected on several occasions, the last in 1972. He finally became NDP Party Parliamentary Leader in 1972 in the face of considerable opposition. By that time, his son Stephen had become active in the Ontario NDP and his father's major confidante in David's leadership battle in 1971 against the more radical so-called Waffle opposition. The elder Lewis's leadership of his party was short-lived, ending with his defeat in the Parliamentary election of 1974.

The Co-operative Commonwealth Federation (CCF), as its name indicates, had started as a federation of already-existing organizations, reflecting the interests of farmers as well as workers and intellectuals. Lewis's work included the development of somewhat greater degree of unity as well as a more urban emphasis. His drive derived from his background and exposure to trade unionism in the model of the British Labour Party as well as his family's commitment to the Bund in Lita.[63] The focus was on achieving political power rather than ideological purity alone. Under Lewis, elements of the CCF joined with the industrial type unions organized in Canada as well as the United States in the late 1930s to form the New Democratic Party (NDP) in the late 1950s. David Lewis's close personal relationship as legal counsel with such unions as the United Steelworkers and United Auto Workers and his personal connection with such leaders as Walter Reuther was crucial in making this connection a viable one.[64]

Lewis devoted his life, and that of his family, to his commitment to democratic socialism, never believing that it would come to power but still believing in the dream that he inherited from his father of working for a world of justice and equality.[65] His Bundist roots were anti-Zionist, and he moved away from this stance only in the post-World War II period. Although not active in the structure of the Jewish community and anticlerical, he was proud of his heritage. Even in his oratory, there was the legacy of the Pale of Settlement, the mixture of pathos and the ever-present opportunity for sinners to repent.[66]

The focus of the Jewish community on immigration was an important issue during the interwar period. The imposition of various discriminatory regulations on immigration grew even more restrictive with the onset of the depression in the 1930s. These policies continued despite the limited efforts of the Canadian Jewish Congress (CJC) resurrected in 1934 in the context of Nazi anti-Semitism. The issuance of the necessary special Orders in Council was met with repeated failure at the hands of the firmly opposed bureaucrats. The search for opportunities for immigration was successful only in rare individual cases with influence brought to bear by the several Jewish members of Parliament. Any tendency to mobilize Jewish public opinion in support of immigration, even as late as 1938 after Kristallnacht, was opposed by these same leaders, hoping that some opportunities still existed with private intercession. The Government remained adamant despite all the efforts of the Jewish community, even when now acting publicly. When confronted with the problems of refugees, Canada cared little and did less. Whether in Quebec or British Canada, few saw Jews as desirable settlers. The particularly active and consistent opposition of the Quebec politicians in the cabinet to any Jewish immigration took precedence. This opposition to Jewish immigration was deeply rooted in the French-Canadian culture.[67]

The anti-Semitism of French Quebec had found increased support in the context of the Jewish quest for official minority status centered around the school question. The publisher Joseph Menard sponsored an anti-Semitic press, becoming increasingly vicious under the editorship of Adrien Arcand. It eventually drew upon caricatures and literature directly derived from Nazi sources.[68] It was based, however, on the long-standing French nationalist rhetoric that had first arisen in the 1900s and had increased in the wake of conscription during World War I. The increasingly Anglophone Jews were easier targets than the more powerful Anglo-Saxon barons themselves. The immigration of poor Jews could also be connected with the peddlers going into the countryside in competition with the French-Canadian merchants. A boycott movement activated by a Catholic priest advocated buying from "their own kind" (*Achat chez nous*). As early as 1932, this boycott movement was tied to parish organizations.[69] Further, Church publications continued to preach that there was no room for the Jew with his liberalism and "materialistic communism." The Jews were an alien element in direct conflict to a mystical form of nationalism connected with a rural and Catholic Quebec.

Anglo-Saxons were also united in opposing immigration on cultural grounds as diluting the British nature of the country. Outside of Quebec, Canada was visibly a British country. By law, Canadians were British subjects, and Britons coming to Canada did not require naturalization. Pressure to assimilate to the British model was overwhelming. The attitude of Anglo-Canada was illustrated by the institution of *numerus clausus,* severely restricting access to university places at McGill as the bastion of the British merchant class.[70] Jewish access to jobs and housing as well as university places were all restricted in Ontario as well as Quebec and throughout Canada. Illustrative of the lack of employment opportunity was the relative absence of Jews in salaried positions versus positions where one could be self-employed such as the private practice of law and medicine.[71]

Immigration during the Depression was considered undesirable; Jewish immigration was particularly undesirable. In the late 1930s, despite the desperate search for refuge, the number of Jews let into Canada remained substantially less than a thousand each year.[72] Canada was second only to the Soviet Union in providing the least aid to Nazi refugees.[73]

During the course of the 1930s, an anti-Semitic, openly Nazi movement was evidenced by the formation of the National Unity Party under Armand. *Swastika Clubs,* made up of youths, acted to prevent access to Jews in beaches and other areas. These activities ceased only with World War II when Armand was interned and his party dissolved.[74] Widespread organized fascism in both Quebec and Ontario gained credence in the political arena in concert with the rise of Fascism and Nazism in Europe. The ethnonationalism of the French Canadian has also been likened to that of the Afrikaner based on language and confessional differences from the ruling British identity. In both instances, a relatively virulent anti-Semitism arose in the 1930s that attracted a mass base. It was in both Canada and South Africa that anti-Semitism was powerfully attached to the process of formation of a sense of racial exclusivity among a beleaguered conquered people.[75] This translated directly into the racially based restriction of Jewish immigration attached not only to East Europeans but to German Jews in their extremity during the 1930s.

The reactivated Canadian Jewish Congress (CJC) came about in 1934 in the context of this revivified anti-Semitism as well as its role in respect to immigration. In 1933, soon after Hitler's accession, protests were organized mainly among the "downtown" element in both Toronto and Montreal. However, the situation was somewhat different from the earlier alignments that separated the "Democratic" and the wealthy elements. The Canadian Jewish Committee, representing the wealthy, joined the other segment. Unlike the disunity experienced during the initial organization of the CJC in 1919 and that experienced during the Montreal School question, there was the beginning of a coalescence of the entire community. The CJC, however, continued to operate with a very limited budget as it organized antidefamation efforts as well as a boycott of German products.[76] In 1939, the accession to the presidency of the CJC by Samuel Bronfman, the wealthy whisky industrialist, was at the initiative of the Labour Zionist leader as an expression of the need for unity of both elements of the community. Bronfman provided the support necessary to make the CJC an increasingly significant factor in achieving the unusual degree of unity of Canadian Jewry.[77].

Illustrative of the opportunities as well as the limits placed on the acculturated generation was the career and life of Abraham Moses Klein. He was intimately involved with all aspects of Canadian Jewish life during this era until his abrupt withdrawal into isolation.

Canadian Literature

Abraham Moses "A. M." Klein sought to incorporate the very essence of Judaic idiom and belief into his work. He was the only poet to bring the full range of traditional Jewish learning to the secular mode of modern poetry.[78] He was a child of both worlds.

A. M. Klein was born in Ratno early in 1909 and was brought to Montreal as an infant in 1910. Ratno was a town of three thousand with a majority Jewish population in Volhynia in a strongly Hassidic environment. His father, Kalman, was a widower with two sons and a daughter when he married, in 1897, a widow with two sons of her own. They had two daughters together before the birth of much younger twin sons. Abraham Moses was the only one surviving of the twins. Klein was thus the youngest child with two doting sisters, several much older half-siblings, and a large extended family. They settled along St. Lawrence Boulevard in the downtown immigrant ghetto.

Kalman became a presser, requiring the lifting of the heavy irons in the stifling sweatshops open to religious Jews. Because of his religious scruples, he remained unemployed for long periods rather than work on the Sabbath. He remained uncritical of conditions he experienced as his lot. Apolitical, Kalman was grateful for the opportunity to live outside of the oppression that Russia represented. He did, however, join the strikes that led to the acceptance of the Amalgamated Garment Workers Union, first in 1917 and then in 1919. The family followed religious rituals consistently, and the boy accompanied his father to the shule every Sabbath.

Enrolled in the local school run by the Protestant Board, he was always the enthusiastic student who would know all the answers. Given a set of *The Book of Knowledge*, he would read it over and over as well as any books available at the Jewish Public Library that he joined at age eleven. Educated with private tutors and at a Talmud Torah, he chose not to pursue rabbinical studies and ceased to be religious. However, his childhood "Yiddish-speaking and Hebrew-thinking" carried into his poetry as he moved into English-speaking literature. His mature poetry reflects his continuing place in the religious and folk tradition of his childhood.[79] Although he was a student of Yiddish literature, he never ventured to work in any language other than English.[80]

His high school friendship with David Lewis and the Lewis family was an introduction to a more secular world. He became a socialist like his friend. Klein entered McGill on a classics scholarship in 1926 when fully 25 percent of the students in the arts faculty were children of immigrants. Latin was his favorite subject from the time he was a freshman. In entering a program of economics and philosophy leading to law, he was following a common pattern among his Jewish peers. An academic career was not an option at this time for a bright Jewish student like Klein. He became known as a skilled debater along with his friend David Lewis. He could quote from the Bible or Talmud in the same breath as Shakespeare and Keats. Joyce's *Ulysses* was to haunt his mind from the time he first read it in 1926. His dream was to write the equivalent book about Montreal as had Joyce about Dublin.[81]

His major paper in political economy as an undergraduate dealt with the strike in 1917 of the Amalgamated Clothing Workers in which his father had participated. He also became a member of the McGill Labour Club and Young Judea, the Zionist youth group. A devotee of Ahad Ha'am, he was committed to the principles of cultural Zionism, to the development of a spiritual center for the renaissance of Jewish creativity. From 1928 to 1932, he was editor of the monthly *Judean* and then educational director of the Zionist Organization of Canada. His real dream was to be a poet, and he associated with a group at McGill that sought to create "the modern movement" in Canadian literature. With David Lewis, he established a literary as well as nonpartisan political journal known as *The McGilliad*. He completed his law degree at the French-speaking Université de Montréal in 1931.[82]

He continued to be a member of a community of writers in Montreal, contributing not only his writing but enhancing the creation of a literary milieu. His eventual literary public was divided. He became known in the United States for his *Jewish* subjects published in such journals as *The Menorah Journal*. Two of his collections of poetry dealing with Jewish subjects were published in the United States. He was described by the critic Ludwig Lewisohn as "the first Jew to contribute authentic poetry to the literatures of English speech." By that it was meant that he did so as a Jew, reflecting the religio-cultural heritage of his people.[83] His more general audience was in the *Canadian Forum* as well as a pair of literary magazines that appeared in Montreal in the early 1940s. The group surrounding those magazines provided him with a congenial setting in which to develop his work beyond his preoccupation with the Jewish community of Montreal.[84] One of his most successful efforts in the immediate postwar era was his *Suite Canadienne*, a set of poems dealing with French Canada published as *The Rocking Chair and Other Poems*, a title evocative of the domestic tranquillity of the French-Canadian farmhouses. It was the only one of his books that was originally published in Canada. It differed from his previous focus on allusions derived from Biblical and Talmudic sources to seek those words common to both English and French, to write in a *bilingual* fashion. He could find some commonality between himself as a member of a beleaguered minority Jew and the Francophone culture that he lived alongside. In these poems, he invested Montreal with some of the qualities of a "fabled city." The positive reception of these poems led to his recognition within the broader Francophone community, reflecting a postwar easing of the relations between the Jews and Catholics in Quebec.[85]

Married, the father of three children as well as caring for his mother, his earnings as a lawyer did not sustain his primary life as a poet even when acclaimed as *Canada's greatest living poet.* Compelled by family considerations to live within the crowded legal fraternity of Montreal, from 1938 on, he supplemented his income by working as a journalist. He was editor of the *Canadian Jewish Chronicle* for almost fifteen years, contributing editorials, book reviews, and literary articles, including translations from the Yiddish and Hebrew.[86] He saw his role to not only convey Jewish issues to the wider community but to bring to the acculturated youth some knowledge of their cultural heritage, hence his commitment to the translations. The tone of his journalistic production was one of morality and passion in the role of a preacher and prophet.[87]

Klein was also employed as a speechwriter by Samuel Bronfman in the latter's role as president of the Canadian Jewish Congress and of Seagram's Distillers. Despite the disparities in politics and status, their relationship represented for both a bridge between their earlier Yiddish backgrounds and the acculturated English-speaking generation. Illustrative of the limits placed on Jews in academia, it was Bronfman who finally secured for Klein his only short-term academic appointment as lecturer in poetry at McGill.[88] It was through his connection with Bronfman that Klein went on a "fact-finding" mission to newly independent Israel that formed the basis for his novel *The Second Scroll*. Klein's relationship with Bronfman was generally one of mutual respect that carried on during the mental illness and withdrawal from public life that lasted the last twenty years of Klein's life after 1952.[89] In 1957, Klein was belatedly recognized by the Royal Society of Canada for his work but was never elected to fellowship to that body nor recognized in other ways until long after he was too ill to enjoy the honors.[90]

The overall problem of his life as well as his work was to bring together the several cultures to which he belonged. "He was engaged in an unending search for a unifying pattern underlying the bewildering multiplicity of the world."[91] There were the several linguistic cultures. There was need to reconcile his familial heritage along with the culture of his English university training as well as the French language of the city and his legal profession.[92] There was the further problem of his life to reconcile his commitment to literature with his search for recognition and income in political and journalistic settings. Despite his difficulties, he was described, even before his death, as "the man who has come closer than any other Canadian poet to greatness."[93] His difficulties as well as his successes illustrate those of his generation of Canadian Jews.

Canadian Zionism

Zionism represents the other secular strand that evolved in this generation. One may recall that the Labour Zionists had been influential in the development of schools in the interwar era. They eventually were able to secure support from their fellow socialists in the CCF for the socialist development of Palestine. The Liberal Party, despite its major, or perhaps because of its consistent support within the Jewish community, might provide sympathy at election time but was not responsive to issues of interest to that community.[94] The Labor Zionists joined together with the much larger and more middle-of-the-road Zionist Organization of Canada (ZOC) and with the religious Zionist Mizrachi to form the United Zionist Council during World War II to lobby the Canadian government to support the Zionist cause. This hard-won unity unique to Canada was one of the last acts of Archie Freiman, the longtime president of the ZOC.[95] Freiman and his wife, Lillian, the founder of the Canadian Hadassah, were the prototype Canadian Zionists of the interwar era.

Lillian Bilsky was born in 1885 in Mattawa, Ontario, as the fifth of eleven children of Moses Bilsky. Her father had been born in Kovno in Lita in 1831. In an extraordinary journey, her father joined her grandfather in Canada in 1845, first in Montreal and then in Ottawa before joining the gold rush to Western Canada in 1861. Discouraged from making his fortune in the gold fields, he then enlisted in the United States Army in San Francisco before returning to Canada and finally marrying in 1874. After leaving the lumber business in Mattawa, he opened a successful jewelry store in Ottawa where he remained for the rest of his life.[96] The Bilsky family became the founders of the Jewish community of Ottawa, taking responsibility for the newer immigrants that began to come to Canada from Eastern Europe, founding the synagogue as well as the Zionist society.[97]

In 1903, Lillian Bilsky married Archibald Jacob Freiman who had come to Ottawa in 1899 from Kingston. He had been born in 1880 in Wirballen in Lita as Aharon Yaacov and came to Canada in 1893, settling in Hamilton. After early religious training in Lithuania, he went to the Hamilton public schools and business college. Starting out as a peddler, he eventually founded what was to be the major department store in Ottawa. The couple continued the family tradition of communal work with her leading a multitude of organizations, particularly in support of soldiers and veterans of World War I. Within the Jewish community, he was president of the synagogue founded by his father-in-law for a quarter century as well as president of the Ottawa Jewish Community Council. It was their joint effort on behalf of Zionism that was a focus of their lives.[98]

Freiman was twenty-one when he attended the convention of the Federation of Zionist Societies in Montreal in 1902, representing Kingston. By 1906, he was president of the Ottawa chapter. By 1912, he was elected one of the vice presidents of the federation. In the aftermath of the retirement of de Sola, Freiman was elected president of the Zionist Federation in 1919. At that time, and until the reorganization of the Canadian Jewish Congress in 1933, the Zionist organization was the only national Jewish body. Under his leadership and that of his wife, a new high level of fund-raising was achieved that made Canada one of the most important per capita sources for support of the Yishuv. Their estate in Ottawa became a place for receptions for visiting Zionist dignitaries as well as governmental officials.[99]

In the immediate post-World War II era, despite valiant efforts of the unified Zionist organization and that of non-Jews enlisted in such efforts, there was little done by Liberal government under Mackenzie King seeking pressure on Britain to relax their blockade on the entry of "displaced persons" refugees into Palestine. In the area of foreign affairs, King did not normally take a stance independent of Britain. In the absence of what he felt was a clear-cut Canadian interest in Palestine, King maintained his ongoing policy of following the lead of Britain.[100] Initiatives for Canada to take a more active role required a realignment in Canadian policy closer to that of the United States. This perforce occurred in the course of Canada's membership, however unsought, on the investigating committee set up by the United Nations (UNSCOP) that then led to a Canadian vote for partition.[101] Later, once Israel had been established and was fighting for its life in May 1948, Canada's support for the British pro-Arab policy was maintained, and Israel was not recognized de facto until Christmas 1948.[102]

The political impotence of the Canadian Zionists belied its relatively widespread support within the entire Canadian Jewish community. The commitment to Zionism had become almost universal within the Canadian Jewry by activities surrounding the plight of the "displaced persons" and the formation of the State of Israel.[103] The Canadian Jewish Congress had Zionism as one of its major tenets. Two of the weeklies, Montreal's *Canadian Jewish Chronicle* under the aegis of A. M. Klein and the *Jewish Standard* published in Toronto, were pro-Zionist with the latter actually founded under Zionist auspices. Both Yiddish dailies *Der*

Keneder Adler in Montreal and *Der Yiddishe Tzurnal* in Toronto
were supportive of Zionism.

Even more significant was the response of Canadian youth
to commitment to possible kibbutz life. Segments of Young
Judea, the youth branch of ZOC, sought to convert it to a more
socialist stance despite the opposition of the parent organization.
Habonim, the youth branch of the Poalei Zion (Labour Zionists)
had been organized in 1935 and had widespread influence among
Jewish youth in Canada as well as the United States in advocacy
of a kibbutz ethos and self-renewal through labor. Mordecai
Richler, growing up in Montreal during the war years, recalls his
membership in Habonim and their march downtown in Montreal
celebrating the positive UN partition vote in November 1947.[104]

4.2.3 The Integrated Generation

Postwar Jewish immigration occurred as part of a far larger
number of other non-British immigrants. To an unusual degree,
this increment in Jewish immigration was made up of Holocaust
survivors. Because of the relatively small base, such survivors
formed a much higher percentage of the total than in the United
States. In addition, a substantial number of immigrants were
Francophones from North Africa. The immigration of these who
were Francophone as well as being more Orthodox Sephardim
has supported the tendency toward bilingualism in the Montreal
Jewish community. This direction was consistent with the goals
of the Quebec government.[1]

In a *Directory of the Canadian Jewish Community* published in
1963 and even later, Montreal was unabashedly described as
the capital city of Jewish Canada.[2] Montreal still continued, for
a time, to be the headquarters of almost all the national Jewish
organizations. For example, although the regional structure
of the Canadian Jewish Congress reflected some increased
decentralization, its headquarters remained in Montreal.[3] Its
historical hegemony however was no longer unquestioned
with the migration of many of the younger Jews to English-
speaking areas of Canada subsequent to the rise of Quebec
separatism.

As elsewhere in North America, the pattern of upward mobility exists in Montreal but to a lesser degree, given the relative recent postwar immigration both of Holocaust survivors and North Africans. As late as 1961, 43 percent of the Jews identified Yiddish as their mother tongue falling to 10 percent only by 1981. The continued relative strength of Yiddish identity reflects the impact of Holocaust survivors and the existence of the Jewish Public Library. With the reduction in the number of working-class Jews in this generation, there were fewer Jews engaged in manufacturing and a far greater representation than the general Canadian population in managerial and professional groups.[4]

Montreal Jewry has always been characterized by a relatively high level of residential density as typical of most ethnic groups in that city. In the postwar era, the area of Jewish settlement had expanded even beyond Outremont toward the western suburbs. The predominant religious identification remained *Orthodox* and *Conservative* with relatively little *Reform*. There continues to be a relatively high degree of adherence to traditional practice such as kashrut and support for Jewish day schools particularly those organized as Talmud Torahs. The YMHA-YWHA in Montreal expanded to include a cultural centre named after Sadye Bronfman, the wife of Seagram's Sam Bronfman. The school problem in Quebec continued with the development of Jewish religious schools now receiving state subsidies at the high school level in return for increased French-based instruction. The conflict within the Jewish community continued over the wisdom of such both in Quebec and Ontario.[5] In 1967, after years of pressure, Jewish members were finally appointed to Montreal's Protestant School Board, which then also later moved to an elective board.[6]

In following the trajectory of the Max Garmaise family of Montreal, there were three children in this generation. The eldest, Golda, trained at Hebrew-speaking Herzylia High School and then at Columbia University and the Jewish Theological Seminary in New York. Married to an American physician in New Jersey, their sons were in finance in New York and London with a daughter trained in law. The youngest child, Gordon, went to McGill before receiving an advanced degree in economics at MIT and has worked as a financial analyst. He lived in Toronto.

In the next generation, his eldest child, in turn, was a professor of economics at UCLA, having trained at Harvard and Stanford. A younger son graduated from Princeton and a daughter was at York University in Toronto.

The second child and elder son, Michael, followed his father's career path at McGill with subsequent training as a notary at Université de Montréal before entering the family practice. Prior to that, he went to Talmud Torah and then received a very uneven education in a very Orthodox yeshivah. He required private tutors in order to qualify for university. In going to McGill, he was joining the overwhelming majority of his peers. There had been a loosening in the 1950s of the quotas limiting Jewish students. Fully a quarter of the students were Jewish. He married, in 1962, Bryna, whose father had come to Montreal from Poland just prior to the outbreak of the Second World War to join his family already settled there. Bryna went to Yiddish school named after Winchevsky sponsored by the Jewish People's Fraternal Order before it was "padlocked" under the law repressing Communist organizations.

Their perginations were also tied to their well-established religious identity. First living in the family neighborhood of Côte-des-Neiges, they then moved to the middle-class Côte Saint-Luc before moving to Westmount. Michael's profession as a notary was idiosyncratic to the legal system of Quebec. He did not feel he could participate in the flight of Anglophones to other parts of Canada. He was able to buy a substantial house in the fashionable Westmont district at a price far below its previous value because of this flight. The family's response to the separatism of the Parti Québécois in the next generation parallels many of the Anglophone Jews of Montreal with the movement of their three children to universities in the United States and then life in Toronto.

Yiddish Literature

The life and career of Ruth Wisse illustrates the continuity with the uniquely Yiddish culture of Montreal expressed into the postwar generation.

Ruth Roskies Wisse's parents met as students at Wilno's Stephen Batory University and married in 1929. Her mother, born in 1906, had grown up in Wilno during the interwar period when it was the center for Yiddish literature and culture. The paternal grandfather was a successful textile merchant in Bialystok in eastern Poland, part of Lita. Leo (Leibl) Roskies, Ruth's father, had earned a degree in chemical engineering and found a job, managing a rubber factory in Czernowitz in what was then northern Romania. Benjamin, the eldest child, was born in 1931 and learned Romanian. Ruth, born in 1936, had a German governess and spoke that language as her mother tongue. Through his business connections, the father was successful in acquiring visas to Canada, thus escaping the fate of his family that remained in Bialystok. The family was four of the 626 Jews admitted to Canada in 1940. Two more children, Eva and David, were born in Montreal during the 1940s.

Benjamin, the elder brother, was nine years old when he came to Montreal and enrolled in an English-speaking Protestant school. He bore the heaviest burden of adaptation to the new environment. His unresolved life problems led to his eventual suicide at age forty-three with serious ongoing impact on his sister. Ruth, also enrolled in the same school, described her unhappy experience with the coldness with which she was received, redeemed by her later enrollment in the Zionist-Labor "Jewish People's School."[7] Its secular faith in social justice and its Litvak dedication to intellectual prowess was fully compatible with her home life. Yiddish was the language of the home, and all roads and stories led back to Vilna. Her mother deliberately moved away from the more fashionable Westmont to the middle-class area of Outremont where she hosted a Yiddish literary salon. After graduation from Yiddish school, Ruth was enrolled in an English-speaking Protestant high school and then in McGill's English Department, graduating in 1957. In 1959, Wisse decided to study Yiddish seriously after meeting Abraham Sutzkever during his tour of Canada. His commitment to the crafting of Yiddish poetry coupled to his life in the Vilna Ghetto went beyond the literary to the very essence of Jewish life.

As a graduate student at Columbia in 1960, Ruth came under the influence of Max Weinreich, the director of YIVO, and his son Uriel, professor of Yiddish language, literature and

culture at Columbia. Her master's thesis dealt with the poetry of
Sutzkever and its need to reflect the highest traditions of aesthetic
sensibility as the only way to adequately represent with integrity
the character of the Shoah. This became her credo in applying
to the analysis of Yiddish literature the high literary standards
normally applied to English. Her doctorate at McGill reviewed
the use of *the fool* in Yiddish and American Jewish writing. She saw
the use of the character as an adaptation and acceptance of the
powerlessness of the Jew. It provided the basis for her continued
political writing, decrying the withdrawal of support from Israel
in pursuit of moral superiority to the possible detriment of its
continued existence.

Her work as a critic and editor of Yiddish writing led to her
eventual appointment in 1992 as the first professor of Yiddish
literature at Harvard. In the tradition of Harry Wolfson, her
appointment to a chair was contingent to a donation, in this
case by Martin Peretz, the publisher of the *New Republic.* Her
joint appointment in Harvard's Department of Comparative
Literature as well as the Department of Near Eastern Languages
reflects the acceptance of Yiddish as one of the living languages
and the Center for Jewish Studies more central to Harvard than
its previous connection with the Semitic Museum.[8]

Canadian Socialism

The other major secular strand derived from Lita within
the Litvak Diaspora is the socialist one. The Co-operative
Commonwealth Federation (CCF) was the heir of the several
radical strands in English-speaking Canada. Its success was
greatest in the Prairie Provinces where it became the majority
party in Saskatchewan in 1944 and, as the second largest party,
the official opposition in the four other western provinces.[9].

The *Regina Manifesto* issued at the outset of the CCF in 1934
was replaced by the *Winnipeg Declaration* in 1956. The latter
avoided the earlier Socialist rhetoric but continued to advocate
public ownership and government regulation of the economy
and increased focus on expenditure for health and social services.
It moved the party from advocating the principle of public

ownership to public "control." Maintained was the central core of commitment: "Society must have a moral purpose and must build a new relationship among men—a relationship based on mutual respect and on equality of opportunity. In such a society everyone will have a sense of worth and belonging, and will be enabled to develop his capacities to the full." The connection was to the underlying religious basis for the ideology, arising from roots in both Social Gospel and Marx and for some, like David Lewis, the Jewish Labor Bund.[10]

The CCF failures in the federal election in 1958 led to commitment to an even closer collaboration with the newly formed Canadian Labor Congress (CLC). This organization reflected the amalgamation of the old Trades and Labor Congress affiliated with the American Federation of Labor and the Canadian Congress of Labor affiliated with the American CIO. The New Democratic Party (NDP) founded in 1961 was an alliance of the socialist base of the CCF and the labor unions as well as middle-class professionals.

Like that of Montreal and Toronto, the character of Winnipeg Jewry has followed a similar pattern of migration away from its proletarian roots toward the managerial and professional classes. This migration was mirrored by the physical migration from the North End to the farther suburbs and to the more fashionable South End. The concentrated Jewish population of the Winnipeg North election district that had, for so long, sent Abraham Heaps to Parliament had become diffused. Nevertheless, for provincial and federal elections, the combination of the now Ukrainian North End and the more Jewish suburbs continued to support the election of NDP candidates.

Particularly noteworthy was the continued presence in this era of the descendants of the secular Yiddishist group of the previous generation. Their ideology was expressed within the New Democratic Party (NDP) that carried on the traditions of Western Prairie socialism.

Illustrative was the career of Saul Cherniack. He was born in Winnipeg in 1917, the son of Alter Cherniack. He attended the Peretz School in which his parents were actively involved. He received a law degree from the University of Manitoba in 1939. In the Canadian army during the war, he became a captain in the Intelligence Corps. He returned to Winnipeg to practice law until 1991. He became Queen's counsel in 1963 and eventually a member of the Privy Council for Canada. He was on the boards of the full range of Winnipeg community activities such as community chest, public library and general hospital. He was similarly president of the range of local Jewish community organizations, with particular emphasis on the Canadian Jewish Congress where he was chairman of the western region and a national vice president and national chairman of the important integration and settlement committee. Noteworthy also was his presidency of the Peretz School parents' association to which his own children went.

In politics, he was successively elected as alderman in the Winnipeg City Council and then as a member of the Greater Winnipeg Metropolitan Council. Elected in 1962 to the Manitoba Legislature from the North End of Winnipeg, he remained a member until 1981. One of the major changes in the Canadian political scene in the early 1970s was the establishment of NDP governments in the three western provinces, with Manitoba the first in 1969.[11] Cherniack became deputy premier as well as minister of finance with the NDP's accession to power in 1969. While in the cabinet, he was particularly involved in the activities leading to the unification of the metropolitan form of government for the Winnipeg area.[12] He attributes his political career to his work with his father canvassing for votes since childhood on behalf of the Independent Labour Party and then the CCF. His membership in the NDP and adherence to its socialist principles was part of his Jewish heritage derived from both his parents from Lita.

Cherniack was most proud of his contribution to establishing laws relating to consumer protection, compensation to victims of crime, and protection of marital property rights. He substituted what had been flat-rate health premiums regardless of income with health financing using the proceeds of the progressive income tax. His work on behalf of consumers led also to the development of Manitoba Hydro that provides the lowest cost clean power supply in North America. Perhaps most interesting was his role representing the NDP in overseeing the activities of the Canadian Security Intelligence Services that brought him in contact with comparable issues of national security in the United States.[13]

Toronto's social character was genteel but thoroughly anti-Semitic expressed in the lack of entry to schools as well as in the restricted residential patterns. During the 1950s, discrimination in housing and employment was chipped away. During this same era, there were two Toronto mayors who were themselves Jewish and active in Jewish causes. More widely diffused throughout the suburbs, Jews were but a small part of the renewed large-scale immigration that transformed the city into a far more cosmopolitan centre. The Jewish population of Metropolitan Toronto doubled during the period between 1941 and 1971 while the number of Italians and "other Europeans" became far larger, displacing the Jews as the largest non-Anglo-Celtic groups. The percentage of those from the British Isles fell from 80 percent in 1941 to 57 percent in 1971, and fell further to below 50 percent in the following decade.[14]

Toronto surpassed Montreal for the first time in the 1970s both in population and as its dominant force in Canadian Jewry. Similar to Montreal, there is no longer the self-conscious working-class culture. The one-third of the Jewish population in owner and managerial positions was triple that of the general population. The occupational structure of the population in both cities showed increased presence in the professions, reflecting increased educational opportunity. However, there were still limited opportunities for employment other than self-employment. There was marked representation in professional groups such as physicians, dentists, and pharmacists. In Toronto, the percentage born in Canada had risen to circa 65 percent in 1961 with only 30 percent reporting Yiddish as their mother tongue.[15]

The move to the suburbs in both cities expanded the number of *Conservative* and *Reform* adherents and a relative diminution of adherents to *Orthodoxy*. The *Reform* movement, represented by the *Holy Blossom Temple* among others, has been more significant in the evolution of the Toronto community than has been its influence in Montreal. Montreal continued to have a relatively "high retention" of ethnic identity even into the third generation evidenced by adherence to ethnic food and customs and obligation to support ethnic causes.[16]

Ontario became the key province in Canada. It was in Ontario that the NDP was to have its eventual greatest success beyond even what had been for the predecessor CCF its base in the Prairie Provinces. In the context of the generally Conservative party dominance of Ontario, the NDP managed to become the official opposition for a short time in 1975. The appeal of democratic socialism in Ontario reflected in large measure the nonconformist Anglo-Celtic religious traditions that characterized that province. Ultimately, the Social Gospel derived from the prophetic Biblical strand supported the feeling also expressed by David Lewis that capitalism was not merely wasteful and outmoded in Marxist terms but actually immoral.

The other strand that expressed itself particularly in Ontario was the attitude of *laborism*, seeking amelioration of conditions rather than overthrow of the system.[17]. This trend manifested itself in the tendency of the NDP to become less doctrinaire and pragmatic in seeking electoral success within the parliamentary system. Its principles were social ownership of basic industries and central planning that was nevertheless responsive to public input.[18]

It was in the arena of the eastern provinces that the Lewis family made its important contribution to socialism in the postwar era. Stephen Lewis, David's eldest son, was elected to the Ontario legislature in 1963 while in his midtwenties and was the Ontario provincial leader of the NDP from 1970 to 1978.[19] Starting at age six, he participated in his first political campaign in 1943 in the Cartier riding in Montreal when his father was defeated by Fred Rose. An only child until age seven, there was a younger brother and twin sisters. He grew up first in Ottawa in a small flat in a working-class district and went to the overwhelmingly Jewish neighborhood public elementary school. His mother maintained the family in the almost-constant absence of his father, caught up as he was in his political activities. Able to read at age three, Stephen was an articulate speaker from the start and a brilliant student. With the agreement of the principal, he would stay home from school several days each week to avoid being bored.

The family moved to Toronto in 1950 where Stephen went to high school before entering the University of Toronto. As a teenager, like his father before him, Stephen shone as a debater and was elected president of the model UN General Assembly. Although a relatively indifferent student at University of Toronto, he became noteworthy when he debated then Senator John Kennedy. Active in politics and the CCF Club on campus, he never wrote the final examination necessary for graduation. All through his growing up, he was immersed in the CCF. As a youngster, he was anointed by Coldwell, the leader of the CCF, to be the first socialist prime minister.[20] He would take on his father in heated political arguments. Like his father, what sustained him was not only the dream of a better society but the inner core of anger and outrage about the way society does work. He identified his life "to be useful, to be part of the struggle . . . to identify causes and fight them."[21].

In the Summer of 1957 when CCF fortunes were at a low ebb, Stephen Lewis was hired for the first time as an organizer to work in the Niagara peninsula area of Ontario. It marked the beginning of his involvement in managing political campaigns that went on during the years when the Ontario CCF was succeeded by the New Democratic Party. He was one of the new breed of young, aggressive members that helped to develop in Ontario a true three-party system.[22] Stephen Lewis's selection as provincial leader of the NDP in 1970 recognized his organizing efforts and an example of the generational transfer of power from the initial socialist generation to the new group, many of whom were connected by family ties.[23] In Stephen's case, those ties extended back several generations to his family's roots in Lita.

During the 1970s, the NDP maintained itself as a significant factor in the provincial legislature. The existence of a democratic socialist entity reflecting over 20 percent of the voters forced the ruling Conservative Party to carry out social reforms to maintain their power.[24] Rather than a sectarian approach, the legislative caucus came to dominate the party to reflect most accurately the political environment of its trade union support. It is not surprising that in Ontario, it acted like the British Labour Party as it was responsive to similar conditions.[25]. Although more successful in Ontario than elsewhere, the NDP was relatively unsuccessful overall in achieving its goal of enlisting union members.[26] At the end of the 1970s, Stephen Lewis withdrew from the Ontario NDP leadership and could not be persuaded to return to Canadian political life as overall leader of the party. He became Canadian Ambassador to the UN and committed to working on behalf of the dispossessed particularly in Africa.[27]

Canadian Literary Life

The Yiddish literary tradition fostered during the interwar era in Montreal had its flowering in English with major contribution to Canadian writing during the post-World War II era. The Montreal writers, Irving Layton and Mordecai Richler, were in some way successors to A. M. Klein.[28] Jewish-Canadian writing, in general, attests to his influence arising out of their commonality of ghetto background and unstable inheritance.[29] Klein's influence was greatest on his successors' poetry. Most closely associated to the Yiddish origins of Klein as well as his belated recognition as a master was Miriam Waddington who was also a poet in her own right.[30]

Miriam Dworkin was born in Winnipeg in 1917, and images from her childhood there live in her mature work despite her transplantation to other places. She finds Manitoba even in other northern places such as Leningrad. Happiness dominates her memories despite being acutely aware of her existence as "an outsider" unlike the prototype Anglo-Canadian.[31] Her father, Isadore Dworkin, had come to Canada in 1910 and founded a meat-curing business in Winnipeg where he married a fellow immigrant. Their home in Winnipeg became a center for Yiddish writers as well as left-wing political activists. Yiddish was the language of the home as well as her early schooling, enabling her later to translate the poems of J. I Segal. While at the Yiddish Peretz School, she was taught in an informal open environment where she was encouraged to question her teachers only to leave in the fifth grade to enter a rigid conservative public school run by *Scots Tories*. During this time, she also attended a progressive summer camp run by the Railwaymen's Union. She described these two widely different aspects as existing side by side, requiring her to devise a third invented world for herself.[32]

In 1931, the family moved to Ottawa where she went to high school and won prizes for her poetry. In 1936, she began studies at the University of Toronto in English literature and continued to publish poetry. She felt ambivalent about her Jewishness in the presence of the injustices she encountered in the anti-Semitism of the Toronto of the 1930s. After graduation, there were no opportunities for her to pursue a career in literature both as a woman and a Jew. She took a diploma in social work at University of Toronto and an advanced social work degree at University of Pennsylvania. She then came to Montreal in 1945 to work as a social worker and teach at McGill's School of Social Work. Her "social poems" reflect her experience with city life and compassion for the squalor she saw in her professional role. Her work in this vein is reminiscent of that of Klein who wrote of poverty as compromising the "holy of holies," the integrity of the individual.[33]

Her first book of poems published in 1945 was succeeded by two more in 1955 and 1958. After a divorce from Waddington, she retained his name and is known as Miriam Waddington. Moving to Toronto in 1960, she was eventually offered a position to teach literature at York University in 1964 where she has continued. The subject of her MA in English literature at University of Toronto was A. M. Klein. As late as 1969, she was criticized by her departmental chairman for placing Klein on the syllabus of a course on literature on the grounds that he was an unknown as well as being a Canadian rather than American or British. She was instrumental in collecting for publication his far-flung poems and other writings. She has compared his withdrawal from society because of mental illness to a Biblical prophet who fell silent when his poetic voice was not heard. Her writings about his novel *The Second Scroll* reflect her own search for identity in the context of her Jewishness and connection with Israel. She continued to publish poetry throughout the 1960s and 1970s, more personal in nature exploring her own loss of love and her divorce. She won the J. I. Segal Prize, named for the poet, on two occasions for the best book in English on Yiddish themes.

Relatively unrecognized, she continued to work independent of any school of poetry. Her work is described to have "a clarity and precision . . . a steadfast knowledge of what it sees and what it hopes to see . . . in order to render it accurately . . . in language."[34] She came to unite her several selves, her Jewish self, her being a woman and a Canadian.[35]

Leonard Cohen, of the younger postwar generation, can epitomize the trajectory from a background in Montreal's Jewish community to the point where, although informed by it, the central concern of his work has moved far outside. Irving Layton was a mentor and friend. Cohen's own *Flowers for Hitler* resembles Klein's poem *The Hitleriad* but also echoes the black romantic *Fleurs du Mal* of Baudelaire. Unlike these other Canadian poets and Cohen's contemporary Mordecai Richler, Cohen's background was not in the immigrant ghetto of *the Main* but that of Westmount. His own family had been the center of the response of those "uptown" Jews that uniquely held to their responsibility for those who came after them.

Lazarus Cohen was the founder of the line in Montreal and the patriarch of the Montreal Jewish Community.[36] He was born in Lita in 1844 to parents "renowned for their piety." Having completed his studies at the famed Voloshin Yeshivah, he emigrated to Canada in 1869. Starting with a general store in Maberly in Ontario, he moved to Montreal in 1883 along with several other families that had originated in Lita and had previously settled in small towns along the St. Lawrence River in Upper Canada.[37] In Montreal, Cohen became successful in a variety of industrial businesses. He was the founder or sustainer of many of the institutions of Montreal Jewry including the McGill College Avenue synagogue and the Baron de Hirsch Institute.[38]

His younger brother, Hirsch, born in 1862, joined him in Montreal in 1889 after having studied in the yeshivot of Vilna and Volozhin. Ordained as rabbi, he became the leading traditional *Orthodox* rabbi of Montreal. He was internationally recognized as one of the leading authorities on issues of Jewish law. Together with his brother, he founded the network of Talmud Torahs in Montreal. He was also a founder of the Religious Zionist *Mizrachi* and the leader of religiously based War Relief Society during the First World War. Hirsch Cohen was the most active propagandist for separate Jewish schools in Quebec in the post-World War I era.

Lazarus's elder son Lyon Cohen was born in 1868 just prior to his father's departure to Canada. He emigrated along with his mother in 1870 to join his father in Ontario. Growing up in Montreal in 1888, he joined his father in their industrial enterprises. In 1906, he himself organized the Freedman Company, one of the largest clothing manufacturers. As such, he took an active role in the Clothing Manufacturers Association of Montreal and thus in the battles in that industry. Despite his role as an employer, he was also the most active person in alleviating conditions for immigrants as president of the Baron de Hirsch Institute. Along with his presidency of the *Shaar Hashomayim* Congregation, he was also an officer of almost every Jewish organization in Montreal and in Canada as a whole including the Zionist Federation as well as the Canadian Jewish Congress. Together with Samuel Jacobs, he founded the English-language *Jewish Times* in 1897.[39]

This was the background that Leonard Cohen alluded to in his early work connected to his Jewish background and to Montreal. Unlike Klein and the culture of the Yiddish poets of the previous generation, Cohen's life was not centered in Jewish tradition. His early poetry dealing with his own life and the Holocaust did show the effect of his heritage. A religious sense seems to pervade his work with the use or even the inversion of Biblical texts such as Exodus. Increasingly important was his connection with the cult of the self and the counter culture of the 1960s.[40] Also unlike Klein, who remained unknown and unrecognized for much of his life, Cohen has become a world figure not unlike the impact of persons such as Bob Dylan in his popularity in the music of the 1960s.[41]

Leonard Cohen was born in 1934 to Nathan Cohen as one of two children. His father managed the clothing factory owned by Leonard's grandfather, Lyon. Leonard attributed as significant to his development the socialist camp he attended one summer where he first learned to play the guitar. He "managed to pay off his old debts to his family and society by attending university."[42] After graduation from McGill in 1955, where he won the prize for creative writing, he went to Columbia University in New York briefly before returning to Montreal. He has never taken an academic post.

With a small legacy, he was able to travel to places such as Cuba as well as Europe, especially the Greek island of Hydra. All of his work revolves around his own personality as an artist, his "life in art."[43] His "coming of age" novel, *The Favourite Game*, published in 1963, dealt with the discovery of a Montreal Jewish boy of his vocation as a poet as well as his sexual initiation. In his *Flowers for Hitler* in 1964, love in nature became death in the ovens of Auschwitz, and previous lyricism becomes irony and sarcasm with the poet separated from the world around him. *Beautiful Losers*, his next novel in 1966, was a "succes du scandale" that continued to project a sense of disillusionment and loss of innocence. It attacked the political and social system and the historical verities of Canada. These were the themes of his highly successful collected poems in 1968 and his record albums and concert performances of the 1960s.[44] In one of his latest works, written when he was fifty and after having spent time in a Zen monastery, he once again returned to biblical syntax and diction, invoking the specifically Jewish tradition, including exploration of the meaning of his own priestly surname.[45]

During the late '60s and '70s, there was emigration from the Montreal Jewish community of Anglophones in response to the threat of an independent Quebec. This accelerated after the rise to power of the separatist Parti Québécois (PQ) in 1976. Jews have continued to adhere to the Liberal Party in Quebec in the absence of any alternative to PQ. Illustrative was that the Liberal Prime Minister Pierre Trudeau represented a predominantly Jewish riding in Montreal. Native-born Ashkenazic Jews are Anglophone by virtue of schooling as well as connection with the other Jewish communities of the rest of Canada as well as the United States. With the reduction of total Jewish population, the percentage of Francophone Sephardim from North Africa has increased with consequent change in the character of the Jewish community. However, English remains the language of community meetings.

Illustrative is the peregination of the Michael Garmaise Family in Montreal in these years. Belonging to the *Conservative* synagogue, *Shaar Hashamayim*, the children of the third generation were all schooled in Jewish day schools. After United Talmud Torah and the Solomon Schechter School run by the **Conservative** movement, they graduated from the Herzlyia High School. The rigorous training offered there in French, Hebrew, and English qualified the only son, Robert, for entry to Harvard and then to Northwestern University Business School. Married to a graduate of the University of Ottawa Law School, they live in Toronto after having lived in the United States. The elder sister, Carole, was married to a fellow lawyer, of Scots extraction from

Saskatchewan. She is the mother of three and counsel to the Toronto General Hospital. The youngest child, Lisa, worked in Seattle for software firm after a period in Boston—for a consulting firm there—and has now relocated to Toronto.

It was no accident that all the siblings of this third generation were living in Ontario rather than Quebec. They have joined the large *brain drain* that has affected the Anglophone community since the Québécois separatist movement gained momentum. The Jewish community of Montreal had long prided itself on being the premier city of Canada. Its cohesiveness in the face of its exclusion from the Anglo British and French Canadian nations became a virtue. It was a North American shtetl confident in its uniqueness. It was Montreal that was the only city in North America other than New York that was on Shalom Aleichem's itinerary when he came to America. The spirit of Reuben Brainen lived on in the Jewish Public Library and in the Sadye Bronfman Center where Yiddish drama is still staged to appreciative audiences. The Bronfmans added to the sense of expansiveness of the Jews of Montreal. Their wealth and the use of their wealth added to the pride felt in the network of community agencies such as the Jewish General Hospital. Created in response to the limitations placed on Jewish physicians, it was the expression of the high quality that could be found within the walls of the shtetl, rather the "ghetto," of Montreal.

Canadian Separatism

The Canadian Jewish Congress has been involved in fostering bilingualism both within the Jewish community and as part of the trend in Quebec. The Cercle Juif de la Langue Francaise (CJLF) is one such activity established in the late 1940s.[46] It is clear that the "splendid isolation" of the past in which the Jewish community had little concourse with French Canadians was not to continue.[47] Efforts at rapprochement in the immediate postwar era were enhanced by the changes in the attitude of the still powerful upper ranks of the clergy with Archbishop Charbonneau a supporter of pluralism. A Comite Saint-Paul was established by the archdiocese to improve relations with the Jews. The public relations committee of the CJC and the B'nai B'rith was the counterpart group from the Jewish community. As an example, it welcomed changes in editorial policy of the major Montreal newspaper *Le Devoir* from what had been an anti-Semitic stance. There was recognition of Jews acting in the interests of bilingualism rather than entirely committed to an Anglophone stance.[48]

David Rome took a particularly active role in this initiative with one of the products a joint book with a French Canadian priest that sought to find commonalities in exploration of some of the differences between the two communities. First published in French in 1986, it then appeared in English translation.[49] In the introduction, the French priest alludes to David Rome's groundbreaking action of speaking in French to group of priests about the relation between Jews and French Quebecers.

David Rome had a far-reaching role while pursuing a wide range of efforts to describe the history of Canadian Jews. He was the leading archivist and student of Jewish life and letters in Canada. He was born in Vilna in 1910 and came to Vancouver in Canada in 1921. He never, however, lost the stamp of his native place. He has epitomized the selfless scholarship of his cultural heritage. Settled in Vancouver, he continued his education with a degree in literature and philosophy from the University of British Columbia in 1936 before a degree in library science in Montreal where he mainly remained for the rest of his life. During 1934-36, he started his literary career by editing the *Jewish Western Bulletin* in Vancouver. He then became the associate editor of the Toronto *Yiddisher Zhurnal* and editor of its English section. From 1943 to 1953, he edited the *Congress Weekly* as press officer of that organization. From 1953 onward, he was editorial director of the Montreal People's Library. He continued to contribute to the full range of Yiddish newspapers in Canada as well as the New York *Forverts*. He was, for a time, the first national director of the Labour Zionist movement.

His major work was as the chief archivist of the Canadian Jewish Congress. He has published several monographs but primarily an extensive series of volumes, documenting Canadian anti-Semitism as well as the evolution of Canadian Jewish life since its eighteenth-century origins. In 1967, he became professor of Jewish studies at McGill and lecturer in History at Concordia University in Montreal.

Among his other activities, he was the first Jewish member of the Quebec Provincial Arts Council.

With urbanization and increased education, the French Canadian majority of Quebec began to question the rule of the church. Movement off the farms led to a high rate of unemployment. The causes of such poverty had previously been attributed to exploitation by the "English," with "the Jew," the stalking horse in the 1930s. The antilabor attitude of the church had changed with more liberal stance toward the Quebec worker arising out of the *Asbestos Strike* in 1949. This could be considered the start of the *Quiet Revolution*.[50]. The secularization of society led to focus on the state as the vehicle for French-Canadian entry into the middle-class professions and the civil service. Ownership by the Quebec government of basic industries, such as utilities and steel, was part of the pattern as well as huge increase in the degree of employment in governmental services.[51]

With secularization, it was no longer only the religious identity but the ethnic, possibly even "racial" identity, that was to take precedence. Language was only the marker for such an identity. Political separation from Confederation was based on a nationalism that focused not merely on adherence to the French language. The Jews experience a sense of danger when a nation-state forms. The question remains whether a Jew, however Francophone, could ever be a "French Canadian." The new term *Québécois* is sometimes used by nationalist politicians in an exclusionary way to delineate "old stock" Francophones identifying their nationalistic membership in Quebec rather than Canada. The role of Francophone Jewish intellectuals in contributing to the culture based on their French linguistic identity remains problematic. It requires transcending the ethnicity of old stock descendents of the original "habitants" and a clear dissociation from the trends of Quebec nationalism that betrays itself in "slips of the tongue" by nationalistic politicians.[52]

Illustrative of both the radical tradition and rare membership in the Francophone majority of Quebec is the long life of Leah Roback whose allegiance to a multitude of causes spanned the century.

Lea Roback was born in 1903 in Montreal, the second in a family of what were eventually nine children. Coming from

Poland, the parents were married in Canada under the auspices of a marriage broker. Her father was religious and would come late to work if necessary in order to fulfill his morning prayers. He much preferred study of his books to his work as a cutter in a men's clothing factory in Montreal. In 1906, the family opened a general store outside of Quebec City in Beauport. Although the only Jewish family in a Francophone and Catholic community, they were accepted. Lea and her elder brother would take a trolley to the English Protestant school in the nearby city. Irrepressible, she spoke Yiddish at home, English at school, and French with her friends. She loved to read and was encouraged to read the range of Yiddish books in the house. Despite their poverty, the children were taught the importance of helping others who were less fortunate that became the focus of Lea's life.

The family came back to Montreal in 1918, and Lea left school to seek work. She acquired a patron who funded her to go to University of Grenoble where she studied French literature while supporting herself by giving English lessons. In 1929, she joined her elder brother at the University of Berlin where he was studying medicine. In the heated politicized atmosphere of Berlin, she joined the Communist party. With the rise of the Nazis, she returned to Montreal in 1932. She remained active in the outlawed Communist Party in Canada and, after a visit to Russia and then the United States, finally returned to Canada in 1935 to find her place in Montreal. She remained there for the rest of her life, carrying out a variety of roles in radical politics. Her first job was campaign manager for Fred Rose in his first run for Parliament. Despite police harassment and attacks by the students at the nearby University of Montreal, she led her mainly Jewish young people to work on his behalf. She then ran the bookstore where Communist literature was sold.

Knowing Yiddish, English, and French, she was hired to be the educational director of the ILGWU in its drive to unionize the garment workers. Particularly important to her were the stories of sexual harassment of the young girls. After a major strike in 1937, the union was recognized as the bargaining agent and a union shop came about. The garment industry was almost entirely Jewish-owned in Montreal. She would not accept racism expressed against the Jewish owners but emphasized that class differences must take precedence in the fight for better working conditions. In turn, she took up for a black worker against the racism of a Jewish owner who refused her a place. With the entry of the Soviet Union into the war, she was assigned to work for development of unions in the war industries. Successful in organizing a union in the RCA plant, she led the union members in interesting themselves in the housing problems of the neighborhood surrounding the plant.

In the cold war era, the union, affiliated with a communist-led UE (United Electrical Workers), lost its accreditation, and Lea was dismissed along with other union leaders. She could not easily get a job or keep one even as a salesperson at Eaton's department store because of suspicion about her political activities. She finally got a job at the Polish embassy, translating documents in light of her knowledge of German, English, and French. She finally left the Communist Party in 1958 after Khrushchev's speech at the Soviet Party Congress but did so without rancor and proud of the work of her lifetime on behalf of unions, of worker rights, and the dispossessed.

Roback then enlisted in 1965 on behalf of the organization for the blind. Retirement in 1975 did not prevent her from continuing to battle for women's rights against violence and the arms race. Even in her new role as a part-time student at the University of Montreal, studying the history of Quebec, she remained an agitator. Yiddish remained her core language and *Yiddishkayt* defined her identity based on the sense of moral responsibility for others conveyed by the term *tzedaka*. There was a basic link between her Jewish background and her progressive ideas. She also identified with the French-Canadian need for recognition as a separate society. She considered herself as a Jew and a Québécois.[53] She received recognition for her commitment to that cause with the award of the L'Ordre of Quebec just prior to her death in 2000.

As in several other countries in the Litvak Diaspora in this generation, there has been recognition within the academic community of Jewish Studies with courses on forty Canadian campuses. McGill has the only actual Department of Jewish Studies. The University of Toronto has developed a major Jewish studies program, and York University in Toronto and Concordia University in Montreal operate a joint Centre for Canadian Jewish studies.[54] Even beyond, the recent increase in public support extended to

Jewish full-day schooling in most of Canada reflects the traditional Canadian relationship of religious education with the state enshrined initially in Confederation. This contrasts with the wall of separation between church and state in the United States.

The total Jewish population in the most recent census of 1991 is 370,000. Canada has become one of the major Jewish communities of the world as Canada itself has developed its own role in the world. Canada prides itself as a multiethnic country in which the Jews are an identifiable group that contributes to the whole. In comparison to those in the United States, Canadian Jews are more "Jewish," that is, they are more likely to speak Yiddish, are more likely to provide more intensive Jewish education, and more likely to be *Orthodox*. These characteristics have been attributed at least in part to the larger percentage of the recently arrived, including Holocaust survivors.[55] They may also, in Montreal, be attributed to the sense of separateness that city has engendered wherein the Jews have been the third part of a community split between the French and British. "The Canadian ideology of multiculturism legitimates and reinforces traits that have long been part of the Jewish experience."[56] To the extent that Canada is indeed a multiethnic country, those differences will remain as a measure of an "integrated" group into this third and subsequent generations.[57]

*   *   *

Notes

4.1 The Character of the Place

1   George Woodcock, *The Canadians*, Cambridge, MA, 1979, 50-52
2   Edgar McInnis, *Canada: A Political and Social History*, Kingston, ON and Montreal, QC, 1967, 5-7
3   Gad Horowitz, *Canadian Labor in Politics*, Toronto, 1968, 10-18
4   Edgar McInnis, op cit, 1967, 63-74)
5   ibid, 114-139
6   ibid, 140-172
7   Michael Brown, ""From Stereotype to Scapegoat: anti-Jewish Sentiment in French Canada from Confederation to World War I," In Moses Rischin, Ed., *The Jews of North America*, Detroit, 1987
8   Joseph Kage, *With Faith and Thanksgiving*, Montreal, 1962, 7
9   Gerald Tulchinsky, *Taking Root*, Hanover, NH, 1993, 8-21
10   Benjamin Sack, *History of the Jews in Canada*, Montreal, 1965, 81-91
11   Gerarld Tulchinsky, op cit, 1993, 24-30
12   Edgar McInnis, op cit, 1967, 230-285
13   Donald Creighton, *Canada's First Century, 1867-1967*, NewYork, 1970, 3-12
14   Michael Brown, "American Connection of Canadian Jews," *AJS Review*, 1978, 3:21
15   Joseph Kage, op cit, 1962, 8-9
16   Jacques Langlais and David Rome, *Jews and French Quebecers*, Waterloo, ON, 1991, 9-11
17   Irving Abella, *A Coat of Many Colors*, Toronto, 1990, 113
18   Joseph Kage, op cit, 1962, 12 n.8
19   Gerald Tulchinsky, op cit, 1993, 49-53
20   Richard Menkis, "Anti-Semitism and Anti-Judaism in Pre-Confederation Canada," In Alan Davies, Ed., *Anti-Semitism in Canada*, Waterloo, ON, 1992
21   Michael Brown, *Jew or Juif*, Philadelphia, 1987, 119-161 passim
22   ibid, 221-228
23   Gerald Tulchinsky, "Goldwin Smith, Victorian Canadian Anti-Semitism," In Alan Davies, Ed., op cit, 1992
24   Morton Weinfeld, *Like Everyone Else butDifferent: The Paradoxical Success of Canadian Jews*, Toronto, 2001, 58
25   Joseph Kage, op cit, 1962, 14-34; Simon Belkin, *Through Narrow Gates*, Montreal, n.d, 24-29

26 Lloyd Gartner, "Jewish Migration en Route from Europe to North America: Traditions and Realities," *Jewish History*, 1986, 1:49

27 Michael Brown, op cit, 1978

28 Robert Harney and Harold Troper, *Immigration: A Portrait of an Urban Experience*, Toronto, 1975, 5

29 Benjamin Sack, op cit, 1965, 211

30 Irving Abella, op cit, 1990, 112

31 Joe King, *From the Ghetto to the Main: The Story of the Jews of Montreal*, Montreal, 2001

32 Simon Belkin, op cit, n.d., 28-35

33 Lloyd Gartner, op cit, 1986

34 Simon Belkin, n.d. op cit, 50-63; Irving Abella, op cit,

35 Simon Belkin n.d, op cit, 75-78

36 Joseph Kage, op cit, 1962, 51

37 ibid, 31-39

38 Irving Abella, op cit, 1990, 83

39 Harold Troper, "Jews and Canadian Immigration Policy," In Moses Rischin, Ed., op cit, 1987

40 Louis Rosenberg, *A Population Study of the Jews of Winnipeg*, Montreal, 1946

41 Jonathan Sarna, "Jewish Immigration to North Ameriaca: The Canadian Experience, 1870-1900," *Jewish Journal of Sociology*, 1976, 18:31

42 Louis Rosenberg and Morton Weinfeld, *Canada's Jews: A Social and Economic Study of the Jews in Canada during the 1930s*, Montreal, 1939

43 David Rome, *Clouds in the Thirties. On Anti-Semitism in Canada 1929-1939*, Montreal, 1979, 81

44 Jonathan Sarna, op cit, 1976

45 David Rome, op cit, 1979, 87-88

46 Michael Brown, op cit, 1987, 250

47 Benjamin Sack, op cit, 1965, 212

48 Gerald Tulchinsky, op cit, 1993, 137

49 ibid, 57-60

50 Benjamin Sacks, op cit, 1965, 184-187

51 Gerald Tulchinsky, op cit, 1993,244-246

52 David Rome, *On the Jewish School Question in Montreal 1903-1931*, 1975, 19-32 Tulchinsky, 1993 p 243-249

54 David Rome, op cit, 1979, 89

55 Gerald Tulchinsky, op cit, 1993, 149

56 Erna Paris, *Jews: An Account of Their Experience in Canada*, Toronto, 1980, 31

57 Gerald Tulchinsky, op cit, 1993, 151

58 Abraham Rhinewine, *Looking Back a Century*, Toronto, 1926

59 Michael Brown, op cit, 1987

60 Erna Paris, op cit, 1980, 33-34

61 Simon Belkin, op cit, n.d, 28-49

62 Harold Troper, op cit, Moses Rischin, Ed., 1987

63 Louis Rosenberg, op cit, 1939, 244

64 Erna Paris, op cit, 1980, 34-39

65 Joseph Kage, op cit, 1962, 54-55, 68-75

4.2 The Evolution in Canada

1 Gerald Tulchinsky, "The Contours of Canadian History," In Robert Brym, Milton Shaffir and Morton Weinfeld, Eds., *The Jews in Canada*, Toronto, 1993

4.2.1. The Immigrant Generation

2 Gerald Tulchinsky, op cit, 1993, 158-163

3 ibid, 131-137

4 Gerald Tulchinsky, op cit, In Robert Brym et al, Eds., 1993

5 Gerald Tulchinsky, op cit, 1993, 172-173

6 ibid, 164-166

7 Joe King, op cit, 2001

8 Bernard Figler, *Sam Jacobs, Member of Parliament*, Ottawa, 1959, 1-17

9 Jack Jedwab, "Uniting Uptowners and Downtowners:Jewish Electorate and Quebec Provincial Politics, 1927-1939," *Canadian Ethnic Studies*, 1986, 18:7

10 Erna Paris, op cit, 1980, 67-83 passim

11 Pierre Anctil, "Introduction," In Simon Belkin, *Le Mouvement Ouvrier Juif au Canada 1904-1920*, Montreal, 1999

12 Geoffrey Wigoder, *New Encyclopedia of Zionism and Israel*, Teaneck, NJ, 1994, 243-244; Gerald Tulchinsky, "Clarence de Sola and Early Zionism in Canada, 1898-1920," In Moses Rischin, Ed., op cit, 1987

13 Pierre Anctil, op cit, 1999,86-94 passim

14 ibid, 101-135 passim

15 David Rome, *The Education Legend of the Migration*, Montreal, 1991, ?

16 David Rome *The First Jewish Literary School*, Montreal, 1988, 20-24

17 ibid, 15-49 passim

18 Pierre Anctil, op cit. 1999. 35?

19 Naomi Caruso, *Folk's Lore. A History of the Jewish Public Library*, Montreal, 1989, 13-15

20 Arthur Hart, *The Jew in Canada*, Toronto and Montreal, 1926,

21 Simon Belkin, "When Brainin was a Montrealer," *Canadian Jewish Yearbook*, 1940-41, 134-138

22 Michael Brown, op cit, 1978

23 Naomi Caruso, op cit, 1989, 53

24 Simon Belkin, op cit, 1940-41, 138-143

25 David Rome, *Men of the Yiddish Press*, Montreal, 1989, 96-126 passim

26 Gerald Tulchinsky, op cit, 1993, 204-212; David Rome, op cit, 1989, 77-96

27 David Rome, op cit, 1991, 66-69

28 Stephen Speisman, *The Jews of Toronto. A History to 1937*, Toronto, 1979, 175-178

29 Louis Rosenberg, *A Population Study of the Winnipeg Jewish Community*, Montreal, 1946

30 Arthur Chiel, *The Jews in Manitoba. A Social History.*, Toronto, 1961, 102-106

31 S. Livinson, "A History of Jewish People's Schools of Montreal," In Arthur Hart, Ed., 1926 op cit

32 Michael Brown, "The Beginnings of Reform Judaism in Canada,: *Jewish Social Studies*, 197, 34:322

33 Bernard Figler, *Rabbi Dr Herman Abramowitz, Lazarus Cohen, Lyon Cohen*, Ottawa, 1968 p1-91; Arthur Hart op cit, 1926, 92

34 Stuart Rosenberg, *Jewish Community in Canada. A History. Vol I*, 1970, 128-129

35 Arthur Hart, op cit, 1926, 130; Stephen Speisman., op cit, 1979, 164-174

36 ibid, 154

37 Arthur Chiel, op cit, 1961, 73-87, 92-102

38 Harvey Herstein, "Jewish Religious Leadership in Winnipeg, 1900-1963," *Jewish Historical Society Journal*, 1978, 2:39

39 Gerald Tulchinsky, op cit, 1993, 262-272; Hannaniah Caiserman, "History of the First Canadian Jewish Congress," In Arthur Hart, Ed., op cit, 1926; Judith Nefsky, "The Pre-History of the Founding of the Canadian Jewish Congress, 1907-1919," *Canadian Jewish Historical Society Journal*, 8:73.1984

4.2.2 The Acculturating Generation

1   Simon Belkin, op cit, n.d., 85

2   Louis Rosenberg, op cit, 1946-47

3   Louis Rosenberg, op cit, 1939, 40-41

4   Louis Rosenberg, op cit, 1947-48

5   Pierre Anctil, "Interlude of Hostility: Judeo-Christian Relations in Quebec in the Interwar Period, 1919-1939," In Alan Davies Ed., op cit, 1992

6   Arthur Chiel, op cit, 1961, 102-107 ibid, 145-154

7   David Rome, op cit, 1979, 100-101

8   Allen Gutkin, *Journey Into Our Heritage*, Toronto, 1980, 190-193

9   Interview with Saul Cherniack Nov 29, 2001

10 Gerald Tulchinsky, *Branching Out*, Toronto, 1998, 7-25 passim

11 David Rome, op cit, 1991, 70-80

12 David Rome, op cit, 1975, 116-136 passim; Gerald Tulchinsky, op cit, 1998, 63-86 passim; Louis Rosenberg, op cit, 1939, 265-270

13 David Roskies, "Yiddish in Montreal: The Utopian Experiment," In Ira Robinson, Pierre Anctil and Mervin Butofsky, Eds., *An Everyday Miracle: Yiddish Culture in Montreal*, Montreal, 1990

14 Louis Rosenberg, op cit, 1939, 217

15 Theodore Norman, *An Outstretched Arm. History of the Jewish Colonization Society*, London, 1985, 95-100

16 Irving Abella, op cit, 1990, 96-99

17 Louis Rosenberg, op cit, 1939, 222

18 Erna Paris, op cit, 1960, 242-262 passim

19 Michael Usiskin, *Uncle Mike's Edenbridge*, Winnipeg, 1983, 143 ibid, 42-51 ibid, 1-15

20 David Rome, op cit, 1988, 60-137 passim

21 Ben Kayfetz, "The Jewish Press in Canada," In Edmond Lipsitz, Ed., *Canada Jewry Today*, Downview, ON, 1989

22 Rebecca Margolis, "Les ecivains Yiddish de Montreal et leur cite," In Pierre Anctil, Ira Robinson and Gerard Bouchard, Eds., *Juifs et Canadiens Francais dans le societe Quebecoise*, Sillary, QC, 2000 ibid

23 Shari Friedman, "Between Two Worlds. The Works of J.I. Segal," In Ira Robinson, Pierre Anctil and Mervin Bukovsky, Eds, op cit, 1990

24 Chaim Spilberg and Yacoov Zipper, *Canadian Jewish Anthology*, Montreal, 1982, 95

MARK N. OZER

25 Irving Massey, *Identity and Community: Reflections on English, Yiddish and French Literature in Canada*, Detroit, 1994, 49-69

26 Ruth Frager, *Sweatshop Strife, Class, Ethnicity and Gender in the Jewish Labour Movemment of Toronto, 1900-1939*, Toronto, 1992, 67-76 ibid,35-52

27 Irving Abella and David Millar, *The Canadian Worker in the Twentieth Century*, Toronto, 1978, 184-194 ibid, 194-195

28 Ruth Frager, op cit, 1992, 85-87 ibid, 11-34

29 Harold Logan, *Trade Unions in Canada: Their Development and Functioning*, Toronto, 1948, 208-211

30 William Rodney, *Soldiers of the International*, Toronto, 1968, 15-27

31 Donald Creighton, op cit, 1970, 158-160

32 Donald Masters, *The Winnipeg General Strike*, Toronto, 1950, 103-112 ;David Bercuson, "The Winnipeg General Strike," In Irving Abella, Ed., *On Strike. Six Key Labour Struggles in Canada 1919-1949*, Toronto, 1974

33 Henry Trachtenberg, "The Winnipeg Jewish Community in the Interwar Period, 1919-1939, Anti-Semitism and Politics," *Canadian Jewish History Journal*, 1980, 4:44.

34 Donald Avery, *"Dangerous Foreigners" European Immigrant Workers and Labour Radicalism in Canada, 1896-1932*, Toronto, 1979, 88

35 Ruth Frager, op cit, 180-201

36 Stuart Rosenberg, op cit, 1970, 189

37 Erna Paris, op cit, 1980, 124-127

38 William Rodney, op cit, 1968, 146-160

39 Erna Paris, op cit, 1980, 167-170

40 Norman Penner, *The Canadian Left*, Scarborough, ON, 1988, 80-160 passim ibid, 243-244

41 Stuart Rosenberg, op cit, 1970, 190

42 Donald Masters, op cit, 1950, 113-127 passim

43 Ivan Avakumovic, *Socialism in Canada :A Study of the CCF-NDP in Federal and Provincial Politics*, Toronto, 1978, 30-43

44 Leo Heaps, *The Rebel in the House*, London, 1970, 1-7; David Lewis, *The Good Fight*, Toronto, 1981, 98-99

45 Donald Masters, op cit, 1950,144-149

46 Walter Young, *Democracy and Discontent*, Toronto, 1969, 57; Norman Penner, op cit, 1977, 143-209 passim

47 James McAllister, *The Government of Edward Schreyer*, Kingston, ON, 1984, 97

48 Walter Young, *The Anatomy of a Party: The National CCF, 1932-1961*, Toronto, 1969, 51-65 passim

49 Gerald Caplan, *Just Causes. Notes of an Unrepentant Socialist*, Toronto, 1993. 20

50 Abraham Ain, 'Swislocz: Portrait of a Jewish Community in Eastern Europe," In Deborah Dash Moore, Ed., *East European Jews in Two Worlds*, Evanston, IL, 1990

51 Cameron Smith, *Unfinished Journey, The Lewis Family*, Toronto, 1989, 154-155

52 David Lewis, op cit, 1981, 2-19; Cameron Smith, op cit, 1989, 147-149

53 David Lewis, op cit, 1981, 37-81, 110-127 passim ibid, 224-232

54 Walter Young, op cit, 1969, 78-79

55 John Morley, *Secular Socialists,: The CCF-NDP in Ontario: A Biography*, Kingston, ON, 1984, 60

56 Gerald Caplan, op cit, 1993, 20

57 Cameron Smith, op cit, 1989, 394

58 Irving Abella and Harold Troper, *None is Too Many, Canada and the Jews of Europe, 1933-1948*, New York, 1982, 1-66

59 Lita-Rose Betcherman, *The Swastika and the Maple Leaf: Fascist Movements in Canada in the Thirties*, Toronto, 1975, 1-31

60 David Rome, *Clouds in the Thirties: On Anti-Semitism in Canada 1929-1939* Section 2, Montreal, 1977, 1-19

61 Pierre Anctil, In Alan Davies, Ed., op cit, 1992

62 David Rome, op cit, 1977, 20-26

63 Erna Paris, op cit, 1960, 49-60

64 Judiith Nefsky, op cit, 1992

65 Lita-Ros Betcherman, op cit 1975, 32-60

66 Milton Shain, "Ethno-nationalism, Anti-Semitism and Identity Politics,: The North American and South African Experiences, 'In Sander Gilman and Milton Shain, Eds., *Jewries at the Frontier: Accommodation, Identity, Conflict*, Urbana, IL, 1999

67 David Rome, *Clouds in the Thirties: On Anti-Semitism in Canada, 1929-1939. Section 4*, Montreal, 1978, 32-52

68 Canadian Jewish Congress, *Pathways to the Present: Canadian Jewry and the Canadian Jewish Congress*, Toronto, 1986 p7

69 Mervin Butovsky, "A.M. Klein: A Jewish Poet in the Modern World," *Jewish Book Annual*, 1988-89, 46:20

70 M.W. Steinberg, "A.M. Klein," In W.H. New, Ed., *Canadian Writers 1920-1959*, 1st Series, Detroit, 1988

71   Urban Caplan, *Like One That Dreamed. A Portrait of A. M. Klein,* Toronto, 1982, 140 ibid, 30-52 ibid, 45-57

72   M.W. Steinberg, op cit, 1975

73   Zailig Pollock, *A.M. Klein. The Story of a Poet,* Toronto, 1994, 149-151

74   Pierre Anctil, "A.M. Klein. The Poet and his Relations with French Quebec," In Moses Rischin, Ed., op cit, 1987

75   M. W, Steinberg and Usher Caplan, Eds., *Beyond Sambation, : Selected essays and Editorials, 1928-1955 A.M. Klein,* Toronto, 1982,

76   Michael Marrus, *Samuel Bronfman. The Life and Times of Seagrams' Mr Sam,* Hanover, NH, 1991, 424-428

77   M. W. Steinberg, op cit, 1988

78   Adam Fuerstenberg, "The Poet and the Tycoon: The Relationship Between A.M. Klein and Samuel Bronfman," *Canadian Jewish Historical Society,* 1981, 7:49.

79   Miriam Waddington, *A.M. Klein,* Toronto, 1970, 1-4

80   Zailig Pollock, op cit, 1994, 3

81   Miriam Waddington, op cit, 1970, ix

82   Tom Marshall, "Introduction," In Tom Marshall, Ed., *A.M. Klein,* Toronto, 1970, xxv

83   David Bercuson, *Canada and the Birth of Israel,* Toronto, 1985, 19-21

84   Bernard Figler, *Lillian and Archie Freiman, Biographies,* Montreal, 1962, 296

85   Irving Abella, op cit, 1990, 114

86   Bernard Figler, op cit, 1962, 11-18 ibid, 18-27 passim ibid, 197-206

100 David Berrcuson, op cit, 1985, 49

101 ibid, 71-73

102 ibid, 185-192

103 Gerald Tulchinsky, op cit, 1998, 246-260.

104 Mordecai Richler, "Montreal 1947: We Danced the Hora in the Middle of the Street," In J.J. Goldberg and Eliot King, Eds., *Builders and Dreamers: Habonim Labor Zionist Youth in North America,* New York, 1993

4.2.3 The Integrated Generation

1   Daniel Elazar and Harold Waller, *Maintaining Consensus: The Canadian Jewish Polity in the post-War World,* Lanham, MD, 1990, 73-89

2   David Rome, Montreal, The Capital City of Jewish Canada," In Eli Gottesman, Ed., *The Canadian Jewish Reference Book and Directory,* Montreal, 1963; Stuart Rosenberg, op cit, 1970, 126

3   ibid, 138-140

4   M. Michael Rosenberg, "The Montreal Jewish Community: A Sociological Profile," In Chaim Spilberg and Yacoov Zipper Eds., op cit,1982

5   A. J. Arnold, "Problems of Jewish Education in Canada," In Eli Gottesman, Ed., op cit, 1963, 264-268

6   Daniel Elazar and Harold Waller, op cit, 1990, 86-88

7   Ruth Wisse, "A Goles Education," *Moment*, 1977, 2: 26

8   Susanne Klingenstein, *Enlarging America, The Cultural Work of Jewish Literary Scholars, 1930-1990*, Syracuse, NY, 1998, 307-345 passim

9   Keith Archer, *Political Choices and Electoral Consequences: A Study of Organized Labour and the New Democratic Party*, Kingston, ON, 1990,17-18

10   Cameron Smith, op cit, 360-361

11   Nelson Wiseman, *Social Democracy in Manitoba: A History of the CCF-NDP*, Winnipeg, 1983, 126; James McAllister, op cit,1984, 120-124; Ivan Avakumovic, op cit, 1978, 248-253

12   James McAllister, op cit, 1984, 74-77

13   Personal communication Saul Cherniack

14   Raymond Breton, Wsevolod Isajiw, Warren Kalbach and Jeffrey Reitz, Eds., *Ethnic Identity and Equality : Varieties of Experience in a Canadian City*, Toronto, 1990, 16-17

15   Daniel Elazar and Harold Waller op cit, 1990, 153-171 passim

16   Raymond Breton et al, op cit, 1990, 82

17   John Morley, op cit, 1984, 125-127

18   ibid,142-144

19   Alan Whitehorn, *Canadian Socialism*, Toronto, 1992, 166-170

20   Cameron Smith, op cit, 1989, 327-350

21   ibid, 349

22   Dan Azoulay, *Keeping the Dream Alive: The Survival of the Ontario CCF-NDP, 1950-1963*, Kingston, ON, 1997, 217-218

23   John Morley, op cit, 1984, 95-100

24   Ivan Avakumovic, op cit, 1978, 273-275

25   John Morley, op cit, 1984, 166-172

26   Keith Archer, op cit, 1990, 35-40

27   Gerard Caplan, op cit, 1993, 17

28   Michael Greenstein, "Nobody Chasing Everyman: Canadian-Jewish Literature," *Jewish Book Annual*, 1993-1994, 51:42

29   Michael Greenstein, *Third Solitudes: Tradition and Discontinuity in Jewish-Canadian Literature*, Kingston, ON, 1989, 1-17 passim

30 Peter Stevens, "Miriam Waddington," In Robert Lecker, Jack David and Ellen Quigley, Eds., *Canadian Writers and Their Works, Poetry Series Vol 5*, Toronto, 1985, 279-324 passim

31 Laurie Ricou, "Miriam Waddington," In W.H. New Ed., op cit, 1988

32 Miriam Waddington, "Introduction," In *The Collected Works of A.M. Klein*, Toronto, 1974

33 Peter Stevens, op cit, 1985, 311

34 ibid, 324

35 Miriam Waddington, "Exile," *Maclean's*, 1974, 87: 40

36 Pierre Anctil, "Les Ecrivains Juives de Montreal," In Pierre Anctil and Gary Caldwell, Eds., *Juifs et Realities Juives au Quebec*, Quebec, 1984, 238

37 Joe King, op cit, 2001

38 Arthur Hart, op cit, 1926, 99

39 ibid.,339

40 Linda Hutcheon, "Leonard Cohen," In Robert Lecker et al. Eds., op cit, 1992, 24

41 Pierre Anctil, op cit, 1984, 240-244

42 Linda Hutcheon, "Leonard Cohen," In Robert Lecker, Jack David and Ellen Quigley, Eds., *Canadian Writers and Their Works, Fiction Series, Vol 10*, Toronto,1989, 25

43 ibid, 26

44 Ira Nadel, Leonard Cohen," In W.H. New, Ed., op cit, 1986

45 Stephen Scobie, *Leonard Cohen*, Vancouver, 1978, 4

46 Daniel Elazar and Harold Waller, op cit, 1990, 73-83

47 Morton Weinfeld, "The Jews of Quebec: An Overview," In Robert Brym, William Shaffir and Morton Weinfeld, Eds., *The Jews of Canada*, Toronto, 1993

48 Jack Jedwab, "The Politics of Dialogue," Ira Robinson and Mervic Burofsky, Eds., *Renewing Our Days: Montreal Jews in the Twentieth Century*, Montreal, 1995

49 Jacques Langlais and David Rome, op cit, 1991

50 Irving Abella, "The Canadian Labour Movement," *Canadian Historical Society*, 1975, 28:3

51 Robert Bothwell, *Canada and Quebec: One Country, Two Histories*, Vancouver, 1995, 60-79 passim

52 Regine Robin, "Francophone Jewish Intellectuals in Present-Day Quebec," In Sander Gilman and Milton Shain, Eds., op cit, 1999

53 Allen Gottheil, *Les Juifs Progressives au Quebec*, Montreal, 1988, 65-103 passim

54 Morton Weinfeld, op cit, 2001, 247
55 ibid, 58
56 ibid, 352
57 William Shaffir, "Canadian Jewry: Some Sociological Observations," In Edmund Lipsitz, Ed., op cit, 1989

CHAPTER 5
SOUTH AFRICA

5.1 The Nature of the Place

5.1.1. A Tribal Society

In 1652, the Dutch East India Company established a settlement at the Cape of Good Hope to provide food for their sailors on the way to the Spice Islands. The origin of the Afrikaner nation is dated from 1657 when the company's servants were first created "free burgers" and given land to cultivate.[1] Soon after the Revocation of the Edict of Nantes in 1685, several parties of Huguenot refugees immigrated to the Cape. Settlers from other Protestant countries such as the German states also came. The economy of the settlement was based upon private ownership of the livestock with the free use of land for grazing. The relatively few local indigenous inhabitants were decimated by smallpox. Labor was provided by imported black slaves.

British control after the Napoleonic Wars maintained the existing stratified society with a ruling white minority. Cape Town became even more important, now as a halfway station to British India. Starting in 1820, attempts were made to settle Britons. English became the official language of the courts and legislature. The British immigrants were the shopkeepers in the towns that began to spring up. The abolition of the slave trade, and then of slavery itself, in 1834 led to other methods for controlling labor.

The more adventurous white frontiersmen extended the areas of settlement by wresting control of grazing lands from the local African tribes. There are no great rivers and transport over great distances under arid conditions made for great regional differences. A tradition of local self-government developed. Central was the temporary organization used to fight the natives. The *commando* was made up of the adult males with their horses and firearms under the direction of an elected commandant. The numerically small, widely dispersed Afrikaner people— descendents of Dutch, French, and German immigrants— gradually developed a group consciousness as an indigenous white "tribe" with the Dutch Reformed religion dominant.[2]

Starting in 1836, several additional parties of Boers (the word meaning farmers) left the eastern districts of the Cape Colony to seek more land beyond the Orange River and the Vaal River on the interior plateau. This large-scale exodus of some fifteen thousand whites, called the Voortrek (Great Trek) became an important milestone of Afrikaner history.[3] There were two Afrikaner republics established: Orange Free State had its capital at Bloemfontein, and the even more northerly, Transvaal Republic had its capital at Pretoria.[4]

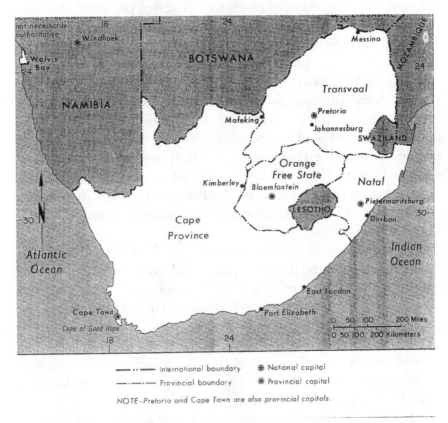

Map 5.1 The Union of South Africa

The constitution founding the Orange Free State in 1854 limited citizenship to white males over eighteen years. It did not include a religious test. English speakers were welcome and were able to rise in politics. English was commonly spoken in the towns and business life although Dutch was the language of the legislature. Black persons were not permitted to own land.[5]

The South African Republic of the Transvaal allowed whites to own large farms as of right; blacks were not permitted to own land. Starting in 1859, the Volksraad (legislature) was elected by white citizens. An independent Voortreker church arose, freed from the Dutch church of the Cape Colony. The Voortrekker church was incorporated into the constitution, and membership in that church a requirement for election to the legislature. Catholics as well as Jews were barred from military posts, the offices of magistrate as well as president and state secretary. Jewish as well as Catholic children and teachers were excluded from state-subsidized schools, and all instruction was required to be given in a "Christian and Protestant spirit" and in Dutch.[6]

The year 1872 saw the establishment of self-government of the Cape Colony with mainly white franchise based upon property qualification. A small number of nonwhites "colored" (people of mixed blood and descendents of the freed slaves) were enfranchised in the Western Cape as well as some Africans in the eastern districts. The Cape Colony legislature, led by Cecil Rhodes as prime minister, represented the diamond-mining interests in conjunction with the association of rural white landowners known as the *Afrikaner Bond*.[7]

The year 1878 marked the beginning of Afrikaner culture with the publication of the first newspaper in Afrikaans. The Afrikaner language was recognized as distinct and not merely a poor variant of the Dutch from which it had been derived. In emphasizing the difference between the "elect" and all others, the neo-Calvinism of the Dutch Reformed Church considered its members as a people one of the "elect." They found a religious basis to justify divisions between nations and races.[8] In its most racist form, it was a Christian nationalism that excluded Jews.

Afrikaner nationalism was articulated in terms of being a distinct people, occupying a distinct fatherland and endowed by God with the destiny to rule Africa and civilize its heathen inhabitants.[9] As a partial expression of this philosophy in the Cape Colony, a series of laws in the 1890s tended to exclude blacks from voting rolls by raising property qualifications as well as excluding any property held communally by tribes from such qualification.[10]

The development of the province of Natal was particularly associated with British immigration starting in 1849-1850. Exclusion of the large number of blacks dated from the outset of self-government in 1865. In the meantime, immigration from India had become significant. The Zulus in the region refused agricultural work as the role of women. The earlier indentured sugarcane workers had been low-caste Hindus from Madras on short-term contracts. Only later provision was made for land allocation after completion of their contracts with the development of a settled Indian population. Other Gujerati traders, mainly Muslim, came on their own. They set up shops in competition with whites in Natal as well as the Afrikaner republics. Indians were restricted in their trading rights and banned as residents in 1890 in the Orange Free State. Persons from India were also subject to a poll tax and could be arbitrarily denied trading licenses in Natal. In response to these activities, Mahatma Gandhi arrived in Natal in 1893 to act as a legal representative of the traders. He set up the Natal Indian Congress and led a protracted passive resistance campaign from 1906 to 1914 before returning to India and his future career. Restrictions of Indian residence, land ownership, and trading rights remained.[11]

The year 1867 saw the discovery of diamonds in the area of what was to become the town of Kimberley just outside the Orange Free State. Mining was to be a fundamental aspect of the South African economy. The mining area known as West Griqualand was annexed to the Cape Colony in 1871 thus coming under British control despite the claims of the adjacent Afrikaner republic. Thousands of fortune hunters poured in both from the Cape Colony and from Europe, including some Jews, the latter almost entirely from England and Germany.

During the next years, consolidation occurred under the auspices of Cecil Rhodes, leading to the foundation of the De Beers diamond-cartel controlling production and the release of diamonds to market. Some of the most prominent owners in the diamond industry were identified as Jews. The diamond industry enriched the few but did not lead to the development of manufacturing or agriculture. The pattern became established in the diamond mines for black workers to be recruited as short-term contract laborers and housed within the mining compounds. Land rights previously held by the natives were overturned as were digging licenses. A "passport" system was instituted to control movement. Blacks were reduced to servitude. All these restrictions were instituted in the name of diamonds having being taken for illicit sale. The relatively few white skilled workers were well paid, establishing the two-tier wage system to be followed in the future. The schools that were established also followed a pattern of racial segregation even in rural areas where there were few white pupils.

With increased white immigration, Cape Town grew into a town of forty-five thousand and Kimberley, the second largest city, had thirty-five thousand people by 1875. The total white population reached two hundred fifty thousand with nonwhites rising more slowly to five hundred thousand. About one-eighth of the Europeans were born outside of Africa.[12]

The finding in 1886 of gold along the Witwatersrand of southern Transvaal was the start of the greatest goldfield in history. The new population led to the establishment of Johannesburg and a line of towns along the *Rand*, both east and west.

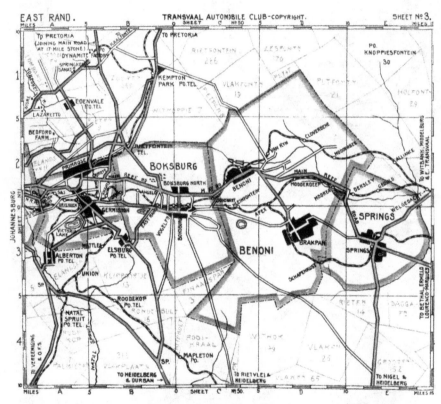

Map 5.2 The East Rand

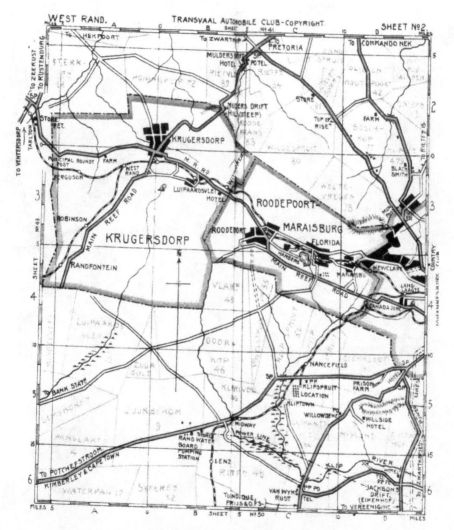

Map 5.3 The West Rand

Immigration, at this time, began to include far larger number of Jews, mainly East European in origin. Some of the Jews who had earlier been prominent in the diamond industry were also active in the organization of the gold mines, along with mainly British foreign investors. The pattern of labor management established in the diamond fields of Kimberley was followed with consolidation of mining companies as deep mines were developed to exploit what was relatively low-grade, ore-bearing rock.

The price of gold was fixed by the international market, and the profits were derived from reducing the cost of labor. There was the use of a large number of short-term unskilled, poorly paid black labor. Their families lived in rural tribal areas. Certain of the supervisory jobs as well as other job classifications were reserved for whites. There was intense competition for these jobs, uniting white workers in support of racial discrimination to protect the jobs they had.[13]

In the Transvaal South African Republic under its President Kruger, it was not enough to be an adult male of European descent to be enfranchised. The *Uitlander*" (foreigner) invasion after the Witwandersrand discoveries in the 1880s exceeded the number of Afrikaner white males in the Transvaal.[14] Initially, Uitlanders could vote only after a five-year delay and a large naturalization fee. In 1890, the waiting period was extended to fourteen years.[15] Petitions for reform were rejected by the Volksraad. The Jameson Raid in 1895 instigated by Rhodes failed to engender the expected uprising of the disenfranchised whites.[16] This abortive attempt to overthrow the Kruger regime strengthened the hatred of the Afrikaner for the British. "Krugerism," with its focus on narrow Afrikaner interests rather than a more broadly based white South African unity, became the ongoing model of political behavior.[17] In 1899, just prior to the outbreak of the South African (Boer) War, recurrent efforts by the Jewish community for removal of their disabilities were unsuccessful, whether carried out independently or as part of a more general effort associated with the Catholics and other Uitlanders.[18]

The ensuing war did not end with the capture of the capital of Pretoria in June 1900 and the exile of Kruger. It continued for two more years with guerrilla raids by Afrikaner commandoes. By 1902, half the white population was either prisoners of war or in concentration camps, the latter filled with the women and children. There was a high death rate. The resultant bitterness was to be one of the foundations of ongoing Afrikaner nationalism.[19]

After the end of the Boer War, the British government made no attempt to alter the political status of the natives. Only in the Cape Colony was there a tradition of inclusion of some segments other than the whites. The political organization of the Union of South Africa in 1910 as a self-governing Dominion confirmed the arrangements compatible with British mining interests and the wishes of the local white electorate. Former Afrikaner generals such as Smuts now held office in the government of the Union that contained the former Afrikaner republics, the Cape Colony, and Natal. A unitary state was created analogous to the other "settler states" of Australia and Canada.[20]

The Convention establishing the Union provided for a central Parliamentary government with what proved to be only some slight safeguard for the voting rights of nonwhites within the former Cape Colony. Even there, the ban on nonwhites taking seats in Parliament continued. Nonwhites could only vote for whites to act as their representatives. The allocation of seats to each province reflected the adult white male population with somewhat greater loading for the generally Afrikaner rural areas versus the English-speaking towns. English and Dutch were to have equal status. The constitution reflected the will of the political leaders of the Transvaal, the richest of the provinces, in disenfranchising blacks. The strength of sectional interests was also reflected in the distribution of governmental offices. The administrative capital was to be Pretoria, with Cape Town the seat of the legislature and Bloemfontein the seat of the judiciary.

Also established was the deep division within the whites. Most of the descendants of the earlier settlers identified themselves as Afrikaners, mainly rural, with their distinct language, religious identity, and historical consciousness forming more than half the white population overall. There were increasingly numerous Afrikaner "poor whites" who owned no land. The nineteenth-century immigrants, mostly British, formed the majority of the whites in Natal and Witwatersrand. Mainly townspeople, they kept aloof from the Afrikaners and newer immigrants—mainly Jewish—who had come to Kimberley and Johannesburg as well as the other older towns.[21]

In 1911, 75 percent of the total population of six million still lived outside of the towns. About half of whites, colored, and Indians lived outside of towns and seven-eighths of Africans. Of the total, two-thirds were of full African descent, a fifth of pure European descent, a tenth were "colored," and a fortieth Indian.[22]. The political groupings were those of the white landowners and middle-class white business class, the increasing Afrikaner white working class and the mining interests with disenfranchisement of the Indians, Africans, and further limitation of the existing rights in Cape Province of the rights of "colored."

The opposition of the blacks to these arrangements led to the formation in 1912 of the African National Congress (ANC). The failure of the British Parliament in London to make any changes in reviewing the constitution disappointed those who saw the British as safeguarding native rights. The only protections ensured were the some greater hurdle to the incorporation into the Union of native areas under British Protectorate such as Bechuanaland and Basutoland.[23] They were to remain separate from the Union but were a source of cheap labor.

Although the population was multiracial and multiethnic, political life failed to reflect that. Indeed segregation and discrimination shaply differentiated the segments of the population into a group of separate "tribes." The Jews saw themselves the beneficiaries of the British in having secured for them the rights they had not previously enjoyed under the Afrikaner Republic in Transvaal. Unlike the Afrikaners, they therefore felt the imperial connection a beneficial one.[24] In the context of the Anglo-Boer War, one of the rabbis living in the Transvaal in 1901 spoke about "the mission of the Israelites to sow the seeds not of discord, but of concord and good feeling. It was part of their mission to promote a better feeling between Briton and Afrikaner."[25] This hope perhaps describes what was to be the position of the Jews, existing only on sufferance between the two white tribes, clinging to their rights. It appeared disadvantageous to the Jews, connected as they were to the British, to see the rivalry develop between these two white groups since the Afrikaners were more numerous and were allocated more representation. The rights of all persons, including even whites, became increasingly subordinate to the *pass laws* and other methods to control the black majority as a labor force as the Nationalist Afrikaners achieved political control in the post-World War II era.

5.1.2. The Existing Jewish Community

The Cape Colony under the auspices of the Dutch East India Company required membership in the Dutch Reformed Church. The British occupation of the Cape Colony opened up opportunity for immigration not only of persons of Jewish birth but those professing that faith. A group of Jewish families came with the 1820s British settlement. Jewish students were enrolled in the South African College, later to become the University of Cape Town. Organized in 1829-1830, there was no religious test for either students or teachers.[26] An act of 1860 empowered the government to appoint Jewish marriage officers. Another act in 1868 proscribed any differentiation on account of religious belief.

Coming from an English background, most of these early immigrants did not feel themselves in an alien environment when living under British rule in South Africa. The pattern of Anglo-Jewry of strong religious loyalty coupled with a considerable degree of social assimilation was maintained. The religious identity was heavily flavored by the British connection with the chief rabbi in London responsible for the selection of ministers and guidance in matters spiritual and ritual.[27]

By 1841, there was the organization of a minyan and a congregation called *Tikvath Israel* in Cape Town otherwise known as the Society of the Jewish Community of the Cape. There was also the purchase of a burial ground. In 1844, the first wedding was performed, notably by a Church of England minister, "leaving out every part objectionable to our religious feelings."[28] The first ritual circumcision was recorded in 1847. In 1849, the first minister arrived from Britain and the first synagogue building opened. Support was tenuous until 1859 and the arrival of Rev. Joel Rabinowitz. He was born in Poland and educated in rabbinical studies there before emigrating to England at age twenty-four. Fluent in English, he had been associated with the Jewish congregation in Birmingham. He was instrumental in bringing about a building specifically designed as a synagogue in 1863 on St. Johns Street. in Cape Town.

The Cape Town Synagogue viewed itself analogous to the role of the Great Synagogue in London in the structure of Anglo-Jewry. With Britain as the mother country, the forms of prayer and custom propagated by the Cape Town Synagogue were those of the Great Synagogue in London. Also around the same time, in 1859, there was organization of the Jewish Philanthropic Society that later became the Jewish Board of Guardians analogous to that in Britain. Under Rabinowitz, a strong pattern of charitable contribution was established among South African Jews not only for coreligionists in the country but for others throughout the world as well as non-Jews.[29]

Mainly of German and English extraction, there were organized Jewish settlers in the Eastern Cape at Grahamstown and Port Elizabeth as well as individual families in many smaller towns. The wool and hide export trade was established in the eastern province of the Cape Colony by the Mosenthal family from Hesse-Cassell in Germany. Their widespread activities led to nearly half the number of Jewish families immigrating between 1845 and 1870. Jewish traders, mainly from that same area in Germany, were found in nearly every village in the Orange Free State. Many took an active role in the local self-government as justices of the peace and members of the legislature. Although influential, there were only several hundred professing Jewish families.[30]

The discovery of diamonds around 1870 led to further immigration with a large contingent from the East End of London. This first wave of immigration to the diamond fields increased the Jewish population in the Cape Colony without affecting the essential Anglo-German character of the community. Although they mainly originated from Eastern Europe, they had become Anglicized in London. Barnett Isaacs was one who became famous for his success in the diamond business. One of the most colorful characters, he took the name of Barney Barnato when he came to the minefields in conjunction with his brother's stage name. The two brothers organized a company that became an important segment of what was to be the De Beers diamond monopoly together with Rhodes. By 1873, a permanent congregation existed and synagogue was built in Kimberley.

In 1882, the first refugees from Eastern Europe began to reach South Africa; they were to become the majority of a much-larger community. Unlike their Anglicized predecessors, the majority spoke Yiddish. They were petty traders and artisans. Starting as peddlers, they ventured into the farming communities where they eventually set up general stores. From the incorporation of Johannesburg among the goldfields of the Rand, Jews comprised about 10 percent of the white population. In 1887, there was an official congregation and burial ground. In the following year the Witwatersrand Goldfields Jewish Association built what was to be the Witwatersrand Hebrew congregation. An additional Johannesburg Hebrew Congregation was also formed, its dedication graced by the presence of President Kruger.[31]

The conflict between the new immigrants and the existing community soon arose over such issues as the provision of kosher meat. The newcomers questioned the piety of the Cape Town Tikvath Israel synagogue—the *English shule*. By 1886, there were meetings to set up a new congregational association in Cape Town. Eventually in 1900, the East Europeans established the New Hebrew Congregation or Roelands St. Synagogue. Differences were less based on fundamental liturgical divergence than personal and cultural attitudes. As evidence, the new synagogue sought its minister from the same pool as its parent congregation, that is, the chief rabbi in London.[32] There was enlargement of the existing communities and the development of many new ones. Johannesburg had the largest proportion of East European Jews. It was where there was the greatest degree of heterogeneity in religious life with three separate synagogues.[33]

5.1.3. The Great Migration

Like all the other countries in the Litvak Diaspora, the relatively small existing Jewish community prior to the great migration was overwhelmed by the magnitude of the East European immigration. Yet the ultimate character of the synthesis was a remarkable degree of persistence of the structure and ethos of the British connection of the existing community. It has been said that South African Jewry was the pouring of Litvak spirit into Anglo-Jewish bottles.

Like the United States and Canada as *New World* countries, East European immigration to South Africa was part of an even larger stream of non-Jewish immigrants coincident with the development of these countries. The East European Jewish stream that came to South Africa was part of a general immigration there, instigated only partially by purely South African opportunities such as the discovery of diamonds and gold. In addition, this immigration was part of the general Jewish immigration that went to the countries throughout the world during this period. The choice of South Africa was made by relatively few in comparison to the number going to the Western Hemisphere.

There was a long distance between Europe and South Africa and no particular encouragement of sponsored immigration. Yet during the years 1880-1910, about forty thousand East European Jews immigrated to South Africa.[34] To a unique degree, the source of these immigrants was a relatively small area within the Pale of Settlement centered around Kovno in Lithuania. In addition to their high percentage, it is estimated that the absolute number coming to South Africa from this relatively small area was second only to the much larger number going to the New World, particularly the United States. South African Jewry was aptly described as a "colony of Lithuania."

There were several specific characteristics of the Lithuanian villages that might be considered as the "push" to immigration. Many of the villages from which Jews emigrated to South Africa were subject to disastrous fires in the years 1881-1884. Although the pogroms of 1881 occurred in the south of Russia, teachers and other persons trained in Lithuania who had gone there were affected. All these factors contributed to the overall sense that emigration was a necessity.

The "pull" of South Africa, per se, has been explained by the rather extraordinary connection between that country and the experience of some of the immigrants from an earlier time. The cholera epidemic of 1868 in the province of Suwalki at the border of Lithuania had brought about the beginnings of emigration to the West. Neustadt-Sugind, the town from which Sammy Marks had come, ultimately sent half its population abroad, the majority to South Africa. Its closeness to the border and the stories of successes by the early emigrants had identified

South Africa as an option at a time when emigration was clearly a high priority.

Samuel Marks seems almost a legendary figure both in respect to the growth of South African Jewry and South Africa. He was unique among the early successful financiers in maintaining his identity with his Litvak roots and the Yiddish culture from which he had come. His signal munificence toward the restoration of the synagogue in his native town was representative of widespread support by South African Litvaks of such activities in their hometowns. Marks's father, Mordecai, became the channel for his son's ongoing benefactions. Marks provided a linkage between the earlier immigrants and the far larger immigration that he helped to foster by his example.

Samuel Marks had been born in 1844 in the Kovno province in the town of Niestadt-Sugind, only one mile from the Prussian border. His father was a poor itinerant tailor who remained in Lita. Marks emigrated to Sheffield in Britain in the 1860s where he married the daughter of one of the leaders of the Sheffield Hebrew Congregation before arriving in the Cape in 1868. Initially a pedlar, Marks came to the Kimberley diamond fields where he became very successful by providing supplies to the miners. He was a pioneer, coming to Kimberley well before there was an organized Jewish community. In the early 1880s, he crossed into the Transvaal, again not as yet settled by organized Orthodox Judaism.[35]

Unassuming and hardworking, he became a close associate of President Kruger of the South African Republic after the discovery of the Witwatersrand goldfields. Kruger found him a shrewd but decent man, "a white man, a kindred spirit." It helped considerably that Marks spoke Afrikaans fluently. Marks pioneered industry in the undeveloped Transvaal. He owned mines for coal as well as copper, diamonds, and gold. He ran model farms and established factories for the manufacture of spirits, glass, and bricks as well as steel.[36] A major legacy was the development in the area of Vereeniging that later evolved into the steel industry near the coal fields. He was opposed to the Uitlander agitation that had led to war. His position aided the bringing about of the peace conference that finally ended the Anglo-Boer War. In recognition of his "elder statesman" status was his appointment as a senator in the first Union Parliament.

Among his other legacies was the establishment of the chair in Hebrew at what was to become the University of Cape Town.

As a forerunner, Marks was also an exemplar of the future South African Jew in terms of being "non-observant Orthodox." The Jewish dietary laws was not strictly enforced in his home. He worked on Saturdays and attended synagogue infrequently. The family celebrated Passover and the High Holidays, but primarily at home. Circumcision took place according to the exact requirements of the law as did *bar mitzvoth*. Judaism was a matter of personal identity rather than religious conviction. He maintained membership in synagogues in Cape Town, Kimberley, Johannesburg as well as Pretoria, the latter his "home" congregation. He was active in strengthening the modernist Anglo-Jewish orientation of that synagogue in recruiting an English minister. He also personally supported a communal school in Pretoria run on secular and modernist lines. Characteristically, he insisted on the school being open to Gentile children as well.

Although not a member of the Jewish Board of Deputies, he intervened with his political friends on behalf of Jewish issues dealing with immigration and rights of licensure. With his pride in his Jewish ancestry went his sense of kinship with the plight of Jews elsewhere, his support for refugees from the pogroms, and his rejection of intermarriage or conversion to Christianity. In his economic success as well as adherence to communal needs, he regarded himself—and was regarded—as an exemplar of the South African of Jewish extraction. Dying in 1920, he essentially founded South African Jewry.[37]

The usual pattern of immigration was of single men who then returned to their native village to bring back a wife, or the brothers and sisters. They were artisans, traders, and workmen. In South Africa, the immigrant tended to carry on along similar lines as artisan, peddler, or shopkeeper. Ten percent of the Suwalki Jews had been engaged in agriculture. A number of farmers were encouraged to go to South Africa where they settled on the land. The self-selection must have included those who were on the whole more venturesome and also those with the more substantial amount of money necessary for the several-week passage to South Africa versus the more heavily traveled and more competitive and thus lower-priced transatlantic route.

During the 1890s, transport to South Africa was smoothed by shipping agents in Lithuania. The normal pattern was of departure from Libau in Latvia to London. Others would steal across the border into Germany. In Britain, like Germany, the local Jewish agencies were active in sending the immigrants onward. For example, the goal of the London-based Jewish Board of Guardians was to minimize the likelihood that the immigrants would remain in Britain. Immigrants were encouraged and, for a time, offered passage to South Africa as one of the more common alternatives to staying in Britain.

The British Wilson Line controlled traffic on the Baltic from Libau that was then coordinated with transshipment of immigrants through London to South Africa via the Union Shipping Line and the Castle Line. These latter two lines had added a number of ships designed to carry steerage immigrant passengers in response to the discovery of the goldfields. The coordination of this effort was enhanced by financial arrangements by these shipping lines and the Poor Jews Temporary Shelter in London where the passengers remained pending embarkation to Africa. These arrangements became even more intimate after the passage of the Aliens Act of 1905 in Britain. Under the provisions of that act, the shipping lines remained responsible for those aliens admitted merely for transshipment elsewhere. A direct subsidy was paid the shelter for room and board as well as other charges.[38]

Illustrative was the pattern of the Cohen family whose founder, Yudel, first immigrated to South Africa from Lita in 1902 immediately after the end of the Boer War. He brought out his wife and their three children in 1905. After spending a week at the Jews' Temporary Shelter in London, they traveled in steerage on a ship of the Union Castle Line. Uncommonly, they landed at Port Elizabeth in the Eastern Cape before moving inland about a hundred miles to a small crossroad village where the father owned a store. Yudel also purchased a two-hundred-acre farm, later to become part of much larger holdings by various members of the family.

The son, David, born in 1895, bought a sheep farm on his own account when he became of age and, in the 1920s, was active in wool dealing. Other members of the family were cattle and leather dealers. David finally married, in 1938, to Phoebe. She had been born in London in 1907 to parents who had emigrated from

Lita somewhat earlier. They had come to South Africa originally in 1913, only to return to England before finally immigrating in 1936. The couple and their children lived in Port Elizabeth while their various farms in the countryside were managed by Afrikaners. Port Elizabeth was somewhat unique in that the Jewish community, although small, had been settled from much earlier times and were heavily involved in agriculture including growing citrus. They were also more integrated into the political life of the province with the Reverend Levy, the local rabbi, on the school board.

During these years, the impact of immigration was even greater for South Africa than the United States. Between 1875 and 1911, its white population trebled, in large part due to immigration. The largest portion of these immigrants was British. However, Jews represented the largest group of the non-British.[39] The first official figure for the Jewish population of all of South Africa in 1904 was circa forty-seven thousand with around twenty-six thousand in the Transvaal, seventeen thousand in Cape Province, around thee thousadn in Orange Free State, and one thousand five hundred in Natal.

Prior to the restrictions imposed in the Immigration Quota Act of 1930, subsequent immigration during the 1920s maintained the relative preponderance of the Litvak component. During that period of Lithuanian independence, over 70 percent were identified as coming from that political entity. The remainder from Latvia and Poland could be identified as coming from the larger cultural entity we have called Litvakia.[40]

Beyond the poverty from which the immigrant came and the wretchedness in which they lived, there were certain values that seemed to continue. Along with their pitiful possessions, they would frequently have books in Hebrew or Yiddish, both sacred and secular. Respect for Jewish learning was instilled by a culture heavily influenced by the Yeshivot through which some had themselves come but more often whose values permeated the culture in whose shadow they had lived.[41] Although the rabbis continued to come mainly from England, Lithuanian Jewry's spiritual tradition was unique in its focus on Torah Lishmah, that is, learning for its own sake. The immigrants from Lita generally maintained their business interests while continuing scholarship. The Haskalah struck deep roots in Litvakia contributing to the Hebrew Enlightenment as well as a hope for betterment of life in the world. There was also a deep feeling for the Jewish national homeland. Lithuanian Jewry had a central place in the movement of national revival from the beginning of the Zionist movement.[42]

The heavy Litvak preponderance gives us a particular opportunity to see how the Litvak characteristics of love of learning, generosity toward charitable causes, organizational complexity, and attachment to Jewish traditions were expressed in this far-off land. The Litvaks were given particularly to educational institution building with the result that South Africa has led in Jewish education. The more secular expressions of the religiously based messianism expressed itself in the commitment to the labour movement in the early days and the singularly strong influence of Zionism. In South Africa, like the other sites for the Litvak Diaspora, these strands evolved differently in the context of the unique character of the country.

5.1.4. The Response to the Migration

Afrikaner and Jew enjoyed a more intimate relationship than Englishman and Jew. The Afrikaner was likely to entertain the Jew as a guest on his farm whereas the relationship with the Englishman was likely to be more formal in a town. The Litvak characteristics of industry and seriousness of purpose were said to fit well with the Afrikaners among which they first settled.[43] The Jews was welcomed in part as the "people of the book" by the Bible-reading Afrikaner farmers. The story of Israelites in their wanderings through the Sinai in search of the promised land and the battles they fought to secure that land resonated in their *Great Trek* and the battles fought against the African tribes.

However, anti-Jewish stereotypes were beginning to be expressed. Aspersions regarding the quality of the immigrants were made by the medical health officer in the Report of the Working of the Immigration Act for the year 1903. In Kimberley, it was common to view Jews as associated with illicit dealing in stolen diamonds. Acceptance of the middle-class Anglo-German Jew and antipathy to the poorer East European Jew was the recurrent theme. Two different stereotypes remained along side each other, that of the middle-class gentleman and the lower-class "cunning knave."[44] The differences between antialienism and anti-Semitism were blurred.

An anti-Jewish tone began to arise particularly in the Transvaal after the discovery of gold in an Afrikaner society bent on maintaining its sovereignty. President Kruger was attacked in election campaign of 1891 on the basis of his association with Jews such as Sammy Marks. In the Cape Colony, the traders such as those for ostrich feathers were seen as cheating the farmer. The Jewish peddlers visiting the farms (*smous*) were seen as sharp dealing and putting the farmers into debt. When the droughts came and farmers were being displaced off the land, the Jews were held responsible.[45] During the 1890s, the focus shifted to criticism of the liquor trade in Johannesburg and the illicit sales to black miners by Jews. The antiliquor crusade led by the churches had established the connection in people's minds of East European immigrants, called *Peruvians* with criminality and disease.[46] That pejorative name was used to describe the poor Jewish immigrant. Its derivation is obscure but attributed to the initials PRU standing for the *Paelischeh und Russiche Verein* (Polish and Russian Worker's Club).[47]. The focus had begun to shift from Jews defined by their religion and social class to their "racial" character.

The Anglo-Boer War was popularized in Britain by the pro-Afrikaner faction as being for the benefit of the international financiers, among whom persons with Jewish names were prominent. These "Randlords" were fabulously wealthy parvenus with large mansions in the center of fashionable London. The caricature of the Jewish capitalist "Goldbug" was personified from 1903 in the hook-nosed *Hoggenheimer*. He was a character of fun in a very popular musical comedy in London and then brought to Cape Town. He became a stock character in political discourse.[48] Condemnation became even more manifest in the post-Boer War era when there was campaign by the Randlords for the introduction of Chinese labor in the mines. By inference, all Jews were so labeled by the caricatures as connected to the *yellow peril*. In addition to the Jewish capitalist, the poor *Peruvians* were the alternative menace as related to criminality such as illegal liquor sales and brothels.

The antialien agitation was not limited to the Afrikaners. The British officials in the Colonial Office were concerned that one should keep the "foreigner" out and let the British in. The linkage by the anti-Semite between the financier, the poor immigrant, and the pedlar was all subsumed by the allegations of criminality and vice. The persistence of these stereotypes and their widespread acceptance is evident in the literary portrayals of Jews in English starting in the 1890s in South Africa.[49] The *Cape Times* regularly would comment in a slanderous fashion on the Jewish identity of persons involved in the law courts. The *Owl* was a Cape Town weekly that regularly published anti-Semitic caricatures focused on the machinations of the De Beers Consolidated Mines.[50]

Yet at the time of the Kishinev pogrom in 1904, there was considerable support throughout the non-Jewish community for relief for the Russian Jews. In contrast to the anti-Semitism, there was a similar conflation of culture and race when emphasizing, as some did, the positive traits of Jewish frugality, hard work and "business insight." In both the positive and negative stereotypes, less distinction was based upon class than before but rather as a people apart.[51]

Before the South African War, there were no restrictions on European immigrants. They were free to enter and reside and follow any occupation. With the further increase in Jewish immigration in the 1890s, questions were raised in the legislature of the Cape Colony about the "needy" and potentially "criminal" nature of the immigrants. In 1897, the *Afrikaner Bond* called for restriction on immigration, concerned that the Afrikaner farmer would be outvoted. In the thinly veiled attack on East European aliens, the representatives of the Bond complained that the need was to take care of their own poor whites rather than those of other countries. Increasingly, those representing rural areas sought to counter the influx of poor Jews functioning as middlemen in the countryside.[52]

The South African War caused an initial exodus of Uitlanders, including the overwhelming majority of the Jews, from the Transvaal to the coastal towns. Return to the former Afrikaner republics, after the war, was controlled by permits issued by the British high commissioner. Although publicly disclaiming any restriction placed on aliens by virtue of their religion or nationality, in his private correspondence, Lord Milner clearly wished to reduce the number of poor Jews.[53]

The East European Jewish immigration was viewed as "alien" by both the predominant Afrikaner and British communities. There were threats of restrictions both on immigration and naturalization. The existing Jewish community organized itself along with the Yiddish-speaking immigrants in defense of their rights. Organized originally as a Zionist Federation, then in the British model as the Jewish Board of Deputies, there was a far-reaching network that knit the small but significant group together.

There had been an ongoing effort to restrict the entry of "Asiatics.," Natal's Immigration Restriction Act of 1897 had applied a literacy test designed to exclude them by the requirement "to sign in the characters of any language of Europe."

The tide of immigration from Eastern Europe was to be adversely affected by the Cape Immigration Restriction Act that took effect in January 1903. Following the pattern of Natal, immigration was prohibited unless "able to sign in the characters of any European language." Although primarily directed against the Indian, curtailment of East European immigration was also clearly intended.[54]

The influential intervention of the Board of Jewish Deputies in London, concerned about the South African-bound immigrants remaining in England, led to Yiddish being recognized as a "European language." However, such a determination was subject to interpretation by immigration officers, and a variable number of persons were denied entry. A deputation was organized by Morris Alexander and David Goldblatt to express the concerns of the Jewish community to the attorney general. Both men were of East European background with Goldblatt particularly associated with the Yiddish-speaking community and Alexander active in a wide range of Jewish communal affairs.

In the 1906 version of the immigration bill, in response to the ongoing efforts of what became the Cape Board of Deputies, the amendment was finally passed to specifically recognize Yiddish "as a European language."[55]

The issue of naturalization closely followed that of immigration. The Cape Board of Deputies next took on the task of supporting naturalization. During and after the Boer War, it was advantageous for those residing in the Cape Colony to acquire British citizenship in contrast to retaining Russian citizenship.[56] On request from the colonial secretary, the newly constituted Board of Deputies took on the role of reviewing naturalization requests by the large number of Jewish applicants. According to the aliens naturalizations acts of 1883 and 1889, naturalization had up till then posed no problem to the Jews based upon the provisos "of good character." Concerned about the large number of Jews being naturalized, the residence requirement was made explicit and determined to be at least two years in 1903. When this requirement did not serve their purposes, it was extended to five years in 1905 with the number naturalized consequently reduced.[57]

The Jewish Board of Deputies of the Transvaal and Natal had been officially organized in July 1903 even before that of Cape Colony that took place in September 1904. The Transvaal Board also took on the issue of naturalization. Samuel Goldreich, the leader of the South African Zionist Federation, had been working with Lord Milner, the British high commissioner, both in establishing naturalization for large number of aliens and in identifying those who would receive the needed permits, enabling them to return to the Transvaal after the end of the war. Goldreich and his followers were opposed to their Zionist Federation being replaced by the new Board of Deputies. There were also differences between the relatively acculturated Anglicized leadership and the Yiddish-speaking East European rank and file on whose behalf they would speak. The residency requirement before enfranchisement was reduced, enabling many Jews to vote in the crucial parliamentary election of 1907. In this election, the principle was established, that has since been maintained throughout its subsequent incarnations, that the Board of Deputies would not intervene in partisan politics but only in watching for the general interests of the Jewish community.[58]

There was a recurrent need for the Board to act on behalf of the interests of the Jewish community as it was not to be conflated on racial lines with the non-European, "Asiatic," Indian population. Once again, the issue of "trading licenses" illustrates how, like the anti-immigration measures, the restrictions were designed to attack both but were ostensibly directed against the Indian. The requirement under the General Dealers' License Act was to keep one's records with the use of "a European language." The board was once again able to get verbal assurances that Yiddish would be so construed by virtue of the lobbying of the Jewish members of the legislature.

With the establishment of the Union in 1910, the immigration laws were again an immediate issue. Afrikaner leaders were in favor of restriction based upon their fear of their constituencies being swamped by these new voters. Finally in 1913, a bill was passed, which maintained a literacy test for which Yiddish was an acceptable language and a right of appeal. This act contained a clause designed to exclude Asiatics but gave considerable latitude to the minister of the interior to exclude others on "economic grounds or on account of the standards and or habits of life to be unsuitable to the requirements of the Union." It is illustrative of the degree that a caste system had become established that the restrictions on immigration of Asiatics were not opposed by the Jewish community on principle but only the conflation of Jews with Asiatics.[59]

It was in the context of these issues that the major change had occurred in the structure of the Jewish community.[60] The deputation organized to protest the language restriction to immigration eventually became established in 1904 as the Cape Colony Board of Deputies. There had been initial opposition by the Reverend Alfred Bender of the Cape Town Hebrew Congregation, the "mother congregation." This opposition persisted even after the formation of the United South African Jewish Board of Deputies in 1912 that united the Boards of the Cape, Natal and Transvaal. Since 1849 and the appointment of the first regular minister of the Cape Town synagogue, the incumbent of that position had become the accepted spokesman for Jewry as well as the liaison with the government. The existence of the Board of Deputies now established a communal voice separate from that of the synagogue. It also acted by open, if not aggressive, communal action rather than the "quiet diplomacy" of the past. This development was strongly supported by the *South African Jewish Chronicle*, the first English-language Jewish newspaper established in 1902 in the model of the London-based *Jewish Chronicle*.[61]

Jewish distinctiveness, both physical and cultural, was reinforced by ghettolike neighborhoods. The alien ambience of a slum area near the waterfront called District Six in Cape Town was an example. The picture was the same in Johannesburg where in 1904, Jews represented about 12 percent of the whites. Most of the newcomers congregated in the poorer sections close to the railway line.

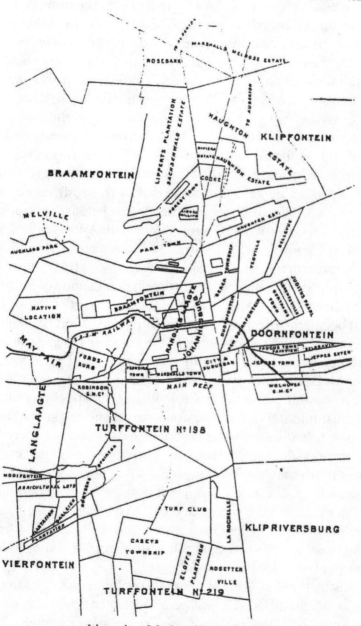

Johannesburg Suburbs and Surrounds, c1920

Map 5.4 The Suburbs of Johannesburg in 1920

The East European Jew had become a symbol of corruption and vice. Images of Fagin were conjured. The agitation against persons from India was also conjoined with the racist arguments against Jews. Nevertheless, there was the feeling that Jews were somehow redeemable, and the second generation seemed to have potential. The children were described by an educator in the Transvaal somewhat patronizingly as intelligent, very musical and "able to make the best of their advantage." There was acknowledgement of Jewish benevolence and commitment to charity as among their positive virtues.[62]

In 1898, a Jewish Lads' Brigade in the British model contributed to the acculturation of the young being raised in South Africa. Although sectarian schooling was provided starting in 1890 under the supervision of the Hebrew Educational Board in Johannesburg, many attended the schools founded by the Catholic Marist Brothers with girls going to convent schools.[63] After the Boer War, state-supported secular education was available along with state support of the Jewish school in Johannesburg. Nevertheless, there were residues of the Christian denominational system within the state system with a requirement for Bible history that presumably was not limited to the *Old Testament*.[4]

In general, the English and German Jews, the first to come, took the lead in forming synagogues and communal associations. The religious identity of South African Jewry was to remain almost entirely as first established under their auspices in accordance with the structure of the United Synagogue and the chief rabbi in London. The earlier settlers remained the dominant social element due to their wealth and standing in the larger community. Most of the Jewish immigrants were desperately poor. The Jewish Helping Hand and Burial Society was one of many arising out of the traditional burial society (*Chevra Kadisha*). This organization and others of the same kind would also provide food in soup kitchens for those whose lives were disrupted by the Boer War. In its management, as elsewhere, friction occurred between the "aristocratic" founders and the "newcomers" who felt that they were being treated in a condescending manner.

The interdependent nature of the relationship between the earlier settlers and the newcomers can be illustrated by the activities of the Jewish Board of Deputies. The very concept of the Board of Deputies and its name were directly patterned after the Anglo-Jewish model of the British Board of Deputies first organized in 1760. Leadership remained with those of Anglo-Jewish origin until the 1930s when the acculturated children of the Yiddish-speaking parents assumed leadership of the communal organizations.[64]

Preservation of one's nationality could be consistent with membership in the larger South African society. There was no overriding South African national identity to which Jews were expected to adhere as part of their acculturation. It was not clear whether a South African identity being forged was to be binational or narrowly Afrikaner. Jews were not politically differentiated on the basis of their religion. Ultimately Jews, unlike the Indian, were accepted as part of the white European population. Unlike the recognition and state support for the distinctiveness of the English and Afrikaner languages and other institutions among the whites, the Jews were expected to acculturate with one or the other of the two groups.[65]

5.2 The Evolution in South Africa

The country was divided, if not rent, into its several tribes. There was never a *melting pot*. Within the basic division between nonwhites and whites, there was the further division within the whites between the two languages and cultures of the British and the Afrikaners. The Afrikaner people primarily feared their absorption by the numerically superior natives by whom they were surrounded. Their fear was also directed at the British government and those who had migrated to South Africa from 1820 onward and finally at all those who were English-speaking. The fear was that the Afrikaner people would have to merge their identity with the rest of the white peoples and so form a broadly based South African nation. The nonwhites were further divided into those who were Indian, the "colored" and the Africans.

The idea that nonwhites would form one nation along with the Afrikaners was never entertained.[1]

Jews were frequently caught between these different "tribes," each pursuing its own interests. Whereas the Jews benefited economically from their hard-won European identity, they were not entirely welcome within either of the white groups. Nor, in light of their own history of oppression, were all Jews entirely comfortable with their membership in the dominant white minority. Despite the cowed silence of Jews as a community, a disproportionate number of individual Jews played a part in transforming South Africa into a more just society. They fought both from within the system as jurists, writers, and members of Parliament and in the "illegal" organizations that were Socialist or Communist or other mass organizations. It was their heritage of East European marginalization, landlessness, and proletarian militancy that created openness to radical positions and empathy with those oppressed.[2]

Although initially connected to the Afrikaner with whose language there were common roots, the increasing urbanization and relative openness of the English-speaking segment led to acculturation of the Jews within that group. It is suggested further that the Jews generally chose to enter the English-speaking sector, at least partially due to the Anglo-Jewish origins of the existing organized Jewish community. The persistence of the Anglo-Jewish forms infused by the Litvak spirit describes South African Jewry.[3] The racial stereotyping inherent in the South African view of the Jew did not lead to assimilation. The Jews remained apart, albeit in the white community.[4] It is not surprising that Zionism had an extraordinary influence in South African Jewry. The tribal nature of South African society identified the Jews as one as well.

5.2.1 The Immigrant Generation

The immigrants mainly made their way to the diamond and gold fields and to the port cities, but to an extraordinary degree, they spread out across the entire country. It was rare for even a small town not to have at least one Jewish family. Despite the differences in climate and social structure, there were some

similarities that aided the Lithuanian immigrant in adapting
to life in South Africa. It was possible to carry on in similar
pursuits such as being an artisan, peddler, and shopkeeper even
farmer. The level of organization of small towns and villages
was similar. Also similar at the outset was the relationship
between the tradesman and the farmer exemplified by the
shtetl where the Jew was the middleman in the marketplace.
The Jews found their niche as small middlemen. Trade with
the farmers either as itinerants or in shops in the small towns
was their special province.

There was a replication of the structure that had been left
behind in Lita. Talmudic study groups in the traditional Litvak
manner were started in Johannesburg. Conspicuous also were
the landsleit associations made up of immigrants from the same
village in Lithuania. The South African Jewish Board of Deputies
during this time, soon after its founding, consisted mainly of
delegates from these "friendly societies." They functioned as
a benevolent association, giving aid to those in need, visiting
the sick, and assisting to bring the families to South Africa. The
societies also would make small interest-free loans that served to
start businesses.[5] Money would be collected to support activities
in the village in Lita from which the members had come. The
names of those societies reflect the predominance of towns of
origin in the Kovno province.[6]

The landsmanshaften carried out religious services in a
variety of settings aside from the established synagogues. For
example, early on, the Litvaks set up their own synagogue in
1893 as the Johannesburg Orthodox Hebrew Congregation.
This tendency to split into various congregations was tied to
the towns of origin. There were, for example, two separate
and antagonistic congregations in Oudtshoorn, a town in
Cape renowned for its ostrich feather industry and its intense
Jewish community. The older synagogue drew its membership
from Shavli, a larger town than the adherents to the other
synagogue who hailed from Kelm.[7]

The development of the East European Jewish community
in South Africa was intimately tied to the activities of
Morris Alexander who became one of its most energetic
advocates.

South African Politics

Morris Alexander, the eldest of three children, was born in 1876 in East Prussia and brought to South Africa in 1881. Living successively in Oudtsdoorn, the ostrich capital, then Cape Town and finally Johannesburg, the family followed their father's business vicissitudes. A serious boy and the mainstay of his mother, *Alec* loved learning for its own sake but was required to leave school at age fourteen to go to work. He worked at a series of jobs in order to earn the money to return to school. He managed to enroll in the South African College in Cape Town where he earned the gold medal as the best all-around student. Armed with a scholarship, he came to England to read law at the Inner Temple and to St John's College at Cambridge. While there, he met Ruth Schechter, the then schoolgirl daughter of the famous Solomon Schechter. Returning to Cape Town in 1900, he started his career as a barrister. Despite the difference in age and temperament, he eventually married Ruth and brought her to Cape Town in 1907. They had several children. As a writer and critic, she went on, in the 1920s and early 1930s, to develop a circle of intellectuals that eventually led to a rupture from her husband and her religion.[8]

Trained in Britain, Alexander was recognized as a leader in the South African Jewish community while remaining responsive to the needs of the Yiddish-speaking immigrants. He was identified with the New Hebrew congregation on Roelands St organized by Lithuanian Jews separate from the original Cape Town synagogue. The deputation he led to the attorney general in reference to the issue of Yiddish literacy ultimately represented thirteen congregations and nine organizations. This deputation was to become the kernel of the later Jewish Board of Deputies.

Alexander went on to be a member of the Cape Assembly in 1908 and, after the Union was established, a member of the Union Parliament in 1910. Starting in 1920, he sat alone as an independent as the sole member of his Constitutional Democratic Party in opposition to discrimination on the basis of creed or color. He joined the United Party in 1933 and was a member of Parliament representing the working-class district of Woodstock in Cape Town until his death in 1946. He was true to the "Cape liberal tradition" of maintaining the rights of the *colored* throughout his career and a supporter of the rights of Indians from the time of Gandhi.[9] For example, in the 1930s, he was one of the few who opposed the removal of the Cape Coloureds from the voting rolls. His stature also contributed to the recognition that the South African Zionist Federation received. His major role was as the spokesman, official or otherwise, of the Jewish community of South Africa throughout his life until his death in 1946.[10]

It is in the Transvaal that the Jewish immigrants had the most impact. They were among the founders of Johannesburg and remained an important influence in its development throughout its history. They were also widely distributed along the *Rand* in the smaller towns that sprang up where gold mines existed.[11] In a predominantly male mining city, the Jews were the first to establish gender balance, reflecting the formation of families. During this first immigrant generation, the East Europeans were mainly the "working poor." As artisans, they could eventually function as petite bourgeoisie with many carpenters, plumbers, and painters becoming small-time builders. Although extremely vulnerable to economic hardship, they were not *Peruvians* involved in the liquor and other illicit occupations. It was necessary to remove the taint of the low-class *Peruvian* from the *South African Jew* who was to be defined as white, English-speaking, and middle class.[12]

In 1918, circa 60 percent of the Jewish population of Johannesburg were either artisans or small shopkeepers. Most lived in slum areas. The immigrants were susceptible to the economic dislocations associated with the price rise of World War I while wages were frozen. The amount of destitution can be gauged by the increase in the activities of the Jewish Helping Hand and Burial Society in aiding the poor. An area of secondary settlement arose in Doornfontein, the first residential suburb of Johannesburg, laid out starting in 1889. The original mansions were abandoned when the mining magnates moved to Parktown after the Boer War. Portions near the railway line later in the 1930s became a slum with the "yards" split up into tin shacks rented to the poor. Many of the residents of Doornfontein were Jews, and one of Johannesburg's earliest synagogues was built there. The main thoroughfare of Beit Street held the kosher butchers and the delicatessens.[13] There were also the boarding houses where the "Kaffiriniks," working in the concession stores on the Rand, would come to eat kosher food on their day off.[14]

The Jewish Labor Movement

In the Cape, the majority of Jewish artisans were tailors, cabinetmakers, carpenters, and bakers. In the period after the Boer War, many also were young men who came from an environment who had thrown themselves into the political struggle to ameliorate the world's ills. They were products of years of intense political activity, particularly in the northwestern provinces of the Pale in Lita where the Bund arose. Their dreams expressed themselves in socialism and the specifically Yiddish-speaking trade union movement exemplified by the Bund. There was recognition of class differences that transcended the old relationship between worker and journeyman. Jewish capitalism was an enemy.[15]

They pioneered in establishing craft unions in the Cape Colony. After the Boer War, the Jewish Tailor's Society was revived and participated in a Political Labor League along with the Jewish Workingmen's Club and the Social Democratic Federation and the Bund. In 1905, Jewish tailors represented 85 percent of the white tailors. The pattern was universal throughout the world of unhygienic working conditions and meager pay. They worked eighteen hours a day with no overtime pay and no days off. Women were paid even less than the men. Still another union, the Operative Tailor's Society of Cape Town, tried to fight for equal pay for equal work in opposition to the frequently Jewish manufacturers who tried to have white and colored tailors compete against each other. The tailors participated in establishing a Factories Act to alleviate working conditions. They also supported the actions of other unions including the 1907 miners' strike.[16]

The bakers were similarly being exploited by their coreligionist bosses. The Bundist organizers started a Jewish Bakers Union and, in 1903, a cooperative bakery. A series of public meetings took place in support of these efforts culminating in a large meeting, celebrating the opening of the cooperative bakery where the crowd was addressed in Yiddish as well as English. Once again,

Jews made up a substantial number of the white bootmakers and established a short-lived union. The Baker's Union as well as the bootmakers were strong supporters of labor political movements in the colony. The Bundist leaders were in the forefront of class solidarity across racial and ethnic lines. Jewish trade unionists were the first to try to unite all nationalities under umbrella union, representing all trades. For example, the Jewish Carpenters Society did not undercut the English Society's rates and refused to act as scabs in strikes.

The British unions, in the tradition of craft unions everywhere, sought to restrict membership and excluded the unskilled. To the contrary, the Jewish trade unionists were the vanguard of the movement to enlist both skilled and unskilled, with the latter including many who were colored. After 1907, the various Jewish labor unions amalgamated with their British and colored counterparts after having pioneered the principle of workers' unity.[17] However, trade unions with mainly Jewish membership, such as the Tailoring Union, continued to conduct its activities only in Yiddish.

Jewish Socialism

During World War I, the existing Labour Party to which many Jewish artisans belonged split on the basis of degree of support of the war. Those opposed founded the War-on-War League, which then was transformed into the Marxist International Socialist League (ISL). The ISL group contained, among others, Israel Israelstam, the doyen of Jewish Socialists.

Israel Israelstam was born in 1870 in Waksne in Lithuania. He came to America at age sixteen where he acquired a fair command of English as well as commitment to Jewish socialism. Coming to South Africa in 1900, he connected to the few members of the Bund from Lithuania who had come over soon after its formation in Vilna in 1897. The Bundist organization became active as Friends of Russian Liberty in Johannesburg in response to the pogroms of 1905. Israelstam urged its members to devote themselves not only to European issues but to the socialist struggle in South Africa. He opposed discrimination based on skin color and attacked Jews who fell prey to this when "they should know that they themselves belonged to a persecuted race." For Israelstam, discrimination against Asiatics, like anti-Semitism, was a result of the capitalist system.[18].

The International Socialist League (ISL) took an active role in organizing workers in the Rand along class rather than racial lines. Its Yiddish-speaking branch (YSB) had particular impact amongst Jewish workers, mainly tailors and shop-keepers. The YSB section of the ISL overcame the language barrier that prevented the full participation of some of its more militant members. Large numbers took part in its activities. It is estimated that five hundred to a thousand were members and an even larger number took part in social and other activities. The YSB was particularly energized by the success of the Bolshevik Revolution and was by far the most active component of the ISL. This nascent political action group supported labor union activities and were allied with the Labour Zionist Poale Zion although the ISL was firmly anti-Zionist in general.[19]

In 1920, a further split occurred when the YSB left the ISL in opposition to participating in parliamentary elections. This stand was apparently consistent with the stance of what was to become the Communist Party of South Africa to which the YSB now contributed its energy. Part of the basis for the revolutionary activity was its Yiddish-speaking identity as differentiated from the English-speaking more middle-class elements. Further, it remained the medium for those Jewish left-wingers who continued to pursue their political commitment in South Africa to the consternation of those aspiring to a middle-class life.

The Yiddish Literary Movement

The connection between labor unions, and socialist political activity did not extend, as it did in the United States, to Yiddish journalism. Despite its relatively small Yiddish-speaking population, there were valiant attempts to maintain a Yiddish press and literary movement. The first Jewish paper in South Africa was a short-lived weekly that appeared in Yiddish in 1890 in Johannesburg under the direction of Nehemia Dov Hoffmann.

The first to bring Yiddish printing to South Africa, he founded the Jewish press.[20] A longer-lasting weekly under the auspices of David Goldblatt, *Der Yiddishe Advocate*, was founded in 1904 in Cape Town. Goldblatt had been introduced to Yiddish journalism in London as a writer for the *Arbeiter-Frynt* (cf Chapter on UK). There also he apparently met Yiddishist Winchevsky. Goldblatt was strongly involved in the developments of the Cape Town Board of Deputies described earlier. His pamphlet, *Yiddish, Is It a European Language?* was instrumental in establishing the language in that category for purposes of immigration. His newspaper lasted until 1914 when Goldblatt departed for the United States. He continued there to be a champion of Yiddish.[21]

Nehemia Hoffmann was born in 1860 on a rented farm in a small village in the province of Kovno. His father was an enlightened Jew. After training in the local school, the boy went on to study modern Hebrew and Yiddish. At age ten, he entered a government school where he learned secular subjects and became proficient in Russian and German while continuing his traditional learning after school. After his *bar mitzvah*, he came under the tutelege of a teacher who was a regular contributor to enlightened Hebrew periodicals. Hoffmann studied astronomy and wrote his first Hebrew article for publication on that subject. At age sixteen, he went to Vilna where he was able to begin to support himself by writing. He published a number of booklets in Hebrew, almost all dealing with science. Hoffmann then edited, in 1886, for a short time one of the leading Hebrew periodicals *HaMagid* to which he had been a contributor. He married a cousin from Neustadt-Sigund from which so many others were to come to South Africa. After a stay in New York as editor of a Yiddish newspaper, he returned to Lithuania and then emigrated to join a brother-in-law, Barnett Millin, in Cape Town.

In 1890, Hoffmann founded the short-lived *Der Afrikaner Israelite* weekly in Johannesburg. He also served as the local correspondent of some of the Hebrew periodicals published in Russia. Some of his articles served to encourage immigration. "This is a wide and large country able to give bread to all its inhabitants with a generous hand. When you come here, don't forget that you are a Jew . . . here a Jew is not ashamed of saying that he is a Jew . . . the freedom and liberty which prevail in the country are enjoyed by all."[22] Hoffmann tried again in 1896 with a weekly in Cape Town called *Der Yiddishe Herald*, also ceasing publication after two years. He stayed active by participating in writing a column for Goldblatt's *Der Yiddishe Advocate*. Later he went on to found other Yiddish weeklies in Cape Town before issuing a monthly *Der Afrikaner* from 1909 to 1914. His memoir, published in 1916, was the first full-length Yiddish book published in South Africa. He died in 1928.[23]

In South Africa, Yiddish was a language under siege. Attacked as a "non-European" language under the various immigration laws, it required almost constant vigilance to ensure its acceptance so as to protect the status of Jews as "Europeans." Despite the activities of such leaders as Morris Alexander, the existing Jewish community itself looked down on Yiddish as part of the picture of *working-class* Jews. Yet despite these efforts, Yiddish persisted and even gave life to a vigorous literature.

The Yiddish literary journals were generally short-lived. However, everything that was written was read, discussed, and criticized with great intensity. One of the longest lasting during this early period was the weekly *Der Afrikaner* published in Johannesburg that started in 1911 and lasted until 1934. It published a number of short stories by Hyman Polsky among others. Polsky went on to become the long-standing editor after the first editor's death.

Hyman Polsky was born in 1871 in a small town in the province of Grodno in the northwest provinces of the Pale. His father had multiple jobs as a shochet, cantor, and bookkeeper. Immigrating to London in 1891, Polsky worked as a tailor's assistant. He longed to be a writer and began a lifelong habit of working on his stories until late in the night after completing his work. He first opened a photographic studio. In 1910, he and his family immigrated to South Africa where he continued his photography while traveling throughout the country. In 1912, he realized his lifelong ambition when he started work as a journalist on the weekly *Der Afrikaner*, founded in Johannesburg by Solomon Vogelson the previous year. The fact that a monthly of the same name had previously been founded by N. D. Hoffmann did not seem to deter Vogelson. He had come to South Africa from the vicinity of Dvinsk before the

Anglo-Boer War. *Der Afrikaner* concentrated on politics, literature, and science and reached a circulation of five thousand at its height. In 1917, it also started an English supplement entitled the *African Jewish World.*[24]

Taking over in 1920, Polsky single-handedly kept it going. He wrote for it as well as serving as editor and publisher. He put together the best of his many short stories in a book published in Warsaw just prior to the start of World War II. All but six copies were lost. It was a bitter blow never to see his work widely circulated in book form during his lifetime. He followed the moralizing tradition in Yiddish literature with punishment of the wicked. Laughter or joy was never unalloyed with tragedy or irony.[25]

The stories by Polsky reflected the struggles and hardships of the immigrant generation. South Africa was far from the land of gold and diamonds for these Jews. They were poor; most remained poor. They had to take jobs no one else wanted. Many had to work running the eating houses for mining workers on behalf of richer Jews or to run the stores that served blacks. It was years passed before they could save the money necessary to bring their wives and children from Europe, and when they did, estrangement had occurred. Many were unable to afford to find wives in Europe and would remain single or intermarried with Afrikaans or black or colored women. Their stories are imbued with a sense of failure in that their religion, values of Yiddish and the culture it represented were to be lost to be replaced by soulless materialism.[26] To an extent unique in South Africa, prosperity must be recognized as tempered by guilt and shame at the injustices to the black laborers by whose toil riches in South Africa were acquired.

These same themes were explored by Morris Hoffman but with greater sensitivity. Born in 1885 in the Vitebsk region, he was the son of a cantor. He was a pupil of Talmud and Hebrew and read modern Hebrew. He went on to master Russian and German in order to read modern literature. His favorite poet was Heine whom he translated into Hebrew. He had written poetry that was published in several outstanding journals before emigrating to South Africa in 1905. He opened a store in the arid wastes near Kimberley where he worked long hours. Despite this, he learned Afrikaans and English from a local priest to whom he taught Hebrew. He committed to memory his favorite English poets as he had those in the languages he had learned earlier. He contributed to literary journals both in Yiddish and Hebrew. In 1935, he published, in Warsaw, a book of his poems. An anthology of his short stories was published posthumously in 1951 *Under Afrikaner Zun (Under African Sun)*.

Hoffman's work emphasizes the tragedy of the idealistic young Lithuanian Jew who succumbs to the primitive South African conditions that crush the visionary, gentle-hearted, and intellectual. He depicts the decay of morals when the immigrant becomes affluent and takes on the characteristics of the Afrikaners with whom he lives. The last vestiges of Jewishness can remain, making the immigrant more sensitive to the pain of servants and employees and to dark-skinned customers.[27]

South African Zionism

To an extent almost unique in the Litvak Diaspora, the Jews of South Africa were identified with Zionism. Like Canada, the formation of the South African Zionist Federation in 1898 preceded any other countrywide Jewish organization.[28] Indeed, its existence, under the direction of Samuel Goldreich, was an obstacle in the development of the Transvaal Board of Deputies and the eventual formation of the unified South African Board in 1912. Its strength as a community-wide effort can also be attributed to the role it took to be concerned with issues directly related to the existence of the community within South Africa itself. Goldreich himself was well connected to Lord Milner and took the role to serve as the "Jewish consulate in South Africa," interacting with governmental policies affecting the lot of Jews in South Africa.

Many of the East European immigrants to South Africa had been members of the Hovevei Zion (Lovers of Zion) societies in Russia, focused on sustaining the struggling agricultural colonies that did exist in Palestine. The year 1896 saw the first society established in Johannesburg by a small number, mainly immigrants from Lita.[29] The organizer, Moshe Weiner from

Wilkomir, was joined by a number of other immigrants, albeit the presiding figures were English Jews. With the emergence of Herzl and the first Zionist Congress in Basle in 1897, the existing society adhered to the new Transvaal Zionist Organization.

To an unusual degree in comparison to Britain, Zionism claimed a number of members of the existing community along with many of the leading rabbis. By 1898, there were five thousand members throughout Transvaal.[30] The outstanding and almost singular exception was that of Reverend Bender, rabbi of the mother congregation in Cape Town. Not until 1926 did the Cape Town Hebrew Congregation become affiliated to the Zionist Federation.[31]

In Cape Town, in 1899, following reports of the second Zionist Congress, the Dorshei Zion Organization was formed. This group emphasized cultural aspects with the formation of a library and, in 1901, the purchase of a building to serve as a meeting place called Zionist Hall. Zionism in Cape Town was energized by the arrival of refugees from the Transvaal during the Anglo-Boer War. The year 1901 also saw the development in Cape Town of a group of women called Bnoth Zion (Daughters of Zion) that was also to persist.

By 1904, the Herzlian focus on "political" action was supplemented by the ideas of practical and cultural Zionism more prevalent among the immigrants from Eastern Europe. A new organization was formed in Johannesburg to take a more active approach to development in Palestine. The Jewish National Fund Club was founded by Benzion S. Hersch, who was to be a commanding figure in the further development of Zionism in South Africa.

Benzion Hersch was born in a town in the Kovno province on the very night when the first Lovers of Zion meeting in that town was taking place. He was so highly dedicated to the Zionist cause that it gave an unusual stature to his life. He arrived in Johannesburg in 1902 after already participating in Zionist work in Lita. The JNF Club was extremely energetic in raising funds. One of its most successful techniques was to invade festivities such as weddings in pursuit of funds. It led to the start of South Africa's repute as being the largest per capita supporter of Zionism. A pattern was established that was to recur for many years. South

Africa surpassed the amounts raised in any other country, second only to the United States. These funds were not raised from the rich alone but from the entire community.

In 1910, Hersch was elected to the executive of the South African Zionist Federation and was joined there by several colleagues of similar immigrant background first enlisted through the JNF Club. He, and others such as Joseph Janower, later the treasurer of the federation, became mainstays for the next generation. Hersch, as head of the editorial board was also primarily responsible for the development of the *Zionist Record*, the organ of the movement. Starting as a monthly in 1908, it became a biweekly in 1924 and a weekly in 1926. In addition to being on the editorial staff, Hersch wrote a column for the paper along with others, including Sarah Gertrude Leibson, later Millin.[32]

The first South African Zionist Conference held in Johannesburg in 1905 brought about a sense of a movement rather than separate societies and individual personalities.[33] To an unusual degree, the South African Zionist Federation maintained its community-wide commitment. The federation encompassed the entire range of the Zionist political spectrum. All that was required was adherence to the Basle Program that had stated "Zionism aims to establish a . . . Home for the Jewish people in Palestine."[34] Zionist ideology pervaded the youth movement as well as Jewish education.

In South Africa it was the norm for Zionism to be the mainstream. Zionism was well represented on the Jewish Board of Deputies. Given traditional nature of South African Orthodoxy, there were not the theological objections of the ultra-Orthodox in terms of messianic eschatology nor of Reform Judaism in terms of the role of the primacy of Jews in the Diaspora. Even more important was the issue of dual loyalty. Jews were perceived, and thus perceived themselves, in South Africa in terms of national identity as much as on the basis of religion. To be a good South African, one should be a good Jew. To be a good Jew, one should be a good Zionist; it was accepted as self-evident.[35]

The Balfour Declaration and the subsequent political developments brought about resurgence of Zionist activity in

South Africa as elsewhere. Several South African connections were helpful in the making of the Balfour Declaration in 1917. One lasting relationship was that of Jan Christian Smuts, who was member of the war cabinet in London and later prime minister in South Africa. Underlying his commitment was his Calvinist Afrikaner upbringing. The philo-Zionism of so-prominent a South African of Afrikaner extraction as well as other politicians of a similar background served to buttress among Jews the particular connection of South African Jewry to Zionism.[36]

5.2.2. The Acculturating Generation

Jewish Immigration continued during the interwar period but to a lesser degree than before the war. A total of only thirty thousand Jews entered South Africa in the years from 1910 to 1948 owing to increasing restriction. In the 1920s, the clause in the Immigration Act that permitted considerable latitude to exclude immigrants was invoked at times to exclude East European Jews. The revolutionary cap of Bolshevism was added to the old image of the inassimilable "Peruvian." On the average, it is calculated that approximately two thousand persons per year entered South Africa during the 1920s. Their distribution continued to reflect the predominance of the Lithuania as a source. Those coming to South Africa in the 1920s came from a Lithuanian Jewish community that had both become more secularized and with an increased national consciousness within the Hebrew Tarbut schools.[1] The political experience of those Jews coming from interwar Lithuania also reflected the almost total absence of the anti-Zionist Bund, much stronger in interwar Poland.[2]

The number of Jews entering either from Eastern Europe or, later, from Germany became successively restricted after 1930. The nationalist government that took power in 1929 introduced the following year the quota bill that essentially sought the cessation of East European immigration. The groundwork had been laid in the previous decade when the common wisdom characterized the Jews as becoming too powerful and, somehow, on basis of eugenics, corrupting the racial stock. The passage of the bill had support from all portions of the political spectrum.

Even the South African Party led by Smuts, the hero of the Jews, supported the passage. Only the Jewish members led by Morris Kentridge protested. The widespread support for the quota bill opened the gates for the anti-Semitism that was to have open political expression in the 1930s.[3]

The rate of urbanization of the white population continued to increase while the urban nonwhite population increased even faster. European immigrants came mainly to the Transvaal where the total white population exceeded one million by 1946. The Jewish population was even more urbanized with movement to the largest cities of Pretoria, Durban, Cape Town, and particularly Johannesburg (in ascending order) in response to the greater opportunities as well as the availability of organized Jewish community life. Johannesburg itself contained about 60 percent of the total. Transvaal province, as a whole, had at 6.5 percent the highest percentage of Jews in relation to total European population. There had been a particular fall in Jewish population in the Orange Free State.[4] Overall in the Union, the white population had risen to 2.3 million, the African had more than doubled to over 7.7 million, and the other nonwhites had also doubled to 1.2 million. The majority of urban population was English speaking, and the overwhelming majority of rural whites were Afrikaan speaking. It is estimated that the white population overall was 55 percent Afrikaan and 45 percent English speaking.[5]

The impact of the restriction of immigration is mirrored in the census of 1936 when, out of a total Jewish population of ninety thousand approximately 25 percent considered Yiddish as their "home language." Just under half and 80 percent of those under thity were born in South Africa. The number of Yiddish speakers continued to fall and was 14 percent of circa of a total of circa one hundred three thousand in 1946.[6]

The close of World War I was marked by two great events that continued to affect the evolution of those coming to South Africa. The Balfour Declaration provided the context for the efforts of mainline Zionists throughout the interwar period. The other major event was the Bolshevik Russian Revolution and the evolution of the Left that provided for many Jews an alternative that reflected a continuity with their roots in Lita.

South African Politics

During the 1920s, the Labour Party ceased to be the expression of socialism. The International Socialist League (ISL) had, at the close of World War I, broken with the Labour Party in order to be aligned with the Communist Third International. Along with the Jewish Socialist Society, the Social Democratic Federation, and the various branches of the Industrial Socialist League, the ISL set up in 1921 a centralized party subject to the discipline of the Comintern International to be called the United Communist Party of South Africa (CPSA). All the delegates and members of the executive were whites although at the public meeting in Cape Town announcing its formation, half the audience was nonwhite. Not to be addressed were the national interests of the Afrikaner, Indian, colored, or Africans but their class interests. The CPSA represented a tiny fractious group but was unique in being open to all races. Their determination was to break through the racial barrier on the basis of class interests, yet they were skeptical about the ability of the nonwhite peasant worker to become a revolutionary. Their main task they thought was to direct the militant white worker against the capitalist system and to transform the race war into a class war by both political and industrial action.[7]

The Labour Party leaders and all those in Parliament were immigrants and unilingual English-speaking. Afrikaners were expected to communicate in English. By upholding British supremacy, Afrikaner workers were alienated while wavering between class and national interests. It alienated Africans by upholding white supremacy. In the election of 1920, Labour was at its height and held the balance of power with Smuts as prime minister. It was less successful in the election called in 1921.[8]

The energy of organized labor was principally directed toward maintaining its monopoly of advantaged slots and thus the membership of the Labour Party was confined mainly to skilled labor. It was cold to the interests of the unskilled and hostile to blacks. A high standard of living in the towns and among some of the whites rested upon a low standard for all others. The ratio of wages ranged from three to ten times greater for the skilled than the unskilled. The postwar Depression in 1921 was the crisis that precipitated the demands of white labor for "civilized" wages in response to the mine owners' push for replacement by lower cost blacks or Asiatics. Their slogan was Workers of the World Unite, and Fight for a White South Africa.

The 1922 strike by the white miners led to violence against scabbing called the Rand Revolt. It was suppressed with heavy loss of life in a military action ordered by Smuts as prime minister. As a result of the disorganization of the unions, the law was passed at the behest of the employers to require conciliation and limit the availability of the strike as a weapon.[9] Smut's party, the South African Party (SAP), was defeated in the subsequent election.

The government elected in 1924 was on the basis of an electoral "pact" between the Nationalist and Labour Party. In forming this "pact," Labour thus identified itself with the white and national aspects of the labor movement. It never again achieved the role it had originally represented in the model of the British Labour Party. Hertzog, the leader of the Nationalist Party in the pact, remained prime minister in various coalitions until 1939. A series of laws were passed to establish a "colour bar," reserving for whites certain employment as well as training opportunities. Monthly passes were used to control entry of blacks to urban areas. The segregation policy then extended to the effective removal of "colored" from voting in the Cape while simultaneously enlarging the European franchise by the removal of property qualifications and the inclusion of women.[10]

The long-time Parliamentary career of Morris Kentridge illustrated the trajectory of Jewish participation in political life, starting with participation in the Labour Party.

Morris Kentridge was born in Lita in 1881, the eldest of five children of a cantor as was his grandfather, hence the derivation of the original family name of Kantorowitz. The father emigrated to Sunderland in England where he served the congregation. The boy was enrolled at St Andrews University at age fourteen as the youngest student and the only Jew. He thrived there in the debating society for the short time he remained. The family then emigrated to South Africa, settling in a small town in Transvaal where the father served as shochet and cantor. Morris remained in England on his own. He eventually was able to join the family just before the end of the Anglo-Boer War in 1902 at the age of twenty-one.

He eventually became a lawyer, settling in Durban in 1909. From the outset, he was active both in the Jewish community in Zionist affairs and in the local politics. He joined the Labour Party in 1909. It was at that time that he changed his name. During the years in Natal, he was elected to the provincial council and, on the Labour ticket, a short time in Parliament in 1914 as a result of a by-election. Moving to Johannesburg in 1917 in pursuit of his political career, he soon became a town councilor. He strongly supported a white municipal employee strike and pioneered municipal social security measures. He eventually returned to Parliament in the Labour landslide of 1920. He was the victor for the Labour party in the working-class constituency of Fordsburg. It was an early suburb laid out in 1893 intended for miners and artisans.[11]

Kentridge was particularly active in establishing rent control during the short time before his defeat in the next election in 1921. He was jailed for a short time in 1922 in the repression that followed the *Rand Revolt*. His original Russian name was invoked as evidence for the Bolshevik nature of the strike actions with widespread editorial comment on the need to curtail Jewish immigration. In 1924, he was reelected for the district of Troyeville, a lower-middle-class area, and remained in Parliament in connection with a number of party labels until 1958.

In 1928, he broke with Creswell, the Labour Party leader who remained part of the pact with the Nationalists. Kentbridge was one of three members associated with the National Council of Labour before joining in 1931 the South African Party of Smuts and then going with him to the United Party.[12] He maintained his ties to trade unionism long after having severed his ties to the Labour Party. Although originally a segregationist, he was more and more an opponent of native repression as well opposing discrimination against Asiatics even when contrary to United Party policy.

In 1930, as one of the few Jewish members, he was the spokesman in the assembly for the Jewish Board of Deputies in opposition to the Immigration Act of 1930 that essentially cut off East European immigration to South Africa. He saw restrictions on immigration even more broadly than a Jewish issue but one that defeated the hope of a "greater South Africa." He was, throughout his career, clearly identified with the Jewish community and Zionism. He, even within the color-bound mainstream of Labour and increasingly repressive attitudes toward race, strove to "ameliorate the lot of the underprivileged, whether white or black, Gentile and Jew; and to help build a United South Africa in which all sections could play their part."[13]

Following the election of 1929, the Nationalists gained power without the need for support from the now far-smaller Labour Party. The Great Depression led to a coalition between Hertzog and Smuts, with the latter as deputy prime minister. The fusion took the name of the United Party (United South African National Party). Their unity was based upon the concept of bilateral development of both white language groups and maintenance of the British connection, however attenuated. White supremacy was a given.

The Nationalist Party in 1934 split, with D. F. Malan taking the leadership of a group committed to a republican political programme.[14] Malan was a former Dutch Reformed minister who had been the first editor of the Cape nationalist newspaper. He saw Afrikaner nationalism as ordained by God.[15]

Founded in 1933, the South African Christian National Socialist Movements was characterized by its "Greyshirts" patterned directly on Hitler. Jews were once again equated on racial terms to Asiatics. Anti-Semitism had now become fully entrenched in Parliamentary white politics. Exacerbated by the entry of German Jews fleeing Nazism, an aliens bill introduced in 1937 effectively ended all Jewish immigration.[16] Jewish immigration from countries such as Germany, not previously restricted, was reduced in the context of the Nazi persecutions and eventually totally cut off by the start of World War II.[17]

The Jewish Press

With the reduction of immigration and the consequent reduction in the use of Yiddish as one's home language, there was a corresponding growth in the significance of the English Jewish press. The original *South African Jewish Chronicle*, founded in 1902, started as a fortnightly, becoming a weekly in 1904. In 1928, it was moved from Johannesburg to Cape Town when it eventually came under the control of the Zionist Federation of Cape Town. It was amalgamated with the *Zionist Record*, and once again published in Johannesburg.[18]

The largest of the local Jewish weeklies during the interwar period under the direction of Leon Feldberg. Leon Feldberg came to South Africa from Lita where his father was rabbi of Krok. The family descended from the Gaon of Vilna. Following family tradition, Feldberg received the Yeshiva training to qualify for the rabbinate. From his teens, he was contributing to the Yiddish press in Lithuania and entered journalism after graduation. He came to South Africa in the postwar period as a minister and Hebrew teacher in the rural community of Bothaville. The opportunity to return to journalism came in 1936 with the foundation of an independent Jewish journal called the *South African Jewish Times*. He surrounded himself with competent writers. Unassociated with any organization or party, it has provided an open forum in the Jewish press. He would encourage controversial issues as a means of increasing the interest in the publication.[19]

Yiddish Literary Life

One of the most stalwart supporters of Yiddish and of labor during this interwar period was Leibl Feldman. Born in 1896 in a town in northern Lithuania, he was the second son of four children. His paternal grandfather was a pious and learned man who, in addition to Talmud, was proficient in several European languages. The father, Joseph Feldman, left for Johannesburg in 1897 where he built up a small produce business along with three of his brothers. He made several trips back home before finally, in 1910, able to bring his wife and four children to South Africa. Traveling via London, like so many others, they stayed at the Jews Temporary Shelter while awaiting the ship to South Africa. Yiddish was their mother tongue. They were firmly against religion and acted on that feeling by refusing to participate in religious services at the shelter.

The family moved to Doornfontein, the centre of Johannesburg's Jewish communal life. Soon after arrival, when enrolled in the Jewish government school, the brothers were registered as Louis and Richard by the headmaster who "disliked Russian names." From their earliest years, the Feldman brothers were devoted to Yiddish. Consistent with his stance, *Louis* retained Leibl as his familiar name all his life. From boyhood, he was a proud and prickly person who held strong opinions to which he adhered consistently.

In 1912, when sixteen, Feldman left school after completing sixth grade. In 1923, he started his own business which grew to be the largest wholesale sweets business in South Africa and also one of the largest tobacco wholesalers. His interests were far beyond trade. Feldman, in opposition to the Zionist Federation, supported the fundraising for Jewish colonization efforts in Birobidjan and the Jewish Workers Club founded at about the same time. Leibl's brother Richard, a partner in his business, also took an active role in politics as a Labour member of the Transvaal provincial council and also a writer. His stories dealt mainly of the relations between blacks and whites.[20]

Despite the limitations in immigration, there was persistence of a Jewish working class well into the 1930s in Johannesburg, particularly in the lower-income areas, such as Doornfontein. About 20 percent were engaged in manual labor, mainly artisans such as mechanics, shoemakers, and tailors. A substantial portion of the largest single group of white-collar workers were employees, not owners. Particularly onerous were the long hours at low rates of pay of the shop assistants, working in the *kaffir* eating houses and concession stores in the mining areas. In 1926, a Reef Shop Assistants Union (Native Trade) was started.[21]

The activities of the Jewish Workers Club in Doornfontein in Johannesburg played a big part in the social and cultural life. Its library was very popular.[22] The Club provided companionship in a setting where there was no need to struggle with a new language. There were drama and choral groups, table tennis, and chess. It cultivated Yiddish as a medium for its cultural activities not only as a reflection of proletarian culture but as a means of political organization, subordinate to the Communist Party. In their

opposition to Zionism, they supported the Soviet province of
Birobidjan. In distinction from Hebrew, Yiddish was not merely
the language of the home but of the masses.[23]

The club followed the ideas of the Yiddishe Literarisher Farein
(Jewish Cultural Federation) for which Feldman was also an
enthusiastic supporter. Founded in 1912 to encourage Yiddish
cultural and literary life, it finally disbanded in 1932. It valiantly
published, intermittently, a literary journal under various names,
the most lasting called *Dorem Afrike* (South Africa).[24] The Kayor
publishing venture founded, in 1949 under its auspices, was
a means for continuing Yiddish literature even into the post-
Holocaust era.

Feldman was active in writing for the various journals
associated with his political and cultural interests. His first
book, *Yidn in Dorem Afrike*, was published in Vilna in 1937. On
his visit there, he met Dr. Max Weinreich and other prominent
Yiddish intellectuals of YIVO. He subsequently wrote books
in Yiddish about the Jews in Johannesburg as well as the town
of Oudtshoorn. Yiddishism and Socialism remained his faith
throughout his life, only seemingly incompatible with his
daily existence as a wealthy man.[25] Within the rather narrow
limits of the South African ethos, he did express his social
consciousness. His was the first large company to establish
a pension scheme for blacks and, at his death in 1975, his
will included a bequest for establishing a trade school for
blacks.

Characteristic of the family interconnections of the
shtetllike community was the recurrent appearance on the
editorial boards of Yiddish journals of the poet Jacob Mordecai
Sherman. Born on a farm in Kovno province in 1885, he was
sent early to various yeshivot. While at the famous *Mussar*
yeshiva of Slobodka, he started reading modern Hebrew and
started writing himself. He came to Transvaal in 1903 and, after
years of wandering, finally found a job that provided him the
leisure to continue writing. His poems as a young man reflect
his deep loneliness and the loss of the ideals he once had.[26]
He was both the author of the first Yiddish novel published in
1956 as *Land Fun Gold und Sunshein* and Feldman's longtime
bookkeeper.[27]

The South African Labor Movement

The post-World War I development of industry in South Africa was aided by protectionist government tariffs as well as direct government ownership of heavy industry such as steel mills.[28] The value of products nearly quadrupled over the period between the wars.[29].

The political experience and class origins of many of the early members of the Jewish Workers Club placed them in the leadership of many of the industrial-type unions that developed. These new unions were built around the unskilled and semiskilled whites and Africans. For the first time, women workers also appeared particularly in the garment industry. These unions differed from the earlier craftlike unions that had contributed to the racial differentiation and had sought to maintain the "color bar." Rather, the mainly Jewish leadership of these new unions sought to break the colour bar in industry and establish the principle of equal pay for equal work. These unions themselves broke the colour bar by opening their membership to colored and Indians albeit in separate sections. For example, the Garment and Furniture Workers Union would hold joint meetings with their African parallels. The African and European Laundry Workers Unions set up a joint executive.[30]

One of the "nonracial" unions that had both whites and nonwhites was the Garment Workers Union led by Solly Sachs. Originally a member of the Jewish Worker's Club and the South African Communist Party, he was expelled after 1931. By then, both had come under the influence of Comintern's instructions with the trend toward *Bolshevization* and focus on the international needs of the Soviet Union.[31]

Emil Solomon "Solly" Sachs was born in Lita in 1900, the second of three sons, the third of five children. He neither spoke nor walked for the first four years but then experienced a sudden awakening. Solly became an outstanding student, the best in the village noted for its students. He would shine in his expounding of Talmud. The father was the black sheep of the most respected families in the district. To the shame of his family, the father was imprisoned for robbery. After release from prison, he emigrated to South Africa.

In 1914, seven years after the father's departure, the family was finally reunited. They finally arrived in CapeTown to find themselves living in a slum called Malay Camp. In three undersized rooms, there was no bathroom or electricity. They arrived to find their father in recurrent trouble with the law. A bootmaker, he did little to support them. The earnings of the two eldest children were all that kept them from abject poverty.

From the start, Solly would fight opposition with a fanatical fury. At school in South Africa during World War I, he refused to accept the teacher's pro-British politics merely based on her demand. To spite her, he organized a pro-German group. He was of medium height with a scholarly stoop. His Slavonic face stood out in the midst of thousands. He was called the Rabbi even after he forsook all religion. The Talmudist in him was ineradicable.[32] He felt that he was absolutely right but was willing to go to any length to accomplish what was practical.

In joining the International Socialist League (ISL) in 1917 and then the Communist Party, Sachs had the feeling that the world would change. Opportunities seemed to exist in the unionization of the black masses. White members of the ISL were the first to bring socialist ideas to the African workers who eventually developed their own indigenous leaders; there was encouragement for the blacks to carry out passive resistance against the "pass" laws similar to that carried out by the Indians in Natal under Gandhi.

Sach's first job at age twelve was as a shop assistant in a black trading store near the mines. He then started his union work in 1920 as secretary of the Reef Shop Assistants Union. From 1926, Sachs was increasingly involved in union matters as a member of the national executive of the nonracial South African Trades and Labour Council (SATLC). In 1927 while studying law at University of Witwatersrand and looking for a part-time job to help support himself, he became secretary of the Middlemen Taylors' Association and, in 1928, that of the trade union called the Witwatersrand Tailors' Association. He never went back to school. With the internecine warfare of the Communist Party between Stalin and Trotsky starting in 1927, the South African Communist

Party began its own purges to the detriment of its activity in that country. Sachs was one of many expelled in 1931.[33]

"Sweating" was widespread in the garment industry with long hours and particularly low-wages-paid women. Most employers were themselves on the edge of bankruptcy. Minimum wage laws were not enforced. The Afrikaner women who had come to the Rand to work in clothing factories were not represented in any existing union organization. Almost all the workers were white, so that racialism was not the problem it was to become. Aside from the Afrikaners, the rest were Jewish. Starting in 1934, the Garment Workers Union representing the factory workers, mainly female, separated from the mostly male tailors' union. The Industrial Council for the Clothing Industry provided a method for resolving disputes in the better economic times of the later 1930s. A closed shop requiring union membership as a condition of employment was established. By this time, the economic issues were no longer the problem but were superceded by the racial and political issues.

Sach's union was unusual in calling two general strikes of the garment industry over wage issues in the early 1930s. He was *banned* from the Rand for twelve months following one of these strikes. He fought this order in the courts as he did whatever and wherever there was a government attack and was successful in all of the twenty such lawsuits by virtue of his perseverance and sense of rectitude about what was legal.[34]

Sachs did not come from the background of the mostly Afrikaner women workers. There were multiple efforts by Afrikaner groups during the 1930s to dislodge Sachs from his position. They called for a crusade "to save the souls of the Afrikaner workers from the corruption of foreigners . . . communists and Jews."[35] The union members stood with him despite all the onslaughts from Afrikaner Nationalism because his energy and skill had won so many benefits for them. Women's wages had risen sevenfold, men's fivefold. The working week had gone form fifty hours to forty hours. He had managed to neutralize some of the racial prejudice by militant trade unionism and socialist education.[36] Nevertheless, his gains against such prejudice were small. In the years just preceding World War II, the number of colored workers began to increase. The Garment Workers' Union tried to recruit them but came in conflict with white hostility. In 1944, when in turn African women were eligible to become members, the colored workers put up strong resistance to their admission.[37]

In 1946, Sachs became a member of the Labour Party and its national treasurer in 1952. He along with others of its progressive wing managed to reverse its-long standing discriminatory attitude toward non-Europeans with a stand for equal pay for equal work regardless of race. In 1952, the government began to proceed against him under the Suppression of Communism Act on the basis of his former membership in the Communist Party. He was forced to resign from his union position and eventually forced into exile in Britain.[38] Race and blood, not the socialist ideals of equality and comradeship would prevail.[39] Coming from difficult home conditions, his intellect was coupled with the messianic drive that originated in his strong religious training in the Lithuanian village where he derived his basic experience.[40]

South African Government

There was Jewish support for the Labour party that continued throughout the 1930s. However, the more normative connection was for the now clearly middle-class Jews to support the centrist South African Party led by Smuts. Later, they followed Smuts into the United Party. The first and only time a Jew entered the cabinet until the 1990s under Mandela was in 1947 under the United Party banner when Dr. Henry Gluckman was minister of health and housing. The career of Dr. Gluckman illustrates the salient degree of acceptance of the acculturated generation into the social as well as political life of the ruling white community.[41]

Born in Lithuanian town of Zager, Henry Gluckman was the eldest of four children. The two sons were born in Lithuania prior to their father's emigration to South Africa. The father, Joseph, had established a small business on the Rand in a town called Randfontein. The family joined him there early in the century. The boy now had to learn English at age of eleven when enrolled in the government school in that town. He went on to secondary school at the famous and long-standing King Edward VII Boy's School in Johannesburg. He had his medical training at the University of London starting in 1912. Commissioned as captain in the South African Medical Corp, he worked in British hospitals while awaiting transport to Africa where the South African contingents were serving. He also had the opportunity to work as a locum tenens in the poor South Wales coal-mining districts.

After the war, he started his medical practice in Johannesburg. He was director of the special treatment center at the Johannesburg Hospital and lecturer on the medical faculty at the University of Witwatersrand and, in 1928, appointed to a consultant position at that same hospital. His specialty in venereal diseases led to his early interest as chairman of the South African Social Hygiene Council and to the interest in public health that was to be the focus of his public life.

He started his parliamentary career in 1938, elected on the United Party ticket from Yeoville, a middle-class constituency in Johannesburg. It was a safe United Party seat in which he was, at times, unopposed. He was a loyal member of Smut's party and, in 1939, part of the small majority that voted for entry of South Africa into World War II on the side of Britain.

A lieutenant colonel, he served as liaison between the Parliament and the South African Medical Services. At his instigation, a National Health Service Commission was established to formulate a national health service for South Africa. As chairman of the commission, he pursued the implementation of its report in 1945 to emphasize health promotion as an integral part of health services. Appointed to the newly established ministry of health and housing in 1947, he was chairman of the National Nutrition Council that pioneered dietary supplementation to the poor. He made the decision to establish a new medical school in Durban for training of non-European doctors.

Much later, his loyalty to Smuts extended to being the chairman of the War Veterans' Foundation that took over the prime minister's farm property as a place of pilgrimage. A high point of the British connection he shared with Smuts was their participation in the royal visit to South Africa in the spring of 1947 of King George VI and his family. He was reelected in the successive general elections of 1943, 1948, and 1953, finally leaving the Parliament in 1958. He represented South Africa in the World Parliamentary Association during those years.

After the 1948 election, he continued as a front bencher of the opposition and maintained his leadership in health promotion in the National War Memorial Health Foundation. The foundation maintained a wide-range health programs such as crèches, community centers, feeding schemes, training facilities, scholarships, and holiday camps for the different racial groups.

He delivered the message on the part of the government of which he was a member from Prime Minister Smuts, supporting the 1947 United Nations resolution establishing a Jewish state. He was particularly involved in the development of the Hebrew University in Jerusalem for the South African component of the new campus on Mount Scopus. He was a member of the executive of the Jewish Board of Deputies and an officer of the South African Zionist Federation. Married to the eldest daughter of the family of merchants of timber and building supplies, he became chairman of the business after the death of his father-in-law. He lived the life of a wealthy man, but the name Zagaren of his country estate retained the name of the village in Lithuania from which he had come.

South African Literature

These same issues of international as well as South African acceptance from humble beginnings was the story of Sarah Gertrude Millin. In addition to her husband's stature as barrister, expert on company law and later supreme court justice was her career as the leading South African writer of the interwar generation. Her identity, however, was above all as a white South African. The sense of dedication she felt for the nation, the white nation as she and others defined it, was the moving force of her life, surpassing any other moral or religious commitments. She was both a symptom and a victim of the course of development of South Africa during her lifetime.[42]

Sarah Leibson Millin was born in 1888 in the same Lithuanian village of Zagar as Henry Gluckman. Isaiah Leibson, her father, was a shy man. His education was limited to Hebrew and the Bible. The mother, Olga Freidmann Liebson, was quite different. Her education was far broader, including Russian as well as other

European languages. She was talkative, colorful, and dramatic—qualities her daughter was to inherit as well as her literary bent. Olga also shared her pride in the family connection with the Vilna Gaon.

Olga's father persuaded Isaiah to join him in emigrating to South Africa. As soon as Olga was well enough to travel after the birth of her daughter, they arrived in Cape Town in August 1888 when Sarah was five months old. Isaiah, unlike his more forceful and impatient father-in-law who was a prospector in the diamond diggings, set himself up as a storekeeper in Beaconsfield, later a part of Kimberley. The eldest brother, Abe, with whom Sara Gertrude remained very close, was born during this era. In 1894, the Leibsons settled in Waldeck's Plant, an area along the Vaal River some distance from Kimberley. The trip there remained in her memory for the rest of her life, including the terror of a boatman whose nose was decayed by syphilis. The alluvial diamond deposits there were becoming worked out, but Isaiah managed to earn a comfortable living There were several more brothers born, and the children played almost entirely among themselves, keeping distinct from the digger's children.

Drunkenness and licentiousness were commonplace coupled with cohabitation between the white diggers and nonwhite women. Miscegenation was an ever-present issue that impinged on the world of the diggings as contrary to the religious teachings of the Dutch Reformed Church, if not yet against the law. The loss of caste and privilege that she saw around her resonated with her awareness of the danger of loss of caste that she and her family could experience as Jews.[43] The concept of being a *stepchild* experienced by the "colored" between the two races was mirrored by her feeling of the Jews being a stepchild torn between being a Jew and South African.[44]

She was sent to school in Kimberley where, in her fierce independence, she herself chose to live in an unsatisfactory situation as a boarder. Illustrative of her pride was, having made the choice, she persisted in it despite its apparent inadequacy. Despite high scores in her examinations and the assurance of a scholarship to college in Cape Town, she turned down the opportunity and remained in Kimberley in order to train as a music teacher. Pride again prevented her from then going on to college and recovering from what now appeared to have been a bad choice. Sarah Gertrude was a voracious reader from childhood and used that method to make up for her deficiencies in the absence of university education. Unable to obtain any instruction in the art of writing, she proceeded on her own. She wrote about her surroundings with particular focus on the evil results of miscegenation. It was in this period that she began to also publish nonfiction pieces in such places as the *Zionist Record*.

The theme of miscegenation was the unifying theme in her fifth novel and most successful book, *God's Stepchildren*, written in 1924. It was a sin that would then afflict each of the subsequent generations of a white missionary who, in his insanity, had defied the color bar. At no point is the attitude of white South Africa questioned, but rather approved, by condemning the original progenitors both black and white. The book made her a literary celebrity in America and confirmed her lifelong ambition to be a writer.[45] Subsequent books established her reputation in Britain and finally in South Africa itself. Her 1982 honorary doctorate from University of Witwatersrand was an important vindication, however late.

Her father had a passion for politics and gloried in the newly discovered political and social freedom of South Africa so different from Lithuania. Similar to the propensities of Sarah Gertrude, Isaiah was pro-Afrikaner during the Boer War and was interned by the British for a short time because of his sympathies. Her pacifism during World War I was strongly confirmed by the death of her beloved doctor brother Abe while protecting his patients on the front lines. She became a firm supporter of Smuts in his role of suppressing the Rand Revolt. In the 1930s, she was now a member of the moneyed class as a result of her own success and that of her husband. In the last years of her life, she became even more clearly a supporter of white South Africa but now in the context of apartheid.[46]

Her childless but apparently loving marriage to the judicious barrister Phillip Millin provided her with the support that balanced her own temperament. She also shared her literary interests with her mother. This habit of discussing literary issues was to continue until Olga's death long after Sarah Gertrude has become acquainted with literary people of standing throughout the world. Sarah Gertrude remained "resolutely, consciously, and defiantly Jewish." In the only book in which Jewish characters appeared, *The Coming of the Lord*, she has the Jewish father character tell his son who is seeking assimilation into the Gentile world that escape is an illusion.[47] Her failure to affect the passage of the Alien's Act that finally cut off German Jewish immigration contributed to the attenuation of her previous hero workshop of Smuts. She had always been supportive of Zionism as something for those unfortunate Jews for whom it was a necessary refuge. Her very negative feelings about Israel in 1949 came about after her visit there. They were colored by personal pique and sadness of the role of her old friend Weizmann as an ignored figurehead in the new country. She believed in a world where there is precedence and order. Her genuine qualities enabled her to enter company of celebrities and footmen in knee breeches at Claridge's, a long way from her origins in Zager.[48]

South African Zionism

During the course of the 1930s, there were several developments within the Jewish community in response to the threats from the active expression of anti-Semitism. One was the reorganization of the South African Jewish Board of Deputies and the other was a new thrust within the Zionist Movement. The two organizations shared the same people so that there was not the problem faced in the United States and Britain where a large anti-Zionist group continued to exist. The Zionist Federation has included the full range of the political spectrum aside from the Revisionists.

The Labour Zionist component had a rejuvenation in the post-World War I immigration. There were some who, although originally Litvak, came to South Africa from Palestine to help form Zeire Zion (the Young of Zion) which favored Hebrew rather than Yiddish and was broadly social democratic rather than doctrinaire Marxist. Its emphasis, however, in terms of the *self-labor* concept of the chalutzim foundered on the availability of black labor as the underpinning of South African life. The Poalei Zion group in Cape Town and Johannesburg managed to unite to form the United Zionist Socialist Party.[49]

Somewhat later, in response to the rise of the Greyshirts, a reservoir had arisen of South African-born Jews with a leftist inclination and liberal outlook on race problems. The clear-cut ideology of Zionist Socialism with its synthesis of Zionism and Socialism received a transfusion of new energy. Louis Pincus became chairman. A new monthly in English and Yiddish called the the *Labour Zionist* was published. This political alignment led to an involvement of Zionist Socialists in the South African political scene different from the traditional activities of the Zionist Federation. For example, the Labour Zionists joined the Jewish Workers' Club on May Day 1943 along with non-Jewish groups such as the Labour Party, South African Trades and Labour Council, and Socialist Party of South Africa. They were particularly involved in the electoral campaigns of Labour Party candidates. In turn, a South African League for Labour Palestine enlisted interest in Labour Palestine among leftists and leading Labour politicians in the country. Although there was closest affinity to the rejuvenated Labour Party progressive wing, they stopped short of affiliation with any political party. One measure of the success of the Socialist Zionists was that the Left movement in the country by 1944 had accepted the principle that "anti-Semitism was automatically reactionary and constituted a direct threat to all progressives."[50]

The youth section of the Labour Zionists went even further in its alignment with other aspects of the Left. A Joint Progressive Youth Committee formed in 1943 aligned them with Jewish Worker's Club but also with the Progressive Asian Club and the Young African League toward a nonracial Socialist South Africa. Most important was the rejuvenation of Zionist youth groups in the period just before the foundation of Israel. By 1945, Zionist youth groups were larger than ever before or since. There were Socialist Youth along with nonparty groups such as Habonim. The latter was becoming more politicized with an expanding core of chalutzim with socialist inclinations.[51] From these as well as ex-servicemen, South African Jewry provided, by far, the largest per capita contribution to the Haganah and particularly to the beginnings of the Israeli Air Force.

In the years just proceeding the establishment of the State of Israel, South Africa continued under Smuts to support political Zionism. South Africa was among the majority voting for partition in the crucial United Nations vote. Just prior to the 1948 election, when Smuts went down to defeat, South Africa was among the first few states to accord recognition to the State of Israel. The crucial watershed for South African Jewry was this 1948 election when the Nationalist Afrikaner Party came to power.

5.2.3. The Apartheid Generation

Under state intervention, urbanization increased for both blacks and whites as the manufacturing component expanded starting in the 1930s. In this area, as in the mining industry, a two-tier system existed. Skilled jobs in manufacturing as well as bureaucracy and professions were reserved for whites, mainly Afrikaner. During the Depression of the 1930s, the price of gold set in international markets rose with resultant benefit to South African mining interests. Extensive black migration to the cities began to take place, including squatter camps on the outskirts.

The Nationalist victory in 1948 was based upon efforts during the 1930s to develop Afrikaner nationalism beyond its rural base. The margin of victory in 1948 was by the votes of the Afrikaner mine workers on the Rand.[1] Its victory in the legislature belied its minority overall but was helped by the premium given the rural voters. The Nationalist Party dominated the South African government for the next generation. Segregation became enshrined as "apartheid." The Nationalists sought to isolate Afrikaners in terms of their identity as a Volk, to maintain exclusivity in the name of an ideology of apartheid.[2] They saw the existence of separate nations and races as foreordained by God.[3]

The United Party, which most Jews supported, was led by Smuts. It had, by its very name and history, attempted to bridge the Afrikaner-British differences but at the price of unity on the color question. It is only by default that white liberals such as Jews expressed themselves within that party. There was never any question about the United Party's commitment to segregation and white supremacy. Its adherents were opposed to the far reaching character of the Nationalist legislative agenda and the degree to which it impinged on liberties of whites. The United Party, in opposition, consistently fought for maintenance of the constitution. It fruitlessly opposed on constitutional grounds the series of laws that delineated rigid residential segregation, registration of persons on the basis of race, and prohibition against miscegenation.

From the beginning of Afrikaner nationalism, one wing had always had the goal of independence from the British Imperial connection. It was finally achieved in 1961 with the foundation of the South African Republic. Steps along the way included a citizenship bill in 1949 that made it considerably harder for immigrants to acquire citizenship. The advantages enjoyed by British subjects over other aliens nearly disappeared. The maintenance of British citizenship became important for those seeking to emigrate in the 1970s. Moreover the state could act to the detriment of individual rights in accomplishing its basic goal of apartheid. This became particularly evident in the segregation of education impinging on traditional church-based responsibility for education of Africans. Segregation within English-speaking universities was put into effect in 1959. There was to be a single-minded commitment to preservation of the white race by a rigid implementation of "separate development" of Bandustans. Criticisms within Afrikaner ranks were more method and timing rather than principle. Only much later with the increased urbanization and sense of self-confidence, there were also factions within Afrikaner society that played a part for seeking a detente with English-speaking whites to create a "white nation" but still on Afrikaner terms.

One goal was to for workers to see themselves in common with members of other classes in one's own racial or linguistic group. The Suppression of Communism Act (1950) was used to eliminate left-wingers, such as Solly Sachs, from the unions, and the Industrial Conciliation Act (1956) prohibited racially mixed unions. There was further entrenchment of the principle of "job reservation." Certain occupations and job categories wee identified on a racial basis. African strikes and African trade unions were forbidden.[4]

The growth in industry during the war had brought about a major increase in nonwhite workers and urban settlements. It was no longer possible to maintain the fiction that nonwhites were transients in the urban areas. The urban "native" population had risen to the point that it was almost equal to white population in the cities. This fact underlay the evolution of United Party, thinking that the fact of economic interdependence would eventually lead to some sort of political recognition albeit hedged by the need for "long period of training."

The African National Congress (ANC) had been a relatively conservative group satisfied with accepting only very limited impact via Native Representative Council. The ANC Youth League organized in 1944 marked a more radical stance in pursuit of African nationalism and non-racial franchise. There was call for a Bill of Rights to abolish all discriminatory legislation that reflected the increasing number of urban nonwhites. This step was unacceptable even to the white liberals who had tried to develop a stance that would merely lead to some relaxation of the colour bar or at least the maintenance of nonwhite voting in the Cape.[5]

South African Politics

In the period after the first Nationalist victory, the means of opposition to these policies were no longer deputations but boycotts, strikes, and civil disobedience.[6] The nonviolent Defiance Campaign carried out by the ANC, the South African Indian Congress (SAIC), and the South African Coloured People's Association (SACPO) started in June 1952. It was during this campaign that Nelson Mandela first assumed leadership. The United Party did not contest the response of the government in its passage of the Public Safety Bill. The government was empowered to declare a state of emergency in the face of civil disobedience.[7] Further, the Criminal Law Amendment Act was to increase even further the punishment, including flogging of those engaged in protest of any laws. Under the wide provisions of the 1950 Suppression of Communism Act, the government could *ban* persons, gatherings, and publications "aiming at bringing about . . . any change . . . by means which include the promotion of disturbance."[8] The role of the radicals following the banning of the South African Communist Party in 1950 is exemplified by the career of Joe Slovo and his family.

Joe Slovo was born in 1926 in Lithuania. His father, Wulfus, left in 1928 to go to Argentina. With the unemployment there in 1929, he then came to South Africa. Joe, his mother, and older sister, Sonia, were finally able to join the father in 1936 in Johannesburg where he had hawked fruit in the streets. They came to Doornfontein to a tin-roofed house on Beit St., the main thoroughfare. The Crystal Bakery and Delicatessen was where his father later worked as a bread deliveryman and his sister as a shop assistant. The boy was sent to the Jewish government school. The family then moved up to Bellevue in a semidetached house opposite their newly acquired fruit store. Slovo completed his primary school education at Yeoville School for boys. In 1938, within two years after their arrival, his mother died in childbirth. Sonia went to work, and the family went downhill literally as well as figuratively to a boarding house in Doornfontein. While living at the rooming house, Slovo left school in the middle of his first year of secondary school to go to work at age fourteen. His father spent a number of short spells imprisoned for nonpayment of debts owed for the bankrupt Bellevue fruit store.

His secondary school teacher, an Irish rebel, enlisted him in the Young Left Book Club. His leaning toward left socialist politics was also formed by the association with the old-time socialists who lived in the boarding house and with the Jewish Workers' Club in Doornfontein. Eventually, Slovo joined the Communist Party and established a cell at his job at a pharmaceutical supply company. He became a member of the National Union of Distributive Workers and embarked on a legal strike in October 1942, which was so successful that he more than tripled his salary. This applied only to the white workers since the blacks did not have the right to strike for economic reasons. After losing several jobs for his organizing activities, at age eighteen he joined the South African Army and fought in Italy. After discharge, he received a scholarship to go to University of Witwatersrand. He qualified as an advocate and practiced law.[9]

The banning of the Communist party in 1950 under the Suppression of Communism Act (SCA) caused it to go underground. Rather than Communist Party of South Africa (CPSA), its new name was changed to the South African Communist Party (SACP) to mark its new status. Slovo's work continued as a member of the Central Committee particularly in association with the ANC. Despite being *banned* in 1954, Slovo was involved in organizing the development of the Freedom Charter with thousands of meetings throughout the country.[10] Slovo was also an active member of the white counterpart Congress of Democrats (COD) supporting the nonviolent Defiance Campaign as were other known Communists.

The Freedom Charter sought a nonracial, democratic system with equal protection under the law. This became the touchstone of the African National Congress in its commitment to a multiracial South Africa. In 1955, there had been a call issued by the ANC to call a Congress of the People. This Congress Alliance included representatives of the various nonwhite organizations that had participated in the Defiance Campaign along with the COD. The Liberal Party, led by Alan Paton, although invited, did not choose to participate.

The success of this undertaking involving three thousand persons led to a police raid on the meeting on June 26-27 at Kliptown near Johannesburg. Even more important was the roundup by the police in December 1956 of circa a hundred fifty persons, most associated with the Congress Alliance that had produced the Freedom Charter. They were accused of trying to overthrow the government by violence; and that this campaign was connected with international communism. The long-lasting *Treason Trial* ended in 1961 with acquittal of all the defendants with both aspects unproven.[11] Among those arrested were Joe Slovo and his wife Ruth along with twenty-one other whites, more than half of whom were Jews. The impact of the *Treason Trial* was far reaching in that it helped create the personal friendships across racial lines that became a core group of activists.[12]

Ruth First was born in 1925 in Johannesburg. Both her parents were radicals. Her father, Julius, had come to South Africa in 1910 from Latvia and her mother, Tillie, from Lithuania in 1901 when aged four. He was chairman of the Communist Party in 1923 and remained a benefactor with the income he earned from ownership of a furniture factory. Tillie was even more dedicated to radical causes and brought her children with her. At age eighteen, Ruth became the lover of an Indian activist with whom she remained connected for the next four years as a living example contravening South African society norms. The passage of the Immorality Act soon after the Nationalist victory made it illegal as well. Soon after, she was married to Joe Slovo with whom she had three daughters.[13] Her refusal to surrender her surname after marrying marked her as a forerunner of the next generation of women.

After graduating from Wits in 1945, Ruth worked as a journalist for the various incarnations of the Communist newspaper whose name continually changed in response to government actions under the SCA.[14] Together, the Slovos shared the exhilaration of breaking the conventions, of living a multiracial life. Ruth First, having been imprisoned in solitary confinement for 116 days in the aftermath of Rivonia, went into exile as well. In reflection of her own thinking, she later—while living in Mozambique—cowrote a biography of the South African feminist and radical Olive Shreiner. She was eventually killed in Mozambique by a letter bomb sent by the South African government. She was, in her own right, an important figure in the movement for racial equality.

In the national election of 1958, the United Party once again failed to unseat the Nationalists who increased their representation in an unprecedented third term in office. After this election, the more liberal members split away to form the Progressive Party in 1959. Drawing upon their United Party roots, they went beyond those roots to advocate the principle of the extension of the franchise to nonwhites albeit on the basis of the "Cape" criteria. The "liberal Cape" concept had always been "vote for all civilized people." In 1978, the Progressive Party finally changed to support universal adult franchise on a common voter's roll.[15]

The Progressive Party now represented the only respectable white option in what was an increasingly wide cleavage between the races. The evolution and continued presence of Helen Suzman, as the sole parliamentary member of the Progressive Party throughout the next era of South African politics, represented the ultimate possibility of a multiracial South Africa.

Helen Suzman was born in Germiston, a mining town just outside of Johannesburg on November 7, 1917, the date she points out, of the Russian Revolution.[16] She was the younger by four years of two girls. Her father, Samuel Gavronsky, had immigrated to South Africa in 1904 when aged seventeen, from a shtetl in Lita near the Latvian border. He had no formal education beyond what was available in the shtetl but became literate in English in South Africa. Together with his elder brother Oscar, he developed a successful cattle and hide business. A total of eight brothers eventually came to South Africa, several of whom worked in the family business that also included a soap factory. Helen's mother died soon after her birth, and she was raised initially by Oscar's wife who was also her mother's sister. Her mother Frieda and aunt Hansa had settled in Kimberley after emigrating from a similar background as Sam Gavronsky. They spoke only Yiddish at home and Helen learned to understand but not speak it. When about five, the family moved to Berea, then a lower-middle-class suburb of Johannesburg. She recalls that there was not a single book in the house. She would long to read as soon as she was able to do so around six or seven. All she could find would be a newspaper or the *Zionist Record*.

Her father remarried when Helen was nine, now to a socially minded Jewish woman who had come to South Africa from England. They moved to a large house in Parktown, the fashionable suburb. As Catholic schools were more willing than Anglican ones to take Jews, she was enrolled in Parktown Convent School starting at age ten. She entered University of Witwatersrand but left before graduation and married at age nineteen to Mosie Suzman, an eminent physician fourteen years her senior. After war service, he became a senior physician at the Johannesburg General Hospital. He was the second youngest son of a family whose father had immigrated in 1889 to found the largest wholesale tobacco company in the country.

She did not recall any discussion about the family background, nor was Judaism a relevant part of her upbringing other than family gatherings for the holidays and attendance at High Holiday services from which she was excused. Yet she felt that her knowledge of the Jewish experience of persecution heightened her awareness of the evils of racial discrimination. She also attributed to her father a commitment to hard work.[6]

She was living the life of a privileged white South African housewife before going back to Wits and eventually becoming, in 1945, a lecturer in economic history. One of her students was Joe Slovo. She became interested in politics and joined the executive council of the Institute of Race Relations. It was her experience in doing work on behalf of the Fagan Commission in 1948 that that brought her into politics. Smuts accepted the recommendation of the commission that there be recognition of the permanent urbanization of black people as a result of the industrialization during the war with the need for adequate housing and other arrangements. This recommendation was rejected by the Nationalist government when it came to power in 1948.

Suzman became involved in United Party organizational politics and in 1952 was the candidate of that party from the northern suburb of Houghton. It was a silk-stocking safe United Party seat with a large Jewish constituency. She was returned for the next thirty-six years, starting in 1961 as a Progressive. Her overriding concern throughout her career was race discrimination. From 1961 to 1974, she was alone in representing her party in Parliament. Her position provided the only way that information detrimental to the apartheid policies of the government could be reported and published. She managed to mitigate some of the excesses of the prisons.

In March 1960, a pass-burning protest took place called by the Pan-African Congress (PAC) the Black Nationalist group that had split off from the ANC. The police shot at those protesting at Sharpeville near Johannesburg and Langa near Cape Town. This "Sharpeville Massacre' had enormous damaging repercussions for South Africa's image abroad with withdrawal of investments and expatriation of capital. It led to a further degree of repression in South Africa itself. A state of emergency was declared, and both the ANC and PAC banned. All meetings were banned, and hundreds were imprisoned.

After the banning of the ANC in 1960, the decision to move to armed resistance was taken by Nelson Mandela. He went underground in 1961, living on a farm purchased by his friends in a place called Rivonia just to the north outside of Johannesburg. The sabotage campaign continued to no great effect aside from providing the justification for the passage of the Sabotage Act, giving wide powers to the minister of justice. It was a legal suppression of due process and a big step toward the police state that South Africa was becoming. The Congress of Democrats was banned in 1962 as were a number of leftist publications. The attack was directed against the whites supporting the black resistance.

The ANC along with the Communist Party made the transition toward the sponsorship of a military organization called Umkhonto we Sizwe (Spear of the Nation in the Zulu language) whose initials were MK. The decision to move to guerrilla war was being debated at Rivonia when the meeting was interrupted by the police raid.[17] The trial of those arrested along with Nelson Mandela resulted in life imprisonment for Mandela along with others. The five white defendants were all Jews. The term *Rivonia's Children* refers to the idea that the raid and the resultant trial destroyed the dream of revolution, the idea of benign radicalism and was coincident with the regime entering into an era of brutality and repression for the next generation.

Although not the most significant of the defendants, Denis Goldberg was the only white among those who were to pay a high price.[18] Denis Goldberg was the son of prominent political activists. He describes himself as a *red diaper baby*.[19] He came from a family where involvement in political activity was taken for granted. Both parents were born in the East End of London although the paternal grandparents had emigrated from Lita. A Socialist from his early years, Goldberg's father joined the merchant marine during World War I as an alternative to fighting in an imperialist war. The report of the Bolshevik Revolution 1917 was, for him, the turning point of his life. He remained in the merchant marine until settling in South Africa in 1929. He was active in trade union work and political work.

Born in 1933, the younger of two brothers, Denis grew up in Cape Town and was the first in his family to attend university. From boyhood, he was interested in the great engineering projects and was in a degree course in civil engineering at the University of Cape Town. He eventually decided that one could not be an apolitical civil engineer in an apartheid society. All decisions seemed political including the need to build a railroad station on the basis of apartheid. The platforms did not follow engineering principles but on the basis that black lines had to go to black townships and white lines to white townships. After graduation in 1955, he was fired from his jobs because of his political work. He was active in the Congress of the People and the Congress of Democrats.[20] He was an early member of MK and involved in the training of recruits. One of the first camps was set up under his leadership in December 1962.[21] Evidence was presented at the trial that he had visited a number of places in Cape Town to buy materials to be used in the making of explosives and was found guilty.

As a white, he remained in a separate prison from Mandela and the others convicted. He was released in an amnesty in 1985 and eventually went to Britain where he lived with his wife and family. He originally came to Israel where his daughter lived in a kibbutz. The other black defendants remained imprisoned in Robben Island until the changes that took place under the Nationalist government in late 1989-1990. At that same time, the bans were lifted that had been placed on the ANC, the Communist Party, and the Pan-African Congress (PAC). Soon thereafter in 1991, the last vestiges of apartheid were legislated out of existence.[22]

Several of the white defendants in the *Rivonia Trial* were acquitted of the charges; others such as Lionel Bernstein escaped. He was on bail for another charge when he and his wife Hilda escaped and went into exile in Britain. Their books and those of others dealing with their imprisonment were important testaments.[23] The book by Albie Sachs, the son of Solly Sachs, became particularly well-known. The police state became the norm. The ANC and the Communist supporters had lost their battle. Any leftist illusions as to the nature of the government had been stripped away. Nevertheless, their influence was profound in the long run. The fact that even a small number of whites was willing to put aside their privileged status and fight alongside blacks for racial justice meant to some such as Mandela the possibility that people should not be judged merely on their skin color.[24] Future battles will arise in South Africa in the 1970s with the Soweto students refusal to have Afrikaans as the language of instruction. Armed resistance came about once again in the 1980s eventually supported by the transfer of the countries surrounding South Africa to African rule and the international isolation of South Africa. Exile in the meantime became a major characteristic of politically active South African Jews as well as the leadership of the ANC.

Having temporarily left the country in 1963, Slovo was not caught up in the Rivonia arrests. He remained abroad, eventually in Mozambique, building up the ANC military wing to which the Communist Party had joined, becoming its chief of staff and the first white to serve on its national executive of the ANC. After contributing to a multiracial transition, Slovo served as minister of housing in the first Mandela government before dying of cancer soon after. In an address to the Jewish Board of Deputies in 1994, he described his religious upbringing as connected to a moral code but it was his Yiddish secular culture that he found his roots.[25]

In 1965, in a self-congratulatory survey of the Jewish community, the author pointed out its great continued success.[26] Given the threat that had seemed inherent in a Nationalist victory, the efforts of the Jewish Board of Deputies had been to develop a reapprochement with those in power. The anti-Semitism that had pervaded the Nationalist rhetoric of the 1930s had seemingly waned somewhat in the name of white solidarity. The Jewish population could no longer be replenished from abroad with the destruction in the Holocaust of the East European reservoir from which it had drawn. Those remnants of European Jewry that remained had not been welcome to South Africa. Indeed some of the support for Israel that had continued under the Nationalist government had been predicated on its value for absorbing immigrants clearly not welcome in South Africa. There were some similarities that the Nationalists chose to see in the fight by Israel for its survival and in its *apartheid* character. The Zionists disputed being so characterized but in a chary fashion. Dr. Malan was welcomed in appearances at Jewish organizations after he made positive statements following a trip to Israel in 1953 and enabled transmittal of funds to aid Israel. It was a double-edged sword in that the Nationalists then held South African Jewry responsible for Israeli opposition to South Africa's apartheid policies in international forums.[27]

The Jewish population had reached its zenith in the range of 118,000. The small communities in the country areas were dwindling away. The drift to the towns was part of a more general phenomenon of South Africa. There had been a transfer of communal leadership to the acculturated generation born in South Africa. Yet there had been maintenance of the religious structure as well as the full range of communal organizations including the development after 1953, of a system of Jewish day schools. What was not discussed in this review was the ever-present issue of race. Although Jews as a group were more positive about blacks than other whites, most Jews were beneficiaries of the ongoing prosperity based on low-paid black labor.

However throughout this period between 1948 and mid-1960s there had been a series of trials and progressively more repressive laws, banning political activities that opposed apartheid. In all these trials, the whites involved had been predominantly Jews. On every level, whether literary, political, or by violent means, the concern for the welfare of the poor—derived from the religious background brought from their roots in Lita—still found expression despite repression in the arid soil of South Africa. Individual Jews more than other whites felt an incompatibility with the righteousness of the racism of the Afrikaner government. In the racist ordering of South African society, the Jewish community as a whole felt threatened; it could be indicted by the Afrikaner government on the basis of some of its members.

The Jewish Board of Deputies throughout this era took the stance that it could not, qua Jewish community, deal with the fundamental moral issue of racial discrimination. Their concern, they said, was preservation of full rights for Jews as members of the white community and the unhindered free existence of a Jewish communal life in which Zionism was central. The actions of Israel at the United Nations in support of sanctions against apartheid were punished by restricting the export to Israel of funds from South Africa in 1961. Hence Zionism and the relations of the South African government to Israel became hostage to the demand of Jewish activists that the board take a more active stand based upon the moral precepts of prophetic Judaism.[28]

Although many radicals and white liberals were Jews, it is equally true that not many Jews were liberals and radicals. There was clearly a divergence between the "communal" more conservative Jews and those who normally remained distant from the Jewish community. The latter were more likely to arise from a tradition as human beings conditioned by their experience as members of a group that has a memory of oppression. In international circles, foremost among those who remained in South Africa to express that moral dilemma was Nadine Gordimer whose writing reflected the transitions in attitude during this era.

South African Literature

Nadine Gordimer was born in 1923, the younger of two daughters, in Springs, a mining town in the East Rand. It had a population, in 1970, of approximately a hundred thousand, 40 percent white. First coal and then gold mining led to an unlovely landscape of mining dumps. At one time, it was considered "the largest single gold mining district in the world." Gordimer wanted to escape and came to Johannesburg where she found a lively cosmopolitan atmosphere. She came to know the black writers associated with the magazine *Drum*. As a white child growing up in South Africa, she described how she came only very slowly to begin to be aware of the African people around her.[29]

Her father, Isadore Gordimer, was a watchmaker who owned a jewelry store in Springs. He had come from Lita at age thirteen just before the Boer War to join his elder brother. Gordimer was made to feel as though he had married above his station in life. His background was never discussed except to be disparaged. He was one of twelve children and brought his nine sisters out to South Africa. Nadine's mother, Nan Meyers, had been born in England of Jewish immigrants settled there for several generations. She came to South Africa at age six with her parents and grew up in Johannesburg. Gordimer describes her father's relatives as strangers. Speaking Afrikaan, they lived in the countryside in Orange Free State. Her mother's family, on the other hand, lived in nearby Johannesburg and was very much part of their lives. Nevertheless, looking back, she identifies—as an adult—with her father. She is short, like her father. She wishes she knew more about his life. Being Jewish was something she was. Given her mother's attitude, they never went to synagogue nor were they involved with the Jewish community in other ways. She attributed her interest and support for the black struggle to her identity as a South African rather than anything specifically Jewish.[30]

She started writing at age nine. She attended a convent school in her town but was kept at home for her health on the pretext of a heart ailment the year she was eleven. She blamed her mother for making her into a "delicate" child unnecessarily. From then until she was sixteen, she was tutored privately. She had no contact with other children and took on the role of an alien observer. Her education as a writer was her intense reading. She spent only a brief time, at age twenty-two, at the University of Witwatersrand as a "general student" since she did not qualify for university entrance. It was then that she first encountered blacks. She married twice with a child in each marriage, first a daughter and then a son. Her first husband was a physician from a Jewish family in Johannesburg and a cousin of Helen Suzman. As a divorcee, she married in 1955 a man from an internationally known German Jewish family. An art dealer, he became head of the Sotheby's branch in South Africa.[31]

She began to publish short stories in the 1940s. Her first novel, in 1953, had the heroine a curious spectator of the world of the blacks. Her second, *A World of Strangers,* in 1958 reflected the unofficial racial mixing in an officially segregated world, the meeting of whites and blacks as humans at a frontier that was not easily crossed, the "no man's land between the black encampment and the white." That has been the theme of her work lasting throughout the apartheid era. She has stayed in South Africa to write about it, but she has done so without being directly affected by the oppressive regime. Like her characters, she has gone on observing. Her detachment was marked in her early stories where her role was as a narrator.[32]

This sense of detachment became less evident as she evolved in the context of her life as a South African. The liberalism of the 1950s ended with the Sharpeville Massacre in 1960 followed by the state of emergency and the outlawing of the black organizations and the exile of the black intellectuals. Gordimer's work during the 1960s dealt with the decline of liberalism, both white and black, and the risks of underground activities in the aftermath of the more and more stringent application of Apartheid. In the 1970s, her work deals with the eventual repossession of the land by the

Africans. *Burger's Daughter*, published in 1979, best illustrates her recurrent theme of "the human conflict between the desire to live a personal, private life and the rival claim of special responsibility to one's fellow men."[33] The heroine, Rosa, is the daughter of a white Communist who has died in jail while serving a life sentence for political activity. She is part of the family ethos where discipline and selflessness as well as austerity are obligatory. She escapes to France to lead a private life but eventually returns to South Africa. The heroine eventually is imprisoned on a political charge in the context of the Soweto Children Uprising of 1976.[34]

The government banned several of Gordimer's books; for example, *Burger's Daughter* was banned for several months after its publication as "obscene, blasphemous, pernicious in the area of race relations . . . and as detrimental to the security of the state." On the other end of the spectrum, radicals would attack her for writing about blacks when she was a white, living in an apartheid society that protected her and her kind. She claims herself to be a radical and disclaims identification with liberals and identified with the ANC at a time when it was an outlawed organization.[35]

South African Exiles

By 1970, the Jewish population remained static circa 116-120,000. The distribution of population remained the same with 65 percent in Transvaal, 28 percent in Cape Province and 6 percent in Natal. Fewer lived in Orange Free State than in 1911. There was a far higher percentage in professional and managerial occupations than the other whites along with a far higher percentage trained in universities. There has been a diminution in rate of population increase in each successive decade, becoming essentially static. The reasons include not only the cessation of immigration and the low birth rate but emigration. There has been ongoing emigration to Israel that was far greater than from other English-speaking countries, second only to Argentina and Russia. One-third of the children living abroad were in Israel. There was also emigration to other English-speaking countries such as Britain and the United States. The erosion of Jewish communal life in South Africa occurred because of emigration, seeking a broader intellectual life as well as the political issues. This emigration has tended to include persons who are relatively young. There is thus a continued trend toward a far larger number of those over sixty as compared to the general white population as well as toward those born in South Africa.[36]

The emigration to Israel was particularly significant because it continued to partake of a degree of idealism that provided an alternative for Jewish youth. Hashomer Hatzair eventually dissolved, in part because its socialism was deemed incompatible with South African government policy.[37] The Habonim movement remained leading to participation in pioneer training in the 1950s and as late as 1960.

The centrality of Zionism as well as Orthodoxy to South African Jewry is illustrated by the trajectory of the Katzenellbogen/Rosenstein family from Lita.

Joel Isaac Katznellenbogen was chief rabbi of a number of small Lithuanian towns, including Neustadt-Sigind from which so many South African Jews had come. One of his sons died in the famous cholera epidemic in Vilna in 1871. The widow continued to manage the family's famous bookstore and publishing house. In turn, one of their sons, Mordecai, continued the publishing of religious books and selling books as well as maintaining a literary discussion group in Vilna. In 1906, one of Mordecai's daughters, Sonya, married Boris (Baruch) Rosenstein who had originated from Bialystok. Their son, Emmanuel, born in Vilna in 1909, came to Cape Town in 1926 at age seventeen to work in the bookstore run by his maternal uncle Beinkenstadt in District Six. Traveling from Danzig to London, he followed the common pattern of remaining in the Jews' Temporary Shelter in London before boarding a Castle Line ship. He eventually trained as a bookkeeper. After several unsuccessful business ventures in Johannesburg, he bought a large and successful cement and tile works that he continued to run with a fellow Litvak until it was sold in 1968.

Emmanuel married, in 1938, a woman born in South Africa whose family had emigrated from Minsk in Belorussia. They settled in the fashionable seaside suburb of Sea Point near Cape Town. Their home was based on traditional Judaism with candles on Friday nights, keeping kashrut and celebrating Passover and the High Holidays. They were otherwise nonobservant members of the Orthodox synagogue in Sea Point. One of their interests was membership in the bowls club. The several colored servants who ran the household were treated with kindness, and the children were raised to respect all people regardless of color. Although not active in politics, they were opposed to the Nationalists and voted for the United Party, but not the Progressive Party of Helen Suzman.

Zionism was a strong factor in their family of four children. The two daughters both emigrated to Israel. The elder son remained in Cape Town as an accountant after attending the Christian Brothers School. The younger son, Neil, born in 1938, trained as a physician at University of Cape Town after also attending the Christian Brothers School and a local heder after school. Unlike his siblings and his parents, he became an observant Jew. He enrolled in the religious Zionist youth group, Bnai Akiva, where he met his wife. After interning in Israel in 1968-69, he moved to the United States where he has been a general surgeon as well as an ardent geneologist with particular expertise in the rabbinic dynasties. Committed to raising his family in an Orthodox setting, he has lived in the model Orthodox community of Elizabeth, New Jersey. Of his five sons, all trained in the yeshivot in their hometown, and the four eldest also attended yeshivot in Israel. The eldest lived in Israel, working with computers; another was an Orthodox rabbi, the first in the family since the death of Reb Joel Isaac in 1890; another studied in a *kollel* in Jerusalem in the same way as his ancestors did in the Jerusalem of Lita.[38]

The story of many families was that of emigration from South Africa of the generation that came of age in the postwar period in light of the actions of the Nationalist government under apartheid. Emigration to other English-speaking countries as well as Israel was the pattern during the 1970s. Coupled with the move abroad was the prior move from the smaller towns on the Rand to Johannesburg.

One such family was the Judakers who had originated in Lita on a farm and mill that remained in the family until the start of World War II. The patriarch of the family remained in Lita but visited in 1932 his children, now all transplanted to South Africa. Joseph Lazarus, the eldest son, was born in 1896. In later life, he fondly recalled his life on the farm, herding sheep and caring for the livestock. He attended the local heder and later studied at a nearby Yeshiva before emigrating to South Africa in 1913 when seventeen. His choice of South Africa was conditioned by the existence of an uncle who had emigrated earlier. Joseph was ultimately responsible for the arrival in South Africa of all his siblings who settled in various towns along the Rand such as Witbank and Johannesburg as well as Port Elizabeth on the Eastern Cape. One sister moved to Israel after only a short time in South Africa. An unmarried brother living in the mining town of Springs on the East Rand was a Yiddish writer. One of his published stories dealt with his own life running a concession store near the mines.

Joseph was the head of his extended family. He settled in Germiston immediately east of Johannesburg on the gold reef. The town was the largest railway junction in South Africa and is now near to the Jan Smuts International Airport. It was also the site of the largest gold refinery in the world. Its population was about two hundred thousand in 1971, slightly more than a third were white. Joseph had several businesses including a haberdashery before selling out in 1936 to manage his real estate interests, mainly commercial property. He died in 1968 in an auto accident.

He married Esther in 1925 who had been born in London's East End in 1900 to immigrant parents from Lita. She had come with her parents to Boksburg on the Reef east of Johannesburg in 1911. Her sister joined Esther in Germiston after marrying the man who ran the Bon Marche store. The Judaker family belonged to the local synagogue and contributed as a matter of course to all the Jewish organizations but were particularly active in the charitable Helping Hand Society. Esther spoke Yiddish fluently, having learned it from her parents. She was active in supporting Jewish charities such as the Jewish Orphanage and Old Age Home. She competed each year and was, one year, a member of the winning team in the South African National Championship as well as, for a term, president of the Southern Transvaal Lawn Bowling Association.

Joseph and Esther lived modestly with a nursemaid when the children were young. Of their three sons. the eldest, born in 1926 was a lawyer in Johannesburg. The youngest, born in 1932 was also a lawyer, first in Johannesburg then in Cape Town. The middle son Leonard, born in 1930, went to the local school where he participated in all sports including rugby, cricket, and soccer and organized the local branch of the Revisionist Betar Zionist youth group. Having been imbued with his father's stories of life on the family farm in Lita, Leonard's interest was to attend an Agricultural College. Unable to attend there, he got a business and accounting degree at the University of Witswatersand. He managed a dairy farm owned by his father near Johannesburg before then becoming a real estate entrepreneur like his father.

Married in 1957, to Betty, they lived luxuriously in Sandston, a wealthy suburb of Johannesburg with their four children. During the 1970s, there was continual talk among Jewish families about emigrating for their future and the future of their children. Despite the inclination of his wife, Leonard wished to leave while his children were young so that they could grow up in their new country. On the basis of his diamond business, he managed to get a visa to the United States. The family moved to Los Angeles in 1978. He chose that place because he knew a family there and the similarity of its climate to that of South Africa. His wife later returned to South Africa, but he and his children have become Americans. He has continued his interest in his family's origins in Lithuania and has managed to reacquire the original family farm there.[39]

There was an entire school of writers in exile. The most prominent of the South African writers working elsewhere was Daniel Jacobson. He became one of the leading British writers as well as retaining his South African and Lithuanian roots. Daniel Jacobson was born in Johannesburg in 1929. His father, Hyman, had come from Latvia and his mother, Leibe, from Lithuania. The maternal grandfather was the rabbi of the shtetl in Lithuania. Invited to come to Cleveland in the United States, he went there in an exploratory journey but returned home. He saw in America the abandonment of the commandments that had formed his life in Lithuania. His death in 1919 enabled the family to leave.

The maternal grandmother, Jacobson's mother and her siblings emigrated to South Africa after the death of the grandfather. Jacobson's mother had been the eldest and was permitted to take private lessons in German and Russian as well as Hebrew. For a short time after arriving in South Africa, she had pursued her education but soon married.

Jacobson was the third of four children and the youngest son. When he was four, the family moved to Kimberley in the diamond district. Jacobson 's sense of landscape derived from his growing up at the edge of the desert. Kimberley, resurrected as "Lyndhurst," has been the site of many of his South African stories. His father had set up a butter and ice factory there. His mother had been very close to her siblings, and Jacobson visited with them in Johannesburg.

He received his education at the University of Witwatersrand, graduating in 1948. He then traveled in Israel to live on a kibbutz and then to England before returning to South Africa in 1951. He began writing in 1953 and then married a non-Jewish woman of British ancestry and moved to London. He has lived in the United States and England since, teaching at various universities but mainly at the University of London.

He describes South Africa as stifling both in its political and cultural terrain. His early writing was set in the semiarid Karoo, the area around Kimberley where he had grown up. He explored the impact of the character of the country on its people, their narrowness and bitterness.[40]His long novel in 1966 *The Beginners* is a saga of three generations of Jewish immigrants and emigrants from South Africa. They must uproot themselves and go to Israel or England in a story that replicates the experience of his own generation. It is the epic culmination of his career as a South African novelist. Many of his protagonists are Jews. In his work, he exposes, like Nadine Gordimer, the helpless and not-quite-honest stance of the South African liberal.[41] Recently, he continued to explore his Lithuanian as well as his South African roots in *Heschel's Kingdom*. He searches for the maternal grandfather whose opportune death saved his mother and her siblings from the Holocaust.[42]

Growing up, Lithuania had seemed to him like a "nowhere" full of hunger and pogroms. His maternal grandmother had been a modern woman, chafing under her religious husband but after arrival in South Africa had become ultrareligious. Her children all abandoned the rules of religion that had seemed so important to their father and now to their mother. He described the transition in South Africa of his mother's eight siblings to a variety of activities including psychoanalysis and even the Nationalist Party. Jacobson, traveling in Lithuania with his own grown son, began to appreciate the existence that had provided the religious structure of his grandparents he had never been able to integrate into his own experience.

Among those who chose exile were not only radicals but many of those who had been hounded out of South Africa in the recurrent arrests. One of those who reflected the actions of many was Ronald Segal who developed and maintained the character of a nonracial South Africa in London. The exiles also reflected the ambiguity of the response of Jews qua Jews to the moral dilemma.

Ronald Segal was born in 1932, the youngest by far of four children, in Cape Town where his father was chairman of the Cape Jewish Board of Deputies. His maternal grandfather had come from Lita to Cape Town at the end of the nineteenth century, settling in Luderitz in South West Africa, then under German control. He came to own a large amount of property in that country. His mother, the eldest, had grown up in Cape Town and was particularly interested in Zionism. His father had come alone to Cape Town as a boy of nine and had a store which later became part of a large nationwide chain, selling to working-class customers. They lived in Fresnaye, one of the fashionable Cape Town suburbs overlooking the sea.

Precocious and argumentative, Segal endured the taunts of schoolmates but maintained his sense of self by his reading and movies. He went to the University of Cape Town where he first learned about the ability of others, including people of colour, to affect his thinking. He became involved in student politics in what was the still a place where nonwhites could enroll.[43] After living in Europe and the United States in pursuit of a graduate degree in English, he decided to return to South Africa in 1956. Using the bequest of a relatively small amount of money from his father's estate, he founded a magazine called *Africa South* with distribution in Britain and the United States as well as at home. Its goal was to provide an intellectual forum, bringing together the various opponents of apartheid. He had the support of the ANC as well as white liberal forces. He managed to continue to publish while the political environment was becoming more and more threatening. He saw the increased powers accorded the government in the name of necessity becoming the road to the police state that South Africa eventually became.

He was involved along with many others in the Treason Trial Defense Fund led by the archbishop of Johannesburg. Although never a Communist, Segal was banned under the Suppression of Communism Act. He was forced to leave South Africa with the crackdown after Sharpeville in 1960. Living in London, he eventually became an editor of a series of books by South African writers.

Among his most biting attacks was on the Jewish community and its willingness to abdicate any responsibility toward a stand against apartheid. The case of Rabbi Ungar was a cause celebre that *Africa South* published. He was a young American-born rabbi of the Port Elizabeth Congregation whose article, "The Abdication of a Community," described the fright and the withdrawal of his congregants occasioned by his sermons attacking government policy. In general, the action of the Board of Deputies and the various rabbis was in inverse relation to the harshness of apartheid. It was most timid during the era when the ideological stance of the government was most obvious in its implementation of the removal of the nonwhites from the cities, the bulldozing of their homes, and the transfer to the townships. Although their resolutions were clearly liberal in their connotation, they were fearful of going beyond the rhetoric that was emanating gradually from the more enlightened Nationalist camp. This became more clear-cut and insistent in the 1980s as a more pragmatic approach began to appear among some of the Nationalists in doing away with the restrictions in light of economic considerations. Several of the rabbis, particularly those from the *Reform* or *Progressive* camp, expressed their condemnation of government policies. Many chose exile in Israel or elsewhere.[44] Although Jews remained the bulwark of the center-left parties such as the Progressive Party, there were some who supported the mainstream National Party now flanked on its right by breakaway segments that were even more openly anti-Semitic.

Zionism and connection to Israel was central to South African Jewry. For many, Israel was the place for refuge for their children. Relations between the two countries had been strained because of Israeli support of United Nations votes in favor of sanctions

against South Africa. In response, the South African government
blocked transfer of funds raised by the Zionist organization.
The response to the internal situation by the Jewish community
were constrained by the fact that connection between Pretoria
and Jerusalem had become close after the 1967 Six-Day War and
even more after 1973 Yom Kippur War when the African nations
that Israel had been cultivating broke relations.[45] The Pretoria-
Jerusalem axis placed the Jewish community in the vise between
the demands, particularly of its youth, to take a moral stand
against the government policy, its own fear of black nationalism
and the newfound alignment of the Afrikaner government with
its own civic religion of Zionism.

A survey of South African Jewry published in 1984 reflected the
nature of the changes as well as ongoing characteristics evident
during the two previous decades. Emigration continued with a peak
in 1977-78 immediately after the Soweto riots and the resultant
government reaction. The overall result has been a continued fall in
the young adult group most likely to propagate. The large number
of Jews in the educated and professional as well as managerial
class continued throughout this period with particularly heavy
representation in those emigrating among the educated.

An example of the exodus of the educated to elsewhere in the
English-speaking world is the Seimon family. Born in 1899 in Lita,
Solly Seimon came to South Africa aged eleven with his teacher
in 1910. His parents and siblings followed in the next years. He
settled in Krugersdorp, a town west of Johannesburg on the Rand.
Named after President Kruger whose statue adorns the town, it is
a pleasant town with parks and trees. Its economy was based on
the gold mines with a population in 1970 approximately eighty-
five thousand, one third white. Seimon married, in the 1920s,
Sophie Braude who had been born in South Africa of immigrant
parents. His crowning achievement was the building of the Hotel
Majestic in the town.

There were three children. The eldest, a daughter, born in
1928, married a pharmacist in Krugersdorp. One of their sons
has remained in Krugersdorp in the family business. Another
moved to Johannesburg as a physician. The youngest son also
lived in Johannesburg where he worked with computers. The
youngest child of the first South African generation, also a

daughter, married a man who ran a bottle store, selling liquor in Krugersdorp. Of their children, one son was a lawyer in Johannesburg; another ran a bottle store while the eldest son, an orthopedic surgeon, joined his uncle Leonard in the United States in 1993.

The son, Leonard was born in 1933. He went to the public high school in Krugersdorp before his medical training at the University of the Witswatersand. After advanced training in the United Kingdom, he settled in Durban where he married Sandra Kaye. Her father, born Sidney Kowalski, had been an accountant for the milling firm making Jungle Oats. Sandra's mother had been a nurse. Sandra attended Durban Girls College, an Anglican school and then the University of Natal. Leonard and Sandra had children. In Durban, all four children attended the Jewish day school, the two girls switching to the Durban Girls College like their mother. Leonard, an orthopedic surgeon, moved with his family to the New York area in 1978 where they have lived since. Sandra's sister and her family moved to the United Kingdom in 1976 but have since moved back to South Africa. Sandra's younger brother and his family also emigrated to the United States in 1988 continuing the persistent pattern of emigration.[46]

The trend toward life in the major urban centers has continued with two-thirds of the Jews now living in Transvaal in the Johannesburg area. Within each of the cities, patterns of residential clustering continued with the northern suburbs of Johannesburg and Sea Point area of Cape Town prime examples.[47] The Jewish Board of Deputies contained representatives of virtually every communal organization and also publishes the monthly *Jewish Affairs*. Starting in 1949, the board established the United Communal Fund to raise money for its own activities along with the Jewish Board of Education responsible for Jewish day schools. The latter has particularly proliferated in tune with a "national-cultural" model which emphasized Zionism and the Hebrew language in reaction to the "national Christian" character of the state schools. The unique quality of the South African Zionist Federation, its deep and widespread roots within South African Jewry has continued. The Israel United Appeal reached 90 percent of South African Jews to a degree unique in the world.[48]

The structure of Anglo-Jewry is reflected in the title of chief rabbi although the incumbent does not have the authority that has traditionally been vested in the British counterpart. The *Orthodoxy* to which the majority adheres also partakes of the British model. The majority of adherents are *nonobservant Orthodox* again in the British model. This model is also compatible with the *Orthodox* mitnagdim tradition of the Litvak. The synagogue has represented the unity of the Jewish community and a large percentage are members, albeit attendance, is limited to the High Holidays and to participation in seder at Passover. The Federation of Synagogues formed in 1933 has achieved a degree of coordination among the seventy or so *Orthodox* congregations in the areas outside of Cape Town. The Western Cape has its own organization called the Cape United Council of Orthodox Hebrew Congregations. Each has its own beth din that functions in the traditional mode in dealing with issues of kashrut, divorce, and conversions.[49]

South African Transition

The 1980s saw a transition to a more open society. The commitment of the ANC to its foundations in the 1950's and its Freedom Charter was highly problematical in light of the more radical black students that had taken control of the movement within South Africa. The old alliance between radicals who happened to be Jews was in the name of universalism. The organizations of Jews for Justice (JFJ) and Jews for Social Justice (JSJ) in Cape Town and Johannesburg respectively reflected the social justice basis of Judaism but did so in terms of their Judaism rather than a role in the universalism of Socialism. Their activities provided some credibility to a role for Jews qua Jews in the new multiracial South Africa.[50]

Contributing to the solution of the unique problem of establishing a transition to a democratic multiracial South Africa has been the extraordinary Truth and Reconciliation Commission (TRC). A forerunner was the Goldstone Commission chaired by Richard Goldstone that dealt with the violence of all segments of South Africa in the period just prior to the elections of 1994 that marked the political transition to the installation of Mandela as president.

Richard Goldstone was born in 1938 in Boksburg, one of the older gold—and coal-mining towns along the Rand between Germiston and Springs. It contains the largest gold mine in the world as well as a number of other factories. Its population in 1970 was approximately 120,000, with one-third being white. His parents had been born in South Africa and his grandparents had come there as children from Lita. He attributed his interest in law to his maternal grandfather near whom he lived as a youngster in Johannesburg. This grandfather encouraged Goldstone to learn about language as well as play chess. Goldstone went to the King Edward VII School in Johannesburg in the British model and then to University of Witwatersrand. While there, he had the opportunity for the first time to meet as fellow students who were blacks whose lives were different from his. He became active in student organizations to oppose these injustices. The fight was particularly against the government's actions in segregating the university system to erase just those opportunities for interracial communication. In 1957, he was a delegate from the National Union of South African Students (NUSAS) to the interracial and international meetings of the World University Service. In his role as a student leader, he also came in contact with those opposing apartheid at meetings at the home of the Anglican Bishop of Johannesburg such as the ANC, the Congress of Democrats, and the South African Indian Congress.

Nevertheless, his last two years of law school were focused on his career. After graduation in 1962 and marriage, he entered a life of lucrative practice of commercial law. The independent judiciary existed in South Africa; and appointments could, at times, include even opponents of the apartheid regime. As a judge on the Transvaal Supreme Court starting in 1980, he would help ameliorate the laws he opposed. His opinion in a case dealing with the Group Areas Act found a basis for following a complicated administrative process rather than the almost automatic expulsions that had been carried out. This decision effectively undercut the entire effort of residential segregation that had been pursued since 1950. In still another case, the banning of literature relating to the ANC that included its Freedom Charter was overturned on the basis that the literature merely mirrored principles widely accepted throughout the world. In these several ways, Goldstone was a member of the judiciary undermining apartheid.

In the years 1985 to 1989, literally thousands of people including children were being held for indefinite periods under a state of emergency. Even more directly, although opposed to the entire system of detention, Goldstone exercised his prerogative as a judge to visit prisons unannounced. He would bring magazines, arrange for family visits, get new clothes for the prisoners.

He had, by 1990, been appointed to the Appellate Supreme Court. That same year, he began to take on a new role. He was appointed to carry out the judicial inquiry concerning police action in firing at a crowd in the township of Sebokeng. This massacre threatened to disrupt the start of negotiations between LeKlerk and Mandela in the spring of 1990. In carrying out this inquiry, the principle had been established of seeking and using evidence to make judgments that were open and clearly based on truth. There was to be no further coverup as had been the practice of the government that had led to the debasement of justice.

After a period of increased violence between all the political factions, a peace accord was established in September 1991. To insure its implementation, a commission was established that came to be called after Goldstone who was its chairperson. In the several years leading to 1994 and the inaugural of Mandela, it provided once again a model of inquiry that received acceptance as being fair and impartial. Indeed it led to the unmasking of the actions of security forces as well as the activities of the ANC and the Inkatha Freedom Party (IFP) that undermined the peace process. Some of the information uncovered made it difficult for those who had carried out abuses under apartheid to request a blanket amnesty as they had hoped. A compromise was reached that led to the formation of the Truth and Reconciliation Commission as an alternative to a blanket amnesty or to the trial and punishment sought by the victims.[51]

The story of the family of Mendel Kaplan exemplified the character of South African Jewry in the postwar generation. Their family pride as well as economic success was coupled with a commitment to the history of the Jewish community and the intellectual life derived from its ancestral roots in Lita. The Kaplan

Centre at University of Cape Town was founded in 1980 within the Department of Hebrew and Jewish Studies. One may recall that the original holder of the chair in Hebrew at the University of Cape Town was Rev. Bender with support from Sammy Marks.

Max Kaplan was born in 1876 in Kovno province. He arrived in Cape Town in 1904 having worked his passage as a sailor from Vladivostok. He had deserted from the Russian military in Siberia. His father was an itinerant preacher. Of the six children, five were to immigrate to South Africa. A blacksmith, he joined his elder brother in the scrap metal business in various sites near Cape Town. He worked mainly in repairing iron bedsteads. He married, in 1904, a fellow immigrant from the same area in Lita who had arrived shortly before. Three boys were born before the mother died of Bright's disease in 1913, and the family moved to Johannesburg, living in one of the worst slums. Desperately poor, Isaac (Ike), the eldest, remained in the Jewish Orphanage until age fourteen while the two younger boys lived with their father. Starting in 1918, Max began to make bedsteads but the business failed. He tried once again to make parts for iron stoves and then managed to construct Johannesburg's first machine to make chain link fencing called African Gate and Fence Works, but he died of heart disease in 1923.

Ike worked helping his father make gates before moving in 1922 to a small town in Transvaal, called Dullstrom, where he worked for an uncle until 1926. While there, he was introduced to literature and music, coming under the tutelege of an exiled educated Englishman. Ike was about to emigrate to Australia when he was hired to manage a general store in Parow, a town on the main rail line on the Cape. He eventually married one of the daughters of the Bloch family, also from Lita, who owned the store. Married in 1933 in the Roelands Street Synagogue in Cape Town, there were two sons born to Ike and his wife, Jessie—Mendel in 1936 and Robert in 1939.

In 1929, Ike started what was to be the family business, the Cape Gate and Wire Works. He initially used methods patterned after the workshop established by his father, Max, earlier in the decade. Ike's younger brother and brother-in-law joined him in the struggle to maintain the business during the Depression.

Initially all the materials had to be imported. The government-owned South African Iron and Steel Works became a source of locally made steel in 1934. The machines they used to make chain link were made by the partners from scrap metal.

The company prospered during World War II and expanded during the post-War period in Parow. The Jewish community in the town had grown to eighty families and built their first synagogue in 1950. The family moved to a Wynberg, a fashionable suburb in Cape Town so that the boys could go to the boys high school there. Mendel graduated from the University of Cape Town in 1959 in economics and law, went to Columbia in New York for a MBA before joining the family firm. The times were not propitious in 1960 during the Depression after the riots at Sharpeville. Robert graduated in 1960 before following his brother at Columbia and joined the family firm, in 1962, now expanded to both Parow and Transvaal. A strong sense of responsibility to his father and the family was the determinant.

During the 1960s, in the wake of the establishment of South Africa as a Republic, Cape Gate and Wire was able to expand by buying manufacturing facilities owned in the Transvaal by foreign companies anxious to leave South Africa. The expansion in their product line and degree of vertical integration of their company was associated with increased wealth. The family became associated with a range of charities, investing in Israel as well as a role in establishing the Kaplan Centre at the University of Cape Town.[52] One of its recent activities has been the celebration of the actions of South African Jews in the Struggle for Democracy and Human Rights in South Africa that documented the role of subsequent generations of Jews in carrying on the traditions they brought from their roots in Lita.[53]

To an extraordinary degree, the Kaplan family represented the character of South African Jewry in their ongoing commitment to remaining in South Africa while maintaining both a connection to Israel and to their Jewish roots in Lita. It was difficult to be sanguine about the continuation of Jewish life in the "new" South Africa. However, to the extent that it remained consistent with its fundamental basis in the culture of Lita in maintaining its sense of community, it can retain its integrity and message for its compatriots.

Chronology of the Apartheid Generation

1948 Establishment of Israel/Recognition by United Party government of Jan Christian Smuts/ Henry Gluckman Minister of Health and Housing / Victory of Nationalist Party

1950s Suppression of Communism Act (SCA) used to control labor unions/ exile of Solly Sachs/Apartheid came into effect with segregation of education and the universities/ Cape Coloureds purged from voting rolls/ Non-violent Defiance Campaign/ white Congress of the People / Freedom Charter by African National Congress/ Arrest of supporters of Freedom Charter/ start of Treason Trial of Joe Slovo and Ruth First/ End of "Liberalism"

1960s Pan-African Congress called pass-burning protests./ Sharpeville Massacre/ State of Emergency/ PAC and ANC banned/ANC underground with program of sabotage MK/ Treason Trial ended with acquittal/ South Africa becomes Republic/ Congress of Democrats banned/ Progressive Party founded/ Rivonia raid and Tria/1 Denis Goldberg imprisoned / Joe Slovo in exile with ANC

1970s Progressive Party supportive of universal suffrage/ Helen Suzman sole member of Parliament/Soweto Children's Uprising / Police State/ Ruth First imprisoned, exiled and killed/ Emigration to Britain, USA, Israel/ Writers in Exile Dan Jacobson and Ronald Segal/ Gordimer's Burger's Daughter

1980s Transition to more open society/ Goldstone Commission/ Peace Accord/Mandela Government/Joe Slovo Minister of Housing

Notes

5.1 The Nature of the Place

1   John H. Wellington, *Southern Africa: A Geographical Study*, Cambridge, 1960, 203

2   T.R.H. Davenport, *South Africa: A Modern History*, Toronto, 1991, 26-31

3   ibid, 44-48

4   Donald Denoon and Balam Nyeko, *Southern Africa Since 1800*, London, 1984, 1-36, 62-71

5   T.R. H. Davenport, op cit 1991, 74-75

6   Louis Herrman, *A History of the Jews in South Africa from the Earliest Times to 1895*, Westport, CT, 1975, 235

7   Donald Denoon and Balam Nyeko, op cit, 1984, 85-95

8   Monica Wilson and Leonard Thompson, *The Oxford History of South Africa*, New York, 1971, 371

9   ibid, 135

10 T.R.H. Davenport, op cit, 1991, 88-98

11 ibid, 239-241

12 John H. Wellington, op cit, 1960, 212

13 Robert Davies, "Mining Capital, the State and Unskilled Whit Workers in South Africa, 1901-1913," *Journal of South African Studies*, 1976, 3:41.

14 Donald Denoon and Balam Nyeko, op cit, 1984, 96-107

15 T.R.H. Davenport, op cit, 1991, 75-87

16 Geoffrey Wheatcroft, *The Randlords*, London, 1985, 181

17 Norman Pollock and Swanzie Agnew, *A Historical Geography of South Africa*, London, 1963, 221

18 Gustav Saron and Louis Holtz, *The Jews in South Africa: A History*, Cape Town, 1955, 196-206 passim

19 Monica Wilson and Leonard Thompson, op cit, 1971, 367

20 Donald Denoon and Balam Nyeko op cit, 1984, 116-136

21 Leonard Thompson, *A History of South Africa*, New Haven, 1995, 112

22 Robert Ross, *A Concise History of South Africa*, Cambridge, 1999, 86

23 T.R.H. Davenport, op cit, 1991, 220-228

24 Belinda Bozzoli, "The Origins, Development and Ideology of Local Manufacturing in South Africa," *Journal of Southern Africa Studies*, 1975, 2:194

25 Gustav Saron and Louis Holtz, op cit, 1955, 212

26 Louis Herrmann, op cit, 1975, 1-8

27 Jack Simons and Ray Simons, *Class and Colour in South Africa, 1850-1950*, London, 1983, 68-69

28 Louis Herrman, "Cape Jewry before 1870," In Gustav Saron and Louis Holtz, Eds, *The Jews in South Africa: A History*, Cape Town, 1955, 10

29 Louis Hermann, op cit, 1975, 192-199

30 Louis Herrman, op cit, 1955, 10-16

31 Louis Herrman, op cit, 1975, 28-240

32 John Simon, "New Archival Material Relating to the Early Development of the South African Jewish Community," In Rueben Musiker and Joseph Sherman, Eds., *Waters Out of the Well*, Johannesburg, 1988

33 Louis Herrman, op cit, 1975, 262-264

34 Chaim Gershater, "From Lithuania to South Africa," In Gustav Saroon and Louis Holtz, Eds., op cit, 1955, 59-84

35 Eric Rosenthal, "On the Diamond Fields," In Gustav Saron and Loouis Holtz, Eds., op cit, 1955, 113

36 Louis Herrman, op cit, 1975, 237-238

37 Robert Mendelsohn, *Sammy Marks: The Uncrowned King of the Transvaal*, Cape Town, 1991, 197-214 passim

38 Aubrey Newman, personal communication 11/22/2001

39 Gustav Saron and Louis Holtz, op cit, 1955, 85

40 Gideon Shimoni, *Jews and Zionism: The South African Experience*, Cape Town, 1980, 6-7

41 Marcia Gitlin, *The Vision Amazing*, Johannesburg, 1950, 12

42 Gustav Saron, "The Making of South African Jewry," In Louis Feldberg, Ed., *South African Jewry, 1965 Edition*, Johannesburg, 1965

43 Daniel Elazar and Peter Medding, *Jewish Communities in Frontier Societies*, New York, 1984, 12-13

44 Milton Shain, *The Roots of Anti-Semitism in South Africa*, Charlottesville, 1994, 12-18

45 ibid, 19-26

46 ibid, 26-34

47 Joseph Sherman, *From a Land Far Off*, Cape Town, 1987, 196 note 18

48 Milton Shain, "Hoggenheimer, The Making of A Myth," *Jewish Affairs*, 1981, 36:112

49 Marcia Leveson, "The Jewish Stereotype in Some South African Fiction," In Reuben Musiker nad Joseph Sherman, Ed., op cit, 1988

50 Milton Shain, *Jewry and Cape Society*, Cape Town, 1983, 1-10

51 ibid, 45-56

52 Gustav Saron and Louis Holtz, op cit, 195, 86-104 passim

53 Diana Cammack, "The Politics of Discontent, The Grievances of the 'Uitlander' Refugees, 1899-1902," *Journal of Southern Africa Studies*, 1982, 8:243

54 Milton Shain, op cit, 1983, 15-45

55 ibid, 93-96

56 Gideon Shimoni, op cit, 1980, 5-6

57 Milton Shain, op cit, 1983, 75-86

58 Gustav Saron and Louis Holtz, op cit, 1955,257-269

59 Gideon Shimoni, op cit, 1980, 89

60 Gustav Saron, "The Cape Board of Deputies is 75 Years Old," *Jewish Affairs*, 1979, 34:57

61 Milton Shain, op cit, 1983, 15-20

62 ibid, 49-69

63 Dora Sowden, "In the Transvaal until 1899," In Gustav Saron and Louis Holtz, Eds, op cit, 1955, 153-164

64 Gideon Shimoni, op cit, 1980, 17

65 Dan Jacobson, "Foreward," In Joseph Sherman, Ed., op cit, 1987

5,2 Evolution in South Africa

5.2.1 The Immigrant Generation

1   Monica Wilson and Leonard Thompson, op cit, 1971, 365

2   Immanuel Suttner, *Cutting Through the Mountain*, New York, 1997, 1-3

3   Gideon Shimoni, op cit, 1980, 4

4   Milton Shain, op cit, 1994, 70-77

5   Nathan Berger, *Chapters From South African History*, Johannesburg, 1982, 81-86

6   Gideon Shimoni, op cit, 1980, 5

7   Gustav Saron, op cit, 1965

8   Baruch Hirson, *The Cape Town Intellectuals*, Johannesburg, 2000, 45-49, 117-121 et passim

9   Gustav Saron, op cit, 1965

10 Enid Alexander, *Morris Alexander, A Biography*, Cape Town: 1953, 1-67 passim

11 Riva Krut, "The Making of the Jewish Community of Johannesburg, 1886-1914," In Belinda Bozzoli, Ed., op cit, 1984

12 Naomi Musiker and Reuben Musiker, *Historical Dictionary of Greater Johannesburg*, Lanham, MD, 1999, 106-107

13 Dora Sowden, op cit, 1955, 149-152

14 Nathan Berger, op cit 1982, 163-166

15 Riva Krut, op cit, 1984

16 Evangelos Mantzaris, "Jewish Trade Unions in Cape Town," *Jewish Social Studies*, 1987, 49: 251

17 ibid

18 Gideon Shimoni, op cit, 1980, 84-85

19 Evangelos Mantzaris, op cit, 1987

20 Joseph Poliva, *A Short History of the Jewish Press and Literature of South Africa*, Johannesburg, 1961

21 Nathan Berger, op cit, 1982, 117-118

22 Gustav Saron, "The Long Road to Unity," In Gustav Saron and Louis Holtz, op cit, 1955

23 Joseph Poliva, *Biography of Nehamiah Dov Hofmann*, Johannesburg,1968

24 Joseph Poliva, op cit, 1961, 19-21

25 Joseph Sherman, op cit, 1987, 17

26 Nathan Berger, op cit, 1982, 118-120

27 Sol Liptzin, *A History of Yiddish Literature*, Middle Village, NY, 1972, 381-382

28 Gideon Shimoni op cit, 1980, 18-26

29 Marcia Gitlin, op cit, 1950, 16

30 ibid, 25-29

31 Gideon Shimoni, op cit, 1980, 52

32 Marcia Gitlin, op cit, 1950, 102-111; Joseph Poliva, op cit, 1961, 17-19; Edgar Bernstein, *My Judaism, My Jews*, Johannesburg, 1962, 174

33 Marcia Gitlin, op cit, 1950, 113-12

34 Gideon Shimoni, op cit, 1980, 28-29

35 ibid, 31-33

36 ibid, 41-49

5.2.2the Acculturating generation

1 Gustav Saron, op cit, 1965

2 Gideon Shimoni, : "Jewish Identity in Lithuania and South Africa." In Sander Gilman and Milton Shain, *Jewries at the Frontier*, Urbana, IL, 1999

3   Milton Shain, op cit, 1994, 114-142 passim
4   H. Sonnabend, "The Social Role of the Jew in South Africa," *Jewish Affairs*, 1948, 14-19
5   John Wellington, op cit, 1960, 212-213
6   Gustav Saron, op cit, 1965
7   Jack Simons and Ray Simons, op cit, 1983, 261-268
8   ibid, 244-250
9   David Yudelman, *The Emergence of Modern South Africa*, Westport, CT, 1983, 190-213 passim
10   Cornelius Kiewiet, *A History of South Africa: Social and Economic*, London, 1957, 212-245 passim
11   Naomi Musiker and Reuben Miusiker, op cit, 1999, 136
12   Morris Kentridge, *I Recall*, Johannesburg, 1959, passim
13   Louis Holtz (L.H.) "A South African Parliamentarian Looks Back," *Jewish Affairs*, 1959, Jewish Affairs, 14: 25
14   T.R.H. Davenport, op cit, 1991, 269-279 passim
15   Robert Ross, op cit, 1999, 108-109
16   Milton Shain, op cit, 1994, 142-148; Gideon Shimoni, op cit, 1980, 97-136 passim
17   Gustav Saron, "Epilogue," In Gustav Saron and Louis Holtz, op cit, 1955, 376-380
18   Joseph Poliva, op cut, 1961, 13-14
19   Edgar Bernstein, op cit, 1962, 175-178
20   Nathan Berger, op cit, 1982, 122-124
21   Taffy Adler, "Lithuania's Diaspora: The Jewish Worker's Club, 1928-1948," *Journal of Southern Africa Studies*, 1979, 6:
22   Nathan Berger, op cit, 1982, 166
23   Taffy Adler, op cit, 1979
24   Joseph Poliva, op cit, 1961, 31,32
25   Joseph Sherman, "Biography," In Leibl Feldman *Oudthoorn, Jerusalem of South Africa*, Johannesburg, 1989
26   Sol Liptzin, op cit, 1972, 382-383
27   Joseph Sherman, op cit, 1989
28   Belinda Bozzoli, op cit, 1975
29   Taffy Adler, op cit, 1979
30   ibid
31   ibid
32   Bernard Sachs, *South African Personalities and Places*, Johannesburg, 1959, 49-51

33   Bernard Sachs, *Mists of Memory*, London, 1973, 29-59 passim

34   Solly Sachs, *Rebel's Daughters*, London, 1957, 17-103 passim

35   Bernard Sachs, *The Road From Sharpesville*, London, 1961, 137

36   Jack Simons and Ray Simons. op cit, 1985, 478-483 passim

37   Bernard Sachs, op cit, 1961, 137-139

38   Naomi Musiker and Reuben Musiker, op cit, 1999, 334-335

39   Bernard Sachs, op cit, 1961, 141-144

40   Bernard Sachs, op cit, 1959, 47

41   Phyllis Lean, "Profile," In Henry Gluckman, *Abiding Values*, Johannesburg, 1970

42   Martin Rubin, *Sarah Gertrude Millin: A South African Life,* Johannesburg, 1977, 11-35 passim

43   Marcia Leveson, "The Enemy Within: Some South African Writers," In Sander Gilman and Milton Shain, Eds., op cit, 1999

44   Lavinia Braun, "Not Gobineau but Heine:-Not Racial Theory but Biblical Theme," *English Studies in Africa*, 1991, 34:27

45   Martin Rubin, op cit, 1977, 72-94 passim

46   ibid, 98-104

47   Marcia Leveson, op cit, 1999

48   Bernard Sachs, op cit, 1959,78-79

49   Gideon Shimoni, op cit, 1980, 175-178 passim

50   ibid, 188-190

51   ibid, 201; Haim Shur, *Shomrim in the Land of Apartheid*, Kibbutz Dalia, 1998, 27-31

5.2.3 The Apartheid Generation

1   David Yudelman, op cit, 1983, 264

2   Saul Dubow, *Racist Segregation and the Origins of Apartheid in South Africa, 1919-1936*, New York, 1989, 1-10

3   G.H. L. LeMay, *The Afrikaners: A Historical Interpretation*, Cambridge, MA, 1995, 200-204

4   David Welsh, "The Political Economy of Afrikaner Nationalism," In Adrian Leftwich, Ed., *South African Economic Growth and Political Change*, New York, 1974

5   Janet Robertson, *Liberalism in South Africa*, 1948-1963, Oxford, 1971, 1-39 passim ibid, 64-82 passim)

6   T. R. H. Davenport, op cit, 1991, 326-336

7   Gideon Shimoni, op cit, 1980, 227

8 Gillian Slovo, *Every Secret Thing*, Boston, 1997, 27-49 passim ibid, 103-111

9 Janet Robertson, op cit, 1972, 171-173

10 Joshua Lazerson, *Against the Tide: Whites in the Struggle Against Apartheid*, Boulder, CO, 1994, 190-192

11 Joe Slovo, *The Unfinished Autobiography*, Melbourne, 1997, 30-34

12 Glenn Frankel, *Rivonia's Children*, New York, 1999, 45-49

13 Helen Suzman, *In No Uncertain Terms*, New York, 1993, 46-64 passim

14 Helen Suzman, op cit, 1993, 6-17 passim; Immanuel Suttner, op cit, 1997, 423-431; Joanna Strangways-Booth, *A Cricket in a Thorn Tree*, Bloomington, IN, 1976, 15-69 pssim

15 Joshua Lazerson, op cit, 1994, 226-235

16 Glenn Frankel, op cit, 1999, 6-7

17 Fran Buntman, "Interview with Denis Goldberg," In op cit, 1998 Immanuel Suttner, Ed.

18 Joshua Lazerson, op cit, 1994, 96-97

19 Heidi Holland, *The Struggle: A History of the African National Congress*, New York, 1990, 143-144

20 G.H.L. LeMay, op cit, 1995, 251-253

21 Hilda Bernstein, *The World That Was Ours*, London, 1989; Albie Sachs, *The Jail Diary of Albie Sachs*, London, 1966; Ruth First, *117 Days*, London, 1965

22 Glenn Frankel, op cit, 1999, 8

23 Immanuel Suttner, op cit, 1997, 221-244

24 Louis Feldberg, *South African Jewry, 1965 Edition*, Johannesburg, 1965, 7-8

25 Gideon Shimoni, op cit, 1980, 206-224 ibid, 272-326

26 Nadine Gordimer, "A South African Childhood: Allusions in a Landscape," *The New Yorker*, April, 16, 1954, 121

27 Immanuel Suttner, op cit, 1997, 108-116

28 Sonya Rudikoff, "Nadine Gordimer," In C. Brian Cox, Ed., *African Writers*, New York, 1997

29 Lionel Abrahams, "Nadine Gordimer: The Transparent Ego," 1960, *English Studies in Africa*, 3: 146.

30 Robert Green, "The Novels of Nadine Gordimer," In Michael Chapman et al, Eds., *Perspectives on South African Literature*, Johannesburg, 1992

31 Paul Scanlon, "Nadine Gordimer," In *South African Writers: Dictionary of Literary Biography*, v225, Detroit, 2000, 184

32 Jannika Hurwitt, "The Art of Fiction LXXXVII: Nadine Gordimer," In Nancy Topping Bazin and Marilyn Dallman Seymour, Eds., *Conversations with Nadine Gordimer,* Jackson, MS, 1990

33 Stuart Buxbaum, The Demographic Structure of the Jewish Community of South Africa, *Jewish Affairs,* 1979, 34:17-20, 67-72

34 Haim Shur, op cit, 1998

35 Rosenstein, 12/4/2001 Personal Communication

36 Leonarrd Judaker, Personal Communication 11/01/2001

37 Sheila Roberts, *Dan Jacobson,* Boston, 1984 ibid, 109-113

38 Dan Jacobson, *Heschel's Kingdom,* Evanston, IL, 1998, 3-8

39 Ronald Segal, *Into Exile,* London, 1963, 9-110 passim

40 Gideon Shimoni, South African Jews and the Apartheid Crisis In David Singer and Ruth Seldin, Eds., *The American Jewish Yearbook,* 1988, Philadelphia, 1988, 26-37

41 Stephen Cohen, "Historical Backgrouund," In Marcus Arkin, Ed., *South African Jewry: A Contemporary Survey,* Cape Town, 1984

42 Tamsen Seimon, Personal Communication, 3/02/2002

43 Allie Dubb, "Demographic Picture," In Marcus Arkin, Ed. Op cit, 1984

44 Marcus Arkin, "The Zionist Dimension," In Marcus Arlkin, Ed., op cit, 1984

45 Jocelyn Hellig, "Religious Dimension," In Marcus Arkin Ed., op cit,1984

46 Sally Frankental and Milton Shain, "Accommodation, Apathy and Activism," *Jewish Quarterly,* 1993, 40: 5

47 Richard Goldstone, *For Humanity,* New Haven, 2000, 2-73 passim

48 Mendel Kaplan with Solomon Kaplan and Marian Robertson, *From the Shtetl to Steelmaking,* 1979 passim

49 Milton Shain et all, *Looking Back, Jews in the Struggle for Democracy and Human Rights in South Africa,* Cape Town, 2001.

SECTION III

THE HEBREW SPEAKING DIASPORA

INTRODUCTION

Support for the development of Jewish life in Zion was one of the responses to the break up of the traditional life of Eastern Europe. The Haskalah's focus on Hebrew, as a secular literary language rather than only for biblical study, served as the forerunner of the national rebirth of both the language and its land. The Renaissance of Hebrew as a modern spoken language was one of the miracles of Zionism that was initiated in Lita.

Starting early in the nineteenth century, there was a strong religiously based immigration to the "holy cities" in Palestine from Lita. Later in that century, there was ongoing tension between the religious and secular strands among the Lovers of Zion and then within the Zionist movement after the advent of Herzl. Reconciliation between traditional religion and Zionism that took place, in Mizrachi and the preaching of Rabbi Abraham Kook, was to a large extent among the non-Hassidic midnagdim. Although many, if not most, of the settlers of the "New Yishuv" were secular, the settlements in Palestine partook of a religious motif of redemption of the Land. In the more recent post-1967 era, the religious strand taken on a greater impact on the total life of Israel with the fusion of Zionism and a sense of redemption.

Support for the Zionist message was variably expressed within segments of the population. It was at times a more middle-class than worker-oriented movement, but the entire international Zionist movement ultimately drew its sustenance from and spoke to the masses of East European Jewry. Particularly salient, in response to the strength of the Jewish Socialist Bund in that same area, was the development of Poalei Tzion (Workers of Zion). This socialist form of Zionism originated in the Pale of Settlement, and particularly in its northwestern provinces that encompassed Lita. This Zionist socialist variant expressed the pervasive commitment to a better world as part of the utopian hopes of the times. It was also part of a Hebraic nationalistic response

561

within the larger socialist movement that took place in Lita with Vilna as its revolutionary center. Its focus on the development of the "new Jew" resonated with the idealism of young people seeking a more specifically Jewish response to modernity. This idealism was coupled with the populist revolutionary strand of the previous revolutionary generation with its emphasis on *productive labor* wherein there was a coupling of "return to the soil" with a return to the Land of Zion. This socialist idealism provided the major direction of the early developments that arose out of the East European sources to create the ethos of the Yishuv. Although their number was relatively small, the *pioneer* element that partook of the revolutionary ferment around 1905 would have the greatest influence in the evolution of the Yishuv and the early State of Israel.

Their commitment to *activism* was also in many ways compatible while also in competition with the other new religion represented by the Bund. The close association of the pioneers of the Second Aliyah with need for self-defense in the pogroms following the aborted revolution of 1905 brought a sense of activism that was to flourish particularly in the Yishuv.

The distinction must be made between Am Israel (the People Israel) and Eretz Israel (the Land of Israel). The Great East European Migration of the people Israel was a "people's movement" that mainly chose places other than a Palestine under Ottoman rule. The modern settlement of the Land of Israel originated with the First Aliyah, amplified by the Second Aliyah, coming during the first decade of the twentieth century while the far-larger migration occurred to the New World. It may be noted that Zionism was the only emigration movement "with a conscious ideology of downward social mobility." With the Balfour Declaration and the British Mandate after World War I, emigration to Palestine became more acceptable as an alternative. The Third Aliyah immediately after World War I had experience of the Russian Revolution and exemplified the religion of labor that formed a basis for the development of the Yishuv. Subsequent migration was further amplified by lack of alternatives elsewhere.

The Zionist groups in the various countries had as their objective "the capture of the community" and the eventual emigration to help settle and strengthen the new Zion. During the interwar era, the battle for community leadership was fought on the issue of religious versus national identity. National identity could be based on Yiddishkayt and Jewish peoplehood as well as Zionism, but both called into question the "bargain of Emancipation" in which the Jewish religious identity, however attenuated, was paramount. The Zionist "capture of the community" was greatest in specific countries such as Canada and South Africa where national identity was coupled with ethno-religious identity. It is particularly from the latter that aliyah to Israel took place among the English-speaking Litvak Diaspora.

The relationship between the State of Israel and its Yiddish-speaking European antecedents is an ambiguous one. A sense of continuity with Yiddish life in the Diaspora exemplified by centers such as Vilna and Warsaw has been problematic. The commitment to the "new Jew" seemed to require a repudiation of the Diaspora and its culture exemplified by both the Yiddish language and its history, culminating in the Holocaust.

The developments in Eastern Europe that found such significant expression in Zionism were significantly modified in the crucible of life in the Yishuv. The initial principles of "productive labor" and Hebrew revival were successful. They, however, evolved in a rocky soil surrounded by enemies. Although rooted in religion, what was primarily a secular movement is once again suffused with theological import. It is our argument that the evolution of the culture of the Land of Israel is an outgrowth of its at least initially strongly Litvak ideological roots interacting with the character of the place.

Israel, as a state, has its own culture that modified its initial roots in the context of the "colonization" of a hostile territory. The settlers reshaped their landscape and were in turn reshaped. The impact of these origins and their evolution in Eretz Israel itself is the story of this section. The character of the Jewish settlement in Zion is not merely a reflection of its early East European sources and those surviving the Holocaust. Zion has had its own evolution in its ingathering of a large number of Jews from elsewhere with particular emphasis on those who formerly lived in Muslim countries. Indeed the ethos of the early settlers is no longer dominant. After 1977, political power shifted.

CHAPTER 6
ISRAEL

6.1 The Nature of the Place

6.1.1 The Historical Land

The country Israel is a function of history as well as geography. The name *Palestine* has had its own complex history. The word derives from the area inhabited in biblical times by the Philistines in the southwestern portion of the coastal plain between Egypt on the south and Syria and Lebanon on the north. Canaan, the land to which Abraham first came and to which Moses led the return of the Hebrews following the Exodus from Egypt, was inhabited by a number of other tribes and was the name of the larger area between the Jordan River and the Mediterranean. The larger area was united for a short time circa 1000 BCE under the House of David with Jerusalem its capital and the site of its temple built by Solomon.

It then split into two: the northern kingdom of *Israel* with Samaria, its capital, was destroyed by the Assyrians in 721 BCE with the dispersal and disappearance of its people encompassing the Ten Tribes. The southern kingdom of *Judea* persisted but was defeated by the Babylonians and the temple of Solomon destroyed in 586 BCE. After the defeat of the Babylonians, there was a return to Jerusalem under the auspices of Cyrus, the king of the Persians, and the building of the Second Temple. Judea was defeated, its name obliterated and Jerusalem and its Second Temple destroyed by the Romans in 70 CE. The Jews were finally dispersed from what was now first called *Palestine* by the Romans under Hadrian after the suppression of Bar Kochba Revolt in 135 CE.

In the fifth-century CE, Helen, the mother of Emperor Constantine, was responsible for identifying the various Christian holy sites related to the life of Jesus and thus connected the *Holy Land* to Christianity. During the next centuries, it was part of the empire ruled from Christian Byzantium. Following the Arab Conquest in the seventh-century CE, Jerusalem was rebuilt and the Mosque of Omar built on the Temple Mount. It marked the site where Mohammed's miraculous ascent to heaven took place. Jerusalem was thus also connected to Islam. After relatively short-term conquest of the *Holy Land* during the crusades circa 1100 CE, the city was once again recaptured by Muslims and by the Ottoman Turks in 1517. During the latter's rule until 1917, the territory was but the southern portion of the province of Syria. Religious Jews, many of whom refugees from the expulsion from Spain (Sephardim), lived mainly in the "holy cities" of Jerusalem, Tiberias, Safed, and Hebron under various restrictions imposed by their Muslim rulers but protected as "people of the holy book."

The British Mandate following World War I reinstated *Palestine* as the name first for the entire area and, following 1922, for the area west of the Jordan River. During this time its inhabitants were *Palestinians*, divided by religion and nationality into Arabs and Jews. For Jews, the term *Eretz Israel* (the Land of Israel) infers by its very title an intimate connection between the land and the people of Israel. Eretz Israel has remained throughout history the land given to Abraham by God and then conquered after the exodus from Egypt. It was the focal point to which daily prayers were directed since the dispersion and the only temporary "exile." It was on the basis of these metaphysical and historical rights as well as the rights of self-determination prevalent in the nineteenth century that Zionism found its power.

During the nineteenth century, the land was deforested and neglected. Its attraction as the site of holy places for Christians and Jews was tempered by the difficulties in travel and the dangers of robbery by the local Muslims. Interest in Palestine increased among the rival European powers during the nineteenth century. The *Eastern Question* dealt with the erosion of Ottoman hegemony and which of the powers would gain from the dismemberment of the sultan's empire. The long-standing French interest on behalf of Roman Catholics derived from the time of Francis I in the sixteenth century. A Latin patriarch, whose position derived from the time of the Latin kingdom of the crusaders, was now newly appointed by Pope Pius IX in 1848. The Russians sought to represent the interests of the Orthodox church with Moscow's claim to be the successor of Byzantium. The Russians represented the interests of the long-extant Greek Orthodox patriarchate of Jerusalem. The British, to counteract the French and Russian influence, assumed responsibility for developing a Protestant presence in the Holy Land. They sought converts from among the non-Muslim inhabitants under the auspices of London Jews Society and the Church Missionary Society.

In 1850, the Russians sought the primacy of the Greek patriarch over the Latin and Armenian churches by ownership of the keys to the Church of the Nativity in Bethlehem and other Christian holy places The Russians then further demanded the right to protect all Orthodox Christians in the Ottoman Empire. In the ensuing diplomatic fight over the "keys," the Crimean War came about with the alignment of France and Britain with the Turks in opposition to the Russians.[1]

During the mid-nineteenth century, Ashkenazi immigrants from Eastern Europe began to outnumber the longstanding Sephardic Jewish community. Motivated by a religious, mystical attachment to the Holy Land, both Hassidim and competing disciples of the Vilna Gaon set up communities in Jerusalem as well as the other "holy cities" of Safed, Hebron, and Tiberias. These communities were supported with alms (halakha) collected in Eastern Europe. Starting in the 1840s, there was a progressive increase in the number of such religiously motivated immigrants. Living in poverty, they were dependent on what was now becoming increasingly insufficient support. The position of these scholars was tenuous in terms of their residence rights as well as their economic status. Rather than submit to Ottoman citizenship and be then subject to the jurisdiction of the Sephardic chief rabbi, they preferred to remain under the protection of the European consuls. The particularly active British consul took on the protection of the Russian Jews living in Jerusalem.

There was clear need to develop a more adequate economic base than dependence on *halakha*. The Paris-based Alliance Israelite Universelle (AIU), under the direction of Charles Netter, founded the first agricultural school at Mikveh Israel just east of Jaffa in 1870. Despite the difficulties of land purchase, Petah Tiqva (Gateway of Hope) was also founded in 1878 near some malarial swamps on the coastal plain adjacent to the Yarkon River.[2]

During this same period, the British began to take a greater interest in this area with the purchase of the Suez Canal and the control of Cyprus. Their objective was to safeguard their imperial interests concerning the route to India while still maintaining the integrity of the Turkish sultan's possessions vis-à-vis the Russians and the French. During this period, a group of English Christians had advocated a Jewish National revival in Palestine. Among them was Laurence Oliphant who had submitted a proposal to Benjamin Disraeli in 1878 and had actually scouted out locations. While working with the Mansion House Fund formed in response to the pogroms of 1881-82, he sought to have some of the emigrants go to Palestine. He enabled several colonies to be founded by direct intervention with the sultan in Constaninople.[3] The meshing of British imperial and philanthropic/humanitarian interest with the growth of Jewish settlement seemed to be a possibly compatible arrangement for the *New Yishuv* of the future.

The geography of the country significantly affected its future political development.

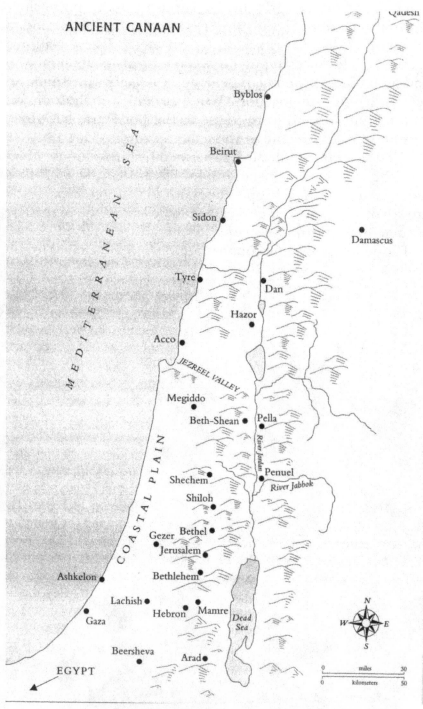

ANCIENT CANAAN

Qadesh

Byblos

Beirut

MEDITERRANEAN SEA

Sidon

Damascus

Tyre

Dan

Hazor

Acco

JEZREEL VALLEY

Megiddo

Beth-Shean

Pella

River Jordan

COASTAL PLAIN

Shechem

Penuel

River Jabbok

Shiloh

Gezer

Bethel

Jerusalem

Ashkelon

Bethlehem

Lachish

Hebron

Mamre

Gaza

Dead Sea

N

W   E

S

Beersheva

Arad

EGYPT

0   miles   30
0   kilometers   50

Map 6.1 Ancient Canaan

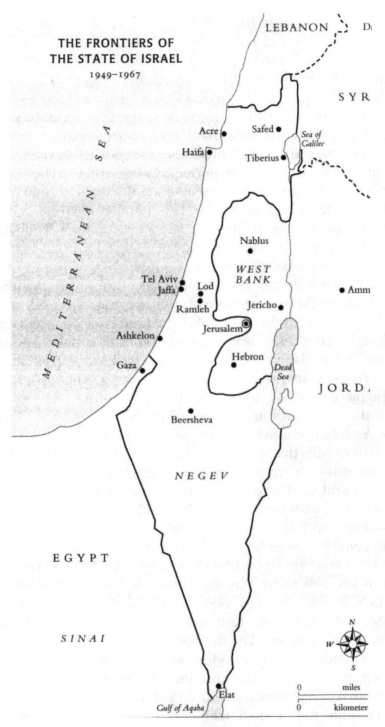

THE FRONTIERS OF
THE STATE OF ISRAEL
1949–1967

LEBANON

D:

SYR

MEDITERRANEAN SEA

Acre

Safed

Sea of
Galilee

Haifa

Tiberius

Nablus

WEST
BANK

Tel Aviv

Jaffa

Lod

Amm

Ramleh

Jericho

Jerusalem

Ashkelon

Hebron

Dead
Sea

Gaza

JORD:

Beersheva

NEGEV

EGYPT

SINAI

N

W

S

0   miles

0   kilometer:

Elat

Gulf of Aqaba

Map 6.2 The Frontiers of the State of Israel

The land available for purchase and Jewish settlement and the eventual political boundaries reflect its physical character. The country is divided into four regions: the coastal plain, the central hills, the Jordan Rift Valley, and the Negev. The coastal plain is interrupted only by bay of Carmel that provided a site for the development of the major port of Haifa. The coastal plain was sparsely populated with swamps infested with malarial mosquitoes. The plain is fertile and humid and traversed by several short streams albeit only two have permanent water flows. The Yarkon River near Jaffa was one of those and was the site of several of the early settlements. Much of the land was untilled and thus available for purchase. Less available were lands held collectively by Arab villagers in the Jaffa, Ramle, Gaza, and Hebron districts.

East of the coastal plain is the central highland region. In the north are the hills and mountains of the Galilee with the inland Sea of Galilee the major source of water. Several valleys run across the highlands with the Valley of Jezreel the largest in the Lower Galilee that runs from the coast plain near Haifa east to the Jordan Valley. The availability of purchase of large blocs of land in this valley from an absentee owner in Beirut was a significant factor in the placement of settlements during the Yishuv.

In the center of the country are the hills of Samaria. There were Arab Muslims living there particularly in hilltop villages in the eastern hills that were relatively free of malaria. There were almond and olive trees and grazing land. Land was owned both privately and by village collectives. Jerusalem was in the center of these hills with Jaffa its port. It was also in the towns such as Jerusalem and Jaffa that the Christian Arab population mainly lived, generally more highly educated than the rural Muslims.

East of the central highlands is the Jordan River Valley. The Jordan River originates in the north around Mt. Hermon on the Lebanese border and then runs though the Huleh Basin to the Sea of Galilee (Lake Kinneret) and thence through the Rift Valley to the Dead Sea. The drainage of the swamps of the Huleh Valley was another major undertaking of the Jewish settlers that freed it from the malarial conditions that prevented settlement. It was not fully accomplished until 1951. In the south is the Negev desert. A portion of the Sinai desert, it runs from the Dead Sea to the Gulf of Aqaba and the Red Sea.[4]

In the absence of a charter establishing sovereignty from the Ottoman government and the inability of conquest, the goal of establishing the Jews in their ancestral land required alternative methods. The method of establishing Jewish sovereignty prior to 1948 was to buy the privately held land and to establish a presence on the land purchased by creating settlements. The further objective was to buy adjoining tracts of land and establish contiguous settlements to develop entire areas of primarily Jewish settlement as an eventual basis for sovereignty in those areas. "Practical" Zionism was characterized by buying and settling "a dunam here, a dunam there" with the *dunam* a measure of land approximating a quarter-acre. Because there was a withholding of land from sale to Jews, the price was artificially high. It is estimated that the price of land was six to ten times that of farmland in the United States.[5]

Much of the privately held land available for purchase was owned by absentee landlords with Arab tenants actually farming on the land. The owners had frequently acquired their land in payment of debts incurred by the previous owners in response to onerous taxation under Ottoman rule. The previous owners remained on the land but now as tenants or sharecroppers and felt themselves to hold title to the use of the land. Purchase by semipublic entities such as the Jewish National Fund from the absentee owners could lead to displacement of the tenants. Intimately tied in to land acquisition was immigration. Both these components were opposed by the Ottoman authorities and, later by the British, in accordance with Arab demands.

6.1.2 The Great Migration

The evolution of the *New Yishuv* in Eretz Israel is a function of its successive waves of immigrants, numbered in terms of surges that occurred. Our focus is on the Ashkenazi immigration and its particular Litvak component ending with the destruction of the core in Lita. Emphasis is on the ideological rather than merely the genetic components of Litvak origin. These ideas are exemplified in the twin strands of the religious traditions and the more secular developments derived from Haskalah. The latter led to a devotion to the use of Hebrew in everyday life and a commitment to making change in the life of Jews in the world expressed in both the return to Zion and a faith in socialism.

The Jewish settlement in the country (Yishuv) and its eventual independence as a Jewish state reflected the number and character of those immigrating. It was to be a cultural or spiritual as well as physical refuge for the renewal of the Jewish people. Initially the number of persons in each aliyah (going up) was small, dwarfed by those going elsewhere in the emigration from the Pale of Settlement throughout the rest of the world. Starting during the interwar period, and subsequently in the aftermath of the Shoah, the rationale for the existence of the state became more primarily a physical refuge as well as a cultural one for the maintenance of the Jewish people.

In the earliest days, immigration was not necessarily one of the imperatives of Zionism. Very few of the Lovers of Zion actually immigrated. For the early Ashkenazi immigrants from Eastern Europe to Eretz Israel, there was considerable movement to and from Russia. It was easier to come and go than crossing the Atlantic. There was frequent disappointment when confronted with the heat and the poverty. Starting in the 1880s, the number immigrating went beyond those who had previously come to Palestine seeking a religious life. Moreover, unlike those going elsewhere, some new immigrants were not seeking an easier life but one that was in response to a new direction.

What was sought was a spiritual renewal of the Jewish people. In 1873, Smolenskin had written *Am Olam* (*The Eternal People*) that argued in favor of the Jews as a nation as an alternative to assimilation. One would need to promote national consciousness and loyalty to one's people with the use of Hebrew as its cement. Although focusing on a "national" spirit, he evoked religion and, particularly the messianic-redemptive component, as having performed in the past such a cementing function.[6] He warned, however, against invoking such settlement "as clearing the way for the Messiah" as needlessly stirring up opposition among the religious who generally opposed the principle that one could force the issue of return.[7]

Eliezer Perelman (Ben Yehuda) wrote in the same Hebrew journal edited by Smolenskin in 1878 "A Worthy Question" that argued not only for restoration in Palestine but the need for a cultural revival by a renewal of the Hebrew as a living language. A Hebrew literature could arise only in a context in which the language was used in daily discourse rather than in the artificial Haskalah literature couched in Hebrew.

In response to the pogroms of 1881-1882, Leo Pinsker, living in Odessa, wrote the pamphlet (interestingly in German) entitled *Autoemancipation* advocating the creation of a nation living on its own soil. Previously committed to assimilation, he now came to advocate the need for a home of one's own. At the outset, that home he thought need not necessarily be Palestine. Later he became one of the leaders of Hovevei Zion, (Lovers of Zion) the movement that sprang up after the pogroms of 1881-1882 in the Pale to sponsor development in Palestine.

A fundamental change had to take place to view Palestine as a place in which one could live and be "productive" rather than only as a place to partake of "holiness."[8] Focus was therefore on agricultural settlement. Much of this thinking arose in the Odessa as an important center for Haskalah.[9] Although the Maskilim of the southern Pale in places such as Odessa as well as those of Lita saw the need for Jewish renewal via settlement on the land, the more traditional Jews of Lita were more attracted by the idea of Jewish revival by settlement on land in Palestine than elsewhere.[10] The *Odessa Committee* of the Lovers of Zion was eventually legalized in 1890 as the Society for Assistance to Jewish Farmers and Artisans in Syria and Palestine.[11]

Although the nationalist message was couched in the use of religious terms such as *redemption* and *Zion*, it did not truly partake of the messianic prophecy in its theological aspects. There was no attempt to calculate the time of eschatological end nor the rebuilding of the temple and the restoration of the sacrificial cult. Indeed Rabbi Isaac Jacob Reines, the founder of the religious Zionist Mizrachi, explicitly separated Zionist activity from the utopian redemption in its theological sense.[12] However one theological concept that would recur that echoed the Bible was that the settlements in Palestine could serve as "cities of refuge" in the case the Jews were no longer able to remain in Europe. Moreover, redemption was to be by one's own efforts rather than by the passive coming of a messiah.[13] To the extent that the

Lovers of Zion were interested in any concrete form of historical messianism, it was in the Return to Zion as exemplified by the actions of Cyrus, the Persian emperor who proclaimed the return after the first period of exile in Babylon in 538 BCE.[14]

Rosh Pinna near Safed in the Galilee in 1882 and *Zikhron Yaacov* near Mt. Carmel in 1883, the latter in honor of the founder of the French Rothschild branch, were founded by Jews already living in Palestine. Under the sponsorship of the Lovers of Zion, the new settlement of *Rishon LeZion* near Jaffa in 1882 was the first to be settled by immigrants from Russia. Rather than merely supporting the settlement of others, the BILU group starting in 1882 consisted of people committed to themselves becoming farmers in Palestine. The term is an acronym representing the Biblical verse Isaiah 2:5 (House of Jacob, come you, and let us go). These young people committed themselves to serve in a model settlement for a period of obligatory service and remain unmarried. The model was established of Jewish nationalists prepared to make personal sacrifices for fulfillment of a Jewish renaissance in the ancient Jewish homeland. Some of their members, with support from the Lovers of Zion, founded *Gedera* in the Judean hills along with renewing the previously abandoned *Petah Tiqva*, the latter a project of a group from Lita, mainly from the Bialystok area.[15]

Unlike the family emigration to other sites in the Litvak Diaspora, those coming to Eretz Israel were more likely young people, unmarried or childless. They were often those who had some education but not fixed on any career. They tended to come from more middle-class families who had become open to newer more secular ideas. The ideology of rebellion was strong with formation of small relatively cohesive groupings that united "in preparation" for aliyah. Their rebelliousness contained an abandonment of their middle-class ways of life. They were able to persist in their sense of differentiation by their migration and the creation of a new form of economic, social, and political life. Although few in number, the self-consciousness of their commitment to agricultural settlement, to labor and to the rejuvenation of Hebrew created the ethos which affected the much larger immigration of more "normal" family groups that followed.[16]

The BILU members, among those coming in the First Aliyah starting in 1881, were irreligious. The Lovers of Zion were split between those who were freethinkers such as Pinsker and Moses Leib Lilienblum and those led by Rabbi Samuel Mohliver. The last sought a religious basis for the Return to Zion. The reconciliation between the intellectuals and the Orthodox that took place was subject to fragmentation and was resolved only by the good offices of men such as Ussiskin who was acceptable to both.[17] The Gedera settlement, as an example, eventually became the exemplar of secular nationalism only when freed from the jurisdiction of the Lovers of Zion.

The ongoing model was that of the "private enterprise" in which each farmer owned his own land, house and equipment although for practical reasons, rather than ideological ones, initially some of the work was done in common. Each of these *moshavot* had a committee responsible for general affairs and the management of such public functions as the synagogue and school. The villages were generally laid out in a linear pattern along a main street analogous to a European village. This arrangement differed from the Arab village in its spaciousness and orderliness.[18]

This First Aliyah totaled thirty thousand Jews and was roughly coterminous with the period of the existence of the Lovers of Zion during the decades of the 1880s and 1890s prior to the First Zionist Congress in 1897. Only 10 percent actually went to the agricultural settlements. Nevertheless, outposts of Jewish settlement developed throughout Palestine. They soon found it necessary to develop defenses against the neighboring Arabs. Since almost all the limited initial capital had been spent in the purchase of land, there was generally not enough capital to maintain the settlers until they became self-supporting. With many of the settlements seeking such support from outside sources, Baron Edmond de Rothschild, the youngest son of the founder of the French Rothschilds, became the major benefactor of the early settlements. Approached by Rabbi Mohliver through the good auspices of the grand rabbi of Paris, Zadoc Kahn, his involvement became a major focus of his life.[19]

Rothschild eventually took financial responsibility for further development of all the established colonies in return for ownership of the land. To safeguard his investment, he appointed managers that controlled the crops to be cultivated and the activities of the settlers.[20] In the search for eventual economic self-sufficiency, the crops changed from cereals to monoculture such as viniculture and fruit orchards including citrus. During the 1890s and the formation of the Jewish Colonization Association (JCA) by Baron de Hirsch, Rothschild became the most active member of the Board of the JCA and continued to take the greatest interest in the activities of the settlements.

Rothschild invested large sums of money as part of a major attempt to provide a viable alternative for those seeking a life outside the Pale of Settlement. Industrial development was exemplified by the operation of the winery in Rishon LeZion that purchased the grapes produced by the other colonies at a subsidized price. The land was fully utilized with the most modern techniques and equipment under the direction of agronomists hired by the baron. Many different options were tried including mulberry trees for silkworms as well as various fruit trees. However, the settlers were left out of the decision-making process and functioned essentially as day laborers. Bureaucratic procedures stifled initiative and led to revolts.[21]

Secular subjects and female education was characteristic of the educational program. Hebrew was taught by *immersion* and became the general language of instruction by 1908. French remained the language of instruction for subjects such as science within these early settlements up to World War I.[22]. Religious observance was maintained to a large part in the colonies and the land was cultivated in accordance with the biblical rules of the "sabbatarian year."[23] New holidays unknown in the Diaspora were introduced such as an extended harvest festival reflecting the increased nationalism and the renewed connection with agriculture.[24]

Jewish immigration in general continued throughout the 1880s at an average pace of one thousand five hundred to two thousand each year aside from a bulge of about five thousand in 1882. Such immigration and settlement occurred despite various obstacles placed by the Ottoman government on land purchases and bans on immigration. Particularly helpful was the ability of the Jews to call upon intervention on their behalf by representatives of the European Powers as well as the lethargy and corruption of the Ottoman authorities. Once again in 1890-91, another bulge occurred following the expulsions from Moscow. The Jewish Colonization Association (JCA) founded by Baron de Hirsch in that year began to sponsor settlement in Palestine along with their other interests in Argentina and Canada. Following the JCA take over of the Rothschild properties in 1900, the administrative system provided greater autonomy for the settlers. Viniculture became less pervasive with greater success with export crops such as oranges and almonds.[25]

Asher Ginzberg (Ahad Ha'am) visiting the settlements in the 1890s found them inadequate in achieving a commitment to a national ideal that he envisaged. Although their number was small and their implementation less than ideal, nevertheless, a new center of Jewish life had been created in Palestine as a counterpoint to those living in the holy cities. In addition to the farming settlements, there was the beginning of Jewish urban settlement outside these holy cities in places such as Jaffa, eventually leading to the foundation of all-Jewish Tel Aviv in 1909.

Theodore Herzl's *The Jewish State,* in 1896, advocated the establishment of an autonomous entity based upon a legal charter rather than the heretofore piecemeal infiltration that he derided. Despite opposition from the wealthy Jews of Western Europe and many in religious circles, Herzl succeeded in bringing the issue to the attention of the Jewish world. The World Zionist Organization (WZO) arose in conjunction with the series of annual Zionist congresses starting in Basle in 1897. The *Basle Program* sought "to create for the Jewish people a home in Palestine secured by public law." Among the organizations set up to implement this goal were the Jewish Colonial Trust to invest in development and the Jewish National Fund (JNF) to buy land.

The urgency of the needs of Russian Jewry and the large scale immigration that was inundating the West after the Kishinev pogrom in 1903 led Herzl to consider other sites The tentative offer by the British of a colony in East Africa in Uganda was accepted by the Zionist Congress in 1903 only with great opposition. Although he was warmly welcomed by the Jewish masses in Eastern Europe, Herzl's diplomatic maneuvering did not lead to the "charter" he sought. Ultimately fruitless were his audiences with the German kaiser, the sultan of Turkey, and even tsarist ministers in St. Petersburg. Nor did he receive the support of the Jewish magnates that he had sought. Rothschild, for one, firmly opposed the activities of Herzl. Unlike the latter, Rothschild had always been circumspect. The open and relatively well organized Zionist activity initiated by Herzl led to even greater restrictions by the Ottoman authorities in Palestine.[26]

The Zionist Congress of 1905 took place after Herzl's untimely death. It occurred in the aftermath of the pogroms following the aborted revolution of 1905 and the increased emigration that followed. The Russian Zionists, Chaim Weizmann among them, reemphasized the need to continue to strengthen the "practical" work being done on the ground in Palestine itself. At this same time, Nachman Syrkin had organized the first Labor Zionist group that, unlike the Bund and other socialist groups concerned with the Jewish worker, saw the need to build a social democratic culture in Palestine as part of the renewal of the Jewish people. There was recognition that the Social Democratic Marxist Revolution in Europe would not necessarily solve the Jewish question. The joining of Marxism and Zionism in the person of Ber Borochov exemplified the orientation of the *Poalei Zion* Russian wing. He connected the evolution of a socialist society in Palestine as a "historical necessity" and not merely based on historical memory.[27] Poalei Zion provided a way for young Jews committed to Socialism and a revolutionary stance in autocratic Russia to reconcile themselves with their Jewish identity. It was this spirit of idealism, of calling forth the Jewish youth to participate in making a just society in Palestine that would provide the spark for a renewed immigration.

The Second Aliyah consisted of some thirty-five thousand that came to Palestine between 1904 and 1914, doubling the Jewish population to about eighty thousand with the 10 percent settled on farms forming as many as twenty-five new settlements.[28] Unlike the previous group of immigrants in the 1880s, those who came to settle on the land were almost entirely secular and imbued with socialist principles. Children of lower-middle-class families, some of those from south Russia were from more assimilated families to whom Russian was their native language. The main contingent came from Lita—eastern Poland, Lithuania and Belorussia—mainly from small towns rather than the cities. Yiddish was their native language. Having come from a traditional Jewish environment, they knew some Hebrew.[28] Their idealism, eagerness for passionate debate as well as sectarianism reflected the character of the shtetls from which they came.[29]

They criticized the earlier settlers for having succumbed to the status of beggars living off the handouts of Rothschild philanthropy not unlike those of the "Old Yishuv" who had depended on alms. The ideology of the new immigrants was one of *Kibbush Ha'avoda* (Conquest by Labor). They sought renewal by physical labor rather than hiring lower-cost Arabs to work the land. Manual labor was one of the vehicles for renewal of the Jew in the new society and had a positive moral value. Worker moshavot were established for the first time such as *Merhavia* by these more idealistic immigrants. Although their absolute number was small, many of the leaders of the Yishuv and the generation that created the state were of this wave. This devotion to "productive work" and the displacement of the Arab brought about the beginnings of even more widespread Arab opposition among the peasant class.[30]

The Palestine Bureau of the World Zionist Organization established farms for training. These farms provided the nucleus of the idea of communal living that was to develop. The idea of worker collective settlements joined together the twin principles of conquest of the soil and that of labor. Land acquired by the Jewish National Fund was leased to worker communes. Starting with *Degania* in the Galilee in 1908, the *kvutzah* exemplified the living of a communal life with everyone receiving an equal salary and profits to be similarly divided. It was the forerunner of the later much larger *kibbutz* style of organization established in the wake of the Third Aliyah. To safeguard the settlements, a Jewish self-defense force came about called *Hashomer* (the Watchman). The latter also applied the principle of "conquest by labor" with self-reliance in security matters rather than the use of Arab guards. The Labor Zionist model of Halutzim (Pioneers) had begun to evolve that was to be the pattern for the next generation.

The Young Turk Revolution of 1908 in Constantinople deposed the sultan. The outbreak of World War I found Turkey allied with Germany against Russia as well as Britain and France. Orders of expulsion were issued for the large number of Jews who were Russian nationals. Even others who had acquired Ottoman citizenship such as David Ben-Gurion and Yitzak Ben-Zvi were nevertheless deported on the basis of their active role in the Zionist movement as leaders of the Poalei Zion. Circa eleven thousand persons were either expelled or left voluntarily by early 1915; many were given asylum by the British in Egypt.

Starting in 1915, disposition of the Ottoman areas in the Middle East was the subject of negotiations between the French and British. The original Sykes-Picot Agreement between Britain and France did not recognize Zionist aims and gave the British less control of Palestine than they came to wish. As an extension of their long-standing interest in Syria, the French claimed its southern segment of Palestine as well. By December 1916, with the advent of Lloyd George as prime minister, there had been a change in the British position regarding the value of Palestine for their imperial interests. In the spring of 1917, a pro-Zionist position was seen by the British as helpful vis-à-vis the French claims in Syria and also helpful in enlisting Jewish support for their war aims in the United States and elsewhere. The Balfour Declaration was finally issued on November 2, 1917 stating the British commitment to the establishment of a "national home for the Jews in Palestine. The relatively ambiguous term *national home* was considered by the Jews and others as a British guarantee of the eventual creation of a Jewish state in Palestine although the caveat existed to protect the rights of the existing inhabitants.[31]

To achieve some measure of participation in the expected British victory, a Jewish Legion was recruited to function within the British army. Although the Legion participated only to a minor degree in the expulsion of the Turks, the important principle had been established that there would be a Jewish fighting force. Veterans of this force settled in Palestine in the early postwar years.[32]

Chaim Weizmann had been instrumental in the course of the war in achieving the political breakthrough that Herzl had been unsuccessful in achieving. The *Balfour Declaration* established a special status for Jews in Eretz Israel under the benevolent auspices of a major power. There were those who viewed the

Declaration as a quasi-messianic occurrence, as a repetition
of history of the act of Cyrus that brought the Jews back from
Babylon.[33] Ultimately the actual implementation would require
the gradual accretion of settlement on the land itself.

The League of Nations gave the British the Mandate for
Palestine, incorporating language supportive of a Jewish home in
that territory. The *Jewish Agency* was recognized as the organization
of the Jewish community in Palestine. By the time of its final
ratification in 1922, the Mandate came to apply only to the
near side of the Jordan. Hussein was the sherif of Mecca and
the Guardian of the Holy Places who had helped the British in
fighting the Turks. The area east of the Jordan River came under
the rule of the Hashemite King Abdullah, the son of Hussein.

In the wake of the Balfour Declaration, the Third Aliyah
lasting from 1919 to 1923 brought thirty-seven thousand new
immigrants. In 1920-21 alone, some ten thousand immigrants
arrived during this first period of unrestricted immigration. The
first wave of Arab rioting occurred in the spring of 1920 and
again in 1921. In 1922, Winston Churchill as, colonial secretary,
issued a White Paper that stressed the restrictive principle of
"absorptive capacity" as limiting immigration. This principle
became ever more stringently applied in response to ongoing
Arab opposition.

Many of the immigrants in this wave were members of Zionist-
Socialist youth organizations. An unusually large number were
unattached young men and women in their twenties.[34] They
differed from those in the previous waves in having received
agricultural training and being more likely to speak Hebrew.
Graduates of the Russian Revolution and the Civil War, they were
the first to settle the then-malarial Jezreel Valley and establish
large-scale kibbutzim. One aspect of their contribution was the
Legion of Labor (Gdud Ha'avoda), an organization of workers
living under communal conditions who constructed roads and
a railroad as well as urban buildings.

Some members founded fairly large scale agricultural
collectives such as *Ein Harod* in the Jezreel Valley, the source of
one of the major kibbutz movements *Hakibbutz Hameu'chad*. (See
Glossary) Fiercely antiauthoritarian, their tenets included that
all were to have an equal share in government. Yet the ethos of

extreme libertarianism also involved rigid principles of behavior that were intolerant of any minority opinion.[35] Others became urban workers as part of a proletariat that began to emerge in centers such as Haifa and Tel Aviv. Still another group in this wave came from a background in the youth movement to form *Hashomer Hatzair* (Young Watchmen). They eventually organized kibbutzim that exemplified a more radical form of communal life with "children's houses," and negation of family life. Their organization established youth groups throughout the Jewish world that provided recruits for the kibbutzim in Palestine.

It was this third wave that established the Jewish labor movement as well as the large scale agricultural collectives. These first waves of immigrants in the Second and Third Aliyah developed the set of values so powerful that they continued to characterize Israeli politics and manners for the next fifty years.[36] *Histradut* (General Federation of Jewish Workers) was founded in 1920 with David Ben-Gurion eventually its secretary general. During the 1920s and 1930s, Histradut provided the entire range of social services including health and education as well as running large-scale industrial enterprises. Although originally many analogies were seen, the socialist model that developed in the Yishuv was not the negation of democracy that Russian Communism clearly became.[37]

The egalitarian ethos of the *New Yishuv* had become established by the 1920s upon which subsequent development was to occur. The Fourth Aliyah of immigration between 1923 and 1927 came mainly from Polish lower-middle-class dispossessed by the Polish anti-Semitic economic policies. Unable to enter the United States due to its restrictive immigration laws, they settled in the towns with Tel Aviv more than doubling its population between 1924 and 1926. An economic depression following real estate speculation caused widespread unemployment and even emigration from Palestine in the late 1920s.

Subsequent immigrants in the 1930s (Fifth Aliyah) was more likely to settle in urban settings and to come as family units. There was a steady immigration from interwar Lithuania conditioned by its widespread Hebrew-speaking school system and commitment to Zionist activity. Overall, the far larger number entering during this period reflected the need of German Jews for safe haven. The year 1935 had been a peak year for immigration with sixty-two thousand entering.

The British White Paper of 1939 restricted Jewish immigration to fifteent thousand per year for the next five years to assure Jewish minority status. This was at the time when all other doors to Jews were closed. Particularly after 1938, the formation of new settlements took on a quasi-military aspect as outposts of the Yishuv in conflict with the Arabs and the British. In general, these events marked the end of the era of cooperation between Great Britain and the Zionist movement that had lasted since the days of Balfour.[38]

Despite some commonality of ideology, the postwar Labour government in Britain maintained the restrictions on immigration.[39] Unrestricted immigration took place only after the formation of the independent state in 1948. By then, with few exceptions, there had been the destruction of the core in Lita in the Shoah/Holocaust.

The Palestine Labour Party (Mapai) formed in 1930 became the party that would eventually found the state. Labor Zionism and the Labor movement came to be synonymous with the governance of the Jewish community in Palestine. The largely Russian figures from the northern Pale of the Second Aliyah ruled Palestinian labor then the Zionist movement and ultimately the State of Israel.

6.1.3. The Response to the Migration

The growth of Palestinian Arab nationalism that has emerged since the end of World War I had paralleled the Zionist developments. The even-wider international Arab response, based on cultural-religious grounds, has transcended the specific concerns of the Palestinians and has made them hostages to its ideology.

Initially, there were few opportunities for the inhabitants to independently express concern to the Ottoman authorities. The governmental policies opposed Jewish settlement albeit tempered by venality and weaknesses of administrative control. Even prior to World War I, the hostile native Arab reaction already encompassed all parts of the country. The newspaper *Filastin* in Jaffa starting in 1911 and the equivalent newspaper *al-Karmil* in Haifa conducted a campaign against the purchase of land by the Jews. Although the number of members of Arab nationalist societies on the eve of the war was tiny, there was both a beginning of opposition to Turkish domination and the expression of opposition to Zionism.

This opposition became more vociferous after the Balfour Declaration and the British conquest. There was the formation of a *Muslim-Christian Association* (MCA) representing the more traditional notables and with support by the British Administration, to counteract the *Zionist Commission*.[40] Efforts initially focused on the abrogation of the Balfour Declaration on the basis of principles of self-determination under provisions of the League of Nations. When these failed, there was refusal to meet with the Zionists, choosing to work only with the British. Widespread public protests were organized in early 1920 on the occasion of the issuance of the public proclamation by the British of their intent to carry out the Balfour Declaration. A series of demonstrations culminated in a riot in Jerusalem in April 1920. Attacks also took place on scattered settlements with the capture of *Tel Hai* in the north the most memorable. The formation of the *Haganah* by Jabotinsky during this time was in line with his general efforts for Jewish self-defense and military action.

The anti-Zionist agitation did not prevent the ratification by the League of Nations of the British Mandate in 1922. The Mandate incorporated even more far-reaching support for the Zionist cause than the original Balfour Declaration in stating that the Jews were in Palestine by right. In turn, the Palestinians boycotted the attempt by the British to set up the institution of self-rule representing both the Arabs and the Jews. In practice, however, there was no boycott of cooperation with the British on lower levels. Arab leaders were not averse to selling land at high prices to the Jews on their own personal behalf whilst demanding the government forbid such sales. A relative acquiescence to the Jewish immigration had come about during the 1920s conditioned by the increased prosperity and the profits made by the rise in the price of land. Nevertheless, the nationalist ideology had been formulated by the urban elite that was to remain their stance from then on.

Its spread to the rural masses came about subsequently by the actions of the *Mufti* of Jerusalem appointed by the British. The appointment of Amin al-Huysayni as "Grand Mufti" paved the way for his presidency of the Supreme Muslim Council. He was thus empowered to deal with all Muslim religious affairs. In that role, he led a propaganda campaign, concerning the danger to the Muslim holy places of the Zionist designs on the Temple Mount. He succeeded in imbuing the masses with a sense of the Zionist threat. These activities led to the August 1929 riots centered originally around the use by the Jews of the *Wailing Wall* of the temple in a demonstration on the *ninth of Av*, the anniversary of the temple's destruction. An Arab counterdemonstration followed as well as attacks on Jews worshipping at the Temple Mount.[41] A large number of religious Jews living in the "holy cities" such as Hebron, in August 1929, were killed.

The subsequent British inquiry led to a recommendation to restrict immigration. The Passfield Report and the subsequent British White Paper emphasized the limited economic capacity of the country and the need to restrict Jewish immigration. It was counteracted only by direct pressure by British Jews on the Labour government (Cf Chapter 3.2.2). Nevertheless, the pattern was established that was to be put into effect following a new series of riots in 1936.[42]

During the 1930s, the Huysayni family led by the Grand Mufti became the Palestine Arab Party, the largest of several political groupings centered about wealthy notables united only in opposing Jewish immigration, land purchase and in their demands for an independent Arab state in Palestine. Because of rivalries, there was no united Arab voice until the end of 1935. In April 1936, assaults took place on Jews with reprisals on the Arabs. The Arab Higher Committee, under the Grand Mufti, united the various groups and called a general strike. The ongoing strike evolved into an armed rebellion with guerrilla warfare that lasted until the fall of 1936. During this time, interest in Palestine was awakened in the surrounding Arab lands including Saudi Arabia. Their intervention was significant in bringing the strike to an end that set a pattern of future Pan-Arab involvement.

A large number of British troops were brought in to restore order. A Royal Commission was appointed in 1936 under Lord

Peel that determined that the Palestine Mandate was unworkable in accordance with the claims of both the Arabs and Jews. The recommendation was for Partition into two states along with a British area safeguarding the Christian holy places and Jerusalem. The principle of partition was accepted by many of the Zionists led by Ben-Gurion and Weizmann but not by the various Arab parties.[43]

In the meantime, land purchases by Jews was restricted and immigration severely curtailed. In 1937, guerrilla bands operated once again under the authority of the Grand Mufti, now exiled to Lebanon. The partition scheme was scuttled. The ensuing White Paper in 1939 confirmed the arrangements for eventual self-government but on the basis of an Arab majority with Jewish immigration limited to fifteen thousand a year. It represented a British withdrawal from the provisions if the Balfour Declaration and the Mandate in face of Arabic opposition.[44]

6.2 The Evolution of the Culture

6.2.1 The Founding Generation

The Jew as a "new man" was one of the aims of the Haskalah. The "new Jew" was connected not only with a sense of self-conscious nationalism but with the Land of Israel. Only there in the land of their fathers could the transformation take place.[1] The existing generation were "the children of the desert." Analogous to those in Exodus, they were condemned to wander for the time needed to rediscover the their strength as a people. There were several pioneers arising out of their East European Litvak background that came to the embryonic *New Yishuv* to form its yet undeveloped ethos.

The Hebrew Language

Born in a village in Lithuania in 1858, Eliezer Perlman adopted what had been his pen name of *Ben-Yehuda* when he moved to

Palestine in 1881. In hebraizing his name, he was the forerunner of what was to be a Zionist passion. His father was a Habad Hassid who died when the boy was five years old. Recognized as a scholar, the boy was sent to yeshivah at age thirteen at Polotsk. There, he came under the influence of a Maskil, Rabbi Blucker, who, although being a great Torah scholar, also introduced his student to the study of Hebrew grammar and translations of secular books such as *Robinson Crusoe*.[2] The young man was then sent for training in the Vilna district where he came under the influence of another Maskil, Samuel Herz Jonas. He was enabled to learn Russian as well as other modern European languages and then enrolled in the Dvinsk gymnasium from which he graduated in 1877. While there, he became involved with the Populists in their focus on the Russian peasant. In his partial dissociation from his Jewish roots, he nevertheless maintained his connection with Hebrew.[3]

The striving for national identity of countries such as Bulgaria in 1878 during the Russo-Turkish War brought him a vision of the equivalent need for a renewal of the Jewish nation in its own land. The Jews had to become again a living nation. The passage in George Eliot's *Daniel Deronda* in 1876 had impact on Ben-Yehuda like many others. "Revive the organic centre . . . Looking toward a land [where] . . . our dispersed people in all the ends of the earth may share the dignity of a national life . . . which will plant the wisdom and skill of our race so that it may be, as of old, a medium of transmission and understanding."[4]

While a medical student in Paris, he published in 1879 in Smolenskin's *Ha-Shahar* the essay "A Worthy Question," which outlined the fundamental principles of spiritual Zionism. Zion was seen as a national center designed to save from assimilation those Jews in the Diaspora. One aspect would be the revival of Hebrew that could come about only if the nation were revived in their homeland. From the start, his nationalism was explicitly territorial and political and not merely one of the "spirit." Influenced by his Populist notions of "going to the people," he sought the further transformation of Hebrew from its use in relatively elite secular settings, characteristic of the Haskalah, to its use in common settings.[5] While visiting Algiers for his health, he observed persons using Hebrew as a spoken language with the Sephardic pronunciation. He chose the Sephardic pronunciation of Hebrew as being closer to the biblical tongue and to differentiate from the Ashkenazi usage in the *Galut* (Exile).[6]

He came to Palestine in the fall of 1881, after marrying his Russian tutor Deborah, the daughter of Samuel Herz Jonas. Their commitment was to use Hebrew alone for all communication. Their son, Ittamar, became the first native Hebrew speaker. After his wife's death due to tuberculosis in 1891, her sister then came to Palestine. Assuming the Hebrew name of Hemda, she became his second wife and long-time collaborator.

In an extraordinarily single-minded way, and despite his physical frailty, he devoted himself to the introduction of Hebrew as the language of instruction in the schools. In his post in the Alliance Israelite Universelle school in Jerusalem he pioneered the *immersion* method of instruction using Hebrew for the teaching of Hebrew. Others in the settlements took up the development of this method and the eventual expansion of the use of Hebrew as the general language of instruction.[7] For example, the school at Rishon LeZion became an all-Hebrew school in 1888. This development led, under the auspices of Menachem Ussishkin, to the commitment of the *Teachers' Association* in 1903-1904 to the use of Hebrew in the settlements.[8] During the succeeding years, city schools, starting in Jaffa, also began to expand their use of Hebrew as the language of instruction. The first Hebrew gymnasium (secondary school) was founded in Jaffa in 1906. The *Herzliya Gymnasium* became a cultural and national symbol. In 1913-1914 Hebrew replaced German as the language of instruction in the technical high school and eventually in the *Technion* (School of Technology).[9] Success in the use of Hebrew as the language of instruction in the schools was the basis for the new generation of native Hebrew speakers.

Perlman was a journalist and editor of the weekly, and then daily *Ha'or*. Unlike the other Hebrew publications focused on literary issues, his newspaper dealt with daily concerns. He was involved in all activities in Eretz Israel to accomplish cultural renewal by supporting work on the land, the use of Hebrew as a living language, and the development of a modern Hebrew unadorned literary style. Such a revival was to lead to the creation of a modern Hebrew literature.[10] He earned the ongoing enmity of the religious people in Jerusalem for his determination to use Hebrew as a secular rather than only as a holy language.

A short-lived society he set up in 1889 was the part of his recurrent efforts to establish Hebrew terms for modern words in daily use and creating a uniform system of pronunciation. It was the forerunner of the *Hebrew Language Academy* that carries on this work even today.[11] Ancient Hebrew roots were given modern forms. Both biblical and postbiblical sources were incorporated. The establishment of Hebrew as a "social" language in daily interactions came about because of the commitment of the pioneers of the Second Aliyah, several of whom already knew some Hebrew. After the Third Aliyah, the founding of the Hebrew-speaking Histradut was the basis for the development of the entire Hebrew-speaking Yishuv.[12] In 1919, a breakthrough occurred when Hebrew was declared as one of the three official languages of the Mandate along with Arabic and English. Ben-Yehudah's work included a pocket dictionary in 1902 that contained Hebrew-Russian-Yiddish and his multivolume *Dictionary of the Hebrew Language*. Started in 1910, it was completed in 1959 long after his death in Eretz Israel in 1922.

Ben-Yehuda was a child of the Haskalah, building on the earlier work of Alexander Mapu and others in Lita to create secular Hebrew as a written language. He applied the Haskalah principle of *self-realization* in his own life work. His scholarly but also practical work initiated an extraordinary renaissance of what has become once again a living language spoken by the modern inhabitants of the Jewish state. Although the development of a Hebrew-speaking society was required to create this achievement, it is also true that the commitment to this one base language was instrumental in the creation of the Yishuv as an entity and, in turn, the State of Israel.[13]

Compatible with the aims of "cultural Zionism" of Ben Yehuda was the influence of Asher Ginsburg (*Ahad Ha'am*) in developing the Yishuv as "a light unto the Diaspora."[14] As editor of *Hashiloah* from 1899 to 1902, Ginsberg had great influence on Hebrew literary style toward greater clarity. In one of his visits to Eretz Israel in 1912, helped rejuvenate the work of Ben Yehuda on establishing commonality of curriculum and Hebrew vocabulary within the schools.[15]

Not given to romantic yearnings, he was by nature a rationalist and a cultural elitist. He had a "distinctly Lithuanian (or mitnagdic) element in his personality, in his patterns of thought and analysis . . . On his emphasis on clarity and consistency." He sought continuity of Jewish thought and thus found value in the Diaspora unlike the more socialistic and Nietzschean models of the "new Jew."[16] After his withdrawal from literary as well as political activity, Ahad Ha'am became almost a mythological figure to whom the leaders of the Yishuv of the Mandate attributed enormous influence and an almost saintly character. Although his adulation waned, it was his principle of the relation of Israel to a continuing Diaspora that eventually received justification.[17] Finally moving to Tel Aviv in 1922, he died there in 1927.

The Redemption of the Land

Menachem (Mendel) Ussishkin was born in August 1863 in Dubrovna in the Mohilev District of Lita. An only son, his father was a Lithuanian Habad Hassid who was described as "God fearing, good hearted, and level headed." His only living sister died as a young woman, leaving him as an only child. Since the father was a wealthy merchant, the family was permitted to move to Moscow in 1871. Ater his bar mitzvah in 1876, he was sent to a secular school for a general education while continuing his Hebrew studies after regular school hours. His tutor in modern Hebrew was one of the leading Maskilim of the day. He was introduced to the leading Hebrew periodicals as well as Hebrew translations of European literature and original Hebrew writings such as those of Mapu. He nevertheless remained committed to his religious studies. As a high school student in 1882, he founded his own *Society for Immigrants to the Land of Israel* from which he dates his service to the Jewish national movement. He took part in the Lovers of Zion movement in raising funds for settlement and, in 1885, elected secretary of their branches in Moscow.

In accordance with his own background, he succeeded in gaining the important endorsement of the Habad Hassid rabbi of this movement with eventual publication of the endorsement in *Hamelitz*. In a similar role, at the Druskenik (near Grodno) Conference in 1887, he was able to reconcile the opposing religious and secular components of the movement. The BILU freethinkers who had settled in Gedera had refused to follow religious traditions and the rabbis such as Mohliver wished to depose their supporter Moshe Lilienblum from his position in the Lovers of Zion directorate

In 1889, Ussishkin became a Moscow representative of the *B'nai Moshe* set up by Ahad Ha'am in support of cultural renewal. That same year, he graduated as an engineer. His honeymoon in 1891 was spent in Palestine on the first of several trips. On his return, he countered the very pessimistic spirit of Ahad Ha'am's article in 1891 by the report of his own visit.[18]

Ussishkin was a delegate to the First Zionist Congress in 1897 as a representative of the Russian Zionists. As a follower of Ahad Ha'am, he was initially opposed to Herzl but became a supporter. A forceful speaker, he was the dominant figure in Russian Zionism. He actively opposed the Uganda Project by organizing the Russian group in opposition.[19] He became closely associated with the Weizmann faction in support of "practical Zionism," following the death of Herzl. Early on, he advocated the recruitment of youth for work on the land that provided the ideas of the Second Aliyah. His commitment to the Hebrew language was evidenced by his leadership in the meeting in 1903 that set standards for use of Hebrew in education. He was also one of the first to recommend the founding of a Hebrew University in Jerusalem.

He finally settled in the Yishuv permanently in 1920, becoming chairman of the Jewish National Fund in 1922. Devoted to the purchase of land for Jewish settlement, the total number of dunams held by JNF increased from 22,000 to 561,000 by the time of his death in 1941. The land was held in perpetuity and leased on the proviso that Jewish workers were to cultivate the land with their own hands. He was firmly opposed to Partition when others came to accept it after the Peel Commission. His Zionism synthesized in his life the several principles of politics, economics, and culture with focus on the sanctity of Jerusalem and the redemption of the *Land* of Israel.

The Haskalah as expressed in the Pale in both Vilna and Odessa has as its goal the entry of Jews into the modern world including a search for a political solution to their existence as a nation. In carrying out what was a secular revolution, the link between their entirely spiritual existence as a nation and the religious tradition tended to be dissolved. The passivity enjoined during the exile had been maintained by the religious tradition. Bringing about the reestablishment of a Jewish Commonwealth in Zion independent of the Messiah was incompatible with many religious traditionalists living in the Palestine of the *Old Yishuv*. There were relatively few religious leaders who saw nationalism as a favorable development for reconciling Torah and Haskalah. Although opposition to "hastening the end" existed among the mitnagdim, it was less highly developed than in Hassid circles.[20] Conflict remained between those who were secular and saw nationalism and Zionism as an alternative to assimilation and those who saw it as the fulfillment of the ancient dream. The latter was the life work of Abraham Isaac Kook.

The Religious Redemption of Israel

Born in Grieve, a town in the northwestern province of Courland in 1864, Abraham Hayim Kook was the descendent of several generations of scholars. The dominant tradition in the home was the austere Torah learning of the mitnagdim. He studied in the traditional heder and under the tutelege of his father, a pious scholar. He was fluent in speaking Hebrew.[21] By age nine, he was described as a "prodigy" and permitted to study alone. At age fifteen, he traveled to another town to study and live the life of Torah. Additional to the traditional Talmudic study, he studied secular subjects as well as Jewish philosophy and mysticism. He became a disciple of Rabbi Salanter of the mussar movement. He went on to become a graduate of the famed yeshivah at Volozhin.[22] Kook was heavily influenced by Rabbi Naphtali Zvi Yehuda (Neziv) Berlin, its head, in the direction of love of Zion and the unity of the Jewish people. These remained the pillars of his mature life. After marriage to the daughter of a leading rabbi, he was appointed rabbi of series of towns in Lita.

During this time, he studied kabbalah and became imbued with mysticism that made him one of its great masters.[23] He also began to develop his synthesis of Orthodoxy and Zionism.[24]

His 1901 essay "The Mission of Israel and its Nationhood" asserted that Jewish nationalism with all its secular aspects is nevertheless the expression of the Jewish relationship with the divine. He identified with the Zionist movement seeing it as the beginning of divine redemption of the Jewish people as foretold in the Bible. He sought within that redemption to express also a return to Torah. He preached that the religious dimension does not consist merely of pietistic emphasis on Sabbath observance and use of *tefillin*. Rather, in line with his kabbalistic thinking, religion extends to the entire range of immediate human endeavor that becomes invested with religious significance.[25] His stance aided in establishing the legitimacy of religious Zionism.

Despite having alternative posts offered in such centers as Vilna and Kovno, Kook became rabbi of Jaffa in Palestine in 1904.[26] The idealistic youth of the Second Aliyah saw religion as tainted with the pietism and obscurantism of the *Old Yishuv* exemplified by those living on alms. Once again in 1909 as in previous *Sabbatical* years, the question was, how one may observe the requirements to leave the land untilled? In direct opposition to most of the other rabbis, Kook found a method to maintain the principle while maintaining control of the hard-won land and its crops by permitting the temporary "sale" of the land to non-Jews.

Stranded in London during World War I, he returned in 1920 to become, under British rule, the first Ashkenazi chief rabbi in Jerusalem. Despite opposition from the extreme anti-Zionist Orthodox, in his role of chief rabbi until his death in 1935, he became emblematic of the unity of Israel rather than narrow sectarianism.[27] He tried to reconcile the two strands of religion and Zionism. Indeed, he preached that one could consider even the devotion of *kibbutzniks* to justice and equality as in itself religious. Their concern with social justice was consistent with the Torah. He maintained that the "divine spark" that led to the social passion was a seed for the future that must be nurtured and made more widespread. Conversely, those who were committed to traditional Judaism must be concerned with social justice as part of their own creed. In his harmonizing view, holiness must include the physical and the intellectual as a basis for the spiritual. The Jewish people need the land to regain their "wholeness."[28] In his dialectical way of thinking, there would ultimately be a synthesis in which the secular strand would become incorporated in what he saw to be the overall divine pattern.[29]

His major educational initiative was founding a yeshivah in Jerusalem reflecting his commitment to Zionism and the inclusion of secular subjects to prepare spiritual leaders in modern times. Graduates played leading roles among religious Halutzim and in the general educational system established after Statehood. This work was to be carried on in the next generation by his son Rabbi Zvi Yehudah Kook.

The Second Aliyah followed the experience of the Kishinev Pogrom of 1903 and the abortive revolution of 1905 and the subsequent pogroms. Almost all the leaders that arose from the Second Aliyah were about the same age, born in the 1880s, and from the small towns in Lita. Almost all had learned Hebrew in the traditional heder. Although they rejected Orthodox Judaism, they were not stridently antireligious. They retained both the strengths and limitations of the shtetl along with the other characteristics of their time. Like the more purely Russian student intelligentsia at the turn of the century, they retained the sectarianism and the idealism, the utter commitment to egalitarian and democratic principles. They were not liberals but Socialists devoted to creating a just society.[30] Unlike the earlier *Lovers of Zion*, they were the *Workers of Zion* (Poalei Zion).

The Religion of Labor

The Palestine Poalei Zion group was part of the larger Socialist movement with membership in the Second Socialist International. Its more ideological Marxist stance initially differed from the *Hapoel Hatzair* (the Young Worker), the nascent labor grouping in Palestine itself. The latter was more "practical" but idealistic, less Marxist and class conscious with A. D. Gordon as their mentor. Both groupings focused on the moral value of manual labor and the importance of such labor in the regeneration of the Jewish people. Yet even when unified in the *Histradut* and later in the

Mapai, the *Hapoel Hatzair* (Cf Glossary) retained their ideological stand toward a more humanistic approach to many issues including the possibility of cooperation with the Arabs and more evolutionary rather than revolutionary activities.[31]

Unlike so many of the other immigrants during this era, Aharon David Gordon was a whole generation older. Born in 1856 in Troynaov Russia, his grandfather had been a noted scholar and his father worked for the leading Jewish notable Baron Joseph Guenzburg, a relative. After a traditional education by tutors, Gordon also studied secular subjects on his own including the philosophers of his time such as Kant, Schopenhauer, and Tolstoy. In addition to his study of the Bible and the Talmud, he had also studied Hassidic literature but was most influenced by the ethical writings of the mussar movement in Lita. He remained as a manager of one of the Guenzburg estates until 1903. Married and with a family, he nevertheless decided to emigrate to Eretz Israel in 1904. He worked as a laborer in the vineyards and orange groves of Petah Tiqva and Rishon LeZion before going to the Galilee in 1912. He eventually settled in Degania near Lake Kinneret where he died in 1922.

Despite his advanced age, he worked in the fields. Coming to live in the land was invested with spiritual significance. Heavily influenced by Tolstoy, he idealized physical labor as a path to spiritual self-improvement for all mankind. Work became really sacred with devotion to it in purity and reverence analogous to the traditional Jew to Torah and prayer.[32] His faith was, having lived in exile cut off from nature, by work on the land itself, one would once again lead a full life, to be "down to earth."[33] This need was particularly true for the Jew who had been exiled both from nature and from Eretz Israel. The religious dimension for Gordon was not because the land was promised in the Bible. Rather because it was in the land of Israel that the Hebrews created their Bible. "Just as an uprooted plant can renew its growth only in that soil to which it is suited, so an exiled people can renew itself only by returning to its natural homeland."[34] The land would ultimately belong to those who worked it, making it fertile and establishing a new more just society.

His writings dealt with renewal as coming for the individual by one's close association with nature rather than overthrow of institutions. His writings had considerable influence on young Jews in a spirit of self-sacrifice in pursuit of a social and national ideal. From 1909 onward, he wrote a series of essays in Hebrew weekly *Hapoel Hatzair* that became the basis for that movement. He opposed the Marxism of the Poalei Zion as being too mechanistic and materialistic as well as internationalistic.[35]

The Hebrew Literary Renaissance

Joseph Hayyim Brenner was born in the Ukraine in 1881, the son of a poor itinerant Hebrew teacher who had traveled to the Ukraine from his native Lita. Like so many others, the father had come to the more prosperous South where a Litvak was valued for his learning. As a prodigy son of a melamed, young Brenner was made to perform feats of scholarship to reflect favorably on his father's reputation. Brenner studied at a yeshivah starting at age fifteen between 1894 and 1897 and then became familiar with secular writers particularly Tolstoy and Dostoevsky. After leaving the yeshivah, he went to Bialystok finding work as a *sofer*, a scribe writing Hebrew scrolls. He became involved with the Bund and continued for a time as editor of its underground Yiddish paper *Der Kampf* before focusing on Hebrew and Zionism. His first book of Hebrew short stories was published in Warsaw in 1900. His first novel was the autobiographical *In Winter* written in 1902-03 and published in the Hebrew journal *HaShiloah*.[36]

Rescued by his Bundist friends from his forced service in the tsarist army, he fled to London in 1902. He remained there until 1908 working as a printer. His plan was to establish a settlement in Palestine or in Russia based on the teachings of Tolstoy. He became active in the Poalei Zion movement and managed almost single-handedly to publish a Hebrew monthly magazine *Hame'orer* (the Awakener). He finally arrived in Eretz Israel in 1909.[37] There he married and had a son. He became editor of the socialist-Zionist Hebrew weekly *Hapoel Hatzair* where he published his own work as well as the essays of Gordon.[38]

During World War I, he taught at the famous Herzliya High School in Tel Aviv, the first secular Hebrew school of its kind in Eretz Israel. He remained both a writer and a worker. In 1920 he went to the Galilee where he worked on road construction and taught

Hebrew to pioneers as a member of the *Ahdut Ha'avodah* movement. Brenner championed the cause of Gordon's redemption by labor and participated in the founding of Histradut in 1921. He founded *Ha'Adamah* (the *Soil*) in 1920 as a literary monthly that continued even after his death. His pessimism about Jewish life when divorced from "the deed" resonated within the Jewish labor union movement in Palestine. He dominated the scene not only as an author but also critic, editor, translator and above all, as a literary personality. His compeers regarded him as a secular servant of God.[39]

His *Russian* background was exemplified in the use of literature to express a social and political stance that projected an underlying spirituality. It is instructive that he chose to translate into Hebrew the works of Tolstoy and Dostoevsky who represented that aspect of Russian culture.[40] In his Hebrew style as well as in his content, he was an innovator. He brought to Hebrew a "novelistic" style.[41] Brenner wrote mainly autobiographical short stories and novels influenced strongly by the antirationalist thinking of Nietzsche and the latter's disciple Mischa Yosef Berdichevsky. His characters were torn from their traditional moorings, struggling to find a new ideology, but who found the Haskalah insufficient. They had left the ghetto only to find Western culture inhospitable and perhaps undesirable.

He had to deal with the discrepancies between the image of Eretz Israel that is held abroad and the "reality" of Palestine. Although everything was hopeless and if one faced those facts, the only honest recourse was to hold onto life against rationality and *nevertheless* build roots.[42] There was his uncompromising almost ruthless denial of utopian hope yet "one must continue." His work may be considered the climax of the evolution of writing in Hebrew in the vein of social realism advocated by Ben Yehuda. Brenner led a secluded ascetic existence and was killed in the disturbances of 1921 around Jaffa. It was consistent with his character that he refused to leave the house where he was in danger, giving up his chance to escape in favor of others.

The story of Brenner's death coupled with his character during life led to his becoming mythologized along with Trumpeldor, the hero of Tel Hai.[43] The story of the latter served to replace the passive martyrdom of those in pogroms in European history willing to die to sanctify God's name with an alternative of fighting against all odds and willingness to die in sanctification of one's *nation*.[44]

6.2.2 The Generation of the Yishuv.

The riots in Jaffa in May 1921 had immediate consequences in the process of separation between the Arabs and Jews. Tel Aviv became a separate municipality with movement of Jews formerly living in Jaffa to new sites in what had been merely an adjacent suburb. This process was emblematic of the developments of the interwar era that led to a consolidation of the Yishuv.[1] The temporary Zionist Commission was succeeded by the Zionist Executive as leadership of the new *Jewish Agency*. The latter was to become the unofficial Jewish government.

The character of the Yishuv, the Jewish settlement, during the period between the Balfour Declaration and statehood was one of consolidation under the auspices of Labor. In accordance with their Russian background, the members of the Second and Third Aliyah came with the experience of a collectivistic rather than individualistic ethos. However, the *Ahdut Ha'avodah Party* (Party of Labour) founded in 1919 differed from the models developed in the Soviet Union. It was more open to the private sector and thus developed a mixed economy although heavily influenced by socialism. Moreover, the party did not have the coercive power. Power had to be responsive to a democratic process. Political dominance came about by virtue of the economic organization that they achieved rather than the obverse.[2]

The Palestine Labor Movement

The Jewish labor movement in Palestine did not arise wholly out of the European rationalist tradition. With its strong ethnic component and nationalist roots, it was shaped by Jewish myth. There were the dreams of messianism, redemption, and the realization of God's kingdom on earth. It was basically a religious movement although anticlerical in line with its other roots in the Hebrew Haskalah. Their faith was millennial, that the realization of the Zionist idea was immanent, that the messiah will come along with the idea of a social revolution. The religious fervor and self-sacrifice that pervaded the Russian revolutionary movement remained one of the drivers of the socialist Zionist enterprise enabling its believers to undergo the privations and struggle.[3]

One of this group that united experience in the traditional shtetl with Zion in his work and his life was Zalman Shazar. He was born in 1889 in Mir, the site of a famous yeshivah in Lita. The name Shazar is actually an acronym derived from the components of the name Schneur Rubashow. The middle name of Schneur reflects the family connection with the Lubavitzer rebbe of Habad. The boy's upbringing was of Talmudic study tempered with Hassidic joy. Zalman learned Bible and Talmud and learned Hebrew grammar from a young poet who also introduced him to Zionism and the writings of Ahad Ha'am.[4] Following his bar mitzvah he decided to pursue secular studies. Already a member of the local Poalei Zion group, he led the Jewish youth of his town in opposition to the Bund. By 1906, despite his youth, he had been a delegate to the secret Poalei Zion conference in Minsk where he met Itzak Ben Zvi. The latter had already settled in Palestine where he organized the self-defense guards for the settlements. Shazar's membership in what was both a socialist and Zionist group was cemented by his exposure to the wretched lives of Jewish weavers. He decided that he could not devote his life to scholarship alone but to the Jewish labor movement.[5]

In 1907, he was arrested while editing the Labor Zionist newspaper in Vilna. After his release he enrolled in the extraordinary nondegree-granting *Academy of Jewish Studies* founded by the famous Baron Guenzburg in St. Petersburg. He studied with men such as Dubnow. He visited Eretz Israel for the first time in 1911 and worked at one of the early communal settlements in the Galilee before returning to Russia. It was during that visit that he first met Berl Katznelson who was to have a major influence on his life. In 1912, just prior to the war, he was enrolled at the University of Freiburg. Shazar spent the war years in the study of history and philosophy in Germany with completion of his studies in 1919 at University of Berlin. During these years he continued his political work as editor of the German Zionist journal and encouraged the development of the Labor Zionist movement there.

He settled in Palestine in 1924 where he worked alongside his wife in Zionist activity. He was appointed to the executive committee of the Histradut and an editor of its newspaper *Davar* from its start in 1925. In his mature work in connection with Zionism, he continued to deal with the issues of messianism exemplified by the Shabbatei Zvi movement.[50] He recalled the time when as a child he first heard the name of this false messiah mentioned by an anti-Zionist in conjunction with the recent appearance of Herzl leading the Jews to the Promised Land.[6] His life and work was devoted to making this new messianic effort come to pass.

In carrying out the messianic impulse in Judaism, it was incumbent to create what would be a *just* commonwealth. Labor Zionism was for Shazar the instrument for accomplishing this mission. His contribution was to embed such a return within a historical and educational context. His role was reflected in his work on *Davar* and as chairman of the Educational Department of the Jewish Agency during the Mandate. He was the first minister of education and culture after independence. His commitment to bringing about unity was fulfilled as the third president of Israel starting in 1962 and ending only in 1973 just before his death in 1974.

Berl Katznelson in turn became one of the spiritual fathers of the reconstructed Zionist culture incorporating items from the past into the new secular ethos. He was born in January 1887 in Bobruisk in Belorussia in Lita. It was a district capital in the Minsk area at the confluence of two rivers that transported the timber that was the main source of livelihood. More than half its forty thousand inhabitants were Jews. The father, Moshe, had traveled to Vilna as a young man in search of an education. There in 1879, he married a daughter of the Strashun family, the founder of the famed library in Vilna. There was a son of that marriage before the wife's death in 1886. He then returned to Bobruisk to marry again.

Berl was the first of five living children of the second marriage. The father was a timber merchant who would travel widely, returning home only twice yearly. There was an extensive library with secular Russian as well as Hebrew and Yiddish works to which the boy had access. Only after firm grounding in Hebrew was he then exposed to Russian. Aged twelve at the time of his father's death, Berl was introduced to the Zionist as well as the revolutionary ferment of his times. He joined the Poalei Zion movement as a follower of Nachman Syrkin. He started out teaching Hebrew literature and Jewish history to poor girls in a school subsidized by the Jewish Society for Propagation of Enlightenment (OPE). He tried unsuccessfully to develop a trade, working as a tinsmith and then foundry worker before sailing for Palestine in 1909.

Soon after his arrival, he met Yosef Brenner. Like Brenner, Berl "shared the uncompromising vision of his people, a sense of doom yet a burgeoning hope."[7] He identified with the "vital spirit" of the people expressed in the unconventional direct approach to human relations and nature as an antidote to the spiritual and highly intellectual life of the Pale of Settlement. Berl also committed himself to the exclusive use of Hebrew. He sought to prove himself as a laborer in the orange groves as part of the proletarian ethos of the Second Aliyah.

He developed the idea of a communal settlement where the members worked for themselves rather than the use of hired help. This was to occur on land that was provided by the Jewish National Fund. For him, work was a path to self-regeneration. Temporarily in *Kinneret* farm in the Galilee, he became a leader of the agricultural workers in a strike against the management. Starting in 1911, he became representative at a conference of agricultural workers in Judea. He led in the development of a sick fund and subsequently became fully involved in practical work on behalf of the agricultural union. He became its spokesman with the Zionist authorities in seeking support for the settlements.

In the wake of the Balfour Declaration, the relatively few survivors of the Second Aliyah were the seed from which there was to be a movement that was both social and national. One result of the enthusiasm attendant to the Declaration was the formation of the Jewish Legion in the British army. It included volunteers from Palestine as well as the Diaspora. Although disappointed in opportunities to act in the liberation of portions such as the Galilee still under Turkish control, it accorded a chance for Katzelson and Ben-Gurion to join together. They became close comrades.

Ben-Gurion led in jettisoning some of the Marxist rhetoric of the Poalei Zion while retaining the connection to the Socialist

Second International and the World Poalei Zion movement. Ahdut Ha'avodah (Unity of Labor) formed in 1919 reflected some of the characteristics of the agricultural union developed by Katznelson. These principles were to build a large-scale pioneering movement based upon workers organized in unions. The organization was designed to incorporate social-economic development but did not yet include the non-Marxist Hapoel Hatzair (Young Worker) nor the newcomers of the Third Aliyah.[8]

In 1920, Katznelson represented the socialist Unity of Labor Party in the formation of a unified group to include both the Hapoel Hatzair and the newcomers. This rapidly growing organization included both city and agricultural laborers in what was called the General Federation of Workers (Histradut). This new labor organization took on the social-economic and national activities of the Unity of Labor Party. The two essentially included the same leadership derived almost entirely of veterans of the Second Aliyah. The party took on the leadership and control of the larger Histradut on the basis of the need for commitment to national rather than narrower trade union goals with David Ben-Gurion eventually becoming secretary of the Histradut.[9]

In 1925, Katznelson became the editor in chief of Davar (the Word) the Histradut daily paper of which Shazar was one of the editors. Davar had a major influence on formulating Jewish public opinion during the Mandate.[55] Katznelson believed in the power of the written word in its literary as well as political aspects with men like the poet Agnon on the staff as well as political correspondents.

As the spiritual leader of the Labour Movement, Katznelson sought to replace conventional religion with spirituality that was a glorification of the pioneering life in Eretz Israel. Yet steeped as he was in links with the Jewish past, he evoked the traditional symbols in reference to the new pioneering life-style. For example, he appreciated the role of the Jewish holidays in the creation of the new Hebraic culture.[56] Although the overriding goal was to shape the image of the Jewish society in the spirit of the socialist ideals, it was unlike what evolved in Russia under the Bolsheviks. The Palestinian model was voluntaristic and pluralistic. Its concern with human values was to a considerable extent the reflection of Katzelson.[10]

The connection with the worldwide Poalei Zion movement was stormy with the Palestinian movement under Ben Gurion establishing its rights to pursue its own unique direction and the primacy of Hebrew vis-à-vis Yiddish. The original hope that the communal way of life exemplified by the kibbutz would be the major mode of organization did not eventually succeed. Further, the Histradut came to include a larger percentage of urban workers reflecting a class interest in socialism. The unification of the Ahdut Ha'avodah and Hapoel Hatzair into the combined Labour party of *Mapai* occurred in 1931. The form was now established by which a Labour party had a dominant position within the Yishuv but one that permitted a mixed economy and democratic opposition all united in the service of socialist-Zionist ideology. The Palestinian labor groups together became the largest single grouping in the World Zionist Organization. Its dominant position in the World Zionist movement enlisted middle-class interests in the Diaspora to support the Yishuv.[11]

The Hebrew Renaissance

In the formation of the Zionist-Socialist ethos of the Yishuv, the role of the intellectual was integral. To a considerable degree, the social-political leadership was itself "intellectual" in that its currency was ideological and at the outset their energies highly focused on cultural activities. During the evolution of the Histradut and its political and economic emphasis, there was a deterioration of that cultural focus. The cultural renaissance intrinsic to Zionism was led by men of Hebrew letters, scholars, and teachers who were not directly tied to the political establishment.[12] Although supportive of the Labor Zionist ethos they were not necessarily socialist but united in the cause of commitment to the Hebrew language. They were self-conscious in their role in the New Yishuv where spiritual achievement arose not from theology but from literature. In line with their roots in the Russian intelligentsia, literature had not merely an aesthetic role but an ethical and social role. *Agudat ha-Sofrim,* the title of the Association of Hebrew Writers, transcends the word *writers* to reflect broader meaning of *men of letters.*

The formation of the Association of Hebrew Writers came about gradually in the 1920s as the writers withdrew from the now more politicized Hapoel Hatzair and founded, in 1922, a more purely literary journal albeit for workers called *Hedim* (Echoes). Its initial developments were particularly encouraged by such Labor ideologues as Katznelson. In the Third and Fourth Aliyah, there was immigration from the previous Hebrew cultural centers such as Warsaw and Odessa to Eretz Israel in the spirit of Ahad Ha'am. The joining of this group with the earlier one provided a more self-consciously literary and less worker-oriented crystallization of the *Agudat ha-Sofrim*. A cultural elite arose separate from but not necessarily antagonistic to the prevalent Labor ideology. Its orientation was not the establishment of an organization devoted to their professional interests as much as spiritual leaders in a cultural mission.[13] One who represented this transfer of the East European intellectual life to the Yishuv was Joseph Klausner.

Joseph Klausner was born near Vilna in Lita in 1874. His father was "religiously observant" with the mother both more devout and committed to a return to Zion. She was, unusual for her time, literate in Yiddish, Hebrew, and German. The boy went to heder for a relatively short time but was strongly influenced by the private instruction by a Maskil who was also a member of the Lovers of Zion. Hebrew was taught as a living language. The family moved to Odessa in 1885. The father eked out a living as a storekeeper and died in 1904. Klausner attended a Hebrew day school where secular subjects were taught and languages such as German and Russian. He was the youngest member in 1891 of a group advocating the revival of Hebrew as a spoken language and spoke only Hebrew to his friends. As early as 1893, he published an article in *Hamelitz* calling for the modernization of the language.[14]

Unable to enter a Russian university due to a *numerus clausus* limiting the number of Jewish students, he studied Semitic languages, philosophy, and history at University of Heidelberg starting in 1897. That same year, he was a delegate to the First Zionist Congress in Basle and to the nearly every succeeding one until 1913. His dissertation in 1901 was on "the messianic idea in Jewish history," a theme he was to return to throughout his life. In 1902, at age twenty-eight, he succeeded Ahad Ha'am as editor of the important Hebrew literary monthly *Ha'Shiloah*, first in Warsaw then Odessa and finally in Eretz Israel until 1926. For a time in Warsaw and Odessa, Bialik was his coeditor. They published the best poetry, fiction, and criticism with such authors as Mendele Mokher Seforim and Brenner. Support for Klausner and the frequently struggling monthly came from Menachem Ussishkin.[15]

He immigrated to Eretz Israel in 1919 to become a leader in what was becoming the center of Hebrew literary and cultural life. There was a commitment to *Hebrew* culture that was created in that language as distinct from other languages, particularly Yiddish.[16] Eventually he became editor of its proceedings and president of the *Va'ad HaLashon* (Academy of the Hebrew Language) whose predecessor was originally founded by Ben Yehuda. He continued the latter's work, broadening the scope of Hebrew to include postbiblical usage. Strongly supportive of the founding of the Hebrew University, he was appointed to the chair in Hebrew Literature but not the well-deserved chair in Jewish History that he had sought. His major work was the *History of Modern Hebrew Literature* starting with the German Haskalah writings in the 1780s and ending in the era of the Russian Haskalah in the 1870s that sought to place Hebrew in the framework of general trends in world literature.

Although he apparently spoke Yiddish as his mother tongue,[17] he did not accept authors such as Mendele in relation to their use of Yiddish.[18] Indeed, in line with his adamant opposition to Yiddish was his success in opposing a chair in Yiddish at the Hebrew University in 1927. The campaign had become a cause celebre analogous to the battle for Hebrew hegemony over other European languages waged just prior to World War I.[19]

His work on Christianity placed Jesus within a Jewish context as a proud Jew who never considered himself other. His exhaustive five-volume work on the period of the Second Commonwealth reflected his focus on the era of Hasmoneans as an era of national glory. He characterized it as an era of messianism in both its religious and political aspects and highly relevant to what he wished to foster in his own time.[20] In the 1930s, he became more clearly identified with the Revisionist Party of Jabotinsky and, for a time, coeditor of its monthly. His militant nationalism was based upon his commitment to a Hebraic Renaissance in consonance with its ancient historical antecedents. He nevertheless, unlike many of the Revisionists, maintained the connection of Jewish messianism and nationalism with the prophetic strand of universalism.[21]

The evolution of Hebrew culture in the context of the Hebrew Renaissance was exemplified by Hayyim Bialik. Not merely the *national poet*, essayist, storywriter, translator, and editor, he exercised a profound influence on modern Hebrew culture. He raised the level of Hebrew poetry to a new plane by both mastery of the language and responding to his own experience.[22]

Hayyim Bialik was born in 1873 in a forest-surrounded village in Volhynia in the northern Ukraine in the context of Hassidic mysticism. He was the second of three surviving children. His father came from scholarly stock and worked in the family timber trade and flour milling until business reverses drove him to keeping a tavern. These first years were recalled by the boy as a lost paradise. When he was six, he came under the care of his pietistic paternal grandfather. He followed the usual pattern of education in the heder, and then, in solitude as a prodigy, after age thirteen in the beth hamidrash (house of study). He reflected, in his early poetry, his childhood sense of poverty and suffering. Yet he also retained his vision of Judaism within the overladen bookshelves of the house of study—the Torah and its students. At the Volozhin yeshivah in Lita in 1890, he began to withdraw from traditional religious thinking to read secular poetry. While there, he wrote his first published poem. Coming under the sway of Ahad Ha'am, he also joined the secret Orthodox Zionist society. Leaving the yeshivah, he continued his secular self-education in Odessa where he was able to have his poem *To the Bird* published.

He initially wrote in the tradition of Haskalah poets such as Judah Leib Gordon whose elegy he composed in 1892. However, he strove to break out of the existing pattern of Hebrew poetry to bring in one's private soul. He allegorized himself as the suffering Jew. As an orphan, he could speak for his orphaned uprooted people. Hope lay only in the distant star of return to Zion. He continued to write nationalist poetry in the 1890s but also now poems of reproof in the tradition of the prophets. In 1900, he then was able to write a series of autobiographical poems that were unique in Hebrew poetry up till then.

As a member of investigatory commission, he was strongly affected by the Kishinev Pogrom of 1903. His famous *City of the Killings* and his later *On the City of Slaughter* reflects this experience. In the former, he castigates the Jews for the lack of self-defense. In the latter, he decries the martyrdom of the Exile to be replaced by the struggle to realize life on earth via Zionism. These calls for action had major impact on East European intelligentsia and were credited with the formation of self-defense groups.[23] In his revival of the biblical prophetic style, angry and critical of the status quo and demanding justice, Bialik was using Hebrew in a revolutionary mode with the very use of the language for such purposes subversive of the traditional political order that reserved the use of Hebrew for religious purposes.[24]

In 1900, Bialik received a teaching position in Odessa where he mainly lived as part of the literary coterie as a writer and a publisher until the Bolshevik Revolution in 1921. During part of this time he edited along with Klausner the poetry and fiction department of the Hebrew monthly *Ha'Shiloah.* He aspired to the revival of a Jewish culture that encompassed the whole of life via the use of the Hebrew language. Hence he labored, during the 1900s, in the creation of *The Book of the Aggadah,* a three-volume compendium of the narrative portions of the Talmud and Midrash.[25] The aim was to collect and choose relevant old Jewish texts and reestablish them in the new modern and secular society.[26] His essays during 1907-1917 dealt with modern Jewish culture and the role of Hebrew literature and the development of the language.

He finally settled in Eretz Israel in 1924. He had visited it for the first time in 1909 and distanced himself even then from the adoration he received as a national poet. Although he had ceased writing, his arrival marked the transfer to Palestine of the Hebrew literary center.[27] Even during his lifetime, his poems were included in the curriculum wherever modern Hebrew was taught. Unpretentious, he was conventional in his manner and dress.[28] He was president of the Hebrew Writers Union and of the Hebrew Language Council. Although he spoke Yiddish as his mother tongue, he rarely used Yiddish words in his poetry.[29]

His work was a watershed in Hebrew poetry. He freed it from the stylized ornate quality of the biblical Hebrew which had limited the creativity of the Haskalah poets. He marked the transition to the conversational verse that would characterize subsequent Palestinian Hebrew poetry. Steeped in Eastern European milieu, he reflects his individual experience as well as that of his generation cast into a secular Jewish world that questions the old values. He both glorified the house of study as the fount of Jewish learning as well as pointing out its inadequacies for the present. He felt himself part of the transition compatible with the nationalist Zionist slogan: "We are the last generation in slavery, the first in freedom." His canonization in the face of other writers of his age lay in his resonance with the history of the Jewish people of this century "the century [sic] of the Holocaust and of rebirth."[30]

Religious Zionism

Alongside the secular Labor Socialist ethos, there were ongoing issues that had surfaced throughout the history of the Zionist settlements. The focus on cultural as well as political development called into question the religious foundation of the Jewish people. In a somewhat defensive posture, Rabbi Kook had provided an overarching synthesis that saw the entire enterprise consistent with the religious impulse. The religious strand of Zionism came into existence in 1902 in Vilna under the leadership of Rabbi Isaac Jacob Reines. Born in 1839 in Lita, Reines trained at the Volozhin yeshivah. He was highly respected in his role as head of the yeshiva in Lida where he had introduced a new more logical format for the study of the Talmud. One of the few Orthodox rabbis in support of Herzl, he had been an early supporter of the Lovers of Zion movement in accordance with Rabbi Samuel Mohliver. The goal of Mizrachi (spiritual center) was to influence the Zionist movement in the direction of Torah observance and other manifestations of *mitzvoth* but to remain part of the Zionist structure.

Starting in 1911, a major impetus to the development of *Mizrachi* came about with the appointment of Meier Berlin (Bar-Ilan) as secretary of the World Mizrachi movement. He was born in Volozhin in Lita in 1880 where his father was head of the famous yeshiva that was the major spiritual center of midnagdic Russian Jewry. Bar-Ilan, in turn, was trained in the leading centers including Telz, Brisk, and Novogrudok as well as his native town. An early member of Mizrachi, he was opposed to the Uganda scheme. He coined the Mizrachi slogan of "The Land of Israel for the people of Israel according to the Torah of Israel." First in Germany, then starting in 1915 in the United States and following 1923 in Jerusalem, he became the representative of the religious Zionist movement in the governance of the Yishuv.

He was a founder and editor of a series of publications including the Mizrachi daily newspaper in Tel Aviv from 1938 to the time of his death in 1949. He initiated the publication of the *Talmudic Encyclopedia*. It is appropriate that the Orthodox university founded in Ramat Gan near Tel Aviv in 1955 by the American Mizrachi movement carries his name. Its purpose is to advance knowledge in both Jewish studies and general studies in accordance with the ideology of "Torah with general knowledge" analogous with Yeshivah University in the United States. It also marked a continuity between higher education in Israel with the great yeshivot of Lita of which Bar-Ilan himself was a direct descendant.

The religious strand was consistent with the Zionist ethos of the Yishuv with the foundation of settlements based on Torah and Labor. The *Hapoel HaMizrachi* was the religious labor expression of their movement in Eretz Israel as well as youth movement in the Diaspora. There was also the development starting in 1920 of its educational system eventually including a network of high schools that were to be the foundation for a resurgent religious character to the state in the next generation.

The Yishuv came to be united in its commitment to the settlement of Jews in the Land of Israel, to a renaissance of Jewish culture and the formation of an autonomous Jewish society. Although there were other trends such as the religious described above and the Revisionist under Jabotinsky, the Zionist-Socialist camp was the dominant one that established the ethos of Yishuv in the period of the British Mandate. There was the establishment of a secular civil religion that drew some of its power from the values and symbols of traditional religion although the latter was generally negated along with the entire experience of "exile." Connection was with the biblical times or with the Second Temple. Traditional holidays such as Passover and Shavuoth were transformed to incorporate nationalistic and agricultural aspects.[31]

Although Katznelson and Ben-Gurion worked together to bring about the social-national ideas of their youth, it was the latter who devoted himself to issues of political organization necessary for the evolution of the Yishuv into a state.

The Jewish State

David Green was born in Plonsk in 1886, a town between Warsaw and the eastern portions of Poland adjoining Lita. It was on a river and on the railroad with about eight to twelve thousand people, more than were half Jews. The grandfather Zvi had taught Hebrew in a school organized by Maskilim and had an extensive library containing works by Plato and Spinoza. He served as an "unlicensed counsel" who earned his living by intervening with the Russian authorities on behalf of clients. The father, Avigdor Green, was a freethinker, the first Jew in town to dress in the European fashion. He was also a leader in collecting money for the local Lovers of Zion society and later became an avid follower of Herzl.

The boy, David, was sickly and short—five foot three inches—with a large head. He was the fourth of what eventually were five living children. He learned Hebrew from his grandfather and father even before entering heder. His first childhood memory was learning Hebrew at his grandfather's knee at age three and he spoke and read Hebrew fluently. Enrolled in the more advanced beth hamidrash, he also read secular books such as *The Love of Zion* by Abraham Mapu as well as books by Harriet Beecher Stowe and Tolstoy. The death of his mother in childbirth when David was eleven was a never-forgotten episode in his life. He was unable to enter a secondary or technical school in Warsaw to prepare for his life in Eretz Israel. In 1905, in continued opposition to the Bund, he joined the recently formed Poalei Zion movement that combined his early Zionism with revolutionary socialism and succeeded in making the Poalei Zionist the leading movement in the town.[32]

In September 1906, he finally arrived in Palestine. He was unusual among the immigrants in being fluent in Hebrew. He was only occasionally able to find work on the farms in competition with cheap Arab labor. The young socialists regarded the Orthodox Jewish colonists already settled on the land as hypocritical, disguising their class interests by their piety.[33] Green suffered from malaria and lack of food. He wandered from settlement to settlement without finding the recognition he craved or a proper role. Nevertheless, that role of agricultural laborer was crucial to his sense of mission. Even as a man of sixty-two, in the first census of the State, he listed himself as an "agricultural laborer."[34]

In 1910 he found his metier when he became a writer for a new Hebrew newspaper for farm workers called *Ahdut* (Unity) and took on his name as Ben-Gurion. The name was that of a popular leader during the last revolt against the Romans. This was the start of his future career as a writer and political organizer. An autodidact par excellence, he read extensively a wide range of subjects and languages even when living in poverty in his early work as a writer. He believed that the Jews could acquire Palestine only by deeds and that the workers would need to be unified. Further, it was his principle that neither the World Poalei Zion nor the World Zionist Organization would dictate to the Palestinian workers.

In pursuit of an opportunity to function in a multiethnic country, he had acquired Turkish citizenship and legal training at law school in Constantinople. With the onset of World War I, despite his citizenship, his newspaper was closed down, and Ben-Gurion deported in 1915. Living in the United States, he toured to recruit settlers to come to Palestine and later to develop a Jewish Legion in the British army. While stationed in Egypt in that army unit, he met Berl Katnelson, his comrade in achieving the unity of Labor that he sought.[35]

Ben-Gurion was appointed in 1921 merely as a member of the secretariat of the newly formed Histradut but went on to become the secretary-general. He was but one member of a leadership collective that would not permit him to function in a dictatorial mode. A Workers Corporation (*Hevrat Ovdim*) became the structure through which Histradut was able to administer a range of enterprises in the national interest for all workers. He sought the primacy of a Labor Zionist approach to the development of the Yishuv rather than one based on private capital investment and in subordination to the World Zionist Organization. The depression after the short-lived speculative boom of Tel Aviv that occurred during the Fourth Aliyah in 1924-1927 seemed to support his concept. In opposition to Jabotinsky and the Revisionists, Ben-Gurion was able to overtake all the other segments of the World Zionist Organization to achieve a plurality of votes for Labor Zionism.

Ben-Gurion became a member of the Zionist Executive of the WZO in 1933 and, in 1935, in coalition with the General Zionists and Mizrachi, chairman of the Zionist Executive and the Jewish Agency Executive. Weizmann once again became president of the World Zionist Organization. Despite significant differences in style and, at times, in their priorities, they continued to work together for the rest of the history of the Yishuv.[36] In light of the British policy of abandonment of the Mandate, Weizmann's faith in the British connection and personal contacts at the high level of government no longer appeared to be a viable method for achieving independence. Ben-Gurion recognized the importance of an alignment with American interests and the importance of mass politics in concert with Abba Hillel Silver yet needed the more polished Weiznann to carry on.

Ben-Gurion had a single-minded set of principles, however pragmatic his actions. These were that Zionism was a revolt against Jewish tradition as expressed in the exile. In order to carry out this revolution, it was necessary to act differently and not merely make pronouncements. It was the Zionist reality on the ground in Palestine that was the crucial factor and not the Zionist activity in the Diaspora. The basis for the new social infrastructure in the Yishuv would be a Labor movement. In its creation, the two aspects of Zionism and Socialism are not merely an aggregate but two halves of the same coin. "Not only need the Jewish people be taken out of Exile, Exile has to be taken out of the Jewish people."[37] To this, he added an identification of the power structures both in the country and the world that could help maintain the viability of the Zionist movement and the state.

A crucial aspect of the Zionist endeavor was the establishment of an independent Jewish economy. The Histradut became the vehicle for industrial development in the national interest. Health care funds as well as educational activities all became part of its mission. Its value was shown when an Arab general strike in conjunction with the 1936 Arab Revolt strengthened rather than disrupted the Yishuv. The 1937 Peel Commission offer of a Jewish State was supported by Ben-Gurion but opposed by many of his colleagues, most particularly Katznelson. The offer of partition was withdrawn and the British, with the rise of Hitler and the need to placate the Arab world, issued the White Paper of 1939. that would make permanent a Jewish minority and an eventual Arab Palestinian State. With the onset of World War II, Ben-Gurion had become the leader of the Yishuv with the objective to maintain immigration, even if illegal, and to develop the military capability as prerequisites for the establishment of an independent state. The Histradut was now instrumental in development of the transition to a war economy.[38]

Hadar is defined as *dignified pride.* That spirit was the objective of Jabotinsky, the antagonist of Ben-Gurion and Labour Zionism. For Jabotinsky, the nation was primary and singular. His own program was militant nationalism undiluted by issues of class and egalitarianism. He had been instrumental in establishing initially the Zion Mule Corps, a service unit in the Gallipoli campaign, and then after the Balfour Declaration, the Jewish Legion. He emphasized the transformation of the Diaspora notion of the passive, nonmilitant Jew. The rifle, with his daily work of comparatively little interest, characterized the Revisionist hero. It was as a nation armed a people defined by discipline, army, and flag.[39] To the contrary, Labour based its image on an independent-working nation, able and willing to defend itself but primarily concerned with its own reconstruction through creative work. Its hero was the pioneer working the soil with a rifle on his shoulder but there only because of necessity.

In delegitimatizing the Revisionists during the 1930s as "fascist" and "irresponsible," Mapai also changed. It became less identified with Labor alone but rather the dominant member of what was now a coalition including the large number of bourgeois immigrants of the Fifth Aliyah of the 1930s. The notion of a nation rather than a class was the basis for the Labour party that would rule in coalition with others including the religious and bourgeois parties for an entire generation of the state.[40]

Jewish Activism

Ownership of Eretz Israel for the Second Aliyah members went beyond merely the historical right to be based upon those who actually work the land and protect it. In Jaffa in 1908, the immigrants, having experienced the pogroms in the Pale, connected the attacks by Arab youths to the same pattern. In contrast to their predecessors, they were not willing to exercise restraint or to request compensation, but rather take the law into their own hands and fight back. What they had been forced to accept in the Pale they regarded as insufferable in Palestine where they felt that they were by right. The formation of *Bar Giora* in 1907, a secret, quasi-miltary organization, was followed by its legal arm of Hashomer.

They brought, from Russia, their revolutionary ideology and practice. The bearing of arms exemplified the new status of Jews in Palestine was what distinguished them from their life in the Pale. Those who were killed "in battle" in 1911 were commemorated in a book called *Yiskor* that evoked the prayers said on behalf of the martyrs. Those who had lived and died as workers and freemen in their new life in Palestine gave their deaths new meaning in the spirit of the Maccabees and Bar Kochba.[41]

Each of the series of Arab attacks during the evolution of the Yishuv led to changes in the settlement policies as well as the growth of Jewish self-defense. The attacks in the Upper Galilee in 1921 led to the development of self-defense within each settlement. Moreover, it aided in the creation of the myth of Tel Hai. The story of the fight to the death of the settlers including Josef Trumpledor marked the idea of the "New Jew ready to fight for his land and die for it."[42] Its anniversary is commemorated as the "day of defense," one of the four anniversaries of historic events officially sanctioned as state holidays and remained part of Zionist teaching of the young until the generation after independence. The countrywide riots in 1929 led to the development of settlement regions, or blocs such as the Jezreel Valley and the Coastal Plain. Foregone was reconstruction of the ancient Jewish presence in Hebron. The 1936 revolt, in turn, led to a "national settlement map." There was the filling in of areas with settlements even during the worst disturbances. The dictum was that no settlements were to be abandoned.[43]

In response to the series of Arab attacks during the Mandatory period, the Jews developed their own self-defense capabilities in the absence of adequate and prompt response by the British forces. Although declared illegal, Haganah (Defense) grew in strength and organization fully authorized by the Jewish community's political leadership. The British, in response to the Arab Revolt of 1936-39, established a paramilitary *Jewish Settlement Police* (JSP). Still another organization was commanded by then Captain Orde Wingate, a strongly committed British Christian Zionist. His *Special Night Squads* (SNS) would carry out raids in the Galilee to protect the pipeline owned by the Iraq Petroleum Company that then ran to Haifa. The SNS were essentially forces of the Haganah. The latter, commanded by Yitzak Sadeh, together with Wingate made units of the Haganah better able to carry out an active form of defense. They learned to intercept the enemy rather than await attack behind trenches and barbed wire. Although soon disbanded, the special squads became an embryonic military force on a countrywide basis. During the course of World War II, the Haganah became a national organization, enlisting almost the entire Jewish population in some capacity or another. It was emerging as a modern militia, an army in the making.[44]

Eliyahu Golomb was the main architect of the Haganah in its development throughout the era of the Yishuv. He was born in Belorussia in Lita in 1893. He came to Eretz Israel in 1909 and was in the Herzylia High School's first graduating class in 1913. One of his classmates was Moshe Sharrett, whose sister Ada became his wife. He organized his fellow graduates into a group for agricultural training and service to the Jewish settlements. He himself went to train at Degania, the first of the kibuttzim. The graduates were the prototypes of what came to be called *Sabras*.

They were characterized by their direct and rough ways, Zionist idealism and Hebrew as their mother language.[45]

At the outbreak of World War I, Golomb opposed the enlistment of Jews into the Turkish army but rather in units of their own. In accordance with these principles, he helped form the Jewish Legion in 1918 and he himself served in it. A new term, *activism,* entered the lexicon of the Yishuv in conjunction with the recruitment. It had the positive connotation as opposed to the passivity of exile of acquiescence with divine judgment. Volunteering for military service symbolized "a new morality that began with the arrival of the first Hebrew worker."[46]Golomb became a friend of Berl Katznelson and helped form the Histradut and, in 1921, Haganah under its auspices. Living in Europe from 1921 to 1924, his job was to purchase arms for Haganah.

The more acceptable response to the dangers of attacks by the Arabs was a self-mastery, a courage that did not recoil from difficulties, not merely physical prowess but perseverance, self-sacrifice, and bravery in one's daily struggle rather than an exhibitionist-type militaristic response.[47] Worker self-defense was acceptable, and the formation of a militia was in accordance with the symbolism of its formation under the auspices of the Unity of Labor Party in 1920. The formation of the Haganah was associated with the myth of Trumpeldor, the one-armed hero who died in the defense of Tel Hai in the spring of 1920. Although not easily defensible, the settlers had committed themselves to its maintenance in tune with "a place once settled is not to be abandoned."[48] Trumpeldor had been an associate of Jabotinsky in the formation of the Jewish Legion but was not a militaristic person. His death and that of his companions was commemorated by Berl Katzelson in the spirit of the workers "loyal and brave, people of labor and peace [who sic] had perished while guarding the motherland." It was a bravery of the right kind in that it was a civilian courage devoid of militarism but integrating modesty, settlement, physical labor, nationalism, and socialism.[49]

The *defensive ethos* became the basis for relationship between the Jews and Arabs after the failure of the British to prevent the disturbances of 1920-1921. The Zionist project was not one of conquest but of settlement. The objective was peace and brotherhood, aspiring to build a socialist society while holding out a hand to fellow workers who might be Arab.[50] The Arab Riot of 1929 seemed to reinforce the import of the self-defense ethos. The major killings occurred in the holy cities where the deeply religious then lived along with their non-Jewish neighbors. Arabs had not attacked where large number of Jews lived or where defenders existed. The strong defense of a kibbutz was held up as a polar opposite to the passivity of the religious students. The obligation was for self-defense is a moral duty but there was still rejection of aggression and militarism. The educational system preached equality, ethics and concern for fellow man. Yet it also preached activism, responsibility to act to make the world better. The image of *defender* was still separated from that of soldier. There were also recognition that an Arab national movement existed that also seemed to include the masses of workers and not merely the upper class.[51]

During the 1930s, Golomb persisted in importing arms and trying to strengthen the organization in response to the deficiencies exposed in the Arab riots of 1929. As a member of the leadership of both the Ahdut Haavodah and the Histradut, he was also in the Mapai and a delegate to the various Zionist Congresses. His stance throughout was that the Haganah should be made up of the Jewish population at large and not an elite fighting force. In the early 1930s, a right-wing Revisionist faction under Jabotinsky broke off in opposition to the Histradut-led main body. The Haganah National Command established in the 1930s included representative of both Histradut and centrist groups, thus isolating the right wing. Golomb, in his role as leader of the Haganah, was opposed to the development of dissident military organizations such as the military arm of the Revisionists.

The initial response of the Haganah to the Arab Rebellion starting in 1936 was "self-restraint." In accordance with the ongoing policy, the Jews were not the aggressors while the Arab attacks were those of "terrorists." The self-image of the Jew as a person of morality was consistent with the entire image of the Yishuv derived from Ahad Ha'am. Yet it violated another of the tenets that in Palestine the Jew would defend himself and not let his blood be shed at will. In response to the Arab use of ambush, it was necessary to "get outside the fence." The transition was from one of defense to attack. Sites were chosen for political purposes in extending the areas of settlement with "stockade and watchtower." It became clearer that ultimately their dependence on the British had to end. For the first time, the ruling Labor group recognized the need for "militarization."[52]

During the Arab Rebellion of 1936-39, Golomb was one of the initiators of the "field units" that were the early effort to organize an activist response to the attacks by the Arabs. It was in conjunction with these units that for the first time that a poem was dedicated to the glorification of a fighting unit and the ethos had shifted to a commitment to an activist stance among the crucial youth movement. These units learned to search for an enemy in various types of terrain, to place an ambush, to carry out a raid. He supported an active defense and reprisals against fighters but, for both moral and tactical reasons, not against the Arab population. New strategic bases were created in which the settlers were both simultaneously fighters and farmers. Not a single settlement was abandoned, and new settlements were added forming contiguous blocs. This entire effort was rooted in the self-defense units first created in the wake of the anti-Jewish riots in the Pale following the Revolutioin of 1905.

During World War II, Golomb supported the formation of a Jewish Brigade in the British army analogous to his experience in the Jewish Legion during the previous war. Consistent throughout were his objectives of strengthening the military skills of the Yishuv. The brigade also served to support illegal immigration and liaison with the survivors of the Holocaust in the displaced person camps. The offensive ethos that he nurtured that emerged during the Arab Rebellion crystallized during World War II and its aftermath in the *Palmach*. Golumb died in 1945 before his work over his lifetime came to fruition.

The Palmach (Striking Unit) was formed from the Haganah in the context of the dangers to the Yishuv in 1941 from the German forces in Africa and the pro-Axis Arabs. It was a commando-type force whose primary purpose was the defense of the Yishuv.[53] In concert with the British, they defeated the Vichy French government of Syria-Lebanon. It was in this action that Moshe Dayan lost his eye. To maintain their structure as a highly trained guerrilla force even after the immediate danger had passed, Palmach units were stationed in kibbutzim throughout the country, mainly associated with the more left-wing grouping later connected to the *Mapam*. They worked half the month and trained the other half. Membership in the reserves after a specified period of active service established the pattern of organizational structure for the Israel Defense Forces for the future. In preparation for a state, what had been formed was the first fully mobilized Jewish army serving under a completely independent Jewish political authority since the days of Bar Kochba revolt against the Romans.

After the end of World War II, and pending the end of the British Mandate, the Haganah carried out illegal immigration of the remnants of European Jewry while also supporting the placement of new strategic settlements as well as attacks on British military installations. The *Hebrew Resistance* united all the fighting organizations across the range of parties. The objectives were now to make British power impossible. Although the Resistance was called off after the blowing up of the *King David Hotel*, the use of force was legitimized in the context of the actual growth of the military arm. Ultimately the British were forced to give up the Mandate. The United Nations vote for partition in November 1947 led to the declaration of the State of Israel on May 15, 1948.[54]

The aim of education of the younger generation was to be both a worker and a fighter. There was a synthesis of nationalist activism and revolutionary rather the previous evolutionary socialism. The story of *Masada*, of heroism even in the case of destruction, was compatible with the importance of the *deed* and those who preferred death over surrender. The youth pilgrimages to Masada took place in the spirit of a poem by Lamdan written in 1937 glorifying the connection to the present. The poem *Masada* alludes to Trumpeldor as the prophet of promise in recognition of the power of the image of Tel Hai. Masada becomes a metaphor for Zion, the high cliff in the difficult struggle for a national revival.

The shift that occurred would be expressed by the generation born and growing up in Palestine as differentiated from their parents familiar with life in the Diaspora. The dominant ideology was negation of the Diaspora. *Sabraism* became the characteristic of a youth movement among the native-born from the kibbutzim, moshavim, and the settled portions of the cities imbued with the culture of the Palmach. The Bible has been taught them without the emphasis on the prophetic teachings but as a heroic epic. From 1937 on, the topic of fighting was being integrated within the value system of the Labor movement. An armed clash seemed inevitable in light of the changes that had come about in the context of the ongoing Arab rebellion in 1936-39. It became accepted that idealistic youth was obligated to fight for the sake of the entire people. They became the heroes of the War of Independence and the early years of the state.[55]

6.2.3. The Generation of the State

The answer to the Holocaust was the Zionist program of independence in one's own land by one's own labor, economy, and weapons. The "new Jew" of Palestine was contrasted to the Jews of the Diaspora seen as passively going to their slaughter. The *Warsaw Ghetto Uprising* and the partisans fighting in the forests were exemplars that belied the weakness from which the Palestinian youth distanced themselves.[1] Jewish independence in Palestine was the war aim that would counteract the genocide that had been inflicted on the Jews by Hitler. That it had to be won by the Jews themselves was the other theme given the lack of intervention by any of the Powers to the genocide as it had been going on.[2]

The Palestinian-born generation took pains to distinguish itself from that of the original immigrants in their walk, in their talk. They seemed to accept the realities of their lives without the self-questioning and struggles that had characterized their parents. They asserted themselves without the conventions of politeness. Ideology was out of date. The focus was on the deed to be performed. Their universe was limited. They were men of action, devoid of intellectual pretensions. The exhibition of human emotions was a sign of weakness. Yet the socialist identity of their legacy served to maintain a sense of differentiation from the pure commitment to violence expressed by the Revisionist military arm. The ideal remained that of a fighter but yet not a soldier.[3]

The War of Independence

The Palmach (acronym for *Plugot Mahaatz* or Assault Companies) would be a major factor in the effectiveness of Israel's military arm in the War of Independence. It was an army of volunteers that reflected and reinforced the social, cultural, and educational pattern of the youth movement. Its organizational structure was similar to the kibbutz with the added component of military training but without the sterility of the barracks-type mentality of most armies. The ideal was "a popular yet resolute army, courageous and well prepared as fighters" that used the partisan groups of the recent war as a model.[4]

Yigal Allon represented the Zionist ideal, the *Sabra* in the kibbutz movement and socialist Zionism. He was born in 1918 on a farm in the Lower Galilee as the youngest of seven children. His grandfather Paicovitch had come to Rosh Pinna from Grodno in Lita in 1882. His father, Reuben, had struck out on his own to develop a farm on land wrested from Baron Rothschild at *Kfar Tabor*.[5] Allon was educated in his native village and then at the *Kadoorie Agricultural School* set up as the Jewish agricultural training center following the bequest of a member of the Iraqi Jewish family.[6] After graduating in 1937, Allon helped organize with his fellow classmates a new Kibbutz *Ginossar* near Lake Kinneret.

During the Arab Rebellion of 1936-39, Allon rose to officer level when serving in the newly created special units of the Haganah with Wingate. He was one of the founders of the Palmach in 1941 and commanded the unit that participated in the successful Allied campaign against the Vichy French in the Levant. As deputy commander and then commander of the Palmach in 1945, he was responsible for planning its training programs and operations. These included combat against Arabic enemy bands, joint activity with the British, and then actions in opposition to British policy in the postwar period. Palmach was also largely responsible for illegal immigration and settlement in prohibited zones. During the War of Independence, Allon commanded operations throughout the country and, more specifically as commander of the southern front, he drove the invading Egyptian army from whole of the Negev. He became the model of the Israeli officer.

The Haganah had been a mainly volunteer force designed to fight against the Arab armed bands but not against the armies of the neighboring Arab states. The latter's threats to invade the Jewish state required a reorganization into became the *Israel Defense Forces* (IDF). Ben-Gurion had taken on the Ministry of Defense in the not-yet-born state. During the spring of 1947, he led the "seminar" during which he identified the deficiencies of the Haganah. One remedy was to exert civilian control in his hands. One step in doing so was to appoint Yigael Yadin, a relative outsider to the chief of operations. He also called on those who were veterans of the British wartime service.[7]

After the dissolution of the Palmach into the IDF, Allon retired to his studies at Hebrew University and Oxford. He then entered politics in opposition to the pro-Soviet policies of Mapam to which he had once belonged. Elected to the Knesset in 1954, he entered the cabinet in 1961 as Minister of Labor. In 1967, he was a member of the inner War Cabinet that mapped out the strategy of the Six-Day War. In the following year, he brought about the formation of the *Israel Labour Party*, becoming deputy prime minister and Minister of Education and Culture.

The process by which the state took over from the Yishuv after the War of Independence required the implementation of the already prepared structure of social and political sovereignty. The military structure necessary to permit independence when faced by the attack of the surrounding Arab nations also drew its strength from the social and political and even cultural character of the Yishuv derived as it was from the Second and Third Aliyah. Despite some deviations, it remained under the control of the political leadership of the Histradut. It was based in the kibbutzim. That ethos of idealism and mutual responsibility nurtured during the interwar era in the new generation was the basis for the military self-emancipation necessary for the community's very continued existence.[8] The transition between the Yishuv and the new state was aided by the maintenance of the Labour Zionist ethos into the early years of the state illustrated by the HaCohen family.

The Israeli Labour Establishment

Mordecai Hillel HaCohen was the founder of the family in Eretz Israel. Born in Mogilev in Lita in 1856, he was taught by tutors in the family compound. Along with his brothers, he was taught Hebrew, the Talmud and the commentaries along with secular subjects and European languages. A well-to-do timber merchant, HaCohen was also an ardent Zionist. He started publishing in Hebrew periodicals at an early age and was on the editorial staff of Smolenskin's *Ha-Shahar* as early as 1876. He was concerned with the need for national unity to counteract the Russian assimilation of the youth as they wandered from traditional observance. He was an early member of the Lovers of Zion movement and visited Palestine for the first time in 1889. As a delegate to the First Zionist Congress in Basle in 1897, he was the first to deliver a speech in Hebrew. His home in Gomel was a center for visitors such as Yosef Brenner. During the summer, Ahad Ha'am and his family, along with Simon Dubnow—the historian of East European Jewry—might share the HaCohen dacha. His elder daughter Rosa married Ahad Ha'am's son.

There were several pogroms in Gomel in 1903 and then again in 1905. There was a relatively well-developed Jewish self-defense force that was attacked by the Russian military. Zionists from the town participated in the Second and Third Aliyah. Indeed the start of the Second Aliyah dates from the arrival of the refugees from the Gomel self-defense group to Eretz Israel in December 1903.[9] HaCohen himself settled with his family in Palestine in 1907. There he continued his literary work along with being one of the organizers of the Association of Hebrew Writers. He was also one of the early builders in the all-Jewish city of Tel Aviv starting in 1909.[10]

David HaCohen, one of his younger sons, was born in Gomel in 1898. After aliyah with his family in 1907, the boy would spend his summer holidays from Herzylia High School in Tel Aviv, working in various settlements. Upperclassmen such as Eliyahu Golomb and Moshe Sharrett had organized themselves as graduates of this premier Hebrew-speaking school to enlist in missions in the national cause. As a Turkish citizen, HaCohen was conscripted into its army during World War I and experienced its harsh military discipline and its corruption. In 1919, he went to London to study at the London School of Economics. There he became a socialist as well as a close friend of Sharrett with whom he shared lodgings. He also remained close to his sister, then living with her husband in the London home of her father-in-law Ahad Ha'am. HaCohen became a close associate of the "brothers-in-law," Sharrett and Golomb along with Dov Hoz who had married Sharett's two sisters. In joining them in their commitment to the Zionism and Socialism, he became associated with Histradut in the Haifa office of the construction firm *Solel Boneh* in 1923.[11]

HaCohen continued Histradut's mission in providing training and jobs in construction to Jews. It became the largest company in the country, employing thousands. The vehicle for employment of Jewish labor on the Mandatory government projects, it enabled the Yishuv to function despite the strike of Arab labor in 1936. The organization was responsible for providing the equipment for the formation of the "tower and stockade" settlements during the era of the White Paper. Solel Boneh was involved in military construction throughout the Middle East during the war, with some members enrolled in the British Royal Engineers.[12] HaCohen was liaison officer between Haganah and the British forces.

Like other leaders of the Yishuv, the British arrested him on Black Saturday, June 29, 1946, to be interned at *Latrun* during the postwar Hebrew Resistance. He was elected to the *Knesset* from its inception in 1949 and was reelected until the end of 1969. As a member of Mapai, he was a loyal follower of Ben-Gurion and chairman of the important Foreign Affairs and Security Committee. He was Israel's first ambassador to Burma and successful in building a relationship between the two countries and with its prime minister U Nu. HaCohen was a member of the inner circle of the Labour Establishment that ruled Israel during its first generation of Statehood. In his entire career, HaCohen has displayed a sense of integrity and devotion to the egalitarian Zionist Socialist creed that exemplifies the evolution of the dream that brought his family from Lita during the Second Aliyah.

After the formation of the state, the dilution of the socialist legacy and the postponement of its accomplishment took place. More urgent were the matters of immigration, defense and "upbuilding the land."[13] In the evolution of the nation-state, there was the submerging of the particular interests of the working class. Labor was but one pillar of the state, albeit the largest. The Jewish state took on a "messianic destiny" in its role in the "ingathering of the exiles" and making the desert bloom. Ben-Gurion would defer social and national redemption until the ingathering of exiles is completed. The army became the embodiment of the pioneer spirit rather than the Labor movement. Emphasis was on state rather than class with an emptying of the socialist content of the concept of *pioneering*.

The Land of Israel

The problem faced by the Zionist ethos was to relate its youth to the issues of historical continuity while establishing the "new Jew." Negation of the Galut (exile) was somehow coupled with the need to provide Jewish continuity.[14] This was solved in part by finding the roots of nationalism in the Jewish religion as evidenced by the Bible. Ben-Gurion stressed the Biblical heritage and negated the 1,900 years from the destruction of the Second Temple and the beginnings of the Zionist return. He promoted the study of archeology and Bible study as reinforcing Jewish attachment and claims to the land. The Bible underwent a secular transformation for its historical and archeological aspects.[15] It was evoked as the history book of the Jewish people. It was also the guidebook to the flora and fauna, to the land of Palestine.[16]

Archeology therefore had an extraordinary appeal both as a pastime and a serious science in enhancing the connection of the State with its roots in the soil. Archeological finds could be related to the country's ancient Jewish past. Interest first surfaced among the settlers with the discovery in 1928 of the mosaic floor of a sixth-century synagogue while digging an irrigation ditch on a kibbutz. Eliezer Sukenik was summoned to evaluate the finding. It was the start of his career as a renowned archeologist.

Eliezer Sukenik was born in 1889 in Bialystok in Lita. He was educated at the Mussar yeshivh at Slobodka in Kovno. The Bialystok pogrom of 1906 caused him to leave his religious studies to join the Poalei Zion and become one of their leading organizers with an emphasis on self-defense groups. He settled in Eretz Israel in 1912 and worked as an algebra teacher. Seeking professional recognition, he came under the patronage of William Albright, the Director of the *American School of Oriental Research.* This led to studies at the University of Berlin and later at Dropsie College in Philadelphia. He received a doctorate based on his work on the *Palestinian synagogue.* Emblematic was his focus on its evolution from the Roman model to become a religious building and even later, the prototype of the Christian church.

The founder of Jewish archeology, he was Professor of Archeology at Hebrew University, and also director of the University *Museum of Jewish Antiquities.* He was instrumental in acquiring part of the Dead Sea Scrolls in 1948 and spent the rest of his career in their study.[17] It was considered particularly symbolic that the first three scrolls were acquired on the very day that the United Nations voted for the re-creation of the Jewish State.[18]

Sukenik's son, Yigal Yadin, formerly the chief of staff of the Israeli army, returned to his family's profession. He led the large-scale excavations by the young generation of the state in a series of important sites. Most important was uncovering Masada, the last Zealot bastion of the Roman wars. Since the 1930s, it became the site of ceremonies of dedication by army recruits as well as youth groups.[19] A Hebrew translation of Josephus Flavius's book *On the Jewish War* in 1923 and the publication of the poem *Masada* by Lamdan in 1927 brought Masada to the attention of the Yishuv. The catch phrase, "Never again shall Masada fall," has remained an Israeli slogan even as great popularity of Lamdan's poem that contained that phrase has faded.

The Zionist collective memory constructs antiquity as the period when the Hebrew nation flourished. The ancient Hebrews were a proud nation rooted in its land. They cultivated the land and were ready to fight for it and, if necessary, to die for it. Focus has been particularly on the period of the Second Temple when Judea waged war against imperial masters such as the Hasmoneans against Hellenist Syria and then against the Romans. The defeat of the Jews by the Romans at Masada and the subsequent defeat of Bar Kochba were the turning point leading to the Exile that remained until the modern State of Israel arose out of the ashes of the Holocaust.[20]

Born in 1917, Yigal Yadin grew up in Jerusalem as the eldest son of Israel's foremost archeologist and of a pioneering kindergarten teacher, both members of the Second Aliyah. The name Yadin replaced Sukenik based on his code name in the Haganah. He and his brother were initially enrolled in an experimental school designed to foster self-reliance and self-expression. He became an active member of the Jewish Boy Scouts. It was on these scouting camping trips that Yadin first visited Masada. He was enrolled in the Haganah in 1933 at sixteen and was trained as an officer at the start of the Arab Rebellion of 1936. During the summer of 1936, he learned how to preempt Arab attacks by "going beyond the fence." He then became an instructor of other Haganah men in the succeeding years. He advanced to commander of the Jerusalem Haganah as well as the British-sponsored Jewish Settlement Police during the late 1930s. He returned to his studies in archeology before being called back to participate in the War of Independence. Primarily a staff rather than a combat officer, he subsequently established the structure of the IDF as a standing army with compulsory military service and the reserve system. In 1952, he left the military once again to return to his studies in archeology at the Hebrew University. He became professor of archaeology there in 1963 and headed its Institute of Archaeology.[21]

Between 1963 and 1965, under Yadin's direction, a large-scale archeological effort began with volunteers from abroad as well as Israel. For Yadin, it was clear that archeological and national interests were intertwined. The myth of Masada, however tenuous, became enshrined by its repetition.[22] The site became even more famous because of the extensive public involvement with the excavation itself. The focus was, however, not on the Herodian palace but on the meager remains of the lives of the *Zealots* who had gone there in their last ditch fight against the Romans. The people of Masada were portrayed as the carriers of a spirit of active heroism, love of freedom, and national dignity. It is the active fight that is emphasized rather than the suicide at the end. It is their readiness to die rather than the mode of death that is made salient.[23]

Masada became particularly important as a counter measure to the image of the Holocaust and the passivity of its victims. The ultimate issue was to die a "dignified death" with one's weapon in hand. Even the suicide was an act of moral integrity, an act of

defiance. The activist idea was that the defenders would fight so as
to exact the highest price possible from their opponents. It was in
the tradition of Masada that Abba Kovner issued his call to arms
in the Vilna Ghetto, the formation of the fighting organization in
the Kovno Ghetto and most important, in relation to the Warsaw
Ghetto Uprising.[24]

The great Zionist ideologues of the previous generation such
as Ahad Ha'am, Bialik, A. D. Gordon, or Joseph Klausner did not
perceive Zionism as encompassing the entirety of Jewish identity.
Zionism was but a tool for the creation of a modern national
framework to bring about a unity of the Jewish people and to
link that people to its historical roots. This was expressed by its
settlement on the land and the use of Hebrew as the national
language. With the realization of the settlement and the revival
of the language, the generation growing up as native-born *Sabras*
would redefine their Jewishness in terms of their Zionism. They
received their cultural vision from writers who negated the
experience of the Exile.

The values of this generation were formed in the youth
movement where they were to continue and complete the
pioneering work. Yet they found their central task in war:
during World War II in acts of rescue and illegal immigration
and then in the wars that established independence
and in the subsequent need to fight to maintain it. The
literary expression of this generation was exemplified by S.
Yizhar.[25]

Israeli Literature

His *Days of Ziklag*, published in 1958, was the exemplary
novel in Hebrew fiction of its decade. Defended by the younger
intellectuals, it was attacked by most of the older critics as lacking
in political correctness as "nihilistic" and denied the Bialik
Prize.[26] Central is the questioning of the older generation and
the metaphor of the *Abedah*, the binding by the father Abraham
of Isaac the son. The sacrifice was transformed in Zionism to
emphasize the voluntary nature of relationship between the
generation of the founding fathers and their Sabra sons.[27]

Covering seven days in the battle for a hill in the Negev during the War of Independence, it reflects the entire struggle to come to terms with the war and the problems of identity, both personal and national. In the tradition of the Yishuv, the narrative is used as an occasion for the discussion of political and moral issues. [28]

Yizhar's characters are idealistic youth dedicated to society and the land but, meeting with the complexities of war, reflect on their feelings of cowardice and fear. Although they have personal doubts, their resolution is in terms of the needs of the collective. Its style also broke new ground in trying to fashion a new Israeli literary Hebrew with previously unused terms and new forms of syntax.[29] Underlying his work is a longing for the primeval earth, the open spaces of the Negev that arises from his generation's close association with the flora and fauna of the land as well as the biblical allusions of the site of Ziklag itself.[30] The place was the site where David had refuge provided by the Philistines when he was a commander of guerrilla forces against Saul. The allusion in the Book of Samuel (1 Sam. 27:6) was that "Ziklag belongs to the kings of Judah to this day."[30]

S. Yizhar was born in Rehovot in 1916 into a family of writers. Coming to Eretz Israel in 1890 from the Ukraine, his father, Zeev Smilansky, settled in Rehovot in 1893 where he owned orange groves and vineyards. Yizhar's great-uncle Moshe contributed to the full range of Hebrew press in Russia and Palestine as well as other countries. He contributed to Hapoel Hatzair, one of the literary organs of the Second Aliyah. He pictured a "wild West" for his East European readers in which Arabs were "noble savages" or naïve victims of civilization analogous to the Indians of James Fenimore Cooper. The Jews were the white colonists.[31] An advocate for Arab-Jewish cooperation, he opposed the Second Aliyah emphasis on exclusively Jewish labor. He was unique in also writing stories of Arab life. Nevertheless, Moshe Smilansky's writings defined for his readers the pioneering experience as a form of religious redemption.[32]

Yizhar in turn taught at the *Ben Shemen* youth village and at a *Rehovot* secondary school and fought in the 1948 War of Independence. He was a member of Knesset in the Mapai-Rafi group in support of Ben-Gurion from its start until 1967. His first story was published in 1938, dealing with his adolescence in the landscape of the orange groves where there were scattered Arab villages.[33] He was the first prose writer born in Palestine to render in lyrical terms a profound awareness of the local landscape. He, like his characters, was rooted in the prestate Yishuv in commitment to the Land and to the Hebrew language.

Yizhar's characters are consistent with the entire literature of the Generation of 1948 with its almost exclusive focus on the communal settlement and its problems. He was one of the *Sabra* generation defined by Hebrew as their native language, writing about life in such places as the youth group, the kibbutz, and the battlefield, whose protagonists were typical Sabras and whose writing was seasoned with Sabra slang and style.[34] There is a sameness in their political and social attitudes. They arise from "a whole cloth of blue and white . . . children born of the sea into a 'youth movement' society."[35] They are, however, torn between the sometimes amoral values of the group, whether the army or the kibbutz, and their own conscience.[36] His characters are reluctant colonizers and conquerors. He exposed the less than heroic qualities of war and the moral corruption inherent in the relationship between the victor and the vanquished.

In two of his stories published in the 1960s, Yizhar represents Palestinians as victims of war. One depicts the deportation of women and children from a village at the end of the War of Independence. In doing so, the Palestinians, rather than the Israeli Jews, seem to take on the universalistic humanistic Jewish moral standards. The author represents the mainstream of Israel thinking of his time in maintaining the commitment to humanistic values.[37]

Following the publication of his *Days of Ziklag*, he ceased his literary career to focus on political topics advocating secular and humanistic values. Indicative was Yizhar's 1958 lecture "Literature in a Turbulent World." He expressed the difference between nineteenh- and twentieth-century literature in terms of his own experience. In the earlier century, there was optimism that the problems present in the social order would be solved. What appeared initially simple and straightforward becomes in this century meaningless and impossible. He questioned the ideology that had served as a basis for action in the past. In response, Ben-Gurion, as part of his dialogue with intellectuals striving to enlist them in the national effort, characteristically challenged the disillusionment being expressed.

This dialogue in which the ruler and the intellectual spoke at cross purposes was the forerunner of the more independent stance of writers in the 1960s in which the latter claimed freedom to differ as inherent in their relationship with politicians.[38]

Holocaust Memory

By the end of 1951, one out of four Israelis was a survivor of the Holocaust reflecting the immigration of approximately 450,000 since the end of the war. Yet there was no talk of the Holocaust and its survivors in the literature of the time nor in the schools. Emblematic was the effort to enlist intellectuals such as writers in 1949 in the cultural absorption of the "human dust." Those contaminated by two thousand years of artificial existence in the Diaspora were to be transformed. Cultural absorption was the imposition of modern Israeli/Palestinian values on the amorphous mass of newcomers.[39] On one hand, the Holocaust provided a legitimization of the Zionist message of the incompatibility of Jewish life in the Diaspora. Further, the formation of the Jewish state was justified by its receptivity of those who did survive. As such the survivors had to be recognized and respected yet there was the need to reconcile the stance of those who died with the heroic image of the Jew in the Yishuv. The ideology of *statism* had, as one of its motifs, the "rejection of the Diaspora," of the passivity of its Jews as compared with the "new Israeli Jew."[40] There was difficulty in dealing with the shame and guilt of both the survivors and those in the Yishuv who had ultimately been powerless as well. This was initially done by emphasizing the few instances of armed revolt.[41]

The decision to recognize the Holocaust was taken only several years after the formation of the state. The Knesset, in 1951, had passed a resolution proclaiming the *twenty-seventh Nissan* as *Holocaust Martyrs and Heroes Remembrance Day*. It occurs in the Spring in association with the Warsaw Ghetto Uprising that started on the eve of Passover. In those early days, the few ceremonies took place in the kibbutzim such as *Yad Mordecai* and the *Martyrs' Forest* in the hills around Jerusalem. Ben-Gurion, for example paid little attention to the Holocaust in his public statements.

It was only in 1959 that the day was set aside by legislation with definite and mandatory guidelines for observance. It is marked by a moment of silence in the model of a day memorializing the soldiers who have died in the wars. The term *heroism* has been transformed to include not only the underground ghetto armies and the partisans in the forests but also the efforts of ghetto Jews to survive, to maintain their dignity.[42]

Yad Vashem (Everlasting Name) is the memorial on Mt. Herzl to the martyrs and heroes of the Holocaust whose building occurred only in 1953. Although it came about at least initially as a result of the exertions of a private citizen, the memorial culture was incorporated within the civil religion of the State. Its foundation in Jerusalem was within the framework of Zionism and in Israel rather than elsewhere in the Diaspora such as Paris where a memorial already existed prior to the Yad Vashem.[43]

The *Eichman* trial in 1961 was the watershed in the connection to be made between Israel and the Holocaust. The opening statement of the prosecutor reflected the Eurocentric view of the Jewish people and related the existence of the Zionist ethos to its European and mainly Litvak roots.[44] The goal of the trial went far beyond the individual in the dock to the recreation of the national and human disaster expressed by the testimony of survivors. It was designed further to bridge the chasm between the generations, to have the young understand what had happened and to diffuse the idea that they had merely "gone like lambs to the slaughter." The real purpose of the trial was for the State of Israel to give voice to the Jewish people in the ideological spirit of Zionism.

In the shift from the statism of Ben-Gurion to a greater identification with the Jewish past, the changing attitude toward the Holocaust was a crucial component. The trial served that role primarily by the opportunity it gave the witnesses to give their testimony. Each individual told a different story of their own survival. In doing so, it provided them an enormous catharsis in speaking about what had been repressed. Moreover, it turned the question back on those who were bystanders. It shifted the guilt they carried for having survived to be shared with those who were equally impotent to change what had happened. By obliterating the boundaries between the bystander and the survivors, it permitted a more genuine encounter with the Shoah to begin.[45]

Among the witnesses testifying at the *Eichman* trial was Abba Kovner who had issued the broadside in the Vilna ghetto that called on the Jews to form a resistance. Born in the Crimea in 1918, Abba Kovner grew up in Vilna. His was the classic appearance of the Jewish intellectual with sharp ascetic melancholy features, flashing eyes, and wavy hair.[46] He was active in the Hashomer Hatzair youth movement and prepared to immigrate to Eretz Israel when the war intervened. He remained in Vilna during the German occupation, first hiding in a convent and then in the Ghetto. His insight to which he gave voice early was that everyone was going to die. It enabled him to envision the possibility of military resistance before others who thought that resistance could bring only catastrophe. He was one of the commanders of the Jewish fighters and then in the forests after the destruction of the Ghetto. Central to his life thereafter was his memory of the half-dead, half-crazed survivor of the mass grave in the Ponar Forest outside Vilna who first brought word of the fate of the Jews being brought there.

One of his poems was published in Eretz Israel in 1943, having been transmitted from his world in the forest. On his arrival in the Yishuv in 1945, many regarded him as the living symbol of Jewish resistance, a spiritual and moral authority. Like some others, he was possessed initially by the idea of revenge.[47] Later, he remained convinced that the foundation of Israel was the climax of Jewish history but did not fall into the simplistic negation of the Diaspora. In further search for unity of the Jewish nation, he also recognized the value of tradition even as he lived a secular life.[48]

He eventually settled in kibbutz *Ein HaHoresh* (Plowman's Spring) where he continued to live for the rest of his life. In central Israel, it had been founded in 1932 by pioneers from Eastern Europe under the auspices of Hashomer Hatzair. During the War of Independence, he was a member of the *Givati Brigade*. He wrote the daily *Battle Sheet* for the troops and functioned as a political officer in the brigade encouraging the writing of battle stories that formed part of what was called *combat heritage*.[49] His experiences during that war were reflected in his prose trilogy published in the 1950s, describing both native-born Sabras and former partisans who fought in the Palmach.

He continued to write poetry dealing with the Holocaust as well as the struggles in Israel in the succeeding decades. He was unique in his personal history of being both a survivor and a fighter both in Lita and in Israel. He played a seminal role in the creation of the Museum of the Diaspora in Tel Aviv (*Beth Hatefutsot*). He was also responsible for the design of one of the Holocaust memorial sites of the Hashomer Hatzair in the kibbutz near Ashkelon, named Yad Moredecai after the leader of the Warsaw revolt. The memorial contains a heroic statue of Mordecai Anielewicz in his Hashomer Hatzair uniform. The museum emphasizes the various outposts of resistance as well as the story of the strong resistance of that very kibbutz in the War of Independence before its capture by the Egyptians.[50] In 1970, Kovner was awarded the Israel Prize and was chairman of the Hebrew Writers Association.

His hope was that the world would be transformed after having experienced the Shoah as he had been transformed. As both a survivor and a poet, he has been able to return recurrently to the subject in a way that few others have been able to do. "In the tradition of the Jewish poet/prophet, he does not write as an individual artist . . . instead he is the voice of a people . . . for whom nationhood is religion and the individual but a fraction of the nation's millennial consciousness."[51]

His poem *The Key Sank*, written in 1950, emulates Bialik in its description of the entry of the Nazis into an East European town, their sealing off of the Jews, the formation of resistance units, the escape of the lone partisan, and the start of the liquidation of the Jews. It is the story of his life and the Vilna ghetto. The ultimate Zionist poem of the Holocaust, the lone surviving partisan, commits himself to return. He is not a defector nor necessarily a redeemer but he is a fighter and goes to a separate Jewish entity to which one can go.[52] In addition to this poem, his legacy includes the posthumous publication of his extraordinary effort to convey the intensity and the breadth of the Holocaust. His *Scrolls of Testimony* was written about the Shaoh to simulate the *megillot* written about previous times of catastrophe for the Jewish people including the lamentations associated with the destruction of the temple, the Book of Esther dealing with the story of Haman. His effort at a liturgy was modeled on the format of the Talmud but had the stories of those who experienced it including the stories of his wife and himself in the Vilna ghetto.[53]

Yiddish Culture

The large number of Holocaust survivors brought about a renewal of Yiddish within the generally Hebrew culture. Abraham Sutkever was the foremost among them. After his miraculous rescue from the forests of Lithuania on the basis of his poetry, he was brought to Moscow to participate in the short period of Soviet support of Jewish heroism. The subject of Jewish resistance was legitimized by his presence in Moscow. In his documentation of his conversations with Yiddish intellectuals, he bore witness to their situation under Stalin and their eventual destruction.[54] After its liberation, he helped discover the materials buried in the Vilna ghetto to record its life. At war's end, he also testified at the Nuremberg Trials.

Abraham Sutzkever came as an "illegal" immigrant to the Yishuv in 1947. He wrote there in 1948 his chronicles of the Vilna ghetto. The *Yiddishe Gas* (Jewish Street) and *Gehymshot* (Secret Town) described the life in the Vilna ghetto and in the sewers beneath the town. Sutzkever continued to write both poetry and prose not only about his life in Eastern Europe but also about life in Israel. His voyage to Israel on the ship *Patria* was described in *Spiritual Soil* where he evokes the story of Homer's *Odysseus*. He accompanied the IDF into Sinai in 1956 and wrote a epic poem of a new covenant based on bravery. His poem about his life in Siberia (*Siber* was published in 1953 with illustrations by Chagall. Throughout his life, he remained concerned about the way words were used and, as in his poems written in the fhetto itself, saw in his precise use of Yiddish a way to maintain its purity in the midst of degradation.[55]

From 1949, he was the editor of the Yiddish literary quarterly *Die Goldene Keyt* (the Golden Chain) published in Tel Aviv. Sponsored by the Histradut, it served as a focus for a wide range of Yiddish writers throughout the world. Emblematic of the final acceptance of Yiddish was the agreement to establish a Chair in Yiddish Literature at the Hebrew University in 1951, so strenuously opposed by Klausner earlier. The Yiddish Writers' Union, founded in 1941, grew in the 1960s to more than 130 members within an active scene of publication of books and periodicals.[56]

The social transformation with the wave of mass immigration and the need for a national ethos based upon the pervasive military preparedness led to the development of a sense of *Isrealiness* that differed from the earlier *Eretz-Israeli* ethos of the Yishuv and early statehood. A cultural transformation occurred during the 1950s with the publication in 1952 of a magazine by a group of students in Jerusalem, *Likrat* (Towards). Edited by Natan Zach, it was the first of a series of little magazines that diverted emphasis from ideology to poetics, from the collective to the individual. Literature no longer could be expected to serve in the furtherance of socialism and the pioneering spirit. For the writer, there was an additional conflict between the "formulated" Hebrew of classical Hebrew fiction as it had evolved from Mendele and the actual spoken Hebrew. The latter "Israeli Hebrew" contained many neologisms as well as borrowings from Arabic, Yiddish, Russian, etc. Spoken Hebrew did not become part of written fiction other than as dialogue. However, the new writers of the next decades discovered the rich pluralism of Israeli society unlike the familiar images of the kibbutz, the farming community and the Little Tel Aviv before 1948. The protagonists are free-floating individuals cut off from the land and the social environment. The new Hebrew/Israeli, both he and she, were more reflective of genuine historical and cultural issues to reflect the growing pluralism of Israeli life.[57]

6.2.4 The Post-Zionist State

The first years of the State were punctuated by almost constant war. Despite the success of the Sinai campaign of 1956, the memory of the Holocaust was renewed in June 1967, the days just prior to the Six-Day War. Comparisons were made between Nasser and Hitler. There was a sense of abandonment and a threat to the existence of the Jewish people. The war that erupted in June 1967 led to the capture of the West Bank and Jerusalem. It led to a sense of messianism and was compared by some to the Six Days of Creation.

Throughout these years of military preoccupation, the person who has exemplified the best qualities of the product of the Yishuv in this generation has been Yitzak Rabin. He was the essence of the native-born *Sabra* in being prickly and undiplomatic on the outside but almost painfully sensitive on the inside.

The Arab-Israeli Wars

Rabin was the chief of staff of the IDF during the Six-Day War of 1967. When receiving an honorary degree at Hebrew University in celebration of the victory, he spoke of the "incomplete joy" of the soldiers. There were not only the glories of the victory but also its price in those killed. There was also compassion for the price paid by their enemies and the awareness that men bound by moral principles were now conquerors. His life exemplified the *Sabra*, the "new Jew" with the unique world view of his first Hebrew generation "as a thinking man sensitive and even fragile, antimilitaristic and . . . a man of conscience."[1] His goal throughout his career, and to which he would eventually give his life, as a soldier and then a politician, was to achieve a peace that would enable Israel to live with its neighbors alongside a Palestinian state.

Yitzak Rabin was born in Jerusalem in 1922, the elder of two children and the only son. His mother, Rosa Cohen, was the niece of Mordecai HaCohen and a cousin of David HaCohen. She, like her cousin David, was born in Gomel where her father, Yitzak, was a successful timber merchant. A rebel, she insisted on attending a Christian girl's school in her town in search of a broad education. After the Russian Revolution, she continued in a revolutionary mode but not as a Bolshevik. Nor did she initially see herself as a Zionist. Encountering a group in Odessa bound for Palestine in 1919, she nevertheless joined them and found herself at the collective settlement *Kvutsat Kinneret* on the Sea of Galilee. Despite her heart disease, she worked as an agricultural laborer. She was visiting her uncle in Jerusalem recovering from a bout of malaria when the Arab disturbances broke out in 1920. She met, at that time, Nehamiah Rabin. He had immigrated to Eretz Israel after having been a member of the American contingent of the Jewish Legion. An immigrant to the United States from the

Ukraine in 1906, he worked as a tailor in Chicago. Active in the tailors' union, he joined the Poalei Zion before being recruited by Yitzak Ben Zvi for the Legion.

The family lived in Tel Aviv. The father worked for the Palestine Electric Company and was active in the metalworkers union. With the mother immersed in community affairs, the father took primary responsibility for family with the children expected to care for themselves as well as help out. While working as an accountant for the Histradut's Solel Boneh, the mother also devoted herself to the poor and the suffering. She was involved in the education of working class children and a member of the Tel Aviv City Council before her untimely death in 1937.[2]

Yitzak Rabin carried, throughout his life, the values of discipline, contempt for any waste, and a deep commitment to public service that characterized his upbringing. His family was rigidly austere. Strongly attracted to the idealistic Zionism of his teachers, Yitzak's commitment was to be an irrigation engineer and work on the land. He had gone to the progressive *School for Workers' Children* and then secondary school in an agricultural settlement near Tel Aviv, both of which his mother had helped found. Also in accordance with his upbringing, in 1937 he went to live at the Kadoorie Agricultural School in the Lower Galilee. He was the outstanding student in his class. It was while there that he began his training as a soldier and came in contact with Yigal Allon and other eventual leaders of the Palmach. Turning down a scholarship to study at the University of California to pursue a career in agricultural engineering, he remained in the Yishuv. Joining the Palmach in 1941, he continued throughout the war to become increasingly involved in its activities. By 1945, he was second in command of the battalion responsible for the North. His first large-scale operation as part of the Hebrew Resistance in the immediate postwar era was the successful raid to free illegal immigrants held at the Athlit Detention Center. He was one of the thousands of Jews arrested by the British on Black Saturday, June 29, 1946. At the time of independence, he was commander of the brigade responsible for the Jerusalem sector. His task was to keep the road open and eventually relieve its siege. It was done but with a loss of life that he never forgot.

His meticulousness in planning, devotion to duty and relatively apolitical stance enabled him to be one of the few Palmach veterans to remain active within the IDF. He held successive appointments as director of training in 1954, chief of operations in 1959, and chief of staff in 1964. In the last role, he was in charge of the revamped IDF that won the Six-Day War.[3] Throughout his career, Rabin was noted for his almost obsessive concern for the safety of those who carried out his orders. The army he had fashioned was not just a military force but a spiritual and moral force "that had earned the right to feel confident in its military prowess without denigrating the virtues of our adversaries or falling into the trap of arrogance." [4]

He was selected by the Labour Party to be the first prime minister of the "sons of the founding generation" but was forced to resign because of American bank account held by his wife contrary to Israeli regulations. He was, thus, not part of the ruling Labor Party leadership at the time of the divisive Yom Kippur War in the Fall of 1973. The Yom Kippur War of 1973 once again brought about the sense of vulnerability that had been belied by the triumphalism of 1967. The rebuilding of the IDF occurred with American aid with Rabin once again prime minister starting in 1974.

In 1977, partially as a result of the near defeat that had occurred in the Yom Kippur War and the breakdown of the original Labour Party with the Movement for Democratic Change under Yigal Yadin, Menachem Begin became the first prime minister of the center-right coalition he headed. It derived its political strength from the Sephardic North African immigrants that felt excluded by the Ashkenazi culture representing the Socialist Zionist ethos. The invasion of Lebanon by Begin's government in 1982 divided the country.[5] Rabin, in opposition to the invasion of Lebanon, maintained his "hawkish" stance while in pursuit of peace. This led eventually to his return to power, the "handshake on the White House Lawn" with the PLO leader Arafat and to the assassination of Rabin by a religious zealot following a peace rally on November 4, 1995.

The Zionist revolution had the aspiration to create the Jewish people anew. Utopian ideals were the motivating slogans that achieved success in achieving its goals of national sovereignty and renewal. What united the disparate elements within Zionism is that it is the movement of the Jewish people seeking to rebuild in Eretz Israel both its national and religious home. The second cornerstone was the commitment to creating Jewish majority in that place. The third cornerstone was the change in the social and economic composition of the Jewish people, to build a working class and a farming class. The fourth was to build a cultural entity based on the Hebrew language. Its success in all these endeavors was an extraordinary one. Yet the disparate elements have become more disparate.

With the establishment of the state and its activities leading to the ingathering of the exiles, the practical stage in the realization of the Zionist idea may have been achieved. The question then remains as to the extent to which realization has solved the existential problems of the Jewish people as it was designed to do. Conversely the question is also the extent to which the State of Israel has a "Jewish" identity in relation to its own character and vis a vis Jews in the Diaspora. The history of the State has been fraught with difficulties and it remains dependent upon the Diaspora for political and financial support, particularly of the United States. In addition, the importance of its role in the maintenance of Jewish life in the Diaspora in terms of its Jewish culture has become more manifest given the rate of assimilation, particularly in the English-speaking countries.[6] The history of Israel since 1967 has continued to evolve in the context of these issues.

The Israeli Intellectual

The writer who best expressed his sources in the Yishuv as transformed in the new generation was Amos Oz. He grew up into literary productivity in the late 1950s and early 1960s as a member of the *Dor Hamedinah* (the State Generation). In addition to the issues that had been present in the earlier years of the Arab refugees, the massive immigration and the unending war, there was an added challenge. That is, in addition to identification with the realization of Zionism, there was an identification with the defeated-undefeated enemy. For Oz and his compeers, there is no question of their Jewish Zionist identity, yet there is an ambivalence about an unabashed affirmation concerning its realization in Israel. Although there remains love for their land, yet it was possible for the first time to criticize aspects without fearing that such criticism could destroy. His "antiheroes" are the most precious sons of the establishment but are unable or unwilling to pass the tests of manliness and heroism. Even as an individual could separate from the collectivity, there was still respect for it and responsibility for its maintenance There is also a clarity of their internal struggle with their *Jewish* heritage in relation to the history of the Diaspora and its continued existence swallowed up in their native-born Zionist *Israeli* heritage.[7]

Amos Oz (Klausner) was born in Jerusalem in 1939. His great-uncle was Joseph Klausner. His father had been born in Odessa where the family had moved from Lita only to return to Vilna after the Bolshevik Revolution. His father went to Vilna University where he graduated in comparative literature. The family emigrated to Palestine in the early 1930s. His parents met as students at Hebrew University where his father was studying for his master's degree. Unable to become a professor in his field of comparative literature, he became a librarian at the Hebrew University and wrote several scholarly books in his field. Although from a distinctly "Lithuanian" mitnagdic background, he grew interested in Hassidism and mysticism. His last work was on the mystical traditions in Peretz's work.[8]

Amos grew up in a Jerusalem that was divided. He changed his name to Oz at age fifteen as part of his rebellion against his father's intellectual world and the suicide of his mother. He moved to kibbutz *Hulda* between Jerusalem and Tel Aviv. Founded in 1909 initially as a agricultural training farm, it was evacuated after a spirited defense during the Arab riots of 1929. It was resettled in 1930 by Gordonian youth movement with which it remained affiliated. Oz graduated from Hebrew University in 1963 and received a master's degree from St. Cross College at Oxford in 1970. After his regular military service from 1957 to 1960, he fought in a tank unit in both the Six-Day War in 1967 and the Yom Kippur War in 1973. Oz continued to live in kibbutz Hulda into the 1980s. Since 1986, he has been a professor at the Ben-Gurion University in Beersheba and has been recognized both in Israel and abroad with a number of prizes.[9]

In the 1960s, Oz was one of the members of the generation in which the new postrealist Hebrew fiction took hold. His first short story collection, *Where the Jackals Howl,* appeared in 1965. His first novel, *Elsewhere Perhaps,* appeared in the next year followed by *My Michael,* his first international success in 1968. His work introduced myth and characters attracted by the remote and faraway. Although Israeli born, writers such as Oz set out to discover their relationship to the past. Their heroes combined the revitalization in Eretz Israel with the traditional exilic heritage of their forefathers and in relation to the Holocaust.

His life and career have represented the role of the intellectual who is thoughtful rather than strident. In his nonfiction, *In the Land of Israel,* published in 1982, he interviewed a variety of people elucidating the country' ideological cross currents. His own position he sees as centrist but "a kind of Zionist Orwell: a complex man obsessed with simple decency and determined above all to tell the truth."[10] Oz remains one of the most affirmatively Zionistic of the intellectuals of Israeli society. His characters abandon, even demolish, Zionist ideals. The demon lies within Zionism, its place in time arising within in the apocalyptic history of the Jews leading up to the Holocaust and its space in the desert.[11] There is a basic conflict between the rational practical policy of the Labor Zionist pioneers ("one dunam at a time") and the passionate irrational vision of the messianic Revisionist.[12]

The Zionist story began to change with the Sinai campaign of 1956. This seemed to be more of a war of choice rather than of survival. Oz protested the war and the values that led up to it in *My Michael.* In the 1970s, a transformation was taking place from Labor Zionism that had stressed humanistic and social-democratic values of the Second and Third Aliyah into a "new Zionism" stressing national-religious values. The formation of the *Gush Emunim,* the weakening of the Labour government, and the rise to power of the Likud marked the break. The pioneers of the Gush Emunim settler movement on the West Bank appear to have stolen the mantle of the youth in the kibbutzim and

Labour. Their threat was to separate Israel out of the union of Jewish tradition and Western humanism.

Amos Oz became the leading spokesperson of the intellectuals opposed to the use of power without clear purpose with the invasion of Lebanon. He has consistently spoken for a humanistic approach to the seemingly unending war. Continuing to live and work in a kibbutz for much of his career, he also remained immersed in its idealistic sources. He harkened back to the well springs of the Zionist socialist dream, to the ethics and ideology of the early Zionists like A. D. Gordon, Katznelson, and even Ben-Gurion.[13]

The impact of the continued occupation of the West Bank post 1967 has reverberated in the writing of the generation that came to maturity in that era. David Grossman alludes to his having been bar mitzvah in 1967 as a crucial aspect of his own personal evolution. In his writing, he represents, for this third generation, the ambition to deal with issue of the Holocaust. His novel breaks with the conventions of realism in order to get at the incapacity of the imagination to comprehend it.[14] In the tradition of east European intelligentsia, the writer is also the intellectual reflecting spiritual values.

David Grossman was born in Jerusalem in 1954. He went to Hebrew University where he received his degree in philosophy and theatre. His early publications dealt with the impact of the occupation of the West Bank and Gaza. The occupation he sees as destructive of both those occupied and the occupiers. This theme was in his novel, *The Smile of the Lamb,* published in Israel in 1983. A later work contained a series of interviews carried out with Palestinians on the twentieth anniversary of the Six-Day War. Its title, *The Yellow Wind* reflects the image of the destruction that can be visited on both.

His second novel, *See Under: Love,* consists of four parts with four different modes of narration.[15] The nine-year-old boy that is the subject of the first part, written in the language of a child who speaks Yiddish as well as Hebrew, is a child of Holocaust survivors living in Jerusalem. He is surrounded by those who do not speak about the unspeakable. In trying to cope with this black hole, he imagines the "Nazi beast" in terms of the children's adventure stories with which he is familiar. The last three sections are the result of the boy, now grown up to be a writer who is a cold and bitter man, trying to imagine what an ancestor Anshel Wasserman experienced in the death camp. The uncle, earlier a writer of Hebrew children's stories, has been broken by his experiences so that he can recite only an endless litany of four words dealing with his Nazi tormentor. Written in colloquial Hebrew, this section is a fantasy about the real-life Jewish writer of children's stories, Bruno Schulz, who was killed in Poland in 1942. In the third section, the uncle—despite his wish to die—stays alive while telling, in his old-fashioned ornate Hebrew of the Haskalah at the turn of the century, the stories he had written that the camp commandant, speaking in educated Hebrew to simulate German, had read as a child. The Hebrew is "studded with scriptural allusions and rabbinical locutions," reflecting its times when the aim was for Hebrew to take its place in the brotherhood of enlightened Western culture.[16] The last section is told in stiff and hyperrational social scientific jargon of an encyclopedia, hence the title of the book, as a counterpoint to the most fantastic portion of the story and results in the suicide of the Nazi commandant.[17] The power of art, of narrative, is to transcend reality.

Grossman's artifice of different languages to express these different sections extends to his more recent books. More specifically, he speaks of the power of language. He explains his overall goal to stake out the individual meaning of words purified from the meanings given to words by the collective bent on the destruction of humanity.

Expression in the variations of Hebrew and Yiddish, such as the work of Grossman, exemplifies the transformation of the languages of the Jews during the last century. The maintenance of the focus on the *word* resonates with the recurrent themes of Jewish life whether in the Hebrew of the Israeli or the Yiddish of Sutzkever in the Vilna ghetto. The twin strands of the secular and the religious have evolved in opposition but are fused now once again in the life of Zion that reflects their common origin in the Pale of Settlement and its spiritual and intellectual center of Vilna, the Jerusalem of Lita.

The early alliance of secular Zionism rooted in Herzl's vision with the religious Zionist movement founded by Rabbi Kook emerged into a nationalism with spiritual overtones. To the adherents of the latter, the independent Israel triumphant in 1967 marked the beginning of God's promise of redemption with the building of a Greater Israel to herald the coming of the Messiah. The conquest of Samaria and Judea and the "redemption" of Jerusalem were seen by religious Zionists as a new stage in the advance toward full sovereignty over the Land of Israel and thus, full redemption. Although Rabin had been originally hailed as an agent of God in 1967, he came to represent for his assassin a treasonous evil for his willingness to consider sharing of the Land of Israel with the Palestinian Arabs.[18]

Zionism claimed religion as secondary to national existence but took on some of the attributes of transformed religious symbols and rituals. Memorials and monuments throughout the country commemorated events in the new Zionist history. The traditional holidays of the Jewish religious calendar were refashioned to reduce, if not eliminate, the religious observances attached. Emphasized were their links to the agricultural cycle of the ancient Hebrews and national survival.[19] The arrangement made was that one could maintain a Jewish identity in Israel without adherence to the Jewish religion. For many if not most Jews, adherence to Zionism generally contributed to and reflected a process of secularization. Religion as expressed in the Diaspora and the *Old Yishuv* was seen as engendering passivity and opposition to modernization.

"Redemptive" Zionism

The religious strand transplanted to Israel has evolved and grown stronger in ways that were unforeseen by the secular founders. For some like Rabbi Abraham Hook, Zionism was seen as a basis for Jewish religious revival. His successors, the religious parties and the rabbinate, claimed increased control over the public expression of religion. *Judaism,* as an essential component of the civil religion of Israel, began to permeate the concept of what it means to be an Israeli. This change reflects the demographics of the large-scale immigration from the more traditional Sephardic Jewish communities. In addition, the Israeli experience of isolation among the nations, of unremitting hostility, has strengthened its sense of difference from other nations. This is to be distinguished from the earlier Zionist goal of being one in a family of nations like others. "Rather than secularism tolerating religion, it is religion that tolerates secularism whereas it affirms traditional religion."[21]

Most serious is the trend toward chauvinism of the expansionists who combine traditional Jewish attitudes of the hostile non-Jew with a faith in God's active intervention. Illustrative of this trend was the impact of the only son of Rabbi Abraham Kook.

Zvi Yehudah Kook was born in the Kovno region in Lita in 1891. He studied at the *Ez Hayyim Yeshiva* in Jerusalem under his father's direction. He studied in Germany and was stranded there by World War I. He joined his father in the administration of the *Yeshivat Merkaz HaRav* and continued as its head after his father's death in 1935. He continued the thinking and methods of education of Rav Abraham Kook and took an active role in the editing and publication of his father's works. His major impact has been his extension of what had been Rabbi Abraham Kook's positive attitude toward the development of the Yishuv. The thinking of Rabbi Zvi Yehudah was now directed toward the support of the existence of the now independent State. He taught that "Torah was . . . fulfilled in a Divinely-chosen land. A divine community with a real government, a real army, a real economy . . . the State of Israel represents an important stage of the Divine historical process."[22]

That discovery of messianic promise in the reality of the culture of the state is consistent with the world view of "modern Orthodoxy" wherein the dynamic of contemporary life can have religious meaning. The influence of the Rabbi Zvi Kook's disciples continued in this vein after the death of their mentor in 1981.

"The [messianic] dream was of utter perfection: the entire Jewish people would reassemble in the undivided Land of Israel reconstituting its life there according to the Torah. This redemption would be a source of blessing for all nations for its redemption would bring about the redemption of the world as s whole." Yet the actual historical occurrence has not fulfilled this dream of several thousand years. Only part of the Jewish people have assembled in what is but a part of the country and only a part of those returning acted in terms of Torah.[23] The messianic ideology as expressed by Rabbi Zvi Yehudah Kook focused on the flourishing of the land and its sovereignty as evidence of redemption with loosening of the connection between national redemption and religious renewal in the pietistic sense.[24]

In the 1950s, a group of highly religious yeshivah students began to study with Rabbi Zvi Yehudah at the Merkaz HaRav. There was the beginning of a transformation of religious Zionism into Zionist religion that led to the formation of Gush Emunim. The leaders were graduates of the *Bnai Akiva* religious youth movement and graduates of a revitalized religious educational strand. Eschatological meaning was assigned to the history of the State from the Holocaust to the Six-Day War. While the government was prepared to accept the partition of the land, God was not so prepared. The result of the Six-Day War was no chance event. For example, it was divine providence that hardened the heart of King Hussein of Jordan when he chose to intervene in the Six-Day War. That action in turn enabled the West Bank and Jerusalem to be liberated. Extraordinary events have occurred and that other momentous events will follow. The sense is that one is living in messianic times in that there is sovereignty of the state and the end of exile through return to the Land of Israel.

Even from the start of the state in 1948, Rabbi Zvi Yehudah preached the divine backing and the inexorability of revival and redemption in the context of the destruction and suffering of the Holocaust.[25] Yet in the transition between father and son there has been the narrowing of the message of Israel from the universal, even cosmic dimension to the particularistic Jewish dimension.[26] Rabbi Zvi Yehuda has preached an intensification of negation of the Galut and an unshakable faith in the "ingathering of the exiles."[27] Like that of his father, his brand of messianism was *active* in that redemptive process is *interactive* dynamic of divine and human actions. When Jews perceive the finger of God in history, they are to take concrete actions to bring about restoration of the conditions preexile. The activism is still bound by the religious tradition but with the understanding that redemption will occur over a period of time and in a natural rather than apocalyptic fashion.[28]

Rabbi Zvi Yehudah Kook was the spiritual guide of Gush Emunim in its settlement of the West Bank despite the opposition of the Labour government. He preached settlement in the territories conquered in 1967. Zionism was part of a new phase in Jewish history in which the people are released from their age-old enforced passivity. Kook's position of "redemptionist-religious Zionism" was in opposition to traditional anti-Zionism of the ultra-Orthodox as well as the secularists' denial of the religious meaning of their undertaking. He translated the ideas of his father into the language of action in the political realm. Settlement on the land would be the vehicle for achieving these goals. "Full sovereignty" was now possible, having been previously blocked by the partition that excluded some of the Land of Israel. Further, the State of Israel is divine, and there must be no retreat from even a kilometer of land thus far conquered.[29]

The Gush Emunim movement presented itself as pioneering religious vanguard within the mainstream of Israeli society. It expressed the quintessential values of Zionism in terms of its focus on settlement of the land albeit now seen as a whole area extending to the Jordan. Its task was to revitalize historical Zionism that had burned out in the 1950s and 1960s in the pursuit of personal and materialistic goals. The settlers adhere to the principles of the kibbutz movement in terms of manual labor and community but based on religious observance. The slogan was "Torah and Labor." This has given them wide support among the general population despite the small number of activists. They also drew support from the Hapoel Mizrachi political party of religious Zionists and the presence of supporters within the National Religious Party, an important member in the successive government coalitions.[30]

Following the accession of the Likud Party to power under Menachem Begin in 1977, these settlers had an even more sympathetic hearing in the government. National goals are clothed with religious rhetoric in a fashion that appears to reflect the stronger religious component in Israeli civic culture.[31] There is identification of the political entity of the State of Israel and the theological one. Israel's wars are not merely carried on for national survival but in opposition to those who oppose the God of Israel. The ideology of messianic determinism has grown more extreme. In becoming "a language of action," it has been deprived of its universalist elements and then of its freedom of individual choice or the actions of the Jewish people per se. In the messianic nature of the quest lies the uncompromising aim of perfection, of perfect peace, on utter harmony, love, and brotherhood and not merely the balance of forces that keep competing interests in check.[32] The original messianic impulse driven into secular expression in Zionism by the Haskalah has now come full circle.

GLOSSARY

Agudat Israel (Association of Israel) is a movement that views the Torah as the only legitimate code of laws binding upon Jews. It is a religiously oriented political party representing the interests of Orthodox Jewry living in Israel and elsewhere. Originally founded in 1912 in Poland in opposition to Zionism, it dissociated itself from the World Zionist Organization in the 1920s. In Palestine in the 1930s and since the Holocaust, it increased its cooperation with the Zionist movement. In Israel, it has formed as a political party and participated in the Knesset and in government coalitions. By so doing, it has required increased adherence to Sabbath observance and other Orthodox principles. It runs its own schools in which religious instruction forms a large part of the curriculum.

Ahdut Haavodah (Unity of Labor) is a Zionist, socialist association of Jewish workers in Palestine founded in 1919 by members of the Poalei Zion Party along with members of the Hapoel Hatzair. It belonged to the World Alliance of Poalei Zion.

Ahdut Haavodah-Poalei Zion is a political party that formed Mapam along with Mifliget Poalim-Hatzair in 1948. Split off to contest elections in the 1960s before forming an Alignment with Mapai in 1965.

Alignment (Maarach) was the political bloc formed by the segments of the Ahdut Haavodah-Poalei Zion that combined with Mapai in 1965, and then with Rafi to form Israel Labor Party in 1968.

Davar (the Word) is the daily newspaper founded in Tel Aviv in 1925 by Histradut and the unofficial organ of the leadrertship and government of Israel when a Labor government ruled it.

Democratic Movement for Change is the political party formed in 1976 by Yigael Yadin to concentrate on domestic political reforms including electoral reforms and budget cuts. It was short-lived after joining the Likud coalition after the 1977 elections.

Gush Emunim (Bloc of the Faithful) is a movement promoting the Jewish settlements in Judea, Samaria and Gaza as a means of promoting retention of these areas particularly in the West Bank. Its founding took place in 1974 in the kibbutz of Kfar Etzion, a West Bank kibbutz captured by the Arabs in 1947 and recovered in the Six-Day War. It began as a faction in the National Religious Party but withdrew from any specific political affiliation.

Haaretz (the Land) is a daily newspaper not affiliated with any political party. First Hebrew language newspaper founded in 1919, published first in Jerusalem and then in Tel Aviv.

Hakibbutz Haartzi was organized in 1927 to reflect a socialist framework associated with the Hashomer Hatzair youth movement and the United Workers party of Mapam.

Hakibbutz HaMeu'chad (United Kibbutz) is the organization founded in 1927 fulfilling the mission of the Ahdut Haavodah within the Mapai and its successor Labor Party.

Halutz (Pioneer) is a term used in the Zionist movement to designate someone devoted to the ideals of building up Jewish Palestine with physical labor, particularly in agriculture.

Hapoel Hatzair (Young Worker) is a Zionist socialist group established by East European pioneers in 1905 that distinguished itself from other socialist groups such as Poalei Zion. It established Degania, the first kibbutz and united in 1930 with Ahdut Haavoda to form Mapai.

Hashomer Hatzair (Young Guard) the youth movement in Israel and abroad that strives to instill national values, Zionist awareness and socialist ideals as well as preparation for kibbutz life.

Herut (Freedom) the political party founded in 1948 by the Irgun descended from the Revisionist movement founded by Jabotinsky during the Yishuv. It advocated militant ultranationalistic action to achieve Jewish statehood. It continued to advocate the right of Jews to settle anywhere in Israel in its historical entirety. Its leader was Menachem Begin who led it to victory for the first time in the elections of 1977 after formation of Likud in 1973.

Irgun (Irgun Zvai Leumi-Etzel) is the Jewish military organization originally founded in 1931. It was primarily made up of members of the Revisionist youth group that remained outside an agreement to join the Haganah in 1937. It continued the ideology of Jabotinsky and, after 1939, took the British to be their main target. Menachem Begin became its commander in 1943. It once again attacked the British starting in 1944. After a short period of unity with the Haganah in the Hebrew Resistance Movement in 1945, it blew up the King David Hotel in July 1946. In 1948, it was disbanded to enter the Israel Defense Forces.

Israel Labor Party was formed in 1968 by the union of Mapai with Rafi and Ahdut Haavoda. United with Mapam in 1969, it retained control of the government until its defeat by Likud in 1977. Its policies are Zionist and socialist.

Mapai (Mifliget Poalei Eretz Israel Workers Party/ Party of Workers in the Land of Israel) originated in 1930; it controlled the Histradut as well as the Jewish agency. From the time of independence until 1965, it won the largest number of seats and formed the government. In 1965, it ran as the Alignment. In 1968, it joined with Rafi to form the Israel Labor party.

Mapam (Mifliget Poalim Hameuhedet-United Workers Party) was organized in 1948 when Hashomer Hatzair merged with radical elements from Ahdut Haavoda. Left-wing socialist-Zionist, Jewish-Arab party, it was more Marxist than Mapai. Split by its pro-Soviet stance, it joined the Alignment in 1969 and maintained the alliance with Labor until 1984 when the latter joined a National Unity Government with Likud.

Mizrahi, founded in 1902, did not see an inherent contradiction between Judaism and Zionism. Along with its labor offshoot Hapoel Hamirachi, it functioned within the Zionist movement. Its principle was adherence to religion and tradition. The two organizations combined in 1955 to form the National Religious Party.

Moshav (Moshav Ovdim) is a cooperative agricultural settlement. Each maintains its own household and farms its own land. The moshav leases its land from public or semipublic agencies. Each family belongs to the cooperative that owns the heavy machinery and deals collectively with marketing and provides services such as education and medical care. Hired labor is forbidden.

National Religious Party (Miflagadatit Leumit-Mafdal) was founded originally by Mizrahi as a religious party combining religious concerns and a moderate socialist orientation within a Zionist framework. Bnai Akiva is its youth group. It has participated in the government under Labor auspices in return for support in religious matters. Its youth faction, after the Six-Day War, became associated informally with the Gush Emunim settlers group.

Poalei Zion (Workers of Zion) is a Zionist socialist workers party. Its platform was influenced by Marxist principles developed along nationalist lines.

Rafi (Reshimat Poalei Israel—Israel Labor list) is a political party founded in 1965 by David Ben-Gurion. It remained in opposition to the government until 1967 when Moshe Dayan, one of its members, joined the government as minister of defense. In 1968, it joined with Mapai to form the Israel Labor Party.

National Religious Party (Miflagadatit Leumit-Mafdal) was founded originally by Mizrahi as a religious party combining religious concerns and a moderate socialist orientation within a Zionist framework. Bnai Akiva is its youth group. It has participated in the government under Labor auspices in return for support in religious matters. Its youth faction, after the Six-

Day War, became associated informally with the Gush Emunim settlers group.

Poalei Zion (Workers of Zion) is a Zionist socialist workers party. Its platform was influenced by Marxist principles developed along nationalist lines.

Rafi (Reshimat Poalei Israel—Israel Labor list) is a political party founded in 1965 by David Ben-Gurion. It remained in opposition to the government until 1967 when Moshe Dayan, one of its members, joined the government as minister of defense. In 1968, it joined with Mapai to form the Israel Labor Party.

658   MARK N. OZER

Notes

6.1   The Nature of the Place

1   Arnold Blumberg, *Zion Before Zionism*, Syracuse, NY, 1985, 45-75 passim
2   Martin Sicker, *Reshaping Palestine*, Westport, CT, 1999, 22-35
3   Ronald Sanders, *Shores of Refuge*, New York, 1988, 117-127
4   Helen Metz, *Israel: A Country Study*, Washington, DC, 1988
5   Baruch Kimmerling, *Zionism and Territory*, Berkeley, CA, 1983, 16-35
6   Eli Lederhendler, "Interpreting Messianic Rhetoric in the Russian Haskalah and Early Zionism," In Jonathan Frankel. Ed., *Jews and Messianism in the Modern Era*, New York, 1991
7   Aviezer Ravitsky, *Messianism, Zionism and Jewish Religious Radicalism*, Chicago, 1996, 36
8   Eliezer Schwied, *The Land of Israel: National Home or Land of Destiny*, London, 1985, 101-107
9   Steven Zipperstein, *The Jews of Odessa, A Cultural History, 1794-1881*, Stanford, 1986
10   Walter Lacquer, *A History of Zionism*, New York, 1989, 69 note
11   Jacob Frumkin, Gregor Aronson and Alexis Goldenweiser, *Russian Jewry, 1860-1917*, New York, 1966, 184-186
12   Aviezer Ravitsky, op cit, 1996, 33-35
13   Eli Lederhendler, op cit, 1991
14   Yaakov Shavit, "Realism and Messianism in Zionism and the Yishuv," In Jonathan Frankel, Ed,. op cit, 1991
15   Martin Sicker, op cit, 1999, 43-46
16   Shmuel Eisenstadt, *Israeli Society*, London, 1967, 9-12
17   Ehud Luz, *Parallels Meet*, Philadelphia, 1988, 70-73
18   Yossi Katz, "Agricultural Settlements in Palestine, 1882-1914, *Jewish Social Studies*, 1988-1993, 50:63
19   Simon Schama, *Two Rothschilds and the Land of Israel*, New York, 1978, 13-24
20   Martin Sicker, op cit, 1999, 50-52; Ran Aaronsohn, *Rothschild and the Early Jewish Colonization in Palestine*, Lanham, MD,2000, 58-67
21   Ran Aaronsohn, op cit, 2000, 68-115
22   Benjamin Harshav, *Language iin Time of Revolution*, Berkeley, CA, 1993,109
23   Ran Aaronsohn, op cit, 2000, 245-248

24 ibid, 247-256

25 Dan Giladi, "The Agronomic Development of the Old Colonies in Palestine, 1882-1914,' In Moshe Ma'oz, Ed., *Studies in Palestine During the Ottoman Period,* Jerusalem, 1975

26 Walter Lacqueur, op cit, 1989, 92-135

27 Shmuel Almog, *Zionism and History,* New York, 1987, 79

28 Simon Schama, 1978, op cit, 137;. Walter Lacqueur, 1989, op cit, 277; Jacob Frumkin, 1966, op cit, 199-201

29 Walter Lacqueur, op cit, 1989, 279

29 ibid, 311

30 ibid, 219-221

31 Martin Sicker, op cit, 1999, 116-137; Jacob Hurewitz, "Britain and Ottoman Palestine; An impressionistic Perspective," In Moshe Ma'oz, Ed., op cit, 1975

32 Howard Sachar, *A History of Israel,* New York, 1976, 112-116

33 Yaakov Shavit, op cit, 1991

34 Amos Elon, *The Israelis,* New York, 1971, 136

35 ibid, 136-137

36 ibid, 145

37 Anita Shapira, "Religious Motuifs of the Labor Movement," In Schmeul Almog, Yehuda Reinharz and Anita Shapira, Eds., *Zionism and Religion,* Hanover, NH, 1988

38 Yehuda Bauer, *From Diplomacy to Resistance,* Philadelphia, 1970, 6-15

39 Christine Collette, "The Utopian Vision s of Labour Zionism British Labour, and the Labour and Socialist International in the 1930s," In Christine Collette and Stephen Bird, Eds., *Jews, Labour and the Left, 1918-1948,* Aldershot, 2000

40 Yehosha Porath, *The Emergence of the Palestinian-Arab National Movement, 1918-1929,* London, 1974, 1-35 passim

41 Yehosha Porath, op cit, 1974, 304-309; Tom Segev, *One Palestine, Complete,* New York, 1999, 307-311

42 Ronald Sander, op cit, 1988, 394-397

43 Jacob Hurewitz, *The Struggle for Palestine,* New York, 1950

44 ibid, 81-107

6.2 The Evolution of the Culture
6.2.1 The Founding Generation

1   Anita Shapira, "Black Night-White Snow: Attitudes of the Palestinian Labour Movement to the Russian Revolution, 1917-1929," In Jonathan Frankel, Ed., *Studies in Contemporary Jewry*, New York, 1997
2   Eliezer Ben-Yehuda, *A Dream Come True*, Boulder, CO, 1993, 19-20
3   Jack Fellman, *The Revival of a Classical Tongue*, The Hague, 1973, 20
4   Martin Gilbert, *Israel*, New York, 1998, 4
5   Shlomo Avineri, *The Making of Modern Zionism*, New York, 1981, 83-87
6   Benjamin Harshav, op cit, 1993, 157-160
7   Jack Fellman, op cit, 1973, 48-54, 94-104
8   Benjamin Harshav, op cit, 1993, 84
9   Jack Fellman, op cit, 1973, 104-111
10   David Patterson, "The Influence of Hebrew Literature on the Growth of Jewish Nationlaism in the Nineteenth Century," In Roland Sussex and J.C. Eade, Eds., *Culture and Nationalism in Nineteenth Century Eastern Europe*, Columbus, OH, 1985
11   Benjamin Harshav, op cit, 1993, 84
12   ibid, 89-92, 146-151
13   ibid, 92
14   Ehud Luz, op cit, 1988, 77-86
15   Jack Fellman, op cit, 1973, 92
16   Anita Schapira, op cit in Jonathan Frankel, Ed., 1997
17   Yossi Goldstein, "Ahad Ha'am in Historical Perspective," In Peter Medding, Ed., *Studies in Contemporary Jewry*, New York, 1992
18   Joseph Klausner, Menachem Ussiskin: *His Life and Work*, New York, 1942, 15-41 passim; Simcha Kling, *The Mighty Warrior: The Life Story of Menachem Ussuskin*, New York, 1965, 1-20
19   Louis Lipsky, *Memoirs in Profile*, Philadelphia, 1975, 120-125
20   Aviezer Ravitzky, op cit, 1996, 10-19
21   Dov Elkins, *Shepherd of Jerusalem*, Northdale, NJ, 1995, 9-14
22   Ehud Luz, op cit, 1988, 11-23; Ben-Zion Bokser, "Introduction," *Rabbi Abraham Isaac Kook*, New York, 1978
24   Jacob Agus, *High Priest of Rebirth*, New York, 1972, 4-28 passim
25   Martin Gordon, "Messianism, Conflicting conceptions, In Shubert Spiro and Yitzhak Pessin, Eds., *Religious Zionism: After 40 Years of Statehood*, Jerusalem, 1989
26   Jacob Agus, op cit, 1972, 57-64
27   ibid, 113-117
28   Eliezer Schweid, op cit, 1985, 171-176

29 Aviezer Ravitsky, op cit, 1996, 112-117 passim

30 Walter Lacqueur, op cit, 1989, 309-312

31 Anita Shapira, *Land and Power*, New York, 1992, 290

32 Shmuel Almog, "The Role of Religious Values in the Second Aliyah," In Schmuel Almong et al, Eds., op cit, 1998

33 Gershion Shaked, *The Shadows Within*, Philadelphia, 1987, 101

34 Eloezer Schweid, op cit, 1985, 161

35 Hannan Hever, "Poetry and Messianism in Palestine Between the Two World Wars," In Jonathan Frankel, Ed., op cit, 1991

36 Alan Mintz, *Banished From their Father's Table*, Bloomington, IN, 1989, 123-149 passim

37 Amos Elon, op cit, 1971, 108-109

38 Tom Segev, op cit, 1999, 174-176

39 Gershon Shaked, *Modern Hebrew Fiction*, Bloomington, IN, 2000, 47-53

40 Shmuel Almog, op cit, 1998

41 Robert Alter, *The Invention of Hebrew Prose*, Seattle, WA, 1988, 50

42 Ben Halpern and Yehuda Reinharz, *Zionism and the Creation of a New Society*, Hanover, NH, 2000, 173-174

43 Tom Segev, op cit, 1999, 182-183

44 Shmuel Almog et al Eds., op cit, 2000, 38

6.2.2 The Generation of the Yishuv

1 Tom Segev, op cit, 1999, 184-185

2 Yonathan Shapiro, *The Formative Years of the Israeli Labour Party*, 1976, London, 4-57

3 Zalman Shazar, *Morning Stars*, Philadelphia, 1967, 79-88

4 ibid, 165-168

5 Abraham Katsh, "Zalman Shazar 1890-1974," *Jewish Book Annual*, 1975, 33:129; Abraham Kariv, "Zalamn Shazar, : The Man and Writer, *Judaism*, 1974, 23: 135

6 Zalman Shazar, op cit, 1967, 42-44

7 Anita Shapira, *Berl, The Biography of a Socialist Zionist*, Cambridge, 1984, 32

8 ibid, 104-112

9 ibid, 47-71 passim

10 ibid, 137-150

11 Shmuel Almog, in Shmuel Almog et al, ed. op cit, 1998

12   Anita Shapira, op cit, 1984, 356-359
13   Yonathan Shapiro, op cit, 1976, 231-251
59   Abraham Cordova and Hanna Herzog, "The Cultural Endeavour of the Labor Movement in Palestine: A Study of the Relationship between Intelligentsia and Intellectuals, *YIVO Annual*, 1978, 17:238
14   ibid
15   Simcha Kling, 1970, *Joseph Kausner*, New York, 17-24
16   ibid, 34-49 passim
17   Zohar Shavit, "The Rise of the Literary Center in Palestine," In Glenda Abramson and Tudor Parfitt, *The Great Transtion*, Totowa, NJ, 1985
18   Benjamin Harshav, op cit, 1993, 86
19   S. Niger. Charney, "Joseph Klausner's 'History of Modern Hebrew Literature' and his Attitude Toward Yiddish," *YIVO Annual*, 1955, 10:197
20   Tom Segev, op cit, 1999, 266-267
21   Simcha Kling, op cit, 1970, 66-93 passim
22   Yaakov Shavit, op cit, 1991
23   David Patterson, *A Phoenix in Fetters*, Savage, MD, 1988, 17-18
24   Dan Miron, "Introduction," In Atar Hadari, Ed., *Songs from Bilaik*, Syracuse, NY, 2000
25   David Aberbach, *Revolutionary Hebrew, Empire and Crisis*, New York, 1998, 117-137
26   Eliezer Schweid, *The Revival of Judaism in the Thought of Bialik*, Jerusalem, 1974
27   Gershon Shaked, op cit, 1987, 104
28   Michael Keren, *Ben Guron and the Intellectuals; Power, Knowledge and Charisma*, DeKalb, IL, 1989, 26
29   Yitzhak Laor, "Scizolingua or How Many Years Can Hebrew Remain Modern? On the Ideological Dictates of the Hebrew Language," In Emily Budick, Ed., *Ideology and Jewish Identity in Israeli and American Literature*, Albany, NY, 2001
30   Louis Lipsky, op cit, 1975, 155-159
31   Gershon Shaked, op cit, 1987, 132
32   Charles Liebman and Eliezer Don-Yehiyaa, *Civil Religion in Israel*, Berkeley, CA, 1983, 25-58 passim
33   Dan Kursman *Ben Gurion, Prophet of Fire*, New York, 1983 p43-73 passim; Michael Bar-Zohar, *Ben Gurion: A Biography*, New York, 1978, 1-11 passim
34   Anita Shapira, op cit, 1998

35 Mitchell Cohen, *Zion and State*, Oxford, 1987, 135
36 Dan Kursman, op cit, 1983, 100-140 passim
37 Michael Bar-Zohar, op cit, 1977, 44-81 passim
38 Shlomo Avineri, op cit, 1981, 216
39 Walter Preuss, *The Labour Movement in Israel*, Jerusalem, 1965, 130-139
42 Myron Aronoff, "Myths, Symbols and Rituals," In Laurence Silberstein, Ed., *New Perspectives on Israeli History*, New York, 1991 Shapira, 1992, 68-82
43 Aharon Kellerman, *Society and Settlement*, Albany, NY, 1993, 24-28
44 Yigal Allon, *The Making of Israel's Army*, London, 1970, 1-14
45 Oz Almog, *The Sabra: The Creation of the 'New Jew*, Berkeley, CA, 2000, 7
46 Anita Shapira, op cit, 1992, 90-91
47 ibid, 81
48 ibid, 99
49 ibid, 98-105
50 ibid, 123
51 ibid, 173-220
52 ibid, 219-257 passim
53 Yehuda Bauer, op cit, 1970, 124-152 passim
54 Yigal Allon, op cit, 1970, 15-29; Anita Shapira, op cit, 1992, 255
5S Schmuel Almog, op cit, 2000

6.2.3 The Generation of the State

1 Anita Shapira, op cit, 1992, 370
2 ibid, 323
3 ibid, 354-370
4 ibid, 304-305
5 Howard Sachar, op cit, 1961, 442-452
6 Tom Segev, op cit, 1999, 283-285
7 Eliot Cohen *Supreme Command*, New York, 2002, 148-172
8 Yehuda Bauer, op cit, 1970, 356-359
9 Benjamin Harshav, op cit, 1993, 155
10 David HaCohen, *Time to Tell*, New York, 1985, 9-11
11 ibid, 18-24
12 ibid, 86-102 passim
13 Mitchell Cohen, op cit, 1987, 204

14   David Hartman, *Israelis and the Jewish Tradition*, New Haven, 2000, 3-8

15   Gershon Shaked, op cit, 1987, 106

16   Anita Shapira, In Shmuel Almog et al. Ed., op cit,1998

17   Neil Silberman, *A Prophet from Amongst You*, Reading, MA, 1993, 5-23

18   Charles Liebman and Eliezer Don-Yehiya, op cit, 1983, 111

19   Amos Alon, op cit, 1971, 280-287

20   Yael Zerubavel, *Recovered Roots*, Chicago, 1995, 22-36

21   Neil Silberman, op cit, 1993, 35-61 passim

22   Nachman Ben-Yehuda, *The Masad Myth: Collective Memory and Mythmaking in Israel*, Madison, WI, 1995, 27-68 passim

23   Yael Zerubavel, op cit, 1995, 62-70

24   Charles Liebman, and Eliezer Don-Yehiya op cit, 1983, 102-104

25   Eliezer Schweid, "The Construction and Deconstruction of Jewish Zionist Identity," In Emily Burdick Ed., op cit, 2001

26   Robert Alter, *After the Tradition. Essays on Modern Jewish Writing*, New York, 1969,186

27   ibid, 210-225

28   Robert Alter, *Hebrew and Modernity*, Bloomington, IN, 1994, 92-94

29   ibid, 82-83; Gershon Shaked, op cit, 2000, 148-149

30   Gershon Shaked, op cit, 1987, 108

31   ibid, 116

32   Gershon Shaked, op cit, 2000, 65-69

33   Menachem Rohshtein, "S. Yizhar: Writer on Native Ground" *Jewish Book Annual*, 1985, 43:154

34   Oz Almog, op cit, 2000, 14

35   Gershon Shaked, op cit, 1987, 170

36   Gershon Shaked, op cit, 2000, 144-149

37   Hannah Hever, *Produciing the Modern Hebrew Canon*, New York, 2002, 113-115

38   Michael Keren, op cit, 1983, 130-136

39   ibid, 124-125

40   Eliezer Don-Yehiya, "Memory and the Political Culture," In Ezra Mendelsohn, Ed., *Studies in Contemporary Jewry*, New York, 1993

41   ina Porat, "Attitudes of the Young in the State of Israel toward the Holocaust and its Survivors," In Laurence Silberstein, Ed., op cit, 1991

42   Tom Segev, T*he Seventh Million*, New York, 1991, 421-445

43 Eliezer Don-Yehiya, op cit, 1993

44 Tom Segev, op cit, 1991, 349

45 Alan Mintz, *Hurban: Responses to Catastrophe in Hebrew Literature*, Syracuse, NY, 1996, 239-243

46 Tom Segev, op cit, 1991, 140

47 ibid, 140-143

48 Irving Greenberg, "Foreward" In Abba Kovner, *Scrolls of Memory*, Philadelphia, 1991, xi

49 Oz Almog, op cit, 2000, 34

50 Tom Segev, op cit, 1991, 447-448

51 Shirley Kaufman, "Introduction," In *A Canopy in the Desert. Selected Poems by Abba Kovner*, Pittsburgh, PA, 1973

52 Alan Mintz, op cit, 1996, 260-263

53 Irving Greenberg, op cit, 2001, xvii-xviii; Abba Kovner, *Scrolls of Testimony*, Philadelphia, 2001, 74-82

54 Ruth Wisse, *Abraham Sutzkever, The Uncrowned Jewish Poet Laureate*, Amherst, MA, 1994

55 ibid,

56 Charles Madison, *Yiddish Literature*, New York, 1968, 500-521 passim; Sol Liptzin, "Yiddish Literature in Israel, The Last Two Decades," *Jewish Book Annual*, 1989-1900, 47:152

57 Gershon Shaked, op cit, 2000, 160-167

6.2.4 The Post-Zionist State

1   Oz Almog, op cit, 2000, 263

2   Dan Kurzman, *Soldier of Peace*, New York, 1998, 37-51; Yitzhak Rabin, *The Rabin Memoirs*, Boston, 1979, 1-6

3   Dan Kurzman, op cit, 1998, 172-230

4   ibid, 232

5   Tom Segev op cit, 1991, 360-403

6   Eliezer Schweid, op cit, 2001

7   ibid

8   Joseph Cohen, *Voices of Israel*, Albany, NY, 1990, 179-185; Amos Oz, *A Tale of Love and Darkness*, New York, 2003, 37

9   Daniel Jones and John Jorgenson, Eds, "Amos Oz" Contemporary Authors New Revision Series v. 65 Detroit, MI: 1998. 190-197.

10 Ibid, 195

11 Joseph Cohen, op cit, 1990, 142

12 Gershon Shaked, op cit, 1987, 177-178

13 Amos Oz, op cit, 2003, 4-18

14 Alan Mintz, "A Famous Israeli Novel," *Commentary*, 1989, 88:56

15 Robert Alter, op cit, 1994, 99-103

16 ibid, 20

17 Alan Mintz, iop cit, 1989

18 Dan Kurzman., op cit, 1998, 484-505

19 Oz Almog, op cit, 2000, 21

20 Simon Herman, *Israelis and Jews, The Continuity of an Identity*, Philadelphia, 1971 p1197-209

21 Charles Liebman and Eliezer Don-Hehiya op cit, 1983, 228

22 Tzvi Fishman, *Torat Eretz Yisrael: The Teachings of HaRav Tzvi Yehuda HaCohen Kook*, Jerusalem, 1991, 104

23 Aviezer Ravitsky, op cit, 1996, 1

24 ibid, 141

25 ibid,126-128

26 ibid, 144

27 Gideon Shimoni, "Reformulations of Zionist Ideology since the Establishment of the State of Israel," In Peter Medding, Ed., *Values, Interests and Identities, Studies in Contemporary Jewry*, New York, 1995

28 Jody Myers, "The Messianic Idea and Zionist Ideologies" In Jonathan Frankel, Ed, op cit, 1991

29 Myron Aronoff, "The Institutionalization and Cooptation of a Charasmatic, Messianic, Religious-Political Revitalization Movement," In David Newman, Ed., *The Impact of Gush Emunim*, New York, 1985

30 Ehud Sprinzak, "The IcebergModel of Political Extremism," In David Newman, Ed., op cit, 1985

31 Janet Aviad, "The Messianism of Gush Emunin," In Jonathan Frankel, Ed., op cit, 1991

32 Aviezer Ravitsky, op cit, 1996, 136-141

INDEX

Z